# Religion & Ethics for A New Age

*Evolutionist Approach*

Emmanuel K. Twesigye

University Press of America,® Inc.
Lanham · New York · Oxford

4720 Boston Way
Lanham, Maryland 20706

12 Hid's Copse Rd.
Cumnor Hill, Oxford OX2 9JJ


Printed in the United States of America
British Library Cataloging in Publication Information Available

**Library of Congress Cataloging-in-Publication Data**

Twesigye, Emmanuel K.
Religion & ethics for a new age : evolutionist approach /
Emmanuel K. Twesigye.
p. cm
Includes bibliographical references and index.
1. Philosophical theology. 2. Christian ethics—Anglican authors.
3. Evolution—Religious aspects—Christianity. I. Title: Religion
and ethics for a new age. II. Title.
BT40 .T94 2001 241—dc21 2001027478 CIP

ISBN 0-7618-2024-8 (pbk. : alk. paper)

∞™ The paper used in this publication meets the minimum
requirements of American National Standard for Information
Sciences—Permanence of Paper for Printed Library Materials,
ANSI Z39.48—1984

**TO**

**Joy**
**Grace**
**Gloria**
**and**
**Peace**
**My Beloved Daughters**

**and**

**All God's Loving Daughters and Sons**

**in**

**This World**

# Contents

# Preface

Religion and rational morality or ethics are positively affirmed to be the ultimate universal common human defining and unique moral, cultural, mental and religious features and activities. This is in addition to the unique human technology of fire-making and usage.

These special or divine intellectual, spiritual and moral activities of the human being arise out of the human being's intrinsic divine essence and attributes. This divine essence that flows into the human being from God and divine attributes which are shared between God and human beings include: spirit, creativity, freedom, mind, moral agency, agape, free forgiveness, justice, knowledge, language and self-transcendence.

The book is grounded within the understanding of God as the *Omnipresent Cosmic Creative Spirit* (*Energy*) and *Mind*. This is the same "Transcendent Mystery" that is "All Encompassing Ultimate Reality" or "Principle of Order, Life and Being" that calls the cosmos and its creatures into being or concrete existence (*Creates*), *Sustains* and *Redeems* them from the omnipresent threat of evil as *chaos* or disorder *(entropy)*, nonexistence *(nothingness* or death) and *meaninglessness*.

To some meaningful degree, God's divine essence and attributes are constantly being revealed to evolutionary finite minds through nature and history. This is more explicitly seen in natural laws and the divine attributes of God as found reflected within human nature as the *imago Dei* (mirror of God) in the world. This is most especially seen in Jesus' moral teachings of agape and nonviolence, and whose moral life was the most perfect *"Mirror of God" (theophany)* in the world and its evolutionary religious and moral history.

Divinity as Mind, Spirit, Self-Consciousness, Creativity, Self-Transcendence, Moral Agency, Compassion and Agape are expressed in the evolutionary human nature of ordinary creatures. They effectively transform the ordinary evolutionary creatures into the extraordinary creatures, the *Homo sapiens* who are God's mirrors (*imago Dei*) and evolutionary representatives in the world. Moses, Jesus and the Buddha provide good examples of this evolutionary manifestation of these divine qualities in both humanity and their moral and spiritual evolution toward purification, perfection, union with God and ultimate personal and collective human fulfillment and happiness.

At this highest level of moral and religious evolution and development, the traditional competing and divisive religious labels and affiliations are both transcended and eternally nullified by God. In God's Kingdom, there are no religious labels or affiliations. Irrespective of creed and religious affiliation, all God's obedient and loving saints are welcome into God's Kingdom and fellowship of love.

As evolutionary minds and spirits in cosmic history and the world, the human beings are also God's special creations. They are specially designed and created by God through the process of biological evolution to become God's special or divine temporal co-creators, co-sustainers and co-redeemers of history and the world. As such, to see a truly obedient human being or saint and their loving and self-sacrificial actions is also to experience a *theophany* or catch a glimpse of God at work in the world! The best example is that of Jesus as the Christ. Other examples include the Buddha, the Hebrew prophets, the saints, Mohandas Gandhi, M.L. King, Mother Teresa and Desmond Tutu.

This book celebrates religion and ethics within the global pluralistic and diverse cultural, religious, social and philosophical contexts. Christianity and science, particularly, human and institutional historical evolution, including cultures, languages, religions and morality are the main fundamental academic contexts for this book.

This new ground breaking and iconoclastic Christian book on religion and ethics has been written in the hope that it will become a positive vehicle for positive academic, theological, spiritual reflection, challenge, reformation and moral transformation. It has been written as an academic tool to effect a long overdue moral and theological reformation and constructive religious revolution within different groups of people, and their respective moral communities or the Church. Is shatters myths and idolatry within the traditional Western patriarchal Christian theology and ethics. That may cause discomfort to some conservative Christians.

The fundamental academic task and primary theological objective for this book has been to make the traditional Christian theology and ethics relevant for our era. I have tried to make traditional Christian dogmas and technical topics understandable and meaningful for today's diverse, scientific, religiously pluralistic and multicultural Global Community. The objective for the book is also to make Christian academic theology and ethics accessible to a great number of people, and not a mere privilege for professional theologians, graduate and advanced college students.

As a result, the usual academic jargon, usually esteemed by the esoteric members of the academe, has been either discarded or kept to the minimum. Some technical terms have been either defined or explained within the text. This approach was considered necessary in order to help the nontechnical readers comprehend the main theological and philosophical content and to follow the theological and philosophical arguments presented in the book.

Accordingly, the traditional mysteries involved in the theological and philosophical debates concerning the problems of the essence and nature of God's radical transcendence, and the inability of the finite human mind and language to both grasp and express it fully, as it really exists in actuality or supernatural essence and infinite mystery, have been simplified and made plain. This task was undertaken in order to make academic Christian theology and ethics more interesting and accessible to college or university students, and the well-educated general reading public.

Therefore, this book can be used as a textbook in Christian theology, religion and Christian ethics for introductory academic courses in these fields. The book can also be used as a text book for well-educated adult classes in Sunday Schools.

The Church should consider this kind of book necessary and commend it to its educated members. The continuing education of the clergy and their congregation members is important if the Church desires to remain relevant. This is essential if the Church wishes to remain a compelling moral force within the contemporary religious global context. This new context for Christian reflection and activity is characterized by pluralism and the moral relativism of the multicultural Global Community of the postmodern era.

The book also offers a necessary Christian, theological, and academic moral constructive response to the serious issues and criticisms of traditional Christian theology, the patriarchal Church and traditional Christian ethics, as raised by people like Mary Daly and the Rt. Rev. John Spong, an Anglican (Episcopalian) Diocesan Bishop of the Diocese of Newark, New Jersey. Bishop Spong criticizes and castigates the traditional Christian Church for being antiquated in its doctrines, and religious language. He also denounces the traditional Christian Church for being fundamentalist, anti-intellectual, dogmatic, homophobic, anti-science and both theologically and morally static in an evolutionary and fast changing world.

This book provides some important responses and commentary on Bishop Spong's radical, but necessary and timely ecclesiastical self-evaluation, and prophetic call for a new theological reformation of the Church and both its ancient and antiquated dogmatic doctrines. Bishop Spong and other progressive thinkers like Hegel, Karl Marx, Alfred North Whitehead, Teilhard de Chardin, Paul Tillich, Karl Rahner and Mary Daly have correctly called for a revamping of the traditional Church's antiquated patriarchal, sexist, racist religious symbols, theological language, dogmatic teachings, moral and social practices.

In response to Bishop Spong's challenge and call for a new Reformation within the Church, this book revamps the antiquated Christian dogmas and misleading classical theological symbols, images and patriarchal language of the Early and Medieval Church. As a result, the book presents the essential new theological and inclusive language, non-sexist or racist symbols, and scientifically grounded paradigms for understanding God's supernatural activities of creation, redemption and heaven or "God's Kingdom." The Church, Christian doctrines and ethics are reconstructed, presented anew and discussed from an inclusive, global, multicultural and pluralist evolutionary Christian perspective.

The traditional Western theological, cultural, patriarchal, moral, and religious global imperialism are rejected. Western theological, moral, linguistic, cultural symbols, epistemology and ideas, no longer consist the universal criteria and measure for truth and divine revelation in history and the world.

It is reaffirmed that God as Spirit, Mind, Goodness, Truth, Creativity, Order, Being and Reality is equally omnipresent in the entire world. Therefore, all of the human history, religions, cultures, languages, scriptures, moral systems and institutions, to some various degree bear the effective presence of God and mediate God's redemptive grace, revelation, and the redemptive holy enlightenment and guidance of the work of God's *Logos* (cf. John 1:1-6) and the Holy Spirit.

However, in order to provide theological continuity, between the new theology of the New Age and the known, as well as pastoral comfort, some traditional important images for God and theological paradigms have been deliberately retained. This includes the paradigm of the Church as a religious, moral or Ecclesial Community of God's obedient people. It is part of God's Kingdom. It is composed of all loving and obedient people as God's moral saints in the world.

The good deeds of unconditional love, mercy, justice, faith and obedience in God, rather than the exclusive Christian sacrament of Baptism, are the true keys and paths to God's Kingdom. These keys of heaven are available to all God's moral saints into inclusive and cosmic God's Kingdom. No qualified person is ever excluded by God from his or her unmerited redemptive grace, unconditional love, life and the Kingdom.

The metaphor of the "*Kingdom of God*" has been deliberately retained in this work. This is necessary in order to provide continuity between the old and new theology and ethics. As a general rule, when the "new wine (teaching) has required new wine- skins (paradigms)," they have been provided as needed! As such, this book does not present a theological revolution against the Church as an institution or its doctrines as Mary Daly's book, *Beyond God the Father* does. Instead, this book presents a theological reformation from within the Church tradition, theology, ethics, hierarchical priesthood and leadership. The success of this reformation will depend on how the Church and the Christian public respond to the contents and -reformulations of doctrines and ethics, such as those in this book.

As an Anglican/Episcopalian priest, theologian, philosopher and ethicist, I have tried to take a theologically justifiable academic stand on some of the sensitive and controversial topics discussed within the book. At the same time, in respect to the Anglican tradition and Aristotle's warning that "virtue lies in the middle of two extremes," I have also tried to maintain the middle ground on many important theological and moral issues.

In addition, I have also sought to provide common ground for the major religions on some selected central moral and theological issues that unite us as intelligent, knowing, thinking, responsible, religious and human beings that are created in God's own image (*imago Dei* or the *Homo Sapiens*).

Consequently, for some religious conservatives, this book will probably appear to be a radical theological and moral deconstructive work. However, this work is a reformist and reconstructive book written from within the mainline Church Christian theological and moral tradition. The book reinterprets old theology and ethics in terms of new inclusive language and contemporary scientific world-view. It has been written by a faith-filled and committed Christian Anglican priest.

Based on the theory of evolution as God's method for the creation of the cosmos and all creatures, including the human beings, I have written this book to reformulate Christian theology and Church doctrines to consistent with that scientific truth. I positively affirm God's continuing revelation and the power of God's unconditional love in both continuing cosmic creation and redemption as inseparable twin processes of God's supernatural simultaneous and coextensive (or coexisting) activities in the world.

Within this academic approach and inclusive theological understanding, the basic epistemological, theological, philosophical, moral and ontological assumption is that God exists eternally as the Cosmic Creative, Sustaining and Redemptive Spirit without gender, color, nationality and human physical features. This is the same nameless Mystery God (*Yahweh*), who revealed himself or herself to Moses, Buddha, Jesus, Muhammad, and other prophets and mystics.

This also the same transcendent Creator-Sustainer-Redeemer God that is worshipped by the Christians, Muslims, Buddhists, Hindus, African Religionists, Native Americans and other religious groups. Essentially, this impartial and nameless God is the cosmic "*Sola Gratia*" (Grace), *Agape* and "*Being*" that is the divine Life-Giving Medium and creative Mystery.

God as the Power of Being, enables life and beings to come into being and have their meaningful and fulfilling existence (cf. Acts 17:16-34). God's *Logos* as God's universal Principle and Medium for God's creation, life, salvation and eschatological divine fulfillment of creatures, is the same Divine Principle that became incarnate in cosmic history in Jesus, the man of Nazareth. That historical divine incarnation of the *Logos* in Jesus did not negate the universality of the *Logos* and God's continuing universal efficacious activities of cosmic creation and redemption through that *Logos* as the Cosmic Christ and Redeemer,

The basic epistemological and pedagogical assumption is that the readers of the book will be those intelligent, well informed, educated, inquiring and open-minded men and women who are already interested in the complex matters of religion, theology, philosophy and ethics from a broad, scientific, intellectual, inclusive and globalist Christian academic perspective. Those people will find plenty of intellectually challenging, interesting and satisfying material and innovative moral and theological arguments to support new post-Darwinian moral and theological positions. Religions and ethics are still in the process of moral and mystical cosmic inclusive evolution toward nonviolence, justice, unconditional love, mutual free acceptance, social harmony and peace as the universal common ground for all moral religions and sound ethical systems. As a result of this continuing moral evolution, God's revelation and guidance of creative-redemptive supernatural grace through the *Logos* and the Holy Spirit, the evils, vices and sins of xenophobia, imperialism, violence, war, tribalism, nationalism, racism and sexism will be finally transcended and overcome by God's obedient, faith-filled and loving people in this world. This movement toward human moral and spiritual perfection is God's work of grace of special creation and redemption of human beings into true free moral agents.

The United Methodist Publishing *Social Principles* and the rest of the of the materials in the appendixes are very important. They clearly illustrate how God's presence and ideal moral values can be reformulated and accessed through different ways today. They are additional moral resources for God's revelation and moral values.

These additional resources include the United Nations' *Universal Declaration of Human Rights*, sermons, commandments and guidelines for peaceful problem solving, and the Lambeth Conference Resolution of the Anglican Bishops concerning sexuality and homosexuality in the Church. These materials provide an illustration of the best religious, theological and moral formulations of practical Christian ethics within a pluralistic contemporary global society.

The feedback from my readers and students have been invaluable. Their questions and comments have led to some modifications of the style, arguments and content of this book to make it simpler and more easily readable.

Footnotes were either removed or incorporated into the main text as part of the improvements suggested by students and other readers. Some essential material from previous chapters is briefly repeated in later chapters so that the readers are not lost in the arguments of the book. The language of the book has been kept free of professional jargon and unnecessary theological or philosophical terminologies. Where these terminologies are used, they are immediately explained in the text.

Despite the past naive and false claims of the arrival of Armageddon and the apocalyptic end of the world, the Third Millennium is here and does not mean that the end of the world is near. Instead this millennium marks a new era of the Reign of God through the Holy Spirit. This is also an exciting era of new human global self-consciousness, new religious awakening, positive creativity, compassion, international cooperation, freedom and peace. God's eschatological Kingdom as God's Reign through the Holy Spirit and the *Logos* requires a new systematic and globally centered modes of thinking, a new inclusive world-view, multiculturalism, and flexible global Christian theology.

This book has been written from this global and pluralist perspective. It is scientifically grounded in the cosmic biological evolution of life, global cultural, philosophical and religious pluralism. The book is intended to serve as a significant Christian academic contribution to the science and technology oriented New Age of global new constructive religious thought, Christian theology, philosophy and ethics.

It is hoped that after the reading the book, the readers will develop some tolerance for different peoples, cultures, and competing alternative religions in the world. And they will be able to recognize this pluralism as constituting different components of God's providence for human freedom, creativity and diversity in the world as his or her Kingdom.

Therefore, welcome to the intellectual, moral and spiritual feast! Read and enjoy the book! It has been specifically researched and written for people like you! The cumbersome notes have been incorporated into the main text in order to make your reading uninterrupted. Nevertheless, the essential depth of the academic content and integrity of the material have been retained. This is because the book is also intended to serve as a textbook for introductory college and university courses in religion, Christian theology and ethics.

I hope that you will find this book interesting, informative, intellectually stimulating, both theologically and morally challenging, academically innovative, and worth reading.

Emmanuel Kalenzi Twesigye
Aden S. & Mollie Wollam Benedicts Professor
of Christian Studies
Ohio Wesleyan University
Dip. Th. (EAU); BA (Hons. MUK); Dip. Ed.(MUK);
MA (Hons. Wheaton); STM (U of the South);
MA & PhD (Vanderbilt U)

Spring 2001

# *Acknowledgements*

I am grateful to the United Methodist Publishing for granting me the permission to reproduce the *Social Principles*. Many thanks are also due to the Reverend Professor Paul Nicely and the Rev. Dr. Thomas Van Brunt for allowing me to publish their sermons on life and ethics in appendixes. These materials provide valuable resources for Christian ethics and moral theology.

I am particularly, grateful to Professor William Louthan, the Provost, Ohio Wesleyan University for the assistance with funds to hire Beatrice T. Twesigye to reread the book manuscript, and make corrections of the serious clerical errors which had occurred during the preparation of the final manuscript version for publication. As a former college professor of biology, she made valuable observations about the material on evolutions and religion. In addition, she also prepared the book index with Gloria Twesigye's assistance. Without their help and the University's fiscal support, this book would not have been published in this form.

I am also indebted to all members of the academic community who have helped to critique the various components of the manuscript. Special appreciation goes to Professor Richard Fusch, Associate Dean of Student Affairs, and Dr. Kathryn Ogletree, Director of Minority Student Affairs, for helping to provide work study students.

I am indebted to my special student assistants and interns who have worked on this book at its various stages. They include: Khadija Garrison, Anita Taylor McGee, Anita Ryan and Lauren Hall. They helped with proofreading the manuscript and copy editing.

Finally, thanks are due to many other people, of whom many are unnamed here, yet whose contributions made this book possible or improved the quality of the book. Thank you.

EKT

# Chapter 1

# Religion, Ethics and Theology In Evolutionary Context: Introduction

*Religion and Ethics for a New Age* is an evolutionist and contemporary academic book in the fields of religion, ethics and Christian theology. The book is grounded in science and religion, reason (intellect) and faith as compatible dimensions of a healthy, well integrated, and holistic human life, thought and experience.

The book is deliberately evolutionist in its scientific, religious, moral, theological, philosophical, academic approach and pluralistic global context. The book has been written within an inclusive, global Christian, theological, moral, cultural, philosophical and broad religious scope and perspective.

## 1. The Nature of the Book

The book has evolved out of a long process of both research and teaching courses in theology, ethics and philosophy at various universities and seminaries, including: Makerere University in East Africa, Fisk University, Memphis State University, Ohio Wesleyan University and The Methodist School of Theology in Ohio.

However, the material in this book has been simplified and modified to make the book appealing to a broader range of audience. It has been written for open-minded well-educated people who are interested in contemporary issues in religion, Christian theology and ethics. As a result of this consideration, and with help from a number of my students, cumbersome footnotes have been eliminated, and academic jargon has been either translated into lay people's terms or left out. The book is specifically written for an inquiring and scientifically thinking people, including university students, religious leaders and scholars.

The book has been designed to answer some tough, perennial, universal and controversial theological-philosophical and ethical questions for people interested in religion, ethics and moral values within the contemporary society. This book is particularly useful for the readers or students who are interested in the discussion or answers concerning the relevance and value of religion in an era of science, global multic-ulturalism and religious pluralism. This book, deals with Christianity, theology and ethics in the age of science and instantaneous global cyberspace, electronic information and the interrelated and interdependent global community made possible by advanced technology and communications.

In this regard, the book provides both a provocative and constructive response to Bishop John Spong of the Episcopal Diocese of Newark in New Jersey, in his vicious criticisms of the traditional Christianity, dogmatic theology, the traditional Christian Church, and his call for "New Reformation." In his call for a "new age" Christian reformation of Christianity and the Church in 1998, Bishop Spong posted twelve theses on the Internet for public theological debate. Bishop Spong posted these theses in the same kind of theological, moral, spiritual, academic and Christian spirit, in which the Reverend Professor Martin Luther (1483-1546) had posted his famous Ninety-Five Theses on the door of a local Catholic parish church in Wittenberg, Germany on October 31, 1517. This was convenient because the parish church was located close to Luther's Franciscan monastery, and the University of Wittenberg where he taught both biblical and systematic theology.

Professor Martin Luther's 95 theses led to an acrimonious theological debate, and religious protests about the order and doctrines of the Church. As a result of the Church hierarchy's fear and resentment of challenge, Professor Luther was excommunicated by the Catholic Church as a rebellious heretic. Luther's devoted followers followed him into "schism" to form the new and reformed Protestant Church of which one branch still proudly bears his name. At the same time, Luther inspired a new universal process of academic questioning of the established chur ches, along with their traditions, dogmatic theological and moral teachings. We, too, are called to continue that kind of critical theological and moral examination of our own religious traditions, institutions and their moral teachings, and call for a reformation or spearhead it, when necessary or when called by God to undertake this task. This book is designed and intended to serve as a humble attempt to accomplish both of those important theological and moral tasks.

## 2. The Constantly Changing Nature of the World, Life, Culture, Knowledge and Technology

With the exception of God, nothing in the world is ever perfect, absolute, static, permanent and changeless. Everything that comes into being, exists in the realm of time or finitude and is completely governed by the laws of chronological time *(chronos)* and change. Things come into being, grow, change, mature, wither, and finally die and decay.

With the reality of death, in time (*chronos*) all created or finite beings eventually grow old, corrode and "die." They disintegrate to release their atomic energy and matter to be recycled by God or nature into new forms of life and beings. This natural process of birth, growth and death is impersonal and universal. It is God's impartial cosmic law (natural law) that governs all things and living beings, including plants, animals and human beings.

Human beings, animals and plants do not die because of the primordial divine punishment due to the supposed original sin that was committed by Adam and Eve in the remote past in the mythological Garden of Eden. Natural death is not a punishment for human sin. On the contrary, natural death is God's design, provision and will for all the created and finite creatures within the cosmos. Therefore, the Church's new theology has to embrace evolution as God's method for the creation of the cosmos and death as a natural process inherent in evolutionary creatures. It is erroneous for religion to reject natural death and portray it as a great evil and a consequence of God's punishment for the primordial human sin.

The traditional theological pivot of the religious myth of Adam and Eve's original sin must be rejected. Adam and Eve's supposed original sin as the historical paradigm for understanding human nature, sin, atonement, soteriology or salvation has led to erroneous and static Christian doctrines which reject science, especially evolution. The Church must repudiate much of St. Paul and Augustine's pessimistic theology of human nature due to the supposed inherited sin and the necessity for the incarnation of God in history through Jesus as the Christ or embodiment of God's redemptive *Logos* (Incarnate Word) in cosmic history.

Human culture, technology, language, philosophy and knowledge exist in a perpetual process of growth and change. Religion, as part of this constantly changing societal phenomena, cannot itself exist alone in some frozen state of unchanging Church or religious community in complete isolation from the surroundings of a dynamic, living social, religious or moral life and culture of that respective society.

The constant religious reformation of world-view, thinking, doctrines, practices, liturgy, canons, creeds, theology and ethics, and the correlative ongoing renewal of faith, meaning for one's own being and consciousness of the miracle of life are essential elements for any religion that seeks to survive and remain relevant through the evolutionary changes of many different ages. That is the testimony of Judaism and correlative survival of the Jews as an identifiable group of people through thousands of years. The Christian Church itself began as a failed attempt to bring a messianic movement and reformation of traditional (Levitical) Judaism. "The messianic Jesus Movement" (Christianity) was both a rejection and modification of the Mosaic tradition by Jesus that initiated the reformation of Judaism.

## 3. Constant Change and the Church's Need For Continuing Self-Reformation

The world, history, knowledge, culture and language being evolutionary and changing, the Church itself needs to keep constantly renewing and reforming itself. This constant ecclesiastical self-study, self-assessment and self-reformation is essential if the Church wants to survive and remain both relevant and meaningful as an institution. The Church that Jesus founded with St. Peter as its head became very different when Saul, a well-educated Pharisee became converted to Christianity.

Saul whose name was changed to Paul after his Christian conversion, employed his Greek philosophy and Roman flexible culture to reform Jewish Christianity. He took the original narrow Jewish sectarian apocalyptic Messianic cult that was centered around Jesus, and which proclaimed that Jesus was the sinless (innocent), rejected and crucified Jewish Messiah (Christ), and effectively transformed it into a universal religion by getting rid of the need for circumcision and observance of the Jewish food taboos.

However, St. Paul retained the Jewish apocalyptic and patriarchal religious heritage. These two elements underlie St. Paul's pastoral letters and theology of the urgency regarding the imminent resurrection of the dead, the return of Christ, God's judgement and the end of the world. Like any Jewish male of his time, St. Paul also strongly believed that women were inferior to men and that God had chosen men as the leaders of his people in the Mosaic Covenant (Judaism/Jewish Church) and the New Covenant (Christian Church).

As a result of his flexible teachings and missionary journeys, St. Paul converted many Greek and Roman "pagans" to Christianity as a new universal religion. Paul also proclaimed that Jesus was the "Son of God" and divine savior of the world. He proclaimed that Jesus was God's agent of redemption and salvation into the heavenly state of "new being" that is characterized by unconditional love, nonviolence, grace, faith, obedience and peace to God. Paul rejected Jewish legalism and both religious and social exclusiveness. His formerly pagan Greek converts understood that Jesus was the "Son of God" in the same manner in which Hercules was the "son of Zeus" within the Greek myths. These "pagan" Greek ideas came to dominate the Hellenistic Christianity. The Apostles and the Nicene Creeds were later formulated within these Greek and Roman pagan cultures, ideas and world-view.

Much of what was taught in these creeds and dogmas of the Church, such as the Virgin Birth of Jesus, the resurrection of Jesus and his ascension into heaven (sky), and his physical return on the cosmic resurrection day to judge the world and establish God's perfect Kingdom on the Earth for the righteous people and punish the evildoers by throwing them into the hellfire or a burning lake, are largely part of this pagan world-view that the pagan Greeks and Romans introduced into Christianity. The African, specifically, the Egyptian mystery cults were also influential in the shaping of Christian theology, particularly as it regards the sacraments of baptism, the Eucharist and holy orders. Mysticism, resurrection and union with God either through holy communion or mental enlightenment is also part of this "pagan heritage." The early Church was more open to change and new ideas even if these ideas come from pagan philosophical and religious sources.

The Church today, should also remain open to science and world cultures as sources of new ideas and truths. God is present in these world cultures, religions, philosophies and sciences in order to effect order, meaning, truth and the needed changes or positive transformation. The Church of God should remain the open medium of God's revelation of new truths, commandments, moral values, societal directions, and nobler goals of inclusiveness, unconditional love, free forgiveness and peace. The Vatican I and II Councils provide ample evidence that the traditional Church must remain self-reforming if it wishes to remain current and relevant for today's world. For instance, Vatican II did away with the popular traditional Catholic Latin mass and the bigoted and exclusive

Christian doctrine of "outside the [Roman Catholic] Church, there is no salvation" (*Extra Ecclesiam Nulla Salus*).

The Vatican II Council was very revolutionary for the Christian Church, global theology and ethics. For instance, the Vatican II *Decree on Non-Christian Religions* positively affirmed the universality of God's redemptive grace in creation and redemption. This declaration reversed the bigoted dogma which taught that there was no salvation outside the Christian (Roman Catholic) Church.

The radical decrees of Vatican II and theological reformation led to the unprecedented global theological flexibility, religious inclusiveness and both soteriological and moral relativism. This is the broad and complex theological context in which there was the historic acceptance that Non-Christian religions, such as Islam, Judaism, Buddhism and Hinduism were accepted as avenues of God's redemptive grace and supernatural salvation. This position did not please the traditionally conservative and exclusivist powerful cardinals and their followers, particularly, the late Archbishop Lefvebre of France.

Nevertheless, this globalist religious position and inclusive theology of salvation, have most effectively transformed the Roman Catholic Church into the unrivaled powerful mainline Christianity in the world. Since then, Roman Catholicism has turned Vatican II decrees into powerful moral and theological tools for interreligious dialogue and ecumenism within the pluralistic world. This is true despite the tragic fact that the ignorant, misinformed, mutually exclusive, and intolerant religious Catholics and Protestants in Northern Ireland, like their missionary converts in Uganda, regard each other as religious enemies.

However, the Catholic Church's process of self-reformation did not begin nor stop with the Vatican II. It began with Peter and Paul as a result of their own missionary activities among the Gentiles (cf. Acts 6, 10, 15 and Gal. 1-6). Like God's own ongoing processes of continuing creation, redemption and revelation, the Church's processes of study, acquisition of new knowledge and truths, and subsequently, effectively carrying out the essential self-reformation, is a constant and an endless religious and revelatory holy task. This tedious and difficult task is God's mandate and duty for the Church, theologians and ethicists.

Accordingly, after an extensive collaborative study by the theologians, ethicists and scientists and having conveyed their recommendations to the Pope, the Roman Pontiff finally acted on behalf of the Church, God and the world, in his official capacity as "the Vicar of Christ on the Earth" to rehabilitate Galileo. On October 31, 1992, Pope John Paul II amazed the world by his ecclesiastical formal reversal of the

Catholic Church's former official rejection and condemnation of the Copernican and Galileo's heliocentric teachings and writings.

The Pope solemnly apologized for the Church's persecution and trial of Galileo. He declared that Galileo's scientific heliocentric (sun-centered) teachings were correct and true. The Pope went on to declare that the Ptolemaic geocentric world-view, which the Church had supported and defended as the [divinely revealed] truth, was wrong ("in error"). This historic official papal declaration effectively put to an end the conflict between science and religion. In addition, the Pope further infallibly declared (*extra cathedra*) that there were two centers of God's revelation in the cosmos. The first universal center of God's revelation was that of nature, which is governed by God's process of natural law. This divine revelation is universally accessible to all intelligent and rational beings through scientific investigation of nature, reason, experimentation and mathematical computations of empirical data. The knowledge and truth established by this scientific method reveals God's works and wonders in cosmic creation.

## 4. Evolution as God's Method for Creation Of the Cosmos and Humanity

In 1996, four years after reversing the Church's past formal condemnation of Galileo and his heliocentric teachings, understandably for most academic theologians, ethicists and scientists, the Pope officially embraced Darwin and evolution. In his official ecclesiastical capacity as the infallible head of the Church and God's Viceroy on Earth, the Roman Catholic Pontiff formally declared that Charles Darwin was correct in his teachings of evolution as the process by which the cosmos and all creatures, including human beings, came into existence. The Pope declared that evolution was not a mere theory, but fact. He also declared that evolution was God's method and process for the supernatural creation of the cosmos, life, creatures and the historical emergence of the unique thinking human beings (the *Homo sapiens* or the *imago Dei*).

Definitely, the acceptance of evolution as God's method for the creation of the cosmos calls for the revamping of traditional doctrines of creation, grace, sin, the fall, human nature, ethics, sacraments, christology, salvation, atonement, heaven and hell. Accordingly, this book has been written from an evolutionist Christian, and global theological perspective in order to meet part of that intellectual, theological moral and religious need.

The second center of God's revelation, according to the Pope, was that of faith and religion. Traditionally, this center is referred to as "special revelation," whereas the first center is referred to as "natural revelation." Special revelation is based on faith in God and historical experiences of the special encounters with the divine mystery in life and the world. For instance, Moses mystically encountered God on the holy Mount Sinai through the divine symbol of the Egyptian Sun-God (*Amun-Ra*) as represented by the setting sun seen through a shrub or the "burning bush" (Exod. 3:1-6).

In historical reality and spiritual experience, this was Moses' transformatory moment of theophany and revelatory inner spiritual of the holy encounter with God and moral enlightenment. He awoke from his moral sleep and apathy. Moses realized he was being moved and called by a higher power, the nameless Transcendent Mystery or God to go back to Egypt on a divine self-sacrificial mission or redemption. On the mountaintop, and in a moment of contemplation, Moses realized that he was the reluctant appointed deliverer of his own people from oppression. This was a moment of great wonder, awe, and the divinizing holy mystery of God's encounter, call and commissioning as the Messiah. This truth is simply communicated in Hebrew Scriptures by the story and metaphor of Moses' encounter with God at Mt. Sinai through the glorious glow of the sunset, which Moses indirectly viewed through the background of a bush.

The sun's natural light became both symbolic and revelatory of God's inner spiritual "guiding light" within the divine media of the mind and spirit which exist in each person as a child of God or *an imago Dei*. This experience become both revelatory of God and transformatory of Moses' own personal moral life, world-view and religion. As a result of the spiritual encounter with God, Moses was transformed from a fearful political refugee and moral skeptic into a prophet, religious leader and "Messiah" or God's chosen "Deliverer" of the Jews from Egypt into freedom. This is still true even when that freedom was of the nomadic life in the waterless hot desert, and journey of faith in quest of "the promised land." This is part of God's explicit or "special revelation" and human subjective spiritual experiential God's revelation, redemption and truth in human history. Its acceptance is based on faith rather than the accuracy of the testimony of history, science or intellectual conviction.

The mystical encounter of light as an external symbol of God's power for human moral and spiritual illumination is universally accessible by human beings by God's unmerited and free redemptive grace. The best recorded examples of this case are those experiences conveyed by God through various means to Moses, Buddha, Jesus and Prophet Muhammad. These human encounters and experiences of the transcendent holy cosmic Mystery clearly illustrate the redemptive efficacy of God's mediated universal power to inspire, guide, protect and deliver God's people from ignorance, oppression, sin and the domination of evil. The sacraments, as part of special revelation and faith, also work in the same mystical and symbolic manner. For instance, baptismal water becomes the symbol for moral and spiritual cleansing, positive transformation and rebirth eternal spiritual life.

Pope John Paul II's 1996 declaration that evolution was God's method for the creation of the universe, including human beings, effectively negated the traditional oppressive myth of Adam and Eve as the cause of the fall of humanity through the original sin. The presumed divine curse of the original sin is hereby exorcized in God's holy name! The curse of the original sin is forever banished from theology, Church, religion and humanity. This process of exorcism should effect liberation for all human beings from the chains of human depravity and corruption that were previously attributed to the defects that were inherited from Adam and Eve's supposed original sin. This is especially important for women who have been oppressed because of Eve's sin.

Therefore, to these vilified and oppressed women as "Eves," I bring and proclaim the good news of God's universal liberation from the destructive chains of patriarchal mythology of male-supremacy, exploitation and dominance based on the supposed curse of Eve by God (cf. Gen. 3). To these male dominated and oppressed people through sexism and discrimination, I proclaim the good news of God's liberation. God assures them that this traditional male oppression of women is due to men's sins of self-deification, male-chauvinism and idolatry, rather than God's will and holy ordinance as some patriarchal male-chauvinistic subordinationists and oppressors of women have blasphemously and erroneously affirmed. That is, that the women are cursed by God and eternally subordinated to the domination of males as their punishment for causing the original sin and evil in God's perfect world (cf. 3:1-24).

To the patriarchal male oppressors of women, God says, "Repent! Live in love, respect, peace and harmony with women as sisters, mothers, lovers and friends rather than as enemies, slaves, servants and sex objects." If one disgraces another person, he or she is also disgraced, because we are all interconnected. What happens to one person in the community indirectly happens to all and will affect all the members of that community in some varying degrees. All human beings are linked together in the common chain of life and God in whom we all share a common bond of both divinity and humanity. In God, all human beings are fellow brothers and sisters, irrespective of who or what they are and where they live.

We can no longer blame Eve, "the Devil" and "the fall" or "original sin" for our moral failures and evil deeds. Human beings are no longer considered born evil in need of the sacrament of holy baptism to wash away the supposed original sin of Eve and Adam, which never really existed. Therefore, Eve and the Devil can no longer serve as the moral and spiritual scapegoats to be blamed for the human temptations, irresponsible misuse of personal freedom and commission of evil. The irresponsible excuse of "the Devil made me do it," is no longer acceptable. However, the expression will remain in use as a metaphor for personal moral irresponsibility, scapegoat, denial of the reality of personal freedom and moral escapism.

Indeed, each person has been liberated to face the reality of the ever-present divine offer of freedom, grace, choice and responsibility in becoming the person God created each person to become. Moral failure and its consequences can no longer be blamed on someone else, Eve, the Devil, the neighbor, the tools, the teacher, the parent, society and God. Ultimately, one has to confront oneself as the real "Devil," and the rebellious and sinful true Adam and Eve. This truth can be morally and spiritually frightening! Nevertheless, this truth will set us free to become God's obedient moral agents in the world in the awareness of our role as God's ambassadors in the cosmos and custodians of God's creation.

A new systematic theology of the Church, soteriology, sacraments and ethics have to be constructed according to evolution as the new truth. This book represents part of this noble effort. However, much of the traditional theology, ecclesiology and sacraments have to be discarded because they assume that perfection lies within the past and that human beings are born corrupt and evil due to the sin of Adam and Eve. In addition, an irresponsible and corrupt society has to invent a new form of Eve and the Devil. New scapegoats to blame, such as the environment (conditioning) or genes (biological determinism) may have to be invented and preached because the human being is the creature that hates himself or herself as he or she really is, morally weak and a sinner. Most human beings are akin to some miserable escapist drug and alcohol addicts who permanently live in a state of denial of the truth and reality of their own tragic condition, while suffering from its ravages.

## 5. Human Ascendence and Access to God Through Many Paths and Sacraments

There are many paths to God. Some of these paths are represented by different religions, philosophies and sacraments. There is no single religion which has a monopoly on God's revelation, knowledge, truth, grace and salvation. Some of the paths to God are well-traveled and reliable, whereas some paths go through snake infested dangerous woods, steep rocky mountains, or hot waterless deserts to the same common destiny, namely, God's Kingdom of Heaven and eternal life. The later, should be avoided, except by the reckless self-sacrificial or suicidal ignorant people. The journey to God does not have to be dangerous and miserable. That sounds more like hell than heaven.

Nevertheless, those who endure these hardships will finally arrive and enter God's Kingdom. It is noteworthy that the manner of the religious quest for the mystical and moral journey of life is also the manner of existence in God's Kingdom itself. This is because the quest for God takes place in God's Kingdom itself.

Amazingly, the moral, spiritual and vision quest for God is the journey of faith which ultimately begins in God and explicitly ends in God having obtained the explicit awareness and knowledge of God's omnipresence and the redemptive indwelling presence of God as "Emmanuel" (God with us). This is also the message of Christmas; to catch the vision of God (*epiphany*) and hope for redemption and survival of humanity through the miraculous birth of a healthy child in the world. Similarly, some people see God in the sunrise and the spring season reminds them of the resurrection and life after death (in the winter). As every winter season is followed by a spring, so must be the case of the human life. Many people reason and believe this to be the case. Human illumination by God and God's revelation are rooted in both the natural as well as the supernatural. The natural embodies and partly reveals the supernatural of which it is the finite medium and expression in the temporal world of time and physical concreteness.

The visionary and the divinely enlightened person gains new moral and spiritual vision and special insight. He or she sees the same world and hears the same voices, but sees more than visual perception and hears more than mere voices. The visual sight conveys to the senses the supernatural mystery and sees God's special activities in the spiritual world and God's miracles where ordinary people see a mere ordinary historical event in the ordinary physical world.

The spiritually illumined (enlightened) person hears God in the wind and through the words of wise people. He or she sees God's message to feed the hungry by looking at any needy and hungry person on the streets or by watching the tragedy of the very sickly and starving African refugees on a local news television broadcast. He or she also looks at evil people and sees demons and looks at obedient people and sees God's saints.

Buddha became the "man who woke up" because he realized that God was not out there in the desert, but within him! Through self-transcendence, Buddha finally realized that his own consciousness and mind were mere supernatural extensions of those of God. He also realized that he was inseparable from God as that Cosmic Consciousness or Mind. Jesus realized the same truth and expressed it in the saying: "My father and I are one." He also added the following statement:"He who has seen me has also seen God my Father" (cf. John 14:8-10).

As such, the quest for God begins with oneself and ends with the awareness of God's indwelling holy presence within oneself. This is more self-evident with the saints in the community in whose holy life, love, good deeds, and wisdom better externally express God's essence and more explicitly reveal God to the world. According to Christianity, by his exemplary and sinless holy life, Jesus performed this revelatory role of God to the world better than any other saint before and after him. As such, to see him was to see God and to imitate his life is also to become reconciled and united with the holy God as our heavenly Father or Mother, and to become a citizen of God's Kingdom.

God's Kingdom and eternal life are not at the destination of the spiritual quest or life. They are the essence of the spiritual quest and the manner of moral life lived by the saint in the world itself. This is akin to love between the lover and the beloved. Love is not a destination of the relationship. It is what is experienced in the ecstasy of the relationship and each other's company.

Love is an open, positive and joyful orientation to be lived and the mystery of a relationship and its experience. True love is not an object or a thing. It is inseparable from the lover and the beloved and their interaction and experience of one another. It is not a tangible thing! Yet, it is the experience of truth and reality that is craved by many human beings. To express true love and to experience it in its purity and fullness of joy is in itself, to experience rapture and life in heaven and heaven's bliss. Love is the sacrament of heaven and to experience it is truly to experience the true joy of heaven and eternal life. Accordingly, in the New Testament God is defined as Agape. Therefore, to be like God is to obey God's definitive universal moral law as revealed through Jesus as the Christ, and practice the moral virtues of agape as the unconditional love, nonviolence and justice for every human being (cf. 1 John 4:7-21).

The various sacraments of the Church function as religious and holy social occasions for both personal and collective love feasts, rituals and experiences of fellowship of one another and with God. The sacraments mediate some effective personal and collective experiences of God's redemptive agape or unconditional love, mystical communion with God, cleansing from sin, union with all the saints and salvation by God.

Accordingly, some of these sacraments are specifically designed to effect a cleansing from sin through repentance, followed by an assurance of incorporation into a loving and beatific mystical union or holy fellowship between God and the obedient and faithful worshipers of God. Baptism, holy communion, holy orders, and confession are the best examples of this case. The most explicit sacrament in this category is that of holy communion. Holy Communion takes place between the worshipers, God and all the saints. In many churches, the one loaf of bread and a communion cup that is shared by many people is the physical representation and social symbol of this mystical union, holy communion and the mutual love between God and the people.

For the traditional Christians, especially the Roman Catholics and some High Church Anglicans, the sacrament of the Eucharist is a central ritual required for the healthy spiritual and moral life of the Christian. This sacrament is required in order to effect a special supernatural processes of human transformation into a divine being through diviniza tion (*theosis*), the acquisition of immortality and salvation. It is believed that when duly consecrated the ordinary elements of bread and wine become efficaciously symbolically transformed by God into the mystical body and blood of Christ. These consecrated holy elements are reverently eaten by the faithful. They are eaten in faith and hope to effect a positive spiritual transformation into a "New Being" and eternal life. This is believed to be the case even when the recipients of these divine elements are physically located here in the world and in this life. God's Kingdom and New Being are believed to be correlative and coextensive with this life in this world, for those saints and the loving people of faith in God.

Through holy consecration, by a duly ordained and church-authorized priest, the ordinary elements of bread and wine are mystically and efficaciously transformed by the power and mystery of God's Holy Spirit into the mystical means of atonement for human sin. They are the mystical and supernatural food and drink that symbolically transform the mortal beings into the special immortal beings. These divinized human beings become like God. They are enabled to transcend the destruction of physical death, by virtue of being mystically united with the risen

Christ and the immortal God. This theology of the Eucharist evolved from both pagan and Jewish religious sources and theologies. The Passover, the day of atonement and sin sacrifice are some Jewish examples of this doctrine.

These are the kinds of holy mysteries and spiritual transcendental experiences which religions affirm to be accessible as God's special revelation and redemptive truth for those people with faith to see them, believe and practice them. Likewise, the scriptures are stories of faith and records of people's special encounters with the Transcendent Holy Mystery. In turn, these stories of the holy encounters with God or the Cosmic Mystery and records of divine messages, laws and directions can also become the inspiration of the readers to encounter the divine mystery in the course of their own experiences or vision of life.

The major world religions' holy scriptures, liturgies, prayers, ethics and traditions mediate divine experience, as they provide the divine light and holy medium for a moral, good, loving, disciplined, prayerful life and the sacred arena for the mystical encounter of the sacred Mystery or God. These holy scriptures also provide stories and myths which enable us to seek a more meaningful re-envisioning and interpretation our own experiences of life, and supernatural activities of the transcendent holy Mystery in order to be enabled to see, read and perceive new divine mea nings in these experiences.

Through self-disciple, renunciation of desire and greed for satisfaction through material things, fasting and contemplative prayer (*Raja Yoga*), Siddhartha was able to transcend the slavery of materialism, and desire for things. He awoke from ignorance and overcame the insatiable desire (*tanha),* and materialism. He was able to transcend them in order to perceive life, history and the world in new theocentric ways like God sees them. By doing so, he became united with God's own infinite cosmic Mind and Spirit in the illumined and blessed state of infinite divine self-transcendent Consciousness (*Nirvana*). This experience of beatitude and blessed enlightenment transformed the contemplative saint (*Bodhisattva*) into the Buddha (the man who woke up), and the incarnation and one of God's authentic self-expressions and revelation of God in the historical and religious processes of the world.

God's supernatural activities, covenants, judgement, moral law and decrees are delivered through the various mediums and agents of divine revelation. These include nature, history, the prophets, messiahs, the Church religious community and the saints. The agents of God's revelation and saints are not limited to any one religion, ethnic or racial group, culture, class, era and nationality. Some examples of these saints, prophets and agents of God's revelation in the world include: Abraham,

Moses, Isaiah, Buddha, Jesus, Muhammad, Paul, Augustine, Thomas Aquinas, Martin Luther, Karl Rahner, Gandhi, W.E.B. DuBois, M.L. King, Malcolm X, Janani Luwum, Julius Nyerere, Mother Teresa, Oscar Romero, Desmond Tutu, and Nelson Mandela. These are men and women who conveyed to the world God's special revelation of love, grace, redemption and transformation into what Paul Tillich correctly called "New Being" (God's Kingdom). God is omnipresent in the whole world and is ever self-disclosing within its history.

The above list contains a few examples of God's special revelation in various places, different eras and developments in both local and global history. Some of these supernatural activities have a broader significance, meaning and value for the different groups of people in the world. But others are very localized and parochial in nature, meaning and application. As a result, they cannot be meaningful or be validly applied to all people of different cultures, religions, nationalities, values or historical experiences. Some of these culturally conditioned revelations of God include food and sex taboos and regulations.

In addition, some of these revelations were specifically cultural and ethnic in scope and value. For instance, the revelation of God through Moses was for a long time understood by most Hebrews to be their own possessions alone. This was essentially the narrow and limited meaning and the value attached the term divine "election." This was specifically in reference to God's election of the Hebrews as God's own special and chosen people of the covenant. The Covenant people became the "insiders and holy members of God's Kingdom" and those people outside the covenant became the "outsiders" or the "unclean Gentiles." The reformers, such as the writer of Job, Ezekiel, Isaiah, Amos, Jesus, Paul, Justin Martyr, Origen and Augustine are examples of those prophets and early religious thinkers and moral teachers who sought to broaden the concept of election and covenant in more inclusive and universalist terms.

## 6. Bishop John Spong's Call for a New Age Reformation

The Rt. Rev. John Spong, an Episcopalian/Anglican bishop, has called for a postmodern complete reformation of the Christian tradition. He is in line with the Judeo-Christian historical process of Church's spread to new cultures, development of and reformation of doctrines and practices, and inculturation in order to meet and effectively minister to the differing spiritual and cultural needs of different cultures and nations in various eras. Martin Luther's German based Protestant Reformation and King Henry VIII's nationalistic English rebellion against the Papal sovereignty and formation of the Anglican Church are good examples.

However, Bishop Spong ignores the self-evident truth and fact that the Roman Catholic Church has undergone so much self-reformation within the past forty years than it had done in most of the second millennium. As the 1992 ecclesiastical apology and radical declaration of Pope John Paul II concerning the Church that erred in 1616 in the condemnation of the scientific discoveries and teachings of Galileo concerning the sun as the center of our solar system and not the Earth as the Church had erroneously taught, indicates that the Church continues the process of self-reforming.

The Pope also stunned the conservative Christian world when in 1996, he further declared that Charles Darwin's teachings on evolution were fact and not mere theory and that both science and religion are valid avenues for God's revelation. The courageous declarations of Pope John Paul 11 clearly indicate to the world that the Roman Catholic Church is taking effective ecclesiastical and moral leadership in the theological reformation of antiquated dogmas, and discarding those in serious error.

Nevertheless, Bishop Spong's call for a new reformation of Christianity is valid and courageous. And it should be taken seriously by the Church and Christian thinkers. It is a theological and moral call for new theology, ethics and a relevant religious language that speaks for the people of today more than those long dead! Bishop Spong provocatively frames his theological theses for universal debate and call for Christian radical theological and moral reformation as follows:

> 1. Theism, as a way of defining God, is dead. So most theological God-talk is today meaningless. A new way to speak of God must be found.
>
> 2. Since God can no longer be conceived in theistic terms, it becomes nonsensical to seek to understand Jesus as the incarnation of the theistic deity. So the Christology of the ages is bankrupt.
>
> 3. The biblical story or the perfect and finished creation from which human beings fell into sin is pre-Darwinian mythology and post-Darwinian nonsense.
>
> 4. The virgin birth, understood as literal biology, makes Christ's divinity, as traditionally impossible.
>
> 5. The miracle stories of the New Testament can no longer be interpreted in a post-Newtonian world as supernatural events performed by an incarnate deity.
>
> 6. The view of the cross as the sacrifice for the sins of the world is a barbarian idea based on primitive concepts of God and must be dismissed.

7. Resurrection is an action of God. Jesus was raised into the meaning of God. It therefore cannot be a physical resuscitation occurring inside human history.

8. The story of the Ascension assumed a three-tiered universe and is therefore not capable of being translated into the concepts of a post-Copernican space age.

9. There is no external, absolute, objective, revealed standard scriptures or universal moral laws of God written on tablets of stone, on the Earth or in Heaven, that govern human ethical culture, religion and conduct in every place and for all time.

10. Prayer cannot be a request made to a theistic deity to act in human history in a particular way.

11. The hope for life after death must be separated forever from the behavior control mentality of reward and punishment. The Church must abandon, therefore, its reliance on guilt as a motivator of behavior.

12. All human beings bear God's image and must be respected for what each person is. Therefore, no external description of one's being, whether based on race, ethnicity, gender or sexual orientation, can properly be used as the basis for either rejection or discrimination. *(Http://www.intac.com/~rollins/jsspong/reform.html)*

Spong's theses and call for a postmodern Christian reformation pose a great theological and moral challenge to the Church and the Christian thinkers. They are definitely timely. They are radical, significant and important for a meaningful relevant and postmodern Christian Church, theology and ethics.

To some extent, Spong's theses should be treated as Martin Luther's ninety-five theses of October 31, 1517 which were posted on the Church door in Wittenberg, Germany near the university where he taught systematic theology. Like Luther, Spong is inviting the scholarly community to debate his theological propositions. Instead of the scholarly debate, Luther was condemned and forced to recant his reformist theological teachings and withdrawal his theses.

However, the impact of Spong's theses on the Church will be very different from that of Luther. The context is different. Luther was a Catholic Priest and the Roman Catholic Church had jurisdiction over him and the university where he taught theology. Secondly, the Roman Catholic Church was also a state established Church in Europe. The Princes of Europe could have easily arrested Luther and executed him on behalf of the Church. Instead, due to the German nationalism, the German Princes sided with Luther and the German Lutheran Protestant Church was born. Thirdly, within the post-Reformation Era, the Christian Church is so fragmented into many different denominations which hardly care about each other's doctrines.

Consequently, outside the academy and the Episcopal or Anglican Church, Bishop Spong's theses may not be read or discussed. There is no central ecclesiastical body to organize a theological debate of Bishop Spong's theses or try him as a heretic. If these theses were contrary to the teachings of the Episcopal Church, then, he would be tried by that body. But, they are not. Therefore, in the absence of the equivalent of the inquisition, Bishop Spong's theses remain mainly radical theological propositions for academic theologians to debate. As such, the next section of this chapter is devoted to the discussion of some of these theses as well as the questions raised by Mary Daly in her book, *Beyond God the Father*. I will state my own theses and outline the assumptions behind the religious-philosophical discussion as well the theological and moral arguments in the rest of this book.

## 7. Theological Axiomatic Principles And Moral Assumptions

As part of a Christian academic theological, moral and religious response to the challenge and criticisms of the Church, traditional Christianity, theology and ethics by radical and reformist Christian thinkers like Bishop Spong, and Mary Daly, and in order to educate the audience beyond my regular students, I have attempted a reformulation of some central traditional Christian theology and ethics within a contemporary evolutionist context. Some conservative Christians may find this task in itself radical and even threatening to their cherished traditional Church and its dogmatic or confessional theology and ethics. They are partly right.

Nevertheless, the intention of this book is to defend those central Christian doctrines that are essential to Christianity. In order to accomplish this task I will suggest an inclusive, globalist and scientifically based new formulation for these doctrines. This theological and moral reconstructive task for theology and ethics will be undertaken within the context of the natural and biological sciences, especially, the biological evolution of all living things from a single celled animal in the water, including the more sophisticated evolutionary, thinking, moral, free and self-transcending animals in the form of the human being (the *Homo sapiens*).

In carrying out the above reconstructive theological and philosophical task and providing some alternative new theological and moral answers to some universally common theological and basic moral problems, I have followed some basic universal theological, philosophical assumptions, moral axioms and social principles for an inclusive global Christian theology and ethics for a new age or the Third Millennium. These moral, theological and philosophical axioms and principles include the following:

1. God is a transcendent cosmic creative, sustaining and redemptive Spirit and not a physical being or tangible object, such as a "Superman," "Wonder-woman," or "Santa Claus." God does not have gender, color, time-span, physical location or spatial limitations.

2. God is a pure energy as a Cosmic Creative Spirit that encompasses and pervades all things. God creates, sustains and transforms the creatures and all creation through the processes of evolution, according to the "natural law."

Natural law functions under the direction and providence of God as its creator. This occurs through the cosmic *Logos*, as God's cosmic principle of: creation, evolution, sustenance, order, life, reality, structure, knowledge, goodness, unconditional love *(agape*), grace, truth, mind, transformation, and redemption (cf. Gen. 1:1-3). Therefore, true love and obedience to God must include justice and the praxis of unconditional love of the neighbor, and respect for nature, and the protection of the environment.

3. God is a self-transcendent, creative mind or knowing spirit that is mirrored in the human beings, mind, spirit, mystery, creativity, love, self-transcendence, freedom, and moral responsibility. Therefore, in order to see, hear, know and understand God, one has to see, hear, know and understand a perfect human being. The authentic human being is the true *"imago Dei,"* and the universal concrete and natural divine medium for God's chosen concrete self-expression and supernatural self-disclosure in this historical and material world.

4. Each loving, intelligent, moral and free being is both an ambassador and incarnation of God in the community, historical process and the world. Jesus and Buddha are the best examples of this God's incarnation as a means of contextual and historical self-communication and self-disclosure in the world, which universally takes place in each intelligent, obedient and moral human being.

5. Apart from God and death for all finite and created beings, there are no universal absolutes. Goodness, love, faith, knowledge and truth are relative since they are conditioned by the local medium and context in which they occur. This includes factors, such as: age, gender, race, culture, world-view, education, religion, intelligence, health, experience, technology, skills, objectives, and history of the person doing the thinking. A fool or an ignorant person will see, perceive and process events and truth differently from the intelligent and wise person!

Therefore, there are no eternal, infallible absolute books or commandments that are revealed to human beings by God. Human beings are essentially finite and conditioned beings that are incapable of apprehending and recording the infinite revelations of God accurately as they are. This is essentially because the nature of the finite mind is to distort complex reality by chopping it into smaller comprehensible units in order to process it. This is analogous to the way that computers narrow down and simplify complex tasks into a series of numbers composed of zeros and ones in order to process the complex reality which is definitely greater than zeros and ones.

Various forms of holy Scriptures are by analogy of the computer also a mere series of zeros and ones to be computed together to arrive at the truth of God's infinite cosmic revelation and supernatural activities in the cosmos. Each set of scriptures is incomplete. It needs the complimentary addition of God's reality, truth and revelation as found in other religious traditions. The various religious traditions and scriptures are component parts of God's giant puzzle of supernatural activities in creation and redemption and self-revelation to the world.

Therefore, all scriptures as God's revelation, including the Torah, Bible (Old and New Testaments) and Qur'an are incomplete and imperfect. They contain cultural and moral biases as well as scientific and historical errors. These holy books were written by the ancient godly human beings in the name of God. These scriptures are not absolute nor universal in scope and application. These holy scriptures provide good spiritual and moral guides to many aspects of life. But they are neither infallible nor inerrant.

6. The saints are God's concrete and historical epiphanies in the world. They manifest God in life, the community (Church), and the historical processes of the world. Therefore, in some figurative sense, to see a saint is to see God. It is also to encounter God's *theophany* or revelation, grace, love and redemption. The saints are God's universal true mirrors of God's essence of love, mercy and humility in the community, history, human evolution and the world.

7. The prophets are men and women who listen to God, obediently respond affirmatively to the divine call to God's special service, and uncompromisingly speak for God in the world and its historical processes. They are witnesses to the holiness and justice. In the name of the holy and just transcendent God, they call the leaders of the world and the religious communities to practice the moral principles of unconditional love, universal free justice and protection for the poor, the orphan, the powerless, the defenseless and the needy. Amos and Jesus provide the

best examples of this case. Jesus' ministry was directed to the poor, the oppressed and the outcasts (cf. Lk. 4:16-21: Matt. 5-7; 25:31-46).

8. God's activities in the cosmos and history are *incognito* and never directly visible. God's cosmic activities are invisibly mediated through nature, the prophets, saints, heroes or heroines, parents or loving people (angels). The invisible God works through the visible moral agents and natural law to effect his or her divine will and to establish his or her ideal and peaceful human community or kingdom.

9. The Messiah or Christ is any obedient, faith-filled, courageous saint of God who is sent to deliver God's people out of moral or physical evil, and threat of destruction. Moses, Buddha and Jesus are such examples of God's Messiahs in the world. The messiahs are many. They are real courageous holy men and not "Gods." Men and women are persuaded to forsake evil and chose the good in order to be saved by God!

10. God does not reveal nor write perfect books in the form of universal holy scriptures. In actuality, there are no perfect, inerrant, eternal and absolute divinely revealed holy books. The Torah, the Bible and Qur'an are books written by "men" and canonized as God's Word (holy Scriptures) by the religious community (Church).

No sacred book is ever literally true and valid in every word, commandment, directive and detail for all time and for every person in the world. The omnipresent cosmic Creator-Redeemer God is alive and continues to reveal and speak his or her living universal Word (*Logos*) of creation and redemption. As such, Jesus could validly, in the name of God, reverse God's laws through Moses.

11. Religion is an essential dimension of human life, co-existence with other beings, and harmonious fellowship with the self, the neighbor and God. It is the varied universal expression of the human spirit, mind, moral consciousness, freedom and self-transcendence.

Religion is a medium for self-contemplation, self-examination, self-empowerment, unconditional love, power of forgiveness, reconciliation, healing, restoration to wholeness, well-being and peace. This is the experience of heaven on the Earth. This supernatural grounding of life is essential in order to live a most meaningful, moral, loving, satisfying and happy life, irrespective of the troubling presence of the reality of evil, uncertainty, transitoriness of all created things, anxiety about the unknown future, pain, suffering and death.

12. Religion and ethics are the universal twin spiritual, moral and cultural avenues of God's judgement and redemption as therapeutic reconciliation with the self, God, the neighbor and the world. Mind (intellect, reason, and intuition), love and faith are God's unmerited free universal endowments of supernatural grace. These divine supernatural

gifts mystically effect God's supernatural process of creation and redemption as both meaningful sustenance and positive transformation of life by God through his agents of natural law, moral agents, the Logos and the Holy Spirit.

13. The moral community, anywhere in the world, is an effective and intrinsic component of the inclusive, universal and redemptive Church of God in the world. This Cosmic Church of God does not require the sacrament of holy baptism as its condition of admission by God. It is an open community of God's people and God's Kingdom which is entered into by virtue of birth as a human being, into the local moral human community.

The members of God's Kingdom experience the redemptive unconditional love and free grace of God through this redemptive Cosmic Church. This is true inasmuch as when one is born or comes into God's community in any part of the world as a new member of the local community is unconditionally welcomed, accepted, loved, protected, and nurtured with diligent tender care, compassion and dedication. Later, when the child grows up and makes mistakes, he or she should be forgiven, and corrected in love. The grace, love, forgiveness and peace of God are mediated to God's people in the world through the obedient, loving, caring and saintly members in any local moral community in the world.

These humble saintly men and women are consecrated by God. They exist as God's true efficacious priests and mediators of God's love, mercy, forgiveness of sins, peace and eternal life in the world. They exist in every human community in the world to effect and mediate God's presence and kingdom in that part of the world. People implicitly know these high-priests of God and seek them out in order to be healed or blessed by God's healing and renewing power which flows through them to bless, heal and positively energize and transform the community and the world into God's Kingdom of love, contentedness and peace.

14. Prayer is not a form of religious magic or a bribe to God. Prayer does not move God to do something (a miracle) for the people as a reward for their faithfulness and devotion. The true worship of God consists of thanksgiving and praise for the supernatural special unmerited gift of life, order, mystery and cosmic beauty in the world. True prayer and worship are also the essential components of a self-conscious process for human self-composure, reflection, spiritual mobilization, recharging, self-refocusing of body, mind, spirit, and energy toward a particular goal and purpose.

Like a powerful laser beam, prayer acts as the focusing spiritual and mental mechanism to harness and channel the human supernatural power in daily life and the world. Prayer acts as the laser beam to heal or to accomplish desired tasks. The collective prayer of God's people can positively affect and transform the community or world history because of its enormous collective power. For instance, the sick can be healed.

15. Faith is the implicit and latent power that exists in each free, intelligent person as the courage to be a finite human being in an indeterminate and changing world. Human life is impoverished if faith as the positive and intrinsic divine power and courage to be human in the absence of guarantees, is lost. Life is lived by faith, if one wishes to be happy. Faith is the necessary courage and guidance to find the ultimate meaning, love and satisfaction in the mysteries and transitoriness of life.

The doctrines of fatalism, determinism and predestination are morally irresponsible religious and intellectual denials of human consequential freedom, openness and the indeterminate nature of most of human choices and their consequences in human life and history.

16. Good deeds and diligent work are part of any true religious tradition. Good deeds as the fruits of divine grace, positive faith and obedience are a universal moral obligation. Thus, good deeds, diligent prayer and obedience are prerequisites of sainthood. To do good deeds of the unmerited grace and unconditional love is to become like God. Good deeds are those deeds which enhance life, beauty, peace, love, justice, forgiveness, reconciliation, compassion, harmony and happiness in the community and the world.

17. Unconditional love (agape) and free forgiveness of sins are the highest universal expressions of holiness and piety. They are the universal manifestations and evidence of the effective presence of God's Kingdom in the world. Christianity is only a more evolved and better religion inasmuch as it is the most open, flexible and inclusive global religion of unconditional love and free forgiveness of sins.

18. Patriarchal symbols, prejudiced and sexist religious language should be both condemned and banned by the caring, loving and the inclusive Church and other religious communities.

Religious, and theological language and religiously compelling symbols are culturally conditioned. Metaphors for God, such as "Father," "Mother," "Ancestor," "Lord," "King," and the like are figurative and symbolic. Unfortunately, many young and ignorant people take them literally as actual physical and descriptive biological categories for God. So are the "Virgin birth," "hell' and "Heaven."

Because of the predominance of patriarchy both in society and religion, the masculine metaphors, images, symbols and terms for God have also become the universal standard in religion, liturgy, scriptures and theology. As a result, despite the acceptance of the inclusive language in many churches as a valid theological policy, terms for God, such as "Father," and "King" are more compelling and preferred by most people over terms such as "Mother" and "Queen" to refer to God. For most people, "God's Kingdom" has more of a religious reassurance of heaven and the expected future perfection than other terms, such as "God's Realm."

However, the nameless and transcendent God does not care which cultural and religious term or symbol we prefer or choose to use for him or her. Nor does God care about human honorific doctrines, such as "the Virgin Birth" in reference to Jesus' sinlessness or unique biological birth.

19. Every human being is born free, incomplete, and open to many competing alternatives to choose from for his or her fulfillment and destiny in life, which he or she must work hard to actualize into a tangible reality. God does not determine the fate of human beings or that of their communities and nations. Human beings are free moral agents who are responsible for what they choose to do or become.

20. The "Devil" does not exist in objective reality. The "Devil" is a powerful symbol and human moral personification of evil, temptation, scapegoat for moral failure, negative principle of life and chaos within the cosmos. For many irresponsible people, the Devil serves as a scapegoat and an excuse for embarrassing moral failure. Courts of law do not accept the plea of "the Devil made me do it!" The Devil is the real culprit that does evil and goes to jail as punishment for misuse of freedom. In true monotheism, there is no room for the Devil as God's adversary.

21. Evil is not a thing. Evil in itself is an absence of goodness, or its diminished expression, such as an imperfection or the corruption of the good thing. Evil is an absence of the goodness and perfection in the same way darkness is the absence of light. Evil is a contrast of essence and existence or what "ought to be" and "what is." Ultimately, moral evil is due to the human freedom, ignorance, hubris and tendency for self-centeredness, greed, selfishness, malice, hate, rebellion, and temptation to deify oneself into God, and refusing to respect or obey the experience, knowledge and directions of other people. This was Adam and Eve's real moral dilemma, and it is still the case for every intelligent and free moral agent (cf. Gen. 3) in the world. They all face the same temptation, namely, to become "like God" or "become God."

22. "The fall of humanity" is not a literal historical event that took place in the remote perfect past. The fall is the religious, theological, and mythological story of a unified human history that originated in a perfect God and became diversified, imperfect and evil as time passed.

However, the fall universally exists in the human consciousness as the acute awareness of moral failure and guilt. The fall exists as the moral and spiritual reality of the unbridgeable gap and sharp contrast of "what is" (existence, actuality and history) and "what ought to be" (essence, ideal, dream, utopia, and hope of perfection in the future).

The fall and guilt are results of human intellect, freedom, moral consciousness, and self-transcendence, as well as the inevitability of human moral failure to do what one knows to be good and morally superior. As such, only the intelligent beings, such as the moral human beings are conscious of moral evil, sin, guilt and powerlessness to stop sinning or doing evil. They explain this human moral addiction to evil in terms of the "fall and loss of God's original grace, not to sin." This leads to the doctrines of predestination, moral determinism, fatalism and the rejection of the reality of the human causal freedom.

Nevertheless, the human consciousness of the fall and imperfection is a good thing since it drives the moral agent to seek perfection and move from existence in evil and imperfection or the way things are to essence or perfection. As such to become loving, just, good, holy and perfect like God.

23. Dualism is a non-Judeo-Christian world-view. It is rooted in the ancient pagan philosophy which divided existence into two opposed systems, realms and two antithetical Gods. The negative and evil realm was considered to be that of the Devil as an ontological negative God. Matter, body, the world, sex, food, drink and money were placed into the realm of the Devil. The positive and the good that remained, namely the mind, spirit, and self-discipline were likewise ontologically placed into the positive realm of God.

In order to transcendent materialism or "ascend" into heaven, or the good and positive realm of God, one had to escape matter and avoid material things such as indulgence in food, drink, drugs, sex, wealth and the like. Fasting, celibacy, poverty, simple living and asceticism were esteemed as moral and religious virtues. As a result, monks and nuns made religious vows to live accordingly.

This dualistic pagan philosophy and doctrine of humanity both tragically and erroneously portrays the human being in a battle ground between God and the Devil (as an evil God). True Christianity is monotheistic and only recognizes the Devil as a metaphor for evil. Matter and creation, including the world, human bodies and sex are proclaimed to be God's good creation and holy gifts to be honored and not misused.

24. Evolution is God's method for the creation of the cosmos. Evolution is God's natural law that impartially governs life, the emergence of plant and animal life including the free minds of the intelligent, moral, religious, knowing, thinking and self-transcending human beings (*Homo sapiens*).

In 1996, Pope John Paul II correctly declared to the world that science, and particularly evolution, is compatible with the Christian Faith. This intellectual, moral, religious and theological awareness calls for a new theology of God, creation, sin, incarnation, christology, sacraments, salvation and ethics.

25. Adam and Eve did not exist as historical beings in history, as the perfect first couple. They are mere religious mythological figures and scapegoats for human moral evil. Women have been tragically vilified and condemned as "Eves," "embodiments of evil" and "devils" by male chauvinists, mainly because of the myth of creation and human fall as found in the Hebrew Bible. The Christian theology that is based on evolution demands that this biblical myth should be discarded and Eve and all women should be exorcized of this mythological fall and Eve's mythical part in it.

26. Based on evolution, there is no "original sin" that was committed by Adam and Eve, since they are mere mythological religious characters. There was no loss of God's "original grace" to humanity. The human perfection does not lie in the past, but rather in the future destiny with God. There is no time when human beings were perfect. God's grace is fully present and available to all obedient human beings. St. Augustine and John Calvin were wrong in their theological and moral assumptions, inasmuch as they assumed that Adam and Eve were real historical beings who had disobeyed God, sinned and lost the grace "not to sin" (*non posse peccare*) which God had given to them to exercise on behalf of all humanity.

27. Men and women are equal representatives of God in the world. They are both made in God's image (*imago Dei*) and possess the power to effect the supernatural activities of God's creative and redemptive work in the world. Discrimination against women is due to sins of ignorance, male chauvinism, sexism, patriarchal oppression, injustice, superstition, and cultural taboos.

Ultimately, there is no valid theological reason why women should not be ordained as priests, bishops and popes within the Roman Catholic Church. Mary, the obedient and loving holy Mother (*Theotokos*) of Jesus as God's Logos incarnate and Mother Teresa could make excellent caring, loving and motherly priests, bishops and popes. That is what true divinity, ministry and priesthood are about. Gender in itself has little to do with true Christian ministry.

28. Goodness is a quality of God, life and reality. Whatever enhances life or exists in purity is good. Good is relative to the person doing the evaluation. What is good according to God or the saint, may be called "evil" by a corrupt person. Whatever endangers life and well-being or

causes exploitation, unnecessary suffering, injustice, oppression, violence, premature death, chaos and the degradation of the environment can be termed evil.

29. Natural death is God's provision for the evolutionary advancement and renewal of life. Matter is recycled by death to create new and better or more advanced creatures, including those with higher intelligence and more sophisticated minds.

Natural, timely, quick and painless death is God's universal will and providence. Therefore, it is good because it is God's holy work. In cases of terminally ill people, euthanasia should be welcome as God's provision for a quick, humane painless and "nature assisted rational death" in which unnecessary suffering is shortened and terminated to allow death take place with dignity. To prevent or terminate some unnecessary pain and suffering is noble, loving and morally justifiable as a good deed.

Religions which reject natural death as evil and propose ways to escape it through the promises of a future physical resurrection may do more harm than good. This life is a good gift to be lived in love, joy, praise and thanksgiving. This is irrespective of the presence of evil or imperfection, pain, suffering, and constant threats of death and nonbeing.

Therefore, a person needs positive faith in an eternal and changeless ultimate reality as the basis of faith and source of the courage to be a finite being, and live meaningfully in an evolutionary, open and transitory life in this ever constantly changing world.

30. Human value, ultimate meaning, and happiness do not consist in power, wealth or accumulation of goods. Buddha, Jesus and the other saints were happy because they were in love, union and fellowship with God. Peace and happiness come from God within and not from external material things, such as sex, food, drink, drugs, wealth, fame or power.

31. Hedonism and materialism such as the indulgence in sex, drugs, alcohol and food can ruin the body, mind, spirit, reputation, family and the community. People have to discipline their own cravings for the sensual and ego satisfaction.

32. Each human moral community effectively constitutes a local community or congregation of God's "Cosmic Church." God's "Cosmic Church" is God's open, inclusive and universal holy arena for human creation and redemption. God's cosmic works in both creation and redemption are limitless and holy mysteries which transcend the human barriers and artificial borders of traditional churches, and religions as both narrowly formulated and defined by human doctrines, creeds and ritual practices (sacraments).

Unlike the exclusive human churches and religions, the interreligious, universal redemptive Church of God is inclusive of all God's obedient and loving saints of every religion, generation, race, color, culture, language, nationality or tribe. It does not require communion or baptism as a prerequisite. Entry into this God's universal, borderless, ever open, inclusive redemptive Church and kingdom only requires unconditional love, justice and good deeds.

33. Sex is God's good gift to humanity to be positively appreciated, respected and celebrated in love. Sexuality, marriage and family are defined by the human culture, religion and laws. God does not care about the individual's sexual orientation, marital status or procedures of human sexual intercourse.

Cultural, moral and religious debates on homosexuality and heterosexuality are not of value or concern to the impartial and unconditionally loving Creator and Redeemer, God. God created both groups of human beings. Unlike prejudiced human beings, God the Creator and Redeemer does not prefer or favor his heterosexual people over the homosexuals. Both groups are God's own creations and subjects of God's own unconditional love, grace and redemption. Sexual orientation and preference is a human cultural preference. God does not prefer one culture, sexual preference or sexual orientation, religious affiliation and doctrine over another. After all, sexual practices and preferences are culturally conditioned, whereas biological sexual orientation is a God-given gift. Since all God's gifts are good, and never evil, therefore, a natural sexual orientation cannot be evil in itself.

34. It is positively theologically affirmed that sin is what is thought and done against God's will, moral law, justice, promotion of love, life and peace. Sin is also the human moral failure to facilitate conditions of justice and perform good and merciful deeds of unconditional love, justice and peace. The majority of human votes can only decree what is good for them or bad according to them. However, the majority vote does not transform what is evil and sinful to become good and holy before God by virtue of their votes. God is not democratic nor is his holy Church and Kingdom based on human values and democracy.

God is not elected by the creatures or people as their God, King or Judge. Therefore, God is not answerable to the creatures who are his or her creation. Accordingly, the holy God does not compromise with the sinners. However, the loving God welcomes and forgives all sinners when they repent of sin and evil and enter his holy Kingdom of love, forgiveness, justice, peace and equality.

35. Men and women of different races, colors, languages, religions, classes, and nationalities are all created in God's own image, that is complex and mosaic in its global human expressions. All human beings are by God's "*a priori*" grace elected by God at the moment of special

creation as potential members of his kingdom. Faith in the goodness of life, obedience, voluntary good works of unconditional love, peace, justice, nonviolence and free forgiveness of sins are the holy laws and manifestations of God's reign and his kingdom, in this world.

36. Sin as hate, is a form of human self-centeredness or hubris, low self-esteem, malice and failure to love is the worst and most destructive evil and sin in the world. It is antithetical to God, and his kingdom as the fellowship of love and peace. Hate is also the source of racism, sexism, injustice, oppression, intolerance, violence, wars and genocide. Slavery, the holocaust, religious wars in the Middle East or Ireland, and wars of genocide in Rwanda, Bosnia and Kosovo are examples of this tragedy.

37. Pain, suffering and death are natural. They are not a result of God's punishment for our sins, or those of the supposed original sin of Adam and Eve that caused the human fall from the supposed primordial human perfection and immortality.

However, saints and sinners suffer and die due to different reasons. The reasons or causes of suffering and death for a saint or martyr are noble, holy, just, self-sacrificial and redemptive for the saint, the community, and the world. Examples are the persecution and martyrdom of Jesus Christ by crucifixion on the cross.

The arrest, trial, imprisonment, (torture and capital punishment of a criminal), are in some cases, forms of freely chosen and self-imposed existential hell. Unlike the atoning and redemptive vicarious pain, suffering and death of the saint, such as that of Jesus, apart from deterrence to crime, the suffering and death of a criminal is of little moral, social and religious value. It neither redeems the criminal nor improves the real moral or religious life of the community. It instills fear, cruelty and anxiety in the community, rather than redeeming love and forgiveness.

38. Hell and heaven are not physical or geographical places that are located in time, space or somewhere within the cosmos. For instance, hell is not located in the volcano, Venus or the Sun, or any other fiery place. Likewise, heaven is not located in any physical place, space or the sky above our heads. On the contrary, heaven and hell are voluntary conditions of life as differing states of human existence. Hell and heaven (God's Kingdom and eternal life) are actual voluntary modes of life, mind, spirit, freedom and existence in this world. They refer to different freely chosen modes of human self-completion through concrete choices made in self-fulfillment, self-actualization in the community, history and the world.

Heaven is wherever God's will and moral law are obeyed and both love and peace prevail. Conversely, hell is the human mode of life that is negatively lived in hate, anger, chaos, misery, violence, war, premature death and destruction. The hellish life is characterized by the intense traumatic experiences of "*angst*" or fear of living, anxiety, malice, fear of death, and destruction.

God does not judge or predetermine and predestine to send people to hell or heaven. Instead, people exercise their free will on how they live life, and by so doing, choose and determine their own fates in life. The doctrines of fatalism, determinism and predestination are false and dangerous. They absolve people of their own responsibility for the ac countability of their freedom and voluntary choices they make, and the volitional deeds they perform in the community and the world.

39. The Creator and Redeemer God is impartial and unconditional in his or her works of unmerited universal free grace in both creation and redemption. As a result, unlike human beings, God does not have any favorite people, political party, political or economic system, gender, holy books or scriptures, religions, messiahs, priests, saints, mediators, languages, cultures, prophets, holy places, sacrifices, and liturgical procedures.

Subsequently, the doctrines of election, covenants, predestination, christology and ecclesiology are often significantly erroneous, divisive, and destructive fraudulent exclusive false religious dogmas. For instance, God is not anymore present in the holy temples and Church buildings than in the bathroom, kitchen, flower garden, ocean beach or the desert. God being an omnipresent, omnidimentional and the transcendent Cosmic Creative Spirit, cannot therefore, be physically limited in the human consecrated temples and other holy places. Wherever God is present, is also Holy Ground and holy temple for prayer and worship. That is everywhere in the cosmos.

As such, all places in the world are essentially sacred and to be kept clean and holy as God's own holy dwelling temple and the Kingdom. The false division of life into the sacred and the secular is a destructive Western religious and political illusion. That is, if this separation is mistaken for real ontological cosmic reality.

Both the secular and the sacred realms are occupied by the same people. The constitutional separation of Church and state is necessary for the protection of the freedom of religion, and diversity of views for all the citizens irrespective of creed and religious affiliation or lack of it. It is not a removal of God from the workplace or the public arena. God being omnipresent cannot be removed from any space or dimension of time. God is even present in the vacuum and black-holes of life and those within the cosmos.

40. The eternal life in God's fellowship with the saints is the positive theological and moral axiomatic affirmation life that is coextensive with heaven as the beatific presence of God's unconditional love, grace, forgiveness and peace. God's Kingdom also exists everywhere and anywhere in the cosmos, wherever God's will, grace, love, free forgiveness of sins and peace are accepted and allowed to reign. These divine values are implanted in the moral and religious community as the normative and fundamental reference, and grounding moral consciousness. They are the normative moral foundations and guides for other values and human laws and cultural or social principles that regulate and govern life. God's Kingdom is open to all obedient and loving saints of God everywhere in the world.

41. God's Kingdom is affirmed to be inclusive of all God's obedient saints of all religions. Like heaven, God's Kingdom transcends the human barriers of race, color, gender, religious affiliation, creeds, human formulations of religious dogmas, marital status, sexual orientation, class, level of technological development, ideology, culture, language and world-view. God's Kingdom is based on the praxis of agape, faith as a positive orientation to the mysteries of life, love, justice and peace.

42. Creeds as mere statements of faith without those good works of love, peace and justice are of no value to God. Jesus said that godliness was universally effectively demonstrated by positive good deeds, such as feeding the hungry, welcoming the stranger, healing the sick, dressing the naked and visiting those in prison (cf. Matt. 25:31-46). These are the universal fruits of the presence of God's redemptive grace in any obedient believer in God and state of saintliness. They are the evidence of a person's citizenship in heaven and God's Kingdom, regardless of religious tradition, race, color, gender and class.

The above material represents some of the main explicit philosophical principles, moral axioms, fundamental theological concepts and assumptions on which this book and various moral and theological arguments are based. The basic assumption is that the human being is born incomplete and becomes a responsible moral agent in the world through the responsible use of freedom to make good or evil (the lesser good and less perfect) choices to complete and actualize one's full potential as a free, creative, responsible, loving and caring human being in the world.

## 8. Humanization, Divinization and God's Kingdom

God's Kingdom and Heaven exist everywhere in the cosmos where God reigns and God's moral law and natural law are obeyed. God's Kingdom exists here on the Earth in the present moment, since natural law and God's moral law are obeyed by many faithful saints of God as the citizens of God's Kingdom, Heaven and eternal life. This is true regardless of whether the human beings are aware of this spiritual reality or not. The spiritually enlightened saints and religious leaders, such as the Buddha and the Christ after their encounter with God realized this to be true and taught it as God's revealed universal truth to their followers (cf. Lk. 17:20-21). Buddha's teaching concerning enlightenment (*Bodhi*) and *Nirvana* are similar to the teachings of Jesus when Jesus declared to his followers that the Kingdom of God was inside them (cf. Lk. 17:21).

In the case of the obedient people, this humanization process as the natural process for the human actualization and fulfillment is also simultaneously, God's correlative and coextensive supernatural process for that human being's special creation by God into a divine being, by divinization (*theosis)* and salvation. At the same time, that is the same process for the damnation of all the disobedient and evildoers in the world. Living, for these people becomes a real nightmare and they try to turn God's world and the Kingdom into hell as they carry out acts of malice, hate, violence and destruction and cause chaos, terrorism and unnecessary suffering and premature deaths in God's Kingdom!

The more hateful and evil people sometimes ignorantly mock the God of love, peace and mercy as they sadistically perpetrate these horrible evils of hate, sexism, racism, intolerance and violence in God's own holy name. Even the self-righteous people sometimes prefer violence and fight the so called "holy wars" (*jihads* and crusades) in mistaken and idolatrous defense of God and religion. A God who needs or prefers to be defended from evil people is a human made idol and not a God that is worthy of human worship and respect. That kind of God is not the Creator-Redeemer and Sustainer God that the monotheistic religious people worship as their God. As such, that kind of God who commands violence and hate is a false dangerous God and an idol that must be rejected and smashed by God's loving people monotheistic people who love a God based state of justice, nonviolence and peace in the world. Jesus and Muhammad set good examples for their own followers by smashing the idols in their respective temples and cleansing them for God's holy monotheistic worship.

The student or reader must remember that this book is intended to be intellectually, religiously, morally and theologically challenging to some unfounded traditional religious beliefs, doctrines and moral theories. It critically examines and analyzes the traditional Christian teachings, doctrines and ethics in order to offer new perspectives and the "New Age" thinking and critique of them. The book attempts to offer some alternative theological and moral perspectives and formulations of the essential Christian truths and values. It accomplishes this important and difficult task in new and more meaningful language and relevant post-Darwinian evolutionary and current scientific world-view. This task is accomplished without losing the unique and central supernatural redemptive spiritual and moral essence of religion, particularly, Christianity.

Finally, I have also included essential material in the appendixes to illustrate that God's presence and ideal moral values can be accessed through different sources, such as the United Nations' *Declaration of Universal Human Rights*, the United Methodists' *Social Principles*, sermons by priests, the documents of Church Conferences, such as that of the Anglican bishops concerning sexuality and homosexuality in the Church. The Seven Principles of *Kwanzaa* have been developed into normative moral principles for building a successful, productive, harmonious and peaceful Afrocentric community.

All the readers of this book are encouraged to read the material on *Kwanzaa* since it very informative on matters of Black holistic spirituality and ethics which operate on the assumption that life cannot be validly separated into the secular realms and the sacred, as the Western systems of religion, politics and ethics dictate. Like Orthodox Judaism, Native American Religion, Buddhism and Hinduism, the African-centered world view holds that the whole realm of life is sacred and constitutes God's Kingdom. All people are called to live each moment and in every place as if they were in the presence of God and live the Kingdom of God.

According to this holistic world-view, the world is God's good world and sacred. All of the world is revelatory of God and serves as holy God's temple. Correlatively, all human beings everywhere are God's children who are constantly also called to live happily together in community as obedient citizens and loving members of the idealized world as a harmonious and peaceful "Beloved Community" or "God's Kingdom." Both this world and this life are special divine gifts to humanity and other creatures so that they could live in love, joy and happiness. Ultimately, our present world is the best of all worlds, and the best existential state of all possible states of creaturely modes of evolutionary being within this evolutionary vast cosmos. As such, God's eschatological (future) Kingdom is already effectively present on the Earth, and within the evolutionary and historical processes of this world.

Therefore, the true mission and task of any redemptive and sound moral philosophy, should be that of moral instruction on how "the good life" is to be found and ethically lived now in the world. All the human beings must be correctly instructed on how best to live together in mutual acceptance, unconditional love, tolerance, harmony and peace on this planet or the Earth, and within this world as God's Kingdom or Heaven. The religious people should be carefully taught on how to live a most satisfying spiritual life within this temporal world and to experience the truly divine personal spiritual reconciliation and fellowship with God and fellow human beings as salvation and the eternal life within the context of the ordinary daily life in "this world as God Kingdom."

By doing so, people learn to have full communion with the neighbor and with God, and thus, live the ordinary life as the effective universal mediation of God's extraordinary supernatural life, salvation and the beatific experience of supernatural life with God, on the Earth as God's Heaven, "Garden of Eden" or "God's Kingdom." This is the unsurpassed achievable heavenly mental and spiritual experience of true contentedness and happiness, such as the state of Nirvana or the *"beatific vision."*

This heavenly, spiritual and mental state is achieved in the world by all God's obedient and faith filled saints, everywhere in the world, and within every era, through diligent good works of unconditional love and justice, prayer and contemplation, like Mother Teresa of Calcutta. These moral and spiritual saints are both morally and spiritually empowered by God's own unmerited free universal gift of supernatural power of redemptive grace, to exercise their true heavenly and supernatural virtues of unconditional love, free forgiveness of offenses, justice for all, happiness, peace, nonviolence, gratitude and thanksgiving.

Accordingly, to see an obedient and loving saint of God at work in the world, is in reality, also to see and experience both God and God's supernatural redemptive in the world. The best traditional examples of this theophany are the Buddha and Jesus. In addition, both the Pope and the Virgin Mary have also served as the mediation of the divine theophany. For many Roman Catholics both the Roman Catholic Church Pontiff (the Pope) as "the Vicar of Christ on the Earth" and the Virgin Mary, as the *Theotokos* or "the Mother of God," have become some additional effective divine vehicles for the meaningful human spiritual encounter with divine and to experience the concreteness of the supernaturally mediated vision of God. God's moral and religious saint is the person who does good because it is good, right and essential for the well-being of the people and the world. The moral saint does what is right because it is right, just, good and a moral obligation and not because of the hope for some divine reward, such as a ticket to Heaven and an entrance permit to God's Kingdom or eternal life.

The saint performs good deeds without counting the cost or expecting any reward from the beneficiaries of the good deeds or expecting God's reward in this life or the one to come, after death. That was the essence of the medieval doctrine of indulgences which Martin Luther and other Protestant reformers found unfounded and repudiated from the Christian doctrines of grace, holiness and salvation. As such, the moral and spiritual saint finds God to be the inspiring "Ultimate Role-Model, Great Teacher" Counselor, "Master" (Lord), and "Friend". The saint seeks to be like God. The moral and spiritual saint is also any diligent moral agent who finds both joy and satisfaction in doing good so as to transform this present moment in this imperfect world into God's perfect Kingdom. The miracles and good deeds of Jesus and those of Mother Teresa provide good examples of this theocratic world-view which proclaims to the skeptics "the good news" that this world is also the sacred Kingdom of God.

Positive and dynamic religious faith is universally an essential prerequisite for religion, love and an open satisfying social life. Faith is the courage to be human and the power for living a finite human life in a capricious world. Faith as positive orientation to life, people and the Cosmic Mystery is the divinely bestowed free gift of God's grace of inner human will power and the moral basis for optimistic and insightful people to believe that this imperfect world, is indeed, the same or coextensive with heavenly God's Kingdom and reign on the Earth. In this respect, faith serves as God's inner call to the faithful people to obey and live a holy life. This is the obedient mode of heavenly life that leads to the voluntary fulfillment of God's commandments of justice and unconditional love.

Therefore, any form of true obedience to God, piety and holiness, irrespective of creed or religious tradition, must inevitably lead to the performance of good works of agape and justice in the world as the essential concrete fruits of true holiness of life and unconditional love. The life of a saint and any truly obedient religious person is externally characterized by self-sacrificial abundant good deeds of socioeconomic justice, agape, nonviolence and peace in the world as God's Kingdom (cf. Matt. 5-7; 25:31-46; Jam. 2:14-26).

Therefore, when human beings hear God's Word (Logos) and obey God's message, implicit moral in nature (natural law) and explicit moral law (commandments and ordinances through the prophets and the Church) and faithfully live according to them in the praxis of agape (unconditional love), justice and nonviolence, they become God's saints and citizens of heaven and God's Kingdom. By their obedience, exercise of God's grace, deep positive faith, prayer and hard work of self-sacrificial good deeds of love and justice, they effectively work to transform this imperfect world into God's perfect temporal Kingdom. This is what realized eschatology is about. God moral saints like Jesus and Buddha came to the realization that God's Kingdom had already dawned on the Earth. This was the central teaching of Jesus as the Christ of God, and the embodiment of God's Logos of God's in humanity and cosmic history (John 1:1-18; Matt 5-7; 25:31-46; Lk. 17:20-21).

## Chapter 2

# Humanity, Religion and Ethics In Global Context

The modern International Community is rapidly becoming closely linked together by technology and the economy into an interdependent, diverse, efficient and well integrated Global Community. This being the case, then, what affects one group of people in one part of the world eventually also affects the people in another part of the world because the different regions of the world are integrated in one Global Community. This is true of the economy, diseases, and abuses of humanrights.

Therefore, the wars of genocide in Rwanda, Sudan, Kosovo and Bosnia could not be ignored by the international community. The Persian Gulf War was fought to prevent Iraq's occupation of Kuwait and possible control the oil trade and flow through the Persian Gulf. Apartheid in South Africa became a global moral and political issue. The Arab-Israeli conflict has become an international moral and political issue that cannot be ignored. Likewise, the past moral issues of the slavery of the Africans and the holocaust of the Jews remain bitter and tragic moral lessons in human history. They compel us to act on behalf of the wronged and injured neighbor to restore justice and well-being, regardless of the cost of this divine and universal moral mandate.

### 1. Globalism and Pluralism

The Global Community is characterized by the complexity of diversity as it manifests itself in cultural, religious, linguistic and political pluralism. Openness to diversity and mutual tolerance are the necessary civic virtues of the Global Community. Cultural, religious and moral relativism is essential components of this Global Community. For instance, the African traditional custom of polygamy is not to be condemned as a moral or social evil. And likewise, the Africans are not supposed to condemn the Western customs of divorce and homosexuality as immoral, unnatural or "anti-traditional biblically based Christianity."

In this global cultural and religious pluralism, God's revelation is overlooked in favor of science, reason, technology and capital investments. The value and influence of religion, culture, theology and ethics are deliberately removed from the public arena and confined to the informal and private affairs. These religious and cultural institutions are marginalized because they are treated with great fear as possible sources of bigotry, mutual intolerance, disagreement, hostility, conflict and violence, as in the cases of the Middle East and Northern Ireland. Subsequently, cultural, religious, moral and linguistic inclusive openness, flexibility, relativism and tolerance are promoted as the ideal civic virtues of the inclusive and diverse Global Community.

The local and national traditional social, cultural, political and economic institutions have had to make the necessary adjustments in order to fit into this new pluralistic Global Community. Similarly, traditional religious institutions must be constructively modified in order face this new challenge of globalism along with its correlative cultural, moral, philosophical and religious pluralism.

In this Global Community, all religions have to compete for converts in a new context in which Christianity and Islam are just a couple of the traditional rivals and usually mutually hostile competitors. Buddhism and Hinduism must be counted as serious additions to the religious options available for people to choose from. In this new pluralistic religious context, a mere dogmatic claim to possess God's exclusive redemptive revelation in the incarnation of God and specially revealed holy scriptures are not enough, since each major world religion claims to possess God's special revelation and holy scriptures.

Therefore, in order to remain meaningful, current, relevant and normative for life within the pluralistic Global community, religion and ethics must be universally both continually reassessed and reformed. This essential academic and religious task must be carried out within the context of the technological and scientific information revolution and synthesis of immense knowledge. Religious and moral self-evaluation and reformation must be continually undertaken in order to remain relevant and sensitive to world religions, cultures, gender and race matters, and issues of local, national and global peace and justice.

This is a nonnegotiable universal moral and divine religious imperative, and the obligatory duty of all God's obedient saints of all religions in the world. This moral and religious duty must be both lovingly and unfailingly accomplished in order for all God's people in the world to live harmoniously and peacefully together, within the inclusive context of the diverse global cultures and human needs of this new millennium.

Christian theology and ethics must also be continually reconsidered and reformulated within the same global context. Traditional values and religious doctrines must be reformulated and restated within the current language, scientific knowledge, openness for diversity, inclusive global cultural and religious tolerance for pluralism as the essential universal pillars, foundation and context for this new global Cyberspace Age.

The ethical, religious and theological formulations of the first and second millenniums are, in most cases, outdated and irrelevant for the intellectually open, spiritually and religiously sophisticated men and women of today. God's cosmic supernatural twin activities of creation and redemption are universally inseparably intertwined and ongoing.

Likewise, God's continuing revelation continues to unfold both in nature and history. As such, God's special revelation did not cease with Moses, or Jesus. Nor did it cease with the Church's canonization of the scriptures as God's "revealed," "spoken" and "written Word" (*Logos*). The cosmic, living God, who is the Cosmic Creator-Redeemer, still reveals himself or herself to the world in creation (nature). God also still speaks his or her creative and redemptive Word (*Logos*) of life, order, guidance, knowledge, truth, salvation and peace in every generation and in every place within the cosmos. God is ever continually creating, sustaining and redeeming the world. This intertwined and inseparable triple dimensional divine process of life takes place simultaneously. Redemption of creation is part of sustenance and simultaneously, the creation of "new being" and "new beings."

Ultimately, according to this global, inclusive, moral, spiritual, religious, theological discourse and reformulation of Christianity and the Church, God's unconditional love and unmerited, redemptive grace in both creation and redemption, are both inseparable and universal in scope. Therefore, no race, ethnic group, gender or class of people is ever disqualified and excluded from God's own universal free activities of unconditional love and unmerited free grace. These inclusive, universal, unconditional, divine activities of love and grace are explicitly manifested in God's processes of "natural law." This is creation through evolution and reproduction; sustenance of life, provision of cosmic order to restrain chaos (entropy), redemption or restoration to wholeness, peace, happiness, and citizenship within God's Kingdom.

## 2. Theology and Ethics in a Global Religious And Cultural Context

The third millennium is a complex era characterized by a pluralistic global context, and an inclusive global religious and cultural background for the study and reformulation of Christian theology and ethics. This is the revolutionary background, context and task of this book.

This complex global context and the natural sciences, particularly, evolution are the fundamental grounding for the present inclusive work on Christianity, religion, theology and ethics for a "New Age" of human inclusiveness, and global interconnectedness. The book has been written for the intellectual and moral citizens of the "New Age" as opposed to the old guard of the past era of exclusive narrow theological formulations of doctrines, moral dogmatic thinking, bigotry, intolerance, religious sectarianism and persecution. In this book, these religious characteristics and practices are both rejected and condemned as moral evils and sins.

The rejection of the Hebrew prophets, Socrates, Jesus and Galileo are cited as some examples of such the traditional religious and community leaders' rejection of truth and God's revelation. The Church mandated brutality of the Inquisition could not suppress the science, logic and the divine truth for ever. With the 1992 official Roman Catholic Church's reversal and apology for the erroneous condemnation of Galileo and his teachings, the Church has finally accepted the universal divine truth that the academic theologians and scientists had already accepted and taught for a long time, even when the Church was opposed to this truth.

Obviously, the Church has no special direct access to God's truth and revelation anymore than the other groups of intelligent and God-fearing scholars of nature, humanity and cosmic history. The study of nature or creation, human nature and history are more reliable sources of the knowledge and truth about God's supernatural activities of free creative and redemptive grace, truths and revelation in the world than the Church and its scriptures by themselves. Faith, scriptures, reason, tradition, history and science constitute an integrated context and system for the discovery, study and understanding of God natural and special revelation.

Based on the intellectual history of the world, it is self-evident that the divine truth cannot be permanently denied or destroyed by such ignorant and narrow minded leaders or bad theologians and moral thinkers. This work is grounded in God's universal, free grace and unconditional love for all human beings. All obedient and loving human beings as *imago Dei* (living mirrors of God), are universally regarded as

God's own adopted children, ambassadors and effective moral, spiritual, creative and physical embodiments and representatives of God in the world, and its evolutionary historical processes.

The human racial, cultural and religious diversities are positively viewed as part of God's supernatural gift through the process of evolution. Diversity provides a necessary contrast and richness that enhances beauty in the world. Diversity also ensures the natural survival of the species. Biological and genetic variation is God's provision for the natural resistance to disease and hence, the survival of all creatures, including the human beings. They are considered to be both good and God's will in creation. As a result, global cultural and religious pluralism, as well as need for love, social harmony, and peaceful human mutual interdependence, are the necessary context in which God's open, universal, inclusive and redemptive Church has been redefined. Both Christian theology and ethics have been reexamined and reformulated in a broader and more inclusive global manner. This is an important and necessary philosophical, theological, moral and religious task.

This radical theological redefinition of God's redemptive Church in a global, inclusive and open manner is consistent with God's own essence of unconditional love (*Agape* cf. 1 John 4:7), unmerited grace (*Sola Gratia)*, and God's free and unrestricted, universal, supernatural activities of both grace and love in creation and redemption. This is the universal self-evident truth that is contained in all sound, moral and redemptive religions. This unlimited, moral, spiritual, religious and theological universal truth is rooted in God's free universal grace, unconditional love, and creative and redemptive activities. These divine moral and religious principles transcend the traditional exclusive, historical Christian Church, and its correlative traditional exclusive soteriological dogmas and sacraments, particularly those of holy baptism and the Eucharist which were traditionally considered to be mandatory for the human attainment of supernatural grace and redemption.

However, like Karl Rahner (*Theological Investigations* and *Foundations of Christian Faith*), St. Thomas Aquinas, found this exclusive dogmatic teaching of the Christian Church to be absurd and theologically problematic. In *the Contra Gentiles,* and several places in the *Summa Theologica*, Aquinas notes that literal and physical insistence on the claims that God's salvation, or the teaching that the entry into God's Kingdom was exclusively for the people who were physically baptized and had received the sacrament of Holy Communion from the Roman Catholic Church, was inconsistent with God's nature as Agape (Unconditional Love) and *Sola Gratia* (Grace). It was also in conflict with God's own free redemptive universal revelation in nature and the natural law. As a result, both Aquinas and Rahner taught a doctrine of God's gifts of effective grace, and supernatural salvation outside the historical Apostolic Catholic Church.

This mode of salvation outside the Church was available through faith, obedience to God, good works and desire for God's salvation (or baptism and the Eucharist). As a Christian philosopher and theologian, Karl Rahner called this wholesome moral life and redemptive spirituality outside the conventional Christian Church, an "anonymous Christianity." Those people who gained entrance and lived in God's Kingdom by means of "anonymous Christianity" were correspondingly also referred to from a Christocentric perspective as the "anonymous Christians." However, if Rahner had written as a Muslim thinker and included the non-Muslims, especially Christians and Jews whom Prophet Muhammad included in God's Kingdom as "the People of the Book," then, he would have referred to them as the "anonymous Muslims," or the "anonymous members of the House of Islam."

In this inclusive soteriological manner, Aquinas and Rahner were able to nullify the traditional exclusive Christian dogma of *Extra Ecclesiam Nulla Salus* (Outside the Church, there is no salvation). They removed the prerequisites of the exclusive sacraments of holy baptism and the Eucharist as conditions for God's salvation and entrance into God's Kingdom. Instead, they replaced them with the universally available conditions of positive faith in God or the Transcendent Mystery, obedience to natural moral law, praxis of unconditional love by the performance of good deeds for the benefit of the neighbor and the community, a virtuous life that is lived according to the moral principles of justice, love, benevolence, nonviolence and peace.

As some prophets, saints and teachers such as Moses, Buddha, Socrates, Plato, Aristotle, Jesus, James, Aquinas, Wesley and Rahner correctly realized and taught, good deeds, moral and spiritual virtues constitute the external visible spiritual condition of the invisible person's soul and inner s spiritual condition. They are the true fruits of God's work in the soul through the permanent divine gifts of God's indwelling grace, the Logos and the Holy Spirit.

Good works of grace and unconditional love are the true, universal, impartial criteria for the true practical measure and universal judgement of any true godliness and sainthood. Any confessions of faith in God, administration of sacraments of baptism and the Eucharist are morally and spiritually barren and worthless, unless they are also accompanied by the necessary fruits of love and grace (cf. Matt. 5-7; 25:31-46; Jam. 2; 1 John 4; 1 Cor. 13). Baptism is supposed to infuse the believer with God's supernatural grace and power to love and do good deeds in the world. It is the good deeds that count, and not the mere administration of sacraments and recitation of creeds or commandments without doing the good works of charity, justice, mercy and love that God demands of all the obedient saints in the world.

Accordingly, in this book, it is both strongly contended and positively affirmed that God's redemptive grace is active in Judaism, Islam, Buddhism, Hinduism, African Religion and Native American Religion as it is in the Christian Church. Ultimately, God's supernatural free activities of cosmic creation and redemption are equally and freely available to all human beings in the world. This availability and access to God's Kingdom is open to all obedient and loving human beings everywhere in the world, both inside and outside the Christian Church. Creation and redemption being inseparable twin activities of God in the world, are both unconditionally effective and accessible to all people everywhere in God's world. They are part of God's Kingdom. This is true irrespective of religious affiliation, creeds and era. They are both impartial and unconditional in nature and cosmic operation as God's universal free gifts for all his or her people.

## 3. The Entire World as God's Global Arena For Creation and Redemption

The cosmic Creator-Redeemer God is an impartial transcendent and an omnipresent cosmic Spirit. Therefore, this omnipresent God is, by essential nature, also ever present in every place, every moment in every age, and in all dimensions of life and reality. This being the case, then the true cosmic Creator-Redeemer God, being transcendent, omnipresent and omnidimensional eternal cosmic Spirit or Creative Energy does not live in special places, such as heaven or the holy mountains, such as Sinai, Kenya, Rwenzori, Kilimanjaro, Tibet, Fungi, or holy rivers like the Nile, Jordan, Ganges, or human-made "holy buildings" like churches, temples, and shrines.

Therefore, to insist that the cosmic Creator-Redeemer God has a particular name, such as "Allah," "Jehovah," and "Yahweh," and only dwells within certain holy places, or to hold the view that God can only be truly worshiped in certain "holy places" in a prescribed manner, and on certain "holy days," is to think of God in anthropomorphic manner and impose human-like finite limitations on God. It is also a sinful human attempt to transform the abstract, invisible Spirit that is the Transcendent Mystery as the Creator-Redeemer God into a mundane, and limited supernatural or magical object of human definition, or creation in his or her own image, and control. The magicians try to harness God's power that is available in the world and use it for their own purposes.

Like many manipulative pious people who worship and pray to God to accomplish some desirable results, the magicians also seek to control God and use God's supernatural power sometimes to do some good and sometimes harm, according to their desired objectives or those of their clients. As a result, these magicians are considered good, if they use God's supernatural power for good deeds, and when they use it negatively, they are considered evil.

This human desire to name God, classify and essentially control and limit God's activities, is a universal human form of self-deification and idolatry. People study, classify and both name things and people in order to control and use them. Likewise, many people also study nature, religion, pray, worship, make sacrifices, and seek God in order to gain access to God's supernatural power (energy) in order to use it like magic so as to achieve some desired goal is a universal phenomenon.

This universal human desire to gain a quick access to knowledge, wealth and supernatural power is rooted in the universal human temptation to overthrow God and become an independent, self-sufficient, all-powerful, rich, happy and self-determining God. Human beings want to control themselves, name and govern others in addition to creation. Name-calling is evidence for this human attempt to name and control other people and things around them.

Accordingly, in the book of Genesis, Adam (Man) names all the things, and later, also names *"the woman" as Eve* ( the Mother of living things). It is implicitly implied by the Yahwist story (myth) that, after the original sin (the fall), *"the man" (Adam)* named *"evil" after Eve*, and blamed women for human temptation, sin and the fall of humanity! This Yahwist account of creation and the fall represents the human egocentric male-chauvinistic negative or misuse of divine power to degrade women and God's good creation. The human being also committed the "original sin" by wishing to "name God" and become God or completely independent of any external dependence or supernatural moral or intellectual direction and physical sustenance.

This male self-deification, chauvinism and idolatrous spirit also underlies much of the Western values and ethics. For instance, the value of a self-sufficient, military superiority, imperialism and various forms of materialistic individualism illustrate this point. Patriarchy is also the foundation of the Western religion and the dualistic world-view that divides the world into two realms. The "sacred realm" was a token realm assigned to God's control and reign as "God's Kingdom" in some far away imaginary place called "heaven." At the same time, the human beings assigned to themselves "secular realm" which was the larger realm. This "secular realm" being equated with the world, was selfishly assigned to the dominion, reign and the "Kingdom of Man!" This is another way for the human being to achieve the divinity and independence from God like the biblical Adam sought to actualize at the beginning of human history (cf. Gen. 3).

Right from the beginning, Adam (man) sought to name creation, creatures, Eve (woman) and God in order to exercise control and domination over them. Magic, sexism, racism, rape, violence, war, murder, genocide, abortion, suicide, slavery, colonialism, imperialism, capitalism, materialism and idolatry are modern examples of this human tendency for self-deification and quest to exercise negative power, or serve as the evil agent of the negative and evil or "the demonic forces" in God's good world.

In short, the inhumane, hateful, unjust, egocentric, rebellious and sinful human being becomes the concrete evil human incarnation of evil forces and negative influence in the human society. By doing so, the rebellious, malicious and evildoers become the real temporal "Devil" in God's good world. This is true in as much as the human being deifies himself or herself, and becomes the temporal evil moral agent for destructive human misuse of both freedom and power, leading to the materialistic domination over things, and the ruthless exploitation of both God's cosmic creation or nature and people.

Even within the Church affairs, where God's reign and Kingdom should be allowed to prevail, human beings have often usurped the central place of God in creation, life, history and human affairs. "Man" or the males have often behaved as gods in the local and international community. They have accomplished this by their creation and institutionalization of the sacredness of the patriarchal societal systems. This is externally expressed by male gods and male-centered religions in which the men were also the exclusive high-priests of their invented major world religions, male gods (God), male symbols or language and curved or sculptured idols. These "Godlike" patriarchs, male popes, priests, kings, pharaohs, emperors and presidents ruled over society in the name of the invisible God of whom they were the divinely chosen, authorized special representatives and visible embodiments.

Within this patriarchal system, the patriarchs or male elders created both the gods and the mental image of God according to their idealized image of maleness including the symbol of ideal "Father," "Patriarch," "King," "Judge," and military commander. In this manner the men created religion and God after their own image, and reversed the process and claimed that God had created them in his own image. As such, what was representative of the ideal "patriarch" or "father," could also be justifiably and validly be said to represent God in the community and the world. Consequently, the male image of God, instead of more loving, creative and self-reproducing female and maternal image of God was institutionalized by men as the symbol for God's essence and concrete self-revelation within the community and the world. The stories of Amen-Ra, Zeus and Jesus provide good examples for this male and patriarchal images of God in religion. This is the kind of anti-female, chauvinistic, corrupt, and idolatrous male-centered religion that Mary Daly correctly viciously attacked, denounced and repudiated in her book, *God Beyond the Father*.

The Roman Catholic Church's doctrines of the papal infallibility and the corresponding Protestant doctrines of the inerrant and infallible holy scriptures, and inflexible human made religious dogmas have sometimes displaced God in religion and the Church. To an outside observer it might appear that among the poorly educated Roman Catholics the Transcendent and holy God has been replaced by a visible patriarch in the form of infallible pope and the Blessed Virgin Mary, whereas among the fundamentalist Protestants, God has been replaced by the fallible "man-made" books as God's inerrant Word. This is idolatry and must be condemned and repudiated from true Christianity.

Furthermore, the exclusion of women from the ordained ministry of Orthodox Judaism, the Roman Catholic Church, the Eastern Orthodox and American Southern Baptist churches is not God's will! It is due to "man-made" (patriarchal) traditions that have sought to empower men and exclude women from positions of power in the home, church, community and the world.

Sometimes, it seems that men have implicitly enthroned themselves in the world, Church and religions as God(s). This happens when God is literary understood as "the Father" and "the Son" within the Christian holy Trinity, which has no female "person." Men (males), as both self-appointed and self-deified gods, have ruled the secular realm or sacred realm as God(s), and have ruled and sometimes terrorized the world, other less powerful men, women, children, and other creatures. Evil men such as Adolph Hitler and Idi Amin are extreme examples of this case of hubris and male-self-deification.

The normal patriarchal power and male hegemony in the world was characterized by the pharaohs of Egypt, popes, the Roman emperors, and divine kings and emperors of China and Japan. What they have done in the past illustrates the universal human temptation of hubris and self-deification into a God. Adam and Eve are mythological examples of what each human being's desires and temptations are like, namely, to become immortal, omniscient and self-determining, just like God. Within this understanding, Jean Sartre was insightful and correct to define the human being as "the being that wishes to become God."

In the *Essence of Christianity*, Feuerbach, himself, said that "Man is God and God is man." This is the kind of crude religious literalism and fundamentalist theological understanding of some poorly educated Christians, who worship the man Jesus as God's actual physical incarnation in history. This is akin to the Greek "pagan" anthropomorphic idea that Zeus could physically disguise himself in many forms and could transform himself into a real man in order to seduce a beautiful woman or carry out another divine mission in the world *incognito*. The attractive simple logic that God has become a man in Jesus could lead to the reverse affirmation that "Man has become God through Jesus-Christ." This is a more sophisticated method for human beings to deify themselves into God(s).

Obviously, such anthropomorphic and crude forms of idolatry fail to take into account the universal reality and truth that human beings are by God's original grace in creation, and in evolution already divine and inseparable from the divinity of God. Human beings are already divine like God whose image they are created. They all share in God's infinite mind, spirit, love, goodness, creativity, moral conscience and they already embody these divine portions and to some various degree mirror God to the world. Nevertheless, God remains infinite and transcendent over all humanity, irrespective of this limited form of gracious free self-projection, divine incarnation and embodiment within humanity.

However, all forms of "a human-made Gods" are mere products of human imagination and mental creation, and therefore, idols. Accordingly, the Hebrew prophets constantly warned the people and their corrupt priests, that to create such gods and worship them, constituted the sin of idolatry and breach of the covenant. Consequently, the second commandment of Moses prohibits both the creation of both mental and physical images of God, since both forms of images constitute idolatry. Likewise, Islam strictly prohibits painting pictures of God in order to avoid idolatry. The Western common form of idolatry includes the child's imagery of God as a fat, kind and generous "White Patriarch" with long gray hair and beard like Santa Claus. Another form of Christian idolatry takes Michelangelo's Sistine Chapel (Vatican) painting of God as a White male as the literal image of God.

This kind of human-made God was correctly understood to be a false God. This kind of "man-made God" was appropriately denounced by Feuerbach, Karl Marx, Nietzsche and Freud as a mere societal illusion, and a creation of human imagination without any reality. They were also correct in their social analysis that this kind of false God and religion associated with it could be harmful for some people. For instance, Marx saw religion as a tool of social control.

Karl Marx correctly viewed the corrupt form of Christianity of his day in negative terms. He viewed religion, particularly the corrupt Western capitalist and feudal Christian Church of his day as the "opium of the masses" that was administered by the bourgeoisie class in order to keep power over the poor masses by keeping their minds focused on a happier life after death. But meanwhile, they were being exploited by the greedy and unjust factory owners who coerced them to work long hours in dangerous conditions for very little pay.

However, the leading Christian thinkers like St. Paul, John, Augustine, Aquinas, Hegel, Kant, Schleiermacher, Soren Kierkegaard, and Karl Rahner, among others, agree that such a God is a mere idol to be rejected by strict monotheists, particularly the Muslims, Jews and Christians. Idols are, by nature, human-made gods. Like their human finite human creators, these idols are limited in terms of space, time and dimensions. A good example of this idol is Whitehead's God that is finite, limited, and ignorant of the future events, and whose consequent pole gets created in the process of cosmic evolutionary history. The other sophisticated human-made idols are those which place God into time and space as the greatest and most powerful of the supernatural beings, spirits of the venerated saints, heroes, heroines, and the ancestors (patriarchs and matriarchs).

Zeus and the Greek Pantheon are the characteristic examples of religious-cultural polytheism, anthropomorphism and idolatry. God and human beings are considered to be the same, except that gods are immortal and more powerful than human beings. Such a view underlies the Christian doctrines of the divine Incarnation and Jesus as the temporal and historical Incarnation of the immortal and invisible God. The perennial human temptation to concretize and limit God's essence either through the doctrines, the incarnations, or covenants, and election is understandable when one realizes that it is very difficult for most people to appreciate the nonphysical and abstract concepts, such as mathematics, theology and philosophy.

Like the Israelites, who, facing serious distress in the desert resorted to worshiping a concrete, visible god in the form of the golden calf for both symbolic control of their own affairs and solace, most unsophisticated religious people also prefer a tangible and a comprehendible "God" for veneration and worship. An idol is any kind of God that the unsophisticated people can see, touch, mentally visualize, understand, name and control. This is as opposed to an invisible, uncontrollable, and abstract transcendent God, who is pure Spirit and Energy, whose presence is a matter of faith, prayer, contemplation, obedience, agape, spiritual power or moral experience, intellect and intuition. As such, like the abstract God of Moses was a problem for the Israelites to accept, the abstract and inclusive Creator-Redeemer God may also become a problem for the more physically oriented people, who wish to impose borders and limitations on God's free grace, love and unmerited activities of cosmic creation and redemption.

The Church's doctrines which try to localize God's presence of the free, universal, divine redemptive grace in the Christian Apostolic Church, and its sacraments of baptism and Eucharist, or preach the bigoted doctrines of "*Extra Ecclesiam Nulla Salus*" (Outside the [Roman] Church, there is no salvation) constitute other common examples of idolatry, as well as dangerous ethnocentrism and religious imperialism. Consequently, many tragic and destructive religious wars of hate and intolerance, such as the jihads and crusades, have been fought in the past. This was largely due to both ignorance and bigotry, these destructive evils of religious pride, division, mutual intolerance, violence and wars continue to plague the world, particularly the Middle East, Northern Ireland, Algeria, Bosnia, Uganda, the Sudan and Nigeria.

Ironically, these destructive wars are fought in the name of the same God! In actuality, religious wars are based on differences in "man-made" false doctrines, anthropomorphic images of the invisible God, and ideology, as opposed to God's will. As such, all wars including religious wars, such as the crusades and jihad are result of human ignorance, sin and rebellion against God's definitive commandment of unconditional love for the neighbor and nonviolence. Except in matters of self-defense and protection of the helpless from harm perpetrated by an evil aggressor, war and all acts of violence are moral evils that must be both rejected and condemned by all just, God-fearing, peace-loving, and caring people in the world, irrespective of creed, ideology, race and nationality.

In the final analysis, it can be morally and logically maintained that violence only begets violence and war. True and lasting peace can only be accomplished through mediation, peaceful dialogue, reconciliation, tolerance of diversity, mutual love and forgiveness. The 1990s Truth Commission in South Africa appointed by the former President Nelson Mandela under the chairmanship of Desmond Tutu, the former Anglican Archbishop of South Africa, provides a good example for Africa, and the rest of the world.

The South African Truth Commission under the good leadership of Desmond Tutu and Mandela has provided to the racist and violent world an ideal moral, social and political paradigm on how to deal with matters of peaceful resolution of the destructive racial conflicts, hate, genocide, and effect both the national reconciliation and healing. Rwanda, Somalia, Liberia, Bosnia, Kosovo, Northern Ireland, the Middle East and the Sudan can learn from Mandela and Tutu of South Africa on how peacefully to handle and resolve their sensitive ethnic and religious issues that cause violence and wars in these places.

Instead of seeking retaliation or revenge for the harm, injustice and other kinds of evil done to him, President Nelson Mandela acted like Jesus. He forgave his enemies ,and sought to promote national reconciliation and as well as both moral and societal healing. Mandela reminds us of the persecution, innocent suffering, and death of Jesus on the cross. Jesus forgave and prayed for his persecutors and executioners, instead of cursing them. Gandhi of India and Martin Luther King of the United States of America (USA) also chose to suffer and protest in a nonviolent manner against injustice. Both succeeded in their objectives despite the suffering they faced. These examples demonstrate that nonviolence is a viable in the mobilization of people for a just cause, peace and harmony.

Military might, violence and war by themselves do not work to bring about permanent conditions of peace and harmony. When the vanquished is able to raise up, they fight back against the aggressor or victor. In his important political work, *The Prince*, Machiavelli correctly theorized that in order to for the victor to maintain power, the opposition party or the conquered group had to be utterly crushed.

In addition, there was a necessity for constant public display of military superiority which had to be maintained with the necessary readiness to detect and quell any potential rebellion on the part of the vanquished party. This may have been a good and pragmatic theory for European conquest, colonialism and imperialism in Africa, Asia and Americas. But even then, it was a costly and brutal policy. This is because violence, as a means to gain power, also requires violence to maintain it. This Western Machiavellian paradigm is brutal, violent, anti-democratic and anti-human rights. Only the wealthy rulers, and evil tyrants like Adolph Hitler, Stalin and Idi Amin would embrace it wholeheartedly. Nevertheless, the Machiavellian strategy failed to work in Poland, Yugoslavia, Northern Ireland, Somalia, Uganda, Angola, Mozambique, Eritrea, South Africa and the Middle East.

Ultimately, all caring and loving religious people have to be taught to accept the unitive universal truth about God and religion, if they sincerely seek the truth, knowledge, redemption and peace from God through religion. The truth must be taught that there is only One, Cosmic Creator-Redeemer God. It is true that all major religions have gained access to various portions of God's infinite revelation, and these portions of God's revelation are both fragmented and incomplete.

All religious traditions have value, inasmuch as they teach nonviolence, peace, respect and love for the neighbor and creation. That is more important than mere religious faith based on the religious propositions formulated in the creeds and doctrines about God. Nevertheless, doctrines are important. Good theology provides the essential theological and moral foundations for a wholesome, and redemptive religion. The doctrines and religious propositions about God must include the main universal attributes of God as the holy, free, cosmic Creator-Redeemer, who is a Transcendent Mystery that can never be completely known by finite human beings, and yet known by many different names of which none is definitive. God must also be affirmed to be essentially transcendent universal, impartial, and nobody's property.

Contrary to the disgraceful doctrines of the Medieval Church, which affirmed that God's redemptive grace and forgiveness of sins could be only found in the Roman Catholic Church, God is a Cosmic Creative and Redemptive Spirit that transcends the exclusive claims and soteriological dogmas of all religions, including those of Christianity. God's redemptive grace can not be limited or be bought with money and penance, as Martin Luther and other Protestant reformers correctly protested.

Ultimately, there is One, true, holy, benevolent, just, and transcendent God who is an impartial cosmic Creator and Redeemer God, that unconditionally cares and loves all human beings. This God cannot be bribed by money (tithe), gold, virginity, sacrifices of cattle and sheep or long prayers. Instead, this holy, just and loving God demands that all the obedient people must also become holy, just, peaceful and loving like him or her. To this end, Jesus taught that God requires that all the obedient saints must unconditionally forgive and love their neighbors as God also unconditionally both forgives and loves them. God also requires that they take care of his or her creation in his or her name (cf. Matt. 5-7; 25:31-46). God is served as one serves both humanity and creation, since both creation and humanity are inseparable from God as their creator (origin), preserver and ultimate destiny.

The natural law as God's universal law of creativity, order, balance and harmony, is to be universally positively accepted as an impartial, good and reliable guide to God's cosmic revelation of knowledge, truth, wonders and cosmic mysteries. Nature or creation are to be positively viewed as God's good "natural revelation," and universal scripture of what God is truly like in his or her essence and works. Life, mind, justice, nonviolence and unconditional love must be positively perceived as God's highest divine gifts to humanity, and the rest of creation. The supernatural gifts of freedom, mind, creativity and moral responsibility are means to accomplish this divine-human task in the world.

God is also both correctly inclusively and positively affirmed to be good, nameless, genderless, colorless and formless transcendent God or Spirit. The transcendent God as the true cosmic Creator and Redeemer-God does not favor any nationality, religion, class, gender, color, race, ethnic or tribal groups of people, culture, language, religion, theological formulations, creeds, and forms of worship. As such, tribal and national gods are human-made idols that are created by human beings to suit and promote their own human pride, bigotry and ethnocentrism. This form of collective ethnocentrism, pride and idolatry is still found in some tribal and ethnic societies and religions. This is especially true for the gods or God worshiped in very exclusive tribalistic or nationalistic and religious groups which exclusively claim to be the exclusively elect or "the covenant people of God."

Therefore, contrary to the exclusive tribal and national gods and religions, in this global and evolutionist, inclusive Christian theological work, the peaceful and orderly global human community is identified as being the same as the one inclusive catholic, nondenominational (interreligious), and redemptive (universal) Church of God that is an open global Church without borders. It constitutes the universal openness and inclusiveness of God's Kingdom on the Earth. In God's inclusive global community or Church, there are no barriers of race, ethnicity, color, gender, age, nationality, class, creed, dogma, religious affiliation, marital status and natural sexual orientation because they have been transcended. God's Kingdom or Reign of unconditional love is based on obedience to God as manifested in a good moral life, and service to God by practicing unconditional love for the neighbor (all human beings).

The saints are also called by God to live a simple mode of holy, loving and altruistic life. That simple, just and saintly mode life must enhance the respect for all life, justice, truth, and the protection of the rest of God's creation. These saints must protest against its exploitation and misuse by greedy capitalists, and pollution and degradation by ignorant farmers in their tillage of land and careless animal grazing. This ideal positive life of obedient service is one that is lived according to the moral-spiritual practical principles of positive faith concerning life in its infinite cosmic mystery, the praxis of unconditional love in relationship to the neighbor and creation, and finally, the observance of the obligations of socioeconomic justice and nonviolence.

Within this global and religiously pluralistic context, each human being is positively viewed as God's special creation who is created in God's own image (*imago Dei*) to become a free, good, holy, thinking, self-transcending spirit, morally conscious, loving, caring, knowing, linguistic, and creative mind (Descartes' *res cogitans*) like God. To this end, each human being is by *a priori* nature a divine being that is akin to God. Each human being is a free, responsible, causal moral agent, creative, intelligent, spirit, mind, and God's adopted child. However, each human being is also a historically evolved knowing and thinking animal (*Homo sapiens*) in accordance with God's creative laws of nature, and the evolutionary biological processes.

Therefore, without any exceptions, including the saints, prophets, and messiahs like Moses, Buddha and Jesus, each human being is intrinsically a complex duality who exists in two distinct, opposed natures. The human being is one composite being made up of both the animal and divine natures. The animal nature makes the human being a member of the animal kingdom. The human being, as an animal, is scientifically viewed as an evolutionary thinking and knowing primate (*Homo sapiens*). At the same time, the endowment of God's free gifts of intellect and spirit are the essence of divine nature. This makes the human being a special self-transcending free spirit, and a creative mind that make him or her akin to God.

By God's own free and unmerited grace and unconditional love, God has chosen and "elected" every obedient and loving human being in the world as an adopted child of God, and a citizen of God's Kingdom. This is true inasmuch as the human being decides to obey God and live according to his or her God-given special divine nature that transcends his or her animal nature which is rooted in greed, and mere personal survival at the expense of the community, virtue, love, order, justice, goodness, peace, and the common good.

Within this moral and global theological understanding, the human being is an important co-creator and co-redeemer with God in the world. God prefers to act incognito in the world through the obedient human beings to effect his or her will in the world's human history. As such, to see God's obedient and true saints at work in the world, such as Moses, Jesus, Buddha, Gandhi, Luther, Pope John XXIII, Martin Luther King, Oscar Romero, Desmond Tutu, Nelson Mandela, Janani Luwum, Julius Nyerere and Mother Teresa is to catch a glimpse of God's *theophany* (God's revelation, vision of glory), and work in the history of the world.

The theocentric and soteriological (redemptive) story of the Passover and the exodus is a good example for this divine intervention according to Judaism. For Christians, the prayerful, holy life of Jesus and innocent death on the cross accomplish this historical divine intervention by God in the world to save sinful human beings. And Buddhists find the life and teachings of Siddhartha as the Buddha the necessary source of God's redemptive *theophany (beatific vision)*, or mental-spiritual enlightenment, and the heavenly beatific union with God (*Nirvana*).

Human beings as authentic, free, obedient, intelligent, loving, just, creative, and responsible moral agents are called to become God's active co-workers and voluntary partners with God in God's own supernatural activities of creation and redemption in the world. Therefore, the saints and all other obedient human beings cannot also become lazy, passive or apathetic observers of life and history and remain faithful to God and the authentic moral agents that God created them to become. Human beings are essentially what they think, choose and actually do. They are their own deeds or actions. They are good, if they do good, and they are evil if they do evil. They are "nothing" if they do "nothing." A life of virtue, justice and good deeds of charity or unconditional love, requires sound moral judgement and hard work. The good deeds of the virtuous, saintly or holy life are those good deeds that promote life, well-being, good health, truth, unconditional love, law and order, justice, harmony, peace and happiness within the local and the Global Community.

Just as the Hebrew prophets stood out against the evils and injustice of their own day, God's saints or other obedient and loving people, cannot become indifferent or hide in the crowd in face of evil. They can never hide or keep quiet in face of evil to save their own lives, or live anonymous lives. Moses, Buddha, Socrates, Jesus, Paul, Luther, Wesley, Gandhi, Martin Luther King, Malcolm X, Tutu, Luwum, Romero and others did not keep quiet when they were required to speak out against evil and injustice in their society. Like the prophets, God's obedient saints are the main characters and players within God's cosmic drama of human creation, positive human transformation, humanization, love, grace, faith, obedience, and redemption.

God's cosmic arena and stage for this supernatural cosmic drama of creation and redemption consists of every human family and moral community in the world. According to this understanding, every human family and each moral community constitutes the essential vehicle and channel for the mediation of God's supernatural grace and the special arena for God's supernatural activities of unconditional love and unmerited universal activities of grace in both creation and redemption. The natural and human social institutions of healthy families and moral communities are also God's natural, evolutionary and social provision for the effective mediation of God's own supernatural and special creation and the correlative spiritual nurture, humanization, protection and redemption of all humanity anywhere in the world.

These God's coextensive supernatural twin processes of creation and redemption take place in the world everywhere irrespective of the variable factors of era, creed, class, color, gender, nationality, race, language, religion, culture and ideology. God's free cosmic activities of creation and redemption are both universal and inseparably intertwined as two sides of the same coin. They are both rooted in God's unmerited universal free grace and unconditional love (Agape).

As such, no human being should try to separate them into two different historical processes or put barriers and conditions on them in order to exclude some people based on the human sinful barriers of prejudice, such as those rooted in racism, sexism, classism, religious bigotry, homophobia, economic and political ideologies. For instance, God does not care about the capitalists more than the communists.

Likewise, God does not care more about the Christians than the Muslims and other non-Christians. The Transcendent Creator-Redeemer God does not favor any religion, economic or political ideology. God is neither a Democrat nor Republican. God is neither White nor Black. God is neither Catholic nor Protestant. God is neither Christian nor Muslim or Buddhist. Similarly, God is neither male nor female. The holy and transcendent God is a holy, creative and redemptive Cosmic Spirit that transcends of all these finite barriers that characterize human beings and divide them. As such, the saints of God are called by God to become like God and by God's power transcend these finite barriers that naturally characterize or classify and divide God's people and the children of God in the temporal and cultural world.

## 4. The Moral Obligations of Agape, Nonviolence and Global Peace

The Christian doctrines of the incarnation affirm that God has become irrevocably permanently incarnate in humanity and inseparably bound with the fate of humanity, history and the world. As such, each human being, and the world (nature and history) have become the holy temples of the incarnate God within the cosmos. Therefore, they also both effectively reveal and express God.

Accordingly, all of God's truly obedient and loving people in the world today are called upon to become his or her true messengers and servants of peace, justice and love in the world. All the obedient human beings, anywhere in the world, are called upon to obey God to become more ethical and morally responsible, than ever before in the recent or remote past. This is the universal, self-evident, inevitable truth and moral human obligation that is required of every obedient and moral human being in the complex technological world of today. This is because human beings now possess the scientific knowledge, powerful nuclear military technology and capability to inflict quick indiscriminate massive harm on others, and even to destroy most higher forms of life.

This planet itself is in danger of human caused destruction. If this occurs, it will be the misinterpreted as the *"parusia"* (return of Christ) and eschatological end of this world that is eagerly expected by many misguided apocalyptic religious fundamentalists, millennarianists and adventists. However, God's will is to save the world and not to destroy it! (Cf. John 3:16-21). Therefore, the caring and obedient religious people have the moral obligation to become more loving, humane, tolerant, nonviolent, peace loving, and environmentalists, if the human species and the whole of life on this planet are to continue to exist and thrive.

In Plato's *Meno* and the *Apology,* Socrates affirms that nobody can make another person more moral and virtuous, or corrupt a truly perfect person. He was partly right. Saints can be corrupted by an immoral society. The ignorant can be taught to become morally conscious, virtuous and moral saints. Socrates was also correct when he taught that there cannot be true virtue, responsible human moral freedom, civic virtues, peace and happiness without the necessary prior acquisition and possession of correct knowledge (information) and truth. Knowledge, correct information and truth are acquired through good education. The correct knowledge of what is true and what is false, what is right and what is wrong, and what is good and what is evil is a necessary prerequisite of living a good and happy life that is rooted in knowledge, wisdom, sound judgement, justice, love, virtue, harmony and peace.

Sound knowledge is the moral basis of any sound moral choices between the conflicting multiple alternative moral choices, actions and destinies. A good education imparts sound knowledge and skills which are the necessary prerequisites for any sound moral thinking, judgment, good moral decisions, virtuous actions and good deeds. Conversely, poor education and ignorance are the sources of vice, poor moral judgement, violence, evil deeds and crime! Without good education, there is no knowledge or the necessary problem solving skills that are required of good moral agents and wise and virtuous people.

From a capitalist, economic, political, intellectual, moral and spiritual perspective, it is self-evident that the community has a moral obligation to invest funds in good education for the young people and to provide job-training skills as effective deterrents to ignorance, vice, laziness, unemployment, crime, and violence in the community and the society as a whole. This is a practical, civic and utilitarian form of ethical theory that works in society regardless of whether the citizens believe in God or not. Crime and violence within the American inner city can be dramatically reduced if more money was spent on education, job-training and employment for the people in the inner city areas than merely building more jails and hiring more judges and police officers! Well educated, morally responsible and employed people do not engage in crimes of violence and vandalism! They are part of the community and they seek to protect it rather than destroy it as it is with the case of criminals and vandals!

The community or society has a moral obligation to provide good role models for the young children to imitate. The young people are the future members of the community and citizens of the nation. They must be adequately educated and trained to assume their proper roles in the society in a professional and responsible manner. Ideal moral and civic virtues must be inculcated into the young people through good education and moral training.

Good, moral, positive and ideal role models are essential for the young people to imitate. This is necessary since they all learn moral values by hearing the words and observing the actions of their own parents, other adults and their own peers, regardless of whether they are good or bad. Parents are the primary moral educators and more influential role models for their own children. Schools, colleges and universities are secondary providers of education. Home-schooling is primary and most important in providing the essential moral and religious foundations for the young and future leaders of the community.

Unfortunately, these essential human institutions often fail to provide good moral education and role models. Broken homes, evil, abusive families and communities often produce broken, evil and abusive people. Children are mirrors of their families and communities in whose image they have been socialized and shaped. The public mass media, especially the television, must provide more educational programs for children and the young viewers. It must also remove the corrupting casual sex and violent programs from the young viewers' programming and computer video games.

This "moral cleansing" includes discarding violent films and cartoons, such as: *Bugs Bunny; The Incredible Hulk; Road Runner; The Power Rangers; The Ninja Turtles; He-Man; Beavis and Butthead*; and *Popeye the Sailor Man.* In the later, Brutal and Popeye are the violent characters that are ever viciously competing, fighting over Oliveoil and deceiving each other in order to win her affection. The mass media, just like the rest of the human institutions, must take its moral responsibility seriously. It should promote positive values, such as nonviolence, creative problem solving through analogue and negotiation and peaceful human coexistence in a world of diversity.

Therefore, no moral and responsible society should ever teach its young to accept that violence and cheating are harmless as long as one finally wins. Instead, the young should be taught that the means are as important as the end, and that greed, cheating, fraud, falsehood, selfishness and fighting are not moral solutions or justified as the means to a noble and desirable end. All forms of violence and killing are wrong and constitute moral evils even when they are necessary and inevitable. This includes murder in the process of self defense. War, murder, abortion, the death penalty and euthanasia are condemned by the Roman Catholic Church as evil and sinful. The Roman Catholic Church views them as a negation of life and goodness. Life is the ultimate gift of God.

These practices of abortion, euthanasia, war, capital punishment, genocide and murder are negatively viewed as negations of life, unnatural, unloving and immoral. The moral and theological position underlying the Roman Catholic doctrines are the assumptions that God is good and whatever this "Good and holy God" has created is good, particularly, the unmerited and special gift of life. God creates life and therefore, God is the only moral authority that can take it away in natural death.

The Roman Catholic position is that these are sinful culturally popular practices, but rejected by the holy Church. Accordingly, the Roman Catholic Church has consistently condemned them. The Church through the papal encyclicals has also declared that these evil and immoral practices should be universally discouraged. Subsequently, Pope John Paul II has condemned these moral evils. He traveled more widely than any of his predecessors on this important global moral crusade. His main purpose for these pastoral travels was to reaffirm traditional Christian values and Church doctrines. His pastoral letters, speeches and encyclicals address these moral issues. In 1993 and 1995, the Roman Catholic Church Pontiff, again, most strongly condemned the practices of abortion, euthanasia and the death penalty in his famous encyclicals, *The Splendor of Truth (Veritas Splendor, October 5, 1993)* and *On the Gospel of Life (Evangelium Vitae, March 25, 1995)*. The Pope declared that these moral and cultural evils should not be practiced by the religious or God-fearing, civilized, well-educated, well-mannered, caring, polite, honest, courageous, loving and peace seeking people.

Killing in self-defense or the defense of a helpless person may be morally justifiable. Likewise, abortion may be morally justified if it is necessary to save the life and health of the mother. Similarly, a terminally ill patient is suffering due to pain that cannot be relieved by the available painkillers should be allowed to die painlessly in both peace and dignity, and among caring family members and friends. In this case, euthanasia is deliverance from evil and therefore, not murder. On the contrary, it is a positive form of God's deliverance from the evils of unnecessary suffering and pain. Jesus' suffering and pain were cut short on the cross by God. This should also be the case true for other people through "euthanasia." If a moral agent has to make a moral choice between two evil alternatives, the lesser harmful of the two evils is the better moral choice. This moral principle applies in the cases of euthanasia and abortion.

People must be taught how to make good and responsiable moral decisions. The parents and other adults within the family and the community are the most influential primary role models and moral teachers for the young people growing up around them in the home and the community. Many young people unconsciously imitate, process, and internalize the values and behavior of their own parents, siblings and peers within the family and the local and Global Community. Subsequently, these children grow up to be like them, and act like them. This is more visible in the poor and crime riddled inner-city families headed by the poorly educated, unemployed and unwedded single parents in some large cities in the world, especially, the slums of Africa, Asia and Latin America.

Due their negative conditioning by their depraved communities, or education, unless there is an early positive moral intervention through the Church, or another caring moral community by providing love, education, better role models, employment and high self-esteem, these children will be lost or grow up to become criminals, such as thieves, prostitutes and drug dealers. The children are the real mirrors of the family and the community. Children reflect moral image of their own parents and peers within the community in which they are born and raised. For instance, sexism and racism are learned from the parents and the community in which the children are born and raised.

The above is true unless there is an external positive moral intervention to halt and reverse this trend. Therefore, the adult members of the family, community and society should by their own good example, words, love, and good deeds teach the young how to live truly a really good, virtuous, honest, productive, nonviolent and peaceful life. Our future is shaped in the home and kindergarten. Therefore, the young and all citizens should be taught to internalize and practice the moral virtues of courage, justice, truth, charity, compassion, caring, honesty, temperance and nonviolence. These values and virtues must be taught as the essential universal moral requisites for happiness and a civilized, humane, peaceful, just and good life. These are the essential moral tools and practical moral principles required to transform this world into what

Jesus called the "Kingdom of God" and Martin Luther King's "Beloved Community."

King's "Beloved Community" or "God's Kingdom" is the ideal godly harmonious human community of unconditional love, justice and peace for all people irrespective of their race, color, religion, nationality, class, gender, and age. In this just and ideal earthly peaceful community, people would live together, irrespective of color, creed, gender, sexual orientation and class. This is also the same ideal community of God that Jesus referred to as "God's Kingdom" or "Heaven." God's loving and obedient people are the saints and effective moral agents of God's reign and Kingdom in this world. They are also the effective historical mediators of God's unconditional love, grace, justice, goodness, salvation and "God's Kingdom" in this world (cf. Mk. 1:14-15; Lk. 17:20-21).

## Chapter 3

# Human Beings as Evolutionary Divine Mind, Spirit And Mystery

The human being is God's special partial embodiment of God's self-consciousness, evolutionary mind, spirit, freedom, moral consciousness and mystery (*imago Dei*). This is both historically projected into matter and concretely or externally manifested in the temporal world (cf. Gen. 1:26-31). At the same time, the human being is also both an animal, by virtue of biological evolution in the world, and simultaneously, a divine being by God's indirect acts of special creation. God's supernatural and special process for the creation of the human being occurs naturally through the apparent ordinary historical evolutionary processes of nature.

Likewise, the ordinary local family and moral or religious human community, universally serve as God's chosen extraordinary universal channel for the mediation of supernatural grace for all humanity in every age, nation and culture, without any regard for religious creed or ideology. The loving, sound human family or any moral community in the world is empowered by God's unconditional love and unmerited free creative and redemptive grace to serve humanity efficaciously as God's "Church" or channel for the creation and redemption of human beings.

## 1. The Human Being as God's Theophany in the World

As a divine being, the human being is like God, in whose image or likeness and mystery he or she has evolved as the Homo Sapiens and has been specially created and divinized by God into an *imago Dei.* Because God is a transcendent and an incomprehensible divine and holy Creative and Redemptive Mystery in the cosmos, the human being having been created in God's own image as an *imago Dei*, is also by essential nature a finite, historical and evolutionary divine mind, spirit and mystery manifested within the temporal world and its evolutionary historical processes. The human being both concretely manifests and reveals the transcendent and invisible God to be fully present in the physical world and its historical processes. The highest expression of this theophany is Jesus as both the Christ and the special redemptive incarnation of God's creative and redemptive *Logos* in the world (cf. John 1:1-18).

Within this understanding, all humanity represents God's own concrete incarnation, embodiment and omnipresence in this world and its natural and historical processes. God's *Logos* or Mind and the Holy Spirit are ever present in the world and its evolutionary processes in order to effect new creation and the positive transformation of some creatures to become more intelligent, free, creative, thinking, spirit or self-transcending in mind and thought, moral agents, responsible moral actors in the world and responsible representatives of God in creation.

God bestows divine attributes of a superior intelligence, great capacity for thought, creativity and problem solving, moral consciousness of right and wrong, a loving and caring spirit, so that the human creation. Most important of all, the human being has been freely endowed with the supernatural gifts of superior intellect or mind, spirit, knowledge, creativity, love, freedom and self-transcendence so that the human being could serve as the mirror of the God and theophany in the world. This being the case, then, it follows that to encounter a saint in the world as a truly godly, intelligent, just, creative, wise and loving being is also to encounter God's mystery and presence in the world. The presence of God's saints and moral agents in the world is both inseparable and coextensive with holy God's presence.

This positive, divine and redemptive presence of God in the world works through God's special chosen saints and other agents in the world. It manifests itself as pure goodness, creativity, creative problem-solving, peacemaking, teaching the ignorant (opening the eyes of the blind), bearing testimony to the truth, socioeconomic justice, healing the sick, taking care of the needy, helping the helpless and defending the powerless, free forgiveness, unconditional love, holiness, humility, nonviolence and heavenly peace. As a result, there are many people in the world who positively testify that they have encountered the redemptive presence of God in the world through godly prophets and saints like Krishna (Hindus), Moses (Jews), the Buddha (Buddhists), Jesus (Christians), Muhammad (Muslims), the Virgin Mary (Christians) and Mother Theresa (Christians and Hindus).

## 2. Adam, Eve and the Original Sin

Contrary to the erroneous, misleading, false and pessimistic teachings of biological determinism, total depravity and divine predestination of St. Paul, Augustine, Aquinas, Calvin and their philosophical-theological followers, human beings are still free to choose to sin or not sin. Only the insane, the young, the drug or alcohol impaired and the psychologically or morally brainwashed, through conditioning and indoctrination, lack moral freedom to choose the right and good thing. Nevertheless, the intoxicated people had the freedom to choose to get drunk or take drugs, and this was not God's doing through an act of predestination.

As Pelagius and Arminius correctly argued, human freedom is central to human moral agency and responsibility. Without human freedom and ability to choose to do the good, as Calvin argued, unless God had willed and predestined them to do so, abrogates human moral agency and responsibility. Since human beings have no real freedom to choose and do good, subsequently, God, Eve, Adam and the imaginary Devil become the scapegoats for the presence of sin and evil in the world.

Paul, Augustine and Calvin's moral teachings on total human depravity and predestination are erroneous and misleading, because they assumed that the Hebrew stories of creation and the fall of humanity as found in the book of Genesis were literal and accurate historical accounts of God's creation of a perfect world in the past. They said that evil, sin and death came into God's perfect world because Adam and Eve were actual people whose rebellion and sin against God caused the loss of the original grace and free will to choose the good. Augustine then reasoned that since Adam and Eve sinned, and lost the grace of God, then all human beings as the descendants of Adam and Eve were also born with a spiritual and moral defect.

Like St. Paul, St. Augustine and Calvin also concluded that all human beings in the world are born with an a priori morally defective and totally depraved human nature due to the inherited original sin of Adam. They also concluded that the Christian sacrament of baptism was necessary to remove this original sin with which every human being is born with and therefore, born condemned by God to death or "hell." This absurd doctrine led to the theological exclusivist dogmatic claim that "Outside the [Roman Catholic] Church, there is no divine salvation" (*Extra Ecclesiam Nulla Salus)*. This dogma has led to the Church's insistence on baptism as a means to salvation and God's Kingdom. This Christian theology prompted some courageous European missionaries to go to Africa, Asia, and America in order to covert and baptize the so called lost people whom they often derogatorily referred to as "pagans" and "heathens." These Christian missionaries truly believed that all the non-Christians would go to hell since Jesus Christ was considered the gate to God, salvation, heaven, eternal life and God's Kingdom (Mtt. 28:18-20).

However, Paul, Augustine and Calvin's assumptions that Adam and Eve were historical beings is false, and since the correlative assumption that God created a perfected world in the past in which there was no death is also false, and since in the evolutionary perspective perfection is in the future, rather than the past as Paul, Augustine and Calvin wrongly believed, therefore, their doctrines on human nature, God, creation, predestination, grace, election, freedom, sin, salvation, sacraments, particularly baptism, are also erroneous, defective and false. For instance, there is no time when the world was perfect and devoid of death as the perishing of any finite beings. Evolution and archeology provide ample evidence for this universal aspect of natural law and its processes.

In an evolutionary perspective, death is the means by which natural selection occurs and guides the evolutionary process upward and toward the emergence of more sophisticated and perfect creatures. Timely death is natural and good. It cleanses the Earth and recycles life to its next higher stage. But St. Paul negatively viewed death within the Hebrew world-view as God's punishment. Sometimes, death is the best thing that can happen. This is more true for conditions of hopelessness and meaninglessness, such as those of painful terminal diseases or irreversible comma. Dr. Jack Kevorkian's advocacy for timely death with dignity has a moral basis that is ignored by the opponents of euthanasia.

Moreover, since there is no original sin as was wrongly assumed by many theologians of the last two millenniums, then it follows that there is no real reason why baptism should be required by God as a means of washing away a nonexistent sin due to a supposed inherited spiritual and moral defect of a mythological Adam and Eve. As a result, the sacrament of baptism is no more efficacious than the religious ritual of circumcision or child naming ceremonies of Africa. These ceremonies and rituals are socially meaningful. But they are not magical devices that can affect

God's will or alter God's relationship or attitude to some individual or groups of people.

Baptism is a naming religious ceremony and initiation rite into the Christian Church. Holy baptism has no magical powers to save sinners of their sins of hate, injustice and disobedience. Each human being still retains God's original grace. Each human being is an Adam and Eve in each moment of choice and freedom exercised for better or worse. Only the obedience and praxis of unconditional love, justice and peace are redemptive for the individual and his or her community. These are the prerequisites for effective citizenship in God's Kingdom and heaven. Conversely, mere pious confessions of faith in God, and performance of religious rituals, such as the sacraments and circumcision, sacrifices, chanting and holy baths are of little moral value in themselves.

Ultimately, no obedient saint of God is ever excluded from God's Kingdom and heaven because he or she was never baptized in the Christian Church! After all, the Christian Church has very often become a moral stumbling block by her vicious sins of division, exclusiveness, bigotry, hate, racism, sexism and pride than a moral instrument to unite, heal society and bring about forgiveness, love, reconciliation and peace in the world. As such, it was appropriate and historically significant that Pope John Paul 11 formally atoned for these sins of the Church and asked for God's and people's forgiveness. The Church failed to exercise the ministry of unconditional love and free forgiveness of sins and offenses.

Unconditional love for the neighbor is what God demands, rather mere confessions of faith, pious creeds, dogmas or statements of doctrines about God, humanity and the world. God does not care about theory or faith without good moral deeds of love, and peace in the world. James and John were more in Jesus' tradition and correct in their teachings than Paul and his followers. Like Jesus, they emphasized the centrality of positive moral action based on faith and unconditional love as the essence of true godliness (cf. Matt. 5-7; 25:31-46; Jam. 2; 1 John 4; 1 Cor. 13). Within the context of human biological and moral evolution, we can reaffirm the importance of human love, freedom, freewill, causal choices and moral responsibility as a reality in the world now. There is no more sound religious justifications for blaming and scapegoating women as "Eves," or the "Devil" and persecuting them for having caused the downfall of humanity.

From this evolutionary perspective, there is no actual historical Adam or Eve who committed the supposed "original sin" against God, and thereby caused the cosmic "human fall" from an "original perfection." In addition, there is no real being called "the Devil" to be blamed for the human moral weakness, yielding to temptations and moral failures. Adam and Eve, the Devil and "original sin" are not real ontological or historical realities. They are mythological scapegoats for human sin and moral failures. The Devil is a mere personification of social, moral and spiritual evil. Accordingly, Jesus could tell Peter that he was "Satan" (cf. Mark 8:31-33).

However, Adam, Eve and the Devil are not sufficient explanations for human moral evil since human beings are free. As a result, those who wish to believe in historical reality of sinful Adam and Eve and the original sin, also believe in biological, moral and spiritual determinism, and deny the reality of human freedom. They affirm that human freedom is an illusion, since they believe that God and the Devil hold human beings in their own power, and play with them as one plays with puppets, by pulling the various strings to make the puppet do what one wants.

This deterministic and predestination understanding of God, and humanity is absurd. It is contrary to the experience of freedom, reason and the primary objectives for teaching, preaching, and punishment of criminals if people are determined and predestined by either Adam and Eve's supposed original sin or God. It would be wrong, evil and immoral for God to punish human beings for the sins of Adam and Eve, or for what he has predestined them to do! Such a God, would be an irresponsible, evil and unloving "Devil" or monster, and the very antithesis of what the Judeo-Christian and Islamic traditions mean by the term "God."

Furthermore, the acceptance of the religious metaphor of the "Devil" as physical or spiritual reality, or the literal acceptance of the mythological "Devil" as a historical reality, does not explain why men oppress and subordinate women to male authority as God's will, or why the Catholic and Baptist Churches have refused to ordain women. St. Paul's subordination of women to the male authority in the Christian Church was erroneously based on the assumption that Eve, a woman, had caused sin and the downfall of all humanity and had become cursed by God (cf Gen. 3). However, this patriarchal Hebrew theology is based on the ancient patriarchal Hebrew religious and moral myth and world-view. It is not based on historical or social reality. In reality, most women are spiritually and morally better than most men! For instance, men are the perpetrators of the destructive moral evils of violence, murders, imperialism and wars in the world. This male violence is characterized by the initial crime of murder where Cain killed Abel, his only brother (Gen. 4).

Therefore, as an Adam or Eve, each human being possesses the really effective and causal freedom as a free, intelligent moral agent. As an intelligent, free and responsible moral agent, the human being is able to choose whether to live according to the higher divine level or at the lower level of nature, which is the animal nature. One can therefore, exist at the animal level. That is at the instinct for violence which is rooted in the natural of the jungle, where "might makes right," and "the survival of the fittest"is the ultimate, natural and impartial ethic. On the other hand, the human being could choose to live according to the divine nature, and accept to become God's moral agent in the cosmos. This obedience requires faith that the faithful moral agent must live according to the divine ethic of grace and agape as concretely characterized by a holy and good life based on the moral principles of benevolence, justice, nonviolence and unconditional love and free forgiveness for offenses.

To live according to the divine nature is good, noble, and morally ideal as the goal of "the good "and "happy life." However, it is not easy. To live faithfully according to the divine-human nature is to become like God! It requires the human being to become God-conscious or to live according to reason, positive faith in God and the goodness of God's creation, agape, compassion, moral conscience, causal freedom, choice for the best possible alternative and full responsibility for one's action in the community and the world.

This human existence at the divine level is possible through God's supernatural power of unconditional love and free redemptive grace. It is God's free universal gift for the divinization of human beings with God's own essence and access to God's universal, omnipresent divinity. This occurs through the free endowments of God's supernatural gifts of a higher intellect, grace, peace, thought, reason (*cogito*), mind, spirit, freedom, creativity, transcendence, universal God-consciousness, moral consciousness and judgement.

Renee Descartes' famous philosophical and metaphysical axiom, "*cogito ergo sum*" (I think, therefore, I am) is the characteristic Western traditional religion, theology, philosophy and ethics. It illustrates the fundamental Neo-Platonic Western understanding of the human being as a *mind or rational individual being*. As an embodied fragment of God's mind, the human being is the being that is demonstrably able to learn new truths, think deep thoughts about the self, God, other people, existence and the world. Descartes provides a good example of how the human being as the *Homo sapiens* (knowing being) or *res cogitans* (thinking thing or being) is fundamentally defined by the divine essence, rather than the animal essence of mere biological existence (*res extensa* or "extended thing") and survival of the strongest.

George Hegel goes even further than Descartes. For Hegel, God as the cosmic Mind, Spirit and Knowing Self-Consciousness is the only reality and truth from which other realities and truths both ultimately originate and return. According to him, God as Mind and Reality is real and not a fantasy. God is not an illusion as Feuerbacher, Marx and Freud later claimed, because God as the rational divine being is the real, and the real is what is rational. For Hegel, the self-transcendent, rational and knowing human being is God in self-projection into matter and self-incarnation into the evolutionary world and its historical processes.

Jesus and Buddha are examples of those people who had finally overcome the illusion of the human separation from God. By their discovery of the secret of contemplative human self-transcendence and union with God in prayer, they effectively negated the doctrines of self-alienation and the false consciousness the "original sin" and "complete separation from God" by sin, finitude and imperfection that led to the human being's universal sense of existential anxiety and dread (*angst*). This existential anxiety was based on this destructive illusion of being separated from God due to sin. The redemptive and heavenly reconciliation with God occurs when the human being comes into the full possession of God's liberating knowledge and redemptive Truth.

This is the universal and free power and process of God's liberating and divinizing supernatural Truth which illumines the seeker's human mind with God's immediate knowledge and the blessedness of the divine encounter of God or the beatific vision. This divine illumination of the human mind through prayer, contemplation and study, dispels human ignorance like the dawning sun dispels darkness or the morning mist. This divine illumination also shutters the illusion of human hubris or self-deification and alienation from God. It effectively bridges the seeming unbridgeable abyss or infinite gulf between the holy transcendent God and the finite sinful humanity. This mental, spiritual, moral and "the Barthian" religious "illusion of the eternal gulf between God and humanity," is overcome when the human being comes to the true realization that he or she is the same as God by virtue of possessing an intrinsic God-consciousness, mind, spirit, freedom and self-transcendence which are cosmic and an inalienable eternal essence of "God himself, herself or itself!"

For Hegel, the dialects of history and evolutionary processes of mind and human-self and God-Consciousness ends when the human being, as the Logos of God incarnate in the world, comes to the final true realization and possession of the absolute truth and knowledge that he or she is the same as the eternal Creator-Redeemer God in self-incarnation and embodiment in the world of matter, flux, change and evolution or "becoming!"

Hegel refers to this beatific stage of God-human reunification as the stage of the "absolute knowledge." This is the end of history and evolution as we know them. This is the adventure of Hegel's monumental philosophical book known as the *Phenomenology of Spirit*. The world and its history are God's arenas for self-creation, embodiment, and incarnation in matter. History is God's process of self-rediscovery through the evolutions of self-consciousness, intellect, spirit, mind, memory, and the knowledge of the self as God in the mode of self-embodiment in matter and incarnation in history.

In this respect, each rational, thinking, altruistic, compassionate and loving human being is a true embodiment of God in the world. Simultaneously, each human being is reflective of God, humanity or self and others to the world. Each authentic human being is an incarnation of the Logos or God and therefore, to some extent, is God incognito in the world and human history. Because human beings possess the divine capacities and the powerful technological means for creation and destruction, rebellious and evil people, such as Hitler and Idi Amin are able to do great harm to people, creation and God's world.

These evil people are the embodiments of rebellion against God's essential goodness, and they become the evil embodiments of negative energy, premature death and destruction in God's good world. Collectively, these evildoers constitute the destructive"power and agency of evil or the Devil" in the world. Evil is a social, negative energy and influence which can be experienced as an external oppressive, spiritual, moral, social, political, military, economic and religious force or influence.

The evil people who rebel against the goodness of God in creation and choose to actualize their potential power in a negative mode are the real devils in God's world. In this understanding, evil is a negative use of God's power and a negative mode of self-actualization in the world by human beings. However, the universal normative principle for God's self-incarnation in the world was positively affirmed by Hegel. He showed that God as the Cosmic Spirit and Mind or the *Logos* was effectively incarnate and embodied within each human being. The goals are love, knowledge and self-recognition as "the other." Martin Buber's "*I and Thou*" would be abrogated once the self has attained sufficient mental, spiritual, and moral positive growth or the fullness of self-development, knowledge, truth, love, and faith. The self must also have the courage to recognize itself as reflected in "the other" or as "the other," in both self-projection, alienation and self-reflection in the mirror of God through our own concrete neighbor and all fellow human beings in the world!

Within this human-self understanding, human beings as the "*imago Dei*" (God's Reflection) are also real temporal mirrors of God in the world. Simultaneously, they are also existential, religious, cultural, moral and psychological mirrors for each other in the community and the world. As a result, some people who do not like or love themselves may also fail to love their own reflections which they may see mirrored back to them through other people. Subsequently, these people may naturally dislike, hate and seek to destroy others, who may unconsciously represent and reflect what they see and hate in themselves. Other people are living mirrors of themselves. Therefore, they may effectively reflect back to these in themselves. It is imperative to note that Jesus' moral and spiritual teaching of agape or unconditional love and free forgiveness must start from the self-disliking or self-hating person before, he or she can truly become liberated to love and forgive others!

A self-hating person is not free to love or forgive anyone else! He or she is like a dead battery which is unable to become the power for starting an automobile, until it has been either recharged or replaced with a new one! No one is able to give to others as free gifts what he or she does not already possess or own. Love, compassion, faith, courage, mercy, forgiveness, wisdom, knowledge, truth, happiness and civic virtues are these special divine treasures which cannot be given away unless the giver already possesses them as divine gifts of obedience.

Within the above context, one can positively affirm that Freud was correct in his projection theory. He correctly observed that people hate what they perceive to be morally, culturally and religiously unacceptable to society as evil. They may secretly do it, despite the society's moral sanction against it. Subsequently, these people may be tormented by their conscience and suffer from painful mental forms of secret guilt of wrong doing. Freud's psychoanalysis theory and therapy were meant to get the "sinner" to accept and "confess" his or her "sins" or moral violations in order to receive healing. In religious terms, this is what is called "absolution" and "remission of sins and guilt." In essence, the psychiatrist in his or her white lab coat had replaced the priest in his black or white clerical robe and white stole.

Freud was also correct in claiming that there is a general tendency for many to unconsciously project externally and see reflections of themselves in the other people! Tragically, some people hate and reject the other people because of what they hate and reject in themselves and yet see reflected in the others. Hating and killing what we hate in ourselves, often leads many of us to hate or desire to kill those people who reflect to us what we hate and desire to kill within us ourselves.

Once we break and destroy the mirrors in which we are negatively self-reflected, we erroneously tend to think that we have also destroyed whatever evil that we hated and sought to destroy in ourselves! That is an illusion and false remedy for the eradication of evil within by extermination of the external mirror and reflection of that evil. Evil remains hidden within us. Nevertheless, we "secretly" know the reality that our moral imperfection and secret sins menacingly lurk within us and our "private affairs." Guilt occurs because we know that we have done wrong. Moral guilt is not due to God's punishment. It is due to the possession of morality, God-consciousness and knowledge of the "good," "right," "just," "loving," and the "beneficial" that human beings sin when they rebel against the good and choose and do what they know to be " malicious" "wrong," "unjust," "evil", "hateful" and "harmful."

This observation is in harmony with the Christian doctrines of the original sin as the human inclination to do what is evil or wrong because it is easier or more convenient or emotionally immediately pleasurable and gratifying option. This is analogous to gravity that makes objects fall to the ground and causes water to flow from a higher plane to a lower one following the path of least resistance. The people who wish to please everybody and hate to go against any path of resistance which requires moral or physical effort also live an evil life since they refuse to resist evil or do the good which requires effort and resistance. God's historical and permanent incarnation in both history and humanity provides and example on how to resist evil. This is especially true for religious teachers and moral thinkers, such as Jesus, St. John, Christian Martyr, Augustine, Aquinas, Hegel, Schleiermarcher, Tillich, and Rahner.

Hegel's theory of mind, intellect, and knowledge as God's attributes are almost reminiscent of Plato's theory of God, mind or Logos and knowledge. For Socrates and Plato human birth is the process of the embodiment of mind and spirit into matter, finitude of time and history. This process of the incarnation of spirit and mind through birth causes the mental trauma which results in a "temporary amnesia." Past forms of existence, history, experience, identity, self-consciousness and knowledge are forgotten.

However, knowledge is recoverable through the process of "recollection." For both Socrates and Plato, the original knowledge which had been forgotten through the trauma of birth, is recovered through the gradual process of education, especially through the Socratic method. That is the dialogical and dialectical method of teaching and learning through the process of questions and answers, followed by discussion or critique by the master (teacher or professor).

Without any exception, each human being has been given God's supernatural gifts of personal causal freedom and the power of grace for self-determination and self-completion into the very being that each person finally becomes. Those people who choose to obey God's invitation to become like him (or her) also choose to live their own lives most fully in accordance with God's will and divine essence. They choose the positive mode of self-determination and self-actualization in the world at the divine level.

These loving and obedient people also effectively become God's living saints, perfect moral agents, and representatives in the world. They are fully enabled by God through positive faith, good intention, agape, and good actions to become a unique moral, social, political, rational, economic, spiritual, religious, linguistic, cultural and technological being. Ultimately, each human being has been created by God through the process of evolution to become God-like (*imago Dei*). This is divine free unmerited choice and special election of the human being by God to become the adopted sons and daughters of God in the world effectively transforms the human being into a divine being in the world. Therefore, according to good theology, by divine adoption the human being is the "Son" or "Daughter of God." He or she is also the specially historically evolved moral agent, concrete representative and temporal ambassador of God in the world. The best example the human being as a divine being and "Son of God" in the world is that of Jesus as the Christ of God. As a result, all Christians are called to imitate his example of obedience to God, moral and prayerful life, praxis of unconditional love and the free forgiveness of sins for everybody including our enemies (cf. Matt. 5-7).

## 3. The Uniqueness of the Human Being: Mind, Divinity, Moral Agency and Evil

Each human being has been created as a special creature in God's own special image (*imago Dei*). This means that even when the human being is biologically and evolutionary related to other animals in the animal kingdom, the human being is also a mind and spiritual being who is related to God and a member of the spiritual Kingdom of God. As an *imago Dei*, the human being is also created to become the child of God and a member of the family and Kingdom of God.

As a result, all obedient, humane, caring, peaceful, just and loving human beings in the world are citizens of the Kingdom of God during this life on the Earth. This is true irrespective of creed, religion, race, color, nationality, tribe, class, language, level of technological development, gender, era, culture, marital state, sexual and ideological orientation. As God's ambassadors in the world, each finite evolutionary human being has also been created in God's own mystery.

Each human being has been created by God as unique and complex creature in order to become an independent intelligent, thinking, free, creative, moral agent as God's own concrete representation and ambassador in God's world of creation, both living and nonliving. The Bible expresses this special human nature and its supernatural abstract qualities in terms of "God's image," whereas Greek philosophy calls this nature rational and political.

The human being's nature is essentially a duality. The human nature as actuality is intrinsically both divine and animal in nature. As such, the human nature as being a duality is simultaneously both rational and irrational, spiritual and material, humane and beastly, and immortal like God and mortal like the rest of the created creatures. The best example of this intrinsic duality of human nature or two natures in one human being are those of Jesus as the Christ. In orthodox Christianity, Jesus as the Christ is considered to be simultaneously both truly God's incarnation in humanity and also truly human. That is, Jesus as the Christ possessed two natures, namely, true divinity and true humanity. The divine nature was eternal and immortal whereas the "human nature" or "animal nature" was finite and mortal. The suffering and death on the cross only applied to the human and mortal nature of Jesus and not to his divine nature which remained immutable, eternal and immortal.

As God's incarnation Jesus was the embodiment of the eternal Logos of God (God's Word), and as a true human being, he was the son of Joseph and Mary or Mr. and Mrs. Joseph. He was born like any other human being, grew up like any other child, and died on the cross at the age of thirty-three like any other criminal or rebellious and nationalistic Jewish political activist who was executed by the Romans by crucifixion.

The eternal God inside Jesus was the Transcendent and Eternal Spirit who is immortal and could not die on the cross. But the animal and human nature as the body of Jesus died on the cross. It was fully subject to the biological processes and natural laws governing pain and death. This is the best example of any true humanity that is completely open and obedient to God's will, holy Spirit, Agape, grace, and activities of creation and redemption in the world.

Like Jesus the Christ, any truly obedient person or saint becomes God's true ambassador and mediator of God's divinity, grace, Agape, and power of God's free forgiveness of sins, healing and restoration of broken lives in the world. True humanity is that which has surrendered to God's Spirit, grace and Agape. It is united with God's divine essence, therefore, transcends duality and the natural barriers which are erected by the animal aspect of the dual human nature. Once human divine self-transcendence is accomplished, the human being becomes a pure temporal (tangible), spiritual or mental medium through which God can be disclosed and mediated to the world and also to be seen (*epiphany*), encountered, talked to, and prayed to! The Church's traditional priesthood serves as this temporal channel of God's mediation of special revelation and redemptive grace!

Jesus, Buddha and the Virgin Mary as the *Theotokos* (Bearer of God) are good examples. The holy saints (Christian) and the holy ancestors within Judaism, and the traditional religions of Africa, Native America and Asia are other examples. Moses, Abraham, Isaac and Jacob are sometimes invoked by believers of Judaism, Islam and Christianity. Is this chain of mediation "pagan" or "idolatrous?" The answer is "no!" There is the danger of cults and abuse which may lead to idolatry. However, Christianity reminds the world that God is truly inseparable from humanity. This is by virtue of God's special creation of the human being in his own image (*imago Dei*), and also by virtue of the affirmation of the doctrines of God's historical incarnation in humanity and cosmic history through Jesus as the Christ and embodiment of the divine Logos.

As such, mainline Christianity affirms that both God and humanity are inseparably bound together with obedient and pure humanity. This is the universal context for the theological incarnational understanding of the human being as the divine creature or historical, evolutionary, spiritual, moral and mental expression of God in cosmic history and creation as the "*imago Dei.*" That is to affirm that the human being as the highly intelligent, thinking, creative, linguistic or communicative, symbolic, moral, humane, forgiving, caring, responsible, and loving creature is the true mirror or concrete reflection and mediation of God in the world.

Because of this human duality as divine and animal, the human being is unlike other creatures in the animal kingdom. Human beings are God's unique mirrors and concrete representatives in cosmic creation. From a theological or religious perspective, human beings are the special creatures in God's creation by God's undeserved free grace, Agape (unconditional Love) and election (being chosen) to become his adopted children and representatives in the world as his Kingdom.

For this purpose, human beings were created as God's work in progress. This partly accounts for their open and incomplete nature. They are God's special evolutionary and historical minds, and spiritual beings in the evolutionary cosmos and its delicate processes. Human beings are created as open and incomplete finite mysteries. All human beings are, by God's design, created with an eternal void or emptiness at the core of their being.

However, Karl Rahner has clearly shown in his many works on grace, such as *The Foundations of Christian Faith; The Hearers of the Word; the Church and Sacraments*; and *Theological Investigations, 25 (vols).* God has created an effective and universal permanent structure of grace and positive orientation to God's Word *(Logos)* of life, revelation and redemption.

This divine structure of supernatural grace within each human being is both spiritual and moral antenna which is *a priori* permanently tuned to God for meaning and fulfilment. This structure makes each human being a religious creature. It recognizes the human inner infinite void at the center of the human being and channels the human being to the infinite Creator-God as the essential eternal source of true human life, fulfillment, meaning, and ultimate happiness. This eternal and infinite void which is experienced at the core of the human existence can only be completely filled by the eternal and infinite God.

God's infinite mystery, agape, grace, service and fellowship are required to fill the human inner void or perceived inner emptiness that is ever yearning to be filled. Yet, this infinite void never gets filled by material things or other acquisitions such as food, wealth, alcohol, drugs, sex, possessions, fame, power and success. This universal human emptiness and void at the center of life cannot be ignored or completely filled with material goods such as wealth, power, sex, food, drink or other hedonistic pleasures. It is an infinite spiritual void which can only be filled by God. Other remedies to fill the void have been unsuccessfully tried. They only lead to addictions, misery and despair. Sometimes, suicide takes place out of this condition of the overwhelming feeling of personal failure, meaningless, hopelessness, depression and desperation.

Human beings as *imago Dei* (God's likeness) are complex mysteries like God in whose image they were created. They are intrinsically born good, open and both positively oriented and attuned to God's infinite mystery, for which they have a permanent affinity and eternal longing. As a result, all human beings need God for meaningful self-fulfillment and completion. This is because of the universal existential structure of God's supernatural grace which has been created within each human being and is universally experienced as the inner eternal void or emptiness at the center of each human being. This inner human void was placed at the core of the human being by God as a permanent antenna of grace to orient each normal human being to the quest for completion and self-fulfillment in God's fellowship, love, grace, acceptance and union.

Human beings are intrinsically religious by essential nature. They need all creatures, because they share in God's own divine nature and attributes. But human beings are not completely divine. They still share and are open to the nature of the other earthly animals, particularly the primates. It was from these primates as the higher life form which had evolved on planet Earth, which God had freely elected and chosen them based on his Agape and purposive universal free redemptive grace *(sola gratia)*. Due to this divine election all human beings have become God's special embodiments of spirit, intelligence, mind, knowledge, truth, freedom, creativity, judgement, moral agency and responsibility in the world. That is, each human being is a true temple or embodiment of God in the world. To some extent, each human being participates in God's direct essence of divinity, creativity, self-transcendence, Agape, healing, freedom, causality and responsibility. As such, to see a true human being, especially a saint, is in some metaphorical and anthropomorphic manner, to see and encounter God!

To this divine goal, through the mediation of natural law, God has both guided and advanced human evolution into the fullness of development of a computer-like biological brain with its amazing neurological wiring, intellect, mind, memory, thinking process, self-contemplation and self-consciousness. This special human brain structure has great capacity for great intelligence and aptitudes. The human brain facilitates the characteristic human full mental unique abilities, such as the rise of mind, intuition, spirit, freedom, language, God-consciousness, moral agency, justice, responsibility, empathy, mercy, compassion, altruism and Agape.

Agape and nonviolence constitute the ultimate twin moral apexes of human moral evolutionary development, humanization and divinization. At this stage of "*anthropogenesis*" and divinization, the natural process of human evolution comes to its apex and completion. At this evolutionary apex, the human being has been elevated and deified into a divine and pure thinking moral agent as spirit and mind that has truly attained pure moral consciousness, self-transcendence, knowledge of the truth and self-realization as a finite part of God's own self-projection and embodiment into matter and the divine creative process of cosmic evolutionary history. The human being and God have become reconciled and become one. Buddha and Jesus testified to the experiential spiritual reality of this beatific or heavenly union of the God and humanity. This is the central essence of the Christian theory of God's Incarnation in the world through Jesus as the embodiment of God.

According to Hegel, this is the moment of divine-self-reconciliation and end of cosmic history. When human beings realize that they are God's creatures, divine mind and spirit in self-alienation and embodiment in fragments of matter, the human alienation that Karl Barth called the gulf between humanity and God will be permanently abridged. Each person will become part of God's self-conscious divine incarnation in the world just as both Buddha and Jesus-Christ came to realize. This will eliminate the traditional duality, gap and alienation between God and humanity; mind and matter; body and spirit; and heaven and the world.

All these realms of duality, conflict and opposition will be reconciled when God's cosmos will be effectively transformed into his perfect single and harmonious inclusive Kingdom again! This is the meaning of the primordial pristine Garden of Eden. God's undivided and harmonious Kingdom as the Garden of Eden contained diversity, but that diversity was unified in the focus on God and God's universal implicit reign through the natural and explicit reign through the written moral law.

These biological systems have by God's design and providence through natural law evolved to the higher level where they are able to support intelligence, complex learning of new things, memory, abstract thinking, freedom, complex spoken or written language, understanding, self-transcendence, moral judgment, free choices, self-consciousness, God-consciousness, moral decisions and responsibility. Being evolutionary, humanity is a not complete or static in its essence and functions. The human being is God's ongoing creation and redemptive project. Self-completion and self-perfection are the essential divine tasks of each person from the moment of birth to death. They are never completed tasks with finished perfect products. As such, life and salvation are from beginning to end, God's supernatural gifts of grace in unconditional love.

This evolutionary task is accomplished through sound education processes and religion. This includes the faith in God's goodness and unconditional love as the basis and context for life and the courage to be human and happy in a constantly changing world and uncertainty. Life and the future are fully open and fluid. Our future and destiny are still waiting to be determined by how we exercise the responsibilities of our causal freedom, now. Due to the reality of the human causal freedom and creativity, all predictions of the future events are only partial in as much as the events that constitute that reality are still indeterminate and subject to change before they occur.

However, it is very troubling for some people to realize that the future is open and determined not by God or the stars at the time of our birth, but rather, by the nature or quality of the daily free choices which we make or fail to make in the present. The choices we make in the present are the real seeds we sow now for the crops or fruits which we harvest in the future! If we sow evil now, we may also reap the fruits of this evil and those negative consequences connected with it, in the future. In this respect, we may introduce evil in God's good world and creation. That is the risk God took when he or she created human beings as his or her free adopted Sons and Daughters, and endowed them with divine essence in the form of freedom, mind, spirit, self-transcendence, creativity, intelligence, and great thinking capacities.

The future and self-creating humanity are part of our contributions to the creative and evolutionary processes. In this respect, we are both God's work in progress. We are also God's co-creators with God in the world and its history.

No person is ever complete at birth. Each person "is born amoral." This is the affirmation of "*tabula rasa moral and spiritual theory*." This "*tabula rasa* moral and spiritual theory" is rooted in the moral theory which teaches that the human being is born free from the traditional, Pauline-Augustinian pessimistic view of human nature for being utterly corrupt and depraved prior to human birth. This erroneous moral theory and faulty traditional theological starting point is based on the false reading of the Genesis stories of creation as historical accounts of God's historical activities in the world. These Genesis accounts of creation and the fall of humanity are mere Hebrew myths and legends of creation and the human fall from perfection and the presence of imperfection in the world.

These religious stories are not history or scientific accounts of creation. They are similar to the stories of creation one finds plentiful in the traditional societies of Africa, India, China, Japan, pre-Colombian America and pagan Europe, particularly in the Greek and Roman myths of creation. St. Paul's and the Augustinian views and teachings of original sin take Adam and Eve as the primordial perfect couple who are created by God. They use their free-will and freedom to disobey God and thus cause the downfall of all humanity.

This "*tabula rasa moral and spiritual theory*" rejects all traditional moral, theological and anthropological doctrines and forms of determinism, fatalism and predestination. It replaces them with freedom, grace and self-determination with the environmental conditions which effect a moral, spiritual and cultural conditioning as a person grows up. Sin and guilt are not part of the DNA (deoxyribonucleic acid) that one inherits. Rather, they are part of the corrupt social and religious environment. Pelagius was correct to reject St. Augustine's pessimistic moral theory rooted in determinism and predestination. He was correct in his affirmation that one can resist both sin and evil given God's sufficient free power of redemptive grace, strict personal discipline, a sound moral education, and good moral upbringing.

However, St. Augustine's Pauline and neo-Platonist pessimistic view of human nature and the world prevailed in the Church. Pelagius and his followers were condemned and silenced as heretics. Since that time, the Christian Church has misleadingly taught that all human beings are to be considered "sinful" and "evil" having "fallen" from God's original state of perfection and supernatural grace. And therefore, having lost the original goodness and perfection, the heavenly state in which the original human beings were supposedly created by God. As a result, both Augustine and John Calvin taught that all human beings now only possess (*posse peccare*) moral defect and spiritual sin and guilt due to the inherited "moral and spiritual pollution of Adam's original sin."

However, within Pelagius' moral theory, a person is born with the divine potential to be transformed into God's true mirror and reflection in the world. This is moral theory is more compatible with evolution than the Augustinian and Pauline one. Nobody is ever born evil or sinful. Each person is born as a clean moral and mental slate on which the society and the individual both write the moral codes that then govern and guide the moral, spiritual and social life of the individual as a knowing, thinking, social, responsible, mature, humane, and free moral agent.

Contrary to the destructive, pessimistic, biological, and deterministic moral teachings of Paul, Augustine and Calvin, God's original grace, unconditional love, mercy and free forgiveness of sins were never lost by Adam and Eve! These are mere mythological figures who never had real historical existence and therefore, could not actually cause the downfall of humanity.

Nevertheless, the human community can cause the downfall of humanity if Adam and Eve are accepted and believed to be real historical beings that cursed humanity with permanent and insurmountable moral imperfection, weakness and predisposition to sin and evil works, rather than good deeds of unconditional love and justice. Deliverance from evil involves mental liberation from the negative, pessimistic oppressive despair associated with the myth of Adam and Eve and the original sin and the fall. As Jesus, St. Paul, Aquinas, Hegel, Wesley and Whitehead correctly taught, God's perfection of humanity consists of the future improvements, and ever beckoning perfection in God.

Human perfection does not lie in any corrupted generations of perfect and sinless people in the past, or the primitive stone-age as non-evolutionists have traditionally both wrongly thought and taught. With the rare exceptions of a few saints like Buddha and Jesus, in reality, human beings have never been perfect. The perfection of humanity lies in the realization that race, gender, color, nationality and class are superficial divisions. Humans must realize that they are all created in God's own image (*imago Dei*) as brothers, sisters, and citizens of God's Kingdom of love, equality, justice and equitable sharing of God's providence in terms of natural resources and human talents.

Ultimately, to be a normal human being is to grow up and fulfill one's divine potential and to become like God. Jesus is the Christian paradigm for obedience, praxis of Agape and human-divinization, or self-deification into God as Agape. That involves the ability to possess divinity in the form of: divine attributes, knowledge, skills, freedom, intellect, mind, spirit, self-transcendence, agape, creativity, forgiveness, moral-consciousness, compassion, language or capacity to speak, and use fire. These divine qualities permit the emergence of more sophisticated, specialized and abstract mental powers of thinking, learning, knowing and decision-making skills. These are acquired through socialization and education as the life-long dual process of humanization and divinization.

As a result, to be fully human also means to learn, acquire and possess correct knowledge, make moral judgment and decisions, and live according to this knowledge and truth. When this happens, then the person is truly God's moral agent and the decisions made according to correct knowledge and truth are also said to be moral, virtuous and good. They are also always godly, hardworking, humane, considerate, caring, peace-loving, loving, forgiving and just. This is possible because they are impartial and just. They also exist and conduct themselves in accordance with sound knowledge and God's truth. In this respect, virtue requires both good and sound knowledge of what is good, and a life which is dedicated to the pursuit of happiness in the knowledge of the good and the "Truth." Here, the "Truth" refers to God as the embodiment of life, order, reality, peace, goodness, justice, love, perfection and happiness.

However, in most cases, human beings are ignorant of the truth. They do not possess perfect knowledge due to the very nature of the human finite mind. The divine embodied mind or finite human mind has an inability to apprehend and comprehend the whole which is the real and correlatively, the truth. Instead, the human mind being finite also essentially concentrates on the more manageable finite fragments of knowledge which the mind can easily apprehend and process. Unfortunately, the finite human mind tends also to treat and process the fragmentary bits of knowledge as the definitive whole and absolute reality. That is an illusion. Great tragedies have occurred in human society and the world because of this erroneous epistemology, falsehood and mental illusion. This was more self evident when some misguided religious people claimed that their fragments of religion, truths and knowledge were absolute because they were God's perfect and inerrant or divine, infallible, definitive universal revelations!

Only the omniscient and Transcendent God is able to possess all the possible knowledge and possess the whole truth. All human claims to possess the infallible totality of knowledge are false and dangerous. This is true, irrespective of whether that claim is made by scientists or the supposed religious infallible authorities such as the holy scriptures, Popes, theologians and prophets!

The tragic examples include the proclamations of the stories of creation as found in the Hebrew Bible in the book of Genesis to be actual records of the primordial historical events within this world. This grave error leads to the tragic dogma which requires the faithful to accept and affirm those mythological stories as God's universal, infallible and inerrant revelation. This is accomplished by proclaiming these myths of creation and the human disobedience, sin and fall of humanity from God's grace and perfection to be history or scientific accounts of how the world originated.

These stories are further used to explain why patriarchal or male-chauvinists treat women as members of an inferior and subordinate class of people in the Church and society instead of equals. These believers then blasphemously claim that this state of affairs is God's decree and holy will, rather than perceiving them as evil and sinful structures to be denounced and dismantled by God's obedient and repentant Church and the moral and just community of democratic or postmodernist civilized men and women.

Consequently, any moral and other practical decisions, whether educational, socioeconomic, political or medical based on such partial knowledge which is unknowingly treated as the whole truth, are bound to error. Subsequently, they cause more harm than good to human beings and the community.

Nevertheless, human beings constantly make important global decisions on the basis of limited fragmentary knowledge, which, in ignorance, is treated as the whole truth. As a consequence, the world is full of evil due to human moral imperfections, ignorance, poor judgment, serious errors, carelessness and accidents. Consequently, if the world today is observed or said to be evil, polluted, and desert, it is not because God made it that way. The world today is in many respects what it is because in the name of God, we have made it what it has now become.

In other words, God created us in his or her own image, entrusted us with his or her creation as his or her intelligent, creative, moral and physical representatives and stewards. Instead, we became greedy, immoral and rebellious against God. As a result, we, too, also became the ruthless masters, exploiters and destroyers of ourselves, one another and God's creation. As a consequence, we have transgressed against God, ourselves and the rest of creation. We have sinned against the Creator-God and abused, injured and tragically marked creation with our own sins and evils of graffiti, aggression, exploitation, pollution, vandalism and destruction.

In short, society and the environment are the external expressions of the human being. As such, they bear the effective testimony to the social and moral values, immorality, imperfection, sin, ignorance, as well as the existence of beauty and goodness. However, whereas moral imperfection, ignorance, prejudice, hate, strife, conflict, and war were prevalent in the past and were tolerated by society, today, these kinds of moral evils and imperfections cannot be tolerated. In the past, these vices, conflicts and wars were generally local problems. But the last two World Wars have indicated that wars are no longer local affairs.

These world wars ended tragically, with the American indiscriminate mass destruction of life and property in Hiroshima and Nagasaki, the two Japanese cities on which the unforgettable deadly nuclear bombs were dropped by American military jets. Whereas the lesson of those cities may be ignored by the simple-minded and immoral warmongers or the prejudiced white-supremacist politicians, it should not be forgotten by those men and women of goodwill and the peacemakers. The western fundamentalist, communist-hating Christians and the ignorant masses are those who do not understand the need for global peace. They hardly understand the danger of nuclear warfare.

Therefore, the environmentalists, and all those who love God and Christ's central moral and religious teaching of unconditional love for all human beings, should work together with all men and women of goodwill to oppose nuclear arms and warfare. These groups should all unite and form a joint moral coalition to protest against the social injustice and the unwise or suicidal nuclear arms race and the nuclear arsenals that endanger and threaten the existence of life and global freedom. Therefore, religious, cultural and ethnic intolerance, hate, bigotry and deadly arms must not be accepted or tolerated by God's obedient people, since they pose great threats to a peaceful society. These vices threaten the mental, moral, spiritual and physical human well-being everywhere.

Ultimately, good theology and ethics should promote peaceful human coexistence on this planet, regardless of creed, race, gender, culture, class and nationality. This can be accomplished by teaching agape, nonviolence and justice for all people as God's children. The very survival and continued existence of life itself on this unique and fragile planet depends on the human praxis of the virtues of agape, peace, tolerance, justice and equity. God's gifts or natural resources are showered on humanity and are not to be fought over and accumulated by the strong or a few privileged individuals; rather, they ought to be shared by all and utilized for the benefit of all God's people.

## 4. The Human Being as God's Unique Creation And Mystery in the Evolutionary Cosmos

The human being is a natural problem solving being by virtue of great intelligence and great capacity for analytical thinking and memory. Many social, political, scientific and technological problems have been already researched and solved.

One of the greatest mysteries still remaining to be probed on planet Earth is the human being. The International Human Genome Project has been charged with this great responsibility. The DNA map and codes of life have been successfully decoded by use of the most sophisticated, fast and powerful computers of the Third Millennium. The essence of the human being is now being investigated by great scholars in both the sciences and the humanities. The human being, having intellectually matured, is now engaged in the self-conscious study and self- analysis. This si essential in order to achieve better self-understanding and develop better medical procedures for the diagnosis of diseases and to prevent them before they strike. Human genetic engineering is ideal when looked a from this medical perspective. Human cloning for infertile couples or those who do not wish to risk inherited diseases should also be considered moral. This is a good reason to support the work of the Human Genome Project and other research projects.

As human beings, we have tried to study everything on this planet and *master it*. We have probed space, other planets, and galaxies. Great astrophysicists like the late Carl Sagan have conducted astronomical research, and tried to make the cosmic mysteries understandable and interesting to the nonscientific community. The heavens have been scanned by special space telescopes and special space-research interstellar spaceships, such as the shuttle and Magellan. The Russians had built *Mir* and the international community late built an international space research laboratory in "the sky" (*the heavens*) above the Earth. All this has been done in the human quest for both knowledge and extraterrestrial life. Humanity has nearly succeeded in its humanistic quest and scientific research objectives. This research has led to the enhancement of both our own knowledge nature and the general improvement of the material quality of human life which advances in modern science and technology have made it possible.

These advances in modern aerodynamics and space science have made it possible for human beings to go into space, walk on the moon, and build space laboratories to manufacture better quality chemicals and medicines in "*zero gravity*" conditions of outer-space. Whereas this has constituted good utilization of technology and the exploitation of the heavens for the benefit and betterment of human kind on Earth or "below," other human forces have been at work to extend the human evils of pollution and warfare into space. Deadly nuclear arms and anti-satellite laser weapons can lead to the destruction of the Earth and pollute the hallowed space or the sky which is lovingly known by many religious people as "heaven" or "the heavens."

Modern science and rapid technological advance have revolutionized electronic communications by proving a quick global "information highway" in the form of the cyberspace and Internet global network. This international linkage of information and research data bases have in turn created great advances in medical technology, medicine, mass food production, the advance has revolutionized housing, water, and transportation which led to better systems. All of these have improved the material quality of our lives by extending the life span from mid the 4Os to mid 70s, just within a few decades, and thus these improvements have to be commended and supported.

It is this very advanced modern technology in the sciences that has also brought about the correlative negative and deadly global threats of advanced military offensive weapons of mass destruction. The biological, chemical and nuclear arms race have become a threat to life, the environment and the well-being of humans. Advances in technology need to be controlled by moral and peace loving world leaders. In the past, military technology made it possible to end World War II sooner before more lives were lost. However, it also created new and more serious threats for misuse and human disaster at the hands of evil dictators and terrorist nations or groups of greedy rogues. Instead of using a gun to rob a bank, these rogues may use a nuclear weapon to hold a nation hostage for huge sums of money or political gain!

Carl Sagan and other physicists of moral conscience have served social prophets called the world leaders , especially, those of major nuclear powers to realize the dangers of nuclear arms and radiation. They also warned of technological misuse for military purposes, instead of building better medical equipment and nuclear reactors to provide cheaper electricity for the poor masses of people in the world. If misused, technology and particularly nuclear arms could lead to the serious global, catastrophic destruction of life, environment, and property.

Nuclear arms could also lead to accidental or suicidal fiery nuclear explosions. In the nuclear explosions' aftermath, there would be massive global radiation contamination, deadly toxic smoke, and radiative dust-storms. These would combine with thick clouds of smoke emitted by billions of burning buildings and green vegetation set ablaze by nuclear explosions to cause further disasters for people and the environment.

Why should we as human beings commit this kind of horrible suicide? Or why should evil leaders and other criminals force to commit suicide? Why should a few individual or even nations be allowed to destroy us and all life on this unique planet? What is there to be gained by going to war in which mutual destruction and no winner is assured? Or one should ask why some intelligent and responsible people should go to war at all? Is warfare and hatred a survival of animality in humanity or a survival of sin in a child of God?

Indeed, these and many other questions should be asked by all intelligent human beings everywhere, regardless of creed, ideology, level of technology, or economic development. Human existence and survival on this ecologically delicate special living planet, the Earth require new moral and scientific thinking, theology, ethics and politics in order to guide and regulate the uses of technology and science for positive ends.

Nuclear arms, instant two-way audio-video telecommunications, supersonic air travel, dwindling natural economic resources, environmental pollution, international trade, and international politics require new global ethics of inclusiveness, understanding of global cultural or racial diversity, religious pluralism, tolerance and peace.

Religious and cultural bigotry have no place in the postmodern global era. Cultural, ethnic, religious strife and conflicts are no longer local affairs. Because of postmodern inclusiveness and pluralism, local matters and conflicts will now become global community affairs. This is because individual affairs are no longer isolated personal incidents to be left to the individual nation's whims. Examples include the cyberspace terrorists who manufacture harmful viruses and unleash them on the Internet to infect and damage millions of computers and cause property and data losses worth billions of dollars. Deadly biological agents or harmful chemicals could also be unleashed into our waters or the air causing great harm to people and the environment. Personal freedom must be regulated to safeguard the public and the world from immoral and irresponsible criminals, terrorists, and the mentally ill.

Personal freedom and private actions are no longer completely separable from the public collective and global affairs. President Clinton and Monica Lewinsky's private affairs in the White House have clearly illustrated that for the world. Human global communications and relationships have become developed to such a high degree that individuals are able to influence global affairs. Moses, Buddha, Jesus, Paul, Augustine, Muhammad, Luther, King Henry VIII, Wesley, Gandhi, Hitler, Stalin, Idi Amin, Reagan, Gorbachev, Princess Diana, and Alan Greenspan are some of these examples. To some varying significance, each major human decision affects not only the individual, but also the family, community, nation and the world.

This includes the decisions which deal with God's creation, such as tree planting, cleaning streams, parks and the preservation of wildlife. Our planet Earth has indeed, become God's new "Noah's Ark" of cosmic salvation of both humanity and the rest of our fellow inhabitants of the Earth, such as the animals and plants. Therefore, each person is analogous to Noah. Rational people cannot afford to let anyone puncture a hole within ozone protective layer by detonating massive nuclear weapons or destroying creation with chemical or biological weapons. We cannot drill a hole in our own corner of the ozone layer or pollute the air and the oceans either in ignorance or greed without setting off a series of disastrous environmental and ecological crisis.

To keep silent in the face of a major evil and disaster, is to condone evil and become an evil accessory to crime, or to become co-conspirator and perpetrator of the disaster. Therefore, all moral and God-fearing people of the world have a moral obligation to denounce the evils and sins committed by evil people, who are hateful, unjust, racist, sexist, corrupt, egocentric, power hungry, greedy and criminals. To keep quiet, and let such evil and demonic people carry out their own evil plans, unchecked, is to both acquiesce and promote evil in God's good world.

Accordingly, faced with the moral crisis posed by President Idi Amin, the evil dictator of Uganda 1971-79, the Most Reverend Janani Luwum, the Anglican Archbishop of Uganda and his supporters, such as Bishop Festo Kivengere, the diocesan Anglican bishop of Kigezi, and his friend, the Rev. Emmanuel K. Twesigye, teacher and Anglican Chaplain at Makerere University and the National Teachers' College, Kyambogo did not keep quiet. They secretly worked together to organize protest groups and undermine President Idi Amin's racist, tribalistic and religious sectarian policies of division, discrimination, Christian persecution and mass murders of those critical of his policies or political opponents.

As a result of this strategic mobilization for Christian moral protest, the various protest acts of a well-mobilized Anglican House (Conference) of Bishops and Church congregation members, President Idi Amin's "reign of terror" and Christian persecution was successfully resisted. Idi Amin was finally overthrown in 1979 by the Ugandan exiles headed by Yoweri Museveni, and the Tanzanian troops deplored by President Julius Nyerere. President Nyerere did not count the cost for waging war against Idi Amin of Uganda. His driving force was his moral commitment to democracy, freedom and human rights in Africa.

The Ugandan Christians were disillusioned when the wealthier and militarily stronger Western Christian nations refused to come and help them get rid of President Idi Amin, a fundamentalist Muslim, who had become an evil dictator and mass murderer of the Ugandan Christians. The Ugandan Christians began to realize that many Western politicians see their own nations' interests in terms of resources and strategic importance, rather than the safeguarding of human-rights and protection of life when it is threatened by evil people, such as the perpetrators of Tutsi genocide in Rwanda in 1994 and the gross abusers of human rights in Liberia, Sierra Leone and the Great Lakes Region in the late 1990s and early period of 2000.

In the case of Uganda, the human cost for the protest and getting rid of President Idi Amin was very high. More than 800,000 people were massacred by Idi Amin over the course of nine brutal years. The Archbishop Janani Luwum was assassinated by President Idi Amin on night of February 16, 1977; Bishop Kivengere and Rev. Twesigye escaped into exile, following the assassination of their leader, and their property were destroyed, and bank accounts were frozen by President Idi Amin.

Likewise, Archbishop Oscar Romero of El Salvador was assassinated in 1988, by the government agents. The government of El Salvador wanted to punish and permanently silence him. The government leaders resented the fact Archbishop Romero bluntly and publically denounced their dictatorship, and exposed to the world, their brutality and massacres of masses of ordinary poor people who had petitioned the government for pieces of land on which to grow their food and cash-crops in order to sustain themselves and their impoverished landless and unemployed families.

As such, silence in the face of moral evil and injustice, amounts to consent to that evil. To be silent in the face of evil is also to participate in it by failure to act positively to either prevent it before it happens or to stop it once it begins. That is why on March 12, 2000, Pope John Paul II, led the Church to repent and atone for its sins of racism, sexism, and violence against, such as the crusades against non-Christian peoples of the world, and racial minorities. Adolf Hitler's racist policies and genocide of the European Jews succeeded because the "Christians" as the "moral majority" either joined Hitler or kept quiet in the face of a great moral and social evil. Therefore, to fail to denounce evil for fear one's own safety and material well-being is moral treason and unfaithfulness to God. Moral apathy and silence in the face of evil is a serious moral failure by God's moral agents. It amounts to moral abdication by God's people of their essential divine given duties to serve as God's concrete custodians of life and creation in the world.

If through apathy and ignorance, we permit evil to occur in the community and the world because of immoral and illogical decisions implemented by our leaders, this will be tantamount to wrongdoing, and participation in evil and sin on our part. It is also both foolish and self-destructive.

For instance, the traditional family institution or its integrity, the community, and the world will all be destroyed by evil and negative forces due to our own moral permissiveness and apathy. This local and global societal evil and disaster can only occur as a self-imposed divine judgement and existential hell. This will be due to our moral evil or failure to restrain the illogical, paranoid, suicidal, bigoted, careless, insane, and irresponsible members of our global community from inflicting harm on themselves, the community, environment and the world.

Therefore, the people of the Third World should be equally concerned about what happens in Washington, D.C. and Moscow. Like the people of the West, they too, are citizens and an integral part of the global community. During the Cold War era, the developing world was used as the battle ground for fighting the indirect wars between the USA and former Soviet Union. The Korean and Vietnam wars, as well as the wars in the Middle East, Angola and South Africa are other examples. Military coups in Uganda and Congo are other tragic examples of this case.

In any case, in terms of military nuclear weapons, the underdeveloped nations should be concerned. For instance, if there was a massive nuclear explosion in the Northern hemisphere, winds would carry nuclear radioactive dust and pollution to these noncombatant developing people in the other hemisphere.

Because of advanced military technology, the Earth is in more danger of being destroyed by irresponsible leaders, anarchist terrorists, immoral suicidal bombers and religious fanatics more than ever before. The destruction of the Earth, although foretold in the Bible (Mk. 13:24-33; Matt. 5:18, 1O:23; Lk. 16:17), can only become a reality soon if human beings fail to love one another, prevent wars and live together in peace. Otherwise, is not God's will to destroy the world.

Therefore, the doomsday cults, such as David Koresh's *Branch Davidians* of Waco Texas, Shoko Asahara's *Aum Shinri Kyo* which killed 12 people and injured more than 5,000 in 1995 poison gas attack on crowded Tokyo train station, and the Ugandan *Movement for the Restoration of the Ten Commandments of God* led by self-consecrated "Bishop" Joseph Kibwetere and the Rev. Dr. Dominic Kataribabo are examples of suicidal apocalyptic doomsday cults and fanatical leaders who could mistakenly kill other people and destroy the world in God's holy name if they gained access to a weapon of mass destruction. For instance, Father Kataribabo used poison, sulphuric acid and gasoline to kill more than 1,000 of the cult members.

On the night of March 17, 2000, more than 534 were burned to death in a deliberately set church fire fueled by gasoline and sulphuric acid in the remote rural town of Kanungu-Rukungiri, South-Western Uganda. The Movement leaders had predicted that the world would end in fire at midnight on December 31, 1999. It did not. The date was then revised to the end of 2000, and finally it was revised to March 17, 2000. Their world ended in an inferno. However, that was a mass suicide and not God's will or doing. That will also be the tragic end of careless apocalyptic politicians who play the deadly military games of war and "Armageddon with nuclear weapons."

The destruction of this world in fiery explosion as God's judgement and punishment in hell for the sinners was that the Gospel would first be preached to every person (creature) in the world (Mk. 13:32; Mtt. 24:14) and to all nations. However, according to David Barret's recent mammoth statistical data, Christianity in all its different thousands of Churches only accounts for just a third of the total population, and was on the decline, and not the increase. The human destruction of the world would negating God's will in creation and sustenance of the world. All human beings are created to live on the Earth. Their main divine mission, moral obligation and destiny is become the stewards and custodians or caretakers of God's creation, and not its destroyers!

It is quite clear and beneficial that instead of seeking to destroy those we call atheists, "communists," or "infidels" we should seek to convert them to God moral obligation of unconditional love. We should also aspire to bring Muslims into the joy and experience of God's unconditional love, free forgiveness of sins, and nonviolence. This is the Christian responsibility and effective witness to God's redemptive mission in the world through Jesus as the Christ. The praxis of love was the primary goal of God's Logos or Christ's mission and incarnation in the world. The Incarnation of God and, symbolically, the unification of God and every human being and God's demonstration of how we should love the neighbor, including the enemy:

> You have heard that it was said, "You shall love your neighbor and hate your enemy." But I say to you, "Love your enemies and pray for those who persecute you, so that you may be sons of your Father who is in heaven; for he makes his sun to rise on the evil and on the good, and sends rain on the just and the unjust . . . ." (Matt. 5:43-48)

It is quite clear that Jesus does not want us to send nuclear bombs and missiles to destroy with fire on those we consider to be evil or unjust. Rather, unlike the followers of Moses, Christians are commanded to neutralize their evil with good deeds of unconditional love and prayer for their conversion, reformation and deliverance from evil and its oppression. Christ's teachings and the imperative Commandment of Agape and nonviolence are the moral and spiritual center and foundations of any true Christianity and definitive Christian ethics or moral values.

The definitive, central moral and spiritual teachings of Jesus Christ are that all human beings should love God and love our neighbor as we love ourselves. This is the moral and intellectual stumbling block of the Christian faith and any truly redemptive Christianity. Even St. Paul, himself, as the basis of much Protestant doctrines, rather than Jesus' own teachings, definitively assured his followers that of all God's supernatural gifts of the Holy Spirit, "*Faith, hope, and agape (unconditional love), all endure, but the greatest of them all is agape*" (1 Cor. 13:14).

Therefore, Christians and other loving, godly and just people in the world have a responsibility to promote unconditional love, nonviolence and global peace. They must seek ideal opportunities to influence society, politics and the world affairs in a positive manner. This is the case, regardless of whether they are in education or politics and government. Some of them may seek the rare opportunity to become the world's leaders of peace and justice, as in the case of Gandhi, Martin Luther King and former Anglican Archbishop Desmond Tutu of South Africa.

Most of these world humanitarian leaders and advocates of international peace and justice have necessarily also become the proponents of disarmament and tolerance for ideological and religious pluralism as the means to establish and maintain meaningful and lasting global peace. They advocate responsible stewardship of money and natural resources. The also support the utilitarian moral principle of using natural resources and money for the maximum benefit of the greatest number of people.

To this end, the national and the United Nations' budgets must shift their respective emphasis from the military to public education, health and effective welfare systems to serve the poor and other less affluent citizens. The Christians have a divine mandate to act in this world as peacemakers and global community builders. To do otherwise is to repudiate God's unconditional redemptive love in Christ that was expressed to this world on the cruel and painful cross. Christians, are also called to bear their own crosses and faithfully follow Christ's teaching and example. If necessary they must to die as witnesses or martyrs for the truth, and thereby mediate God's salvation for the world which was originally ushered into the world *incognito, in the incarnation or birth, life, ministry and innocent death of Jesus Christ on the cross.*

Because this divine redemptive mission in cosmic history was incognito, it is thus a matter of faith, rather than knowledge and evidence. Accordingly, the New Testament is the major statement of this Christian faith. Like the Apostles and Nicene creeds which were developed later as baptismal covenants to be recited by those adults coming to be baptized or initiated into the holy mysteries of God's salvation in Jesus as the Christ, the whole of the New Testament is a testimony of faith about Jesus as the Christ of God or the divinely chosen redemptive agent of God's eschatological salvation. The New Testament also shows Jesus as the divine agent for the establishment of the Kingdom of God in the world. This is characteristic of the "the messianic secret" as found in the Gospel of St. Mark.

Mark was concerned with providing a convincing answer to the difficult question regarding the messiahship of Jesus in light of the fact that Jews had rejected him as their expected Messiah (Christ) whereas Christians affirmed that he was in fact the Christ or the messiah. His answer was that Jesus did not come as a messianic king to restore the kingdom of David, and nor did he drive out the Roman occupying imperial forces as a Hebrew messiah would have been expected to do.

However, Jesus came as God's spiritual and messiah, historically established in the world God's moral and spiritual Kingdom of Love and nonviolence.

According to St. Mark's Gospel, Jesus' messiahship was a divine secret or incognito, and it was only accessible through the deep religious faith and repentance! (cf. Mk. 1:14-16). Repentance meant denouncing evil habits and accepting to be transformed by God into new beings who would obey God's commandments of justice, peace and unconditional love. Because of the power of the indwelling Holy Spirit and faith in the universal need and efficacy of God's free redemptive grace and unconditional love, they would be able to love their fellow human beings as they loved themselves.

As a result, these loving and obedient Christian believers would be able to understand that if God had indeed loved the world unconditionally, and sent his "Beloved Son" as a sin sacrifice in order to "redeem" or "save" this world, then as his beloved creation, he does not desire its destruction by disobedient and evil human beings. Subsequently, these obedient and loving Christians and other God-fearing men and women of good will, irrespective of their religious denomination or religion, cannot afford to stand still and let people like Adolf Hitler, Idi Amin, Saddam Hussein, former President Ronald Reagan or George Bush, endanger its very own existence by their ideological and military crusades in the world. It is insignificant whether their acts are in the name of racial superiority or ideological supremacy, such as capitalism as opposed to communism, or religious bigotry.

Ultimately, God acted in unconditional love in Christ in order to save this world. Subsequently, we, too, have to act in love for our fellow human being so as to save them from evil, hatred, oppression, cruelty, warfare and self-destruction. obedience to the commandment of unconditional love and nonviolence calls us to oppose the nuclear arms race and the militarization of oceans and space. In the final analysis, the same measure of unconditional love we express to our neighbor and the goodwill we extend in peace to all human beings are directly returned to us in the same or greater measure. As such, the unconditional love and peace we extend to our neighbors around the globe are extended to ourselves in a reflected manner, just as the boomerang goes out and eventually returns to its thrower.

By the same analogy, we will also receive what we extend to others around us; if it is evil that we express to others, it will also be generously reciprocated with greater evil. Therefore, as Christians, let us sow the seeds of love and peace on this ever "shrinking globe" and pray that God will bless it to yield the traits of love and global peace which we desperately need today.

Consequently, what humanity needs today is not more money, knowledge and technology. Instead, the world needs more love, compassion, tolerance, forgiveness, human caring, understanding and peace both nationally and internationally. This is extremely important for mere knowledge and nuclear technology, for without human love and care to direct and safeguard its humanitarian usage, it will soon prove tragic and suicidal for humanity and this planet. Since the greatest good and value of any knowledge, skill, science and technology is the enhancement of human survival and well-being of the human being, it seems that in the recent advances made in the sciences and technology, the necessary moral teaching required to govern ethical usage has lagged far behind. The cloning and gene-therapy technology are good examples here.

Animal and human cloning have raised serious ethical and theological issues such as the human acquisition of the Godlike power to create new life forms and alter the existing ones according to the human ideals and purposes. The scientific breakthroughs and advanced technology have tended to master the inventor. The human being has sometimes become the servant of technology rather than its creator, controller and master. Moreover, with increased knowledge and better technology, the human being has tended to deify himself or herself into God. This is idolatry. Sartre's definition of the human being as the creature that wants to become God is quite applicable in this case.

When the human being has utilized technology to play the role of God in the word, the results of misuse of technology have been tragic. Hazardous chemicals and radiative industrial waste have become a great problem. The disposal of this toxic and non-biodegradable material has become a great environmental problem in the Western industrialized nations of the world. The Third World is beginning to experience the same problems as it tries to industrialize.

Automobile and factory emission gases have polluted the air we breathe. These gases have coalesced in the air to form acid rain, which has ruined buildings, forests and farms. Industrial waste has been dumped into streams, rivers, lakes and oceans. Because of these actions, industrial waste and agricultural chemicals, such as fertilizers and insecticides, have become major environmental pollutants.

These gases and chemicals have contaminated our water supply by polluting the air, clouds, rivers, lakes, and oceans. Acid rain has killed essential vegetation, corroded buildings and national monuments. Unless this trend is halted, we will face a deadly global environmental crisis. Some man-made chemicals have even eaten holes in the ozone layer, leaving us exposed to the sun's cancer-causing radioactive rays. Nevertheless, driven by greed for profit and economic success, industries continue to manufacture these chemicals, and we buy them even when we know the great harm caused on a global scale. Therefore, at this point, one should stop and pose a vital question about our nature as human beings. What kind of creature or being is the human being? In traditional terms, the infinite question has been put as follows: "What is Man [humanity]?"

## 5. Quest for Human Essence And Ultimate Meaning

The universal existential question has been: "What is man [humanity]?" or "What is a human being?" or "What am I?" This perennial existential human question has always been asked by each individual and groups of thinking human beings everywhere in the world. The Hebrew Psalmist answered the question as follows:

> What is man [humankind]?
> That you should think of him?
> He is a mere mortal.
> Why should you care about him?
> Yet you made him just a little lower to yourself.
> You crowned him with glory and honor.
> You appointed him the ruler over everything you made.
> You placed him over all creation.
> You placed him over sheep and cattle;
> and the wild animals too.
> You also placed him over birds and the fish,
> and all the creatures in the seas. (Ps. 8:4-8)

The Psalmist has both theocentrically and correctly defined the human being as a special religious or God-centered creature of God who is akin to God. The purpose of the human being is identified with that of being God's ruler or custodian of all creation. That is the meaning and purpose of the evolution of the human being, divine human election, and possession of God's incarnate mind, spirit, freedom, thinking capacities, and creativity.

However, there are still many people who feel that the question has not been fully answered. They are particularly perplexed by the presence of evil, innocent suffering, pain and death. The infinite question which has not had satisfactory answers because there is no finite answer which cans satisfy the infinite question. Accordingly, the Psalmist also says:

> O Lord, you have always been our home.
> You tell man to return to what he was.
> You change him back to dust.
> A thousand years to you are like one day.
> They are like yesterday, already gone,
> like a short hour in the night.
> You sweep us away like a flood;
> Our lives are short just like a dream.
> We are like weeds that sprout in the morning.
> That grow and burst into bloom [in the warm sun].
> Then dry up and die in the evening.
> Our life span is seventy years;
> eighty years if you make us strong.
> Yet all they bring us is trouble and sorrow.
> Life passes quickly, and we soon gone.
> Therefore, teach us to number the days of our life
> so that we may become wise [in how we live].
> Fill us each morning with your constant love [Agape],
> so that we may sing and be happy all our lives.
> Give us now as much happiness as the sadness you gave us
> during our years of misery.
> Lord our God may your blessings be with us.
> Lord, give us success in all we do! (Ps. 90)

Obviously, the Psalmist is distressed because of the finitude and transitoriness of life and the pain it causes those who are alive. The Psalmist does not blame God for death. Death is accepted as God's providence. What the psalmist is praying for is a life filled with happiness! Buddha himself answered the same human existential question about suffering and death by saying that life has an intrinsic quality which is that of suffering and sadness (*Dukkha*). Buddha called for faith to accept the mode of life in the world as that of suffering and death. Jesus echoed the same truth when he called his disciples and told them:

> Pick up pick your cross and follow me. Whoever loses his or her life for my sake will regain it. And whoever rejects me and tries to save his or her own life will lose it. What does it profit a person to gain the whole world and loses his or her life? (cf. Mk. 8:34-36)

This Christian invitation to carry the cross or suffer as part of one's religious and moral calling and mission in the world, is significantly clear. This is especially when one realizes that the cross was the Roman instrument of torture, a slow, painful death. It was meant to be a deterrent to crime and uprising! But, for Christians, the cross and suffering become the symbols of self-discipline, obedience to God, self-renunciation, self-sacrifice, atonement, unconditional love for God and the neighbor, forgiveness of sins, and eternal life.

The early Church was characterized by courage, faith, suffering self-sacrificial death and martyrdom. Today, anybody who stands for peace and justice for all people, or socioeconomic justice and equity in a capitalist, greedy society, will also be rejected and persecuted like Jesus and the prophets were. Jesus, Gandhi, Martin Luther King, and Malcolm X are examples of men who were rejected and killed by hateful men because they demanded equality and socioeconomic justice for all people without discrimination on the basis of color, race, class, gender, ideology or religious basis.

Ironically, some people call themselves Christians, and yet they hate and discriminate against other people on the basis of color, race, nationality, class, gender and ideology! That is truly what it means to be an "anti-Christ." This is the case since Jesus taught and commanded his followers to love other people without any conditions!

However, the underlying question remains, namely, "what is humanity?" And why should we value human beings to the degree that we are commanded by Christ to love and forgive them unconditionally? The question of "what is man or humanity?" is central to any system of sound religion and ethics. It also underlies the human quest for the meaning of life. In short, this question underlies the other universal human existential or ultimate questions of humanity and the human condition.

This has been the universal case, regardless of era, technological and economic level of development, creed, ideology, race, color, nationality, and gender and socioeconomic status. The *Homo sapiens* as the thinking and knowing creature we call "the human(e) beings" become the religious and moral agents as soon as those thinking creatures either implicitly or explicitly ask what Paul Tillich called "the ultimate questions of concern." According to Tillich and Sam Keen, the universal ultimate questions of life and concern include the following:

1. "Who am I?" and "Why am I here?" "How do I know?"
2. "What am I?" "Am I just a body? Or an eternal fragment of God's mind and spirit in a finite and mortal body?"
3. "Where did I come from?"
4. "Why are there different races and colors of people?"
5. "Are some people better than others?" "Why?" "How?"
6. "What is my future?"
7. "Why am I here?"
8. "Why is there evil?"
9. "How do I live *the good life?*"
10. "What are the normative rules of life?"
11. "Who are my friends and allies?"
12. "Who are my enemies to fight or avoid?
13. "How do I know the good?"
14. "Why do good people suffer?"
15. "Why is there pain and death?"
16. "Is death the ultimate end of my life?" "Or is there life after death?"
17. "What will happen to me when I die?" Will I get reincarnated into another body or being?"
18. "If God loves us, why does he let us die?
19. "If God is loving and powerful, why is there evil and death?"
20. "Does God have some favorites? Who are they? Why?"

As a free thinking, intelligent and self-transcending creature, the human being is indeed the creature that is endlessly engaged in self-questioning, self-contemplation, and self-study. In this process, the human being has infinite questions of himself or herself. But, in this human self-contemplation and self-study process, if any person asks the above questions or similar ones, that person has already embarked on a moral and spiritual quest for meaning, God, salvation and happiness.

These ultimate questions are posed in the quest for a person's true identity and meaning. The origins and destiny are ultimately universally located in God. These questions are also the ultimate questions of the meaning of life. It is important how one answers the question regarding whether human life has any special meaning. If human life has no special meaning, then the hedonistic principle of "*let us eat, drink and make love for tomorrow we die"* (Eccl. 2:24) becomes the normative principle of life, particularly in politics, economics, religion and ethics. Apart from God as the purposive creator who gives human life its purpose and transcendent value as God's Child and representative in the world, the human life in itself, apart from the mind (*nous* and *logos*) which is part of God's essence that is embodied in finite matter (or the human body), does not have any separate value and meaning from that of other creatures! The only difference would be that the human being is merely more intelligent and capable of achieving a better life than the other animals! Their destiny would be the same-- namely, eternal death!

These are the existential and universal human questions which Paul Tillich correctly characterized as the human existential questions of ultimate concern. As such, they also require ultimate answers. To this end, they require religious and philosophical answers in reassurance of personal identity and meaning. Helpful answers are those dealing with the human existential condition in which the correlative ultimate questions for meaning and God are both raised and formulated.

According to Karl Rahner, Karl Barth, Paul Tillich and other major thinkers, the task of good theology is to provide sound religious answers, which correlate with these existential questions of human life and human nature itself. These ultimate questions of the human nature and finite human life have to be answered in light of God's reality, agape and redemptive grace.

The existential, religious answers are to provide meaning to human life that is lived the world and simultaneously in the true presence of an eternal, loving, Creator God who gives meaning to human life as its ultimate source, grounding, and final destiny. In this Judeo-Christian understanding, the human being is a special creature or creation of God living in the world created by God and the final future resting place of the human being, also being God.

This understanding of the human being is certainly the one supported by the Bible. For instance, according to the "Priestly ("P") account of creation" in the biblical book of Genesis 1:26-27, we read that God created humankind (Adam) and that both male and female were created in God's image to have dominion over the rest of God's creation as God's own representatives and stewards.

In this Priestly account of creation, as well as the "Yahwist ("J") account of creation" which is found in Genesis 2:4 and 4:2, the human being is a special creature of God. The human being is created as one person who possesses two different natures. The first nature is both creaturely and beastly. It is shared with the other animals and living beings in the world. It is symbolized by the body, the senses and physical matter.

The human body, like that of the animals, is created out of star dust and Earth elements, such as iron, calcium, zinc, water, acids and proteins. The bible simply calls this "dust, "clay, or "Earth (*adamah*)." This body is the temple of God's dwelling as mind, spirit and Agape. The second nature is divine. It is symbolized by God's image, mind, spirit, soul and Agape. According to the New Testament, God is Agape, and the human being who exercises Agape is the true temple and embodiment of God (Agape) in the world.

Accordingly, in the Biblical second creation account, we read that God breathed his spirit of life into Adam's body which was made of dust, and subsequently, Adam became a living soul (Gen. 2:7). It is also to be noted that Adam became a living soul even when he still possessed the physical body constituting of dust to which it was destined to return at death.

This divine spirit, which is said to have been breathed into the human being by God, is a good symbol for the divine qualities which are found in the human being. There is great truth in this in that God and the human being share certain qualities, such as spirit, intelligence, knowledge, justice, love, sense of holiness, creativity, and an awareness of order and beauty. However, unlike God, the human being remains finite, temporal, material and as such, subject to the corrosion of time, death and decay just like the rest of God's creation. Christians also believe that God has, in Christ, become a human being by virtue of the Incarnation. If this belief is true, then it also follows that in Christ, human beings have also become one with God or become God. The Russian and Eastern Orthodox Churches have taught this doctrine, and the Christian Mystical tradition has historically taught that human beings can become divinized or deified into union with God.

This is accomplished through obedience, and the various mystical processes. These include the rigorous ascetic stages of self-purification, purgation, enlightenment or illumination by God and divinization as union with God. Illumination and union with God are what Buddha called the state of "*Nirvana*." The followers of Buddha also called this stage the attainment of "*Buddha Consciousness*."

In the "Yahwist" or second Biblical account of the creation of human-kind, we also find that our human nature is still not as pure as God had either originally created it or had intended it to be. This defect in our nature is explained in terms of human sin. More specifically, it is disobedience against God's guiding moral law or commandments as divinely proposed direction for human life that leads to and the subsequent human self-autonomy, self-centeredness, selfishness, greed, envy, hatred and murder (Gen. 3-4).

This observation is true, regardless of whether we believe in a literal and historical creation of Adam and Eve or affirm God's creation through evolution. The presence of sin and evil in the world are a universal reality. This is true, regardless of whether we believe in God's original creation of a perfect Adam and Eve as adults, who in personal freedom of choice, voluntarily sinned and caused the downfall of humanity, or whether we believe in a biological and historical evolution of humanity.

Spontaneous creation of human beings by God, or a slow divine process of human creation through evolution, does not account for human sin, greed, hate and moral evil. In both cases, human beings would sin and become morally imperfect as long as they had the freedom to choose and do as they pleased! Human disobedience of God's commandments of Agape and nonviolence and the human misuse of causal freedom, account for most moral and social evils in the human community and tragic hateful acts of violence in the world.

Human moral imperfection is taught by all religions along with the various creation and fall accounts. Many of them greatly vary from those found in the book of Genesis, while others may even sound almost similar to those in Genesis. In all cases, the human problem is that of disobedience against God's given moral law for human life. The results of this sin, generally, include loss of love for the neighbor, hatred, strife and murder or death.

This means that even if God had intended for us to live together happily in a community, by our own sin and disobedience to God, we would have invented a way to kill off those we dislike. And thereby, disrupt societal harmony peace and thus defy God-given immortality for all human beings. The high number of crimes involving bodily harm and homicide provide is ample evidence that human beings do not generally desire a good, happy and long life for all members of their own kind. Even some governments even try to eliminate those people they regard as a danger to their national security and to their fellow citizens.

Subsequently, the unjustifiable state capital punishment and clandestine killings of opponents by secret police agents can amount to a form of state terrorism for many citizens. Such acts, are a negation of the state's very reason for being there, namely, to protect the life and property of her citizens. This remains true whether the citizen is law abiding or not.

Therefore, criminals are still human beings with constitutional rights to life and state protection of that life and their property. The fact that states have abused their powers is evidence that human sin and imperfection have infiltrated all human institutions, including politics, government, the judiciary system, police departments and even the Church. In short, wherever human beings are found, one can also expect to find human imperfection and sin in terms of corruption, defective products, envy, malice, plots, gossip, hatred, strife, and murder.

This is why dangerous nuclear weapons, in the hands of such imperfect creatures as the ones described above, pose a great danger not just to the nation possessing them and its antagonists, but to the whole world. For instance, imagine a quietly insane president who wants to commit suicide, and in doing so, takes down the whole world with him! He could do great global damage with nuclear weapons in such a short time, before those around him realize that he is mentally ill, and therefore, not to be obeyed.

A general or tactical commander of a nuclear missile submarine could become mentally unbalanced and set off nuclear missiles in paranoia, just as guns in the hands of the insane have left us with periodic mass murders in public places. Nuclear weapons in the hands of many imperfect and retaliatory violent human beings or governments are also going to leave this planet in a tragic state, unless the international community polices those nations that may be tempted to use these weapons to settle border disputes with their neighbors. Just like the dinosaurs disappeared from the face of the Earth, irresponsible use of technology and militarism can also lead to human self-destruction and extinction. Irresponsible use of nuclear and mass chemical or biological weapons can destroy the Earth and its creatures, turn it into a quiet lifeless radioactive dessert, filled with only shambles and desolate ruins of cities and wasteland of farms.

It is not surprising, therefore, that because of the evil inherent in the human being, the first great attraction for any new technology and invention is the possible military use. The value of the new technology is perceived in terms of the mass killing capacity and great destructive scale. The tragic truth is that the technological military potential in terms of the great magnitude killing power is sought to kill off our fellow human beings and therefore, morally evil and objectionable to all peace-loving people.

These people see the other people as the devil and the enemy. They are like Paul Jean Sartre who affirmed that the "Devil is the other people." If human beings become ethnocentric, paranoid, exclusive and xenophobic, then they will also correlatively negatively view and perceive "the other people" or the other group, including the other gender, race, color, class, tribe, religion, nationality and culture as the enemy to be sought out, neutralized or destroyed. To this end, the greater the killing power of the weapon at a long distance, the greater the value that is placed on such a strategic weapon by the military strategists and war-mongers of the world. This is why the international ballistic missiles have been deployed by the USA and Russian governments. Therefore, one is forced to ask about what kind of great advancement we, as human beings, would have made if the funds invested in creating sophisticated human killing (strategic) weapons had instead been made in agriculture or medical research. The world and humanity would have been better off this way than at the present moment, when some governments spend a greater portion of the national budgets making or buying deadly arms than on either education or social welfare. The priority here seems to be killing human beings rather than either saving or serving them.

When Aristotle defined the human being as a "political animal," he had in mind the *polis* (the orderly political community) as the center of human life and activities. What Aristotle had in mind was the essence of the human being which was a result of membership within the moral, political and humane community. The human being was more of a product of the socialization or humanization process. This is an educational and humanizing process through which a civilized human organization or community, transforms the new members of its community into civilized beings. These are the people who are:

1. Well educated (informed and knowledgeable)
2. Cultured or civil
3. Linguistic
4. Social
5. Peaceful-loving and nonviolent
6. Skilled or technological
7. Economically productive (hard-working)
8. Virtuous (just, moderate, humane and compassionate)
9. Religious
10. Reliable

11. Honest (Trustworthy)
12. Independent free thinkers
13. Problem solvers
14. Courageous (brave)
15. Wise
16. Seekers after Truth
17. Patriotic
18. Morally responsible citizens
19. Politically active in the community
20. Law abiding.

According to Moses, Plato, and Aristotle, the state and its related institutions have been willfully established for the purpose of collective, peaceful, self-governing, and non-deadly power struggle and dominance for either the strongest or the most warlike. Indeed, before Aristotle, Plato had advanced the idea of a philosopher-king in order to ensure that the political leader was knowledgeable in the common good and would not abuse his important office for self-gratification, oppression of his opponents, or to inflict harm and evil on the people he ruled through ignorance and bad decisions.

## 6. Human Knowledge, Free Choice, Responsibility and Virtue

Human beings are free moral agents, and therefore, responsible for the consequences of their own free choices. Because correct knowledge and freedom are the essential prerequisites for sound moral agency, such as sound moral judgement and free choice for any moral deed. Both correct knowledge and freedom are the basis of moral responsibility for one's choices and actions.

Therefore, very young children and the insane are neither morally accountable nor legally held responsible for their good or evil actions. They are amoral beings like the animals. As a result, their parents or guardians are held accountable for the actions of their young children and pets. Similarly, animals being incapable of the knowledge of good and evil and lacking both a higher intellect and moral reasoning, they are also devoid of the moral freedom to sin or not to sin; to do good or to do evil. Animals may be externally conditioned through a process of reward and punishments to be useful and perform the tasks that we consider to be good, and moral, nevertheless, these animals are still amoral. As soon as the conditioning fails due to lack of positive reinforcements, the performance of these tasks also ceases.

Unfortunately, some poorly socialized and irresponsible materialistic human beings, behave almost like these conditioned and programmed animals. They are deontological in their moral theory. They do good because of the expected rewards by society, such as praise by friends, promotion by the boss, pay-raise for a good job, or the religious expectation of God's reward with eternal life and happiness in heaven after death.

These kinds of people are poor moral agents. Their good deeds do not come from a mature and internalized healthy moral conscience characterized by the spiritual or moral richness and goodness flowing from an inner positive life, as in the case of teleological ethics. Rather, they are conditioned and determined by external factors, such as rewards and fear of being caught and punished for doing evil or public moral infraction. This is the deontological moral dilemma. When the parents, police, God and the other external moral authorities are not physically present to enforce their will, or watching by hidden cameras or other electronic surveillance systems designed to catch criminals in the act, and punish the evildoers, the irresponsible moral agent or actor may decide not to do the good moral deed, nor follow the stated rules, laws and acceptable codes of personal or professional conduct.

This is in contrast to a well socialized and responsible moral agent, who operates on a teleological ethical moral system. This is because the mature moral actor and saintly persons do not derive their moral authority for good deeds from external authorities, such as parents, police, laws and fear of either jail or hell-fire. On the contrary, in the case, the moral agent's moral authority and reference comes from within. Moral conscience rooted in the power of agape (unconditional love), courage, benevolence, hardwork, truth, goodness and socioeconomic justice, is well formed and highly developed as an effective internal moral agency that serves the moral agent as a reliable authoritative moral reference and guide.

However, because such a well-formed and developed reliable moral conscience is rare, the Roman Catholic Church has justifiably taught that in the case of conflict between the moral teachings of the Church and an individual's personal conscience, then, the moral agent should follow the teachings of the Church. Similarly, the Evangelical Protestants have taught that the authority of the holy scriptures are supreme and should judge and guide personal conscience. As a result, they Evangelicals condemn and moral practices, such as abortion and homosexuality as moral evils, even if some Christians and churches accept them and teach their members the virtues of acceptance of moral relativity, diversity and the pluralism of moral theories and practices.

When the internalized moral values and codes of conduct are violated, the moral agent feels a sense of moral guilt as personal punishment for the moral violation and failure to live according to the internally established moral ideals, virtues and social standards. These are the kinds of men and women who stop at the traffic lights at midnight when there is no other car in sight and there is no police-officer to impose a fine on the person, should he or she drive through the stop light. Those who depend on external moral authority to do good, will shoplift, if no one is watching and will not meet the contractual obligations if they suspect that their clients do not know all aspects of the work to be done. An example here is a car-repair technician who does half a job on each car to be serviced, and yet still charges for a complete repair job including the work not performed, such as changing the oil-filter or replacing worn out parts with new ones, which have been included in the bill..

In general, animals predictably function according to their innate biological instincts as the mechanism for survival which regulate the animals' behavior for feeding, reproduction and running away from predators. Human beings who only live at this biological level, also live like mere beasts, and sin against God and the moral community. This is due to the fact that human beings are more than mere evolutionary animals. They are God's special thinking, creative and moral divine beings as created minds, spirits and God's concrete ambassadors or representatives in the temporal world.

As God's finite and partial incarnation in the world, the human being possess the divine and supernatural virtues of knowledge, reason/thought, moral consciousness, justice, truth telling, goodness, unconditional love, peace, creativity, mercy, free forgiveness, and nonviolence. These attributes are associated with God because they part of God's own essence. As such, it can only be deduced that these divine attributes and virtues come from God, and like a stream from a mountaintop, they flow from God's essence toward humanity through the mediation of the Logos and the Holy Spirit that are omnipresent in God's creation and the world. However, these special God's free universal supernatural gifts from God into humanity, because the human being is akin to God, and therefore, to some finite degree capable of sharing in God's own essence, especially, transcendence, creativity and infinite mystery.

The prophets and the writers of the Hebrew Bible also intuitively assumed that knowledge and wisdom were divine virtues. They were God's special gifts to chosen people, such as the saints, prophets and deserving leaders of God's people, such Moses, David and Solomon. Conversely, ignorance and foolishness or stupidity were regarded as moral and spiritual evils and vices. Ignorance and stupidity became the negative and evil sources of secondary evils and sins, such as injustice, malice, hate, violence, murder, disease, poverty, suffering, disbelief and atheism (cf. Ps. 14).

According to St. Paul, ignorance was a consequence of the original sin of Adam and Eve. Paul affirmed that ignorance led to other sins like idolatry, pride, stupidity and homosexuality (cf. Rom. 1:17-32). However, St. Paul was mistaken in his teaching since Adam and Eve's original temptation was to eat the forbidden fruit of the tree of immortal life and the knowledge of good and evil, so as to become omniscient, wise and immortal like God (cf. Gen. 3:1ff).

For both Plato, and Socrates, a good person was one who was free, knowledgeable and virtuous. For these thinkers, virtue itself was considered to be a product of correct knowledge, wisdom and self-discipline aimed at life according to one's knowledge. Subsequently, according to the Hebrew and Christian Bible, the universal fundamental, human moral and spiritual problem is that of hubris and sin of idolatrous, self-deification into God and the subsequent disobedience to God's moral law or God's reign and Kingdom. According to Moses and Jesus, the cure for the moral evil and sin was human repentance and obedience to God's will and moral law.

However, for the Greek philosophers and moral teachers such as Socrates and Plato, the fundamental universal human evil, vice and moral imperfections were attributed to human ignorance. For these Greeks there was no concept of sin and guilt before God. Rather than sin and moral weakness to choose and do the good, even if it were known as the Hebrew prophets and Jesus preached, for the Greeks, it was affirmed that it was the lack of the knowledge of the good that was required to make men and women virtuous and wise citizens. It was assumed that knowledge in itself was a divine powerful essence that those who possessed it were transformed into wise, humane, civilized, just and virtuous people. Therefore, for both Socrates and Plato, good moral education was the prescribed cure for human moral evil.

Unfortunately, this is not entirely true. Knowledge by itself does not translate into virtue and morality as Socrates taught. For instance, there are some doctors and nurses who smoke, despite their correct knowledge that smoking is harmful to the smoker and those around him or her. Again, there are so many overweight nurses in our American hospitals, despite the fact that they know that overeating and overweight are harmful. Likewise, most people know that unprotected sexual intercourse will lead to unwanted pregnancies and sexually transmitted diseases; yet, they knowingly engage in unprotected sexual intercourse, and then, suffer the consequences.

Therefore, as both a philosopher and an educator, I only partly agree with Socrates and Plato that good moral education will enable many humans to become wise, responsible, virtuous, humane, just and "civilized people." Good education is what makes people become more aware of the importance of their freedom, the consequences of their free moral decisions, choices and actions. A well educated person becomes aware that he or she is a local and global moral agent, and that each moral action has both local and global implications. Human beings are now both locally and globally interconnected by instant electronic audio-visual "virtual reality" and "cyberspace communications."

In the postmodern era of high-technological cyberspace communications and "virtual reality," distance or space and time have been transcended by the human being. The Earth has indeed become a real "global village." As a result, all human beings on this Earth are now socially, economically, politically and morally interconnected. Thus, what one person does in one part of the global community can have serious local and global implications. Some examples are the actions of Moses, Buddha, Jesus, Muhammad, Marx, Hitler, Idi Amin, Gorbachev, Mother Theresa, Pope John Paul XXIII and Saddam Hussein.

Other examples of global interconnectedness include the prices of stocks and commodities which are traded worldwide through global computer networks and the "World-Wide Web" (WWW). When markets in one part of the global community go down, the other parts of the world respond the same way within a few hours. The stocks, securities and commodities markets on Hong Kong affect the markets in Tokyo, London and New York. Wars in the Persian Gulf also affect the prices of oil, gasoline, heating, food and transportation of goods worldwide. As such, each person must be an advocate of peace, since war has not local but global consequences beyond the primary combatants and their respective nations!

In addition, pollution from war has a serious global effect beyond the nations engaged in war. The winds and water transport the pollution to the rest of the noncombatant nations and their environment. Refugees also become an additional international problem. Animals and the environment in the war-torn areas also get destroyed as innocent casualties of war. All people must be educated about the real dangers of war and violence to the health of the citizens of the world and the environment as a whole. People and their leaders must be educated and trained to value peace and peaceful resolution of conflicts and how to avoid the threats of violence and war as methods of conflict resolution. Violence to promote peace since it begets destructive counter-violence. This is the tragic case in the Middle East, Africa and former Soviet Union.

The violent or revolutionary rise and tragic fall of the communist former Soviet Union should remain a postmodern humbling lesson of time and processes of birth and death of empires and nations in human history. This is a good example of how in the present, as in the past, empires still rise and fall with time, ideologies and personalities. Arrogance, bankruptcy, moral decadence, internal strife, repression and the corruption of leaders and the military are some of the major causes of the fall of these empires. Finally, the oppressed people rise in mass in quest for freedom and self-determination, and the empires collapse, unless they resort to the Machiavellian extreme repression and brutality.

The fall of mighty repressive empires provides an important lesson that human freedom cannot be denied indefinitely. Freedom is essential for true happiness and any full realization of the human being's authentic nature as a free divine being and responsible moral agent in the world. Freedom is a universal divine given human right that is required for the human being's completion of the coextensive dual processes of meaningful humanization and divinization through volitional choices and moral deeds of self-determination, self-actualization and fulfillment in the community and the world, both as a child of God and citizen of God's Kingdom.

The Kingdom of God in the world operates on the basis of grace and persuasion. It requires people to utilize their freedom responsibly in unconditional love. God's Kingdom and true godliness require human freedom since it is the universal basis for meaningful active faith and obedience to God. Human obedience is demonstrated in positive use of personal freedom and knowledge to effect responsible choice to do good deeds irrespective of the cost, truth, nonviolence, justice, peace and free forgiveness for all human beings in the world. These good deeds are the external and universal manifestations of true obedience to God, evidence of any truly redemptive practical faith in God, agape, godliness and the effective presence of the rule of God or the "Kingdom of God" in the community and the world.

Like intellect, freedom is another of God's divinizing special gifts that is universally freely bestowed by God on every human being in the world. As such, to deny a person being the exercise of freedom is to take away that person's right to act as an authentic human being and to actualize oneself into a complete, satisfied and happy person. The removal of human freedom through detention and imprisonment is a severe form of punishment that should only be reserved for the very dangerous criminals, such as the violent armed robbers, murderers and rapists. Human freedom cannot be indefinitely repressed or denied to any people, regardless of how helpless and docile they may seem to the intimidating evil oppressors or dominant power. Therefore, it is a matter of sound moral judgement based on the self-evident truth and common sense that human freedom, religion, democracy and human rights must be respected by any state government, Church or human community that wishes to be respected and last long!

Ultimately, since the human being is, by intrinsic nature, a free moral and religious being, any complete, meaningful and sound liberal arts education must also include sound, civic and good moral education. This is essential in order to promote the moral use of personal freedom. Moral education is also a prerequisite for civic awareness of essential civic virtues and moral responsibilities which are inseparable from the good, productive and happy human personal and professional life within the community. The ideal life of a well educated and socialized person is that who is positive, productive, law-abiding, happy and peaceful. These are the essential qualities of a well adjusted, moral and useful citizen of the community. A well educated person is one who has gained the necessary knowledge, virtues, socioeconomic and moral or social skills that enable him or her to value membership in a just, productive, democratic, harmonious, peaceful and civilized, humane and nonviolent community. Such a person must also seek to create this community, if it did not already exist.

All citizens and members of such a community must be trained in the responsible management of their God given gifts, including freedom, creativity and natural resources. All citizens of the community must also be trained in the art and skills of time management, managing anger or aggression, and peaceful effective methods for creative problem solving and peaceful conflict resolution. The members of the community must be instructed in creative moral reasoning, peaceful coexistence with others, sharing resources, interpersonal relationships, nonviolent problem solving, responsibilities for making good choices, beneficial wise decisions and carrying good actions.

However, as a Christian, I am also acutely aware that a good education alone does not have the power to transform human nature from an evil one to a good one. This is necessarily true, because this human fundamental transformation calls for a supernatural transformation of the human being which can only be effected by the holy, loving Creator, Sustainer and Redeemer God. Only the Creator God can effect this kind of total transformation of a person from a lost sinner into a redeemed saint and child of God. This because redemption or positive transformation of sinners constitutes a secondary act of new creation, healing and restoration of "broken people" to wholeness.

This is true inasmuch as the human redemption or salvation is the restoration of the human being to the original divinely intended existential state of wholeness, holiness, love, harmony, and happiness as the state of contentedness and peace. This divinization process by which God redeems and restores the sinner, is also commonly known in Evangelical churches as being "born again" or "being saved." This is because only God as the loving, benevolent Creator and Sustainer can also mercifully and effectively save or redeem the human beings from evil and self-destruction. These divine activities are made possible by God's own grace and essential nature as both "*Agape*" (Unconditional Love) and "*Sola Gratia*" (Gracious and Compassionate).

Chapter 4

# Divine Attributes And Unique Nature of Humanity

The human being is a special and unique evolutionary intelligent, thinking, self-conscious moral divine being and the only linguistic and religious being within God's vast cosmic creation. This is because only the human being is truly both animal by evolution and divine or akin to God by God's special creation in God's own image *(imago Dei)*. There is no question that the human being has been regarded as a special creature by all people irrespective of era, creed, ideology, level of technological development, race, color, and education. This is a well-documented fact from the ancient Egyptian and Babylonian civilizations, through the Bible, and from Greek civilizations up to the present time.

## 1. Human Beings as God's Special Elect And Sinful Representatives in the World

Without exception, all human beings in the world have always thought of themselves as the unique and true elect children of God. Traditionally all human beings have often thought of God as their heavenly or primordial ancestor or Patriarch. For instance, the writer of the Gospel according St. Luke traces Jesus' biological genealogy through

Joseph to "Adam the son of God" (Lk. 3:23-38). Adam becomes the first "son of God."

Therefore, the children of Adam also become the children of God! They are a "Community of God's People." As a result, human beings everywhere in the world have often sinfully and ethnocentrically exclusively considered themselves the only unique and special children of God. The terms such as the "elect" and "Covenant people of God" have been sometimes been used to convey that concept. However, in academic theological terms these designations simply affirm that all human beings possess God's special endowed divine gifts in order to become divine beings and God's representatives as the temporal masters of the world (creation) on God's behalf (cf. Gen. 1:26-31).

The other human unique features are empirical, and can be objectively observed and studied scientifically by any interested scholar. For instance, human beings are biologically classified as mammals belonging to the rest of the "animal kingdom" on the Earth, and from which we are supposed to have originally evolved. We are, however, physically, socially, intellectually, spiritually, morally, linguistically, and culturally quite different from them. This is an obvious observation which cannot be refuted by any intelligent thinking and observant human being.

This dual nature of the human being as both a divine being and an animal or beastly being, has plagued human civilization with savage vandalism, senseless warfare, crime and violence of all kinds, including that in intimate relationships, family spats, and entertainment. Whereas today we enjoy rough games such as wrestling, boxing, American football, and bullfighting, the ancient Romans enjoyed deadly games.

The gladiators fought ferocious beasts to the delight of the spectators. During the era of Christian persecution, crowds came to be entertained by watching unarmed Christian men and women being thrown into the arena to fight hungry lions with bare hands. The "pagan crowds" were delighted as these Christians were torn to pieces and eaten alive by these hungry animals. An evil, sadistic and tragic aspect of human nature is symbolized by the crowds who shouted with delight, as the hungry animals ferociously tore the poor defenseless men and women to pieces, one after the other.

This kind of sadistic human delight in cruelty is a continuing aspect of the animal nature which has not yet fully evolved into the divine aspects of the human essence, namely agape and nonviolence. This animal nature within humanity delights in beastly pleasures or actions and savage games. It also finds pleasure in war, pornography, violent sex, rape, violent movies or cartoons, wrestling or other violent forms of entertainment. Deadly nationalistic and tribal wars that are often fought for the sake of asserting the exclusive territorial rights or dominance over a certain territory are clear examples of the "animality" still surviving within the human being.

Sometimes, it is even difficult to tell whether the human being is less savage and beastly than the wild beasts themselves. These beasts rarely kill off their own kind in senseless jungle wars. They probably know better how to follow the natural laws than the human beings. The natural law includes the instinct that the animals of the same kind must flock together for mutual protection and survival, rather killing each other. Even when the males fight for mating rights, it is a means of ensuring that the strongest and most health genes are passed on to the species' offspring, thus, ensuring their good health and chance for survival in the wild, where there is no medical attention for the weak and the sick animals.

In this manner, "the jungle ethic" or natural law ensures a peaceful animal community conducive to mutual protection and the survival of the species. Survival and community constitute the first law of nature. As a result, some animals live in fairly well organized communities in order to ensure their own survival, whereas the less social ones live alone, also to ensure their own survival ability, especially when food is scarce. The well-being and survival of each animal is closely tied in together with the survival of one's own species. For instance, when there is an elephant hunter who hunts elephants for sport or their expensive tusks, the safety of each elephant is at stake. Subsequently, in the presence of the enemy, strong bull elephants try to protect the herd. They try to ensure their own species' survival by charging the armed enemy, even at the cost of their own lives. This is also true for most nations and groups of people. Unfortunately, in this case, the enemy is in most cases perceived to be the other people.

Subsequently, there have been family feuds, tribal wars, regional civil wars, international wars, racial and color prejudice, ethnic strife, racial conflicts, violence and genocide. Therefore, what humanity needs are both to bridge and heal all these unnecessary human divisions, strife, and conflicts so as to create a new positive global human self-identity as "Humankind and Global Citizens." This global awareness and international human identity would naturally neutralize the narrow local loyalties of tribe, region, and nation by focusing the local attention to the wider international scene. This would also mean that to ensure the survival of one's own offspring, one would also have to ensure the survival of the other creatures and the planet itself. This requires the protection of the delicate planetary systems of ecological balances of life and the environment.

This is a justified shift in priorities and concern, because of the new modern technological shift from the local community and state of affairs to the global one. This means that for anyone to survive, all human beings and the planet Earth must also survive. This is the basic moral guide for modern technology its users. Advances in technology and communications have transformed the previous expansive world into a closely linked human "Global Community."

Consequently, each individual life has become internationally linked to all humanity. Therefore, whatever affects one human being eventually affects all. Likewise, when there is a contagious disease on one part of the globe it will infect the people in other parts of the globe due to fast means air and land travel around the world. Therefore, individuals, like nations, are now more closely linked together than ever before. This makes it difficult for one group of people to survive alone without the other. This is why to love our neighbor is coextensively also to love ourselves and ultimately to ensure our own survival in the human community and the world. Those who sow the seeds of love also gain the fruits of love when it is returned.

Hopefully, gone forever are the days when "primitive" and ignorant tribal groups thought of themselves as the total humanity. They thought of themselves as the very chosen children of God living at the very center of the universe. We do not find such exclusive tribal claims only in the Bible (Gen. 12:1-3). We also find them in other tribal Creation and Election Myths such as those found among the Jews, Chinese, Japanese and African people, particularly the "Bantu" (People). This kind of exclusive claim to humanity of one group of people at the exclusion of others, particularly the strangers and foreigners, has been the background to "tribalism" in modern Africa and the political instability prevailing there. In the West, it has led to wars such as the Second World War which was directly linked to Adolf Hitler and his ethnocentric and racist Nazi Party. In the USA, Northern Ireland, Lebanon, Israel, and South Africa, there are still ethnic and racial armed conflicts which flare up now and again.

The ruthless repression of the Black people, who are the majority in South Africa by a minority White group is the clearest contemporary example of this problem of destructive societal systematic racism. The problem becomes even more complex when the dominant group claims that it is because of God's election or gracious choice that it happens to have become the privileged group in power. This scenario is made more complicated when the dominant group claims exclusive divine election and supremacy over the other people as its subjects by divine will and God given right.

In South Africa and North America, some White racists and white-supremacists claimed that God had chosen them to rule over the nonwhite people. The Tutsi (cattle-keepers)of Rwanda had ruled over the Bahutu (agriculturalists) by divine right until 1994 when the Bahutu rebelled and carried out a bloody genocide of the Tutsi ruling elite ethnic group. Except for the neighboring Uganda, the rest of the world watched in horror but refused to intervene. This was partly because they did not approve of the Tutsi domination of the majority Bahutu. But by failing to intervene and prevent a horrible moral evil of genocide, they also failed to act as responsible moral agents and defenders of human rights, justice, democracy and peace in the world.

The advocates of divine favoritism and God's election of some people to have more intelligence and govern the less intelligent include most European supremacists, imperialists and colonialists of the nineteenth and twentieth centuries. These people claimed that God had endowed them with the special gift of beauty and intelligence. As the prejudiced authors of the infamous *Bell Curve* have clearly illustrated in this era, racism can invade the academy and research data and interpretation. It shows we can erroneously believe that the white skin color is some kind of visible and reliable eternal evidence of superior intelligence.

Conversely, it also clearly illustrates how some racist, color-prejudiced people could just accept and believe that the black color is a reliable, external evidence of inferior intelligence and intrinsic genetic orientation to a life of laziness, violence and crime. The external color was taken as sufficient evidence of the internal intellectual power, superiority and great capacities. These racists believed they were given the divine choice for royalty and governing of the majority who happened to be Black (and were considered ugly because of the black skin, kinky hair, thick lips, and flat noses).

The recent fascist-like trends in the former White minority ruled South Africa remind us of Hitler, and the cruel manner in which he sent millions of Jews to the gas chambers, as the world kept silent. This time, the world intervened with trade sanctions when the White Afrikaners began to systematically exterminate the Black people. Nelson Mandela was released from jail in 1990 after twenty-seven years of political imprisonment. In 1994, Mandela was elected the first Black President of South Africa in the first democratic elections ever held in that country. Prior to that period, democracy was only permitted for the White minority citizens of that country.

Why did it take the death of many thousands of innocent people to do what was right and moral? The moral problems of White racism, Western capitalism and greed for African resources, and imperialism compromised the principles of democracy, justice and human rights in South Africa, Angola, Congo and Kenya.

The innate beast inside us seems not to have changed since the ancient Roman days. Although the nature of cruel games, the technology of weapons, and the arena contestants have changed, human beings themselves have not changed and still enjoy watching simulated war games, but prefer seeing real wars, and the suffering of others. This remains enjoyable for many people as long as those suffering are others and not themselves or their close friends and family members.

Therefore, sadism, hate, injustice, bigotry, prejudice and love of violence are major human evils and sins against God and fellow human beings. Unfortunately, some of these evils are embedded in the animal aspect of human nature which by evolution we share with the other nonthinking and amoral animals! We must find a means in the divine aspect of human nature to transcend these major negative characteristics of the human being which are rooted in the animal nature.

It is a moral imperative to find the ethical means by which we can transcend the atavistic animal nature within us. Unless we find a constructive and effective way to counteract and neutralize it, the animal nature can lead to the very extinction of the human species through some self-destructive fatal act of violence and misuse of technology. This is scary. We have nuclear, biological and chemical weapons of mass destruction which can fall into the wrong hands. Terrorists and psychopathic mass murderers can get hold of these weapons and threaten to blackmail the world, or seek to inflict pain and punishment on a group of people out of their intense dislike or fear. This can also happen in times of international disagreement, strife, and armed conflict.

However, miscalculation can lead to unexpected counter retaliations and mutual destruction at a higher level, which is never taken into account before the onset of the conflicts. This is how minor wars have in the past led to greater wars, and how international wars have started in minor diplomatic disagreements which have kept on growing into a full military hurricane. This also illustrates the capricious nature of the human being and how futile it is for the human social scientists to try to predict all future human behavior, both individual and corporate.

## 2. The Unique Physical Features Of the Human Being

The human being has a very unique and characteristic feature of being bipedal and upright in posture. This upright posture is very advantageous because it frees the hands to do work. Definitely, this is one of the main distinguishing features between the human being and the rest of the animals, especially the primates that so closely resemble the human beings.

The other primates may occasionally walk on two legs and even use their hands to manipulate tools. But unlike the human being, the usual posture of these creatures is walking on four legs or using their long, strong arms to swing from branch to branch and from tree to tree. While we are better at walking, these primates are better runners and tree climbers. Their own way of life and survival require such abilities, whereas they are not for the human beings.

In addition, the human movable thumb is unique among the other primates. This again enables the human being to make better tools and utilize the hand better and more efficiently. Therefore, unlike the clumsy chimpanzees, the human being can more successfully undertake and accomplish fine, delicate and complex tasks that require agility and good hand coordination, such as writing, curving, painting, building, or using small hand-held tools like the surgeon's scalpel or the seamstress' needle. The human being's larger brain and higher intellect are the greatest human unique asserts which the movable thumb merely compliments.

Since the human being is bipedal and upright in posture, in order to remain well balanced on the two feet, the large head with its two ears has top of the shoulders in order to retain balance. The ears not only provide auditory functions, they also provide information to the brain regarding body position, angle and balance. Moreover, the human upright posture with the eyes located close to the top of the head provides a great advantage to the human being in terms of sight and personal safety. Most animals try to stand on their hinder legs or climb trees and stand on higher ground in order to gain a similar advantage. Except for the very tall animals, such as the giraffes and elephants, the human being can see much further from his normal walking position than most of the other animals, including the lower primates which also try walking on two legs.

Subsequently, most animals try to stand on their hind legs so as to see more clearly above the tall grass. In some cases, some animals even climb trees or high ground so as to survey carefully the territory around them for enemies or food, which they cannot do from under the grass or on lower ground. Some animals, like monkeys and other primates, have been known to keep one of their members on guard high up in a tree or on higher ground while the others remain on the ground feeding until it is their turn to keep watch. This is also true of some human beings during wartime. In this respect, animals and human beings desire the same things; namely, good vision, security, and advance warning when there is trouble or danger coming.

Animals are better than human beings at using natural instincts and senses to "smell or sense trouble" coming. The animals have keener senses of smell, taste, hearing, and sight. For instance, some people keep watch dogs to hear for them and see what the people are unable to see. Dogs sound a warning alarm by barking at the intruder. With our modern powerful telescopes, binoculars, and smoke detectors, we can very easily compensate for this deficit. However, we can never carry these gadgets around with us everywhere and at all times!

Whereas it is true that unlike the other animals, our advanced technology allows us to dominate and shape our own environment to our own particular taste, it remains also true that we are still creatures of our environment. Therefore, we are subject to the natural laws that govern all natural life of which we are an integral part. Moreover, there is a limit on how far we can go without destroying our own environment, and subsequently, causing our own destruction along with it since our own existence is essentially dependent on our physical and biological environment.

This does not mean that we return to the pre-scientific era when the human being behaved like the rest of the animals around him or her, and therefore, logically sought to live in harmony with nature and the given surrounding environment by making adjustments to the weather and the local conditions. However, in contrast today, we seek to adapt the environment to our needs and tastes, rather than adapting ourselves to its ways. This is why the human being is found on every continent, regardless of weather.

Human beings are characteristically hairless on most of the body, unlike the other mammals which are entirely covered with thick coats of fur to protect them from the elements as well as the other hazards of living in the jungle, such as insect bites, scratches and cuts. Being hairless on most of the body seems to be a unique, expensive feature of the human being. It is an expensive feature in that most of the earnings of "civilized people" in our society seem to go for expensive clothes, lavish food and elaborate housing!

Indeed, this natural nakedness of the human being seems to be one of the great driving sources for human inventions, moral codes, social etiquette, religious inspiration, love, romance, elaborate dressing, and housing arrangements, including "bathroom taboos," some being for the "ladies" and others for "gentlemen." The idea behind privacy and that which should not be done in a public place, is based on moral conventions regarding what are considered decent public actions which the public has a right to know, and private actions which the public has right to know or inquire into. For instance, a person's sex orientation and sex life are personal and private matters, unless for some justifiable reason the person wishes to disclose these private matters to the public. But, he or she should not get surprised if he or she gets rejected because of that disclosure of personal affairs to the public. This is particularly true for the homosexuals within the USA military. They may by law be discharged for such revelations of private affairs.

In this moral and cultural convention, if anyone has to see the other naked, it should be a member of the same gender! The implication underlying this understanding in this case is that public nakedness is bad and should not be tolerated among people of different genders. Again, one has got to go further than this and speculate that in some people's mind nudity can only mean sexual immorality, and therefore, that it is to be rejected as sinful. The same gender bathrooms also ignore the possibility of homosexuality and threat of same sex rape! Fortunately, these homosexual problems and threats of same sex rapes are not the norms. They are the exceptions, although they are important in moral considerations.

However, sin does nor consist in the exposure of the naked body or the genitals. Instead sin is in the motive and mind of those either exposing them or looking at the natural body with lust and "dirty thoughts." For instance, we are all born naked. That is not evil or sinful. It does not seem to bother either God or those present at birth that both the mother and the baby are exposed. Why is this the case, we might ask?

It is because the attention of those present at birth is not focused on the genitalia for its sexual appeal, but as an organ of child birth.

I have visited to some parts of tribal Africa where Western dress is still frowned upon. In the hot tropical climate and in the absence of air conditioners, it makes great sense to walk naked or put on minimum clothing! After all, the popular Biblical account of human creation in the book of Genesis tells us that when God first created human beings, they were naked, yet sinless and without shame (Gen. 2: 21-26; 3:4-11.) The divine intention was that human beings would be free and naked in the Garden of Eden. It was after they sinned against God that they became embarrassed about their own identity, nakedness, sexuality and mutual relationships. They began to blame one another for their own sins and guilt. And they were ashamed of themselves and of each other.

Nevertheless, I was embarrassed to see young women's exposed breasts heaving up and down as these young women happily walked about doing their daily work! This was because I was from another culture. These traditional Masai women do not regard exposed breasts as an indecent or sinful sexual exposure or an invitation to sexual activity. Indeed, the evidence is that they are still expected to be virgins when they get married. Disaster still befalls those who are not found to be virgins and great shame is felt by their families for not having kept their daughters virtuous.

Ironically, being fully clothed maybe a sign of wealth and a certain socioeconomic status. But it has little to do with sexual morality! This is because clothing can be quickly discarded by those intending to engage in sexual intercourse! It does not deter them. It may instead invite sexual curiosity and lust. Yet, we still ethnocentrically condemn as immoral and "uncivilized" those "tribal people" in some parts of Africa and other parts of the world, who insist on going either naked or with scant clothing! Isn't this a form of protection of our own sexual lewdness and guilt on others who may be completely innocent?

Unfortunately, this seems also to be the other unique trait of the human being; namely, that we often deny the evil in us, and project it on those we dislike. As a consequence, we often hate and persecute other people for what we hate in ourselves but see in them. For instance, we often find it easy to blame others for the evil we do, whereas we take all the credit for the good we do, even that done by others!

Subsequently, like escapism and self-deception, both fraud and plagiarism are also uniquely human moral evil characteristics of decent and dishonesty. Some human beings try to take advantage of other people's ideas and works and pass them onto others deceptively as their own! This is often in an attempt to look better than they are in the judgement of other people. This is obviously a case of an ethical dilemma created by moral self-deception, fraud, intellectual theft, academic dishonesty and criminal behavior.

## 3. The Intellectual, Moral and Spiritual Uniqueness of the Human Being

In the West, particularly within the Greek world-view, the human being is perceived in terms of mind (*nous*), intellect and thought *(cogito)*. The human being is a free rational being (*res cogitans*) or a free self-thinking "bio-intellectual machine!" St. Paul, Augustine, Aquinas, Descartes, Hegel and Kant are good examples of this Greek rationalism, idealism and dualism.

However, for some other people like the Hebrews, Africans, Hindus and the Buddhists, the human being is essentially a divine spirit. This human spirit is created by God (the Cosmic Creative and Sustaining Eternal Spirit), and then, incarnated into matter or the human body for its physical existence and concrete external self-expression within the physical world. But at death, this divine finite spirit leaves the human body to exist within a spiritual world with God. This is the supposed goal of humanity as the realm of immortality and heavenly bliss. Like the Greek world-view, it is also static, dualistic and non-evolutionary.

From an evolutionary perspective, we have already seen that the human being has a distinctively and characteristically large, round skull protectively housing a very large brain. The huge brain is one of the greatest unique features of the human being, distinguishing humans from non-humans by virtue of enabling the humans to possess a much higher and greater intellectual capability for abstract thinking, memory, freedom, moral responsibility, and self-transcendence.

This human intellectual power enables the human being to possess an infinite curiosity for knowledge, higher abilities of thinking or data collection, a scientific analysis for cause and effect. Great intelligence also leads to great capacity for memory which serves as data storage for both processed and unprocessed data, and systematic storage for later retrieval when needed in analyzing and solving new problems.

This distinctive human intellectual characteristic is so basic in understanding the human being that a skeptic like the great French philosopher Rene Descartes was able to prove his own existence and that of God merely on the basis of thinking. His great proof for his own existence and indirectly for all human beings was: "I think, therefore, I am" (*cogito ergo sum)*. This is a classic example of Western individualism, dualism and idealism. There is little room for community and subjective experience in terms of relationships, love, peace and harmony. Thinking is an individualistic process which excludes the other people and the community. In this Greek system, God cannot be experienced as Agape or forgiving compassionate Father or Mother. God can only be experienced as Mind and Truth.

However, Descartes' understanding of thinking includes human self-awareness or self-consciousness, reason or logic, and understanding. If this is the case, then, as far as we know, human beings are the only true thinkers or rational beings. Non-human or artificial intelligence in the form of sophisticated computers lack self-consciousness and understanding. They are computing machines with no powers of intuition, subjective self-awareness, and moral conscience.

In this respect, animals are closer to human beings and true intelligence than computers with their high speed computing artificial intelligence. Animals such as chimpanzees, dolphins, elephants, dogs, and parrots possess a sophisticated degree of intelligence. They have limited capacity for data processing, decision-making, and memory.

The animals, particularly the higher primates, such as the baboons, monkeys, chimpanzees and gorillas, seem to exhibit some human-like forms of intelligence. They even have similar behavior, community and crude forms of governance with laws and punishments for the "criminals" or violators of the animal society's norms.

Some of these animal societies are patriarchal, and others are matriarchal, as in the case of hyenas, elephants and Bonobo Chimpanzees. Matriarchal societies are more orderly, cooperative, peaceful and social. The patriarchal animal societies are just like the human societies. They are full of competition, greed, hostility, alliances, violence and wars! The larger and stronger male gets the harem, and the weaker ones are destined to become permanent bachelors! The patriarchal animal society resembles the Nietzschean ethics! This relates to his idea of the *Ubermensch* as the unrestrained powerful individual with a will to absolute power, who will rape, robe, pillage and kill at will!

Nevertheless, this animal intelligence is at a very rudimentary evolutionary and limited level. In addition, there is no evidence so far that these animals are getting more intelligent in terms of brain structural change and increase. Since thinking is a complex functional structure of the brain, as well as a result of good education and training, it seems unlikely that even if we gave these animals the best of the human education, they would become human. This is a basic anthropological and theological assumption. Certainly, some animals have been trained for human entertainment and to act in circuses, but apart from this sophisticated training and conditioning, these animals remain mere tamed beasts. For instance, they can neither think analytically nor speak. If they did, then they would truly become human, regardless of their physical form or looks.

Thinking and creativity are major human qualities in themselves. For instance, in traditional Christian theology and philosophy, God is known as the Creator and the Omniscient. This is also true in most world religions, particularly in Judeo-Christianity, Islam, and the African traditional religion. Saint Thomas probably speaks for most Christians when he defines and describes God as "Pure Intellect," "the Omniscient," and "the Omnipotent."

If this Thomistic characterization of God is correct and true to God`s essence and reality, then it follows that the human intellectual activity and the essentially correlated thinking processes, and the acquisition of knowledge and subsequent mental or skilled creativity are divine attributes found in the human being. In other words, by an intellectual activity, the human being participates in God's divinity and God's own transcendental, eternal dimension, traditionally and variously known as "spirit" or "mind."

This takes us back to the biblical book of Genesis, which states that God made human beings, both male and female, in "his" own image (Gen. 1:27), or that God breathed his life-giving breath into Adam and "he became a living soul" (Gen. 2:7). In this biblical understanding, the divine quality God imparted to the human being that makes the human being more Godlike or in God's image, is the intellect or the soul. No other creature is referred to as an *imago Dei* (God's image) apart from the human being, who is endowed with God's own special breath, or spirit for his/her uniqueness of being and special position of moral responsibility and creativity in God's cosmos.

Unfortunately, according to the Bible, it is also this divine quality found in the human being in the form of intellect, thinking, and creativity that led to the human being's disobedience and rebellion against God's moral and natural laws. The human being acted in favor of an unrestricted human independence and experimental search for more empirical and moral knowledge so as "to be like God." That is, to know the good and the evil, and also to gain the secret key to eternal life, and therefore, become immortal and live forever like the Immortal, and Eternal God (cf. Gen 3:1-7).

This is the spirit that still drives us on in quest of knowledge and truth about the nature of the universe, God and our own lives. It motivates us to study theology, the sciences and to do further experiments as we conduct empirical research to unlock more of the secrets of life. This process of cosmic and self-study has enabled us to live longer and better lives. Nevertheless, we are still searching for eternal life, perfection, peace and enduring wholesome sources of happiness.

However, we must remember that Adam's disobedience and forbidden experiment in search of divinity and immortality only brought the depressing knowledge and cognitive awareness the reality of death and inevitability for all living beings. The attainment of knowledge led to the discovery of truth and the reality of human finitude and the definitive reality of death for all living creatures, including human beings. This knowledge and the alarming discovery of the reality of death were more shocking because it negated the positively desired secret or knowledge and attainment of human divinity, immortality and eternal life. Like every finite and intelligent human being, Adam and Eve feared death and sought to "deathless" like the Immortal and eternal God, which most religious human beings desperately desire to become. That was the temptation of Adam and Eve and it is the temptation of every normal human being. Hubris and idolatrous human self-deification into the immortal and all-knowing God through the attainment of knowledge and truth is still the major universal temptation of most human beings (cf. Gen. 3:5).

## 4. Original Sin as Religious Myth and Metaphor

Within evolution, there are no historical Adam and Eve as original two perfect adults who were created by God in the beginning. Therefore, within theology based on science and evolution, there are no historical or original perfect people that were originally created in a state of perfection by God, that later sinned and caused the supposed cosmic evil and imperfection through the "original sin" of hubris and rebellion against God's will and cosmic moral law.

This being the case, then, the term "original sin," or the "Fall of humanity," is understood to be metaphor for evil in the world and part of religious mythology and moral cosmology, rather than that of actual cosmic history. Accordingly, the Genesis stories of creation, the fall, Noah's flood and Tower of Babel are all understood and explained from that academic theological perspective.

Therefore, within an evolutionist academic theology and ethics, these religious terms can be correctly viewed as religious parables and moral metaphors for an evolutionary imperfect humanity and imperfect world. The human being as an evolutionary thinking mind and spirit (*Homo Sapiens*), is a moral being that is also universally acutely aware of his or her uniqueness of moral and spiritual predicament. The more intelligent human being as a responsible moral agent has more troubling moral awareness of one's own as well-being as the corporate human existential moral condition needing serious improvement, positive transformation or "redemption."

The moral saint being more acutely aware of the great gap between reality/existence or "***what is***," and "***what ought to be***" or the ideal, may sometimes despair at the prevailing human predicament. The prophet may conclude that the state of moral and spiritual finitude and imperfection requires a supernatural reversal or deliverance from evil in order to prevent human self-destruction. Therefore, the prophet may call for God's direct and active moral and spiritual intervention. Such a call for God's moral, spiritual, military, political, and socioeconomic intervention in the world to get rid of human moral evil and imperfection is abundantly found among the Hebrew prophets as recorded in the Hebrew Bible.

A broader list of well-known examples of the prophetic voice includes Noah, Abraham, Moses, Isaiah, Jeremiah, Amos, John the Baptist, Jesus, Paul, Augustine, Aquinas, Luther, Calvin, John Wesley, Oscar Romero, Desmond Tutu, Janani Luwum, Mother Teresa, M.L. King and recently, Bishop John Spong, who has called for a new reformation of the Church and the inclusion of the gays and lesbians within the Church and its ordained ministry.

It is self-evident that the human being lives in a constant moral and intellectual struggle to overcome the limitations of ignorance and moral imperfection, more particularly those vices that destructively manifest themselves externally in the form of socioeconomic injustice, crime, intolerance of diversity, violence and war. Prophets are essential in calling the world to honor these practical noble moral virtues and principles of agape and socioeconomic justice.

Ultimately, within this new evolutionist theological and moral understanding, the terms "original sin" and "the Fall" are to be correctly understood as Christian mythological and metaphorical terms employed to describe the negative universal reality of the present state of world-affairs. Therefore, the world's religious myths, including the popular biblical stories of the creation of Adam and Eve, and all other kinds of "metaphors" for the "original sin" and "the Fall of humanity," do not literally refer to any actual historical events that took place in the world at creation or the beginning of cosmic history, as the Church has erroneously taught in the past. But rather, these important religious myths or legends, metaphors, and valuable moral stories correctly refer to the prevailing negative moral or religious state of world affairs as seen in the world today. They are moral and religious commentaries, and descriptive moral and religious stories about the people and the world both in historical and current perspectives.

In short, both the "original sin" and "the Fall," correctly refer to the negative experiential aspects of humanity, community or society, history and the world in their present conditions of imperfection and moral failure. "The Fall" effectively conveys the visual imagery of the world and its institutions for being both unstable, and unreliable as support systems for human maximum self-fulfillment and happiness. It also conveys the moral theory and deterministic theological view that it is because of past and present human moral failure, rebellion and sin against God's cosmic moral law in nature, that these changing human institutions are imperfect, and constantly threatened by strong internal and external destructive forces of evil, transitoriness or impermanence, chaos, violence, war, scarcity of resources, hunger, disease, poverty, ignorance, crime, bigotry, intolerance, rebellion, brutality, hate, suffering, pain and death.

With this kind of litany of evils, many people conclude that *this world is not what it ought to be*. This observation and conclusion constitute what has been traditionally referred to as "*the Fall of humanity*." These are the Hebrew myths and stories of creation and the sinful rebellion of Adam and Eve against God expressed in the biblical book of Genesis (Gen. 2-3). These popular biblical myths are not historical accounts of creation and the fall of humanity and the world from an assumed original perfection. Instead, they are moral observations and statements about the world as it existed then and now.

Each person serves as both an original Adam and Eve within this dramatization of God's activities of creation and redemption. For instance, the Early Church incorporated Jesus and Mary as the perfect moral characters that reversed the original sin of Adam and Eve in the original Garden of Eden, by their own obedience to God's will. Similarly, each human being is called upon either to identify with either Adam and Eve's life of rebellion against God, or to identify with Mary and Jesus, and their model life of holy obedience to God's will for their own lives and both moral and social conduct within the community and the world.

Therefore, one could validly argue that Adam's disobedience and experiments brought into the world an empirical knowledge of death and the truth of the reality of finitude due to the finite nature of human existence. Adam's attempt to become immortal and omniscient like God, instead brought the disturbing truth of human finitude and morality. This was by virtue of "eating the fruit of knowledge and wisdom." Unfortunately, for Adam and Eve, the knowledge gained was that of the reality of death for all creatures and the inevitability of human suffering, aging, and death, just like any other creature that God had made.

Like all modern research data and knowledge today, Adam's discovery was both significant and traumatic. It shattered their innocence and caused existential anxiety *(angst)* due to the awareness of the human being's finite nature and its limited achievements, duration, and temporal, composite constitution dissolved into its original constitutive elements by time, and ultimately by death. As a result, the natural phenomenon of death was rejected. Immortality, resurrection, eternal life, medicine, healing and longevity were positively viewed as God's special rewards and blessings for his obedient people and the saints.

Death was negatively viewed as the human being's chief enemy and greatest evil. Therefore, it was to be rejected and fought against by all means possible. Suicide, abortion, euthanasia and capital punishment were all condemned as evil and sinful because they implied an acceptance of death of human life as a good thing, depending on the situation and circumstances. Subsequently, all the major religions focus on this human weakness and despair in the face of the unescapable radical threat of death. They and try to look for ways to either escape it or overcome it with God's help. This is what they teach as the reliable path to God and salvation.

In most religious teachings about God's supernatural salvation, there is a high degree of emphasis on God's free saving grace as a required divine supernatural power or spiritual or moral special energy. In doctrines of "hard determinism" and extreme predestination, such as those of Augustine and Calvin, God must give the person the necessary grace in order to be saved or redeemed. Otherwise, it is pessimistically believed that Adam and Eve lost the redemptive grace as God's original free will and power to obey God, choose the good, do the good as opposed to evil, and be saved!

What these different groups of moral pessimists, determinists and predestinationists need to hear proclaimed and to know is the *Good News* of God's liberation and redemption from hopeless and despair due to the supposed lack of true freedom for effective and true self-determination. The good news from the benevolent, loving Creator and Redeemer God is that: *YOU ARE FREE. THERE IS NO "ORIGINAL SIN!" ADAM DID NOT LOSE GOD'S GRACE OR CAUSE THE FALL OF HUMANITY! ADAM AND EVE NEVER EXISTED! THEY ARE MERE RELIGIOUS, MYTHOLOGICAL FIGURES IN ANCIENT HEBREW LEGENDS*!

Therefore, all human beings still have God's efficacious original grace and supernatural power to choose to love and obey God. Human beings are both an Adam and Eve in each moment of their usage of free will to judge alternatives or truths, make choices, decisions and implement them. They have the God's free redemptive power of faith, grace and the praxis of love to be transformed, redeemed, spared or saved from the eternal destruction of death. The human response to God's invitation of grace is voluntary and personal. It is not coerced by God!

Within the traditional doctrines of soteriology (redemption or salvation), Christianity is a classic example of redemptive religion. This is self-evident when we look at the Christian doctrines of Christ's atonement for universal sin. By God's free redemptive grace, unconditional for all human beings in the world despite their sins and moral evils, and by Christ's obedience to God in his own innocent and vicarious self-sacrificial death for sin on the cross, and *on behalf of all sinners in the world or all human beings*, Jesus has permanently effected a valid and efficacious universal atonement for all human sins in every age.

The Christian Church has also taught that all those who believe in this Good News of God's redemptive action in human history through Jesus as the Christ and follow the teaching of Christ and hope for a general resurrection of all those who have died, will also be resurrected and rewarded by God with eternal life on the eschatological day of judgement (cf. Matt. 7:31-46). Accordingly, those who have obeyed and done good works of justice and unconditional love for the neighbor will be judged and found by God to be morally upright and worthy of God's Kingdom and heaven.

This is the desired goal of all religious people, namely, to live eternally with God in heaven. On the contrary, the wicked ones and all evildoers or those people who had faith alone (*sola fide)*, but lacked the necessary fruits of obedience, God's grace for moral and spiritual sanctification and perfection, are like the tree without fruits which God cursed, and will go into eternal punishment known as "hell" (cf. Matt. 5-6; 7:13-23; 25:31-46; John 1-3; 14-16; Jam. 2:1-26; 1 John 4:7-21).

Like creation, the supernatural salvation is God's work of agape and free redemptive grace from the beginning to end. All that the human being can do is to accept God's free gift of redemptive grace, obey and cooperate with God through faith and do the good works of unconditional love, free forgiveness of sins and peace in the world. This is necessary and has to be done as part of human obedience and positive response to God's invitation to salvation, fellowship of agape, peace and citizenship in God's Kingdom.

This means that one can live simultaneously in God's supernatural Kingdom of Agape and Peace, and yet still live in the world of hate, intolerance, strife and conflict due to human misuse of personal freedom and rejection to live by the redemptive principles of unconditional love, free forgiveness and nonviolence! As such, it is the collective effort of God's obedient saints that is able to positively transform this world into God's Kingdom of love. This is as opposed to the dominion of evil and sin. God's saints negate and neutralize the destructive and evil rule of hateful, greedy evildoers who are the real devils that constantly work to transform this God's good world into some kind of evil place and "existential hell" by their misuse of freedom and the God-given talents and negative uses of knowledge and specialized skills.

However, this characterization of human freedom, infinite curiosity and search for knowledge as the possible venues for human sin and rebellion against God's natural and moral laws does not mean that we should discard science and technology in order to live in conformity with natural laws. It simply means that we should not destroy the natural foundation of human society.

The ecological balance and the natural environment on which both animals and plants live must be protected. Human beings and the nonhuman creatures need a healthy environment. Their lives and ours depend on it for food, rain, and the air we all need to breathe. An example of the destruction of the environment is the expanding desert in

Africa due to deforestation. The immediate consequences have included drought, famine and human starvation due to lack of water and food. Even the animals, including valuable livestock, such as cattle, goats and camels have died for lack of both water and adequate grass or food to eat.

This African drought and famine are directly linked to human sin and disobedience against God's moral and natural laws governing correct interaction between the human being and the rest of nature. For instance, in traditional Africa, the traditional religion taught that one had to pray to God (as the God of the forest) for permission to cut down a big tree.

This traditional African respect for the environment and caution in dealing with it was due the fact that the African religion teaches that big trees are the temples of God and the departed ancestral spirits. Therefore, they are sacred to both God and the ancestors, particularly, since most big trees surrounding the homestead happened also to be planted over the ancestral tombs or protected the family burial grounds.

However, when the Western Christian Missionaries arrived in Africa, they condemned the African traditional religion as "paganism" and its doctrines as "superstition." This was especially severe when it came to the African Religious teaching on the respect and sanctity of all God's creation or the environment. The African Traditional Religion taught that God was in nature and nature was God's universal habitation.

Accordingly, the African Religion taught that huge trees could not be cut down because they were the temples of God and the sacred habitation of the ancestral spirits. The missionaries scoffed at this African doctrine and called it baseless African pagan superstition and pre-scientific, primitive ignorance.

In this Western Christian crusade against the African Traditional Religion which was summarily dismissed and condemned as paganism, some Christian Missionaries are even known to have killed some of these venerated and revered beliefs by cutting down the trees in the presence of their disbelieving and horrified African converts. The European missionaries encouraged the cutting down of the African sacred trees and groves in order to demonstrate to them the folly of the African beliefs! This is the Western source and grounding of the present African evils of deforestation and decertification. Likewise, Islam encouraged the same destructive concepts as Christianity. After all, Arabs were themselves desert dwellers and did not appreciate African forests. Like the Europeans, they encouraged the Africans to get rid of the forests and jungles.

The African Muslims and Christian converts soon learned convincingly from their Arab and Western Christian missionary teachers that trees were only useful as sources of firewood and timber. They learned that the trees were not the sacred habitation of God and the ancestral spirits. Unfortunately, from the Western Christian missionaries, these Africans also learned to disrespect God and their ancestor, and to cut down the sacred trees and sacred groves with impunity. The Africans indiscriminately cut down these ancient trees to sell to the West and firewood for cooking. There was also increasing demand for them to be shipped to the West and the new urban and missionary centers in Africa.

Soon, the trees in many African countries were cut down for commercial timber and cheap fuel for cooking, and none were planted to replace them. Most trees and forests were gone and the hillsides were bare. The rain-water eroded the top soil and the poor tropical soil was gradually become sandy and agriculturally unproductive! Alas, to the African horror, the ancestral spirits and God's punishment and vengeance for disobedience had visibly descended upon them with great destruction! The Africans were being collectively punished for disobedience, rebellion against God, and the ecological sins of having cut down the life-giving and rain-giving sacred groves and ancestral trees!

Now, the vital fertility of the soil, seasonal rains, planting and harvesting rhythms had ceased. Food had also vanished, along with the vanishing trees, forests and the rains they brought to the area! The tropical sun now baked the bare soil into hot sand. Then, the ever hungry African goats and cattle had also eaten the unprotected grass and remaining vegetation, leaving the land bare and lifeless. The cattle had also trampled the dry soil to sand and dust! Africa had now inherited a desert sand and famine, instead of a heaven of plenty which both the Arab missionaries of Islam and the Western missionaries of Christianity had vigorously preached!

Therefore, for the adherents of the Traditional African Religion, this desertification and famine have bee taken as proofs that God and the African ancestral spirits live in forests and big trees of Africa and they should not be carelessly cut down by greedy and "irreligious" Christians and Muslims. Since the Christians had disrespectfully cut down these forests and the big trees indiscriminately, they believed that God and the angry ancestors were now punishing the whole continent by inflicting unprecedented, prolonged years of drought, the drying up of streams and water-holes, shortage of human and animal food, and subsequently, unprecedented mass starvation and deaths of both people and wild life.

Therefore, human thinking, technology, and rational knowledge have not always brought about good consequences. In many cases incompetence, bad decisions, greed for quick profit, and human misuse of knowledge and technology have resulted in harmful consequences and the premature death rather than enhanced and improved human life. Subsequently, human reason and intellect, unaided by God's eternal vision and wisdom, are bound to endure short-sightedness always present in all human knowledge due to human finitude and inability to see the whole in terms of past, present, and future.

Since only the eternal God is able to scan the eternal stretch at a single glance in all these dimensions of knowledge in terms of past, present, and future contingent events, then only God can possess all the knowledge of all events past, present, and still yet to occur. Consequently, human knowledge is always partial and imperfect. This is as true in the humanities as it is true in the sciences. Even scientific knowledge is partial and relative to change and improvement as we learn more about ourselves, the observers and the phenomena or nature we observe.

New theories replace the antiquated ones, and new truths are revealed which have always been present but hidden from us largely due to our natural intellectual limitations and imperfection of both our present scientific theories and research instruments. And the more we know, the more we realize how little we know and how much more there is still to know. Here, a good analogy would probably be that human beings are like small children playing with water buckets on the beach of the cosmic ocean of the infinite knowledge. Or, that if we only came down each day, we would have the whole sea contained in our water buckets!

What is probably the most surprising and perplexing mystery about human beings is that although we have sent probes into outer space, made trips to walk on the moon, or worked in the shuttle or space laboratories, and although we have made a plane that goes around the world without stopping or refueling on the way, we still have not yet learned enough about ourselves as human beings, nor have we learned to live together in mutual respect and peace.

Regrettably, as essentially and intrinsically moral, intelligent and rational beings, we still live irrational lives and do stupid things together or individually which do not show any evidence of rationality or wisdom, which we claim to possess as our chief "trademark" or characteristic as human beings. What then, is wrong with us? Why are most human beings prone to violence, hate, injustice and evil more than doing what is loving, just, noble, virtuous, compassionate, peaceful and good?

This very puzzling question will take us to the very next ultimate question of human existence, puzzle of religion, theology, philosophy and ethics. This is the question of the existence of the holy, good, benevolent omnipotent Creator God and the problems of the human being's moral imperfection, rebellion, evil-deeds and destruction of God's good world and creation.

There are many religious, theological, philosophical and cultural theories and answers to why there is human moral and spiritual imperfection and evil in the world. The next several parts of the book will discuss some of these theories and answers and evaluate them in terms of human causal freedom, free-will, societal values, moral education, and ultimately, the teachings of Jesus concerning God's free redemptive grace, unconditional love, free forgiveness of sins, and need for diligent practice of nonviolence if peace and God's Kingdom are to prevail in this world, "as it is in heaven." According to Jesus, the human being is also God's child who is like God his or her "Father" (*Abba*). The human being is also as much an active participant in God's supernatural process of forgiving the offenses and sins of people. Therefore, the human being is God's local supernatural agent for both healing and redeeming the world from evil in cooperation with God.

The obedient human being as God's representative in the world is also God's commissioned special missionary in the world. He or she is the real temporal partner and active co-creator and co-redeemer of the world. The human being also serves as the finite mediator and high priest for the world. The self-transcendent, intelligent, and free human being, accepts his or her natural role as an evolutionary moral agent and the *Homo sapiens,* therefore, the human being thinks, speaks and benevolently acts on behalf of the unthinking and silent creation and the cosmos.

Therefore, the human being as God's ambassador in the world, and simultaneously, as the representative and high-priest of creation to God, prays to God on behalf of other less intelligent creatures and nonliving things within the cosmos, and in turn mediates God to them. As the human being thinks deep thoughts about the cosmos, worships God, prays and intercedes for the world, he or she becomes the local living extension of the cosmic Logos and God incarnate in humanity.

According to the Christian tradition and its exclusive doctrines of the divine Incarnation and soteriology (salvation), this divine theophany and heavenly divine reality were best historically manifested in Jesus as the Christ of God. However, the same redemptive divine reality was equally manifested in the Buddha and Krishna according to the Buddhist and the Hindu traditions. Ultimately, God has not left any human community without his redemptive unconditional love, unmerited grace, supernatural revelation and salvation. Contrary to many religious exclusive traditions, no human being or special community of God's people is ever favored at the expense of others, or excluded by God from these free divine universal activities of God's cosmic creation and redemption.

# Chapter 5

# Human Beings' Freedom, Moral Conflict And Spiritual Dilemma

The intelligent and knowing human being (*Homo sapiens*) is a free moral agent in the world. A person with a well-developed moral conscience, living anywhere in the world, and in any age also experiences hubris, self-interest and some serious inner moral conflict and spiritual dilemma. This is true irrespective of creed, culture, class, nationality, gender and religious affiliation.

The moral crisis occurs when the well-formed conscience that is grounded in well-learned and internalized moral codes and sound values is deliberately forced to violate its constitute moral principles in order to gain some political, economic, social or other benefit or for fear of offending important people of a different moral opinion. Inevitably, when a moral agent's conscience and the moral choices made or actions performed are in irreconcilable conflict with his or her conscience, this leads to a spiritual dilemma. Similarly, a conflict of interests causes serious moral and spiritual dilemmas for many people in the work-place and the community.

## 1. Conscience, Moral Conflict and Spiritual Dilemma

Mature and responsible moral agents operate on the basis of an internal teleological moral system. This is as opposed to a deontological moral system which requires an external moral authority, such as God, the police, parents and supervisors, for its effective enforcement and observance. Those who operate on the basis of the teleological moral system are morally governed and guided by a well formed and developed moral conscience with an internalized system of moral values and ideal moral codes of conduct. It is internally enforced by a well-formed moral conscience and God's Holy Spirit that dwells within each person as a moral agent or the *imago Dei.*

Therefore, when the moral agent makes a moral choice and performs a deed that is in direct conflict with one's conscience, then, a serious state of a personal inner moral conflict and spiritual dilemma may arise and cause intense guilt and misery. For instance, a person who sleeps with the boss in order to get a job, promotion or a pay raise, may become very miserable after the event. This is due to personal moral self-judgement and the rise of an inner moral conflict, guilt and experience of a spiritual dilemma. Subsequently, in the USA charges of sexual harassment may be filed as a consequence of this immoral event and the person's need to resolve the torment of the inner moral conflict and guilt associated with the undesirable immoral occurrence.

When there are no clear guidelines for what is right and wrong, the moral agent may very acutely experience moral conflict about the many conflicting possible alternatives available of which only one can be chosen at any given time. This is more troubling when all of the possible alternative choices are not perfect or ideal and may have some serious negative consequences, despite the advantages. In addition, intense guilt may be felt at the innermost core of one's being and a hellish torment may also result due to a secret sin and moral infraction.

Guilt often arises due to the consciousness of the moral failure. This may include the failure to do the maximum good possible in any given particular situation. This constitutes the universality of human moral imperfection and sense of the "*original sin.*" This is due the human intellect, thought, knowledge and moral agency and the human capacity to know the contrast and gap between perfection and imperfection. This is concretely visible in the world in terms of "*what ought to be*" (the ideal) and "*what is*" (reality).

The human experience of guilt and anguish due to moral failures and sins which have been committed produce the spiritual suffering and existential hell, unless confessed and atoned for in a both culturally and religiously prescribed manner. For the Roman Catholics and the

Anglicans, this may require confession to be made to God through a priest and absolution of sins to be declared by the priest on God's behalf.

Deep faith as a positive orientation to life and the divine cosmic mysteries is required for the penitent sinner to accept that his or her sins have been forgiven by God. Martin Luther who lacked such a faith in connection with the sacrament of confession, never had the desired spiritual "feeling" of healing or redemptive experience from the burdens of sin and guilt as they were removed by God through the sacrament of confession. Luther mistakenly concluded that God did not forgive human sins through the mediation of the Church and its sacerdotal priests since he did not feel forgiven after sacramental confessions.

As a result, he agitated for theological and ecclesiastical reformation of the Roman Catholic Church. Luther demanded the removal of moral and spiritual abuses from the Church's practices and doctrines. He also condemned the sale of indulgences for forgiveness of sins as a false Church doctrine, since only God could forgive sins based on his grace, and both the sinner's faith (*sola fide*) and confession of sins.

Instead of the anticipated reformation, Luther was requested to recant and withdraw his Ninety Five Theses. When he refused to do so, he was excommunicated. Subsequently, he started the mass German patriotic peasant rebellion against the Roman Catholic Church. He established a Protestant Church through this ecclesiastical rebellion known as the "Protestant Reformation." His famous Ninety-Five Theses formed the basis of his reformation. They were grounded in Luther's own spiritual experience, moral and soteriological theology which led to his rejection of the traditional Catholic theological and moral theory of sin and atonement through the traditional Catholic Church's hierarchical institutional sacerdotal (priestly) mediation of God's redemptive grace, Church and forgiveness of sins.

As a diligent monk and Franciscan priest, Luther had failed to gain the essential moral and spiritual assurance of God's forgiveness. He had failed to experience or "feel" God's grace and deliverance from his sins through the Church's established sacramental procedures for the removal of personal guilt due to those sins through the Church's traditional channels of sacramental confession and absolution. Later, through the study of the Pauline Epistles, especially the letters to the Romans and Galatians, he reached the conclusion that sinners are justified before God by faith alone (*sola fide*) and not by good works. This divine atonement and remission of sins are made possible by God's grace alone *(sola gratia*) through the Incarnation, life, work and innocent death of Jesus

Christ on the cross. For Luther, faith alone justifies the sinner before God. That is, faith unites the believer with God's redemptive mission as it was both historically manifested to the world and accomplished through the work of Jesus Christ on the cross.

However, regardless of religious tradition, moral theory and doctrine of sin and God's free forgiveness (or atonement), human guilt universally exists. Guilt exists as human being's self moral judgement, self-condemnation and self-punishment. This process is coextensive with God's inner administration of divine holy judgement and justice through the human being's well-formed and highly a developed personal intrinsic divine instrument of moral conscience. This is universally the case although human conscience is finite, imperfect and conditioned by local factors, such as family, community, neighborhood, religion, culture, gender, class, education, age, law, era, science, heathy, nationality and socioeconomic conditions.

Nevertheless, properly morally, spiritually and socialized and well educated normal human being is that person who has become morally mature, law-abiding, skilled, benevolent, caring, nonviolent, just, humane, considerate and fully responsible for his or her own use of freedom. He or she has learned to deal with conflicts as part of a moral or social life, and resolve them in a peaceful manner. The moral and well-educated person has attained the skills for making well-informed, sound moral choices that benefit the majority of the people within the community, enhance beauty, harmony and peace within the community, and both preserve and protect the environment and the world from abuses, exploitation, pollution and degradation. The well socialized and educated moral agent recognizes the inevitability of conflict with the self and the community as a natural aspect of evolutionary life. Life and reality are composed of some contrasting intrinsic competing multiplicities of potentiality seeking to become fulfilled as concrete reality in a unified event.

The moral agent is constantly faced with competing alternatives to choose from. This in itself is a permanent source of contrast, frustration, and conflict within the moral agent's mind, choices, deeds, history and the world. For instance, those who choose to get married and choose from many suitors often wonder what life would have been like if they had chosen someone else for a mate. Those who cannot accept what choice they made often become dissatisfied and miserable because they convince themselves that life would have been better with a different partner. Some divorces and other social evils are rooted in this moral and mental illusion which suggests that "grass is greener on the other side of the fence." Ignorance, greed, envy and self-interest are vices rooted in this destructive epistemological, social and moral illusion. It is a source of moral and spiritual dissatisfaction and dilemma.

In short, the human being is a free moral agent, who is universally acutely aware of his or her innermost moral dualism, conflict and guilt. It is also because the human being (*Homo sapiens)* is an intelligent, knowing, thinking, judging and responsible moral agent. As a result, the human being experiences a unique personal moral conflict and spiritual struggle in choosing between good and evil. The human mind is the battle ground for both the perceived good and evil in the world. This is due to the nature and reality of human freedom, intellect, knowledge and moral consciousness of both good and evil. Since the world is experienced in a contrasting dualistic and subjective mode, this subjective dualism also affects the human being's knowledge, consciousness, mind, spirit and self-identity, as either a wise and good person or a foolish evildoer. St. Paul and St. Augustine's experiences and writings best illustrate this universal human condition and experience of inner spiritual, moral dualism, and dilemma due to guilt, and despair (*angst*).

Both Paul and Augustine, attributed to Adam and Eve's "original sin," and "the fall," of humanity from God's grace and perfection to the state of sin and imperfection. For Paul and Augustine "original sin" constitutes the universal experience of a human moral and spiritual dilemma (cf. Rom. 5). This is the moral and spiritual dilemma of human imperfection. The human moral and spiritual dilemma, which Paul Tillich called "the human predicament," is characterized by anxiety due to the human moral and spiritual dualism. There is an irreconcilable intrinsic conflict between good and evil. There is also existential anxiety due to the human moral failure to choose or do the right thing, and subsequently, a tormenting sense of guilt. Being Neoplatonists, they attributed this subjective experience of spiritual struggle and moral division, which are experienced deep within, to results of their own modes of existence as physical realities and embodiments of the spirit and mind. These dualists called the mind and spirit good and rejected the body or "flesh" and its senses as evil.

These Church Fathers and other religious Neoplatonists were unanimous that the bodily senses caused serious evils and conflict within the moral agents. They observed that the body's senses and physical needs caused insatiable craving for physical and sensual pleasures, such as food, sex, material possessions and comfort. Furthermore, the religious people viewed these bodily pleasures as false sources of true happiness and false remedies for human existential anxiety. They both rejected and condemned them as hedonistic goals dictated by the body desire and illusion of truth and happiness. For them, only God was the universal, reliable and true source of ultimate, most meaningful and lasting human happiness and peace!

Naturally, all human beings experience some distressing degree of personal, moral and spiritual struggle and failure. Human beings are aware of their own spiritual imperfection, wrongdoing, omission of choosing or doing the maximum good. The human being is also aware of his or her sins against both God the creator and fellow human beings (the neighbor). As a result, the normal moral people experience personal moral guilt for this spiritual and moral evil or imperfection. Human beings have also sought to escape or remove it through repentance. Sacrificial atonement and a voluntary personal life of more strict moral and rigorous spiritual self-discipline, such as the performance of abundant good deeds of unconditional love, contemplative prayer and meditation.

## 2. Possession of the Knowledge of the Good And Evil as the Secret to "Become God"

Unlike the amoral animals, the human being is intrinsically a moral, religious and spiritual being that is able to face moral dilemmas, because he or she is akin to the holy God as the heavenly Father or Mother. The human being essentially experiences guilt due to an intrinsic acute consciousness of sin and moral failure. This is largely due to the fact that in creation, only the human being is essentially the most highly intelligent, free, thinking creature, possessing knowledge, including that what is good or right, and what is wrong, evil and destructive.

Since according to most traditional religious beliefs, God's secret knowledge of divinity and immortality were hidden from mortal human beings, then it follows that the human beings could gain access to this forbidden knowledge by research or studying God's self-revelation through his works in nature. In ancient times, the Oriental, African and Babylonian practices were theocentric. Today, some people refer to these theocentric practices as mere superstitions regarding nature, particularly, water, sky, sun, planets, stars, trees and beliefs in the powers of magic. In some of these ancient religious systems, it was also thought and hoped that there might be some herbal cure of death as a fatal moral disease. This is illustrated by the biblical account of creation and fall in which the "secret tree of eternal life" or divinity, omniscience and immortality plays a central role in the natural world as the Garden of Eden (cf. Gen. 2-3).

In addition to the herbs which were used for medicine and healing, in some ancient cultures it was also believed that by eating some magical fruits from the special mythological trees of the knowledge of eternal life and immortality or divinity, human beings would also become omniscient and immortal like God. Christmas trees, the mistletoe and the evergreens still symbolize some aspects of these primitive beliefs today. Later, Christians declared to the world that by participation in the sacrament of the holy Eucharist as "the eating the body" and "drinking the blood" of Jesus as the crucified and risen Christ, the believers would have eternal life because the body and blood of Christ were the food of eternal life and God given free universal antidotes against the human sin and death.

According to the *"Yahwist"* ("J") anthropomorphic account of creation (Gen. 2-3), the primordial human temptation (Adamic or original sin) was "to become omniscient and immortal or to become God!" They wanted to "possess the divinizing knowledge of what was good and what was evil" and to determine how to live the good life in the world. There is no reference to God as the Creator, Redeemer and source of guidance, or moral laws on how to live, or virtues based on sound divine knowledge and values.

The common theological perception was that to be Godlike, one had to possess the secret knowledge of what is good and what is evil, and how the universe operated. The human being having acquired this divine essence and knowledge of the good and evil, in metaphorical and mythical language is said to "have eaten the forbidden fruit of the tree of knowledge, divinity and eternal life." This acquired divine knowledge and truth lead to the human divinization and simultaneously, rebellion against God's rule "without the human being's informed personal consent," loss of innocence and automatic natural citizenship in God's Kingdom" or "heaven."

Now the human "being has to work hard" at self-discipline, conscious personal obedience to God and earn his or her return to "paradise" (the Garden of Eden) or God's Kingdom (Heaven), by renouncing the evils of disbelief, disobedience, egocentricity, hubris or pride and self-deification into a false God. The human being has to renounce idolatry, and the destructive insatiable desire for sex, drugs, alcohol, food, or greed for money, wealth, material possessions and other physical things which clog spiritual and moral life as false offers of salvation and happiness.

These are false remedies for the troubling inner, infinite void and ever yearning spiritual emptiness experienced at the center of human life that is ever calling for filling. This is a bottomless void. It is a feeling of emptiness and infinite or abyss which is existentially experienced by many human beings at the center of their humanity and the life they lead. It cannot be filled by sex, liquor, drugs, money, fame, power, possessions and wealth. These are false remedies and illusions of happiness, fulfillment, satisfaction and peace. In themselves they are incapable of filling the spiritual void, and thus, provide the essential true and lasting happiness to the rich and the powerful people of the world. Princess Diana discovered that sex, power, money, beauty, food and fame could never be sufficient as sources of lasting happiness. She died a tragic death, still trying hard to fill her inner void and life with sex and romance as a source of happiness. This was in sharp contrast to Mother Teresa, who died peacefully in her mature years, having found happiness, peace and satisfying love (agape) in the fellowship and union with God.

The universal human experience of the inner human emptiness and spiritual void is an existential reality. It is not an illusion, imaginary, or state of neurosis and paranoia to be diagnosed and treated by psychiatrists. On the contrary, spiritual emptiness exists as a result of human alienation from God's infinite love and grace which are required to fill that infinite void at the center of human life and existence. Buddha, Socrates, Moses, Jesus and Gandhi discovered that the secret for lasting human happiness does not lie in the accumulation of material possessions and wealth. On the contrary, they discovered the secret to God and lasting happiness in self-discipline, self-renunciation, obedience, self-sacrificial good works on behalf of others, prayerful life and the diligent contemplation of God. That involves the renunciation of ego or self, and the rejection of power, material desire for wealth, pride and autonomy from God's will and the Kingdom. This process of self-crucifixion or self-purgation of all barriers and moral and spiritual impurities, finally leads to spiritual enlightenment, and a beatific union with God in mind, spirit and will.

Ultimately, regardless of the goal and mode of life chosen, the human being is by functional definition, "a thinking, free moral agent in the world." That is, the human being possesses an "*a priori*" intrinsic freedom and an intellectual capacity to choose to act and live according to what he or she knows to be both good and right moral principles; that is, to act and live in accordance with the knowledge of the good or to act and live in a very contrary manner to what he or she knows to be right and good for lack of goodwill, courage and moral integrity.

The human possesses an insatiable desire and craving (*tanha*) for self-fulfillment and happiness. Other animals are primarily governed by their natural instincts, particularly, those of security and survival, including correct food, mating behavior, protection of the offspring, and interaction with others. For the human beings, the culturally established moral, religious and legal codes largely govern the human beings behavior and actions. In addition, the human being has a moral understanding and some knowledge of what is right and wrong. Yet, the human being can knowingly and deliberately choose both to rebel against God's good moral guidance (commandments) and consciously choose to do evil.

Whereas social norms and moral codes are in many literate societies written down in a legal code and used to enforce the desirable moral behavior in a given society, the moral interpretation of that code may vary from person to person depending on family background, education, personal moral stand, and personal conscience. This was the case with the Mosaic Law. It was originally written down by Moses whose moral code was made up of the Ten Commandments given to the Jewish people in God's holy name. However, the code was, later, expanded until it numbered about 613 commandments. In turn, these commandments were expanded and commented on by the Rabbis, the Jewish moral teachers and religious leaders, until they filled many volumes of the *Talmud* and the *Mishnar*.

Nevertheless, this did not prevent Jesus and the prophets from denouncing these traditional religious moral teachers as hypocrites and dangerous blind guides of the ignorant masses. Jesus condemned the religiously zealous Pharisees as unspiritual and immoral because they failed to see the divine love and holiness behind the Mosaic code that they observed. They just observed the "letter of the law" and failed in comprehending God's redemptive love that was the grounding of this explicit divine moral law.

As a result, these Mosaic laws became a significant religious, moral and cultural burden for the ordinary people whom the Pharisees derogatorily referred to as the "common people" or "sinners." The poor and uneducated class of people did not observe the Mosaic law and its cumbersome rituals for cleanliness. They also failed to appreciate the Mosaic Law as God's moral and true path to divine illumination, equality, human rights, righteousness (virtuous), holiness, justice, a good life, happiness, and a peaceful life or divine redemption.

However, instead of offering thanksgiving and praise to God in appreciation of God's providence in giving them the natural and explicit moral law to guide them into truth and a righteous path of goodness, justice and peace, these sinful people complained about the burden of keeping God's moral law! As a result, these moral rebellious and sinners rejected God's law. Instead, they preferred the easier life of unrestricted pleasures, sin, violence, self-indulgence and moral corruption. This was easier to accomplish when compared to that of life lived according to the moral code of self-sacrificial purity, justice, nonviolence, and love for their neighbors which was negatively looked at as the burden of the law. This is because these people failed to understand that the moral law was God's concrete means for God's concrete provision and mediation of his unconditional love, rule and the establishment of his concrete kingdom on the Earth through the societal love, peace and harmony within the community and the world.

The practice of the Mosaic Law led to the obedient moral agent's appreciation of God's moral guidance to a harmonious life of virtue, goodness, justice and peace. For this devoted religious group, the Mosaic Law contained the essential guidelines and moral principles of God's reliable moral holy path to guide them to God's moral and spiritual perfection, harmony and peace. God's moral law as given through Moses was also God's societal means to protect and save people from pain, guilt, and the anguish of moral evil or sin, and injustice.

Because human beings are intelligent, free, knowledgeable, and moral agents and finite creatures, they are also able to suffer mental or spiritual pain when they knowingly do what is wrong, instead of doing what is right and good. The human defiant immoral acts that are due to the human being's knowingly doing evil are universally common among rebellious or evil human beings. It is called "sin." This is the essential meaning of the theological terms "original sin" and the "the fall of humanity." This human moral deficiency is universally condemned as moral evil to be rejected and corrected by society through education, moral training, religion, ethics, codification of laws and punishment of the lawbreakers and moral offenders. In religion, this human moral evil deed or act is referred to as sin. And sin or evil deeds hurt the perpetrators, the victims and ultimately, evil-deeds injure the whole society by disrupting social networks, order, harmony and peace.

Evil-doers are sinners who promote vice, injustice, hate and violence in the community. This is one of the main reasons why the society must fight evil and transform evil-doers into the doers of good deeds. The society must formulate, codify, and enforce social moral norms and moral laws, if it has to continue to exist as a society and not a mere collection of autonomous individuals and groups of people with nothing in common and without the bond or restraint of the common good or law and order. Such a collection of unrelated people is not a society or community. It is crowd or a mere irresponsible and destructive mob in a state of anarchy.

The human being's cost for doing evil or committing sin is great. It includes personal guilt and the destruction of the self, the community and the world. In some cases, immediate physical harm and chaos may result from doing evil. However, sometimes evil consequences are indirect and delay in becoming externally visible in the world. Nevertheless, there are immediate consequences such as a fine, jail sentence, deadly venereal diseases in cases of sexual sin, death (in cases of drugs), broken families, divorces, loss of job and property, and the like. The principle of *Karma* or cause and effect affirms that each negative or evil deed has a tendency to produce an equal or greater negative societal evil effect in return.

Ultimately, people reap what they sow although the book of Job contradicts this moral theory. Job's sufferings were due to his righteousness and not his sins and evil-deeds. The prophets and Jesus follow into this mystery of why evil and suffering afflicts good people! Nevertheless, the general observation confirms that in most cases, the moral theory as grounded in the universal natural law of causality or "cause and effect" holds true in most cases and real normal conditions of human life.

That is the affirmation that the good deed is like a good seed or good fruit tree which Jesus commended for "begetting a good yield." As a result, Jesus affirmed that true prophets, and the true obedient saints of God, would be judged by their quality and quantity of the abundance of their fruits or good deeds (Matt. 7:14-23). On the final day of judgement, God will also judge the people according to their concrete actions as opposed to their confessions of faith and creeds which had no correlative good deeds (Matt. 25:31-46). And because there are more evil-doers in the world than those who do good deeds, the world itself appears to be evil. Nevertheless, the world having been created by a good-loving God cannot be an evil entity. The world is essentially good. It is often transformed into an evil place by evil people who live in it and pollute it with the evil deeds of hate, injustice, violence and destruction.

However, human beings, having great capacity for both doing good and evil, and having real freedom to choose being otherwise grounded in human selfishness or self-interest and self-centeredness, more often choose to do evil more than good, thus causing moral evil and imbalances in the essentially God's good world. This is not God's fault or failure to create more perfect people and a better world. Rather, it is good evidence that the human being's actions are indeed free and cause real positive or negative consequences in the local community, society and the world. As such, the human being should accept freedom and responsibility for their actions.

The "*law of karma*" or the moral principle which teaches that what "we sow is what we reap" has universal moral validity, irrespective of era, culture and creed. This universal principle of moral causality in the world is self-evident in much of the history of our world. History clearly illustrates that human freedom, choices and deeds have some corresponding physical, social and moral consequences. Evil men like Adolph Hitler and Idi Amin illustrate this point very clearly. Just like a farmer sows wheat, and reaps wheat, and sows corn and also reaps corn, human deeds also lead to correlative consequences. Good deeds lead to a good and happy community while evil-deeds lead to discord, violence and misery. Just like the farmer who sows corn does not harvest rice or beans, instead of corn, likewise, if human beings sow the seeds of moral evil and violence, similarly, they will reap the harvest of hate, violence, war and destruction. The sowers of moral evil cannot reap the harvest of goodness and peace.

When people as the moral agents in the local community and the world sow the seeds of goodness and righteousness, they also reap the corresponding good fruits of goodness, righteousness joy, peace and happiness. The fruits of these good deeds are good. They bring us joy and happiness together with those connected with us, such as friends, colleagues, neighbors, and relatives. Evil spreads like cancer in the body. Goodness and justice are the effective antidote to moral evil and its destructiveness.

Therefore, it is encouraging to learn from the Bible that although the wicked and evildoers have always abounded in the world, and even when they completely outnumbered the saints and the morally upright people, evil never prevailed for long. Justice, order and peace would always be reestablished after some time of suffering, war and chaos. Peace, goodness and happiness are the ultimate goals of many people even when they do evil and fail to accomplish those noble and ethical goals through their own egocentric, selfish, misguided, violent and unethical methods.

According to the national and world history, it has always been through the dedicated work and self-sacrifice of those few saints of God, and all the obedient children or just and loving servants of God in the local community, that the world has been redeemed from evil, chaos, injustice, hate, violence, and division. Therefore, it is continuously transformed into a good, just and ideal peaceful community of God's people. This is how God's Kingdom is concretely and historically established on the Earth. For instance, the Biblical story of Noah's faithfulness in a land full of sin, corruption, and evil is one such great example. We also have the story of Lot concerning Sodom and Gomorrah, and how God promised to spare the evil city if a few holy people would be found in it.

We also have the examples of the prophets and the saints who worked hard to positively transform and redeem for God the people of their own age. Gautama Siddhartha in India who came to be known as Buddha, Socrates the Greek moral philosopher, Abraham, Moses, King David, John the Baptist, Jesus the Deliverer (Messiah or Christ), and Prophet Muhammad of the Middle East are some good examples of non-Christian saints and prophets, although most of them have been accepted by Judaism, Christianity and Islam. However, they are God's non-Christian obedient saints in the world. They are the true obedient saints whose personal holiness, moral uprightness, courage, exemplary life and moral teaching have served to change, reshape and transform the world morally, religiously, socially, and politically.

Communism thrived because of its focus on the disillusionment due to the religion's moral failure to practice the moral teachings of socioeconomic justice and unconditional love for the neighbor. Karl Marx emphatically rejected unjust and oppressive modes of Western capitalist Christianity as corrupt and evil. Marxist intellectuals correctly repudiated the corrupt capitalistic form of Christianity as "the opium of the people." This is the kind of corrupt and dysfunctional Christianity which was associated with the rich and powerful ruling group who exploited the poor laborers in the factories. This form of corrupt Christianity compromised the teachings of Jesus on materialism and the definitive commandment of Agape.

To this extent, the silent masses in the face of evil are guilty of complicity. For instance, some morally irresponsible Christian ministers preached to the African slaves in America and the exploited, working masses in Europe, that it was noble and virtuous to be obedient to their masters or superiors. They were taught that as Christians they should have faith in the goodness of God's providence and put their hopes of a reward in God in heaven during the future life after death! This was as opposed to focusing on the real misery in this present life in which they were being oppressed and exploited by the ruling, rich elite class which owned the means of production and the religion-political machinery power, and used its coercive force to enforce their economic and political will on the helpless poor masses.

However, even these Marxists had to come up with a practical form of a moral code for their society. Remarkably, even when they had done away with the idea of God and religion, the two foundations of most moral codes, they still looked to religion and scriptures for ideals that were finally incorporated into the "utopia." The goal of establishing a just, crime less and egalitarian communist society on the Earth was the inversion of the Christian concept of heaven. This Communist Utopia was in essence God's Kingdom on the Earth, which would be established through human efforts and revolutions by the oppressed poor masses of the world. This Kingdom was completely humanistic and utilitarian. It was God's Kingdom on the Earth without God or the human corrupt, oppressive and tyrants for leaders.

This observation is of great importance for it reveals the deep intrinsic moral essence of the human being's basic nature as a moral agent or an *imago Dei.* The Marxist experiment proves that human values and sense of morality are not mere results of human religious sentiments and illusory beliefs in a nonexistent God, as Feuerbach, Nietzsche and Freud have erroneously claimed in their influential atheistic writings. On the contrary, these ideas and doctrines show that human beings are, by essential nature, both intrinsically moral and spiritual (religious) beings. Religion and spiritual values are both simultaneously natural and supernatural aspects of the human being, who is both simultaneously a divine being and an evolutionary animal. These dual natures of humanity are realities that are best manifested in Jesus as the incarnation of God (cf. John 1-3).

Likewise, the acute moral consciousness of sin and guilt are neither mental illusions nor mental disorders to be treated with antidepressants, such as prozac or tranquilizers. Sin and guilt cannot be ignored or be effectively cured by psychoanalysis and psychiatric therapy! Instead, problems of sin and guilt need a moral and spiritual treatment and cure that can be provided by a redemptive religion and spirituality. This is because human beings are by essential nature also the most highly intellectually and spiritually evolved, are the Godlike creatures that are the free, self-transcending, spiritual and moral agents in the world. This is made possible because they possess the intellect, creativity knowledge, and the capacity to judge between right and wrong, and to choose and either do good or evil.

Religion is helpful in ethics and moral values. Nevertheless, it is not necessarily the essential basis for sound and good moral judgement, justice, democracy, human rights and good deeds. On the contrary, religion by itself has sometimes led to the abuses of human rights, restrictions of freedom and stifled the intellectual quest for the scientific truth and liberal arts education. Socrates and Jesus were executed as criminals by the religious establishment of their time. The past controversy over the teaching of evolution and its restrictions in many American schools is such an example. Like the past jihads, the crusades and the inquisitions, religion has led to bigotry, falsehood, intolerance, violence, wars, evil and immoral deeds in human history.

Therefore, sound moral judgement requires more than religious faith in God alone. Good moral thinking and judgement must be grounded in a well-formed moral conscience, internalized or teleological moral values, sound reasoning skills, wisdom, courage, freedom to make the best choices available, good or noble intentions and correct knowledge.

Good, sound and redemptive religion can enhance human moral sensitivity but some religions have been known to teach that which is ethically questionable and even evil. Thus, religion by itself cannot always be taken as a reliable, infallible and correct moral guide. This includes the holy Scriptures, including the Bible and the Qur'an, irrespective of the fact that many Christians and Muslims, exclusively claim that these sacred books are God's inspired, inerrant, and infallible direct redemptive revelations. However, these are false claims since nobody has ever seen God, and God does not write books which contradict his or her explicit universal and infallible revelation in both nature and the cosmos. For instance, the biblical book of Joshua seems to praise as ethical and holy what we would condemn today as genocide.

Similarly, the crude Mosaic doctrine of "tooth for a tooth and an eye for an eye" *(lex talionis)* appears to be violent and unethical to us today. Fortunately, Jesus rejected this law of violence and reversed the Mosaic Law of equal retaliation form of justice. He replaced it with the moral obligations for the praxis of mercy, nonviolence, forgiveness and the commandment to "love your neighbor" and "forgive those who wrong you," including one's enemies (Matt. 5-7). As such, true Christianity is centered on these moral principles of God in Christ. That makes Christianity an essentially compassionate and nonviolent as a religion as a moral way of life or path to God, salvation, a good life and happiness.

However, Islam, Judaism, and some fundamentalist Christian groups still insist on violence and retaliation as divine justice and proper responses to evil or when wronged. However, only the good deed can produce good whereas evil generally produces more evil. Similarly, violence only leads to more violence and will not lead to lasting peace. Those who are defeated in the war soon regroup to reorganize themselves for a more effective reversal of the humiliation suffered in the war when they were defeated. Only peace negotiations and treaties can lead to meaningful terms of peace.

Subsequently, peace obtained by war or other forms of violence is an illusion. Peace established through violence or war has to be constantly maintained through continued violence or threat of violence if it is to endure. This is currently the case in Northern Ireland, Eastern Europe (Bosnia, Serbia, Kosovo and Yugoslavia), Israel, Lebanon, and Africa's Great Lakes Region (Congo, Uganda and Rwanda). In these cases, intense heavily armed police patrols or military intimidation or coercion are required, if "military peace" is to endure. The conquered people never give up the military struggle to regain their lost freedom, unless there is either mutual shared political and economic power, or the conquered people got nearly exterminated, as was the case of the North American Indians.

Christianity itself has had its own bad record of violence and bloodshed. For instance, the infamous crusades were Christian military attempts at exterminating the Muslims in order to liberate Jerusalem from the Muslim occupation and reestablish Christianity. This was no better than the Islamic Jihad of which we now repudiate as state-sponsored terrorism. The infamous inquisition was another Christian moral and religious authoritarianism, which in reality, amounted to a Christian reign of terror. In this era, freedom of scientific research and academic expression were severely curbed by the church and the State. For instance, Galileo was forced to recant his scientific findings and teacings or be executed!

Therefore, there is a great danger when we allow religion to dictate moral absolute values and to regulate what can be taught or researched into and published. Indeed, it was because of Christianity's failure to address the moral, social, and economic problems created by the industrial revolution in Europe, that Marx and Engels became disillusioned with "capitalist religion" (Christianity), and perceived it to be a mere societal tranquillizing drug, the "opium of the oppressed" poor masses. Marxism was formulated as a better and more humane alternative system of socioeconomic justice and human liberation from oppression than Christianity.

Religion (Christianity) a the drug to keep the masses happy in their state of ignorance and capitalist exploitation by the rich, was according to Marx, administered to the unsuspecting poor masses by the Christian Church which was the tool of the ruling class. If Marx had written his material in the 20th century, he would have used the example of the missionary Church in colonial Africa and America as an additional illustration. Marxism has offered a great challenge to Christianity to become more just, constructive and practical in its own ethical teachings. This is especially true in respect to Christian obedience and the implementation of Christ's essential commandment of socioeconomic justice and the ethic of nonviolence as the universal praxis of the unconditional love for the neighbor (cf. Matt. 25:31-46).

Jesus the Christ as the founder of Christianity had a ministry which was devoted to the oppressed, the disenfranchised poor masses and the outcasts. He also healed their diseases free of charge, and fed them when they were hungry. He never sent them away ill and hungry. This example in itself is very revolutionary. Yet, Christian churches spend most of their time today ministering to the rich and less time is given to the poor. This is because the pledges and generous donations of the rich support the Church personnel and their pastoral functions within the Church, the community and the world. The poor and the needy who are served as the beneficiaries of the Church, lacking in wealth and the power it confers, also do not have voice within the Church affairs.

Like in the rest of the capitalist world, in the Church, the poor are often excluded from the Church's governance, oppressed and voiceless. This is mainly because they do not give the money that supports the Church ministry, or pay the pastor's middle class income stipend! It is still true in the Church that whoever pays the minister's salary "calls the tune" or sets the minister's agenda! This is tragic, but that is the case. Jesus never got paid by his poor audience. But today, the minister, like other professionals, has to live by his own training and professional occupation. This means that some churches have to become business-like in order to afford to hire a well-trained professional minister, and to provide adequate support for his or her ministry.

As result of the clerical professionalization, the role of the Church has become very bureaucratic, business-like, mundane in scope and administration. Some ministers have become greedy and their main concerns have become Church business and making "big money" than taking care of the poor, the needy, the sick or seeking justice and speaking out on behalf of the voiceless and the oppressed people in the world.

The pastoral and prophetic aspects of the Church have been dropped because they do not bring money into the church treasury, and instead, infuriate the public. Prophets got killed by their audiences, and were not paid by the people to whom God had sent them to minister his Word! In some cases, this would displease the minister's rich congregation members who are doing the exploitation and the oppression, and subsequently, there is more temptation to keep quiet so as not to be fired. To these kinds of worldly, materialistic, greedy and money-loving ministers, Jesus would have probably said the following:

> Hypocrites! Lovers of money more than God's work which you so profess to love and do! Go away from my sight. Go into the eternal punishment prepared for the Devil and his followers who cleverly disguised themselves as the children of God, but in honesty, they were greedy, ravenous wolves in sheep's clothing. You can fool human beings, but you cannot fool God. Hypocrites, you will truly get what you deserve. (My own *Paraphrase of Jesus' sayings in the Gospels*.)

It is by now probably clear to the reader that what is basically wrong with the human being is sin and moral evil. This problem is so great that there is no easy solution or simple cure for it. If there had been an easy cure for the human moral crisis the world would not be in such a mess as it is in right now.

Some philosophers have prescribed various ethical remedies and theologians have prescribed various confessional rites and absolution. Nevertheless, these ecclesiastical ritual formulations have failed to work for the majority of the evildoers and sinners. Judiciary systems have also tried various laws and punishments in order to deter crime and restrain evildoers or reform them. Instead, the jails have become filled, mostly, with the poor who cannot afford the high cost of hiring competent attorneys to defend them. As a result, the poor and the poorly educated constitute the majority of the prison population, and those who are put to death for violent crimes, such as murder.

Ironically, the jails have sadly become evil schools for producing more sophisticated criminal behavior, and as such, they have become a failure, if viewed as a form of punishment meant to deter crime or reform criminals. The reformation and rehabilitation of the criminals has largely failed to work, and yet we cannot sentence to death people for the annoying petty crimes, such as pickpocketing, fraud, theft, and burglaries. It is also known that a prison sentence or even a death penalty does not effectively deter crime. So, what do we do about chronic evildoers and habitual criminals? Do we kill them (capital punishment) or keep in them in jail? Who pays the jail bill?

## 3. Moral Obligation to Prevent Evil: Injustice, Hate, Crime and Violence

Crime prevention is not matter of the police and the government alone. Crime prevention is a civic moral duty of every citizen in the community. No law-abiding citizens should overlook the evil deeds of criminals in the community. To do so, would be to aid and abet crime. Eventually, crime would overtake that community and make life miserable for all those who dwell there, both the innocent and the guilty.

This is what has happened in some inner city neighborhoods where the criminals and gangsters have been allowed to takeover and control life in those areas of the city. The results have been tragic. Violent crimes, such as rape, drive-by shootings, murder, burglary, armed robbery, drug-peddling and prostitution have become the way of life there! The innocent and the guilty alike are all terrorized by armed and violent criminals!

This is what happens when good people are apathetic or too cowardly to fight evil and crime in their communities! They become the victims of the evil and crime when they are too scared or indifferent to fight it! Cowardice and apathy are vices which encourage crime and evil. Moral courage to confront evil and injustice and fight them is both moral virtue and true godliness. That is the main feature of God's saint, irrespective of creed, color, nationality, class and historical era. Gandhi, Dietrich Bonhoeffer, Martin Luther King, and the Archbishop Janani Luwum of Uganda, who was brutally murdered by Idi Amin's forces in 1977, and Oscar Romero of El Salvador, who was assassinated by government troops in 1980, are all good examples of moral courage, faith in the goodness of God in creation, and the saintly crusade against evil, injustice, human-rights abuse, tyranny, racism and violence in the world. Most of us know that we have a moral obligation to do good and to stop others from harming us and our society through doing evil or committing crime. This obligation extends from our immediate neighbor to our leaders as well as the people of other nations.

However, the fundamental moral and political problem arises when an ethical individual knows that some powerful leader or person is planning evil, such as building a powerful biological, chemical or nuclear bomb in order to blast some hated group. Timothy McVeigh, who bombed the Oklahoma Federal Building in 1995 and killed many preschool children, government workers and many other innocent people, is an example of these evil people. He was trained by the USA to kill the enemy, when the enemy was still clearly defined as "the communists!"

Since the so called "evil empire" or former Soviet Union no longer exists as the scapegoat for evil in the world and the enemy to be destroyed, what new enemies are we going to invent? Is this why Saddam Hussein has become a new focus of the USA and the Western allies? He is not the greatest threat to world peace. Nevertheless, in the absence of a major enemy to focus aggression on, he became the convenient tool for the Western military and ideological focus, aggression and a scapegoat for new global and societal evils, such as biochemical warfare and international terrorism!

Human beings seem to be essentially violent beings. They become unified together as a viable community or nation despite some internal problems, and thrive when they have some external common enemies to fight. In religion, the Devil and demons provide the ideal outlet and target for this human aggression, blame and scapegoating. Women, ethnic and racial minorities have also been demonized and dehumanized so as to serve in this role. As a result, during the World War II, about 6 million Jews were exterminated during the Nazi vilification and mass murders of the Jews, the homosexuals, gypsies, the handicapped and the Christian leaders who dared to oppose and denounce this genocide as a moral evil.

It is self-evident that the majority of the people in the world have an intrinsic, ontological, dualistic world-view. As a result of this inherent and unconscious ontological binary or dualistic mental structure, human beings automatically process data in this distorted world-view of reality according to this inherent binary and dualistic mental processor. As a result, the finite human minds tend to view reality in a exclusive dualism or permanent bipolar epistemological system which is deduced to be true for a bipolar ontological reality. This is illustrated by an apparently mutually exclusive pair of opposites such as: body and mind, spirit and matter, weak and strong, alive and dead, black and white, male and female, single and married, young and old, boys and girls, hot and cold, good and evil, God and Devil, heaven and hell, birth and death, tall and short, pregnant or not pregnant, north and south, positive and negative, and alive and not alive. This dualism may be an illusion, since matter and mind are different states of existence, such as that of matter and energy.

However, in traditional metaphysics and ontology (understanding of reality), in the above pairs of opposites, there is no middle ground allowed! For instance, one is either pregnant or not. There is no middle ground of being just a little pregnant! Likewise, regardless of size, the compass always points north, unless there is a magnetic interference. It maintains a contrasting bipolar system, regardless of the size of the magnet or campus. The middle ground is completely eliminated to create a dualistic world.

Likewise, some dualistic thinkers also argue that in order for goodness to exist, evil must exist also as the contrast to goodness! In this human limited thinking and epistemology, goodness and evil exist as the necessary background context to judge goodness and evil. But this is false epistemological assumption. The brightness of the sun does not need darkness to be known as such or to blind the person who dares look at the sun directly for a prolonged period. Epistemological dualism leads to destructive moral dualism, such as racism, sexism and religious soteriological exclusivism as in the case of the pre-Vatican II Roman Catholic doctrines of Church and salvation. People were considered to be heading to hell if they were not baptized members of the Roman Catholic church.

The pre-Vatican II Roman Catholic Church doctrines were ethnocentric, conservative and exclusionary. They dogmatically affirmed that either you were in the Catholic Church and saved or you were outside the Church and perishing, even when you did not realize it at the time! Purgatory was believed to be "the half way house" or station between heaven and hell. It was the extended post-death ecclesiastical station for further purification of some deserving sinners before finally becoming pure enough and qualifying for entrance into God's Kingdom or heaven. Purgatory was God's second chance for less sinful sinners to repent, work and atone for their sins. Notably, their friends and relatives could help them accomplish this task faster and easier by holding special prayers and Mass for them and even by performing good deeds on their behalf. Monetary offering was also accepted as part of this "indulgence." In the Medieval Church, certificates of merit (indulgences) were given to indicate that God's supernatural grace and absolution of sins were given to those contributing money for Church building projects and works for charity. Martin Luther and other Protestant reformers denounced this Church practice as spiritual corruption and sale of God's grace and salvation.

In addition, the Western dualistic form of logic, which excludes the reality of the middle, has done a great harm in religion, ethics, economics, philosophy and society. Truth is not always subject to the following Western dualism and the correlative common form of fallacious logic and dualistic epistemology which excludes the middle: *(1) Either P or Q (2) Not P (3) Therefore: Q*. In this setting, P and Q can stand for various variables or opposed elements in society. This setting creates possibilities for interesting arguments. For instance, imagine the following scenarios where P and Q stand for the following variables:

*(1) P = Friend and Q = Enemy (2) P = White and Q = Black*
*(3) P = God and Q = Devil (4) P = Heaven and Q = Hell*
*(5) P = Capitalism and Q = Communism (6) P = Male and Q= Female.*

The fallacy of this dualism is self-evident. Duality is real, such as male and female and Black and White. However, the excluded existence of the middle is misleading. When it is applied to all matters of life and reality, it becomes false. As a matter of fact, in some cases, the middle ground represents the greatest numbers of people and degrees of reality. This is illustrated by the fallacy of the Western stereotypical racism that almost exclusively portrays people in terms of "black" and "white." The majority of the people in the world are neither white nor black. The world's majority people are brown. This is because China and India have the highest concentration of the world's populations.

The brown people constitute a large middle category which American traditional racial dualism has no room for. As a result, they are sometimes ignored or grouped with the Whites and at other times with the Blacks depending on the situation or person doing the classification. This confusion is not a moral issue since the DNA scientific human genetic analysis has eliminated race as a biological factor and focuses on individual variation of groups and individuals within the human race.

In the case of communism and capitalism, there is a middle ground in the form of socialism. This again accounts for most people in the world, particularly, those in Africa and Asia. Heaven and hell are conditions of existence, which can exist simultaneously, in the same community or even person! As regards friends and enemies, there is no reason to assume that those who are not yet friends are enemies! That is a destructive and false world-view.

The majority of the people and nations would simply be among the neutral political category. These are just examples to illustrate how western traditional logic has been responsible for creating false enemies among nonaligned neutral nations. During the "cold war" many nations of Africa and Asia refused to be aligned to the West or the East. This was partly due to self-interest in hope to benefit both from the "Communist Block" as well as the Western capitalist nations.

During the Cold War, the African, Arab, Asian and Latin American nations benefitted both politically and economically by playing the Soviet Union over the USA! However, they also realized that the idea of alignment was politically unwise and unpractical for most of the poor and developing nations of the world. Nevertheless, many Western instigated military coups took place in Africa and Latin America in order to curb the perceived threat of communism in those nations that practiced benign traditional forms of socialism.

In these non-Western community oriented nations, there was a positive appreciation of communism as a more effective form of traditional socialism. Capitalism was negatively viewed as a mode of life that was too individualistic and anti-community and antisocial in its values. Liberation movements in the Third World deliberately employed Marxism as the positive tool of social analysis and model for economic self-development. Marxism was also adopted as a tool for developing a new liberation theology in a non-Western context of poverty, neocolonialism and the oppression by minority regimes of a few Western supported local capitalists and rich land owners.

The above indicates that we have a major moral dilemma. The moral problem can, be simply stated as follows: "How does one individual who may be morally upright and peace-loving stop the President from doing evil?" This is a serious problem, since the President may be supported by a naive majority but surrounded by greedy and evil influential advisers. This is the kind of situation where democracy can become a source of great harm. Democracy becomes evil when the voting masses are either ignorant of the good or corrupt and evil. This was the case with Hitler's fascist and Nazi Germany. Whitesupremacy and racism led to genocide.

Nevertheless, one can still validly ask about what the few morally upright people could do in this state of affairs. For instance, should the upright try to kill an evil ruler, like Hitler or Idi Amin, in their ideal moral efforts to get rid of an evil regime or evil ruler supported by an ignorant or an evil majority? In other words, is it morally correct and acceptable to use violence to get rid of violence, or to use an evil method to get rid of the greater evil? Can one truly get rid of violence or evil through committing more violence? There is no "good violence" or "good evil" since violence tends to result in destruction and death.

However, the Christians believe that some self-sacrificial death may be necessarily in order to get rid of violence and evil. This is why the martyrs or people who have courageously died for their religious faith are universally celebrated as God's saints and the innocent and painful death of Jesus on cross is celebrated as "Good Friday" and as God's cosmic provision for atonement for all human sins. Nevertheless, the Christians can only affirm the goodness and atoning value of Jesus' death on the cross, from the perspective of the resurrection. That is, the belief that in Jesus' death on the cross, God tricked death, hooked and effectively destroyed death's power and dominion over human life by the resurrection of Jesus on the third day.

Otherwise, violence and peace, life and death, good and evil being the opposites, cannot be easily reconciled or collapsed into goodness, although religious people affirm that God has the power to transform evil into good. However, for most people or finite moral agents, only good comes out of something good whereas evil comes out of something evil! However, there is nothing that is ever completely evil! As both Augustine and Thomas Aquinas correctly observed, evil is not something in itself, the same way the Devil is not something itself. Evil is a mere corruption of the good or deprivation and degradation of the goodness in something that already exists as good. Likewise, "the Devil is a mere personification of evil." This means that in actuality any human being who becomes the agent or channel for the mediation of evil in the community and the world, is the real Devil in the community and the world! Evil friends, and supervisors and teachers are conduits of evil in the community and the world. Hitler and Idi Amin are recent historical examples of such devils in local and global history.

Undoubtedly, the question of evil and whether good can come out of evil actions or deeds, is a great moral puzzle. For instance, Christians have traditionally positively affirmed that the tragic crucifixion of Jesus and painful death on the cross were good since they were the perfect human sacrifice and atonement for cosmic human sin. They also affirm that they were also the means by which God forgave human sins and conferred salvation on all humankind.

Subsequently, the Friday on which Jesus was crucified and died on the cross is know as "the Good Friday" and that week is also correspondingly known as the "the Holy week." Within this understanding, only the good Creator-Redeemer God can redeem and effectively transform evil and into goodness. Otherwise, evil begets evil and good begets goodness. Therefore, morally upright people and God's obedient saints cannot keep quiet or faith to act appropriately when evil is being done and masses of innocent people are being killed. In this case, the lesser evil should be done even by those who hate evil in order to stop a greater evil from happening. This should be the guiding moral principle in matters of this nature and other similar ones involving the taking of a human life, such as the death penalty and abortion.

Nevertheless, the present and future human moral condition remains imperfect and a great problem. It is difficult to arouse compassion, empathy, love and concern for the poor and the needy, and to mobilize positive action by all morally upright men and women, everywhere, regardless of creed, ideology, color, or race. This is because of the world's moral crisis which urgently requires a united, global, effective remedy if the human species and the world are to continue to survive in a meaningful existence and relationship.

Sometimes, one is led almost to despair when one realizes that some leaders of great nations are also very capable of great evil deeds rooted in ignorance, racism, intolerance, bigotry, imperialism and corruption. This accounts for wars in Eastern Europe, and most coups in "the Developing World" or the "Third World," and particularly, Africa. Men like Idi Amin (Uganda), Bokassa (Central African Republic), Mobutu Seseko (late dictator of former Zaire), and Arap Moi (Kenya) have been accused of great felonious crimes while they were self-declared life presidents of their impoverished and mismanaged nations. The Slobodan Milosovic, the Serbian evil dictator in former Yugoslavia provides a similar example in the case of Europe.

However, the religious and ethnic wars in the Middle East and the former Soviet Union, particularly in Bosnia and Kosovo clearly indicate that corruption, totalitarianism, religious intolerance, ethnic wars and genocide are not limited to Africa and poor nations. They are global evils and threats to global peace. The international community should work through the United Nations agencies to put these evils to an end, by promoting global ethics rooted in tolerance for religious, cultural, economic, political, racial and ethnic diversity and pluralism.

The evil perpetrated by hateful, power-seeking, greedy, immoral national leaders, such as Hitler and Idi Amin, the deposed former president of Uganda, leaves us wondering whether Plato was not right and prophetic when he declared that there will not be peace on the Earth until more "philosophers become rulers and rulers become philosophers." By a philosopher king, Plato had in mind a person who was the most educated, knowledgeable, virtuous, just, and skilled in ruling. This kind of national leader was in essence more of a national moral teacher, role-model, and guide. The closest recent examples that come to mind are India's Mahatma Mohandas Gandhi, and Tanzania's former President Julius Nyerere who is known to his people by the honorific Swahili title of "*Mwalimu*" (Professor, Teacher or Rabbi).

Both of these national leaders were nationalists who brought independence to their own respective colonized nations. Interestingly, Gandhi refused to become the first President of the newly independent India. He also refused to immerse himself in the materialism and luxury which the departing colonial British left behind. This was great evidence that Gandhi's moral crusade and nationalistic fight for the Indian independence was rooted in moral principles rather than greed for power, fame and wealth. He believed that it is just and moral for nations to govern themselves for the general welfare and common good of their local citizens. Gandhi did not fight for India's independence for personal gain.

Gandhi put first the interests of his fellow citizens and the nation, whereas many corrupt national leaders in Africa, Asia and Latin America often seek to serve their own interests first. This is also true at levels of government. Many corrupt cabinet ministers, judges and police officers solicit and accept bribes so as to subvert the justice of which they are supposed to be the impartial enforcers and custodians! Mobutu serves as an example of the most corrupt African head of state in Africa.

In 1997, Laurent Kabila with the help of Uganda and Rwanda got rid of him. However, they replaced him with a corrupt government which soon got into trouble with Rwanda and Uganda due to corruption and repression of some its citizens, the Banyamulenge. Ironically, in African politics, the liberator of today has often become the dictator of tomorrow. Therefore, true African liberation will occur in the future when there is both democracy and a pan-African socioeconomic integration and unity of the currently impoverished African nations.

Julius Nyerere became the first President of his nation, Tanzania. He refused to accept a huge salary, a huge mansion and an expensive Presidential limousine while his country remained poor. Instead, he lived simply like his people. He tried hard to teach the people how to live a simple life together happily in collective villages. In these collective villages the people were provided with clean water, electricity, and educational and medical services more readily by the Tanzanian government. He called this African "socialist" experiment "*Ujamaa*" (Unity). Unfortunately, this "*Ujamaa*" experiment failed because of human selfishness and evil. For instance, the people felt that they did not have to work hard on the newly introduced cooperative farms in "*Ujamaa*" villages. They became lazy and passed time in idleness instead of doing creative farming on these collective farms, as they did on personal farms.

Consequently, the results of collective farms were disastrous. There was not enough food grown on the *Ujamaa* farms. Subsequently, there was inadequate food to feed the people in the new collective villages. As a result, President Nyerere was painfully forced to abandon this socioeconomic experiment and "philosophical idealism." Nyerere became a naive victim of human moral evil and sin. He had underestimated the destructiveness of moral evil and the human capacity for greed, selfishness, envy, laziness and malice. To his disappointment, he later discovered that these people were most eager to work for personal individual profit rather than a collective one. African communalism and socialism masked an intense personal interest and greed that had been often publicly condemned as "witchcraft" and "antisocial" moral evil.

Subsequently, Nyerere tried to utilize the individual's self interest and profit drive in order to motivate people to produce enough food to feed the people in the village and urban areas. At the same time, Nyerere also tried to prevent corruption in his government and the private sectors. Remarkably, he accomplished this difficult task by curbing the excessive greed for individual's personal gain at the expense of other people and the nation. He set a good personal example for the other African leaders to follow.

In order to provide free medical services, and subsidized education, governments have to tax people and businesses. President Nyerere highly taxed the businesses and the rich people in order to provide needed essential human services in rural areas and to uplift the poor. Consequently, though Tanzania still remains one of the poorest and least developed nations in Africa, it has one of the best literacy rates in the whole of Africa. Tanzania also remains one of the least corrupt nations in Africa, while Nigeria, Kenya and Uganda serve as examples of corrupt post-colonial African nations.

Furthermore, Tanzania has also been one of the most stable and peaceful nations in the whole of modern Africa. For instance, the neighboring state of Uganda has experienced several civil wars, coups, political repression and mass murders under Idi Amin and the five successive presidents. Tanzania on the other hand, under president Nyerere, acted as the peacemaker and guarantor of peace in Uganda 1979-85. In 1979, President Nyerere helped the Ugandan exiles led by Yoweri Museveni to drive out President Idi Amin in the name of human rights, dignity, morality, and East African peace.

It is remarkable, therefore, that the other national leaders just watched in amazement while Idi Amin grossly abused human rights in Uganda. The persecution and mass massacres of educated Ugandans, estimated at about one million people, spread over the eight years "of his reign of terror." President Nyerere got so disgusted and morally indignant that he unilaterally decided to act positively in order to get rid of President General Idi Amin. He subsequently put an end to the gross abuses of human rights, mass arrests of innocent civilians and mass murders that were being committed by Idi Amin across the border. President Nyerere's war against the murderous President Idi Amin of Uganda is a good example of the "just war theory" at work and the moral and constructive use of military power and force to defend the helpless neighbor, curb violence, restore human rights and establish peace.

President Nyerere acted nobly in obedience to unconditional love and justice for the neighbor. Tanzania being a developing poor nation, Nyerere did not have much money for the task, nor did he have anything to gain personally by intervening in the tragic Ugandan affairs. It was because of his moral consciousness, commitment to justice and respect for human rights that he intervened in the Ugandan affairs and sponsored armed liberation movements in Zimbabwe (Rhodesia) South Africa, Namibia, Angola and Mozambique. He also had faith, courage, and goodness which were required to undertake this noble moral task for the redemption of Uganda. This is also the practical moral thinking and action that has deeply grounded his support for African freedom fighters and liberation movements in Southern Africa.

Nyerere was consistent on moral and political issues regarding the respect and the protection of human rights and justice. He was a very staunch supporter of Bishop Tutu and Nelson Mandela's moral call to the

West to stop supporting the evils of white racism and apartheid in South Africa. Many Western nations were supporting the Minority White government in South Africa out of economic selfishness, moral indifference, and greed for minerals, wealth, cheap labor (slave labor), and profitable investments.

The moral call is to put human rights and welfare before the cheap acquisition of wealth and profit at the expense of other human beings' degradation, exploitation, oppression, and even extermination. Clearly, this ill-gotten wealth is a disgrace and an offense to both humanity and God. Unfortunately, this is the kind of socioeconomic evil which absolute capitalism is capable of inducing in most human beings who find it difficult to say "no" to the temptation of easy money and quick wealth. Indeed, there are just a few people who get wealthy by doing good deeds. It seems that the drug-dealers, pimps and thieves often get rich before honest businessmen and women can make significant profit on honest business and investments! Subsequently, in some poorer urban communities, there is a great temptation to steal, cheat, sell drugs or sex, and commit armed robberies, in order to get rich quickly.

However, the society that allows its members to indulge in such evils, crimes and immorality will eventually destroy itself. This is because evil is conducive to violence and death, whereas the society's well being and survival requires the creation of harmonious socioeconomic networks and healthy social relations grounded in mutual love and trust. Therefore, the human being's welfare, future existence and total survival cannot be assured by the modern advances in science, medicine, and technology alone. As we have already seen, the major human problem is the human being himself or herself.

In other words, the major global, moral or ethical problem is that of the human being's moral and spiritual dilemma arising out of human casual freedom, greed, power, diversity of moral choices, conflicting values and diverse pluralistic actions. The human moral problem has grown into a global crisis. This is mainly due to  of the human being's advanced technology in the biogenetic and nuclear fields. Humanity now possesses the technological capacity and DNA information to clone itself and through genetic manipulation transform into a super human race, and alter the nature of other creatures through genetic engineering by selective crossbreeding and cloning. Most frighteningly for many people, the human being also has the great technological capacity for destroying himself or herself. Humanity possesses the capacity for mass suicide and also to destroy most of the planet Earth, along with life and everything on it. Tragically, that would be the end of known major biological forms of life on the universe, since within the known galaxies, intelligent forms of life are only found on the planet Earth. Therefore, life on the Earth must be protected at all costs. Life, mind and consciousness are God's supernatural gifts bestowed on the cosmos.

## 4. Moral Problems of War: The "Just War Theory" And Weapons of Mass Destruction

All wars and different forms of violence are evil. This is true regardless of whether they are offensive or defensive, "justified" or unjustified, they are all destructive to life, property, community and the environment. This is the truth irrespective of whether it is in reference to a "just war," or "holy war," such as the jihads and crusades of the past. Today, we look at these "holy wars" with disdain and see very little holiness in them.

According to our more humane values today, these wars were largely unjustified. When strictly examined, they fail to meet the high moral and military requirements for the "just war theory." Nevertheless, the religious leaders of that era thought differently about war and violence. They mistakenly fought the so called holy wars and killed people in God's holy name as a religious moral obligation for the saints of God. Ultimately, all wars are violent, bloody, destructive of human life and evil. War and violence are incompatible with God as definitively revealed in Jesus Christ through both through his teachings and on the cross as Agape, Compassionate and forgiving God without any conditions (cf. John 3:16-21; 1 John 3:7-21).

If God preferred a "holy war" instead of persuasion and peace, the same holy and just God could have sent his saints and the prophets as his armed and trained holy warriors, commandos and moral crusaders to fight against evildoers. Instead, God sent Jesus to persuade sinners to repent their hateful and evil ways and to observe the commandment of unconditional love and free forgiveness of sins. God's law of unconditional love is God's effective and persuasive means of rule over his Kingdom on the Earth and within the hearts of all obedient believers in the moral teachings of Jesus as the Christ of God. This is in contrast with Islam which accepts the holy war (*jihad*) a moral obligation for all obedient Muslims.

The Christian *just war theory* was originally formulated by St. Augustine, then later, modified by St. Thomas Aquinas. However, over the years the theory has been both expanded and modified by some other major Christian thinkers and ethicists, including M.L. King. The moral theory deplores war and violence. However, it permits the use of a limited form of violence as a last resort, when all other options have been sufficiently tried and have failed to work. Whereas Jesus taught the absoluteness of nonviolence and pacifism in the form of unconditional love (Agape), free forgiveness of sins, offenses and turning the other cheek (Matt. 5-7), the Christian "just war theory" modifies these teachings of Jesus to fit the reality of the present world in which Christians now live. As a result, it allows a limited use of violence in self-defense or defense of the neighbor in the name of unconditional love, justice and peace. This applies both to the private as well as the national and international public affairs.

The "just war theory" was designed to minimize the brutality and destructiveness of conflict, violence and wars within a violent society. It was formulated within the context of the violent and uncaring criminal elements within the community, who must be restrained by the use of reasonable force. The just war theory limits the uses of military force or violence by nations to resolve conflicts or punish the rogue nations. Instead, it seeks to promote peace through negotiation and peaceful resolution of conflicts. It also promotes true and lasting peace by setting high and strict military requirements, moral guidelines, humane and ideal political and military principles and guidelines, to be followed before, during and after the conduct of an inevitable war. These strict moral guidelines for fighting a "just war" based on the "just war theory" include the following moral criteria and military principles:

1. The war must be declared as a *last resort*. All other peaceful means to resolve the conflict must have been exhausted. They must have been well-developed, fully implemented and given sufficient time to work. If these peaceful measures, such as international economic sanctions fail, and there is no other means left untried to effect a peaceful resolution of the conflict, then war or violence may become the justifiable last resort to end the conflict or stop aggression or oppression.

2. The war must be declared by the constitutional legitimate authority or the right person who is empowered to do so by the nation and its laws or constitution. For example, in the case of the USA, the President or Congress are the ones authorized to declare war, and not the military generals or powerful senior senators. In other countries, the respective

heads of states, kings and emperors are constitutionally empowered to declare war on behalf of their nations.

3. The war must be limited in scope and winnable. The war must not be declared or fought, unless there is a high degree for military success and resolution of the conflict as a result of the war.

4. The war must be quick and not protracted. (Protracted wars cause unnecessary pain and suffering to the combatants, and the general civilian population of all the nations engaged in war.)

5. The war must be defensive and not an offensive one. A just war must not initiate an attack on the enemy. It must be defensive.

6. The main intention of the just war must not be either retaliation or punishment. The intention must be self-defense, liberation of an oppressed weaker nation or to facilitate love and establish an enduring peace-treaty following a military victory.

7. If the war is offensive, it must be for the purpose of defending and liberation of a militarily weaker nation (or group) which had been unjustly invaded and overrun by a militarily superior one.

8. The weapons used to wage war must be appropriate and proportional to the scale of the war being fought. Weapons must be chosen according the nature and scale of the war.

*The appropriate weapons of war must be able to distinguish between the military personnel and the civilian noncombatants.* Noncombatants should not be targeted. Weapons of indiscriminate mass destruction, such as nuclear, chemical and biological bombs and "carpet bombing," do not meet this criteria.

9. Excessive force must not be used. Only that force necessary in order to facilitate the surrender of the offenders, or victory is both justified and permitted.

10. War prisoners should neither be mistreated nor tortured or executed. The war prisoners must be fed and well-cared for. They must be given good medical care, and treated for their medical injuries. They must be released at the end of the war, and be assisted in their return to their home countries.

11. The war must be fought according to international conventional laws, (i.e. humanely and with love.) Cease-fire and negotiation of peace and surrender terms must be facilitated as soon as the opportunity arises. The restoration or establishment of lasting peace is the goal and measure of the success of the just war, as opposed to the vengeance, retribution or punishment and deterrence to future wars or international crime.

Nevertheless, irrespective of the above principles and limitations of war by the "just war theory," all wars are to be condemned as evil and to be prevented. Even the "just wars" are still violent, destructive to human life, property, the economy, the community, health and the environment. Consequently, wars are major destructive evils and causes of suffering, especially by refugees. Therefore, all wars must be prevented and denounced when they happen, by all God's obedient and loving people.

Furthermore, the new technological and biological powerful weapons of indiscriminate mass killing and destruction are dangerous to all. These include chemical, biological and nuclear weapons. Some people have naively believed that nuclear weapons are necessary for world peace since they are good deterrents of war. The former United States President Ronald Reagan naively believed in the use of limited strategic nuclear weapons to win a nuclear war. This is both morally irresponsible and suicidal. There is no need to take unnecessary military risks to fight "a mutually assured destruction" nuclear war in which there is no winner, since all are losers.

In short, apathy and the human moral failure to prevent moral evil in the community and the world leads to the prevalence of evil in the local community, society and the world. For instance, unchecked drug trafficking in a local community brings the other crimes of prostitution, robbery, violence and murder. The moral evils of human hate and greed lead to injustice, destructive acts of intolerance against the people of different races, gender, sexual orientation, cultures and religions. Greed, intolerance and injustice have in the past tragically led to racial and religious wars and many unnecessary deaths in the quest for mutual extermination of each other as enemies! Nuclear weapons and other weapons of mass destruction have made war an unacceptable global menace. The weapons of mass destruction can tragically lead to the humanity's mass suicide and extinction of life on this special living planet.

After humanity has carelessly committed suicide in mutually assured destructive nuclear or biochemical wars, the gruesome doomsday cult prophesies will have become fulfilled. Doomsday cults like the Ugandan Movement for the Restoration of the Ten Commandments of God, which is responsible for more than one thousand deaths of its followers including the 534 people who were burned in a church on March 17, 2000 and Heaven's Gate cult whose apocalyptic members committed suicide on March 23, 1997 will have triumphed in their predictions of the fiery end of the world, as a tragic human story. It is also possible that in God's divine loving, forgiving, redemptive grace, he or she will create another human life-form that will evolve better moral values of love and nonviolence, and therefore, be able to avoid a similar history and tragic end. The ethics of agape and nonviolence are the only assurance in teaching human beings to shun the evil inclination of hate, violence and self-destruction.

Therefore, the human potential for mass suicidal self-destruction in a nuclear war and fiery holocaust along with the rest of God's creation is a moral evil to be prevented. Nuclear, biological and chemical weapons pose a serious threat for the destruction of God's goodness in creation, sustenance, and redemption. As a result, sound systems of ethics, religion and morality should be developed to negate and neutralize the human moral sin and evil and their destructive results of selfishness, egocentr-icity, bigotry, intolerance, pride, envy, hatred, malice, murder, war, and suicide.

Accordingly, some modern orthodox Christian theologians, such as Paul Tillich and Karl Rahner, this state of disobedience, hatred, fear, despair, war, and death is identified with hell. If hell includes a real fire, then, the nuclear holocaust may become the literal hellfire, kindled on the Earth by sinful human beings through the destructive evils of greed, hate, injustice and violence, rather than the merciful and redemptive loving God. That would become the ultimate punishment for human collective sins of disobedience against God's law of unconditional love, free forgiveness and nonviolence.

Human moral evils of hate and sadism lead to human suffering and death. The morally deviant and mentally sick people have a distorted view of a good life in the world, goodness, happiness and self-enjoyment. Lacking in moral restraint, conscience, love, and empathy, they perform horrible and morally reprehensible acts in order to enjoy the short, transient, "evil, sadistic pleasure" of seeing one's enemies suffer and cringe with pain or die a slow, painful death. Therefore, caring religious institutions and the people of moral conscience and have must courage to protest moral evil and corruption to end suffering. Therefore, churches and governments must promote democracy and respect for human rights as outlined in the *United Nations Universal Declaration of Human Rights* of 1948 (see Appendix A).

Instead of democracy, equality and justice for all under the law, within the *Shari'a* (Islamic religious law) based Islamic nations, there is state terrorism against local human rights activists and foreigners who support democracy and change within these totalitarian and self-styled "God-fearing and theocratic nations."

Furthermore, religious bigotry and intolerance which are associated with religious fundamentalism and ignorance can lead to destructive acts of bloody crusades, such as the bombing of the US Embassies of Nairobi in Kenya, and Dar-es-Salaam in Tanzania on August 7, 1998. This is reminiscent of the destructive crusades and jihads of the past two millenniums in which religion was employed as a social and cultural force for military, economic and political mobilization of troops to conquer, convert, kill, enslave, and exploit the people of different religions, and cultures. The crusades and jihads of the past era were also disguised racial, cultural, economic, political and imperialist wars of expansionism. This partly explains why Christianity remained yoked to Latin and English, whereas Islam also remained chained to Arabic both in language and cultural values. Accordingly, Muslims worship in Arabic while facing Mecca in Saudi Arabia, take Arab names, such as "Muhammad," and observe Arabic and other Semitic food taboos, such as the avoidance of pork.

Ultimately, true democracy cannot be built on religion. This is because the traditional and conservative religious exclusive values by are nature antithetical to true democracy. This is irrespective of whether that religion is Christianity, Islam or Judaism. Unlike democratic institutions which are flexible and inclusive all religions tend to be irrational, exclusive, intolerant, and fanatical in their dogmatic beliefs, laws and values. All these religions embody the evil seeds of bigotry, intolerance, exclusiveness, persecution, violence, jihads or crusades and bloodshed in the name of God. The Bible and Qur'an testify to this truth.

The prophets were persecuted because they did not conform to the traditional religious norms. They broke existing religious laws as God's revelation, and supposed infallible and eternal Word or moral code of God. Jesus was persecuted, arrested and crucified as a lawbreaker and blasphemer. Prophet Muhammad had to flee from Mecca to Medina because of his monotheistic teachings which were in opposition to the traditional values, idolatry and lucrative trade in idols. Most important of all, religion is not democratic because the God of worship is not a democratic King. God's Word is God's Law and non-negotiable. As such, scriptures and the commandments having been canonized and declared to be God's Word, they have become the infallible and inerrant Word of God that cannot be negotiated or compromised without sinning against the holy God as its author. All these religions which teach theses beliefs to be true for God and the scriptures, such as Islam and some Christian denominations can not become democratic.

The Puritans and other Pilgrims came to America in order to escape religious intolerance and persecution in Europe. Subsequently, from their own history, and experience, the American Founding Fathers insightfully decided that for all different people's views, rights and religions would be equally protected. In order to protect the freedoms of speech, religion and democracy, there was need for a constitutional separation of Church and State.

Consequently, the Constitution and laws of the USA effectively guarantee the essential freedom of the press, association, religion and speech. These constitutional rights and guarantees of freedom for all citizens are the essential solid foundations and sound pillars for any true and enduring systems of democracy, humane governance, benevolent, open, tolerant and peaceful society. Any truly beneficial religion must both embody and promote these essential human rights and values as part of its principles, creeds and doctrines.

To this end, the papal encyclicals and the United Methodist Church in America had provided the guiding light and example by the clear formulation of the moral *Social Principles* (see Appendix B). These moral principles address all major contemporary moral issues and social problems. Topics of moral debate, including Christian perspectives on war, abortion and homosexuality are definitively addressed from a compassionate yet Christian moral point of view. The holy Scriptures, reason, tradition and experience serve as the main foundations and effective normative guides for this applied Christian public moral theology and ethics.

On May 12, 2000, during the Methodist Worldwide Conference (May 2-12) held in Cleveland, Ohio, the Methodist Church apologized for the sins of racism against the Blacks and held a symbolic reconciliation service. This was reminiscent of Pope John Paul's service of atonement and apology for the Church's sin held on March 12, 2000, during the Lent season, as the Church formal period for self-examination, atonement and repentance of sins. The new millennium must become more humane, tolerant, just and peaceful in order to negate and redeem the past era of ethnocentrism, nationalism, colonialism, militarism, imperialism, white-supremacy, racism, slave-trade, tribalism, sexism, aggression, bigotry, intolerance, violence, war and genocide.

Regardless of Christian denomination, Pope John Paul II's encyclicals, particularly, *Evangelium Vitae* (1995), and the United Methodist

Church's moral and *Social Principles* are excellent Christian references and moral guides for Christians who wish to find God in the workplace and other public arenas of human social life. However, for the conservative American Southern Baptists, they will find the resolutions of the Southern Baptist Convention of June 13, 2000 in Florida very significant and the authoritative source for religious and moral guidance in the Church and society. These resolutions which constitute the revised document of the Southern Baptist Convention *Faith and Message* explicitly condemn several cultural and moral practices, such as homosexuality, abortion, racism, and women's ordination for being anti-Biblical and sinful.

The strongly worded negative affirmation that women are subordinate by God's ordinance to their husbands was consistent with their domestic treatment of women as domestic servants for the men. They also affirm that all Christians, regardless of gender, age, race, class and nationality are called to God's ministry. However, the resolution specifies that only the males are called by God to exercise the ministry of ordained pastor.

Like in the Roman Catholic Church, this Southern Baptist Convention resolution officially excludes women from the Church's ordained ministry, hierarchy and top leadership. The Convention, again officially condemned racism as a sin. At the last Convention, the Church had apologized for the sins of slavery of the Africans. Similarly, on March 12, 2000 Pope John Paul II also apologized for the sins of Christian ethnocentrism, racism, sexism, injustice, violence, slavery and the oppression of racial minorities and the Africans.

The traditionalists and conservatives within the Roman Catholic Church were in opposition of the Pope's atonement and apology for the sins of the Church because it undermined the traditional Catholic dogma of the infallibility of the Church in matters of faith and doctrine and moral teachings. The conservatives could not intellectually reconcile dogma, God's continuing revelation, and reality. Yet, they were reluctant to see the truth and reality testified to, as opposed to the long cherished, but errant or false dogmas of the Church and the ecclesiastical traditions. That is, Church dogma and tradition can be erroneous, sinful, evil and false or distortions and misrepresentations of God's essence, will, moral law and revelation in the world. Most creationists and religious fundamentalists are guilty of this misrepresentation of God's nature and God's free cosmic creative and redemptive activities of God's own unmerited supernatural grace and unconditional love in the world.

Therefore, all mature, just, loving and morally responsible Christians must learn from history in order to repent of past sins and avoid the past moral failures and mistakes of the Church. The United Methodist, Roman Catholic and the Southern Baptist churches provide some good examples to follow. They also challenge dilligent Christians not to conform to the prevailing cultures and values of the world, unless those cultures and moral values are in conformity with God's commandments, the Holy Scriptures and God's definitive revelation in the Divine Incarnation, life and teachings of Jesus as the Christ of God.

# Chapter 6

# Problems of a Loving Good God: The Reality of Evil and Death In God's Kingdom

The evolutionary human being as a knowing, and thinking finite being (*Homo sapiens*), possesses the troubling special knowledge and acute awareness of his or her finitude and the absoluteness of death any time in the future. Therefore, unlike any other creatures in God's cosmos and temporal Kingdom, the human being possesses the traumatic knowledge of the universal inevitability of human suffering and death.

This knowledge of the universal existential state of finitude, together with the human beings' divine capacity for self-transcendence and self-consciousness as a finite creature make the human being anxious and fearful of life in this world. As a result, the transitoriness of the finite of this human knowledge and acute awareness of finitude and impermanence of life, all normal human beings experience existential anxiety due to finitude that makes suffering, pain and death essential attributes of any creaturely natural life everywhere within God's created cosmos or Kingdom.

## 1. The Human Experience of the Threat of Evil And Need for God's Intervention or Salvation

Due to the universal existential reality of evil as chaos, pain, loss, suffering and death in the world, all human beings exist in a state of existential condition of predicament and existential anxiety (*angst*). There are anxiety and fears of the unknown future, suffering, pain, death and annihilation into nothingness. For most people death is the greatest evil. That is why Christianity centers around the painful death on the cross and final resurrection of Jesus-Christ. The doctrine of the resurrection is a positive Christian metaphor, myth of human immortality and creedal affirmation of God's triumph over death and evil. This is because human beings being thinking and self-transcending finite creatures, and dreading both suffering and death, wrongly identify death as the ultimate evil and enemy of life and all humanity.

Because of this universal human experience of finitude and reality of the troubling consciousness of this existential threat of evil in the form of suffering and death, all human beings consciously live in the predicament of finitude and "*angst.*" As a result, most human beings have the intrinsic need to escape from this existential human condition of *angst.* They seek to escape from the perceived evil and the imperfect life in this world, in which they feel threatened, endangered, helpless and unable to save themselves. Consequently, most of these human beings are unable to accept the truth that this world is God's world and Kingdom. They prefer to believe that God's Kingdom is somewhere else in space (sky) or on another planet where there are perfection, immortality, peace and happiness.

It is due to the presence of evil that all human beings live in some kind of implicit and explicit forms of quest of security, happiness and peace as God's salvation or reward for having lived an obedient, virtuous and just life. To this end, human beings often mentally construct and seek the supernatural intervention of an eternal, omnipotent, omniscient, merciful, loving and benevolent cosmic Creator-Sustainer-Redeemer God for being the necessary cosmic power that is powerful enough and able to save them from the constant threat of chaos, pain, suffering and death. This is one of the main reasons why religion is preoccupied with evil as sin, guilt, death and salvation as God's gift of a supernatural escape from suffering and death. The Passover in Judaism and the cross of Jesus in Christianity offer clear examples of this theology and religious worldview of the past.

Any religion which would positively affirm natural death as God's will and a natural event to be celebrated would be intellectually true and prophetic. However, it would have only a few followers. Ancient Judaism provides such a positive example of this wholesome doctrine (cf. *Ecclesiastes* and *Job*). The error of identifying natural death with ultimate evil has led the world into escapism and the invention of false religions which promise immortality to finite human beings whose nature is to be born and eventually die like any other of God's creatures in the world. Therefore, the teachings of religion concerning natural death as an evil constitute a serious misunderstanding and an erroneous rejection of natural death, regardless of whether it is for plants, animals, human beings, planets and stars, as being part of God's original will. Like the mythological "Devil," evil is not a self-existing reality or ontological object, as dualism simplistically affirms. On the contrary, evil is manifested by the contrast between "what is" (actuality) as opposed to "what ought to be" (potentiality). In this sense, evil is an imperfection or privation of the maximum goodness possible in any given situation, and the constant threat of chaos and death in God's creation and the world, which are self-evident universal realities. These cosmic realities are part of an evolutionary life, creatures and the world.

Imperfection, pain and death are intrinsic in the natural process of cosmic evolution. This is true despite the fact, that evolution itself is God's own chosen method for the creation of the cosmos, life and all living things, including animals and human beings. This does not make God a creator of evil. Rather, this process affirms God as Creator, Sustainer and Redeemer of creatures and creation from the threat of chaos as the physical material resistance to the maintenance of order (entropy) in the world.

Within this evolutionist understanding of the world, the fundamental cosmic amazing miracle of God consists in the prevalence of order, ecological balance, evolution of life, mind, reason, unconditional love, spirit, self-consciousness, creaturely freedom, justice, responsibility and God-consciousness on the planet Earth. These are divine characteristics are still in the process of evolution toward perfection.

Therefore, contrary to the world's traditional erroneous religious teachings and dogmas, the world has never been either perfect or free from chaos, evil, change, pain and death. Evil as a corruption of the good, is ontological reality. There is also a mental construction of evil as imperfection in the mental ideal of the good or what ought to be. Imperfection in the good as the corrosion of the perfect is part of the mystery regarding the coexistence of good and evil, perfection and imperfection. As a result, good and evil mutually appear as overlapping existential realms of human mental and physical experience. It is also both experienced as a reality within the human historical and evolutionary modes of life.

This reality is a universal intrinsic component of the evolutionary finite creatures including the human life. The human being's supernatural gift of self-transcendence leads to the human being's own intellectual awareness of his or her own imperfection and incompleteness as a dependent being that will finally grow old, wither, die and decay. This is part of this reality of the coexistence of good and evil as an intertwined process of finite life due to finitude. In this respect, the consciousness of finitude, inevitability of pain and death is a matter of the human being's possession of mind, intellect, reason, spirit, knowledge, freedom and self-transcendence as a divine being.

Therefore, according to both the intellectual understanding of the Oriental monist philosophy and Western monotheistic religions (Judaism, Christianity and Islam), evil is also a matter of duality and mutual contrast, in the same way light and darkness exist in mutual contrast and tension. The oriental philosophers solved the problem of good and evil, and light and darkness in their affirmation of the mutual existence of the "*yin*" and "*yang*." This is also true of life and death, as two dimensions of matter, being, and states of consciousness for any intelligent, thinking and self-transcendent beings.

The state of being alive, loved, healthy, at peace with oneself, the neighbor, God and creation is both simultaneous and coextensive with the state of contentedness, blessedness and happiness, which is the state of ideal human perfection, life in heaven or God's Kingdom and full self-consciousness as a child of God or a being that has become truly divine like God. This is the state of *Nirvana* or heaven where the human's mind and self-consciousness has overcome evil and death by having become united with the immortal and eternal God.

## 2. The Reality of Chaos, and Death as God's Will

Contrary to the religious and biblical myths of the primordial existence of an original perfect and deathless creation as the primordial will of God for the world, evolutionary theology and philosophy positively affirms that human perfection is a future event still to be actualized by God in collaboration with obedient, humane and loving humanity. Evolutionary theology, philosophy and science stand uneasily together, united in opposition to the biblical literalists and other traditional religious myths, doctrines and revelations of God which teach the reality of a historical past perfect creation and the historical reality of the human original sin or the primordial rebellion against God's rule and "the fall" that resulted in the entrance of death into the world as God's punishment for human sin.

Death is traditionally perceived as the greatest evil and human enemy because of its power for annihilation of life. Death is not correctly perceived as a natural phenomenon and pat of God's impartial natural law the governs all life including the human mortal life, and that is the manner in which God had intended and created it, right from the beginning. Within the Judeo-Christian tradition (Judaism, Christianity and Islam), death has been rejected and misconstrued as being due to the mythological human original misuse of God's free gifts of grace and causal freedom. Rather than accepting natural death as both good and as God's providential will for all finite creatures, instead it is rejected as being either good or a natural component of God's original will and primordial plan for finite creation.

As a consequence, the Judeo-Christian religions often become escapist, anti-intellectual, anti-science and evil when they rejects God's will, truth and the universal gift of God's supernatural life. This supernatural free gift of life for all creatures in the world is also universally characterized by finitude. That is, all living creatures come into being within time and they also wither, die, decay and cease to exist after some duration of time. Some living being live longer than others, but they are all governed by time (*chronos)* and eventually die or perish in time. This is also true for all evolutionary beings including the stars and planets. Since they, too, came into being in time, they will also perish in time. It is a matter of time. This includes our sun as a star and its solar system, including the Earth and life on it. After some billions of years, nothing that exists today will remain. The death of all things is a cosmic truth and an absolute certainty, based on natural law and the function of time.

The realization of this truth causes great dread and existential anxiety to all intelligent, knowing, self-transcending, thinking, and self-contemplating finite beings, particularly, the human being as the *Homo sapiens* and the most intelligent and self-conscious being within the known cosmos. Death becomes the greatest omnipresent enemy to be feared, fought and avoided by most human beings. For most lay people, religion serves as the supernatural means provided by God to escape from the fear and power of death. The Christian dogmas and doctrines of the resurrection and the elements of the Eucharist as food for eternal life provide good examples to illustrate this salvific function of religion.

The human religious rejection of both finitude and finite life occurs when scared and anxious human beings and their human-made cultures and religions systematically reject the reality of death, natural truth or natural law as the universal and explicit revelation of God's truth and activities through nature. These include the existential realities of finitude, corrosion, decay and disintegration of creatures to create room for new ones. It also includes pain, the birth and death of all living organisms including all human being. Then, these escapist religions having rejected human mortality and the finality of death, erroneously seek to save people from the joys of life in this evolutionary and changing world by seeking to escape from the imperfect life in this world, without realizing that in actuality, this world is correlative and coextensive with God's Kingdom. That is, without the cosmos, there is no God's Kingdom for the human beings to inherit!

This apparent universal human rejection of life in the world is grounded in the human intellect, mind, self-consciousness, self-transcendence and existential anxiety resulting from the natural fear of pain and death. As a result, God's Kingdom and salvation, for most religious people, becomes the quest for immortality and resurrection after death.

This religious rejection of death is the essence of most of the religious myths that strongly affirm that death in the world was unnatural event that was caused by the sinful and rebellious human beings. As a result, there are many religious myths in the world that positively affirm that death is God's punishment and therefore, a direct result of the primordial human beings' "original rebellion" against God's sovereignty and universal moral law or commandments (cf. Gen. 3).

Why would God be so cruel to his creatures? Capital punishment for human disobedience would make God immoral, a cosmic evil and revengeful tyrant, rather than the loving and benevolent Creator-Redeemer God of the Judeo-Christian tradition. That kind if blood thirsty and unforgiving God would be antithetical to God as *Abba* and Agape as was revealed in the teachings and life of Jesus as the Christ (cf. Matt. 5-7; 1 John 4:7-21).

God's supposed explicit universal moral law in nature or commandment is also the mythological grounding of some systems of religious ethics. It is the grounding of the promise and dream or hope for the perfection of humanity, creation, and immortality or a longer life-span of human life as potential components of life in utopia (the Garden of Eden) or heaven, whose actuality was dependent on free human choice, in the past rather than the future. What these religious prophets, thinkers and religious teachers did not realize was that in actuality, the past is universally characterized by imperfection, chaos and death.

As regards, human beings, the evolutionary past is characterized by a lower form of primitive life and not perfection or immortality, as non-scientifically based religious dogmas, traditions, and myths of creation and the fall erroneously affirm (cf. Gen. 1-3). Thomas Hobbes was correct when he characterized the life in the past and according to untamed nature, being short and brutal. Savage tribal wars, feudalism, cannibalism, human sacrifice, slavery, crusades, jihads, sexism, racism and genocide are records of the human past.

The future has a promise for global peace that is grounded in common global human citizenship, equality, cooperation and mutual tolerance despite gender, culture, language, religion, class, color and nationality. This is the direction of human civilization, electronic communications, politics and trade. It is also the eventual goal and destiny of human evolution of global inclusive human identity as one common race, mutual interdependence, peaceful human minds, inclusive moral consciousness, justice and peace within the context of the diversity of the global human self-consciousness as fellow brothers and sisters.

Within an evolutionary and historical reality of the world, there is no time when chaos or evil and death were not present in the natural cosmic processes of creation and evolution. As such, death is natural. Death is not evil if it occurs in a natural manner. Natural death is part of God's will as embodied in natural law, and the intrinsic constitution and nature of all finite or created things. That means that, apart from the immortal God, the rest of creation, having a beginning (birth) in time, will also have an end (death) in time. The end or death may take a very long time to occur, such as the death of our sun, and the correlative destruction of our solar system, including all life forms on the Earth. Nevertheless, it is an assured reality that will take place in the distant future.

Indeed, chaos, entropy, death and evolution are part of the cosmic creative processes which have made possible the emergence of life, complex life-forms and mind (the human being). If death did not exist, there would not be any room for the evolution of life and its ascent to perfection in the self-realization of the deifying supernatural development of mind, freedom, spirit, self-transcendence and divinity.

Within this scientific and correlative systematic theological understanding, death is positively understood as God's provision of universal natural system to serve as the purifier, recycling mechanism and perfecter of all forms of life. In that sense, death is not evil. It is God's natural providence for the essential process for the improvement, purification and renewal of creation. The improvement of life takes place through the selective process of evolution, to improve life and create more complex forms of life.

However, most people and their religions mistakenly classify the natural processes as evil, including: chaos, pain suffering, aging, death, decay and disintegration. This kind of erroneous classification of God's good or neutral process of creation through evolution, death and recycling of matter and life to create new and better ones, creates serious moral, spiritual, philosophical, religious, social, cultural, theological and medical problems. The more serious of these is the denial of death as both a reality and God's provision for the end of one life and beginning or nurture of other forms of life. For instance, people kill animals and plants in order to eat them.

Life feeds on itself. Without the death of some animals or plants, it would be difficult to nurture and maintain a healthy life either among animals or people. Even the vegetarians kill plant life in order to maintain their own lives. Seeds themselves are the embodiments of a future plant life! They are alive even when they look dry and dead! What they need is good soil and water to spring back to life. Jesus recognized this reality when he employed the parable of the mustard seed to teach about the implicit nature of God's Kingdom in the world (Lk. 13:18-19).

The problem of the existence of evil in the world as a reality and not a mere illusion (*mara*) creates serious moral, religious, philosophical, theological and existential problems for most religious and nonreligious human beings in the course of life in the world.

The reality of evil is a major source of moral and religious skepticism about the existence of a loving, good Creator-Redemptive God, and atheism as the conclusion that such a loving and good Creator-Redeemer God is a mere religious myth and illusion and does not exist in actuality. Evil poses a great moral dilemma and challenge to religion, theology, philosophy, ethics, law and society. The dualistic explanation of evil as a creation of the Devil is not acceptable in strict monotheistic religious and philosophical systems, including Christianity.

## 3. Evil, Devil and the Seven Deadly Sins

The complex theological and moral issues of God's goodness and omnipotence have become major problems because of the presence of imperfection and evil in the world which God himself created. The devil did not create the evil in the world. This is true since there is no ontological Devil. Within non-dualistic systems of monotheism, there is no "Devil" as a real external evil moral agent who is opposed to God, as in Oriental dualistic systems. According to good theology and philosophy, the Devil is a mere personification of evil as a personal scapegoat for moral and spiritual failures. The "Devil" is the sinful and rebellious aspect of humanity or people who are evildoers or tempt others to do evil.

There is a universal problem of theodicy or meaning of suffering and evil. There is the problem of explaining the reality and negative presence of evil in the world. The goodness of God and God's power of creation and redemption need an explanation because of evil. None of them is very satisfactory for all people at any given time. The book of Job also tried and failed to resolve this troubling problem of evil and left it as God's mystery. Job affirmed his faith in the goodness of God by simply affirming that: "God gives and God takes away! Thanks be to God (cf. Job 1:21)." Job's story shows that suffering, pain and death are not due to human sin. They are part of moral and spiritual trial and purification. Jesus' fasting, temptations, persecution and final death on the painful cross are good examples of this truth. Suffering is not God's punishment for sin. In most cases, pain and suffering are due to natural causes. Nevertheless, there is suffering, pain and death, that are due to sin. Examples include capital punishment for murder and catching a deadly sexually transmitted diseases, such as AIDS due to sexual immorality.

The Christians themselves did not understand that death as occurrence was God's will and mystery. Most of them fell into the error of Greek dualism and Hebrew patriarchal sexism. They blamed evil, sin and death on the Devil and women as "Eves." However, other Christians were influenced by Greek dualism and as a result, they blamed evil and sin on the senses of the body. This was particularly the case with sexual sins, gluttony, laziness and quest for material accumulation of things as a source of pleasure and happiness. The traditional list of the seven deadly sins came into being and included the sins of "ego." They are:

| | | | |
|---|---|---|---|
| 1. Pride (*Hubris*) | 3. Lust | 5. Gluttony | 7. Laziness |
| 2. Covetousness | 4. Envy | 6 Anger | |

These seven deadly sins are themselves too narrow and inadequate to define evil in society and the world. For instance, they omit hate and failure to love the neighbor and injustice. Yet, these are the most deadly and destructive spiritual, moral and social evils in any community and nation. Racism, sexism, intolerance, injustice, violence, slavery, murders, genocide and wars are rooted in the failure to love the neighbor and forgive offenses without any prior conditions, as commanded by Jesus.

Christ's central and definitive commandment to love the neighbor without conditions has been rejected by many Christians in favor of returning to the Mosaic law of *lex talionis* (proportional retaliation and violence), which Jesus had rejected. By so doing, these Christians have inadvertently rejected the true essence of Christianity. They have opted for the form of Christianity as a Christendom devoid of the essence and spirituality of Jesus Christ as its founder. In this understanding, most Christians who affirm that the essence of Christianity is faith and confession of Jesus-Christ as Lord and savior, apart from doing the will of God and fulfilling Christ's obligatory commandment to love God and the neighbor without conditions are corrupt and non-redemptive (cf. Matt. 5-7; 25:31-46; 1 Cor. 13; Jam. 2; 1 John 4:7-21).

Gandhi may have been aware of the hypocrisy of Western Christianity inasmuch as it rejected the central commandment of love and justice when he formulated his own seven deadly sins. It is of a universal moral, religious and societal significance that he formulated them as follows:

1. Wealth without work.
2. Pleasure without conscience.
3. Knowledge without character.
4. Commerce without sacrifice.
5. Science without humanity.
6. Worship without sacrifice.
7. Politics without principles.

As part of the British colonial subjects, Gandhi came to realize that the Christians of the West did not always live by a moral conscience and moral ideals based on the love, justice, equality, nonviolence and peace as the teachings of Jesus Christ which the European missionaries preached in Africa, India and other parts of the European colonial empire. The local people were often despised and discriminated against by the European Christian missionaries and their colonial government administrative colleagues.

In the perspective of the local people, the Europeans were members of the same race, religion, clubs and socioeconomic class, regardless of whether they were missionaries, traders, tourists of colonial government agents. They all despised the local people and treated them as inferior beings. In South Africa, this white-supremacy and racism resulted in tragedy of apartheid. Many Africans died as a result of white police brutality, torture, lynching and mass massacres. Gandhi had lived in South Africa and witnessed this oppression, abuse of power and horrible crimes of hate and genocide that were committed by the white- supremacist minority regime government against the majority of local people just because they were non-White and non-European.

## 4. The Problem of Human Causal Freedom, God's Holy Omnipotence, And the Presence of Evil in the World

Traditionally, Plato formulated the universal problem of the theodicy in terms of the dilemma of affirming the goodness of a loving and omnipotent God in the face of the reality of evil in the world as follows:

*A. Either God is both good and loving, but powerless and unable to remove evil from the world;*

*OR*

*B. God is omnipotent, but both non-loving or non-benevolent and therefore, creates evil or permits it to exist since there is evil in the world, and he has not removed it by his omnipotence.*

For Plato, God could not be both loving or good, and at the same time, be the omnipotent cosmic creator of this universe, since there is evil and innocent suffering in it this world. He could not accept Job's statement of faith in God's goodness while there is unnecessary loss of life and human suffering. What is the value and meaning of such suffering and death? Christians also traditionally positively affirm the suffering of Jesus had a universal meaning and value. What about our own suffering and deaths? Do they matter? Do they have some value? Do they have any meaning? People constantly ask these kinds of questions.

Paul Tillich called true faith and dynamic power as "the courage to be human." Faith in the goodness of God and life enabled the human being to face life and all its uncertainties in the hope that it will be an enjoyable experience and a source of joy and happiness. By faith in God's goodness, the human being is able to transcend and overcome *angst* as the paralysis of existential anxiety, and the dread of and fear to be a mortal being for fear of pain, suffering and death.

Those people who have ever lost loved ones either to disease such as cancer, or violence such as murder and unnecessary wars, have similar questions. In his pain on the cross, Jesus also asked why God had forsaken him. The question of evil and the existence of God arises when there is injustice, unnecessary pain, suffering and premature death. It does not have good answers. It can only be effectively resolved by what Soren Kierkegaard called "a leap of faith." No intellectual answers can solve the human existential predicament of finitude. Traditional answers do not satisfy the mind and the spirit concerning the human dilemma of the reality of evil, pain and suffering in the world, if God is loving and omnipotent and does exist as both creator and redeemer from evil.

Why should good people suffer at the hands of evil and violent hateful people? Why should God not intervene on behalf of the innocent? Why should he not intervene when a helpless child or person is being abused, raped or killed? How can a loving and omnipotent God turn away at such a moment when he is needed most? Why should God allow for his obedient servants (laity, nuns, priests, bishops and archbishops) to be persecuted and killed? Why should God allow religious wars (crusades and jihads) to be fought in his holy name? These and other questions pose a great challenge to religion and religious leaders, in times of great tragedies, loss and violent crimes.

However, the Oriental thinkers viewed evil differently. They called it an illusion (*Mara*) and distortion of reality by the self-centered proud human beings and finite minds. The Greek humanistic world-view which was characterized by Protagras' *Homo mensura* theory as the human-centered moral theory and anthropocentric world-view affirms that: "Man is the Measure of all things." This idolatrous, humanistic, secular world-view and moral theory substitutes the human being for God as the center of the cosmos and as the ultimate measure of all things and values.

In this secular humanism, what is good is what is pleasurable, profitable and beneficial for the human being. God, the environment and other creatures are not taken into account! This position is also characterized by "*objectivism*." Objectivism affirms that greed and self-interest are the real criteria for personal judgement of what is good and what is evil! That valuation or measurement of what is good and evil is almost *completely determined and subjectively correlative to the interests and needs of that particular individual*. There is no valid universal or objective method to accomplish this subjective task.

Without a unifying singularity of God as the universal reference and ultimate measure for goodness and value, there is no universal standard to measure value, goodness, and evil. Each human being becomes his or her own God and ultimate measure of value, goodness, and evil! The results are confusion and conflicting claims of value, goodness and evil! That is the essence of the Hebrew story of the Tower of Babel (Confusion). The human beings wanted to reach heaven and become gods, and when they arrived, they got confused and could not understand each other or cooperate anymore! Each person had become a god and in the process had become separated from the true God and fellow human beings (cf. Gen. 11).

The human being wishes to become like God and even to become God by himself or herself. The human being desires to become transcendent and unlimited by anything. This is the real Adamic or original sin. The human being does not wish to live a life that has any forms of limitations. Accordingly, what limits human freedom, such as nature, laws, aging, pain and death or pain, were erroneously categorized as evil!

However, nature, pain and death in themselves are not evil! They are only considered evil when they affect us in what we consider to be painful or negative! In this case, the real problem of physical and natural evil is a human existential problem! It is a problem because the human being is threatened with pain, loss and death or annihilation!

If the human being were God, then the question of evil would never arise! This universal human problem arose because there is evil in the world. God's goodness, providence, and redemption from evil and chaos are not always visible to some people in the world. Consequently, they doubt God's Unconditional love, providence, omnipotence and goodness in creation and the world as God's good Kingdom. These kinds of people, including Plato, fail to take into account human free will, freedom, choice and causal efficacy of the human being in the world.

False assumptions and faulty premises about God and human nature have, in the past, caused many problems in religion, ethics, theology and philosophy. The problem of affirming the goodness of an omnipotent loving God in the face of evil, innocent suffering and premature deaths in the world is a serious problem for many people. In the Hebrew Scriptures, the Book of Job deals with this universal problem of theodicy. In Hebrew theology and philosophy, disease, pain, physical evils and premature death were considered to be God's punishment for the human moral evil and sin.

However, this religious and theological doctrine and explanation did not satisfy human intellect. There were good and innocent people who suffered pain from horrible diseases or died prematurely because of murder or accidents. Was God punishing them for their secret sins or the sins of other people? Would it be right or just for God to punish people for the crimes and sins committed by other people? Wouldn't that be injustice and evil on the part of God? Even the morally imperfect human forms of justice attempts to investigate crimes and try subjects of evil deeds and crimes in law courts to ensure that the criminals are convicted and punished while the innocent are set free. To punish as innocent person for a crime he or she did not commit is considered a tragic travesty of justice and a great moral evil. The holy God cannot be expected to be less just and less morally perfect than the morally imperfect and sinful human beings.

The problem of innocent suffering of obedient, God-fearing, righteous or morally perfect people like Job, is an illustration of this universal problem of human existence and theodicy, or the problem of finding meaning in the face of evil, suffering and death. Some of these faulty and false assumptions which have led to fatalism and predestination can be effectively nullified by counter arguments and propositions about the essence of God, humanity, the cosmos and its evolutionary history. These theological, moral and philosophical counter arguments include the following axiomatic affirmations and propositions:

I. 1. The assumption of the dogmatic doctrines of fatalism and prede stination by God or other forces are based on the false assumptions that there is no human causal power, freedom and self-determination because the future is already determined and fixed by God. These kinds of erroneous and horrible pessimistic doctrines of God and human nature affirm that there is no real freedom for human beings. Human life is fixed by God or fate depending on the date of his or her birth and what star happened to be in the sky! Stars have little to do with human nature. They are not intelligent objects or gods, as the ancient pre-scientific people believed. Astrologers are not accurate forecasters of the future. Human life is not fixed at birth.

I. 2. Human beings are free, despite the natural and human-made cultural, legal and other conventional societal limits. These include gender, race, color, culture, religion, class and nationality. But these are not evil in themselves. Racism and sexism are due to misunderstanding and misuse of these natural forms of identity. For instance, there is no gender or race which is better than another. There is also no culture or religion which is better than another! However, we have been negatively conditioned to think that our race, culture and religion are better than those of other people!

I. 3. This feeling of racial and other forms of superiority over other people is a source of major evils in the world. It constitutes the moral and spiritual evil or sins of pride (*hubris*), ethnocentrism, bigotry and racism! Our cultures, races, and religions can even be idolatrously elevated to the level of divinity itself! Jihads, crusades, ethnic and racial wars have been fought because of this form of nationalism and idolatry. Hitler, who tried to create a super White race and to exterminate those considered being racially inferior, is a good illustration of this form of human-self-deification, idolatry, white-supremacy, violence, genocide and war.

I. 4. The individual is also shaped and conditioned by the environment in which he or she grows up. But that is not predestination. The genetic engineers may have a better method of predestination of the biologically engineered child by tampering with DNA or cloning the desirable traits. But the clone will still have sufficient freedom to deviate from the original in the same way in which biological twins who constitute nature's human clones, may vary in behavior depending on the environment and cultural or societal conditioning.

II. 1. Original sin by Adam and Eve in the primordial Garden of Eden and the supposed result of the permanent loss of perfection and God's supernatural grace as the power to choose the good and do it! This was the kind of false and erroneous assumption made by St. Paul, Augustine, Calvin and Luther.

II. 2. "Original sin" or "congenital moral or spiritual corruption and depravity" is a basic, wrong theological assumption and erroneous moral theory because there were no original historical perfect people in the form of Adam and Eve. There has never been a single historical person who was perfect and then, due to temptation sinned against God and lost God's supernatural grace on behalf of all humanity. Evolution puts human perfection in the future, rather than in the mythological historical past.

II. 3. By accepting biological and historical evolution as God's method for creating the universe, including the human beings, the myths of Adam and Eve cease to become meaningful as historical and theological descriptions of the perfect world prior to the fall. The fall becomes the universal human awareness of the guilt due to sin as a result of spiritual and moral failure.

II. 4. The fall of humanity is the historical and evolutionary transition between human essence and existence. It is the transition from the primordial perfection of the human essence as was conceived and existed in pure perfection of God's mind, to the historical and concrete human evolutionary emergence and imperfect mode of human choices in the process of self-actualization and existence in the historical process of this material world. The fall is not an actual historical event which took place in time, space and human history.

II. 5. On the contrary, the fall is the universal human awareness or consciousness and acute troubling knowledge of the existence of a big gap "between what ought to be" and "the reality of what is." That gap between what ought to be and the actuality of what is constitutes moral, spiritual and physical imperfection and the fall! It is not God's doing. Nor is it the supposed work of the Devil. On the contrary, it is a result of human misuse of freedom to rebel against God's moral law in nature, the sacred scriptures and ignorance.

II. 6. The fall is a religious and theological metaphor for the universal existential condition of moral and spiritual imperfection, and guilt for moral failures in which the human being finds himself or herself in the present. It is a universal human condition of living life in a less perfect mode in which there is guilt due to the awareness of moral or spiritual failure which has created *the gap between essence (what ought to be) and existence (what is)*.

II. 7. Based on the above philosophical-theological understanding, the biblical stories of creation, human temptation, rebellion, the fall or sin against God, judgement and punishment by God, are descriptive of the human condition in the present moment. The human sinful mode of existence is self-alienation from God's fellowship and the Kingdom of God as the primordial Garden of Eden! Rebellious and sinful people are expelled from God's holy fellowship and Kingdom. This fellowship with God and the Kingdom of God are symbolized by the Garden of Eden.

II. 8. This moral failure is both personal and collective. As such, without a historical Adam and Eve, there is still guilt of sin and spiritual and moral failure. This guilt can be oppressive enough to cause anxiety, fear, dread of life and despair (*angst*). That form of *existential hell* is painful enough to require redemption or liberation from it! That liberation from evil and oppression by sin and guilt is truly called supernatural salvation.

III. 1. There is the assumption that human freedom is an illusion rather than a causal reality. This is in order to affirm predestination or the doctrine that God out of providence plans a detailed course of a person's life and destiny. This is a false and dangerous assumption. In actuality, human beings are within some *a priori* natural limits (IQ, gender, age, sexual orientation or race), truly free to fulfil themselves and complete their own nature and seal their own destiny through the exercise of their freedom, and free-will in order to choose and do good or evil. Each human being is born incomplete and open and ready for education and self-development of one's potential into reality so as to effect self-fulfillment and self-completion.

III. 2. Freedom and free choices and actions are needed to complete the identity and destiny of the individual person. In this sense, each person is a real historical Adam or Eve in this world. What people voluntarily choose and do with their freedom and lives has great consequences on themselves, other people and the world.

III. 3. Ultimately, the free human exercise of personal freedom, choices and actions, to some significant degree, determine and shape person's future and destiny, the person's community, nation and the world. But even then, these factors do not eliminate human freedom as the power for self-determination or self-creation and transformation of the self, the community and the world. Because of human freedom and intellect, human beings are special true causal moral agents in creation, and also effectively function like God in the world!

III. 4. When human beings are obedient, they act in God's name. When they are in rebellion against God, they declare themselves Gods and try to displace the true Creator-Redeemer God from the center of life and moral values! This act of human self-deification into God is the true essence of the universal human temptation and the biblical "Adamic sin" of hubris and idolatry (cf. Gen. 2-3). The results are tragic. They include premature death, conflicts with one another, envy, greed, murder, hate, guilt, destruction of the environment, sexism and oppression of women.

III. 5. Adam and Eve exist inside each individual. Therefore, each time we make a choice and do it, we are exercising our God given freedom, grace and choices for ourselves, families, the neighbor, the nation and the world. Environmental protection or destruction is directly linked to our choices and actions in the world. For instance, if we choose to buy and drive big cars, this decision has tremendous consequences on the environment. This leads to the characteristic capitalist consumption of the natural resources, energy consumption, minerals, and the car and factory emissions which pollute the air, water and the soil!

III. 6. In the moral theory of freedom, there is the awareness of the "universal law of cause and effect" or the "*law of Karma.*" Good choices lead to good actions and evil choices lead to evil actions in the world. These repeated processes due to freedom lead to the accumulation of either good or evil in the world. This accumulated human moral evil may be mistaken for a devil an external evil power. But it is a result of human moral evil and corruption in life! That is not God's doing, nor the Devil's evil creation!

III. 7. Apart from the human being as a free moral agent in the world, there is no other source of moral evil and imperfection. In this respect, Sartre was correct to assert that the "Devil is the other people." However, Sartre was wrong to exclude himself from the devil! He also correctly viewed the idolatrous nature of the human being and defined "the human being as the creature that wants to become God."

IV. 1. The assumption that the future is defined and absolutely fixed by God or fate, and therefore, unchangeable by human beings is at the heart of beliefs in fatalism and predestination. This is a false assumption. Human freedom is real and causal. The past is fixed and unchangeable. But the future is open and not fixed as fatalists falsely and erroneously claim. The future is to some great degree voluntarily chosen and determined by what the respective individual freely chooses or omits in the present moment.

IV. 2. Human beings are shaped by their choices in freedom and the concrete actions which they voluntarily choose to perform in the world. The prophets and Jesus assumed that human beings were completely free in their choices and actions.

IV. 3. Therefore, all "normal human beings" (moral agents) were also completely held accountable for their use of freedom, free will and evil or sinful choices and the consequences for these evil or sinful choices. As a result, the prophets, including John the Baptist and Jesus called people to repent of sins and change from their evil and sinful ways, and live a holy, loving, just and peaceful life in obedience to God's moral law and commandments. The moral laws of God and the commandments are universally revealed by God through nature and God's *Logos* which is incarnate in the human mind, conscience, scriptures and nature.

IV. 4. However, although the human life and the future events are open and subject to change, at birth there are certain natural limitations which God and nature impose on human freedom. These include gender, race, culture, class, environment, and mental and physical aptitudes. Nevertheless, they can be transcended. This is the testimony of Buddha, Moses, Jesus, Gandhi, Martin Luther King, and Mother Teresa. Mother Teresa was a poor, small and short woman, but that did not stop her from founding the *Society for Daughters of Charity* which is a very influential worldwide charitable organization.

IV. 5. The natural barriers and limits of body size, height, culture, language, race, gender, color and class can all be transcended by those who use their superior gifts of intellect, minds, agape, goodwill and creativity. The future is open and not completely determined by God or other supernatural forces. Stars have little to do with human freedom and choices, which are both free, despite finitude and boundaries imposed by human societal conditioning, physical and intellectual limitations.

IV. 6. Therefore, in their extreme forms, the doctrines of fatalism and predestination constitute moral irresponsibility, and irrational escapism from the reality of freedom and the moral responsibility for making free choices. This moral irresponsibility and religious escapism leads many human beings to reject the reality of freedom as an illusion. They argue that human beings are like robots carrying out actions according to the programming of God or natural law.

IV. 7. Augustinian and Calvinist doctrines of double predestination and the traditional Oriental forms of pessimistic fatalism are examples of this hard, physical, biological, moral and spiritual determinism. These kinds of people seek to evade the responsibility for their causal freedom by blaming evil choices on the mythological "original sin" of Adam and Eve or temptation of the nonexistent mythological scapegoat called the Devil. This irresponsible moral escapism sometimes takes this following crude moral form: "*The Devil made me do it!*" But law courts know better! In a just society where laws protect society from criminals and where misuse of freedom is punished by having it revoked in the name of God, the real "devil" is the evildoer who is sent to jail!

IV. 8. The Greeks blamed misfortunes (disasters) on the alleged "bad stars" or "fate." The Chinese took astrology and human fate so seriously that only the state licensed astrologers were allowed to practice divinization and forecasting the future as was read in the stars or human hands! The Chinese thought the future was completely fixed by external supernatural forces, such as the star that appeared during the time of one's birth, that the future could also be read in these stars and be accurately predicted since the future was determined and fixed. All that one needs was a good diviner or visionary to foresee the future and provide future events as future history and not as mere probabilities.

IV. 9. In both predestination and fatalism, the freedom of human causal agencies through free will and volitional choices and free actions which causes ambiguity, caprice and uncertainties in life is rejected in favor of total or "hard determinism." Biological, cultural, environmental, mental, physical, racial and religious forms of determinism have tried to advance arguments for determinism and predestination. But all of them have failed to eliminate the uncertainties of future events due to the reality of human freedom and its unpredictable causal power as major factors that unpredictably shape and determine future events!

IV. 10. Therefore, it was erroneously believed that the stars were divinities which functioned as fixed living maps of human lives and events within states and empires. As a result, the stars were both valued as divinities and feared as evil portents in the sky and causes of evil among individuals, society, nations and the world! It was erroneously believed that these stars sealed human fate and determined events in the world.

IV. 11. The mortals were considered to be finite, powerless and completely helpless unless God, or a god, intervened on their behalf to save them from the tragedies of fate. All human beings as predestined and powerless mortals were considered to be completely at the mercy of these gods, and they were supposed to be powerless to change the events and course of their lives or that of their nations! Within these "pagan" systems of thought, world-view and ethics, there was complete predestination by God or the stars as gods. Human freedom was an illusion. Human beings were like puppets on God's string. They just moved and acted as divinely decreed by God or fate!

IV. 12. Characteristically, the Christians within the Calvinistic tradition reject freedom and God's free universal grace and salvation. Then, they attribute human fate to God and his activities of selective election. Following Augustine and Calvin's teachings on utter depravity and moral corruption of human nature which they attribute to the fall of Adam and Eve, they affirm that God's grace to choose and do good was permanently lost by Adam's choice to misuse his freedom and free will to disobey God's moral law. As a result, God elects a few of those to be saved and the masses are to be damned in hell.

IV. 13. Subsequently, God freely endows his free gift of grace to those elected to be saved. This process of divine predestination is double in that God elects some people to be saved and others to be damned in hell. Since God's grace is affirmed to be irresistible, once elected by God to salvation, the person remains God's saint through perseverance of grace!

IV. 14. However, the damnation of the masses (*massa damnata)* is for those people who are not predestined by God to salvation, but it is considered to be God's eternal punishment for the alleged original disobedience and the original sin of Adam and Eve. The refutation to these erroneous doctrines lies in evolution as God's historical method for creating the universe and humanity. That means that Adam and Eve are nonexistent and non-historical people. They are only mythological scapegoats for human moral evil and imperfection.

IV. 15. Both scientifically, or historically and theologically, there are no real or actual primordial disobedient human beings or couple called Adam and Eve (Evil!) who caused the moral imperfection and spiritual downfall of the whole human race. Each person is ultimately responsible for his or her volitional exercise of personal freedom and intellect as God's supernatural gifts for meaningful free choices and volitional free good or evil actions in self-determination and self-fulfillment.

V. 1. There is also the false assumption that if God is omnipotent and good, then there cannot be any real human freedom or events which are truly independent of God's power. This assumption of freedom as an illusion affirms that human beings are akin to God's biological robots that are a priori programmed to live the lives they choose to live. Therefore, all events in the world are both directly or caused by God's omnipotence as the cosmic creator of everything. As such, not only are human life and history predetermined and fixed by God, the evil in the world is also attributed to God as the creator of all things. This moral theory fails to take human freedom and its causality as a reality or creates problems by the denial of this self-evident empirical reality.

V. 2. Since God is both good and holy, and evil is the opposite of both goodness and holiness, God could not negate his own essence of goodness and holiness by creating evil in the world. Evil as defined by both Augustine and Thomas Aquinas as "the privation of the good" is essentially a mere corruption and imperfection of the good things which God has created. Moral evil is the creation of evil human beings who use their freedom to choose "the less perfect alternatives" and "do evil or the imperfect as the lesser of the good actions in the world!"

V. 3. Human causal freedom, and reason or higher intellect, are God's special supernatural gifts which he has bequeathed to all humanity in order to make humans divine beings as his adopted sons and daughters and the beneficiaries of his Kingdom as his cosmic creation. As such, human causal freedom does not negate God's omnipotence and goodness. They both divinize the human being into a Godlike creature. But because of the human being's sin or misuse of freedom and creative powers, and the subsequent human choices to do the lesser good or evil, there exists the problem of moral evil and vice in the world. It is a human creation, rather than that of God, who is holy, good and perfect.

V. 4. This moral evil is particularly experienced in the form of human greed, self-deification, materialism, intolerance, hate, malice, envy, conflict, violence, war and chaos in the world, instead of unconditional love (Agape), harmony and peaceful co-existence as God's universal will and decree!

V. 5. Human freedom is powerful enough to negate God's will in the world. Through human rebellion against God's moral law and holy commandments of God's Kingdom, the human being is able to create evil in the world and negatively transform God's Garden of Eden into a desert and also transform God's Kingdom into an evil place of innocent suffering and premature death.

V. 6. In actuality, human moral evil and sin can't transform God's good world and the Kingdom into a kind of "existential hell!" This is why God's redemptive agents continually come to call sinful and rebellious people to repentance and urge them to return to a positive good holy life of love, forgiveness, and obedience to God's commandments and reign of his Kingdom. All this depends on the positive affirmation of the reality of human free will and freedom to hear God's Word and repent of evil and live a changed life which is in accordance with God's will and decrees or commandments.

Ultimately, within the mainline Christian theological and moral teachings, there is the conscious recognition or affirmation of the existential reality of freedom, goodness and imperfection or evil in the world. However, very often the human being is too preoccupied with evil in the world to appreciate and enjoy goodness and beautiful things that God provides in the natural world! Because of this human pessimism, negative orientation and preoccupation with the existence of evil in the world, the human being has suffered from great pain caused by the fear of life and the world.

This was the kind of "*angst*" that Martin Heidegger and Paul Tillich called various names including "existential anxiety," "dread," "guilt," "human finitude," "human predicament," and "the human condition." This kind of paranoia leads to human existential paralysis and despair, instead of enjoying life and the world as God's supernatural undeserved free gifts! Consequently, many people are dualists, just like the ancient Greeks. Therefore, they also tend to view the world both negatively and pessimistically as the real domain (kingdom) of evil and "the Devil," instead of correctly seeing it as God's good creation and as the "Kingdom of God!"

Tragically, the more paranoid and misguided people refuse to live fully in this world, the more they seek to escape or flee from the realities of this world into another mythological world called heaven, supposedly located in the blue sky or celestial space above. For these scriptural literalists and fundamentalists, the new millennium represents the end of the world and the establishment of God's Kingdom. For these unsophisticated people, "heaven" and "hell" exist as real geographical places in time, space and history. For instance, "heaven" is supposed to be a place which they expect to be better than the one they now inhabit, namely, the Earth! Other people scoff and say quietly to themselves:

> Let those ignorant and religious fanatic people go to heaven! Let them join God either on Mars or Venus! Let them leave us in peace to enjoy this world which God has given us! Most of us prefer to drive our cars and live here on Earth than join God in the mythological "heaven" which they preach and where there is no fun!

> If this world is hell, then, I prefer it to your kind of heaven! I know that I am right! Have you ever thought that the world could be heaven and that each person is God? At least, I feel like God! My mind is very creative! (A comment by a student during a debate on God in my course, *Critical Issues in Religion and Ethics*, fall semester, 1997, at Ohio Wesleyan University).

Religious fanatics and millenarians abound in the West, particularly, in the USA. Some of them are dangerous both to themselves and those around them. The Reverend Jim Jones and his paranoid apocalyptic followers who committed mass suicide in Jones' Town, Guiana in the early 1980s, or David Koresh and his armed followers who died in Waco (Texas) in an inferno in 1993 at their "messianic and heavenly compound," are examples of the dangerous ones.

The various white-supremacist groups, such as the "Identity Church" and the Japanese Dooms' Day cult that released poison gas on the Tokyo train in mid 1990s, are other examples. Professor Theodore Kancyzanski, the "unabomber" and "technological terrorist" of intellectuals and engineers, is the opposite of the nonviolent and anti-technological Amish. In contrast, Kancyzanski, the former mathematics professor, is solitary, anti-technology and violent.

The tragedy of Marshall Applewhite and his followers, who committed suicide in 1996 during the appearance of the Haile-Borp comet in the hopes of going to heaven through the transportation of the comet, are examples of the extreme fundamentalists and scriptural literalists within this group of religious irrational fanatics.

The universal awareness of insecurity arising out of human wickedness and moral evil has led many to question the goodness of God, given the axiomatic Christian dogma that God is by essential nature and attributes, the loving, omnipotent Creator, Preserver and Redeemer of the world. Many great theologians and philosophers have, for a long time, battled with this question of evil in the world. Some thinkers, such as Feuerbach, Nietzsche and Marx, have sided with Plato, and said that God cannot be both simultaneously pure goodness and loving omnipotent Creator since God's creation does not manifest pure goodness, and human beings are terrorized by the threats of evil, chaos, disease, suffering and death. They argue that the presence of evil in the world and a variety of both physical and moral imperfections effectively negate both God's goodness and perfection in the world.

Furthermore, they also argue that the idea that God is both the loving and good omnipotent Creator is based more on mere blind faith than the actual examination of nature, history and religious experience and doctrines about God. Some of these thinkers have even concluded that God does not actually exist. Nietzsche affirmed that the world was a mere self-creative and ordering blind force. Evolution is said to be a mere process of life following chance and environmental factors, rather than being God's method for creating life. Evolution is impersonal and wasteful of life in order to perfect itself. For him and other non-theistic evolutionists, God does not design and create life, if he does, he could not be called good or moral, since evolution follows the brutal jungle law of "the survival of the fittest."

However, there are also some other thinkers like Moses, Aristotle, Augustine, Aquinas, Descartes, Spinoza, Hegel, Kant, Kierkegaard, Buber, Whitehead, Niebuhr, Tillich, and Rahner, who see moral evil as a result of human moral freedom and not God's will. They also see nature as God's ordained impartial process for the evolution of life.

Most of these thinkers have tried to solve this apparent contradiction of the presence of evil in God's good world by putting both the problem and the blame on the human being as God's free moral agent in the world. Because of the human moral agency and causal freedom, the human being, like God, is able to create great evil in God's world as well as do good. However, these people argue that the human being has misused his or her unique position and freedom to do evil in the world, and therefore, misrepresents both God and God's essential goodness and perfection. This shift of the problem of evil in the world from God to the human being is valid in as much as the human being is the concrete, intelligent, free, moral, and effective or consequential representative of God in creation with the supernaturally endowed powers to think, judge, make moral choices, and implement them in the world in God's name and on his or her behalf.

To this end, this moral theory also requires that the human being be accepted not just as God's image, but also as a true child of God and as such, a Co-Creator with God, the eternal or heavenly Father and Mother of the human being. Furthermore, just as human parents are not tried and convicted for the crimes and evils perpetrated by their own children, similarly, God should not be tried or convicted for the evils and crimes committed by the free moral agents as his adopted children.

Ultimately, "most defenders of God's goodness, love and human freedom" argue that the human beings are moral agents who are fully free and responsible beings that should be held accountable for they have failed to do, done and created in God's world. This is because the human moral defects are not due to God's defective creation of the human being and human misuse of freedom. They are directly due to the human being's moral agency as an intelligent, thinking, moral, responsible, living, free, judging, and independent special creature created for a special purpose and mission in the world.

Therefore, God made no mistakes, nor did he or she do evil to create a free moral human being to take care of his or her creation on his or her behalf. However, the human being made a terrible moral mistake to choose to serve his or her own material self-interest rather than that of the creator of the world. Subsequently, human moral evil and the world's major problems are directly rooted in this human moral evil or greed and self interest. The other evils are mere offshoots and expressions of this basic human moral problem of egocentrism and the exclusion of others unless they enhance the clearly preconceived self-interest and personal gain.

Subsequently, this solution of evil is more Christian and traditional than that proposed by Whitehead. Whitehead speculated that God is neither omnipotent nor perfect since he or she never controls the creative process. On the contrary, God is said to persuade the free moral agents to actualize themselves according to the highest possibilities for the best outcome, which is itself not fully known by God until it has actually occurred! That is also the denial that God is not omniscient. And, with this denial of God's omnipotence and omniscience, Whitehead thought that he had creatively solved the problem involved in the religious and philosophical debate of the presence of evil in the world in the presence of a good, omnipotent God who is also the omniscient.

The absurdity of this Whiteheadian solution of evil lies in the affirmation that God is not the knowing powerful Creator, but rather, the weak and ignorant architect working from the limitations of time, space and knowledge, just like finite human "creators." Whereas such a finite, ignorant, and weak God may provide a plausible intellectual explanation for physical evil in the world such as malformed creatures, imperfections, earthquakes, and some diseases, it is a very weak one when it comes to human moral evil. This is the case since the blame is left on God for failing to provide a suitable or an irresistible moral persuasion to choose the good and do it, rather than choosing evil.

Moreover, religiously, Whitehead's weak, imperfect and finite God is very unattractive because he or she is neither the purposeful, loving, mighty, and cosmic Creator nor is he or she powerful enough to redeem the human being from both moral and physical evil that ever plagues finite humanity.

Nevertheless, for finite human minds in quest for the infinite through the mediation of the finite intellectual means, Whitehead provides some satisfactory answers by "creating" the infinite Creator God in the "human finite image" so as to render him or her apprehensible and understandable to finite minds. "Anthropomorphism" as the human temptation to view God in human terms or create a mental image of God as a "White," strong and elderly patriarch ("Father"), has been the downfall of religion and the perennial source of idols and idolatry both intellectual and religious expressions. For centuries, such idolatrous anthropomorphism has for centuries led to the resistance against women's ordination in the Christian Church.

The popular metaphor of "God as Father" (*Abba*) was taken both erroneously and literally as a biological and cultural definition and description of God, as a male being! This blasphemous and idolatrous assertion about God, completely ignored the fact that God was a transcendent creative Cosmic Spirit, Conscious Energy or Mind that completely transcended the finite human categories of time, gender, color, ethnicity, language, mind, location and physicality. Moses had correctly forbidden the creation of images of God. This includes physical, mental, linguistic, artistic and symbolic images.

Michelangelo's rendition of the creation and the painting of the picture of God as a super, bearded, White male has been instrumental in some people's minds for what God looks like. Other people just substitute the Greek Zeus with "God the Father" in the Christian concept of God, the Greek Hercules or Egyptian "Osiris" with Jesus and Europa, or Isis with Mary as "the *Theotokos*" or "the Virgin Mother of God!" All this is idolatrous anthropomorphism which was correctly denounced by Prophet Muhammad, who re-instituted strict monotheism devoid of priesthood and human mediators for fear that these people would be worshiped as God or gods by the superstitious people who were accustomed to polytheism or the worship of many gods and idols.

Whereas Christianity claims to be a monotheistic religion, it borders on both idolatry and polytheism. The crude affirmation in some Churches that Jesus, the man of Nazareth, was God is such an idolatrous example! A God who gets born and dies like any other human being is not the eternal God and the cosmic Creator, Sustainer and Redeemer! Such a God is not the God worshiped in monotheistic religions, such as Judaism, Christianity and Islam. Furthermore, Jesus as "the Christ," "messiah," "deliverer," or "liberator" of human beings from evil and oppression, like Moses, Prophet Muhammad, Gandhi, King and Nelson Mandela, does not have to become worshiped as the God who had sent him to liberate his oppressed people!

The relationship between Jesus and God has been the subject of controversy and heresies within the Christian history. Therefore, the Apostles and the Nicene creeds should be viewed as answers which satisfied the ancient Christian thinkers, but need revision and reformation within today's world-view, evolutionary anthropology, physics, theology and ethics. The "Jesus Seminar" has done a needed task to reformulate the image of "Jesus of history" and "Jesus of faith" and Christian myths based on the new interpretation of the New Testament in its historical and theological context.

## 5. Human Moral Conscience and Religion

The human being is also, by unique nature, a religious creature. Therefore, to be an authentic human being, one also has to be religious. This religiosity may be either affirmed by going to religious activities such as worship, fellowship, meditation, or prayer, or may be denied by becoming anti-religious, atheistic, and agnostic.

Nevertheless, in both cases, whether in the denial or affirmation of religion, there is a fundamental affirmation of the underlying essential religious element. Religion is the universal basic constitutive component of the human being. This is what is being consciously questioned. This is analogous to when a child grows up and questions whether the people that claim to be his or her mother and father are in essence his or her own real biological parents. This is because of the human unique mental qualities of free thinking, self-reflection, self-transcendence and doubting the self, God and the empirical data or truth based on the senses, as well as that based on logic and imagination alone!

Likewise, it is also because to be human, is also both correlatively and coextensively to become an intelligent and free moral agent. In other words, to be a human being is also both to be correlatively moral and coextensively religious. This human-divine essence accounts for the fact that all known human beings have an established religion of one kind or another. This is universally true.

Characteristically, the former atheistic Soviet communist Messianic leaders themselves, whose teachings and practices were interpreted as the very rejection of organized traditional Christianity and other forms of religion, have ironically created a new kind of civil and secular state religion. They quietly, institutionally assumed the divine authority and messiahship which was the previously denounced traditional role of religion!

Communist leaders, such as Stalin of the former Soviet Union and Mao Tse Tung of China, had taken the place of Jesus Christ. They had become the national deliverers or messiahs from socioeconomic and political evils of Western capitalist exploitation. Patriotic hymns were also sung by the enthusiastic masses. Stalin and Mao became Christ-like figures for the former Soviet and Chinese forms of communism.

This universal religious phenomenon cannot therefore be a mere moral or social accident or just a universal coincidence. On the contrary, what is self-evident here is the irrefutable evidence to support the claim that religion is an intrinsic essential feature of finite human beings found on planet Earth, and that it is an essential manifestation of any being or creature that possesses human qualities.

Consequently, religion and religious sentiments in any recognizable form constitute the main essential unique feature of a human being which no other animal is known or observed to possess. Not even the most intelligent primates have been seen to practice some form of rudimentary religion, whereas in other respects, they seem to have some fundamental forms of human institutions, such as social organization with a single leader, social hierarchy, punishment systems, and feeding and mating rules. These same animals appear to be completely devoid of religion since it requires an intellectual and spiritual capacity for self-transcendence and the awareness of the Divine Mystery that is variously referred to as Creator, Deity and God.

For most religious people, this Cosmic Creative Power and Mystery known simply as God has been extremely revered and personalized as a benevolent, loving and caring heavenly parent known to many as "Father" (Abba) and to others as Redeemer and Lord. It is this native and redemptive mystery that is both feared and loved as the Almighty God, the Creator, Preserver and Redeemer of the world of which the human being is the central created symbol and cosmic representative to God. And as such, whatever happens to the human beings also happens to the world of which he or she is the spiritual and intellectual embodiment and symbol. Likewise, whatever the human being does has a correlative cosmic significance for both God and the world.

Following *the law of Karma* or the law of cause and effect, good moral actions have good and positive consequences for the world and all the people and creatures in it, whereas evil moral deeds cause negative and destructive consequences for the human beings, the environment and the creatures in the world. This is not God's will. As such, evil in the world is not a result of God's will in creation, predestination, punishment for sinners or the work of the mythological Devil as the scapegoat for the evil.

Ultimately, cosmic moral evil is the creation of free disobedient, greedy, self-centered and evil intelligent beings, particularly, the imperfect human beings as God's sinful moral agents in the world. In reality, moral evil is neither the creation of God nor the devil, although duelists prefer to blame it on a mythological Devil or women (Eve) as the ontological scapegoat for evil in God's good world. Eve (women) serves a traditional patriarchal moral theory for the explanation of the presence of temptation, moral failure and evil in the male dominated world.

However, within a monotheistic and non-dualistic theological and moral context, there is no real ontological Devil. An evil person is the real devil in god's good world! The evil person's evil deeds create more evil in the world in terms of physical, moral and spiritual evil. Since human beings are social, physical, mental, spiritual and moral beings, when they become evil, they also create evils at those respective levels and dimensions of society, body (physical), mind, spirit and intellect. Freedom and its misuse are the tools and media for the societal human evil. But, when freedom is positively utilized, it is the avenue for goodness and divinization!

Subsequently, since the human being is both divine and creative, heavenly and earthly, spirit and matter, human and animal, and the divine representative on the Earth. The human being is also the unique finite cosmic created and divinely elected representative of God to the world, and the world's high-priest or mediator to God. This is because of the essential need of mutual and meaningful representation between God and the created world. The essential dual nature of the human being endows the human being with divine essence.

This divinity in humanity provides the human being with the intrinsic, special, supernatural capacity to communicate with God as readily as he or she communicates with the rest of nature. This special structure of the human being was correctly defined by Karl Rahner in his mammoth collected works, *Theological Investigations*, as "*the supernatural existential.*"

Rahner identified this special feature of the human being as God's permanent, free and universal efficacious supernatural gift of God's agape, prevenient and redemptive grace. These divine attributes are built in each human being by God at creation. They are God's "divine hardware, operating systems and software" that transform the human being into an *imago Dei*, a Child of God, a moral agent, a religious being and free moral representative of God in cosmic creation.

These divine attributes enable the human being to be like God and to serve as the temple and embodiment of God and his creative and redemptive activities in the world. As such, each human being is not just God's representative in the world, but is also God's incarnation in the world! According to this understanding, each human being, and not just Jesus as the Christ, is essentially, a divine incarnation of the *Logos* in the world. To that extent, each person has the power of God to create, heal, forgive sins and redeem the world from self-destruction which is caused by sin, hate, greed, idolatry and disobedience against God's moral law and Christ's commandment of agape. They need more faith and prayer.

As a result, the human being is by nature the cosmic divine priest and mediator between God and creation of which the human being is a key constitutive component. Subsequently, the human beings as Cosmic Priests, come to God in prayer to intercede for the atonement and forgiveness of the sins of the world committed by sinful, disobedient, egocentric, immoral human beings (cf. Matt.6:9-15). They also help to pray for more seasonable weather in times of drought or too much rain, storms, thunder, hurricanes, and destructive floods. The human being also brings back God's message of warning, absolution for those repenting of their sins, love, hope, patience and benediction or blessings.

Despite the fact that the human being is morally imperfect, he or she is nevertheless the very elected and chosen divine vessel for God's concrete representation and activity in God's processes of creation and redemption of the world. As such, the human being is both a co-creator and co-redeemer with God in the world and its historical processes. The human being is not just a mirror of God in the world, but is in reality God's actual creative and redemptive representative, agent and medium of these activities both in the community and the world.

This is, indeed, a great responsibility. As a result, unless the human acts in the community and history in God's name, God does not act either until he has found another willing agent to do his work. For instance, Moses was God's chosen deliverer for the people of Israel. Joshua could not have done it. In any case, God's activities must be mediated by humanity in his dealings with human affairs, or become personally incarnated in humanity in order to effect human affairs at the human level, within their culture, world-view, religion and language.

Ultimately, the human being is the divine concrete or physical divine representative in the world through whom God operates to effect his or her divine, creative, and redemptive primordial purpose in the world. At a physical and cultural level, this makes sense. One can argue that God being nonphysical can only work through an intelligent, moral, and free agent to do his or her work in the human community, history and physical world, where action on matter requires another equivalent form of matter to act physically to move it in concrete time and space.

On the other hand, another person could also counter argue that there is the realization and documented evidence that the mind actually controls and moves matter according to the mental will. Since God is mind, he can also by his supernatural power and energy move matter around without needing physical arms and hands in order to do so! After all, human beings have also invented machines which can do physical work through verbal and electronic commands! This paradigm can explain how God can function as a the Cosmic Creative Force or Energy or Spirit and effectively accomplish the task by mere use of mind and energy to organize and move matter around as needed for creation.

Subsequently, we do not usually see things moving by themselves from place to place by God's spiritual command. Instead, what we usually see are men and women doing things in God's name, such as healing, senseless killings of human beings in war, punishment, murders and elective abortions. This is because obedient and moral human eyes, ears, hands, and feet are also the eyes, ears, hands and feet of the divine and as such, the divine instruments for God's own work in the world. This is exactly Paul's meaning when he declared to the Greeks of Corinth that Christians are a new creation and God's ambassadors of reconciliation and peace in the world:

> Therefore, if anyone is in Christ, he is a new creation; the old has passed away; behold, the new has come. All this is from God, who, through Christ, reconciled us to himself and gave us the ministry of himself, not counting their trespasses against them, and entrusting to us the message (Gospel) of reconciliation. So we are ambassadors for Christ, God making his appeal through us. Therefore, we beseech you on behalf of Christ, be reconciled to God. (II Cor. 5:17-20)

It is clear and obvious that God works through human beings in order to effect his or her divine purpose and carry out his or her work in the world. Therefore, without us as his or her intelligent and moral agents, God would be limited and even powerless in what he or she can do on this temporal human history. This is by virtue of the reality of the human casual freedom and volitional moral deeds, which have transformed this planet Earth into what it is, especially now.

For instance, God did not build "the skyscrapers" in New York, Chicago, Tokyo, Hong Kong, Boston, Atlanta or Johannesburg. Human beings did it. They also built the great Egyptian pyramids in Africa and the imposing medieval cathedrals in Europe before modern technology had come into being! This fact does not necessarily mean that human beings can save themselves from moral and spiritual evil, or that God is limited or powerless to save humanity and the world. God works incognito both in cosmic history and in human affairs. God works by the method of persuasion through the small inner voice of reason and warning, rather than by coercion, manipulation, threats of violence and show of force.

God prefers to treat human beings as his children and responsible agents in the world. As such, there is an actual need for cooperation and teamwork between God and humanity in the world to effect God's processes of creation, redemption, love, justice, harmony and peace. It also affirms that human beings are intelligent, creative, and moral representatives of the invisible, infinite, eternal, and immaterial God in the visible, finite, temporal, material and physical or concrete world. Indeed, it was for the sake of this special divine purpose that God created a special creature in the form of the human being at the very apex of creation and evolution.

Therefore, in the present world, God is still actively creating some new things, fulfilling and redeeming the old ones in the moral and free matters involving moral intelligence, knowledge, judgement, calculations and the like. The primary instrument of God's activity and intervention is the human being. For instance, when we pray for the homeless to find food, clothing, and a warm shelter, we never intend or expect God to answer in a "supernatural manner" by sending these things from the sky or to make them just pop up from nowhere!

Even the most naive religious person knows that for this kind of prayer, the divine answer has to be sought here on Earth through the work of other godly, loving, humanitarian and generous human beings. These are the real angels through whom God performs his miracles in the special need of his needy people through the loving compassionate and charitable people in the community and the world. This is the essence of Jesus' parable of the Good Samaritan (cf. Lk. 10:25-37).

However, this does not mean or imply that we have to draw the naive, atheistic conclusion about God and prayer. Although God is not compelled to do our will because we have prayed, God answers prayer within his freedom of "*kairos*" or right time for action. It will rain regardless of whether we pray or not. But that should not bring us to the fallacious or absurd conclusion that since prayer to God is answered in many cases through the work of other human beings that then human beings are either God or Gods! This was the kind of mistaken atheistic conclusion reached by great philosophers like Feuerbach and Marx and great social scientists like Durkheim and Freud.

These and other scholars have reached the absurd conclusion that God is just the glorified, idealized, magnified, and deified human moral self-abstraction and self-projection in the sky or heaven, and subsequently worshiped as God. So that in reality, it is God that has been essentially created by "Man in his own (male) image," and not the reverse.

Subsequently, according to these scholars, the worship of God by human beings becomes a mere human activity of self-deification, self-immortalization, and self-glorification; ultimately, human worship becomes mere collective self-idealization and self-worship.

Whereas this atheistic explanation of God may sound morally correct, and therefore plausible, it fails to account for creation itself and the orderly cosmos which cannot be a result of a mere accident or a result of mere cosmic blind creative forces. Even then, as soon as one admits the existence of an eternal force being involved in the origination of the Cosmos, one is no longer an atheist but a theist!

This can be said affirmatively to be necessarily true. This is the case, since by "God," most philosophers and theologians mean the existence and presence of this external force that is responsible for the origination or creation of this universe. The mode of origination or creation can be logically and scientifically compatible with the theory of biological evolution without negating the fact that God is the ultimate source and creator of the universe.

Consequently, the spiritually and religiously destructive fundamentalist, naive Christian insistence that for God to be the Creator and Redeemer, one has to take the biblical book of Genesis as an accurate, literal, and historical record of how the universe originated is intellectually, scientifically, theologically and historically absurd. It is also spiritually and religiously dangerous. This is necessarily the case, because this kind of religious controversy is rooted in deliberate religious bigotry and ignorance in the name of God who is also affirmed to be omniscient, yet the ground of anti-intellectualism, anti-science, new knowledge, "positive" progress, and the social change that comes along with it.

For instance, a literal belief in the book of Genesis would also require a pre-scientific cosmology in which the universe is constituted of one, big, dome-like structure which is rooted in the sea beyond the horizon for support. And below the dome or sky (heaven), is the flat Earth which is thought of as the center of the universe, being the dwelling place of the humankind, with God watching over humanity from the advantageous height of "heaven" in the sky above the Earth. As such, tops of mountains were also considered to be the holy dwelling places of since they "touched heaven" or the sky.

Furthermore, God and his or her heavenly dwelling place was thought to be "heaven." Interestingly, this "heaven" was anthropomorphically placed high above in the "sky." "Sky" was another word for "heaven." In the Hebrew account of creation, God as the cosmic creative Spirit (Vital Force) is placed just above the cosmic preexisting water and chaotic matter. Some of this water was also thought to be located above in the sky. From this ocean above the "Earth's dome," it was believed that God fetches some water which he pours down below as rain to water the plants and gardens in the world.

In the absence of good science and understanding of how rain and floods occurred, ancient people attributed them to God. Unfailing, seasonal rain was needed to water the gardens. It was considered good and God's blessing. But too much rain and subsequent destructive floods were considered to be God's punishment or evil caused by enemies through magic and witchcraft.

In the semi desert lands of the Middle East, rain and clean drinking were scarce. Water symbolized life both in the natural and supernatural sense. It preserved life and cleansed people from dirt or dust. As a result, it became the baptismal symbol for repentance, spiritual and moral cleansing. It became the Christian ritual and spiritual symbol for the purification from "original sin." In any case, water in the form of snow and rain were valuable as God's holy water which he poured down to cleanse and nurture the earth and provide drink for both humankind and the wild life. The dead are also supposed to go below the earth into "*Sheol*" or "*Hell*" to live a shadowy, meaningless ghostly life.

Subsequently, Noah's flood could only take place in such a small, flat, limited world, since we are told that it covered the entire world and that all life was destroyed except for that which was preserved in the Ark. If the entire known world did flood, it must have been a local, geographically defined flat world in the Middle East which excluded much of the present world that was only discovered in the fifteenth and sixteenth centuries by the Portuguese and Spanish sea-goers and wealth-seekers in Africa, India, and the Americas.

These unknown distant lands were not part of Noah's world, which is said to have been destroyed by floods due to too much rain. Therefore, they could not have been covered by Noah's flood, since it is said to have covered the world (as they knew it) and there was no way to know it. These distant and vast lands and the animals that inhabited them were still unknown! The polar bears and kangaroos in Australia were still unknown and therefore, they could not have been gathered by Noah to saved, since outside Noah's boat of salvation, everything is said to have perished! Moreover, Noah could not have seen the flood covering these foreign and distant lands from the security of his watchtower or window in his small Ark to verify that the flood had covered the entire Earth.

Furthermore, it is inconceivable that all the world's animals and their food and water could have, in any way, fit into Noah's Ark, which was a mere 450 feet in length, 75 feet in width and 45 feet in height. In this kind of limited space, there is not even enough space for one elephant and all the necessary hay and water for it to last even a week, since on the average, an adult elephant consumes more than two tons of vegetation in one day and drinks between 5-10 gallons of water!

In addition, we are still in the process of learning about the different types of species of animals, insects and plants. New species are still being discovered by scientists in the course of their research. It is very surprising, therefore, that we are told that a pair of each kind of "unclean animals" and "seven pairs of clean animals" were gathered from the world by Noah and preserved in the Ark for more than forty days.

All the necessary food stuff and fresh water for these animals would also have been collected and stored aboard the small boat. This would have been made more difficult by the fact that food and water would continue to be required during the flood and long after it until there was sufficient new vegetation and other new life forms on the land to support these animals! Even then, the carnivorous animals would have required more game on Noah's "houseboat" to hunt while on the boat and afterwards more than the boat could have supported!

Therefore, a naive literal interpretation or literal belief in the story of Adam and Eve or Noah and the cosmic flood is intellectually and spiritually absurd and religiously tragic. A literal explanation of Noah's flood story as an actual record of a historical event is like reading "poetry as prose" and "myth" or "story as history!" This is the confusion between "denotation" and "connotation," and "myth" and "history." Confusing "story" with "history" is like confusing fiction with nonfiction. Confusing "parables" or "myths or legends" and history is a serious mistake indeed! Confusing the stories of creation and the fall in the Bible with history is as absurd as confusing the Greek myths of Zeus and the pantheon of gods at holy Mount Olympus with actual Greek history and politics!

Likewise, reading the story of Noah's flood literally as sacred history is a such a serious mistake. It fails to take into account the great universal moral value in it as a parable of human universal sin and moral evil. It shows the whole world deserves God's righteous judgement and the just sentence of death in punishment for hubris and the correlative sins of treason and rebellion against God's moral law, reign and the Kingdom.

However, because of God's unmerited grace, Agape and mercy, and through the righteousness of a few individuals, the world is always spared from his anger and redeemed by God's free redemptive grace and Agape from destruction. These righteous people exist in a scattered manner. They exist here and there like islands in the flood of destructive evil and corruption, the divine sentence is commuted and those who heed the warning gain salvation.

Therefore, for anyone, especially an educated or thinking adult, to understand or interpret the Genesis prophetic moral warning as most effectively communicated in a parabolic moral story of Noah's flood, is like taking literally the fairy tale of Snow White and the Seven Dwarfs or Jesus' parable of the Good Samaritan.

Subsequently, going to look for the historical and archeological remains of Noah's Ark is absurd. Such actions could be due to ignorance and intellectual failure to understand that Noah's story of the flood is a non-historical, religious, mythological story or parable like those employed by Jesus to teach about sin and God's Kingdom. Jesus' parables include "the farmer (sower)," who sowed seed on four types of soil, "the Good Samaritan," "Lazarus and the indigent and homeless beggar" and "the Kingdom of God and the mustard seed." These parables, stories and religious myths are non-historical. Their message is eternal in terms of moral values, spirituality and how to live the good life here in the world.

Within this religious context, going to look for Noah's houseboat (Ark of salvation) is like going to look for the forest where "Snow White" met "the Seven Dwarfs," or to look for the specific road and the inn to which the Good Samaritan took the neglected victim of armed robbery for both shelter and treatment, or to look for the descendants of the Good Samaritan in order to reward them for the good that their ancestors did.

In the same way, we cannot go to look for Noah's Ark and biological descendants. Similarly, we cannot go back to the Middle East or Africa to look for the parabolic, primordial, "heavenly" Garden of Eden where Adam was created. Nevertheless, according to the theory of evolution, the Garden of Eden is to be found in the East African, beautiful Savanna with its abundant wild life and good climate. This is the place where the original human being originated or was created by God.

For this natural and wonderful revelation, some of us cry out in joyful praise and thanksgiving to God saying: "THANKS BE TO GOD!" But others disbelieve not just because of prejudice that nothing good or of value can come from Africa except natural raw materials, but also because the idea that God could have chosen to create the human being by way of evolution is simply objectionable. During a conversation on evolution, I was told by a concerned and irritated religious friend that: "*You came from God! You did not come from a monkey*!"

This statement reveals not only an ignorance of theology, but also a lack of sound knowledge regarding evolution as God's method for creating the cosmos. It reveals a serious misunderstanding of the essence of God, humanity and creation. The truth is that even monkeys were, like us, created by God! They are part of God's beloved creation and the world. They, too, are included in this famous hymn of praise for God and creation:

1. Praise to the Lord,
   the Almighty,
   the King of creation;
   O my soul, praise him,
   for he is thy health and salvation:
     Join the great throng,
     Psaltery, organ, and song,
     Sounding in glad adoration.

2. Praise to the Lord;
   over all things
   he gloriously reigneth:
   Borne as on eagle-wings,
   safely his saints sustaineth.
     Hast thou not seen
     How all thou needest hath been
     Granted in what he ordaineth?

3. Praise to the Lord,
   who doth prosper thy way
   and defend thee;
   Surely his goodness and mercy
   shall ever attend thee;
     Ponder anew
     What the Almighty can do,
     Who with his love doth befriend thee.

4. Praise to the Lord!
O let all that is in me adore him!
All that hath breath
join with Abraham's seed to adore him!
Let the "Amen"
Sum all our praises again
Now as we worship before him. Amen.
(Joachim Neander, 1680; *based on Psalms* 103 and 150).

Ultimately, true prayer is that of praise for creation, sustenance and redemption. According to sound religion, theology and religious ethics, God is "functionally defined" as "the ultimate Creator, Sustainer, cosmic ordering Principle that resists chaos and entropy. *God as the "All-Encompassing" Cosmic-Creator and Sustainer is analogous to a woman that is perpetually pregnant.*

As "Mother", God is the Cosmic and Infinite Medium of the emergence and existence of reality, creation, order, mind, life, spirit, meaning, love, happiness, peace, creativity and the ultimate meaning for human existence. As "Cosmic Mother" (and" Father"), God is the Transcendent Cosmic Spirit and life giving ("animating") omnipresent cosmic Reality who is the all-inclusive and living embodiment of the cosmos. In this understanding, it is God that is the ultimate source of life, embodiment of goodness, and destiny of all creatures, particularly, the human beings as historical embodiments of portions of God's eternal mind and spirit.

Within this global and inclusive and systematic theological perspective, God is the Creative Principle, Reality and Energy that initiated the "*big bang,*" and guided the evolution of life and creatures as the historical means of his creation as viewed from the human perspective of linear time or *chronos*. In God's eternity, there is only singularity. There is no present, past and future as in the human linear time or chronos, which is characterized by finite progression of events and history.

In God's eternity, everything is present in singularity as the eternal *single moment is the eternal now*! *Kairos* is God's right time for action in this non-chronological time of God. God contains chronos, but is not subject to its limitation of duration, space, distance, and speed! These finite dimensions do not define or determine God's actions. God's actions are determined by God's own freedom of Agape, grace, creativity, redemption and compassion.

True prayer is that of thanksgiving and not of petition! Petition requires God to act on the behalf of the creature. That sounds like magic or blackmailing God into action! Jesus affirmed that God hears prayers even before they are uttered by human beings. This is why silence before God is an effective form of prayer and listening to God's answer for prayer or communication to the self and the world. The prophets and saints found time for silence before God, as did Jesus and the Buddha. Monastic orders encourage this form of silence as a means to communicate with God at the level of spirit and mind where words are inadequate as tools for communication!

God is the Cosmic Mystery that created us or brought us into being as historical spirits and minds in his creation. God is the source of humanity regardless of whether or not human beings have been created by God indirectly through the amazing gradual process of biological evolution. It is a marvel that human beings and apes are, according to DNA, more than 99% biologically akin and yet very different in intelligence, behavior, technology and culture due to that remaining difference of less than one percent.

Ultimately, it does not really matter whether God's creation of the human being occurred in a more direct act of creation through a mere verbal command or molding clay and breathing life into it as the myths found in the Hebrew Bible suggest (Gen. 2:4-26). In terms of theology, God's intention was to create living human beings as the biblical accounts of Creation would suggest, if understood literally as history. It is a fact that we are now here as intelligent creatures. As such, what really matters then is that we are now here on this unique planet Earth, and that we are endowed with supernatural powers which distinguish us and set us apart from the rest of creation of which we are a part.

However, a literal reading of the Yahwist account of creation has an effect of creating a patriarchal system in which the man is Godlike and the woman is created as a secondary creature for the sake of the male. It is the male giving birth to the female through "*God's primordial biological process of human cloning,*" in as much as Eve as an adult person who is miraculously cloned from Adam's rib by God! (Gen. 2:21-25). Interestingly, God had to use anaesthesia to put Adam in a sleeping state while he operated on him to get a rib from which he cloned Eve. God as the primordial surgeon and biological genetic engineer is quite medically astounding!

Nevertheless, what is important is our special qualities that make us human and how we use them to actualize fully our divinely endowed full potential as authentic human beings. This human *self-actualization* is desired in order to live a more meaningful, and humane fellowship with other human beings, God, and the rest of God's creation on which he or she shares a symbolic relationship of mutual interdependence and coexistence.

This mutual coexistence of the human being also illustrates the very essential importance of the presence of the intelligent, spiritual and moral human being in material, non-moral, and non-thinking creation. We have already seen how this special nature and God-given human supernatural qualities force the human being into becoming "the divine Cosmic Priest and Mediator" representing creation and the world to God and God's word, love, holiness, care, and justice to the world. The biblical story of Noah's obedience and righteousness that saved the world from destruction in punishment for human evil clearly illustrates this very symbolic and priestly relationship between the human being and nature of the world.

Accordingly, Noah's story is not history, but an appropriate prophetic, environmentalist, moral and religious story about the world now. It states that the global human moral evil has a corresponding destructive global consequences on both humanity and the environment. Human moral evil and wickedness during the days of Noah were so great that it polluted all God's creation. The human being as the representative of God in creation and the mediator, and high-priest of creation who prays to God on behalf of creation has a central role to play in matters of creation, redemption and well-being of people, the environment and its preservation. Therefore, the story of Noah and punishment foreseen have to be viewed within this context:

> This is the story of Noah. He had three sons; Shem, Ham, and Japheth. Noah had no faults and was the only good man of his time. He lived in fellowship with God, but everyone else was evil in God's sight, and violence had spread everywhere.
>
> God looked at the world and saw that it was evil, for the people were living evil lives. God said to Noah: "I have decided to put an end to all humankind. I will destroy them completely, because the world is full of their violent deeds. Build a boat for yourself out of good timber; make rooms in it and cover it with tar inside and out. Make it 45O feet long, 75 feet wide, and 45 feet high.
>
> I am going to send a flood on earth to destroy every living being. Everything on earth will die but I will make a covenant with you. Go into the boat, with your wife, your sons, and their wives. Take into the boat with you a male and female of every kind of animal and every kind of bird. In order to keep them alive, take all kinds of food for you and for them. Noah did everything that God commanded. (Gen. 6:5-22)

This biblical story of redemption for all the species of animals makes it explicitly clear that God is interested in the salvation of human beings and animals. This is true even when God wishes to punish the world because of human moral evil and sin. At the same time, God's redemptive grace, mercy and unconditional love temper his divine justice with compassion and forgiveness. As a result, God seeks to punish human sin and sinners without destroying the world and all the different forms of life in it.

Ultimately, Noah is a theological and moral story with a universal religious meaning for humanity and the human being's role in the degradation or preservation of wild-life and the environment. Noah is a theological and moral ideal personification and symbol for any individual human obedience to God. He represents the ideal human ethical purity and righteousness that are the universal essential divine instruments for God's reign (Kingdom) and redemption of the world. Likewise, all human good deeds of self-sacrificial unconditional love, justice, mercy and peace come together to constitute a supernatural "lifeboat" for God's redemption and Kingdom in the world of sinners.

The parable of Noah and the flood is a theological illustration for teaching of the redemptive value of human faith, obedience in God's redemptive Agape, holiness, justice, grace, and interest in saving all the animal species. It is the effective religious and moral dramatization of the gravity of human sin and God's punishment as its consequence on the human community, nonhuman creatures and the world. Noah's story ends with the sign of the rainbow and God's promise never to destroy the world. This is clear theological indication that the story is more about the reality of God's unmerited mercy and his free universal saving grace for the world, more than about the history of sin and God's destruction of the world. It is concrete divine salvation in the surrounding sea of human moral evil, injustice, corruption, sin, and death.

However, those who seek the literal meaning of Noah's story in history do harm, by destroying the ethical value, moral meaning, and teaching of this story or parable as it would be simply dismissed as mere fable since the boat mentioned above is not even large enough to house one blue whale and all its required food for forty days.

Moreover, there is no way Noah would have gone to all parts of the globe to gather all the species of animals, insects, microorganism, and plant varieties in order to obey the divine command to preserve a pair of each creature. And if he could provide the space required to house all of these creatures and the required supply, it would have been greater than the size of Palestine itself.

## 6. God's Divine Incarnation in the World And Deification of the Human Being

Mainline Christianity affirms that God is omnipresent and has also, through the Logos, become historically incarnate in the world, its history and processes. Above all, God has, through the Logos (the Word), become incarnate in all humanity. This is what is symbolized by the doctrine of Jesus Christ as the Incarnation of the Logos and as the historical, perfect embodiment of Agape or God in the historical world, and particularly, within the human moral and spiritual or religious affairs.

Since God has become inseparably united with each human being by virtue of the incarnation, then perfect humanity such as that of Jesus or Buddha has also become the holy temple or medium for God's embodiment (incarnation), divine manifestation or self-revelation (*theophany*), and activities of creation, redemption or healing and restoration in the world and human history! Jesus was the best and perfect example of what any true human being can become and do in God's holy service in the world.

Like Jesus the Christ, each obedient and loving human being is also a true divine agent of God's creation and redemption in the world. He or she is like Christ, a true son and daughter of God! (cf. 1 John 1:1-18). All those obedient and loving people who possess unwavering faith in God are empowered by God's grace and their faith to do the very things which Jesus had done and possibly even exceed them.

In essence, in the Christian orthodox doctrine of the Incarnation as taught in Catholic, Anglican, and Eastern Orthodox Church dogmatic theologies, God became a human being in Jesus as the Christ so that the human being might symbolically also become God by virtue of this divine Incarnation. It is both positively and unequivocally affirmed that the Incarnation became permanently and irrevocably united with humanity in the person of Jesus Christ who is truly both God and human in permanent dual natures, coexisting harmoniously in the one person of Jesus Christ.

This Incarnational theology, though radical sounding, actually appears to be in line with the natural dual nature of the human being which is already described above as both divine and human, image of God and creature, and breath of God and dust. The Incarnational theology is also well founded in the New Testament, most especially in the Gospel of

John which identifies Jesus Christ with the eternal Logos (Word) of God who was God's very medium or principle of creation. St. John writes:

> Before the world was created, the Word already existed; he was with God, and he was the same as God. From the very beginning the Word was with God. Through him God made all things; not one thing was made without him. The Word was the source of life, and this life brought light to mankind. The light shines in the darkness, and darkness has never put it out.
>
> God sent his messenger, a man named John, who came to tell people about the light, so that all should hear the message and believe. He himself was not the light that comes into the world and shines on all mankind. (John 1:1-6)

John goes on to describe this divine and creative preexistent Logos or Word of God in the following divine redemptive terms:

> The Word was in the world, and though God made the world through him, yet the world did not recognize him. He came to his own people; they did not receive him. Some, however, did receive him and believed in him; so he gave them the right to become God's children. They did not become God's children by natural means; that is, by being born as children of a human father; God Himself was their Father.
>
> The Word became a human being, and full of grace and truth, lived among us. We saw his glory, the glory which he received as the Father's only Son. (John 1:12-14)

According to this biblical passage and teaching, Jesus as the Christ and the eternal creative Word *(Logos)* of God did not just become a human being, he also gave the supernatural power to all those who believed in him to become like himself. That is, they could become God's own children. In short, the believers in Christ have been given the power to become God. As children of God, the children have to be like their own Father both in essence and being. However, it is still difficult for most of us to accept the fact that in Christ, we have become like God our heavenly Parent, for this sounds like some kind of terrible blasphemy.

Ironically, this is the very kind of blasphemy of which Jesus, himself, was accused. Ultimately, he was put to death for it. But, as we know, he was innocent of this charge of blasphemy, because what he taught about himself and human nature was the truth. And since the world could not accept the truth that he taught, the religious leaders sought to get rid of him together with his followers. As a result, religion itself cannot have the unchallenged claim to the divine truth or revelation since it rejected the ultimate revelation of God and the divine truth in the person, life, and teaching of Jesus as the Christ.

This is still the main source of confusion, disobedience and evil in the world. The world still reflects God's revealed truth through the prophets, Jesus Christ, the prayer life of the saints, and the godly sermons of each age and generation. The disobedience constitutes spiritual, moral, political, and socioeconomic darkness and chaos in the world. This has sometimes led many to complete despair and skepticism as to whether God is in actual control of the world, and if so, whether this God is holy, benevolent, and loving, since the world seems to be engulfed in chaos and destructive evil, of which the human evil is the most deadly. Thus, the world is still in need of God's redemptive activity, regardless of the previous entry of God's Messiah to save the world.

It is true that evil and darkness seem to abound and threaten the very existence of all human and nonhuman life on this fragile planet. However, we should always remember that as long as we are Christian, peace loving, and obedient to God as God's ambassadors of love and peace in this deeply troubled world, there will always be the guiding divine light just like a lighthouse of God's eternal and universal light of salvation and peace. This is God's redemptive mission in the world that is accomplished through his saints. This work of God is carried out in the amidst of great storms of cosmic evil, turbulence, hatred, war, despair, and destruction. This is the eternal light of the redemptive God which has always shined in the cosmic darkness to drive away the primordial darkness of nothingness, chaos and lawlessness.

Subsequently, in the book of Genesis, we read that before God created anything, there was darkness and chaos and that God's creative word brought light into this primordial darkness and order into the prevailing chaos. Consequently, if the book of Genesis is correct in its affirmation, then it also follows that without God's continuing activities of both creation and redemption, the world and the entire cosmos would cease to exist. Without God as the ultimate reality, the cosmos and its natural laws vanish and return back into the primordial darkness and chaos or "nothingness" from which God had originally both created and redeemed them.

Fortunately, the Christian doctrine affirms that by the act of the Incarnation, God has not merely "come down" into the concrete material world and cosmic history in the "form," "embodiment" and "medium" of the human being. Rather, God has also become irrevocably unified with humanity itself by becoming a human being in Jesus Christ; as such, God has also in the act become inseparably bound not just with humanity, but with the created concrete world or Cosmos itself of which the human being is an integral part.

Therefore, the dissolution of the cosmos itself would also, to some extent, lead to the dissolution of God, since God has become inseparably bound with his or her creation through the Incarnation process. The Incarnation means not just mere human deification but also divine light, peace, and salvation into the world.

It is not surprising, therefore, to find that Christmas is a holiday which is observed almost universally, regardless of creed and political ideology. For instance, the former and good willed Soviet leader Mikhaill Gorbachev's 1987 New Years' greeting and message reveals that even those previously misunderstood as non-Christian communist nations, implicitly knew God and valued peace. They also valued this season as a time to reflect about the true meaning of humanity and mutual, peaceful co-existence. Gorbachev's message was reported by the New Year's day issues of major newspapers; one of them, the Tennessean, reported it as follows:

> Gorbachev told his countrymen that they must work much harder in the new year in order to overcome economic stagnation. He spoke of the overriding need for Americans and Soviets to learn how to "live in peace on this tiny and very fragile planet."

Gorbachev addressed the Soviet nation for eighty-one and a half minutes on television on New Year's Eve shortly before midnight. In 1986, Gorbachev told the Soviet people that the world and all people had become increasingly aware of the menace of war. He said:

> "Never before has the earth, our home, been subjected to such a danger," he said. "We are sincerely extending a hand of friendship and cooperation to all who favor immediate negotiations on the complete ending of nuclear tests, who favor immediate reduction and full destruction of nuclear weapons." . . . Gorbachev wished peace and prosperity to the American people . . . and said the realities of the nuclear age mean the superpowers must learn to live together. (*Tennessean*, Front page news, December 31, 1986).

One can hardly tell that this was a message from a Soviet Communist leader. It sounded similar to that of Pope John Paul II, as delivered both on Christmas Day and New Year's Day of 1887. In his message, the Pontiff called for global prayers of peace and denounced the destructive build-up of nuclear and other weapons of mass destruction. In fact, it was largely due to Gorbachev's initiative of global peace and call for reduction in nuclear weapons that finally led to the December 1987 Summit in Washington, D.C., and the historical Intermediate Nuclear Freeze [INF] Treaty.

For Christians, Christmastide is the special time to reflect on the angelic message of God's cosmic peace: "Glory to God in the highest, Peace on Earth and Goodwill toward all men and women" (Lk. 2:8-14). Indeed, Gorbachev's message was Christian! It was similar to the familiar Christmas prayers for goodwill and peace on the Earth. An example of these prayers is the Christmas bidding prayer which is read in many Episcopal/Anglican Churches on Christmas Day. It reads:

> Hear people of God; in this Christmas Season, let it be our duty and delight to hear once more the message of the angels, calling us to go to Bethlehem and see the son of God lying in a manger.
>
> Let us hear and heed in Holy Scripture the story of God's loving purpose from the time of our rebellion against him until the glorious redemption brought to us by his holy child Jesus, and let us make this place glad with our carols of praise.
>
> But first, let us pray for the needs of his whole world, for peace and justice on the earth, for the unity and mission of the Church for which Jesus Christ died, and especially for his Church in our country and city.
>
> And because he particularly loves them, let us remember in his name the poor and the helpless, the cold, the hungry and the oppressed, the sick and those who mourn, the lonely and the unloved, the aged and little children, as well as all those who do not know and love the Lord Jesus Christ.
>
> Finally, let us remember before God, his pure and lovely Mother, and that whole multitude which no one can number, whose hope was in the Word made flesh, and with whom, in Jesus, we are made one for evermore. (*The Episcopalian*, December Issue, 1987)

The Episcopal Church prayer for the international human family also echoes the same themes and messages:

> O God, you made us in your own image and redeemed us through Jesus your Son; look with compassion on the whole human family; take away the arrogance and hatred which infect our tears; break down the walls that separate us in bonds of love; and work through our struggle and confusion to accomplish your purposes on earth; that, in your good time, all nations and races may serve you in harmony around your heavenly throne; through Jesus Christ our Lord. Amen. (*Episcopal Book of Common Prayer*, p. 257)

This prayer portrays the world as God's Global Community. It prays for all people to live together in peaceful and loving relationships as members of God's loving "human family." This Christian invitation to a live a life of agape, free acceptance of all people as brothers and sisters, and to live a life of nonviolence requires great personal faith, self-sacrifice, obedience and God's power of grace in order to effect moral perfection. This calls for self-sacrifice, repentance and obedience within the Christian. Living truly according to God's will is difficult.

Nevertheless, because of the love, self-sacrificial service, dedication, faithfulness, and obedience of the few saints of God in the form of humble, godly men and women in the world, the world will be saved. God will redeem and save the world from evil and self-destruction by the virtue and work of these few saints who are ever interceding for the world and its sinful people before God's throne of grace and salvation. They do so for the world's salvation from an evil and suicidal course to self-destruction in a nuclear holocaust, disastrously detonated by the evil and hellish consuming fires of greed, bigotry, and hatred. But, because God has "come down" into our world of humanity and its human affairs, God will also find a way to avert and save us from evil and self-destructive egocentrism and hatred.

However, since we also have become like God in ourselves, by virtue of the Incarnation, therefore, we have also been given divine supernatural powers to act definitively in the world and to intervene in human and global affairs on God's behalf. Therefore, as the *Homo sapiens* who are the intelligent, free, knowing, thinking and moral agents in the world, we have God's special mandate to act in God's name to stop the evil of nuclear weapons, war, genocide, global suicide, and self-destruction. As God's own children, we have the power to accomplish all this for the praise and glory of God, and also in practical obedience to God's commandment of love.

The definitive commandment of Agape requires all human beings to love God and the neighbor in the same way in which they love themselves. Since most of us seek to live a satisfying, good life, we must also become aware that this is also the primary wish and priority of everyone else. This realization brings us to the acute awareness for the practical and moral need to cooperate and work together for the common good.

Ultimately, as intelligent, loving, social, peaceful and obedient moral agents, human beings everywhere in the world must unite and cooperate with all men and women in the world of good will in order to accomplish this priority goal, regardless of creed, race, color, or socioeconomic status. This is necessarily the case because fulfillment, peace and happiness represent the highest common good sought after by every living thing. This is particularly true for the human beings because of their higher intelligence. They are able to systematically search for the most meaningful, beneficial, satisfying, and happy forms of life.

Being social beings, the most satisfying mode of human life is also found within a life that is lived socially in love and peace. This kind of fulfilling life is found within the collective harmonious, moral, caring, just and peaceful communities in this world. Therefore, each person be taught how to find his or her true meaningful self-expression and fulfillment within mutually receptive social and loving fellowships with other people and in union with God. Within this context, God serves as the essential benevolent Center, Source and Guarantor of social order, love, justice, well-being, peace and happiness within this ideal human community as Heaven and God's Kingdom on the Earth. God's Kingdom and Heaven are here within God's saints and their loving activities. That was the teaching of Jesus (Lk. 17:20-21) and the Buddha.

## Chapter 7

# The Human Community As God's Arena for Creation And Redemption: Sex, Community and Humanity

God works *incognito* through the natural processes of evolution and history to effect the supernatural creation of humanity. The human community is God's universal divine arena for the supernatural activities of unmerited free grace and unconditional love in both supernatural creation and redemption. God's special creation and redemption of human beings take place naturally through the healthy and morally sound family, community and nation. Each moral community constitutes God's own universal and inclusive redemptive "Church." It is God's providential and effective channel for mediation of unconditional love, language, identity, moral consciousness, values, work-skills, knowledge, truth, freedom, responsibility, goodness, happiness and peace.

### 1. Good Works of Unconditional Love As God's Work (*Opus Dei*)

The intelligent human life (*Homo Sapiens*) is both simultaneously God's most wonderful supernatural product and special natural gift to the cosmos. The human life is a natural product of God's design to be accomplished through both the biological evolutionary process, and sexual reproduction within the moral and social context of a loving and responsible family.

God works *incognito* through this evolutionary and historical world. Through the processes of evolution and history God acts in this world both in a supernatural manner and through the natural law. God works through the ordinary human love and social activities of free and loving human beings to effect his or her divine activities of human creation and redemption. This supernatural process takes place quietly within the social context of free, moral and self-determining members of the loving family and responsible local community.

In this indirect manner and through these moral agents, God works *incognito* within the human society and history to create human beings as his or her special creatures in the world. Through this same medium, God also works within the world and the human community both to sustain and redeem human beings from sin and evil. That is, the human family and local community are God's arenas for God's supernatural activities of both special creation and redemption of human beings.

In this respect, the local family and the community are called to serve as God's primary redemptive "Church" in the world. The conventional Church is secondary. God's universal primary supernatural activities in the world are carried out incognito through the seeming ordinary processes of nature or natural law, and the correlative natural institutions, such as the human family and the human community. As such, God's supernatural creative and redemptive grace is universal and free.

Therefore, these divine activities cannot be limited to the Christian Church or any single group of people as God's own favored and chosen or elect people. God is impartial and just. God has no favorite religion or nationality of any people. God as the Creator and "Father" or "Mother" of all human beings, unconditionally loves all human beings. Therefore, God never excludes anybody from his or her supernatural activities of grace, such as creation, healing, forgiveness of sins, salvation, eternal life and Kingdom or heaven.

God, the cosmic Creator and Redeemer, is inseparable from natural law, good works of the prophets and obedient saints, as God's free and intelligent moral agents, temporal representatives in physical creation, minds and concrete ambassadors in the world. For most people, God is a good God because he or she has created the good cosmos, life, mind, spirit, beauty, mysteries and order. God's goodness and love sustain and redeem the cosmos from the evil threats of entropy, chaos and nonbeing.

All positive activities which are life enhancing, good, virtuous, loving and caring human works of compassion, charity, healing, peace, creativity, reproduction, order, and technological improvement to enhance of beauty in the world are part of God's work. These good human works are both correlative and coextensive with God's own indirect and mediated supernatural activities (*Opus Dei*) of creation and redemption of the world. This means that all good human works are both noble and sacred in nature, origin and benefit to the community and the world. This is the universal positive affirmation that all forms of good works constitute a ministry of service to God and God's people. For instance, a person can effectively serve God by doing garden or farm work, whereas another person can also serve God by taking up the ministry of healing as a doctor or nurse, while another can serve God by joining the ordained ministry, or joining the convent or monastery as a contemplative.

All these forms of service are valid and equal before God. God does not favor the ministry of preaching or administration of sacraments over that of healing or growing food to feed God's creatures and people in the cities. Another person may equally serve God by building good roads to transport God's people around the Earth. St. Paul evaluated these divine gifts and modes of service, and concluded that they all stem from the same supernatural source in God's Holy Spirit.

However, despite St. Paul's value and emphasis on the need for faith as a means of salvation (*sola fide*), Paul was convinced beyond any doubt that the practice of agape (unconditional love) was the highest divine gift. Like St. James (Jam. 2:12-16), St. Paul was also sure it was not faith, but rather the praxis of agape that was the definitive work of God that transcended all other divine gifts and ministries (cf. Cor. 12-13). Since God also is defined in the New Testament as Agape (1 John 3:7), then, it also follows that all works of agape are, therefore, to be regarded with reverence as a manifestation of God in human history.

As such, whoever performs the good and self-sacrificial works of agape (unconditional love) becomes like Jesus the Christ and God. He or she becomes the local extension of God's redemptive work in Christ. He or she unites with Jesus the Christ in obedience to God and joins in the divine redemptive mission in the world. He or she has also become God's moral saint and the effective local concrete divine agent for the societal divine mediation of God's love, grace and salvation in the community.

Ultimately, God's work in the temporal world and human history is carried out both indirectly and incognito through the impersonal processes of the natural law, and more intimately through the obedient people of God or the saints. At a personal, social and historical level, God carries out his or her special activities through the works of inspired, well-motivated, intelligent, visionary, skilled, talented, obedient and loving human beings who serve as the holy saints and concrete representatives of God in cosmic creation or the world and it's complex evolutionary and historical processes.

God's supernatural works in the physical and temporal world are performed naturally through the loving, skilled and obedient people to perform miracles in the world, and to provide the world with his guiding lights (luminaries). As a result, the works of God's obedient saints like Buddha, the messiahs, and prophets like Moses, Jesus, and Muhammad are in this theological, philosophical and anthropological understanding also positively affirmed and proclaimed to the world as God's real supernatural redemptive work in human history and the world. Ultimately, God creates and redeems his people through his obedient and loving people or servants.

Therefore, the loving and good activities of any free, obedient moral agents and saints of God in the world, are also essentially both correlatively and coextensively, God's mediated loving, creative and redemptive supernatural activities in the world. In other words, the ordinary works of nature (natural law) and those of obedient, just and loving human beings are both spontaneously and simultaneously, the works of God. That is, God and nature, God and humanity are inseparably intertwined and the same applies to their good activities in the world. Accordingly, we talk of God's unconditional love, forgiveness, peace and justice because we have either experienced them or hope to experience them through our interaction with God's people in the world.

## 2. God, Evolution and Community

All universal forms of meaningful human evolutionary life and authentic modes of human existence emerge and take place within the social and interactive ideal existential context. This ideal existential context consists of any peaceful community that is truly loving, caring and peaceful. At the "micro" level, the community consists of the ideal human family which is the basis of sound, peaceful and enduring human community or society. At the macro level, the human community consists of the state, nation, and ultimately, the global human community.

Furthermore, every human community serves as God's concrete agent and embodiment of freedom, creativity, reproduction (human creation), identity, love, protection, moral law, values, guidance (redemption), fulfillment, fellowship and happiness. In addition, each respective community everywhere in the world, also both defines and declares God's moral law to the people.

The obedient and moral community accomplishes this special divine moral and redemptive task by formulations of laws and instituting customs that set limits on human causal freedom, and setting guiding moral principles to direct and regulate the Godlike human powers for infinite creativity. This is done in order to avoid the human's potential for creation of negative things, chaos, discord, imbalance and evil in God's balanced and good world.

All human communities impose limits on human freedom and creativity in order to promote order, harmony, peace, fellowship and happiness in the community. This heavenly mode of the blessed state of life in love, peace and fellowship with the neighbor and God is possible everywhere in this world. This is because this world is both correlative and coextensive with God's Kingdom, and heaven, for all the obedient, moral, caring, loving and responsible members of the community and the world, in which we live.

In other words, for God's obedient people or saints, life in this world is also to be positively experienced and valued as one would in God's Kingdom and heaven, for that is the true spiritual and moral state of this world as God both intended and created it. That is, we all live in God's Kingdom and heaven. Unlike most intellectually satisfied or naive people, Aken Aton, Moses, Plato, Buddha and Jesus realized this truth, namely, that God's Kingdom was truly present in the world and was manifested in the lives and works of his obedient saints.

For instance, Siddhartha became the Buddha or the man who woke up from spiritual ignorance through the realization that despite the finitude of humanity and suffering, this life and the world were God's gifts. This spiritual and moral enlightenment liberated him from the chains of desire for material satisfaction, which is rooted in the ignorance of the universal attainment of mental and spiritual forms of satisfaction and happiness through prayer and contemplation (*Raja Yoga*). Jesus also engaged in a self-disciplined life of prayer (contemplation), good works (*Karma Yoga*) of unconditional love and forgiveness of sins (*Bakti Yoga*).

Jesus positively affirmed the universal reality of human moral and spiritual union with God through faith, prayer, obedience and good works (Matt. 5-7; 25:31-46). Accordingly, he declared: "The Father and I are one" (John 14:15). Like Buddha, Socrates and Plato, Jesus also taught that people should know the Truth, and the Truth would set them free (*Jnana Yoga*). As such, the teachings of Buddha and those of Jesus are not mutually exclusive, nor do they negate each other. On the contrary, the religious and moral teachings of both Jesus and Buddha complement each other and together provide a more meaningful and comprehensive moral and spiritual regiment of self-discipline and paths for the attainment of moral and spiritual enlightenment, well-being, mystical union with God, peace and happiness.

## 3. The Human Community as God's Universal Medium and Agent Of Human Creation and Redemption

Human beings and their communities are results of both the mediated and indirect special evolutionary creative processes of God, through the complex laws of nature, evolution, culture, mind and divine revelation. In both the theological and philosophical language, I will define human beings as "God's own voluntary, partial embodiments or incarnations of portions of his or her mind, freedom, spirit, creativity, love, grace, power, intellect, truth, self-transcendence, and moral consciousness."

Within this Hegelian evolutionist and dialectical paradigm, and philosophical-theological understanding, each obedient or authentic human being is by essential nature as an *imago Dei* (God's image cf. Gen. 1:26-31), also God's true incarnation that are best manifested in men like obedient Jesus the Christ, Krishna and Buddha. As such, to see a truly obedient and loving saint of God in the world, such as Jesus, Buddha and Mother Teresa, is truly to catch a spiritual and mystical glimpse of God in the community, history and the world. These saints as the true *imago Dei* also effectively manifest God glory (*theophany*). Through their lives and work, we see the glorious reflection of the eternal invisible perfect, loving and the benevolent creative-redemptive cosmic Spirit that we call God.

Each human being is both an evolutionary special creation of God, and the social product of the local community. No human being ever got created and redeemed by God outside the concrete human community. Because of the diversity and variations of the human communities in the world, human beings also vary in their cultures, religions, world-view, history, concepts of God and historical experiences of life.

This universal phenomenon of human racial diversity, cultural and religious pluralism is natural and normal. Ultimately, biological, racial, cultural, linguistic, and religious diversity is good, and exists as God's universal will. Diversity universally exists as God's judgement and rejection of the life-negating monolithic structures, despite the fact that many human beings prefer these ethnocentric and monolithic structures. Tribalism, ethnic nationalism, nepotism, racism, and bigoted exclusivist religious doctrines which claim that only members of that religion will go to heaven, are rooted in this idolatrous quest for monolithic structures as the ideal. Exclusive doctrines of election, covenant, Church and salvation for Christians only, are examples of this tragic, monolithic teachings.

Ultimately, it is due to human sins and evils of xenophobia, ethnocentrism, imperialism, sexism and racism, that most Western Christians have in the past erroneously taught that only baptized Christians were God's redeemed children and heirs of God's salvation as eternal life and the kingdom. Fortunately, Vatican II rejected this traditional teaching, and by its "*Decree on Non-Christian Religions,*" positively reaffirmed the existence of the universality of God's efficacious redemptive grace, and the correlative existence of God's supernatural salvation and his Kingdom, both within and outside the traditional Christian Church. This ecclesiastical, historical, radical declaration recognized non-Christian religions like Hinduism and Buddhism as valid and efficacious arenas of God's universal supernatural activities of free redemptive grace and salvation.

Within this inclusive, Christian systematic and global soteriological (redemptive) theological and evolutionist religious context, any moral human community constitutes the authentic and efficacious medium of grace as the true universal supernatural arena for God's mediated and indirect supernatural creative and redemptive activities. Therefore, the moral human community anywhere in the world must be positively viewed as God's unconditional free stage of God's comic activities of grace, particularly those dealing with the creation of human beings, providence, love, protection, morality, sin, evil, guilt and redemption. Within this setting, any human moral community constitutes the true, universal (catholic), and inclusive redemptive Church through God's universal and eternal Logos-Christ.

It is this same eternal Logos that serves as God's principle agent for cosmic creation, life, mind, evolution, sustenance of creation, order, positive transformation and deliverance from evil or redemption. This Logos or Word of God is omnipresent in the world and is incarnate in each person, but was more visibly active in the lives of Buddha and Jesus-Christ (cf. John 1-3; 14-15). Each human being and community are God's embodiment and indirect manifestations of God (*theophany*) to the world. Sometimes God's own light, glory, love, grace and power are not clearly revealed and communicated to the world through human beings and the community due to human disobedience, sin, and evil or moral failure to do the good. God's *theophany* is seen in the world through people like Moses, Jesus, Buddha and the saints because of their faith and obedience to God's commandments of love, justice, simplicity, humility, benevolence, and self-sacrificial good works.

Accordingly, each moral human community in the world is "God's moral agent." Therefore, it can either positively or negatively serves as God's concrete moral and social arena, as well as being the tangible temporal moral agency for historical creative and redemptive of human beings. It also serves as the normative and "deontological" or external source, embodiment and enforcer of religion, culture, normative values, laws and customs that are necessary for the guidance and protection of all the citizens of the community.

However, the ideal moral position is the "teleological one." This is the internalized ideal moral state of the individual's inner state of ecstasy due to the attainment of a mature or higher state of moral and spiritual consciousness of God and divine mental illumination or spiritual enlightenment. This heavenly state or *"Nirvana"* comes from the immediate and direct human spiritual and encounter and intuitive mental apprehension of the infinite Mystery (God) as the cosmic Infinite Unconditional Love (Agape), pure supernatural experiential presence of contentedness and peace within the saint's contemplative life, mind and soul. This is the "*kairotic moment*" of life, the *beatific vision* and eternal life as life lived in love, nonviolence, justice, and complete union and loving fellowship with both God and one's fellow human beings. Buddha called this experience of "*Nirvana*" or "heaven." Religious people seek this same experience of heaven through good deeds, faith, worship, sacraments, contemplation, prayer and reading the scriptures, and some less religious people seek the same heavenly experience through food, alcohol, mind altering drugs and sex.

The second category of spiritual quest for fulfillment through physical things is not satisfactory. It provides false temporary physical pleasures as permanent remedies and cures for a spiritual craving, and indirect quest for God's infinite love and peace. This physical hedonistic and capitalist method of spiritual quest for fulfillment, often leads to materialism, accumulation of things, and ultimately, leads to tragic addiction to sex, food and drugs. It also leads to the heightened sense of the insatiable desire (*Tanha*) or craving for constant physical indulgence and satisfaction in material things. As such, true fulfillment is only attainable through a non-materialistic, simple, self-disciplined life of meaningful work, positive faith, love, prayer, and contemplation.

In this ideal moral state, the human being as a free, intelligent, responsible, self-disciplined, critically thinking, well-informed, self-regulating moral agent has reached the highest moral level of moral education, in which the positive moral and civic virtues have been correctly learned and internalized. The individual as a self-policing and morally responsible moral agent seeks to do the good and right thing. The responsible moral agent does not do good because the community or the external moral authority, such as God, the Church, the law courts, police, government, parents, peers and tradition require it. Rather, as both a religious and moral saint, he or she seeks to do the good because it the right and correct thing to do in that situation. The potential consequences of the moral action are seriously taken into account before the action is carried out. If the consequences are perceived to be negative and harmful to the individual, the community or the environment (God's creation), then, that action is judged to be evil or harmful.

However, for the less morally responsible and immature people, the community and its laws are the necessary moral guides to ensure the enduring existence of the ideal societal conditions of order, harmony, good deeds, civility, peace and happiness for the individuals and their respective communities. As a result, the responsible moral community also universally serves as God's moral agent by disciplining and punishing the disobedient, criminal and sinful members of the community. The moral community has also the universal and inescapable intrinsic, societal, moral obligation to serve as God's redemptive and forgiving community or God's inclusive "Cosmic Church." They accomplish this divine task through the mediation of God's own mercy, forgiving and transforming and redemptive grace. This is achieved through the peaceful mediation of conflicts, restoration of the alienated through moral education, rehabilitation and purgatory-like reformatory schools and jails or other correctional institutions.

"Existential hell" as a permanent excommunication and banishment from the community through life imprisonment or capital punishment, is likewise, often carried out by many communities. These kinds of moral judgements and sentences are often pronounced in God's name and ceremonially imposed by judges, or other authorized members of the community, upon notorious sinners or criminals and non-reformable people, such as serial rapists, and murderers.

Ultimately, the moral community, by essential divine and normative moral nature, also effectively functions as God in regard to the functions which we attribute to God as "creator," "protector," "provider," "sustain er," "redeemer," "lawgiver," "judge," and "the source of reward or blessing for the obedient saints." The moral community serves as God's arena and concrete medium for God's supernatural provision, sustenance and fulfillment of these essential human needs for security, peace, as well as social, physical, emotional, spiritual, moral and economic well-being!

In anthropomorphic and concrete imagery of God, one can say that the moral, creative, caring, loving, peaceful, protective, happy, enduring and redemptive community is in this sense, both symbolic of God and heaven for its obedient, humane, nonviolent, just, caring and loving members! For that matter, Buddhists and Christians have consciously deified their founders and worshiped them as God!

Therefore, if the respective local community fails to meet these essential human, physical, social and spiritual needs, its members negatively feel spiritually abandoned by God. As a result, the deprived people experience both degradation and dehumanization. They feel both rejected by God and the human community. As a result, they negatively experience life and the world in which they live. For them, this life and world are experienced as if they were in "hell," or suffering some kind of divine punishment for their sins and those of their own ancestors. In many cases, this is the kind of negative experience of life and the world that results into *angst* as existential anxiety, despair and suicide. Suicide is an attempt to escape from life because it is, at that time (either due to great depression, terminal disease or pain), perceived to have become too painful and unbearable.

It is this kind of extreme *angst* and pessimism about life, humanity, and the world that characterizes much of the Western theistic and atheistic forms of existentialism as found thinkers like Dostoevsky, Kafka, Kierkegaard, Nietzsche, Jaspers, Heidegger, Sartre, Camus, Buber and Tillich. It is also the same kind of erroneous, pessimistic world-view and anthropology that created the spiritual and societal moral trauma of a supposed historical human fall from the "original perfection" and the supposed consequent universal "original sin."

This erroneous assumption of the primordial human perfection, disobedience, and "original sin" led to the wrong assumption that all human beings now exist in an imperfect state of "fallenness" and alienation from God's original love, grace and fellowship. The result being that human beings are estranged from both God and one another. They live in self-estrangement and live the imperfect life of unhappiness. They also erroneously perceive that this is an evil world from which they need to be redeemed by God. Christians have added another erroneous and false soteriological dogma which teaches that only those who believe in Jesus and get baptized into the Christian Church, are the only people who will be redeemed by God from evil, death and destruction.

## 4. The Loving Human Community as God's Inclusive and Universal Redemptive Church

Within the evolutionary and global scientific context and understanding, the moral human community is God's one, true, universal (catholic), inclusive, and redemptive Church. The theological Christian positive affirmation of the community as God's redemptive Church is consistent with God's will and supernatural activities through the historical evolutionary process of the world. It is also consistent with any coherent, systematic, inclusive Christian, global philosophical-theological approach of this book on Christian theology and ethics.

All authentic modes of human existence are positively viewed as essential components of God's redemptive work in the world and the Church. They are all positively affirmed to be the historically and locally God-given media for human creation and redemption of all the loving and obedient members of those communities and systems of human life. This is true, inasmuch as these cultural and religious media are the fundamental sources of human values, culture, language, civilization, identity, truth, love, self-fulfillment, meaning, security, peace and the promises or hope for happiness.

In order to accomplish this universal divine task for the humanization and redemption of their respective members, these human-divine institutions are expected to meet an acceptable degree of some visible and universal measurable moral criteria. For instance, they must be intrinsically caring, just, social, loving, humanely interrelational and mutually interdependent. This prior existence of caring and loving people gets coextensively institutionalized in the form of a caring, loving and peaceful human family, community, nation and the Global Community. However, as time passes, the institutions takeover the role of creating and shaping the cultures, values, religions, conscience, skills, technology and destiny of their respective members.

The universal truth about humanity can be stated in new evolutionist and contemporary moral, philosophical and theological terms as follows: "*No human being is ever created or redeemed by God in isolation of other people and the community.*" Without the evolution of the human family and the community, there is no individual human being.

According to this anthropological and theological understanding, the human being and community are inseparable. Each human being as a moral agent has many essential needs. He or she needs nurture, education and socialization (inculturation) or humanization, personal experiential existence within a caring, moral, cultural and social community. These needs need to be met prior to the special creation or divinization and redemption of the individual as a responsible moral agent, productive and reliable member of that respective human community or social institution. One gets his or her identity in terms of genetic, cultural, social, linguistic, moral and religious inheritance from the human community in which he or she is born or becomes an adopted member.

This argument or observation is almost analogous to that of the chicken and the egg. This is in terms of relationships and existence based on chronological time. What came first? The egg of the chicken? This puzzle of chronological linear time and relationships applies to other dimensions of life, such as "lover," "love" and "the beloved." Is love the cause of the relationship between the lover and the beloved or a result of the relationship between the two people? Does the sequence matter?

For some Western individualistic thinkers like Locke and Hobbes who wish to view the community as a convention and a contractual society created by individuals, may wish to assert the primacy of the individual over the community. However, for the traditional Africans, Asians and Native Americans, the existence of the community is prior to the creation, and existence of the respective individual members of the community who constitute it. The analogy is that of the body and its constitutive individual cells. At anytime, the various individual cells may be die and be replaced by the body as it creates new cells.

Likewise, the human community one created, in turn, it gives birth to its respective members, nurtures and protects them from physical harm, moral and spiritual evil. A person without a community is both socially and morally lost. He or she is like a single buffalo that has become lost and separated from the security of the herd. Regardless of its strength, the buffalo without a herd is vulnerable to predators, even small ones, such as packs of wolves.

Traditionally, this universal truth, regarding the social nature of creation and salvation in community was only vaguely taught. In this partial, and yet exclusive form, it was both taught and affirmed by the dogmatic Catholic teachings on Church, sacraments and salvation. This famous soteriological teaching, and the affirmation of Christ and the Church as the only and exclusive embodiment, source and mediation of God's supernatural salvation in the world was definitely and provocatively formulated as: "*Extra Ecclesiam Nulla Salus*" (*Outside the [Roman Catholic] Church, there is no salvation).* Fortunately, this bigoted Christian exclusive doctrine was rejected by the reformist Catholic Church Council of the Vatican II of 1963-65. The theologians of Vatican II led by Karl Rahner correctly affirmed the inclusion of all obedient and loving non-Christians among God's redeemed saints, true citizens of God's Kingdom, heaven, salvation and eternal life.

Therefore, this anachronistic traditional dogma of the Church, sacraments and salvation, can be more inclusively and theocentrically reformulated as: "Outside the loving and peaceful human community, there is no salvation." The *Logos* remains the active agent of God's universal activities creation and redemption. Moreover, God both creates and redeems all human beings, through the special media of the loving family and the community.

The loving community is God's inclusive universal creative and redemptive medium or the true "One, Catholic (universal) Church of God." One enters this inclusive Church by virtue of birth into the human community. One accepts the obligation of this membership by living a peaceful, productive and humane life in practical acceptance and obedience of God's implicit universal divine moral commandment "to love the neighbor without condition" and "to do the necessary good works" of unconditional love, grace, justice, as an essential requirement of moral obedience, active faith in God's cosmic goodness, justice, unmerited grace and unconditional love.

In the same way in which the human being is both animal and divine, human communities are likewise, both human and divine correlative as well as coextensive special institutions. The special institutions of the human family and the human community are God's special arenas of God's universal free creative and redemptive grace. In the context of the family and community, God indirectly creates each human being and provides for his or her well-being through the natural love and obedience of the parents, relatives and the caring or supportive members of the community.

Therefore, what parents and members of the community fail to perform in love for the child, as God's child, extends the conditions of sin, hell and misery for the child as both a human being and a child of God. This is because the human beings as God's ambassadors and free moral agents are the agents and effective concrete mediators of God's grace, love, peace, life, creativity, goodness and God's Kingdom within the family, the community and the world. Hell is the result of human free will, negative choice, rebellion against God's will, and general moral failure of this human moral agency and special divine mandate.

This complex human and divine nature of the family and all human communities is as true for the Church as it is for the family, community and the state. All these special cultural, supernatural and societal institutions are universal. They exist in many, and different locally appropriate cultural forms. Despite their diversity, differences, imperfections and pluralism, they were indirectly universally established by God in human moral and cultural evolutionary stages of the evolution of mind, self-consciousness, culture, religion and morality.

This evolutionary process was accomplished through human moral agency and mediation (inspiration) of both the divine "*Logos*" (Word of God) and the Holy Spirit. As such, all these human-divine institutions, including all religions and churches are by intrinsic nature and constitution evolutionary and imperfect. They are as perfect or imperfect just like the very human beings who instituted them in the society in God's name. To make them special, the primordial human founders of these institutions "theologically endowed them with both divine authority and supernatural origin." These people accomplished this complex and delicate religious task through the employment of myth, story, poetry and parables. Through the societal and pedagogical devise of story and mythology, human beings were led to accept the non-verifiable dogmatic claim and positive affirmation that God "himself" had directly founded those institutions in the ancient times.

It was also in this mythological manner that Jesus was declared, by his human followers or the early Church, to be born of a Virgin because he was "the eternal Son of God" and "God incarnate in humanity." This doctrine became popular with many early Church superstitious Christians. The more intellectually sophisticated Greeks rejected Christianity on the intellectual basis that they found these teachings illogical, contradictory and absurd.

Being well educated in both Hebrew theology and Greek philosophy, St. Paul tried the art of logic and philosophy to reason with them in hope to convert them to Christianity. Paul tried to win them by using Greek philosophy and logic. He wanted to convince them through reason to accept that Jesus was the incarnation of God who died to provide atonement for human sins and that he rose again to life on the third day. Paul tried to convince them to accept the "Good News" (Gospel) that they could gain immortality by accepting his teaching, and getting baptized in the name of the risen Jesus as their Lord and savior. Nevertheless, Paul was unsuccessful in his missionary work to these Greek philosophers (Acts 17). They found it absurd that Paul taught that the natural corruptible body could become immortal through a ritual of baptism.

As a result, St. Paul concluded that only faith (*sola fide*) would lead people to salvation since no intelligent people could rationally accept the central Christian doctrine or teaching that Jesus was the special historical incarnation of God and the agent of God's supernatural salvation in the world. Unfortunately, this Pauline doctrine has had serious negative consequences for the Christian Church. There were many Christians, like Tertullian, Anselm, and Luther, who erroneously believed that Christians should not emphasize the central role of reason in faith and Christianity.

There were also some other Christian thinkers, like Origen, Clement, Augustine, Aquinas and Descartes, who maintained that the mind and reason were part of God's own divine essence, and therefore, were superior to the gift of faith. These proponents of the divine minds and intellect also positively affirmed that like the senses, the proper exercise of faith had to be also governed by reason through sound logic and both critical and analytical thought. In this process, the entertainment of doubt and experimentation to verify empirical or revealed truth were considered to be part of Christianity and not the enemy of true religious faith. Religious faith was the grounding and starting point for early science and research, such as that of Aquinas, Copernicus, Kepler, Mendel and Einstein. Charles Darwin himself was a man of great Christian faith. He was buried in St. Paul's Cathedral, London after his death.

Therefore, unlike the Catholic seminaries which embrace philosophy as an inseparable part of theology and sound Christian ministerial education, most Protestants being Pauline in theology, omit courses in philosophy in most of their traditional seminaries. They reject the fundamental epistemological importance and moral essence of teaching philosophy as a core part of the seminary education and sound theological training for the ordained Christian ministry. As a result, Protestant scholars have not done a good job in the research fields of theology and ethics. As a result, the leading scholars in these areas are Catholics and Protestants who trained in nondenominational universities.

In general, the ancient Christians were still influenced by their own "pagan" world-view and background from which they had been recently converted. Their primitive world-view, values, education, culture, language, expectations, technology, philosophy and theology are alien to us today. We cannot accept their primitive world-view, culture, values and theology as our own today. Their values were good and appropriate guides for them in their era, cultural and religious context. Therefore, to adopt those antiquated moral values and religious codes for our communities today would be to disobey God's revelation for us today and return the past. Behold, the past is gone, and God is creating new life and new things today. We are to seek God's will and revelation for us today, as they did in their own age. The answers of the past are no longer valid for today or tomorrow.

To the discomfort of many conservative, exclusivist and bigoted religious people, it must be pointed out that this affirmation of religious relativism does not exclude any supposedly specially revealed and redemptive favored religions, including the Christian Church. Western Christian missionary activities based on this theology are misguided, ethnocentric, religious and cultural forms of imperialists. Apart from agape and free forgiveness of sins, Christianity has no special message for the world. Yet, missionary Christianity never emphasizes these central tenets of Christianity. Instead, missionary Christianity preaches Christian "traditions of men" and the Western culture!

Jesus rejected much of the traditional Judaism on the basis that it was composed of mere traditions of men (Mk.7). Jesus would do the same with today's corrupt expressions of Christianity and Islam. Any form of Christianity that is devoid of its essential authentic center in the moral and spiritual teachings of Jesus Christ's definitive commandment of unconditional love for God, the neighbor and free extension of forgiveness of sins, is both a false Christianity, and harmful religion. Such a Christian tradition has lost its moral and spiritual foundation, center, objective, message (God News), and has become corrupted into a mere "Christendom" as Soren Kierkegaard correctly called it.

Accordingly, the observation of universal religious imperfection as well as spiritual, moral, epistemological and soteriological relativism includes Judaism, Christianity and Islam, which ethnocentrically claim to be the specially revealed and redemptive religions of God. Each one of these three revealed religions exclusively claims to be special historical institution of God's direct, special, and exclusive redemptive revelation. For instance, the foundation of Judaism by God is through the Covenant of Moses with the Hebrews; Christianity is founded through the Covenant of Jesus and his atoning death on the cross, and finally, Islam is founded by God through Prophet Muhammad the human agent that recited the holy Qur'an as God supposedly dictated it from heaven through the angel Gabriel.

Within this academic context, all these exclusive religious dogmatic claims are treated as both idolatry and false claims to the possession of absolute divine revelation as immutable truths. These mutually exclusive dogmatic religious claims to possess God's universal and definitive immutable revelation and redemptive truth is the fundamental basis of the Christian and Islamic dangerous forms of religious fundamentalism, bigotry, mutual intolerance and bloodshed.

For the intelligent, open-minded, loving and rational people, anywhere in the world, it should be a self-evident universal truth that God has neither favorite people nor any rejected people. It is very clear that God has no favorite or preferred race of people, nationality, language, culture, religions, religious sects or denominations, liturgical forms of worship and form of sacred texts as divinely inspired and revealed scriptures! The holy Bible is not more preferred by God than the holy Qur'an or the Veda. The Bible has no advantage over the Qur'an before God and nor does the Qur'an and its devoted followers have any advantage before Allah as the Almighty God, "the Compassionate" cosmic "Judge" and "the Merciful Redeemer" of all obedient human beings.

The creation of all human beings, the universal implicit societal moral and spiritual awareness and need for peace (*salaam*, *shalom* or *neema/mirembe* or *obusingye*) as an obligatory universal basic religious teaching, and the presence of love-inspiring teachings are due to God's nature, will and revelation. These teachings transcend human cultures, families, communities, sacred texts and religions. The loving, harmonious and peaceful human community is coextensive with both the true redemptive Church and God's Kingdom in the world. It is also the very definitive universal arena of God's activities of unmerited supernatural grace, and unconditional love in historical, social, and natural as well as special acts of human creation and redemption in the world.

Without the existence of a sound, healthy, caring, loving and peaceful human family and community, there can never be any authentic human beings who are happy, law-abiding, humane, just, caring, loving, responsible and free moral agents. These noble and ideal, civic, moral virtues are inseparable from the families and communities which embody and mediate them to their respective obedient members. These noble ideals, values and both moral and spiritual virtues cannot be effectively mediated by God through a social, moral, spiritual, cultural and linguistic vacuum. On the contrary, they are both universally and supernaturally decreed by God as his or her will. However, they are concretely both imperfectly and universally mediated naturally through the gradual historical evolution of mind, God or moral consciousness which are coextensive with the emergence of the respective local cultural and religious institutions.

Ultimately, all good societal, cultural, religious, moral and spiritual values are learned in a stable, loving and peaceful family and the supportive community in which the family is located. Accordingly, unlike Judaism, Christianity, and Islam, the ancient Africans, Native Americans and Hindus of India correctly viewed the omnipresence of God in the universe including God's incarnate presence in every human being. Understandably, members of these non-Western religions both reverently and correctly regarded every human being as both a supernatural spiritual being and child of God. As a result, they treated every person as a religious being who was created with an intrinsic knowledge of God and needed to be nurtured in that implicit God-consciousness and reverence for all life and creation as part of God's revelation and divine mystery, as opposed to being converted to a new religion.

## 5. The Human Family and Community As Agents of God's Supernatural Creation and Redemption

God's supernatural activities of creation and redemption take place locally, within the context of the loving family and peaceful community. This is the place where the newborn encounters both God and humanity. This is where human beings as agents of God's creation and redemption are most effective. They can save the child or even rebel and kill it before or after birth!

St. Matthew's Gospel reports that Joseph and Mary, Jesus' parents, went to Egypt in a voluntary exile, in order to ensure the safety of their son (Matt. 2:13-15). This is an example of how God works through the family to protect children through the moral, benevolent, and self-sacrificial or any good actions of their parents. Parents, relatives, and other loving adults are God's guardian angels for the young!

Most religious people are theologically anthropomorphic. That is, they talk about God as if God were some kind of mighty king or supernatural human being, such as "Superman," living high in the sky (heaven) or on the tops of high mountains. The wise and great womanizing God, in the form of Zeus, was an anthropomorphic Greek mythological rendition of such a God! The anachronistic Christian christological myths and superstitious ancient doctrines of Jesus as the physical incarnation of God in time, history and the world as Messiah or Savior of the Jews from the Roman occupation, moral evil, disease and the scourge of death, have to be rejected and revamped for today's age.

These mythological Christian doctrines include the literal Virgin Birth, and the idolatrous view that Jesus is God, or was the divine Christ who was the true physical historical manifestation of the invisible God or the physical incarnation of the eternal God into the finitude of humanity, limitations of linear chronological time, and cosmic history is another concrete anthropomorphic example. The Jesus Movement, like Strauss and Bultmann before them, wishes to demythologize the Christian doctrines and thereby liberate Christianity from the chains of superstition and false doctrines.

Many poorly educated fundamentalist clergy, uninstructed laity, and other religiously misguided Christians erroneously believe that the scriptures are the inspired, literal, and inerrant or infallible Written Word (Logos) of God. As a result, most of these people often literally read the scriptures as an accurate record and history of God's activities in the world. They interpret the biblical mythological stories of creation, Noah's flood, Job and the myths of Jesus' Virgin Birth as history.

Subsequently, these Christian literalists regard Jesus as God's physical incarnation in the man Jesus-Christ, and therefore, make it difficult to have a meaningful ecumenical and interfaith theological dialogue. This is especially true when it comes to an interreligious dialogue with the more radical monotheistic Muslims and Jews who regard the traditional Christian doctrines of the divine Incarnation and God's definitive universal self-revelation in the man Jesus of Nazareth as dangerous religious myths of human self-deification, blasphemy and idolatry. The Christian doctrine of the Holy Trinity where God is worshiped as God the Father, God the Son and God the Holy Spirit as one Godhead that eternally consists in three equal and inseparable divine persons, becomes terribly confusing to many scholars, religious leaders and lay people. It is rejected by both Judaism and Islam in the name of true monotheism.

As a result of the Christian doctrines of the divine Incarnation, many Christians seem to prefer to "worship a man" called "Jesus as God," and ignore the rest of the complications of this form of idolatry. No man can ever truly become the eternal God. Nevertheless, this human desire for self-deification and immortality remain the universal human temptations. This is due to divine nature of human intellect, self-transcendence, divine nature, sin of hubris, self-deification and idolatry! Within Christianity, this human desire for self-deification is best expressed in the doctrine of the God's Incarnation. This doctrine teaches that God has become a human being through the person of Jesus the Christ (cf. John 1-3).

Conversely, through the Divine Incarnation, the human being has also become divinized to become reconciled and united with God, or "has become God." This is the essence of the Christian doctrine of the "Hypostatic Union" as a theory of the Incarnation. In short, in Divine Incarnation, the human being as the *imago Dei* (subject) has become unified and identical with its own "object" (God) of reflection. As such, Jesus taught that to serve humanity is to serve God (cf. Matt. 25:31-46).

In reality, each normal human being both explicitly and implicitly desires to become God and attain God's unlimited power. This divinity and power are desired and sought by the human being in order to control time, govern his or her life and determine his or her destiny. Human being seek God's power in order to control life, and also attain the unlimited capacity to exercise power over other people, society, history and determine cosmic events. The popularity of the energy theory as found among the "New Age" people is a result of this quest for divine power or energy, as well as the desire to become God! Evil tyrants like Adolph Hitler and Idi Amin are recent examples of this hubris and quest to control the world's affairs!

## 6. Patriarchal Communities: Male Self-Deification And Oppression of Women

God created both male and female in his or her own image (Gen. 1:26-31) to represent God in the world. This "priestly" account of creation has received less attention by those who prefer to exclude women from power, ordination and Church leadership. They prefer the "Yahw ist" anthropomorphic and patriarchal account of creation where Adam is created first and Eve is created out of Adam (Gen. 2-3), and subsequently sins against God.

However, Adam's original sin was that of self-deification into God through knowledge. Instead, he gained the knowledge of his own mortality and the inevitability of death! God never dies, yet Jesus and Buddha both died like any other mortals in the world and human history! That does not seem to worry those who worship these men. To appeal to salvation by faith alone (*sola fide)* was designed by St. Paul in order to overcome this intellectual hurdle of reason. Since then, Christians like Augustine, Anselm, Luther and Kierkegaard have reaffirmed that Pauline doctrine of "salvation by faith alone."

Nevertheless, Jesus affirmed that salvation was through obedience and good works of unconditional love for the neighbor, rather than faith which is devoid of obedience and the necessary good works of grace and love (cf. Matt. 5-7; 25:31-46).

However, for many less sophisticated children, Santa Claus, the loving parents and other adults in the community are considered to be like God. In this case, the metaphor of "God as Father" is concretely understood. "God as father" stands for their real fathers! If their fathers have been abusive parents, then God is feared, and later rejected as an angry, even an abusive or "rapist God" as Mary Daly has put in her book, *Beyond God the Father*.

According to Piaget, this is the elementary religious level. It is the physical, literalist level and "concretization" of the abstract spiritual matters. At this level of religious development God is conceived to be a real physical object. God as "Our Father" is perceived to be a real strong White man with a long gray beard just like Santa Claus! Likewise, "Heaven" is thought to be a really good place and hell is a lake of fire, such a volcano! The statues of saints are also viewed as real gods. They have no sense of idolatry or polytheism as problems. They are also completely dualistic. Things are either good or bad (evil).

Unfortunately, many adults never seem to outgrow this dualistic, physicalist, literalist, and childish religious evolutionary stage of moral, spiritual development! These are the same people who treat the stories and myths of creation and Noah's flood in Genesis as literal history! Within the respective local family and community, in which one is born, one learns to love God and other people by being accepted, loved, and cared for by the parents and people within their community. One never learns to love without being first accepted and loved by others, especially by their parents and other members of the child's family.

For the child, these caring and loving people may be mistakenly perceived to be some kind of Gods! They have the power of life over the child. They provide love, nurturing, security, peace, values and company. Later, the child projects all these emotional sentiments, needs, ideals and values on a supernatural external moral force, principle, "Super Man" and divine authority that we call God! If the child's experience of his or her father was positive, then God will also be positively anthropomorphically and symbolically accepted as "God as the Father."

God as the benevolent "Cosmic Father" or "Patriarch" may be loved and worshiped without shame, fear of "being raped," or judgement by God as an evil male supernatural being. "God the Father" may be positively imagined as a loving, compassionate, provider, protector, sustainer, redeemer (deliverer) from evil and predicament. Unfortunately, for a person who has been abused and raped by his or her father, the metaphor of God as Father may bring the association of horror, rape, abuse, injustice and violence to be negatively projected to "God the Father," and the patriarchal priesthood. In this case, the metaphor for God as the "the Loving Cosmic Mother" is better, reassuring and redemptive for those who have been abused and traumatized by their own imperfect or evil earthly fathers. For them, the term "mother" may be associated with compassion, unconditional love, acceptance, forgiveness and healing.

Apart from Freud's works, there is enough research data in psychology and psychiatry to demonstrate that people's experiences affect their social, religious, moral and psychological attitudes towards other people, religion and God. If children and young adults' experiences of their fathers have been negative, traumatic, and violent such as those of physical and mental abuse and rape, it is understandable that the image and metaphor for God as "God the Father" may be violently rejected, feared and hated.

Perceiving God as a supernatural male being may, in some cases, be negatively viewed as another potential male oppressor, abuser, and "rapist!" Mary Daly's book, *Beyond God the Father* is an extreme example of this theological and philosophical feminist paradigm and rejection of any male references and metaphors for the holy, loving and benevolent Cosmic Creative and Redemptive God. Mary Daly equates maleness with rape and other serious evils in the world, such as sexism, racism, imperialism, violence and war. Consequently, as an angry, anti-patriarchal and radical feminist, Mary Daly calls for "the castration of God the Father."

Daly's anti-patriarchal radical feminist liberation theology provides some graphic material and detailed illustration of the serious nature of the negative and sexist social, moral, spiritual, religious and theological dilemmas which have been created by the male dominated traditional language, theology, christology, ecclesiology, ethics and world-view. The mythological story of Eve, temptation and the original sin and human fall from perfection into imperfection as a result of her moral weakness and rebellion against God is at the center of this oppressive patriarchal hierarchy which Mary Daly rejects in both the traditional patriarchal society and the Church and seeks to destroy through her method of "castration of God" and the cultural and religious patriarchal structures in this male-dominated world. Daly also seeks to exorcize the curse imposed on Eve by "God the Father" which subordinated all women to men as God's will and moral law (cf. Gen. 3: 1-16).

An extreme example of this religious and theological discrimination, exclusion and oppression of women by the sexist Christian Church, is the traditional doctrine which excluded women from ordination to the Catholic priesthood on the theological grounds that "God the Father" is male, Jesus was male and all of his original twelve disciples, who were later ordained and commissioned as his Apostles, were all males (cf. John 20:17-23).

As a result, the traditional Christian Church as a historical, Christocentric (Christ-centered), and Apostolic religious institution, is inherently male-centered or patriarchal in its original founding, structure, clerical hierarchy, language, theology and doctrines. Women's ordination, liberation theology and feminist theological contributions to scholarly debate and discourse are beginning to bring about positive changes within this conservative, and traditionally male dominated or patriarchal religious institution.

The exclusively male Christian priesthood was also traced back to the patriarchal Hebrew male priesthood and the Levitical codes of purity and holiness. This kind of theology ignored the fact that Greeks, Europeans and Africans were not part of the twelve apostles, and yet they have been ordained into Christ's Church as priests, bishops and even popes. Jesus was not an Italian or a White Anglo-Saxon! He neither knew any Latin nor English, which now dominate the Christian Church liturgy, scriptures and theological formulations. This inculturation and contextualization of Christianity is correct and essential in order to render Christianity more meaningful and relevant for a culturally diverse and religiously pluralistic global human community, living in today's inclusive and pluralistic world.

However, despite Christianity's efforts to become a universal and inclusive religion as St. Paul's theological and pastoral letters to the Gentile Churches he had founded clearly demonstrate, Paul and traditional Christianity failed to incorporate women at all levels of the Church's ministry as equal partners in God's work and as equal citizens of God's family and kingdom. As a patriarchal Jew, St. Paul did not feel the need to treat women as his equals in the new Church. He still subordinated women to men as it was practiced within"Orthodox Judaism" of that time (cf. 1 Cor. 12-14).

Unfortunately, St. Paul's writings and those of his followers have been widely used by Christians to exclude women from ordination and leadership of the Catholic Church and many conservative Protestant churches. For instance, the USA Southern Baptist Convention of 1998 in Salt Lake city, Utah, reemphasized the Pauline doctrine of the subordination of women to male authority within the home and the Church. Unlike St. Paul, Jesus himself had ministered to women and empowered them to become his transformed followers.

The paradigm of the self-sacrificial faith, obedience of Mary the Mother of Jesus, Martha, Mary Magdalene and others was not emphasized. In general observation, most male theologians and thinkers failed to see how women played a central role in the life of Jesus and his earthly ministry. Ultimately, the first witness and Apostle of the risen Christ is Mary Magdalene. She brought the good news of the resurrection to the rest of the Apostles who were in hiding for fear of persecution. Mary Daly has a good reason to reject patriarchal Christianity as the corruption of the teachings of Jesus. In this respect, Jesus rejected the prevailing Mosaic traditions that ostracized and oppressed women.

Contrary to the teachings of both traditional theology and Mary Daly, God's true liberation and salvation as an empowering positive human transformation to live a happy (contented) life of agape, peace and good works, remains the universal religious truth which transcends all religions and doctrines. This state of salvation, fellowship of wholeness, mutual human free acceptance, love, contentedness, peace, harmony, happiness and blessedness as God's Kingdom is both analogous and coextensive with the loving and inclusive human family and the community.

The caring, nurturing and peaceful family and human community coalesce and together constitute the temporal and concrete God's arena for historical, social, religious, economic, political, cultural, moral and physical processes of God's human biological (physical) creation and redemption from evil. As such, there cannot be any true humanity outside the context of a loving family and a supportive, moral, peaceful and caring community.

Dysfunctional families and conflict riddled communities generally produce dysfunctional, hostile, criminal-minded, maladjusted, angry and violent adults. Most of the inner city crimes in America are committed by people who have grown up in such homes. Family psychologists, psychiatrists and therapists have begun to accept the truth based on common sense, intuition and plenty of research data which indicate that traumatized, abusive and broken homes also generally produce some traumatized , criminally-oriented, and social misfits for children.

Subsequently, these unfortunate children, and other abused people, may also suffer for life from the effects of sexual, physical and mental abuse, divorce, poverty, drug abuse, poor role models, poor education, deprivation of love, violence and neglect. This socioeconomic, moral, social and spiritual deprivation may lead the deprived person to a life of insatiable craving, a restless and frustrated life of unfulfilled inner spiritual and moral emptiness, addictions, *angst*, existential anxiety, depression, despair, neurosis, and contemplation of suicide and misery. This is largely due to the fact that human desires and craving have been left unmet and uncontrolled. As a result, they have become physically oriented to the quest for the ultimate personal meaning and satisfaction in material things, such as food, wealth or money, drugs, alcohol, sex, power, aggression and violence.

Violence within urban, poor communities is one outlet and an external manifestation of this problem. Destructive wars and deadly violence within poor and repressive nations of Africa, Latin America, Asia and former Soviet Union is another expression of this societal moral problem, and public or collective spiritual crisis. The destructive genocidal wars of "ethnic cleansing" in Bosnia, Kosovo and Rwanda are clear illustrations of this societal moral problem of unfulfilled material needs, frustration, social and spiritual or moral confusion, and ethnic violence. Muslim Croations and Tutsis became the scapegoats for physical, social, moral and spiritual evils in the case of Bosnia and Rwanda, in the same way Adolph Hitler singled out Jews as the scapegoats for Europe's problems, while in Uganda, President Idi Amin blamed Asians for Uganda's problems, and expelled them from the country in 1972.

These are examples of tragic moral confusion in the world. In these examples, there is a fundamental confusion between the physical and spiritual natures, needs, fulfillment, and ultimate destinies. There is a lack of faith and clarity that the essential needs of the human being, and different modes of human existence, can only be completely and permanently fulfilled by God, who works incognito through the moral and peaceful human community to minister to all his obedient people. The Western prevailing form of materialism tends to fuse the spiritual aspects of humanity into the physical and materialist aspects and subsequently, to direct them toward the physical and materialist abundance of worldly goods created and promoted by capitalism as a means and goal of success and happiness for all humanity. This is erroneous, tragic and misleading to humanity.

Contrary to the misleading and destructive false promises of materialism and capitalist advertising designed to promote and cater for Western materialism and consumerism, the ultimate and authentic human value, meaning, reason for being, fulfillment and happiness do not consist in material things or the attainment and great accumulation of material things or objects (food, luxurious houses, cars, planes, boats, clothing, jewelry, gold, and the like), money and other kinds of material wealth.

The true, ultimate human spiritual and moral completion, self-fulfillment, destiny, meaning and happiness do not consist in physical or material means, and abundance of material goods and wealth because the material things cannot fulfill a spiritual void. This is the real essence of idolatry, hedonism, capitalism and Western materialism, which attempt to negate and nullify the teachings of Buddha and Jesus, which emphasize simple living, sacrificial self-denial, fasting and renunciation of desire for material possessions, and the craving for sensual pleasures of the body.

Accordingly, the capitalist and material false advertising that buying a new and larger car, or buying a larger house will make you happy promotes idolatry and misery. This is true inasmuch as the public is told that true happiness is found in buying and accumulating things or the attainment of wealth! This is the essence of the prevailing Western religious idolatry of socioeconomic ideology of capitalism and the correlative system of materialism. In addition to human "thingfication" or materialization, and degradation, capitalist materialism also degrades the basic institutions of the human family and the sanctity of the human community as the universal arena of God's natural and supernal activities in history and the world.

The family and the human community also constitute the divine arena of the human being's own creation and redemption. The family and the community provide the biological environment for marriage and reproduction. They also provide the social environment for socialization or humanization, sin, and salvation. In other words, the individual is the direct creation of the community. Each respective community creates its own unique members according to its own physical, cultural, moral, religious, and linguistic image, including values and world-view.

Contrary to the traditional bigoted and exclusivist teachings of Christianity and Islam as God's only revealed and redemptive religions, in reality, the African Religion, Hinduism and Native American Religion, are likewise, revelatory of God and redemptive religions for their loving, humane, peaceful and devoted practitioners. These religions reveal God's holiness, universal will for people to love one another, share the Earth's resources and live together in harmony, mutual respect and peace. As such, they provide an efficacious path to God's redemptive truth, universal revelation in nature, knowledge, salvation, moral law, order, peace and citizenship in God's Kingdom.

These "nature-based" and theocentric religions form a religious continuum with those religions like Judaism, Christianity and Islam, which claim to be based on God's special revelation. These religions which claim to be based on special revelation ignore the fact that nature is itself God's most complex visible universal supernatural revelation. Therefore, Judaism, Christianity and Islam are themselves the beneficiary reformations and literary evolutionary improvements nature religions. The two categories of religion are inseparable components of the same inclusive divine universal complex phenomenon of God's universal revelation and supernatural activities of God's universal free redemptive grace in creation and redemption. These divine universal activities are universally carried out in the world by God everywhere according to his or her will and timetable *(kairos)*.

God is ever tirelessly working incognito through us and around us through nature, and obedient skilled people. God works in human history through the prophets, and all obedient saints. Locally, God works to accomplish extraordinary things through the seemingly ordinary historical, religious and cultural processes and heritage. As a result, God's special revelation to the Jews was mediated through the ordinary processes of the local Hebrew patriarchal culture, history, language, prophets and world-view. This divine revelation is local and culturally conditioned so that God could directly design it for the ancient patriarchal Hebrew people. It was not designed to speak to the Greeks or the Europeans, and other foreigners.

Jesus, as the Christ of God, and St. Paul, his disciple, tried to modify God's revelation to the Jews through Moses, so as to make them universally applicable. That meant expunging the strict Mosaic laws regarding retaliation, ceremonial cleanliness, food taboos, circumcision, ceremonial cleanliness, ethnic discrimination (segregation), exclusive doctrines of the Jewish election, covenant, ritual sacrifice in the temple for atonement, and whatever was exclusively Jewish culture. As a result of this reformation, the new religious community (New covenant or Christian Church [*ekklesia]*) that was Jesus or Christ-centered, rather than the Hebrew Moses-centered one (Old Covenant or Hebrew *ekklesia*) became known as "Christianity." Therefore, Christianity only makes sense when it is viewed within the context of Judaism and the Mosaic Covenant.

However, due to the complex nature of the Christocentric Christian doctrines, Christianity has become exclusive in terms its of claims of special revelation and salvation based on the doctrine of God's special incarnation in Jesus as the cosmic Christ and redeemer of the entire world (John 1-3). The Pauline doctrines of religious and cultural purgation, Hellenization, universalization of Christianity, and reformation of both Judaism and the Hebrew culture to make it compatible with Christianity has advantages for the promotion of Christianity into the only God ordained, redemptive and universal religion.

After Emperor Constantine's famous edict of the legalization of Christianity as the Empire's official religion in 313 CE, Christianity quickly grew into a major world religion. In this process, Christianity was also negatively transformed a morally pure and persecuted minority religion into a powerful, materialistic and corrupt majority religion.

Christianity as an established imperial religion, soon became more concerned with access to power and wealth than the moral and spiritual exercise of unconditional love, justice and nonviolence. It also ceased to care about the protection of the needy and the weak. Christianity became transformed into the unloving, "capitalistic," imperialistic, sexist, racist, anti-Jewish, militaristic, violent and an intolerant powerful religion that was closely associated with the activities and power of the Roman Empire. Correlatively, the power of the Pope as the Bishop of Rome soon became parallel and similar to that of the Roman Emperor. Later, the Pope became more powerful than the Roman Emperor and subordinated the emperors and kings and other rulers to the power of the Pope and the Roman Catholic Church.

Therefore, it obvious that the Church did not only subordinate women to its power, it also subordinated men, including emperors and kings to its dominion. This Church domination of people and their institutions was carried out in the name of God the Father and his Son, Jesus the Christ. For instance, women were not traditionally ordained into the priesthood of the mainline Christian churches. This was because God and Christ were considered to be real males. Subsequently, it was theologically asserted by the patriarchal Church that only suitable males could legitimately be ordained into the priesthood because they were the only ones qualified to represent God and Christ at the Eucharist and within God's holy community or the Church.

Later, some of these rulers, such as King Henry III rebelled against the oppressive power of the Pope and the Roman Catholic Church which he headed. Prior to that, Martin Luther, a German nationalist Roman Catholic Franciscan priest and professor of systematic theology had already in 1517, revolted against the Roman Catholic Church power and rejected the supremacy of the Pope as the global head of the Christian Church and Mediator between God and all the people in the world. Recently, Mary Daly as an angry Roman Catholic women was also seeking to create a reformation of the Roman Catholic Church in which women would attain moral, social and spiritual equality to men.

However, there are many Christians who cherish St. Paul's anti-women and anti-Judaic writings in the New Testament (cf. 1 Cor. 14) and have erroneously accepted them as part of God's inspired and inerrant holy Scriptures, and God's universal, eternal truth and special revelation. As a result, they are reluctant to accept women as equals of men who can be validly ordained to serve as God's priests and ministers within God's holy Church. The Roman Catholic Church and the US Southern Baptist churches are major examples of this sexism and discrimination against women based on what is claimed to be God's revelation, holy Scriptures, and Church patriarchal tradition. Likewise, Islam as God's special revelation to the nomadic and patriarchal Arabs in the patriarchal society of ancient Arabia, was mediated through Arabic language, patriarchal and sexist Arabic culture, as God's redemptive revelation for Arabs.

Like the rest of the revelation of God, Jesus' mission and teachings were also distorted by his male-chauvinistic followers, and the patriarchal Church. The patriarchal, historical Church was established by the Apostles as its founding twelve patriarchs. The essence of Christ's message of universal, unconditional love and free forgiveness was corrupted in the same way the ancient Hebrew patriarchal and sexist society had already corrupted the revelation of God through Moses, which Jesus was compelled to purify. Contrary to the claims of Muslims of the eternal perfection, inerrancy and infallibility of the Qur'an as God's direct verbal dictation through the angel Gabriel, God's divine revelation to the Arabs through the Prophet Muhammad was also distorted by the local patriarchal and sexist culture of the Arabs.

Unfortunately, in all of these cultural cases of distortion of God's inclusive universal will and revelation for the world, the local cultural distortions of God's revelation was projected to the local people and the world as part of God's inerrant and infallible revelation and eternal truths! Despite some crude anthropomorphic mental and pictorial images of God as a some kind of benevolent Patriarch or "Superman," in actuality, God as a genderless and colorless Spirit is not a Jew, Christian, Arab, Greek, European powerful male or an African Patriarch or Matriarch. That would an idol and not the truly transcendent God that transcends the finite barriers of matter, gender, culture, nationality, language, time and space.

The universal good news for all people that is proclaimed in this book is that God transcends all these kinds of finite categories and limitations of human divisions and barriers of gender, race, color, class, nationality, culture, language, religion and political ideology. God does not favor one gender, culture, language, race, tribe, nationality, language and mode of worship over another. The transcendent Creator-Redeemer God does not favor any written scriptures or formulation of doctrines concerning his essence, grace, works of unconditional love in both cosmic creation and redemption.

Ultimately, all that God cares about is that, irrespective of religious affiliation, culture, gender, color, race, nationality, class, level of technological development, marital state, sexual orientation, and age, all free, intelligent and morally thinking human beings should freely come to the voluntary redemptive decision of positive practical faith. This is an important and positive religious efficacious, free spiritual and moral decision of faith, obedience and love. This decision is made in practical faith, obedience and voluntary response to God's universal redemptive grace through the mediation of God's creative-redemptive universal power of his Logos and the Holy Spirit. It is both a moral and religious or spiritual significant decision that is made to love the neighbor, and obey God's moral law.

The success of this moral and spiritual decision and the new moral life that is based on it, requires moral and spiritual conversion and transformation. This is because it requires a new self-image as well as a new form of moral inner positive vision of the self, the neighbor, and God as inseparable moral or social references. Obedience to God's universal commandment of agape also implicitly mandates that the people who obey definitive, universal redemptive God's commandment of unconditional love must first learn to love themselves.

Then, these obedient people are enabled by God's free power of unconditional love and free unmerited grace to exercise that same unmerited supernatural gift of God's unconditional love to their neighbors, and God's creation. They are also enabled to love God and other people, as they love themselves following God's own example as seen in Jesus as the Christ. God has already provided an inclusive and universal example of unconditional love as he or she freely and unconditionally loves each human being in the world, and values him or her as his or her special creation in the world, and as a citizen of God's Kingdom.

This global human mode of ethnic pluralism and diversity of people, cultures, religions and ideas are results of God's will and natural law. They are also consistent with God's creation and command to reproduce, multiply, and create cultures, civilizations and technology to subdue, tame and control nature of God's behalf (cf. Gen. 1:26-31). However, through the historical, cultural, religious and biological human evolution, the human community does not only create human beings in God's image, but also creates them in its very own respective own image. Like God, the community permanently stamps all its own individual members or groups with an indelible "racial" or cultural image and distinctive identity.

The local community's specific image, in which its human members are created and shaped, includes the following: culture, language, religion, race, ethnic group or tribe, nationality, class, normative values, gender roles, philosophy, world-view, education, political structure, ideology, technology, and economic condition. Within this theological-philosophical and religious anthropology and metaphysics, it is self-evident that God and community are co-equal forces in God's processes of creation and shaping the human being into what he or she is now. As a result, we have some idea and stereotypes of what various groups of people, such as men, women, homosexuals, Africans, Native Americans, Indians, Chinese, Japanese, Arabs, Jews, Muslims, and communists are like!

Accordingly, most atheists argue that there is no reality in the cosmos that is identifiable as the eternal Creator God. They maintain that all there is, and what we call God is in actuality is nature, human beings and the community in their intertwined complicated processes of creation, sustenance, perfection (redemption) and fulfillment of the human being. They further argue that God is in this respect, the triple combination of humanity, the human community and nature which have been mythologized and projected externally into the sky, and internally into the human consciousness, as well as culture, history, myths and religion as the invisible, loving, holy, perfect and transcendent cosmic Creator, Sustainer and Redeemer God.

Consequently, each human being in the world bears the inseparable dual stamps of both God and the local community. These stamps of images of God and humanity vary from place to place, culture to culture, continent to continent, depending on the *a priori* (given or already existing) biological, ethnic (racial), cultural, religious and other environmental variables at work within the respective local community, nationality or race, in which the individual happens to be delivered into this world. As the delivery system, the community is here as God's medium through which human beings are delivered into the world and cared for until they exit this temporal world, and return to their spiritual state. This is the same as returning to the "All Encompassing Cosmic

Spirit" or the "Ultimate Origin," which is only to be found in the eternal God who is "the *Alpha* and the *Omega*" or the beginning and the end of the human process.

True humanity cannot exist in a cultural or social vacuum. This is partly due to the universal human factor that by nature, all normal human beings are social and incomplete at birth. For instance, human values, culture, skills and language are not innate or present in human nature or acquired immediately after birth. These are acquired through a long process of socialization and education that last a life-time. These processes by which children acquire these human qualities and basic human values can therefore, be correctly described as the humanization and divinization twin processes. This is true in as much as the divine qualities and virtues, such as the knowledge of the good or truth, unconditional love, justice, nonviolence, compassion and free forgiveness of sins, including those of the enemies are present.

However, whereas this is to affirm that human beings "are made" or "processed into caring people by society," this affirmation does not constitute a denial of the humanity to the unborn and those not yet fully socialized by society. They possess the full potential to become fully human and humane like Buddha or Jesus. This position holds that human beings, the way we know them in this world, are a direct result of their own parental, socioeconomic and cultural heritage. The parental heritage constitutes the human biological heritage whereas the social heritage constitutes the cultural heritage or the humanization qualities that we sometimes refer to simply as civilization.

This intrinsic universal and *a priori* human dual heritage is expressed most clearly in both African social ontology and existential philosophy. As Professor John Mbiti correctly affirms in his famous book, *African Religions and Philosophy*, there is an intrinsically universal bipolar African social ontological and philosophical existential axiom.

This social ontological and anthropological African axiom both positively affirms and teaches that "*because we are, therefore, I am; and since I am, therefore, we are.*" This is another way to affirm that both the individual and the community are mutually interdependent on each other, although for any given particular individual, the community's existence in an expressive condition of love, tolerance, security, openness, freedom, peace and well-being are an *a priori* prerequisite condition for one's creation and humanization as a complete and authentic human being, and true "*imago Dei.*"

However, the human community is imperfect. As such, all human beings in the world, are to some varying degrees, existing in the ongoing creative evolutionary processes of God, and therefore, exist as both imperfect and incomplete creatures, just like their own respective parents and communities that create them. As evolutionary, historical and self-transcendent intelligent incomplete beings in the world, all human beings in the world are acutely aware of their own incompleteness and the need to seek God the Ultimate Creator, and Redeemer or Fulfiller to save them from their incompleteness which is experienced as an eternal inner emptiness and gaping void at the center of one's being.

In spite of the human desperate attempts to fill this in gaping emptiness or abyss with drugs, alcohol, food, sex, material possessions and the like, they fail to fill this inner gaping void with those expensive material things. This is because the inner human emptiness is a spiritual void which can only be effectively and permanently filled by "spiritual things" or the infinite God.

Ultimately, the universal human existential emptiness that is experienced at the center of the human being is not a human defect. It is God's universal provision of grace to lead all human beings seek God as the only ultimate cosmic moral and spiritual power or Spirit that can completely satisfy spiritual craving and fill the infinite emptiness with unconditional love, forgiveness, satisfaction, truth, and true and lasting happiness. Drugs, food, booze and sex offer only temporary and false remedies. As result, they lead to addiction, disease, crime, depression, anxiety, despair, *angst,* misery and premature death.

God, as the holy, creative, infinite and redemptive eternal Cosmic Spirit is the power and infinite "Object" that is good, and big enough to fill the infinite void at the center of the human being. This was the redemptive truth and "Good News" which both Buddha and Jesus discovered and sought to declare (reveal) to the world through their own lives and teachings. Some people are positively socialized and taught to both obey and seek God for their ultimate fulfillment through unconditional love, and good deeds on behalf of their neighbor and creation. These faithful and obedient saints of God find their ultimate satisfaction and personal fulfillment in the knowledge and service of God.

It is in the infinite loving and benevolent God that all human beings in the world are predestined by God's grace in both mental and spiritual *a priori* orientation in creation in both God's own image and divinity, to seek God for their own meaningful destiny.

God as Agape and *Sola Gratia* (Unconditional Grace) as well as the human ultimate destiny also embodies the essential human ultimate meaning for their own lives, love, forgiveness, grace, and eternal life. God as the loving, benevolent and gracious Cosmic Creator, Sustainer and Redeemer also embodies all personal human worth, value, goodness, truth, moral guidance in the Logos and Holy Spirit, reason for being and happiness in the ordinary and yet redemptive supernatural divine process of God in the world.

This supernatural beatific state is attained on the Earth and in the course of this life by the faithful and obedient saints of God. It is attained anywhere, both inside and outside the traditional Christian Church and with or without the aid of any religion. It is both universally and supernaturally conferred by God through the obedient people, or the saints' own process of performance, the self-sacrificial benevolent and agapic acts of obedience in implicit faith and concrete acceptance to become God's partners and ambassadors in the world.

This divine redemptive and transformatory supernatural process can be realized anywhere in the world by the saints' own free practical obedience to practice God's universal moral obligation of unconditional love for the neighbor and creation, and serve them in unconditional love, and free forgiveness. And truly serve them with humility and respect as they would serve God. This service to humanity is service to God. It is universally redemptive. It is the practical demonstration of true obedience to God and diligent praxis of agape. This is what it means to be God's saint and servant in the world. This is also the mission of God's obedient Church.

Caring and diligent service to humanity anywhere in the world constitutes obedient faith in God, godliness, good works of saintliness, and a positive mode of redeemed life (cf. Matt. 5-7; 25:31-46). This is particularly the case when this service to humanity has been rendered in the spirit of unconditional love. This implicit practical faith in the Cosmic Creator, moral obedience and diligent praxis of agape is both correlative and coextensive with free moral and spiritual acceptance, and practical fulfillment the commandment of unconditional love and service of God.

This is due to the efficacious universal supernatural unmerited free creative and redemptive activities of God's Logos (Word or Christ), and the Holy Spirit which are truly universal, omnipresent, and effectively incarnate in every person in the world, as they were efficaciously and divinely present and incarnate in God's obedient saints like Jesus, Buddha, and Krishna. Conversely, very often, human beings are also often both consciously and unconsciously negatively socialized into negative (sinful) modes of life that are imperfect, unloving, uncaring, selfish, hateful, racist and sexist.

Nevertheless, an imperfect community is still preferable to none at all. This is because it is better to live as an imperfect human being or sinner than not to live at all. It also preferable to live as an imperfect human being than a perfect, but amoral animal, such as a dog, cat, cow and the like. The human community is special and divine instrument despite its corruption and imperfection. Ultimately both the human family and community constitute God's universal sacred arena for both human creation and redemption.

As a result, if a human child is abandoned at birth and brought up by nonhuman creatures, that child will never grow up into a authentic or full human being despite of its human biological heritage and physical features. Similarly, when human beings bring up a nonhuman child, such as a chimpanzee or a monkey, it will not grow up into a human being! This is because of the dual heritage requirement, namely, the cultural or environmental and biological forms of heritage in order to complete the creation process of a given creature in raising the human being.

Subsequently, any defect in either one of these dual heritages will also cause the creature to be defective in development or growth. For instance, if there is a biological defect in heredity regarding physical or mental condition, the child will either die or be born with these defects. Similarly, at the cultural level, an evil-filled society also has an evil-filled culture of defective and depraved moral values which are passed onto the young people. This evil heritage is unconsciously inherited by the young people through education, imitation of role-models and as they are both socialized and integrated into the life, values and culture of the respective society. Some examples of evils inherited through an evil culture and corrupt forms of religion include color and racial prejudice, sexism, various forms of bigotry, intolerance, hatred, classism, xenophobia, ethnocentrism, war-mongering, and unwholesome sex norms.

Consequently, it can be said that an evil culture will also produce evil people, and that since culture is also a human creation, evil people create an evil culture. Therefore, the culturally inherited human evil is also in turn passed down to the offspring in the form of culture, education, and even religion. Fortunately, God's redemptive work in Jesus Christ seeks to challenge the individual and institutional evils in order to redeem both the individuals and their evil (or fallen) structures are both distorted from their true essence and functions because they have become riddled by evil and sin.

God works through the media of the family and community. This is because human beings are intrinsically social and cultural beings. This is true both in their creation and redemption. Therefore, an individual is lost without loving family and the community. As such, both the community and the individual must be created, redeemed and saved together. One of these two elements cannot exist by itself without the existence of the other, since the individual and the community are inseparable. The human being cannot exist without the human community. Conversely, the human community cannot exist without the individuals who constitute it as its members. The existence of one presupposes the prior existence of the other for its own essential existential grounding, basis and context of coming into existence. This is almost analogous to the "chicken and egg" argument regarding to what comes first. I will call this problem the "correlational theory of creation and existence."

## 7. Sex, Family and Community

Sex is God's good and supernatural gift to humanity for self-reproduction (self-cloning). Sexual intercourse between two mature people who love one another can, in some cases, serve as a momentary glimpse at heavenly ecstasy! The lover (subject) and the beloved (object) have become united as "one entity."

However, human sex constitutes the special, carefully guarded, socially and legally regulated gate of human life, creativity, *eros* or sexual love and fulfillment. Sex is God's natural as well as supernatural provision for the creation of all human as well as the other kinds of animal evolutionary biological life in the world.

Myths of virgin births, including those of Buddha and Jesus were invented by primitive societies because they constituted the means to deify "men" into gods by their devoted human followers. This task of deification was carried out in order to defy both evil and death for their masters and simultaneously, for them. This was done mythologically by faith, mystical, spiritual and mental self-transmutation of themselves into gods either through the doctrines of union with the eternal Creator God as in the case of mysticism or through the resurrection of the dead, as in the case of Christianity. This is why St. Paul's "fundamentalist theology" was centered on the power of the axiomatic, literal and historical resurrection of Jesus which formed the basis for the Christian Church.

St. Paul's theology for the deification of Jesus into divinity and immortality through the doctrine of the resurrection constitutes the theology of salvation, atonement and human immortality or deification by God through the victory of God over death and the promise of resurrection for all human beings (cf. 1 Cor. 15). Other religious and

Christian thinkers tried to deify their founders through supernatural births or incarnations of God. Therefore, doctrines of Virgin Birth and immaculate conception are not a matter of historical events and miracles. Rather, they are crude theological, spiritual, mythological, anthropomorphic, and religious symbolic methods for affirming divinity and holiness of a religious founder like Buddha and Jesus, while simultaneously denying human imperfection, sin, finitude, and death that characterize ordinary human life and historical creaturely existence in this world.

However, contrary to the negative teachings of dualism concerning human sexuality, sex in itself is God's wonderful gift to humanity, as well as all his or her more advanced creatures. As such, when used according to God's will, sex is good and cannot be evil as both St. Paul, Augustine and their dualistic followers either implicitly or explicitly taught. This destructive erroneous moral theory and Church teaching was based on Christianity's own inherent dualism. This dualism is intrinsic in traditional Christian theology and ethics because these are deeply rooted in Greek philosophical dualism.

Correctly understood, both sex and eros are good, and to be celebrated with both joy and respect. They are God's natural means through which God both continually and universally creates human beings as special and divine beings through the ordinary and natural medium and mediation of the human family and community. The nuclear family is the basic organic unit or component of any given community, whether local or global. Whereas an individual's existence is of great importance, it is like that of an atom unrelated to others whose great importance lies in the relationship capacity and possibility to join with others to form larger clusters, such as molecules. The family is the molecule equivalent in human relationships.

In the family unit, different individuals of different sexes who are not closely related by blood kinship voluntarily enter a legal and religious marriage bond based on mutual love, friendship, and desire to live together as husband and wife. Furthermore, they wish to bring up their offspring together in the sanctity and loving protection of their home. The Hebrew Bible makes it quite clear that, in the beginning, God created humankind in his own image (*imago Dei*). He created them both male and female, in his own image (Gen. 1:27) and wedded (blessed) them (Gen. 1:28). He also commanded them to reproduce ("clone themselves") and "multiply and fill the Earth" with other human beings through their offspring. From this passage one can, therefore, conclude that homosexual relationships are excluded from the marriage bond.

Marriage was established as a sexual bond between a man and a woman; and it was for the sake of producing and rearing of the children.

However, according to the second account of creation ("J" or *Yahwist)*, marriage is said primarily to be for the sake of avoiding "loneliness which is considered not to be good." God is said to have "cloned Eve from Adam's rib." After the successful operation, God brought Eve to Adam as a "suitable a marriage partner" (cf. Gen. 2:18). A "suitable partner" for marriage is considered on the basis of biological, social, spiritual and mental compatibility with the intended mate. Marriage is a means of providing an ideal companionship, love, and "suitable help" (Gen. 2:17-25). This creation and marriage account does not include the objective of producing children as the primary reason for marriage, sex and companionship. Therefore, if marriage was theologically and morally valid only for the sake of child bearing, then, it would most logically follow that all heterosexual sex and marriages which no longer lead to reproduction would have been considered immoral and proscribed!

This biblical account may be used to provide a needed theological basis for the Church's acceptance of committed homosexual relationships or marriages as meaningful legal, sexual and social bonds that provide essential companionship, sexual fulfillment and eliminate the evil of loneliness! After all, this is the main reason why those who are either struck by the misfortune of being biologically incapable of reproduction (barren or impotent), or have already passed the child bearing years, still get married, if they are single, or stay married if they are already married!

Accordingly, Bishop John Spong of the Episcopal Diocese of New Newark, New Jersey, advocates for gay rights and inclusion of practicing homosexuals within the priesthood of the Episcopal Church, and the rest of God's ecclesial community, as an essential, practical expression of agape and true forgiveness.

Bishop Spong both courageously and convincingly argues that obedient, loving and academically well-grounded ethicists and theologians should see God's agape and inclusive grace in broader terms. A true understanding of God's unconditional love, and free grace can be positively demonstrated to be inclusive of all gays and their natural biological homosexual orientation and natural sexuality based on this mode of ones's God-given nature.

The Christian gay-rights advocates call upon the Church and the moral theologians to remove their heterosexual bias and prejudice against homosexuality as an immoral sexual that should be morally rejected.

Based on both biology and natural law, the homosexual person is God's own beloved child like anyone else. He or she that has been created with a hormonal imbalance. In some cases, this condition may become an untreatable inherited genetic or natural defect. This constitutes a natural state which naturally leads to a non-traditional sexual orientation to seek sexual consolation, companionship, fulfillment and satisfaction with people of the same gender, instead of seeking sexual fulfillment in a mutually loving relationship with a mature person of the opposite sex.

Since no medical treatment, social ostracism, psychological counseling, societal censorship, physical harassment, persecution, and religious or cultural threats of excommunication or damnation by God, in the supposedly unquenchable fires or hell, have been able to cure or permanently correct the problem of homosexual orientation, then, in that case, it is part of God's natural law. That being the case, it also naturally follows that there should be no ecclesiastical theological, moral or spiritual discrimination and objection to this natural human social and sexual need for fulfillment and suitable companionship. According to the Hebrew creation stories and the fall of humanity, both natural sexual fulfillment and guard from loneliness are part of God's primordial will prior to the human sin, rebellion, fall, guilt and shame (cf. Gen. 1-3).

According to the Yahwist mythological story of creation (Gen. 2-3), the real functional reason why a woman (Eve) was created was because the man (Adam) was lonely (Gen. 2:18). God is reported to have said: "It is not good for the man to be alone; I will make him a suitable partner" (Gen 2:18).

Within this understanding, the primary function of marriage is not reproduction as some Christian leaders, particularly the American Southern Baptists, and the Roman Catholic Church have in the past erroneously taught. Rather, the true and primary function of sex and marriage is God's universal provision for *eros*, social and sexual fulfillment, fellowship, support, protection, and the essential removal of loneliness! However, the Priestly story of creation seems to emphasize the command for humanity to reproduce and fill the earth (Gen. 2:25-31), tame and to rule over creation in God's name. Both of these commandments have been already over full-filled!

Ultimately, the Earth is already overpopulated and there is need for control of human population growth if the natural resources of the Earth are to be conserved and managed well to support life and all creatures as God intended. This demographic reality necessarily eliminates the need for marriage to serve as the reproductive means to populate the Earth. With revolutionary reproductive technologies and human cloning, the function to reproduce and fill the Earth can easily and most efficiently be achieved through well controlled, sanitary and more convenient genetically improved incubators and "baby-factories!"

Women are no longer derogatorily and degradingly considered being mere "natural baby factories," "baby-sitters," "natural cooks," and "housekeepers!" These patriarchal views of the past led to the oppression of women, as well as both religious and socioeconomic discrimination against them. Fortunately, in the third millennium, women have finally become legally equal to men both in the home and within the work-place. However, gender equality does not mean that men and women are the same. That was not God's intention in creation of men and women.

The USA affirmative action and anti-discrimination laws were essential in order bring about gender and racial equality in the work-place. In many Western countries, women and racial minorities have achieved both legal and socioeconomic equality with White males who had traditionally dominated the political and economic affairs of the Western nations, as well as those of the global community. Nevertheless, mere legal equality without the essential cultural and social equality of men and women and the moral acceptance of people of all races as equals remains a mere utopian ideal and tantalizing dream for the oppressed.

Significant changes in human society and gender roles are usually slow to emerge. This is understandable because those in power and the traditional beneficiaries of such power generally resist any attempts to give up some of these privileges and to share their power with others. Marxism and the threat of communism was important in forcing the Western powers to change and adopt more democratic socioeconomic principles that would benefit the majority within the middle class. This strategy was designed in order to foil the popular intellectual socioeconomic appeal of both Marxism and communism.

In part, it was the Western fear of communism that led to the United Nations Declaration of the Universal Human Rights of 1948. This intrinsic Western desire to survive and resist both Marxism and communism also led to the Western desire to introduce innovations in education, politics, philosophy and governance in order to become more democratic and humane. Eventually, this strategic move led to the increased holistic and inclusive liberal arts education for men and women, and the emergence of Civil Rights movements of the 1960s and 70s. These educational, political and social movements led to the emergence of effective liberation theologies in both universities and seminaries, increased popularity of women's studies or feminism, and the correlative awareness of the need for racial and gender equality.

In addition, advanced technology and household gadgets, as well as these movements and ideas, have combined in various forms to effect the liberation of both men and women from much of the past evils of prejudice associated with racism and sexism. For instance, the invention of tractors and combine harvesters rendered much of the need for cheap slave-labor on the cotton, corn, and wheat farms obsolete. That explains why today's slave-like illegal migrant seasonal farm workers still come from Mexico to harvest those crops such as oranges, tomatoes, strawberries, and vegetables which machines cannot yet harvest effectively.

In the case of sexism and the traditional sex roles, advancement in science and technology have inadvertently enabled the contemporary gender and sex revolution to occur. Biology has revealed that women are human beings like men.

Therefore, apart from size and the essential reproductive differences, women are equal to men. Women are capable of doing the same office work as men and doing so with equal excellence, and sometimes, even outperforming their male counterparts. Furthermore, in its various forms, technology has also very significantly contributed to the accelerated process for the liberation of men and women from traditional gender roles, work within the home, and professional careers outside the home. Technology has caused this revolution by providing birth control devises as well as simplifying work through mechanization and automation.

Moreover, technology has actually made men and women equal in the work-place. This has been accomplished this important transformation of society by providing affordable and easy to use utility machines, such as dishwashers, microwaves, vacuum cleaners, lawn-mowers, laundry machines and driers which simplify the tedious housekeeping chores. Technology has made it possible for both men and women to share housekeeping chores and to work outside the home as equal partners and professionals.

## 8. Traditional Values, Freedom, Rebellion and Hedonism

Traditional moral and social values were for Jews, Muslims and Christians are deontological. They are externally derived from the moral authority of God's revelation. This revelation was based on nature, the Ten Commandments of Moses and the holy Scriptures: the *Torah* (Judaism), the *Qur'an* (Islam) and the *Bible* (Christianity).

Consequently, traditionally, the Christian Church leaders and moral theologians who are opposed to homosexuality, point out that in order to fulfill Adam's social and sexual need, God created Eve, a woman. God did not create another man for him. God is supposed to have instituted heterosexuality by having created and provided an attractive woman (Eve) for Adam's sexual fulfillment, and personal relationship. This mythological story is always cited as the theological and moral basis heterosexuality as the universal cultural, religious and normative principle governing marriage, and all other forms of human sexual relationships.

However, the mythological story was itself a creation of patriarchal heterosexual males to justify their moral subordination of women (Gen. 3) and rejection of homosexuality (Gen. 17-18; Lev. 18). Life being theocentric, this ancient patriarchal form of sexism, and prejudice against homosexuality was formulated and codified in God's name as God's eternal will and revelation. The Catholic Church hierarchy and leaders of the American Baptist Church have also constantly affirmed this ancient Hebrew mythical religious material to be God's will and moral revelation to guide the Church today.

According to this ancient Hebrew, heterosexual and patriarchal moral story of Genesis, both of Adam and Eve were naked and free with each other until the barrier of sin, guilt and the consequent human evil made Adam and Eve, and symbolically all human beings, uncomfortable with each other's presence and deeds. They began to blame each other for their misuse of their own freedom to rebel against God's moral law (commandments), and to be ashamed of each other's moral and physical imperfections. Obviously, this patriarchal mythological story of creation and the fall was created by males to justify their domination and oppression of women as God's will and curse for their supposed primordial initiation of both the human rebellion against God and the cosmic fall from God's original perfection (cf. Gen. 3:1-24).

Based on this popular, patriarchal, Hebrew tradition of creation and the fall, it was due to hubris and human temptation to become like God, and subsequent rebellion against God's moral law, misuse of freedom and voluntary sin that the barrier expressed itself in shame and embarrassment about each other. As a result, they invented masks in the form of clothing made of leaves in order to hide from each other, and later to hide from God (Gen.3).

Adam found his egocentrism expressed in male-chauvinism, domination and patriarchal expression of both moral and social evil in the oppression of Eve. Human evil had truly begun with this primordial couple. It is not surprising, therefore, that their own children, Cain and Abel, became evil themselves. They became bitter rivals who were envious of each other. They hated each other despite the fact they were brothers, and the only children in the family. They had everything in the world to gain as their God-given inheritance. Yet, Cain was blinded and consumed by hate for Abel, his brother. Cain did not want to share the world and God with Abel.

Subsequently, out of greed, envy, malice, hate and intolerance for competition, Cain most tragically killed Abel, his only brother! Sadly, the story attributes this murder to religion and different lifestyles. Cain was an agriculturalist who sacrificed wheat to God for an offering, whereas Abel was an "animal farmer" whose animal sacrifice is said to have been more pleasing to God than Cain's burnt cereal sacrifice! Obviously, the moral message of this story warns about the danger which differences in religion, concepts of God and socioeconomic styles can bring into both the human community and within God's global community.

Those religious fundamentalists or people that speak of returning to the wholistic "biblical family values" as the ideal moral foundation of a good family and society should be morally resisted by the more inclusive and enlightened moral agents within the contemporary society. The biblical family values are antiquated and meaningless for today's global pluralistic world which values cultural and religious diversity. These ancient Hebrew biblical values are rooted in an ethnocentric, xenophobic, sexist, racist, homophobic, tribal, nonscientific and patriarchal non-technological society of three thousand years ago.

Bishop John Spong, and others who preach unconditional love and tolerance as God's universal will in creation and redemption, are correct in repudiating these restrictive and punitive ancient Hebrew biblical values and sex taboos as norms for today's Christian ethics and morality. This is essential in order to reform the traditional exclusive Church. This is a moral and theological prerequisite position if the Church has to become effective in its mission to proclaim to the world today, God's unconditional love for all people.

This message of God's unconditional love and redemption has to be proclaimed to a diverse and culturally pluralistic people, irrespective of both *who* and *what* they are. This action and proclamation will positively transform the Christian Church into an open and tolerant proclaimer of true Christianity as God's good news of redemption for the culturally diverse, divided, quarrelsome, hateful and intolerant world.

Those who advocate a return to "biblical family values" are also often the conservative or poorly educated people that seem not to be aware of the fact that in reality there a very few ideal or sound families and good role models for modern families to be found in the Bible. For instance, the Hebrew families were patriarchal and often polygamous. In addition, Adam blames his God-given wife, Eve, for his own moral failure and sin against God. This in itself proves that marriages are unstable institutions that even if they were God-made (arranged) as in the case of Adam and Eve, they would still fail due to human imperfection.

Tragically, the first recorded murder takes place within the primordial human family! Out of Envy, Cain killed his brother, Abel. This was prophetic of what other human families were to be like. It is a parable concerning the universal truth and disturbing existential phenomenon of the reality of the universal human moral, social, and societal imperfection, strife, jealousy, envy, hate, violence, shame and guilt.

As a result of hate, strife and rivalry, murder especially, fratricide, and infanticide seem to have been common in many ancient communities. In many African societies, these crimes were taboo and abominations to God, the holy ancestors, and the theocentric and moral community. However, when these moral failures and violations occurred, the offender and his or community had to be purified from moral and ritual pollution and their negative social, spiritual and health consequences.

The offender and his or her community had to repent and perform acts of contrition and atonement. In order to accomplish this task, the "penitent offenders" were required perform atonement in the form of a sin-offering (sacrifice) to God, the ancestors, and the community. The offenders were also required to pay reparations to the aggrieved party as part of one's own repentance (penance) or "self-purgation" of sin or evil, restitution, atonement and symbolic public punishment. This was necessary in order for the individual and his or her community to be spared from God's justice and subsequent retaliation in the form of misfortune, disease, loss and other kinds of suffering.

In some cases of more heinous moral evils and crimes, such as murder, the murderer could not be allowed to provide a substitutionary sacrifice. In that case, the murder had to be executed in order to cleanse the community of the evil committed and the moral, spiritual and physical pollution it had brought upon the respective community. It was strongly believed that if this was not done, then the holy and just God would punish both the evildoer along with his and her respective community. Both the evildoer and the uncaring immoral community would be punished by God for lack of respect for life and moral failure to punish the sinner as an irresponsible, unholy, antisocial evildoer and criminal.

From an evolutionist theological and globalist moral perspective, the story of Adam's sin and Cain's murder of his brother also indicates the Hebrew anthropology and theology that Adam's sin was inherited by his son Cain. Therefore, this story is a Hebrew universal religious affirmation that due to the original sin of Adam and Eve, who were considered to be the universal human ancestors, and correlatively, all humanity as the supposed offspring of Adam and Eve, was also affirmed to be morally and spiritually contaminated by Adam's original sin.

All human beings, as the supposed descendants of Adam and Eve, are also supposed to be all born with Adam's sin. Sin and moral failure were considered to be universal as the hereditary moral and spiritual defects legacy of Adam and Eve. This was the ancient people's prescientific, mythological and crude theological, biological and anthropological explanation for the universal human orientation toward the misuse of freedom and evil. It explained the human being's self-destructive negative inclination and vices of selfishness, greed, egocentrism, hubris (excessive pride), envy, and hatred, malice, graffiti and vandalism.

Sin as a moral theory also explained the human family and community problems of strife, conflict and violence. The conclusion was that without "the fear of God" and God's retribution or punishment for sins, evil deeds and injustice would prevail in the world, and human community and society would be impossible. Humanity without the fear of God or atheism was also considered evil and demonic, since it was considered to be humanity without the necessary moral virtues of unconditional love, justice, nonviolence (*ahimsa*) and free forgiveness which are the grounding for a peaceful community and harmonious coexistence with other people or creatures in God's world.

Nevertheless, the family home is also the beloved primary place within the community that one both calls home and feels most at home. The family environment as a home, is ideally the safe place and arena of unconditional mutual love, free acceptance, forgiveness, shelter, security or protection, peace and healing. One may have many good friends, but they do not replace the real need for having close family members such as mother, father, and brothers and sisters. Friendship will last as long as both of you work at the relationship, whereas being a family member within a given community is an involuntary and an "*a priori*" act of God. It is not chosen by the individual.

The individual is "thrown by God" into being and is created within a specific community through the prevailing local cultural and technological reproductive processes. Membership in both the family and the community is essentially an "*a priori*" as an already given set of biological and cultural heritage, and as a human right. This essential human membership to the moral, caring, loving and peaceful community is a necessary prerequisite or prior condition for any meaningful human relationships, proper humanization or socialization, well-being and joyfulness due to the happy experience of the family, community and the world as God's perfect and beatific kingdom.

Indeed, we have no choice of where and when we are born. In other words, we cannot choose to be born in a certain family, ethnic group, nation, or race. Similarly, since we cannot choose our own parents, and we have no control over our own respective given biological or physical heritage, such as color, gender, height, race, athletic aptitudes and intelligence. Therefore, we have to accept ourselves, parents, and other family members, and the given condition of our being members of a human family. We have to accept and love ourselves as we are, and likewise, be able to love others as they are, without any prior conditions. This unconditional love may then produce the positive results of positive transformation and good works which are correlative to love.

However, if we fail to love and forgive ourselves without condition, we will not be able to love other people. If we impose conditions of conduct and perfection that must be met first before we can love ourselves or other people, we may never be able to love. Likewise, if we impose conditions of forgiveness before we can extend our forgiveness to the offenders and sinners, then it is most likely that we will never be able to forgive or love fully ourselves or anyone else. This is partly because God's commandment compels us to love and forgive without conditions.

Unconditional love and forgiveness are free, and unmerited. Imposing prior conditions on love and forgiveness means the love and forgiveness are both earned or merited as rewards. That negates the teachings of Jesus and God's commandment of unconditional love and free forgiveness of sins (Matt. 5-7). In addition, it is also because we may unrealistically set our conditions, standards and expectations too high to be met. In any case, if God had also imposed such conditions as prerequisites before we could merit his or her love and forgiveness, we would never have attained them, since we are both morally and spiritually imperfect and sin constantly.

Therefore, we are commanded by God through Jesus the Christ to extend our love to all without condition, beginning with the members of our family, neighbors and members of our local community. Our main goal should be to promote a peaceful and inclusive global world-view. The objective is to teach a world-view in which all human beings as moral agents and spiritual beings, are universally positively viewed as interrelated members of God's one inclusive global family, or God's Kingdom.

Through the diligent praxis of agape, we gain God's (Agape) liberation from evil and become like God (cf. I John 4:7-21). We experience the divine redemptive and healing power of God's unconditional love, unmerited grace, and peace through the healing knowledge of God's moral law and practical obedience to its moral guidance or divine imperatives.

There is need for inclusive moral and global social awareness of all God's people and the correlative acceptance of all loving, just and obedient people as the redeemed members of God's one universal inclusive family and fellowship of love which we idealize as heaven or God's Kingdom. This ideal and inclusive fellowship of God's people and the harmonious global community is a religious, spiritual, moral and socioeconomic utopia which we assign many different favorite names. These names depend on local language, world-view, culture, class, historical experiences, expectations in ideal and religious affiliation.

The list of these names for a redeemed and ideal state of peaceful life in fellowship with God and the neighbor include "paradise," "the Garden of Eden," "the redeemed Church," "heaven," "*Nirvana*," "Happy Hunting Grounds," and "God's Kingdom." Buddha and Jesus are examples of men who "woke up to God's redemptive truth," became filled with the joy of God's inclusive redemptive grace and unconditional universal love.

Enlightened and mystically united with God, they were enabled by their self-purification of their bodies, minds and spirit through self-discipline, meditation and prayer to become completely open to God and to become united with God in his free gifts of knowledge, truth, grace, unconditional love, and eternal life. This spiritual and mental ascent and deifying union with God, conferred on them and their followers the necessary divine power needed to live this mortal life most fully in maximum divine contentedness, happiness and peace that derives from perfect fellowship with God, creation and the good deeds of unconditional love for the neighbor.

Jesus and Buddha show us the best examples of how we can become united with God. They provide concrete examples and steps to take on the spiritual journey to God. We need self-disciple rooted in faith, love, justice, good works, prayer, and contemplation. Diligent prayer, contemplation and self-discipline can lead into the interior of our innermost being. Deep within the infinite void and infiniteness of God within our being, there we can encounter God's holy redemptive presence, mystery, union with God, joy and heavenly peace. Within the interior of our being, through contemplative prayer and silence we can truly discover the indwelling Holy Spirit and God's supernatural gifts of truth, transcendental peace, the eternal life through beatific fellowship and mystical union with God.

This *theophany* and divinizing mystical union with God and experience of heaven and eternal life can be truly realized by each person when they seek God within the interior of their own lives as the true holy temple of God and God's throne within each person, as the incarnation of God and *imago Dei* in the temporal world. Within this beatific interior divine presence, God's reign, fellowship of love and union with God, the believer, saint, worshiper or contemplator becomes part of God's eternal life and the kingdom. The citizen of God's Kingdom becomes fully liberated from the physical world and its desires, and to harness God's divinizing power of grace, unconditional power of God's love, spirit, forgiveness and peace.

However, the saint is urged by God to return to the real world in order to bear testimony of God's goodness, unconditional love, free grace, forgiveness of sins and the moral obligation for nonviolence, and living together in harmony, love and peace as God's children.

It is this mystical discovery of God, within and the appropriation of God's indwelling divine essence and attributes, that we become enlightened by God and attain the beatific vision and happiness that come from being united with God. Within this state of union, Siddhartha became the Buddha and Jesus became the Christ and Son of God. He was also able to say, "The father and I are one" (John 15-15). Jesus also explicitly taught his disciples to obey his moral and spiritual teachings and practice them in order to become the obedient and redeemed sons and daughters of God. This is to be "born again" of God's Word of light and spirit (John 1-3).

To become divinized and united with God is also to become the authentic human being as God intended the human being to be. Good examples are Jesus, Buddha, and Mother Teresa. To be like God is to become enabled to transcend human sins and limitations of finitude, hubris and idolatrous human self-deification, greed, selfishness, sinful exclusiveness and quest to prevail over human idolatrous and self-deifying sinful desire to become the God that imposes limitations on the transcendent Creator and Redeemer-God's own free universal creative and redemptive grace.

Finite, sinful and unloving human beings always seek special privileges for themselves at the expense of others. To this unethical and selfish end, these evildoers and sinners also seek to enlist God's help.

They seek to impose limits on God's free universal activities of unmerited grace both in universal creation and redemption.

Many conservative religious people also desire to impose barriers in the form of prerequisites of partisan and sectarian conditions of faith, creeds and hard work before sinners can become eligible for God's grace, mercy, love and redemption from the threats of physical, social, economic, moral and spiritual evils, chaos, anxiety, destruction by a premature death and eventual sinking into both oblivion and non-being. Consequently, we become empowered to love and forgive each other unconditionally, as we often try to do within our immediate family members and close relatives. Indeed, in Jesus the Christ, our big Brother and Redeemer, we all have become closely related as brothers and sisters, since all the other barriers of race, color, nationality, economic status, and ideology have been transcended by all those who are obedient to God.

The human family is a very important primary human institution. It is the foundation of all human communities, societies, nations, and their correlative values. It is also important because of its function as God's universal primary divine provision and ideal means for creating new human beings into the world. It is also through the family that God acts to provide humanity with his love through the loving tender care of mother, father, and other family members. We have also already seen above, according to the Bible, God created the first couple and entrusted it with the divine responsibility of reproducing themselves through nature's evolutionary and cloning process to fill the world with God's supernatural gift of intelligent life, historical self-transcending spirits, and mind.

The world is already filled with people and other creatures. Therefore, we have done a very good job of self-reproduction and multiplying the human population. In many cases, this has been accomplished as a moral and religious duty in fulfillment of God's will and commandment to reproduce and fill the Earth (cf. Gen. 1:26-31). Having accomplished this divine task for self-reproduction, now God's original commandment "to reproduce and multiply" (Gen. 1:26-31) no longer applies to all cases of sexual intercourse and marriage. Instead, we now have the moral obligation to practice birth-control and the overpopulation of world and destruction the Earth's environment through overpopulation and degradation.

Therefore, today, it is considered by some governments a moral obligation to impose birth-control on humanity and to conserve the Earth's essential natural resources. The Earth and its resources are not capable of sustaining unlimited populations of hundreds of billions of people. Today, this is taking place in Africa, Asia and Latin America where there is increasing population, deforestation and overgrazing and desertification leading to both shortages of food, firewood, rain and subsequently, hunger for the poor masses.

Unplanned and uncontrolled careless human self-reproduction can destroy the environment and intelligent life on this planet by depleting it of all its essential natural resources needed to support an already overcrowded planet. Therefore, individual family planning, state population control and management by requiring proper child spacing, are now urgent, necessary and new universal moral obligations. The adoption of this moral and demographic position essential in order to ensure the continued well being, dignity and good care of all human beings, both born and not yet born.

Nevertheless, most Christian moral theologians and ethicists and Church leaders, such as Pope John Paul II, appropriately warn us that in our zeal for population control, human beings should never become selfish, and inhumane. For instance, the traditional Christian leaders and their followers strongly condemn Christians who advocate abortion, murder, capital punishment and active euthanasia as either a form of birth control, or the mercy killing of the terminally ill, and those born with serious defects. They also both condemn irresponsible casual sex and oppose abortion as a means of solving the problem of sexual promiscuity and unplanned pregnancies.

These moral and religious conservative people reject the morality and legality of "Roe vs. Wade" of 1973 and seek to reverse it. They resent the fact that "Roe vs. Wade" granted women the legal and moral right to privacy and choice regarding whether to carry any pregnancy to full term and bear a child or to have abortion performed on demand. This means that the rights of the unborn are secondary to the rights of the mothers.

Many radical feminists and "pro-abortion" (pro-choice) people argue that when the life of the mother is in any way endangered by pregnancy, including health, profession, education, reputation, social or fiscal well-being, then the mother's interests and rights bear more weight and the pregnancy may be terminated unless it is in the third trimester. These religious and moral conservatives also condemn public policies in countries like China and India for encouraging abortion as a population and birth control mechanism. In addition, India is condemned for encouraging the medical use of ultrasound and other *in utero* gender determination tests in order to abort female fetuses.

Indeed, most of these conservative moralists, preachers and religious leaders affirm that in biological actuality, and God's natural law, there is no such thing as "unplanned" or "unwanted pregnancies." They base this on the assumption and affirmation that the moral primary normal function of sexual activity is reproduction within the context of marriage, and the traditional patriarchal family structure. As a result, sex acts not intended for reproduction or enhancement of the heterosexual marriage bond are rejected and condemned as immoral and evil forms of self-indulgence and abuse of sex as God had created and intended it.

The Roman Catholic Church strongly condemns the following sexual practices as moral evils and mortal sins: bestiality, rape, pornography, virtual sex, prostitution, incest, homosexuality, masturbation, anal and oral intercourse. This is in addition to the condemnation of sex outside the marriage bond.

The Catholic Church also condemns sex for "pleasure alone" in-itself as mere recreation. It rejects sexual activity that has no other higher moral or spiritual purpose, such as reproduction, as moral evil and a pervasion of human sexuality as was intended by God in creation. This kind of casual human sexuality is regarded as evidence of moral irresponsibility, sin and societal moral decadence. The Evangelicals, such as the Baptists strongly agree with conservative Catholic position of family values and sexuality. As a result, there is a strong condemnation of abortion and homosexuality within these churches.

According to traditional Christian moral teachings or ethics and doctrines, each time normal human beings engage in this procreative activity, they should expect to see a beginning of another human life in the form of conception! This is mainly why the Roman Catholic Church and some conservative Protestant churches vigorously condemn all forms of casual sex not intended for reproduction, such as prostitution, homosexuality, virtual, anal and oral sex as serious forms sexual perversion, sins, crimes and abominations to be avoided by morally upright people.

Accordingly, most of these conservative Christians are actively seeking to a legal ban of abortion and these kinds of sexual acts as immorality, sins or evils and unacceptable sexual practices. The lists include: pornography, casual sex, prostitution, sex out of the marriage sacramental bond, sex for pleasure, masturbation (sex with oneself), bestiality (sex with an animal), homosexuality (same gender sex), sodomy or anal sexual intercourse and birth control devices. These moral theologians and ethicists argue that it is because of human moral evil, sin, and perversion that human beings have largely separated sexual activity from its primary function as procreation within the society and legally approved bond of marriage.

Moral theologians and ethicists make the moral judgement that it is because of human sin and moral evil, including immoral Christian teachers and their lustful and sinful followers, that sex has become another human recreational activity and capitalist commodity. They observe that some people have even supported legal prostitution and sex for advertising of all kinds of goods!

According to these moral traditionalists and religious conservatives, the "post-Christian" Western society's moral relativism has destroyed the sanctity of sex within the traditional marriage bond. They lament that Hollywood's films and sex industry have tragically transformed sex into another valuable capitalist form of goods to be packaged and sold or bought at will. Casual sellers and buyers of sex take various forms. Prostitution, pornography, advertising and merchandise are common examples that are justifiably cited. The more sophisticated realize that the exploitation and misuse of sex can take many different forms that should be correctly identified and condemned.

However, most of the sermons and literature are directed against the more visible and prevalent hedonistic forms of some casual sexual relationships, cohabitation, divorce and homosexuality. Ultimately, these moralists and religious people condemn all forms of sexual activity engaged in primarily for its own sake as a source of pleasure of a recreational activity. That is to behave like animals "in heat," rather than rational, responsible and moral people.

From a conservative religious and moral perspective, it can be observed that there is a need for many people to return to what Aristotle called "the virtue of moderation." Definitely, there is virtue and goodness which are found in "the virtue of moderation," including matters of sex, drink, food, work and exercise. For instance, those who lose moral, spiritual and physical self-discipline and control become degraded when they are controlled by their sexual or other physical desires, instincts and drives like the unintelligent, non-thinking and amoral animals. If this happens, then those people may behave like the amoral and unthinking instinct driven animals. In this existential crude form, human beings degrade themselves as they surrender their reason, intellect, dignity and moral responsibility and choose to live as some animals.

In some cases, some people have sacrificed careers, education, money, integrity, health and lives in order to satisfy their "lower animal nature" at the level of sex. This occurs even among the rich, educated and the most powerful human beings, such as the USA presidents! The case of Monica Lewinsky is a good example. Nevertheless, there is nothing extraordinary about sex! As we know, it is natural. Even unintelligent trees, insects, and animals such as dogs and cats do it by natural instinct! As such, it is more divine to control one's animal instincts and cravings for food, sex, drink, aggression and violence than to yield and do them, like unthinking, dumb beasts and plants!

Within this moral context, it is therefore, amazing that many young and morally immature and irresponsible teenage students on many college and university campuses engage in risky sexual and self-destructive behavior. Some of the college freshmen being away from their watchful parents, having gained their moral and sexual freedom for the first time, behave as amoral wild animals. That is, they surrender their bodies to the control and direction of their hormones and sex-drives, rather than their minds. Some of them become infamous "sex machines" and main bearers of sexually transmitted diseases on their respective campuses.

Many of these teenage undergraduates, especially some males who see themselves as "studs," glamorize indiscriminate sex as a "sexual conquest," and the "binge drinking" of alcoholic beverages until they almost pass out or can't tell right from wrong and good from evil. At this point, these kinds of people, irrespective of their age, occupation and intellect, have actually degraded themselves to the instinctual sexual level of the unthinking and amoral beasts in heat, during the mating season. Under the influence of alcohol or drugs, many college students engage in highly risky sexual behaviors and female students become pregnant. Sexually transmitted diseases also become a problem on many college campuses as result of irresponsible overindulgence in drugs and sex.

It is obvious why this materialistic and self-destructive hedonistic mode of human life is negatively viewed as immoral. It is a great moral evil for the intelligent beings to behave like non-intelligent, and non-thinking amoral beasts. Human beings are intelligent, responsible, free and thinking moral agents, whereas most other animals are not. Therefore, it is a moral crime for the knowing and intelligent being or moral agent to surrender his or her mental faculties through the use of drugs and alcohol.

When the surrender of the moral agency happens, the community should come in to help and discipline the undisciplined member of their community. This is the function of a caring and responsible community. The community should never allow its members to degrade themselves and other people by sinking morally lower to the level of shameless and guiltless amoral animals. Emotions and hormones should never be allowed to control and govern an intelligent moral agent. To allow natural desires of the body, hormones and physical instincts to control the mind, is to surrender one's humanity, intellect and moral agency.

This moral irresponsibility also leads to the loss of human privileges such as freedom and respect. Jail sentencing of offenders, evildoers and criminals is the best expression of this societal disapproval and censorship of irresponsible moral behavior that trivializes the intellect and civic virtues, or abuses freedom and moral responsibility. These are real negative social and legal consequences for any person who chooses to live according to his or her animal nature. The debased form of human form of life rejects the person's divine and higher level of positive self-actualization in accordance with the moral guidance of the of the intellect or enlightened mind (reason) and the noble virtues of wisdom and self-control!

As a result, some parents and other concerned people have made the sad observations that on some weekends, some undisciplined college fraternities, and occasionally, the sororities are more like animal zoos when it comes to food, sex, and alcoholic drinks, rather than college. Nevertheless, there are many college and university residential campuses where academic work, sound education, moral training in civic virtues and preparation for future leadership are the main priorities.

However, many teenagers express varying degrees of moral rebellion against traditional moral conventions and religious values. This leads some of them to indulge in the "forbidden fruit (s)" of sex, alcoholic drinks and drugs. In this moral and religious rebellion and hedonistic experimentation of life, the body and all its sensory sexual pleasures, they abdicate the moral guidance of reason, and allow feelings, pleasures and sexual drives to direct them. As result, many of them have become careless pleasure-seekers and irresponsible hedonists.

Correspondingly, sexually transmitted diseases and abortions are common within this group, particularly, on college and university coeducational campuses. College freshmen and sophomores are disproportionately represented within this category. This is partly due to the fact they have not yet learned to use their newly acquired freedom and moral autonomy in more creative, positive and responsible ways. Having been deontological in their moral orientation and there being no fear and supervision of parents at college. As a result, binge drinking of alcoholic beverages, illicit drugs, laziness, sexual promiscuity, shoplifting, cheating on homework assignments, loud-music, depression and attempted suicides are also serious problems within this college group. Some people grow-up thinking that this kind of life is acceptable.

Hollywood films and popular entertainment reinforces this kind of hedonistic world-view.

In some cases, some important leaders and successful people have been humiliated by scandals that have brought them down to the ordinary moral level of the common prostitutes, pimps, drug abusers, and criminals. The traditional, Christian, dualistic, moral theologians may erroneously attribute this moral rebellion to temptation by the Devil. However, this excuse does not work since the Devil is a nonentity. The "Devil" being a mere metaphorical and anthropomorphic dualistic personification and symbolization of human moral evil, misuse of human causal freedom, and human moral failure to live according to reason, the good, virtue, self-disciple and sound moral judgement is a mere scapegoat for these moral and spiritual failures. The human body and its sensual desires are not the Devil.

It is also at this animal level of crude sexual drives that the mighty and the humble have been equalized in sin. Indeed, the Bible is clear that even great kings like David and the wise Solomon ceased to be either holy or wise when it came to sexual sins. King David fell in love with the naked and physically attractive Bathsheeba whom he secretly saw from the height of his palace balcony, and subsequently arranged to have her husband killed at the war front in order to marry her. On the other hand, King Solomon, who was known for great intelligence and wisdom, is reported to have amassed about a thousand women for his harem! Finally, Samson's tragic story also teaches us how sexual craving, moral failure to control one's sex drive, indiscipline and sin can lead even a holy man to both sin and premature death (cf. Judg. 16).

Like Samson, many Church leaders, politicians and professionals have been blackmailed. In some cases, they have also become publicly embarrassed or disgraced because of irresponsible indulgence in sex. The famous cases of the Rev. Jim Baker, Jimmy Swargart, Gary Hart, O.J. Simpson, Prince Charles and Princess Diana, Anita Hill and Judge Clarence Thomas, and more graphically, the cases of President Bill Clinton Paula Jones, and finally, the media sensationalized drama of the sex scandal between President Clinton and Monica Lewinsky, the young White House intern, are examples of this sensitive moral issue of sex.

However, the Christians must remember that Jesus never judged or rejected the sinners, such as the prostitutes and greedy tax-collectors. Instead, he extended God's unconditional love and free forgiveness of sins. This is illustrated by a woman who was caught in adultery (cf. John 8:1-11). Jesus did not condemn her. In this manner, Jesus has set very high standards for his obedient followers and the Church. God's saints and the Church are called by God to become like Jesus in the world. They are God's instruments of unconditional love, free forgiveness of sins, healing, peace and reconciliation of sinners tormented by guilt. God's forgiveness, free redemptive and healing love must be unconditionally extended to all sinners, including those who are guilty of sexual sins and moral failures. The loving and merciful God forgives all sins of all the repentant people. God's Church must do the same.

# Chapter 8

# Creation and Redemption: God, Church, Sex And Community

Sex is universally regarded as a very sensitive social, religious and moral subject. Sex and its morally acceptable normal biological functions and societal expressions are essentially supernatural, social and private. These complex natural and supernatural functions take place within the social and biological context of the community as God's sacred arena of creation, humanization and divinization of the evolutionary human beings. Each human community represents God's own true Creation Covenant. Ultimately, the human community constitutes God's universal Creative and "Redemptive Church" or "Ecclesial Community."

## 1. Marriage and Sex as God's Supernatural Medium For Creation of New Life: A Global Moral View

Traditionally, sex has been universally religiously perceived, and positively morally affirmed as God's good supernatural universal free gift for the creatures' natural self-reproduction. This remains the central teaching of most religions, including traditional Christianity, Judaism and Islam. This theocentric and natural moral theory of sex is grounded in both the natural law and God's special revelation (cf. Gen. 1:26-31) as its essential foundations and supporting twin pillars.

In addition, sex also gives God's creatures their direct natural definitive biological identity and function. Gender provides both cultural and social identity within the family, community and the world. For instance, in most traditional rural African and Asian cultures and societies, women serve the roles of full-time mothers and housewives.

The females as mothers give birth and take care of the young children, whereas the males as husbands and fathers are the main breadwinners for the family. In the developing countries, very often these men leave their villages and travel to the cities in search of employment. They try to earn money to supplement the income from the family farm or small business. This is not easy. There are very few available jobs in the African and Asian cities where unemployment is often more than 70 per cent. As a result, prostitution and other crimes are also very common.

In sound a religion and good principles of ethics, sex is celebrated as God's special supernatural gift for the creation of new life from the existing living things. Therefore, the apparently ordinary sex is simultaneously both God's supernatural and natural biological provision for the creation of new life including both human and nonhuman living beings. Within this theocentric understanding of nature (ontology) and Christian theological and ethical understanding of humanity (anthropology), sex is properly understood as God's supernatural gift for the continuing divine process of creation and evolution of new life and more intelligent higher beings, such as the human beings.

Accordingly, in this evolutionist work and Christian understanding, sex is also positively affirmed as the natural and supernatural means by which God creates all human beings. That is the main reason why the Roman Catholic Church has consistently condemned in *vitro fertilization*, and genetic engineering and the cloning of people. The Roman Church condemns these reproductive technologies as unacceptable unnatural means of reproduction where the medical technocrat plays the role of God in the selection of desirable traits to be inherited and the undesirable ones to be liquidated.

Traditionally, heterosexuality has been both universally and traditionally regarded as the correct and acceptable conventional moral means for personal sexual expression and fulfillment. This takes place within the social, religious, legal and moral context of the community and its moral codes and laws. This is accomplished through the institution of marriage or other suitable, legal, committed and loving sexual arrangements. Marriages in the West have tended to be monogamous, whereas in Africa and the Muslim countries, they were polygamous.

Because sexuality was culturally social, nearly all marriages in traditional African and Asian societies were also arranged by the families and other members of the community. Sex and marriage had little to do with romantic love or mere sexual fulfillment. They dealt with the fundamental social relationships within the family and between families linked through the marriage alliances. The children born were also members of the whole community and not the property of the parents! The whole community or village served as an extended family for the young children. The traditional African saying that "it takes a village to raise a child" was true. Each responsible woman was a considered as a "surrogate mother" to each child. Likewise, each man was a "surrogate father" to each child. The village children also regarded each other as brothers and sisters.

This practice provided the essential loving and peaceful environment for the positive nurture and growth of children as well adjusted, social, loyal, virtuous and peace-loving citizens of the respective community. This is mainly why African citizenship and loyalty to the local village, clan and tribe are often considered to be more important, in much of Africa and Asia, than the citizenship and loyalty to the larger community, such as nation, regional grouping and the Global Community, such as the United Nations. In the case of Africa, tribalism has seriously hindered both the needed national unity and the Pan-African Unity and integration of the feudalist African fragmented and ethnically feuding nations into a new major political world power and an economically viable block, namely, a "United States of Africa."

In these traditional African and Arab countries, the traditional marriage customs encourage men to marry several wives at the same time. For economic, social, political, religious and cultural reasons, in these countries, polygamous marriages were considered politically, socially and morally ideal, practical and more economically preferred forms of permanent marriages and sexual arrangements. For that matter, the rich and famous King Solomon who is reported in the Hebrew Bible to have had seven hundred wives and three hundred concubines. Yet, he was blessed by God and esteemed as the wisest man. God did not direct him to divorce his many wives and remain with one so as to be righteous or holy. Polygamy is not a sin or a moral evil before God. It is a mere human cultural and social preference.

Obviously, according to a good Christian theology and ethics God is not interested in the trivial issues of life or bothered by the different major socioeconomic issues of the various societies' family structures, such as polygamy or monogamy and celibacy. Before God all people are essentially equal. This is true regardless of their social, marital, economic and political status in the community and the world. God is just and impartial. Therefore, God is not impressed by self-serving human deeds of pride and egocentric heroism. On the contrary, God is interested in the nature and quality of interpersonal or social relationships. Consequently, God is interested in the central moral and interrelational issues of justice, love and peace within the family and the community.

Therefore, contrary to the claims of many conservative Western Evangelical Christians that God has eternally and universally decreed the sanctity of monogamous heterosexual marriages by virtue of God's creation and wedding of Adam and Eve (Gen. 1:25-31), in reality, God does not prefer monogamy to polygamy. Nor does God prefer married people to the celibate ones, or the celibate to the married people! Likewise, God does not prefer the heterosexual people to the homosexuals! And unlike most people, God is impartial and unconditionally loves people regardless of their gender and sexual orientation. This is God's universal and unconditional redemptive love at work in the community and the evolutionary moral consciousness and history of the world.

The human beings and both their cultures and religions have specific preferences and biases. In order to sanctify and universalize these local cultural and religious moral and cultural preferences, these preferences and prejudices are normatively ascribed to God's essence and revelation. Then, they are imposed on the world as God's holy will, revelation and universally binding divine eternal moral law. As God's moral law or revelation, it is sometimes dramatized in holy activities in the world. A good example is the biblical story of the destruction of Sodom and Gomorrah as sinful and homosexual communities (Gen. 19).

However, this story reflects the Hebrew cultural bias and religious condemnation of homosexuality. It is not about sexual immorality as a whole. For instance, Lot suggests giving to the men of Sodom his virgin daughters so that they could be raped! That is a worse moral evil than that of homosexuality! Nevertheless, Lot wants to protect his male guests from being raped by the men of Sodom, but has no hesitation about offering his own virgin daughters to be raped by the men.

Obviously, this story is a Hebrew moral and cultural condemnation of homosexuality in favor of heterosexuality. Lot's story of visiting anonymous angels disguised as men and the destruction of the cities of the hedonistic Sodom and Gomorrah is not a story about God's condemnation of urban life or homosexuality. It is not a biblical story about sexual morality as a whole. It is not a story about marriage, virginity or sexual activity outside marriage. Lot's story is not concerned about these moral components of sexual morality and family life.

Lot's story is only concerned with the moral evils of homosexuality and the possible rape of his male guests by the men of Sodom. The story makes it implicitly clear that the men of Sodom found his male guests more sexually appealing than Lot's virgin daughters. This is a historically influential anti-homosexual Hebrew moral and religious story. Later, this story served as the moral foundation and theological basis for Moses' legislation against homosexuality, and the stipulation of capital punishment for such a homosexual practice as a Hebrew cultural and religious taboo or abomination (cf. Lev. 18:20).

Unfortunately, St. Paul being a patriarchal Jew inadvertently introduced into Christianity and its scriptures the traditional Hebrew cultural bias and religious abhorrence for homosexuality as a sin and abomination before God (cf. Rom. 1:17-32). This cultural bias against homosexuality was imported into Christianity in the name of God. This was done in the same way St. Paul reproduced the traditional Hebrew bias against women into the Christianity and the Church.

Nevertheless, St. Paul was a religious liberal who was eager to do away with other Hebrew cultural taboos, such as the food prohibitions, ritual circumcision and ceremonial laws concerning ritual cleanliness and holiness. As such, if Paul had not been Jewish in culture and religious upbringing, he could have also done away with the prohibition against homosexuality and the subordination of women. Liberation from the Mosaic Law and the reformation of Judaism remained incomplete despite the efforts of Jesus, Paul, James, John, Tertullian, Athanasius, Justin Martyr, Augustine and other early Christian thinkers and reformers.

However, since St. Paul did not complete the initial Christian reformation or complete the separation of Christianity from Judaism, today's Church can complete it. The Church can go further than Paul and Martin Luther did. In the name of God and the risen Christ, the Church can remove the current oppressive prohibitions against homosexuality. This reformation can be carried out in the same way in which it has done with the passages prohibiting women's ordination and the exercise of leadership within God's Church (cf. 1 Cor. 13:34-35; 1 Tim. 2:9-14; 3:1-13). Obviously, St. Paul introduced into Christianity the same kind of strict patriarchal and anti-homosexual sexual values, taboos and prejudices which he had internalized and inherited as an active conservative Hebrew, religious fundamentalist and self-righteous Pharisee.

As a consequence, a true Christian reformation of Judaism must be based on the exemplary life, ministry and inclusive moral teachings of Jesus as the Christ (cf. Matt. 5-7), instead of being based on those popular teachings and writings of St. Paul, which most Protestants find more intriguing than the teachings of Jesus the Christ. One of the main problems is that whereas St. Paul was not an eyewitness of Christ, he actually wrote the earliest influential material in the New Testament.

The Pauline material constitutes more than a quarter of the New Testament, whereas Jesus himself wrote nothing. Jesus' immediate followers, such as the Twelve Apostles also wrote very little. This was mainly due to the fact that they were largely ignorant and uneducated simple men. For instance, James and Simon Peter, who later became the successor of Jesus and the first Pope, were simple fishermen before they became Jesus' disciples.

Later, the apostles became the celebrated apostles and founders of the Early Church. They are the first Christian bishops of the Christian Church. The Church was largely a Church of the marginalized, disenfranchised, uneducated, ignorant and simple poor people. This remained generally true until 313 C.E. when the Emperor Constantine became converted to Christianity and transformed it from a persecuted minority religion into an established official religion of the Roman Empire. This is when Sunday became a public holiday.

The apostles were apocalyptic in their world-view and expected the end of the world to take place within their own lifetime. They expected the immediate return of Christ as the eschatological Lord and King of God's Kingdom. As such, they saw no good reason to hire secretaries and dictate them the teachings of Christ in a systematic manner, as they remembered them. This would have been essential if the teachings of Jesus had to be reported accurately and for them to serve as the essential moral foundation and theological guides for the Church which they had founded. This task was left to others, especially St. Paul who was better educated in the Hebrew Law, scriptures, and Hellenistic philosophy.

It is self-evident that the twelve apostles despised Paul who had persecuted Christianity before his conversion, and was an outsider who did not know the original teachings of Jesus. Paul had also rejected the Mosaic Law which they still observed as Jews and good members of Judaism. The apostles did not wish to start a new religion. They saw the teachings of Jesus as a reformation of Judaism.

However, St. Paul, being better educated, also better understood that Jesus's teachings constituted a new inclusive religion in which the Gentiles could feel at home. He saw very clearly that Jesus' teachings shifted the religious moral emphasis from God's impartial justice, holiness and righteousness as observing the Mosaic Law to a new inclusive global and inclusive ethic of agape and righteousness as the performance of good self-sacrificial and unconditional deeds of agape as deeds of mercy, unmerited grace, free forgiveness, nonviolence and promotion of peace and harmony in a violent, greedy and materialistic world. The Pauline perspective of Christ's teachings effectively broadened and transformed those original narrow Jewish teachings into a new inclusive global religion, namely, Christianity. A Jewish based form of primitive Christianity which taught that Jesus was a prophet, rabbi and Jewish Messiah died out.

The Pauline and John based Gentile form of Christianity soon transformed Jesus into a God and the doctrine of the Holy Trinity began to emerge (cf. John 1:1-18). As a result, after this long process of the Christians' deification of Jesus, for these Christians, Jesus' teachings also became correspondingly viewed as "God's immutable revelation" and "new universal moral law" and definitive religious and exclusive moral path back to God and salvation.

Those people who held this moral and theological doctrine, began to teach that outside Christ and his Church, nobody could ever be saved by God. This doctrine dominated Christianity and its moral and theological teachings. They also inspired European racial and religious ethnocentrism, white-supremacy, European imperialism and missionary activities in Africa, Asia and the newly discovered "New World" of North and South America. This view was revamped by Vatican II (1962-65). By that time, it had already caused great cultural, religious, moral and theology discrimination and intolerance to these non-Western people. The teachings of Jesus and St. Paul provided the moral guidelines in the case of missionary activities and religious doctrines within this new global religious arena with its new challenge of pluralistic and conflicting cultural ideals and strongly rooted local traditional religious values.

However, being Jews, both Jesus and Paul were conditioned and shaped by the Mosaic Law, the Hebrew patriarchal culture and values regarding sexual morality, ritual purity, gender roles in both society and religion. Accordingly, although Jesus ministered to many women with respect and sensitivity, he did not include any woman among his chosen inner circle of the twelve apostles whose successors are known as bishops. Similarly, St. Paul excluded them from the ordained ministry of the churches which he had founded among the Gentiles. As a result, there are some churches, such as the Roman Catholic Church and the [American] Southern Baptist Convention still prohibit the ordination of women into the holy orders of their respective churches. Clearly, this exclusion of women is both morally and theologically unjustified within today's global cultural, inclusive religious and moral context.

Ultimately, both Jesus and Paul excluded women from the ordained ministry of their time due to a local Hebrew patriarchal cultural value and consideration for local cultural appropriateness and effectiveness of their ministry to their local audiences rather than God's universal revelation and immutable Christian theological teaching of Christ. Oppressive patriarchy in both Church and global social culture is due to serious sins and cultural evils of sexism and idolatrous male self-deification than God's universal will and moral law in both creation and redemption. Therefore, any religious myth or doctrine that teaches patriarchy as good and the subordination of women by men as God's will or holy ordinance, must be considered as an evil to be exorcized from religion and people's consciousness because it is antithetical to God's moral essence as pure goodness, justice and Agape.

Another example of culture, religion and sexuality in conflict is the practice of celibacy and monasticism. For instance, the Roman Catholic Church extols the virtues of virginity and celibacy over good marriages. Conversely, within the patriarchal systems of Islam and the Traditional African Religion, celibacy is despised as vice or an abnormality. Instead, they extol the virtues of polygamous marriages or the "possession of many wives and children" as evidence of God's favor and blessings.

Therefore, whereas many Africans are Roman Catholics, they generally also reject the traditional Catholic ethic of celibate nuns, monks and priests! As a result, there is a great shortage of Roman Catholic priests, particularly in these countries. Those Africans who positively answer the call to the priesthood sometimes leave the priesthood in order to get married. However, some of those who stay, often secretly take concubines and produce children out of wedlock. They do this in quest for the traditional African religious, social and personal sexual satisfaction and biological fulfillment. This human mission as the reason for being, is traditionally accomplished through sexual the sacred act of sexual intercourse and self-reproduction. For these African Catholic priests, the reproduction of children is both culturally and religiously considered being more important and sacred than the vow of celibacy which they made at their ordination to the priesthood. According to the African Traditional Religion and culture, not having children is considered to be a misfortune due to some hidden sin, and therefore, both a social and religious disgrace.

In traditional Africa, having many healthy children was considered to be an indication of God's favor and blessings. Similarly, having many wives and wealth was evidence of God's many blessings. Many wives were essential for providing cheap farm labor as well as producing many children for the same purpose.

In addition, According to African Traditional Religion, personal immortality was gained through the bearing of many children. This was achieved through memory and offering sacrifices to the dead ancestors as well as through genetic survival through one's own biological descendants. Before the Western Human Genome Project and its validation of the fact that the DNA transmission confers some form of reincarnation and limited immortality to the parents, the Africans knew it. They had already institutionalized and implemented this spiritual-biological theory of immortality through the practice of polygamy and having many children.

Like the ancient Hebrews, the Asians, and Native Americans, the ancient Africans believed that sex was God's sacred gift for reproduction. They also believed that a person would be remembered and immortalized through having children and many descendants. Children were also valuable as a free labor source, and insurance of care and protection during the old age. In the absence of modern provisions for "social security" and "public welfare assistance," the children were the real means for medical insurance, "social security" and the "welfare system." Accordingly, within these societies, it was understandable that nonreproductive sex, such as homosexuality, prostitution, adultery, fornication, bestiality, incest, rape, masturbation, oral and anal sex (sodomy), along with other forms of casual and recreational sex, were condemned as abominations and proscribed by religious and state laws.

It is a well-established fact that sex is also a serious potential source of competition, conflicts and aggression within the family, community and the world. Therefore, the subject of sex was universally censored by the community and religion. Sex and related issues were heavily regulated by religion or the Church and the laws of most states. Most of the religious laws and commandments that define and regulate sexuality, such as those of Hammurabi, Moses, Jesus and Prophet Muhammad, were all issued to the people in the holy name of God. They were proclaimed to be God's universal and immutable laws to be obeyed everywhere in the community by all the obedient and God-fearing people.

Those who violated God's moral laws through Moses were judged to be guilty of a capital offense. Very often, they were summarily tried in public, sentenced to death and immediately executed by the mobs or other religious or state representatives. The Mosaic Law and the stipulations of death-penalty for incest, adultery, homosexuality and bestiality were attributed to the eternal God as his absolute universal moral law and immutable holy revelation. Essentially, Jesus was persecuted and finally executed mainly because of his teachings, disrespect and public violations of the Mosaic law.

## 2. God, Church, Sex and Controversy Of Homosexuality

Like most of the Western world, in the United States, sex has become a source of moral confusion, serious theological debates and religious conflicts. This undesirable state of affairs has led to serious social, political and religious debate, conflict and division. In some cases, there have been serious grievances, and quest for legal and political state intervention.

The primary causes of this violent controversy and the corresponding religious and political uproar is the topic of homosexuality. It has led to the acrimonious debates on the morality and legal validity of homosexuality, and the proposed Church blessings of gay and lesbian marriages. These ferocious debates have also included sensitive moral issues of extramarital sexual activity, sex among consenting unmarried adults, euthanasia, and "abortion on demand," irrespective of the term of pregnancy. The conservatives have used the Bible as the moral basis for their condemnation of homosexuality and its practice.

The American Episcopal Church has been nearly split into two over the acceptance of homosexual practice and the ordination of non-celibate homosexuals. Bishop John Spong's enthusiastic theological, ecclesiastical formal and pastoral support for homosexuality has upset many Christians in America, including those in his own Diocese of Newark in New Jersey. The conservative members of his diocese had tried unsuccessfully to get rid of him and were relieved when he retired in 2000 and went to Harvard Divinity School in Cambridge.

Bishop Spong, an outspoken Episcopalian liberal bishop from the USA, antagonized many conservative Anglican bishops from Africa and Asia when he enthusiastically proposed the Anglican Church's acceptance of homosexuality at the 1998 Anglican Bishops' Lambeth Conference in England. He strongly promoted the issue of homosexuality despite the fact that the majority of the Anglican bishops were opposed to the acceptance of the homosexual practice as "a pagan" and an immoral sexual practice that is inherently antithetical to true Christianity and any obedient and biblically based Christian Church.

Nevertheless, the Anglican Bishops' Committee on Sexuality debated the topic of homosexuality, and some American bishops' positive affirmation of homosexuality nearly alienated most the African evangelical bishops who are traditionally both biblically and theologically conservative. At the same time, though economically poor, and politically powerless at the Lambeth Conference, these conservative African bishops constitute a regional majority of the all bishops within the Anglican Communion.

Despite being bishops of very impoverished dioceses in the poor and developing countries of the world, the African and Asian evangelical bishops have a strong prophetic Christian voice that cannot be ignored. For instance, at the Lambeth Conference of 1998, the African voting bishops numbered more than 234 as compared to 177 from North America. Furthermore, Christianity is growing faster in Africa whereas on the decline in the West. Therefore, in the future the most active and influential Anglicans and Roman Catholics will probably be also located within these conservative and evangelical churches of Africa. For that matter, Africa may produce one of the key popes of the new millennium.

Having failed to resolve the debate on homosexuality or stop the ban on its practices within the Anglican Communion, many liberal Episcopalian bishops (Anglican bishops in the USA) got angry and resorted to some unorthodox economic, religious, academic and political bullying of their Third World bishops as some methods to force the Anglican Church to lift the ban on the practices of homosexuality. However, the African and Asian conservatives were not for sale. They responded by putting pressure on the Western and North American bishops to accept the Anglican resolution condemning homosexuality as a sin or force the Anglican Communion to split over the issue.

The conservatives consistently argued that homosexuality was both a heinous sin and moral evil condemned by God through the holy Scriptures. The liberals were contending that the prohibitions of homosexuality were based on an ancient religious superstition and ignorance concerning biological factors involved in human nature and sexuality. The conservatives condemned the Western Church for reviving the ancient Greek pagan practices of homosexuality that had been condemned by St. Paul (cf. Rom. 1: 17-32), and the traditional Church.

Subsequently, on Saturday 29 January 2000, in Singapore, the conservative Archbishops Moses Tay of the South-East Asia Anglican Province, and Emmanuel Kolini of the Rwanda Anglican Province, along with Bishop John Ruchayana of Shyira Diocese in Rwanda, serving as the representatives of the conservative wing of the Anglican Communion, consecrated and ordained the Reverends Charles H. Murphy III and John H. Rodgers of the United States as Missionary Bishops for the USA. This was in protest against the acceptance of the practices of homosexuality within the Episcopal Church by both the lay people and the clergy.

The Episcopal Church in the United States had rejected the Lambeth condemnation of homosexuality as a sin and many dioceses were ordaining non-celibate homosexuals to the priesthood and considering to approve proposals to wed homosexual couples within the Church and to extend to them the same benefits as those traditionally enjoyed by the heterosexual couples. Some Episcopalians have left the denomination in protest, and joined the Roman Catholic Church which still condemns homosexuality as a sin, moral evil and sexual pervasion.

The above is just one of the examples of how these issues on sexuality have caused serious controversy, moral confusion, theological debate and division within the Christian Church. The United Methodist Conferences and Conventions of 1996 and 2000, and the Presbyterian Synods of 1997 and 2000, also vigorously debated the controversial topic of homosexuality in their churches. They too, rejected it for being incompatible with the scriptures and banned its practice for both the laity and the clergy within their churches.

Between May 2-12, 2000, the Worldwide Methodist Conference meeting in Cleveland, Ohio, by a great majority of two to one, the delegates reaffirmed the Methodist Church's previous condemnations of homosexuality and ban of homosexuality and homosexual marriages. These practices were declared to be incompatible with the scriptures and the Christian Church's teaching. As in the case of the Anglican bishops at the Lambeth Conference in 1998, the evangelical and conservative African and Asian Methodist delegates were also in this debate straightforward and uncompromising their strong rejection and condemnation of the practice of homosexuality. They declared homosexuality to be an unnatural sexual act, sinful moral social and evil, anti-biblical and a great abomination before both God and humanity.

Similarly, on June 14, 2000, the Southern Baptist Convention meeting in Florida, also passed a strong resolution condemning the cultural practice of homosexuality as a sin against God. This resolution was included in the revised document on the *Southern Baptist Convention Faith and Message.* On May 31, 2000, the Rev. Phil Hart, a United Methodist minister was ousted from his Church in Columbus, Ohio for having disclosed that he was gay. The 970 Clergy Assembly of the West Ohio United Methodist Conference debated the Rev. Hart's case for about 40 minutes and overwhelmingly voted to dismiss him as a minister of the United Methodist Church. His homosexual lifestyle was in conflict with the Church moral and social principles as outlined in *The Book of Discipline.* It is self-evident that matters of homosexuality will continue to become a serious local and international moral issue of controversy and debate in these churches until the sexual cultural practice of homosexuality is accepted by the Church.

However, this kind of Christianity that has been converted by the local culture and shaped into its own image, instead of the reverse, will continue to be challenged by some Christian thinkers, prophets, saints and evangelists. It is exactly this kind of Church that Soren Kierkegaard denounced in his writings (*Either/Or; The Postscript Fragment; Fear and Trembling;* and *Training in Christianity*) as a form of "Western paganism" and a mere cultural Christendom. The Catholic Church has also consistently condemned homosexual practices, yet without condemning the natural homosexual orientation. Traditionally, the Church did not accept the idea that people could be encouraged to act upon their inborn homosexual orientation, since that homosexual orientation was negatively viewed as a defect in nature, and therefore, to be corrected. As a result, the mainline Church has traditionally encouraged counseling, medical treatment, and celibacy as the morally acceptable recommended Christian moral and pastoral solutions for dealing with persons born with a natural homosexual orientation.

Nevertheless, in its appropriate societal, cultural, religious and conventional moral expression, sex is not a matter of mere personal likes and dislikes as a just private affair, as some people sometimes mistakenly believe or affirm. In its true universal existential social reality, sex is complex and multidimensional in both function and expression. Sex is personal, social, legal, political, economic and religious in both practice and consequences. As such, sex is controlled by the laws of the state, Church and the community. Both the state and the Church regulate the practice of sex and license those qualified to engage in it because it is the foundation of the society, Church, values and relationship.

The moral and socially appropriate expressions and acceptable objects of sex, age, and medical condition are defined by the law. In order to protect the various categories of people from harm and exploitation, most nations have enacted laws which protect the sexual exploitation of the severely mentally disabled, the unconscious, minors and the elderly people. They also prohibit close relatives people, such as parents and their children from engaging in sexual intercourse. For instance, laws prohibit sex or marriage between a man and his sister, mother, grandmother, and other close relatives. This is defined as an immoral sexual and deviant social act that constitutes "incest." This sexual crime and pervasion is censored by most human cultures, and may be punishable by law in many states and nations of the world. There are also moral laws prohibiting bestiality (sexual intercourse between people and animals, such as dogs, cows, pigs, sheep, horses and the like) as an immoral, unnatural and abominable act.

Mental competency for consent for sex is required among adults, prior to lawful sexual intercourse. This means that the adults must be free from drugs, excessive alcohol or other substances that inhibit mental capacity. Consent obtained while the person is under the influence of drugs or other serious mental disability is legally and morally considered to be uninformed, involuntary, incompetent. It is nonbinding. It is also rejected by the law courts in case of a law suit. As a result, the person engaging in sex with such a mentally incapacitated person will be charged with the crime of rape! This is the same for a person who engages in sex with a mentally disabled person, a minor, or a subordinate whose job (or grade) is threatened by a refusal to engage in such a coerced sexual act. Sexual harassment and rape do not have to be accomplished by physical force, as some people have wrongly assumed.

According to the traditional Christian moral teachings and family values, sex is God's sacred gift for the primary function of reproduction. The joy of sexual intercourse was designed to make the reproductive act pleasurable. Marriage and the family were the necessary and morally acceptable contexts for sexual activity, reproduction and the rearing of children. As such, to be born out of wedlock was considered a great moral and social evil as well as a sin before God. Derogatory terms like "bastard" and "illegitimate" were used to refer to those children born out of wedlock and they still carry serious social stigma in many societies.

According to the traditional conservative Protestant and Catholic Church's moral teachings, doctrines and sexual ethics, the human sexual acts were only considered morally acceptable if they were designed and intended to produce children within the context of marriage. As a result, all sexual acts whose goal was sexual pleasure and gratification were condemned as immoral. There could not be any moral justification for the separation of sexual intercourse from its divine and natural purpose, namely, reproduction.

The U.S. Southern Baptist Convention, and the Roman Catholic Church condemn sexual intercourse outside the context and contract of marriage as sins of adultery and fornication. They also condemn other sexual practices including: homosexuality (same sex intercourse), bestiality (sex with animals), masturbation (sex with oneself or other objects), and abortion. The Catholic Church recognizes a homosexual orientation as a natural biological condition. Nevertheless, the Catholic Church reaffirms the traditional teaching that the homosexual orientation as a natural sexual orientation to seek sexual fulfillment from the people of the same gender is in itself a result of a defect. It is considered to be biological error that has occurred in God's mediated process of natural law in the creation of that particular individual. As such, a homosexual orientation is negatively viewed as a condition of deficiency which must not be acted upon in a sexual manner. It is either to be resisted or corrected and transformed into heterosexuality through therapy and counseling. It was biologically and medically attributed to hormonal imbalance and cultural conditioning.

Therefore, the Catholic Church still promotes the traditional solutions to homosexual orientation. It prescribes the traditional and controversial remedies of medical treatment, sexual abstinence and celibacy for those with this orientation. Gene therapy, hormonal treatment and counseling are recommended. Ultimately, the Catholic Church still regards it as a grave sin for anybody to act in a homosexual manner, either by voluntary choice or natural inclination. This position seems to be based on the ancient Hebrew, cultural, and religious inflexible moral doctrines of the ancient times, whereas the Catholic Church also affirms that natural law is God's universal and permanent moral law to govern the universe.

In general, the normative moral argument against homosexuality is grounded in the antiquated religious and cultural texts of Moses (cf. Lev. 18-22). These texts are not Christian. In addition, these Hebrew scriptures do not represent our cultures, religious codes, moral and sexual practices for us today. In a contextual revelation by God within a Hebrew culture and moral application, these Hebrew scriptures and moral codes were only binding on the Jews of a past era for whom God had culturally designed them, and appropriately revealed them through Moses, and the subsequent Hebrew prophets.

As a result, Mosaic Judaism is no longer binding on modern Jews themselves. As God's eschatological prophet, liberal religious reformer and moral teacher, Jesus both revised and reversed what was considered to be God's absolute revelation and the moral laws as revealed through Moses. For instance, Jesus rejected the deeply entrenched violence in the world as sanctioned by the Mosaic Law and the traditional practice of retaliation (*lex talionis*) as both justice and deterrent punishment for crimes of violence. He repudiated it along with any Mosaic laws that justified it in the name of God. Subsequently, Jesus replaced the Mosaic moral principle of "*lex talionis*" (equal retaliation) with the normative moral principle of agape as the unconditional love and free forgiveness for the neighbor (all human beings).

According to Jesus, the neighbor includes the enemy, the homosexuals and people of different races or cultures, and the people of different religions and ideologies. They are all to be accepted, forgiven and loved without any prior conditions. Jesus also promised to send the gift of God's Holy Spirit as a teacher that would continue to teach his followers new truths and revelations from God as they unfolded and became disclosed to the people in a particular historical time within the historical and evolutionary process in the world.

In this respect, we cannot refer back to Moses for normative and guiding principles regarding the moral life of Christians and the life of the Church today. Rather, we have to pray for the continuing revelation of God through the Holy Spirit and also refer to the teachings of Jesus Christ, especially his normative universal moral and redemptive principle of unconditional love for all human beings. Ultimately, God still speaks his or her holy Word to the world. Through the *Logos* and the Holy Spirit, the living cosmic creator and redeemer God continues to create, redeem the world, and reveal new truths and moral law to serve the beckoning light and moral guidance for the evolutionary life of the Church and the moral community.

Without this moral evolution and divine guidance, the Christian Church would have reverted to the Mosaic law and would have remained a mere sect of Judaism. The admission of the "gentiles" to the Church, the continuing universalization and reformation of the Church, including the inclusive language for God, and the ordination of women as ministers, priests and bishops within God's holy Church, are evidence of God's continuing revelation through the Holy Spirit and God's ongoing redemptive supernatural activities in the world.

The full acceptance of the homosexuals and their homosexual lifestyles, including the same sex marriages and the ordination of practicing homosexuals as priests and ministers in God's Church, is another moral and serious religious challenge to the religious community or the Church. However, this serious moral and religious challenge of either inclusion or exclusion of the homosexuals from God's redemptive Church, as the holy community (fellowship) of God's people, can be resolved through the unconditional full acceptance of the homosexuals and their sexuality on the basis of Christ's obligatory commandment of unconditional love and free forgiveness for all human beings without any conditions.

In addition, it could also probably be convincingly argued that from a biological, theological and moral perspective, the case of homosexual orientation should be redefined in biological terms as well as the natural law. From this triple foundation, one would probably argue that based on both the natural law and biology, the homosexual is not responsible for his or her natural condition as an *a priori* biological homosexual orientation. One can argue that based on nature and biology, a homosexual orientation can be determined to be "natural." Therefore, not to be condemned, when it is acted upon for sexual fulfillment with another consenting adult of a similar homosexual orientation. In this understanding, homosexuality can be said to occur naturally among the heterosexual evolutionary processes as "a natural variant" as opposed to treating it as "a defect" or a "biological glitch" and a sexual malfunction due to a hormonal imbalance or other medical or cultural problems.

Since we are all created by God through the mediation of natural law and evolution, it is amazing that most of the time, God's laws function well as intended by God. It is a miracle that God's cosmic laws of creativity or the natural law functions well most of the time. God's automated natural law is impartial. It does not discriminate against people who become homosexuals or those are born with disabilities. It functions mechanically in the cosmos according to God's general design and will. God corrects it or intervenes on behalf of some creatures. That divine intervention in the cosmic evolutionary or historical processes as well as the creatures' response to God's work of deliverance or salvation is called "*kairos*." Within this understanding, *kairos* is the negation of deism as the teaching that God created the universe a long time ago and left it to be operated by the cosmic laws of nature and evolution.

Therefore, in the case of humanity, God's natural law constitutes the person's own DNA as the person's unique bluepoint or map of what he she may become. Yet, God's active creative and redemptive presence are present as *kairos* through moral agency, freedom, spirit, intellect, self-transcendence, knowledge, grace, choice, agape, benevolence, good deeds of altruism and the experience of forgiveness. As such, the human DNA as the special human bluepoint determines human biological nature and some forms of biologically based behavior, such as sexual orientation and some genetically related diseases, but does not explain every aspect of human behavior, choices and uses or misuses of freedom. In other words, biology is not destiny.

Biology can be radically modified and redirected by other factors, such as religion, nutrition, education, socioeconomic class, personal discipline, exercise, habits or lifestyle and the environment. Therefore, the human being remains an open and incomplete mystery that changes constantly with each new choice made or not made, and with the actions carried out or omitted. As such, time, environment, choices, history, resources, technology and the community have as much influence on the shaping the nature and destiny of a person as the inherited DNA or the biological factors.

This is also the general environmental and biological background and context in which the controversial debate on homosexuality takes place. The biological determinists affirm that homosexuality is genetic and therefore, God's work to be accepted unconditionally. However, the environmentalists and cultural relativists counter argue that homosexuality is a matter of cultural conditioning and can be effectively transformed into heterosexuality.

The biological determinists counter argue that the homosexuals did not create themselves or freely choose their sexual orientation. They argue that the good, holy God and nature are responsible for that good creation of God. They also argue that since no treatment or counseling has effectively permanently reversed the natural condition of homosexual orientation, it should be accepted as natural and as God's will for those people. They strongly advocate for the homosexuals to be allowed legal sexual fulfillment with other consenting adults of a similar sexual orientation and for the Church to grant them God's blessings as it does to the heterosexual couples who request the Church and God's blessing of their lifelong companionship and sexual union.

The advocates of homosexuality and the wedding of the homosexual couples argue that apart from the begetting of children, the homosexual couples are equivalents of the heterosexual couples in terms of love and companionship, and that the same legal and economic benefits and protections should be extended to these homosexual couples in the same way in which they are extended to the heterosexual couples. As a result, many universities and major companies in the USA have extended the traditional family insurance coverage and other benefits to committed same sex couples and households. Due to the great mounting pressure, mainline liberal American Protestant churches, such as the Episcopal, United Methodist and Presbyterian churches are likely to follow this popular cultural trend and wed homosexual couples.

Like in the cases of the traditional sexual practices of heterosexuality, the advocates for homosexuality should place emphasis on homosexual marriages for committed and monogamous couples based on "right companionship to remove loneliness" (cf. Gen. 2:18). Accordingly, emphasis should be placed on the psychological and social suitability of the couple as mates and quality of their relationship. This includes the nature of commitment to a monogamous sexual relationship, rather than sexual orientation or the biological sex of the couples, since this homosexual marriage is for companionship as opposed to the heterosexual marriage where "the marriage between a man and woman" is traditionally socially designed and biologically intended for reproduction.

Therefore, it can be both morally and socially validly contended that in essence, the homosexual marriages functionally serve the same needs and support roles as the marriages of heterosexual couples who have past the childbearing age or those who do not intend to have any children, or those who cannot have children. Consequently, the moral, cultural, social disdain and religious traditional fear and rejection of homosexual sexual activity and marriage based on the traditional theological and social argument that homosexuality is unnatural because it does not lead to the reproduction of children is no longer a valid argument today, since the world is already overpopulated. Such an argument and objections to homosexuality are based on the traditional, cultural and religious prejudice against homosexuality or sexual relationships. Therefore, they are groundless. They are neither theologically sound nor morally justifiable today.

The above objection to homosexuality is based on the false ancient premise that today's marriages are still required to fulfill God's primordial commandment for reproduction and filling the Earth (Gen. 1:26-31). The Earth is already filled and even overpopulated! This being the case, then what the Earth really needs today is family planning and birth-control, instead of more children!

Therefore, homosexual relationships and marriages should be positively viewed as God's natural provision to the world with a good and effective solution for natural family planning and birth-control! Moreover, objections against homosexual activity also ignore the biological reality that some people are naturally born with a permanent sexual orientation to seek and have sexual pleasure and fulfillment with people of the same sex. In a simple manner, this fulfills the natural law.

The traditional objections against homosexuality often ignore the great importance of right companionship as a primary social and sexual role of marriage, apart from reproduction. If this were not the case, then those people who are unable to reproduce would not have been allowed to get married. All marriages would also become subject to voluntary dissolution after menopause or when the duties of reproduction and childbearing were completed! However, that is not the case. Indeed, such a law would be immoral and unacceptable. Therefore, loving, committed and discreet sexual activities between consenting and responsible adults should never be the business of other people, unless laws are violated.

In order to avoid destructive prejudice and violence, people's sexual affairs must be treated as private matters, and should remain a private affair, even if they have a social aspect and public consequences. Revelations of personal sexual matters outside the confidentiality of the of the sacramental confession and professional medical treatment can bring unpleasant and severe social, economic, legal, religious and political consequences. President William Clinton and Monica Lewinsky's widely publicized sexual scandal provides clear evidence for this important social and moral lesson. Indeed, many societies in Africa and Asia traditionally prohibited casual conversations or talk about personal sexual matters in the public. Even sexual organs could not be publicly named. In these societies, there were many sexual taboos which were designed to protect the sanctity of sex as God's sacred gift for the creation of new life. Accordingly, in Rwanda and Burundi the word for God (*Imaana)* and the word for the woman's reproductive organ (*imana*) are almost the same.

It should be understood that public revelation of these sexual matters will cause embarrassment, loss of dignity, loss of a job and the related benefits. Societal intolerance against the homosexuals in the USA, including those in the military where homosexuality is officially banned, led President Bill Clinton to devise the practical moral principle of "don't ask and don't tell." This moral principle is based on the existential reality of what happens in the military and other places when people learn that one of their own members if a homosexual. This is also true in the traditional Church community. Gay clergy and laity are marginalized or even ostracized by the mainline Church authorities and membership.

In any case, if the homosexual person is regarded as the unfortunate victim of God's creative process, he or she should not be doubly traumatized by God's own loving and redemptive community, such as the Church. The homosexual should not be rejected and ostracized from God's redemptive community or the Church instead of being redeemed, consoled and ministered. After all, Jesus's own ministry was directed to the outcasts of society and the religious community (Church) of his time. He embraced the prostitutes, tax-collectors, sinners and lepers who were rejected and thrown away by the religious community of his time.

The Pharisees as the self-elected moral and religious police of Jesus' time made sure that these religious and social outcasts were kept out of the temple for fear of ritual defilement from these "sinners" and ritually unclean people. Yet Jesus associated with them and ministered to them. He restored them to wholeness, God's fellowship and fullness of life within the community. The Church must follow the example of Jesus the Christ and welcome today's outcasts and the untouchables, such as the homosexuals, the victims of AIDS, the unemployed, the homeless, drug addicts, single teen-mothers and the prostitutes.

The Church should embrace them and their families in order to minister to them more effectively, bring God's unconditional love and salvation. Therefore, God's loving and obedient people cannot validly argue that the homosexuals should be excluded from the Kingdom of God due to God's own mistake that had occurred in God's indirect and mediated process of the act of creation through the natural law and biological evolution! The more loving and caring Christian response should be the inclusion and pastoral care for the homosexual persons as God own redeemed non-heterosexual children and true members of God's community.

The antiquated moral codes of sexual ethics and family must be carefully studied, appropriately revised and amended in order to remove the ancient and the Victorian puritanical moral and social moral ideals and the destructive traditional stigma attached to the homosexual committed relationships and non-traditional alternative marriage models and structures, such as those of working single parents. This acceptance of these non-traditional family structures will enable the community to devise more appropriate new structures of support for the people within those institutions. As the institutions change, so must the means of delivery for the socioeconomic support services and Christian ministries to meet the essential needs of the people and serve them more meaningfully and effectively. Otherwise, the Church may be ignored as an irrelevant and meaningless ancient religious system.

The American Catholic Bishops have voiced their strong opposition to this Vatican position on sexuality. On September 30, 1997, the American Catholic bishops released a pastoral letter as an official Church document which called for a Christian sympathetic understanding on matters of homosexuality, acceptance and the inclusion of the gays and lesbians within the Christian Church community. However, this ecclesiastical pastoral statement did not accept homosexuality as a valid sexual practice based on the natural state of an *a priori* homosexual orientation as an acceptable and good creation of God.

In actuality, the Catholic bishops' pastoral letter maintained the *status quo* on regarding the traditional moral debate on homosexuality and natural sexual orientation. The Roman Catholic Church rejected the idea of the natural homosexual orientation as a theological grounding and ethical justification for homosexuality. Natural homosexual orientation did not meet the necessary moral, theological, cultural and biological qualifications be accepted on the basis of the natural law alone. For instance, it neither negated nor reversed the existing papal encyclicals in their strong official ecclesiastical condemnations of all homosexual practices as "unnatural," "moral evil," "a biological defect," "sexual aberration" and a "mortal [deadly] sin."

The fundamental rationale and logic behind this moral papal position and traditional ecclesiastical teaching is that it is "unnatural," or against the norm, and not intended to produce an offspring within the context of holy matrimony. Arguments based on genetic or natural disposition in the form of homosexual orientation as a justification for homosexuality are rejected by the traditional moral theologians. They are also rejected by the conservative Christian and Muslim religious leaders in favor of counseling and medical treatment for homosexuals. They also advocate celibacy for those people who cannot be cured of homosexuality through traditional medical intervention and therapy.

According to this position, a natural homosexual orientation is a natural biological defect that is analogous to being born with an eyesight defect, such as myopia. The person born with the natural defect of myopia as a natural condition obviously has a serious natural eyesight deficiency. Naturally, the person rejects the natural defect and its limitations. Subsequently, the person seeks a medical correction of this defect by going to an eye doctor for proper eye corrective treatment. Surgery or prescription of corrective lens may provide the desired remedy, despite the inconvenience! The person born with the correctable eye defect does not stumble about blind on the moral justification based on natural law. That is, he or she does not claim the natural right to remain nearsighted or blind.

The non-biological determinists argue that biology is not destiny in the case of near vision nor should be in the case of an inborn case of homosexual orientation. Similarly, the traditional moral theologians and ethicists prefer medical intervention and therapy for the homosexuals, as people born with a natural defect and hormonal imbalance. These moral theorists contend that homosexuality is unacceptable natural defect in the human being and needs corrective treatment rather than moral, cultural and religious acceptance as a normal occurrence. As a result, they strongly affirm and teach that homosexuality is inconsistent with the scriptures, traditional Christian ethics, authentic Christian doctrine, and natural law. This is the position that the Anglican, Methodist, the Roman Catholic and the Southern Baptist Convention have officially taken and affirmed in their official statements on faith, morals and Christian practice as of 2000. These ecclesiastical resolutions and documents claim to provide the necessary moral guidance for the Church and Christians into the third millennium.

However, there are many moral and religious dissenters within these churches. There are many liberal moral theologians, liberal ethicists, liberationist theologians, radical feminists, and other well educated Christians who are supporters of homosexuality. They contend that it is both a natural and morally acceptable sexual practice for those who are born with this natural condition. They also affirm that it is a genetic condition which cannot be medically treated. They argue that treatment for homosexuality does not work, since it is irreversible or a medical disease to be treated. If a homosexual orientation is biologically established as a natural, genetic and as an irreversible inherited condition, rather than a mere cultural choice and a freely chosen sexual preference, then it must be positively embraced and affirmed as God's will in creation.

This kind of liberal moral position will inevitably offend and alienate many conservative, traditional and literalists among the Christians, Jews and Muslims. However, the question remains as to whether it would offend God who is the unconditionally loving Creator, Sustainer and Redeemer of all human beings. Jesus as the Christ of God condemned the Pharisees of his day for their legalistic observation of the religious law at the expense of human compassion, mercy, unconditional love and free forgiveness. The lepers, outcasts and prostitutes were unconditionally accepted as God's children, and were effectively rehabilitated by Jesus.

The AIDS' victims and homosexuals are in many societies analogous the lepers and outcasts of Jesus's own time. Undoubtedly, Jesus would welcome them and seek to minister to them as God's persecuted and suffering children. His Church cannot afford to negate Jesus' essential example and at the same time remain faithful to him and his redemptive mission in the world. Jesus was condemned for his association with those supposed to be sinners, impure and outcasts of his own time. His followers and his Church should continue his noble example in every culture, age and religious context. Jesus reversed the laws of Moses to include the outcasts, and so should be the obedient and inclusive Christian Church of God through the mediation of Jesus Christ.

As an irreversible, inborn and genetic condition, the homosexual orientation becomes part of God's natural law. In this naturalistic, nonjudgemental scientific understanding and positive affirmation of nature and God's natural law, homosexuality itself ceases to be an evil defect to be corrected. Instead, it is treated as an amoral variation within the natural law and evolution. As God's work, it is unconditionally accepted and positively affirmed and celebrated as good, since it is God's work.

However, according to many hardline, pessimistic, conservative religious people and traditional moralists, such as the Southern Baptist Convention, the Roman Catholics, the conservative Republicans and Christian ethicists, uncompromisingly reject homosexuality as a sin and social evil to be eradicated from the society. They regard it as being a freely chosen, immoral and culturally conditioned evil sexual practice.

This has been especially true for those people who belong to the "Moral Majority" conservative group of Jerry Falwell, Oral Roberts, and Pat Robertson, as well as those leaders of the American Constitution

Committee that sponsored the American Leadership Conference on May 8-10, 1998 in Washington, DC. They affirm that today's major threats to the traditional family unit and moral values include homosexuality, divorce, casual sex, abortion, drug addiction and child abuse. They preach that these moral and social evils are rooted in the sexual revolution of the 1960s and 70s, the challenge and rejection of patriarchal religious values, and the subsequent liberalization of sexual values, standards, gender roles and family values. They maintain that this sexual revolution destroyed that sanctity of sex within the holy confines of the family institution.

These conservatives condemn the societal decadence and moral sexual rebellion. They condemn the acceptance of casual divorce or dissolutions of the marriage bond. They blame the breakdown in the traditional family values on several factors, particularly, the societal acceptance of homosexuality as an alternative sexual life to heterosexuality, abortion on demand as a legal human right for women, casual sex out of the marriage bond (fornication and adultery), cohabitation or living in sexual relations out of the traditional sanctity of wedlock, and producing children and rearing them in poverty in a crime-riddled innercity environment.

This is particularly the case in the innercity communities of American metropolitan cities. They make the observation that this moral phenomenon is made worse by the fact that there many children born out of wedlock to poorly educated teenage mothers. They see many young males within these underclass single-female headed households who are raised without the discipline of fathers, and the beneficial societal presence of other good role-models for the young to emulate, turn to criminals, such as drug-dealers and gangsters for their role models. These conservatives lament that this societal acceptance of sex between unmarried people and living together in such sexual unions have led to sexual immorality as a normal way of life on college and university campuses and beyond.

The political, social, sexual revolution and liberation of the 1960s has effectively changed societal sexual norms and weakened family values. This sexual liberation from the traditional sexual norms that prohibited premarital and extramarital sexual activities has effectively undermined the sanctity of sex and marriage. Casual sex has led to a high rate of abortions, and serious sexually transmitted diseases. In addition, casual sex has also led to increasingly great numbers of women to become defiant of the restrictive traditional family values and sex norms. Many of these self-confessed "feminists" are choosing to have children out of wedlock, and subsequently, proceed to raise their children as single mothers.

For instance, by 1986, it was estimated that of all the Black children being raised in this country (USA), about 60 percent of them were being raised by single parents! And this trend was on the increase until mid 1990, when it began to decline slightly. Whereas the figure for the Black children born out of wedlock had climbed to more than 70% in the 1990s, in the same period, it had also rocked skyward for Whites to more than 30%. As a result of this problem, in 2000, the low income White communities and some suburbs were also beginning to experience the similar dynamics such as family instability, poverty, vandalism, violence, murders, crime and other dynamics which are associated with "problem children" who are raised by single parents or working parents in great hardship due to socioeconomic deprivation, poverty, and both undisciplined and dysfunctional families!

Violence and shootings of students and teachers in some urban and suburban schools in the American South and Midwest are of the 1990s provide evidence for this fact. Columbine High School in the suburbs of Denver shocked the world because some angry, violent and suicidal students had built bombs capable of demolishing most of the main school building and killing hundreds of students. Fortunately, the bombs did not go off and many students were killed and others injured as the suicidal students shot students randomly with their assault semiautomatic rifles and handguns. This is a serious symptom of dysfunctional families and a loud cry for help for families and schools as they raise the future citizens of our respective nations.

## 3. The Separation of Sex from Reproduction, Debates on Homosexuality and Salvation

It has been already pointed out that sexuality is a sensitive moral issue, especially the topic of homosexuality. Some moral and religious support for homosexuality include the argument and important observation that not all morally acceptable forms and cases of natural sexual intercourse are intended to lead to reproduction. Sexual intercourse among those who have past the child-bearing years do not do so with the intention of producing a baby, nor would that be a desirable event at their age and declining health. The popular usage of birth-control among the married couples is also another form of evidence of this truth.

Nevertheless, the Catholic Church has consistently maintained that sex for pleasure alone or recreation in any form, including consorting with prostitutes, pornography (mental sex), "virtual sex," "phone sex," adultery, fornication, bestiality, incest, rape, masturbation, anal sex, oral sex, and homosexual sex, are all condemned by the traditional moral teachings and doctrines of most Christian churches and the major world religions. One of the most sensitive sexual practices and moral problems that is currently vigorously debated in both the mainline Christian Church and Western society has been that of homosexuality and its controversy. This moral issue has nearly caused schisms within the Episcopal, Presbyterian, and the Methodist churches along the traditional morality and doctrines which condemn homosexuality as a sin and an abomination before God and the moral human community.

The official minutes, proceedings and journals of the 1996-2000 annual mainline Protestant Church conferences, senates and conventions in America extensively document this heated ecclesiastical moral debate and doctrinal controversy on this sensitive moral issue of homosexuality as a practice within the Christian community. At the time of writing, the mainline Christian churches, including the congregations and the Church leaders were still divided over this issue of homosexuality. Only the United Church of Christ (UCC) accepts the practice of homosexuality, including the ordination of practicing homosexuals, and Church blessings of homosexual marriages as valid alternative forms of sexual relationships.

Nevertheless, within these churches, there are many Christians, including bishops and the clergy, who believe that homosexuality is not a sin nor a moral social or cultural evil. They reject the traditional moral arguments and biblical passages employed to condemn homosexuality as a sin. They argue that the Old Testament passages and immoral injunctions are antiquated and culturally irrelevant ancient Hebrew cultural and moral material that both belong to the primitive Hebrew past. They contend that this Old Testament and laws are not binding God's eternal, universal revelation and the immutable truth as God's will and moral law for all people in all cultures and in all times. Bishop John Spong is the most radical spokesperson of this liberal moral tradition in the Church.

The radical cultural and Christian moral relativists, such as Bishop Spong, also actively support the ordination of practicing homosexuals and gay marriages as a sound pastoral position, natural and human right for those people who are born with a homosexual natural orientation. In this scenario, the Church accepts the inclusion of the homosexuals in the same way they accepted the inclusion of Blacks who were previously regarded as subhuman and immoral creatures lacking in intelligence, beauty, work ethic, honesty, and personal moral responsibility.

However, unlike matters of race and gender, from a traditional religious and conservative Christian perspective, homosexuality is not a matter of human rights. To treat homosexuality debates in the Church as a civil right is to ignore the central theological and real moral issue of homosexuality by confusing it with sexual politics and human rights. From that perspective, to equate homosexuality with a mere human right and equality between the heterosexuals and the homosexuals in the workplace and Church is considered erroneous moral reasoning and bad theology. It is rejected as making the error of confusing moral debate on homosexuality with politics. And then confusing politics with religion, and biology with ethics.

The traditional theological and moral position strongly affirms that all sound religious teachings, sound formulations of Christian doctrine, and true moral values are not based on mere human conventions, popular cultures and the democratic majority vote! The moral argument is that all human beings are by nature morally defective (fallen) creatures and sinners, who love the sensual pleasures of sin and evil deeds more than the delight in the goodness of God. As such, being creatures that are considered to be voluntarily oriented to evil and sin. As such, these morally imperfect human beings could not be expected to vote against their own personal interests, namely, their sinful ways, culturally and morally corrupt sexual practices. The religious and moral conservatives often cite the biblical story of the destruction of Sodom and Gomorrah as God's rejection, condemnation and destruction of the majority of the sinners in the world (cf. Gen. 18:16-19,29).

The cities of Sodom and Gomorrah also represent an alien moral and sexual culture which was in opposition and conflict to that of the Hebrews. For the conservatives, Sodom, Gomorrah and the Greek pagan sexual values and hedonistic philosophy have triumphed over the Hebrew puritanical sexual values and ritual holiness. For traditional Hebrews, this state of affairs would have been morally and religiously denounced as forsaking God's holy covenant and call to holiness.

According to the Hebrew prophets, the temptation to follow popular cultural practices poses a constant moral and religious danger of idolatry violation of God's moral law, the Ten Commandments and the covenant. The worship of fertility and sex gods, as Baal, Aphrodite and Eros are some examples. This is why the Hebrew Religion (Judaism) became corrupted from time to time when the priests wanted to accommodate the popular cultural elements which the Israelites had borrowed from their pagan and idolatrous neighbors!

God constantly sends his or her holy prophets to condemn corrupt forms of Judaism, and to purify God's people from the sins of pride, greed, materialism, immorality and idolatry. That is still true today. The only difference is that we do not have enough courageous prophets who come in the name of God to purify Christianity from paganism and corrupt practices which were borrowed from "the ancient or modern pagans and atheists!"

Christians, especially the Protestants teach that the Bible is the fundamental religious and moral principle for their doctrines and practices in matters of morality. The Bible is very harsh on homosexuality, adultery and fornication. The seventh commandment of Moses prohibits adultery and fornication. The Bible also explicitly condemns the practice of homosexuality along with the despicable acts of bestiality. According to the Mosaic Law, the punishment prescribed for sexual moral violations and aberrations or sins was death (Lev. 20:12; 15-16).

Many traditional Christian leaders and moral theologians constantly remind the Church during the debate on homosexuality that we also have the example of Sodom and Gomorrah, where homosexuality was both condoned by the society and culturally practiced. They point out that these cities were finally severely punished by God and destroyed by his holy and purifying fires of purgatory and hell. There are few Christian and Muslim fundamentalist extremists who would like to arrest the homosexuals and set them ablaze in the name of God, just like God is supposed to have done to the homosexuals of Sodom and Gomorrah.

Within this traditional, strict biblical and religious context, it is easy to see why and how some conservative and many traditional Christian moralists have in the past negatively regarded AIDS (Acquired Immunological Deficiency Syndrome) which they at first associated with homosexuality and illegal intravenous drug usage as today's divine punishment on a society which permitted sexual immorality and drug abuse. "The Moral Majority" and Evangelical preachers almost sounded like the ancient Hebrew prophets when they claimed that AIDS was God's warning to the world to repent.

Like the Hebrew "prophets," some Christian ministers have insisted that AIDS was God's collective punishment for a sinful and sexually promiscuous immoral society. These religious moralists contended that

God was punishing the corrupt world for its corrupt sexual practices and immoral teachings, which sought to justify adultery, fornication, pornography and homosexuality as acceptable popular cultural practices which had to be accepted by the Church as part of its pastoral ministry to its sinful members.

These preachers also pointed out that HIV and AIDS were originally God's punishment on the homosexuals and the non-homosexuals, including innocent children, because the non-homosexuals either condoned homosexuality or did nothing to eradicate homosexuality as a moral and social abomination to God. Most of these preachers had observed that, unlike Africa where the HIV is primarily a heterosexually transmitted disease, within the United States of America, AIDS was originally considered a disease that was primarily associated with certain religiously condemned and publicly unaccepted life styles, such as those of homosexuality, sexual promiscuity and intravenous drug abuse.

Thus, in order to eradicate the scourge of AIDS, these Christian moralists declared their moral crusade and Christian mission being God's mandate to evangelize and convert the homosexuals whom they considered moral perverts and the breakers of God's moral law in both nature and according to Moses (Lev. 18) and Paul (Rom. 1: 17-32). It was this spirit that during the Anglican Bishops' Conference at Lambeth in 1998, a Nigerian bishop was reported to have tried to exorcize an evil spirit of homosexuality from a North American bishop who is a very strong advocate for the acceptance of homosexuality within the Anglican Church. These Christian conservatives see their mission in global terms, including converting Jews and Muslims to Christianity. They are also mounting crusades to convert drug abusers, adulterers, fornicators, prostitutes and the homosexuals. They condemn polygamy and sex out of marriage. They advocate the holiness and moral virtues of monogamy and sexual abstinence for all the unmarried people.

These "religious moral crusaders" have consistently rejected the teaching that promotes the use of condoms to prevent unwanted pregnancies and deadly sexually diseases, including the AIDS causing virus (HIV). They prefer celibacy and the moral ban on sexual activity outside the marriage bond. In general, these traditionalist Christian moralists and preachers have consistently called the nation to be reconverted from what they see as a prevailing destructive culture of "secularism," hedonism and sexual vice. This includes casual sex, premarital sex, adultery, prostitution, homosexuality, divorce, teen pregnancies, abortion and pornography. They preached the urgent need to repent and return to the traditional norms of chastity, monogamy, and lifetime faithfulness to the marriage vows.

In the USA, casual sex and adultery have become rampant. On college and university campuses, unprotected casual sex has in the past led to many serious kinds of venereal diseases, quarrels, and divorces. In addition, unprotected sex in the era of AIDS may tragically lead to a painful and premature horrible form of death. It is the ideal time for the Church to become a prophetic, courageous moral conscience and guide for the world into the new age of human evolution.

The new age of instant information requires each human being to become a well-developed, teleologically morally grounded and responsible moral agent. It is a good time to extol the virtues of chastity and abstinence from casual sexual relations as both a sound moral habit and a wise healthcare practice. To this end, Pope John Paul II has provided the necessary prophetic voice and moral guidance by his encyclicals, particularly, the *Evangelium Vitae (The Gospel of Life).* The United Methodists have also provided an excellent Protestant oriented moral guide to the same goal in their *Social Principles.* The more conservative Christians may find the *Southern Baptist Convention Faith and Message (2000)* the ideal moral guide.

In this religious quest for Western moral reformation and movement to return to the traditional ethics of sexuality, fulfillment and true happiness have to be redefined. They have to be explained as states of the mind, peace and contentedness that comes from within through the art of mental and spiritual self-discipline, rather than coming from external sources, such as the abundance if material possessions, food, drink, alcohol, drugs and sex. As we know, the rich people have a lot of money or wealth and material possessions, likewise, prostitutes engage in plenty of sexual activities. Nevertheless, most of these rich people and prostitutes or "sex workers" are not happy or satisfied. This is because any lasting and true human happiness does not consist in nor derive from the external material things, such as plenty of money or wealth, alcohol, drugs, food and sex.

On the contrary, these material things are temporary and false materialistic remedies for an inner spiritual crisis or predicament. Material things are incapable of filling an insatiable spiritual and material craving (*tanha*) that resides within the infinite void at the core of the human being. It is this craving that causes spiritual and moral crises for the human being and the community. The human spiritual and moral crisis expresses itself as an overwhelming inner state of emptiness, existential anxiety (dread), moral and spiritual crisis (*angst*).

Human made false remedies for finitude and *angst* are unable to cure the human ontological (existential) anxiety and moral predicament. Idolatry and false religions and various addictions, such as those of sex, food, alcohol, drugs, power, fame, and wealth also fail to provide a lasting remedy which they promise. Therefore, any true and lasting happiness must be found in God and rooted in agape and a disciplined virtuous life. Discipline and virtue include the successful mastery of the desires of the body by our disciplined minds. The human will must also had to be trained and directed toward positive self-fulfillment in a wholesome simple life with the fellowship of love.

This is a universally available positive condition of human, social and loving existence. It is an achievable self-disciplined simple social life that is open to all human beings in the world. This redeemed and redemptive mode of a self-disciplined, social, loving and simple life is deliberately and consciously daily lived. It may be achieved within the monastery, convent, ordinary local community and anywhere in the world. It is lived in simplicity both individually and collectively within the community. The peace of mind, contentedness, spiritual tranquility, reconciliation, and unity with God, the neighbor and creation are both directly and indirectly mediated and achieved through contemplative prayer, love, positive faith (optimism and openness to cosmic mystery), appreciation of cosmic wonders of creation, obedience and dedicated to one's duties.

Finding pleasure, ultimate meaning, fulfillment and satisfaction in one's work in the classroom, laboratory, kitchen, garden, camping, family, friends, Church and creativity are part of this natural and yet supernatural fulfillment, happiness and peace. When we are able to see the omnipresent miracles of God's activities in the seemingly ordinary daily life, evolutionary and historical processes of the world around us, and appreciate them, then, we are also able to see God's world and creation as the wonderful arena of God's cosmic free activities in creation and redemption.

We also become enabled by God's power of grace to see God's miracles and mysteries within this life and cosmos through the indwelling Holy Spirit and the sharpened human inner spiritual vision of intuition and insight. Through this profound spiritual vision, contemplative human beings everywhere in the world are able to see and appreciate the wonders of God's gentle hand at work in his or her supernatural activities of cosmic creation, sustenance and redemption.

People are also able to hear clearly and positively respond to God's omnipresent, yet silent inner Voice (*Logos*) of God's creativity and redemption constantly at work within each human being. They are also able to see God's Word (*Logos*) at work within the cosmos, incognito, in the apparently ordinary, mundane and natural processes of daily life in the world to effect divine creativity, positive transformation and the divinization of the evolutionary creatures, the human beings, into divine knowing and thinking, free, self-transcending minds and historical divine spirits in the world.

With the attainment of this knowledge and truth, the human beings have through this self-knowledge as divine beings and as the children of God truly ascended to God in heaven and become filled with God's grace, love, knowledge and truth of the beatific vision! They have become like God and attained union with God. At this level of *theosis* or divinization, Jesus could validly affirm that he was in God and God was in him or that those who saw him had seen God. The possibility of the human encounter and union with God was testified to by the prophets, mystics and saints, of whom the most famous include Moses, Isaiah, Amos, Jesus, Buddha, Muhammad, Paul, John the Evangelist, Augustine, Mister Eckert, Gandhi, Martin Luther and Martin Luther King.

Ultimately, this fulfilling moral life is lived simply by a conscious adoption of a positive style of life that is simple, loving, non-materialistic, honest, clean, prudent, simple, loving, social, caring, holy and stress-free contemplative life. It must embody, practice and extol the virtues of the spirit, unconditional love, forgiveness, peace and harmony, as opposed to a life based on the hedonistic sensory transient pleasures of the body, especially wealth, food, drink, drugs, and sex. Even the animals by natural instinct do these things in moderation as required by the body's essential needs and seasonal sexual drive to mate and reproduce to ensure the continuity and survival of the species. As result, for most less intelligent creatures, life centers around three innate basic principles: food, reproduction (sex) and safety.

However, unlike the less intelligent animals which function on the basis of biological drives and instincts, the human beings being more intelligent and free, are capable of misusing both the natural drives for food and sex. They often transform these natural drives into hedonistic sources of sensuous pleasure and false happiness. Consequently, all human communities and societies have developed locally appropriate controls, norms, values, customs, taboos, cultures, social boundaries and laws to guide wholesome behaviors, relationships and social interaction.

This religious, moral and social codification of moral values and laws is, particularly, strict and definite in matters that are associated with food, drink, sex, and the treatment of relatives, strangers, animals and plants. This codification of laws makes life in community possible.

In some ancient patriarchal societies, these legal, cultural and religious societal regulations were often designed and formulated in the holy name of God. The moral laws, including those of Moses, Jesus and Muhammad, were formulated on God's behalf by the male elders (patriarchs) as God's local representatives in the community. Subsequently, these moral codes were universally ceremoniously imposed on the members of the community in the holy name of the Creator-Redeemer-God as God's absolute universal moral law to be obeyed by all the chosen and faithful people of God's Community (Covenant or Kingdom). Moses, Jesus and Muhammad are good examples of this religious moral tradition and codification of moral laws in the holy name of the Transcendent Cosmic Creator and Redemptive God.

## 4. Sex, Moral Laws and Taboos

Since sex is the means of God's creation of new creatures, it is regarded as a special divine instrument for God's creative purposes, rather an instrument for human joy and recreational activities for mere sensual pleasures. As a result, the Roman Catholic Church has traditionally condemned sexual activities outside marriage and sexual activity for the purpose of pleasure and self-enjoyment in itself as sinful. As such, the Catholic Church condemns abortion as a heinous sin of murder and misuse of sex. Sex is viewed as God's sacred provision for reproduction or creation of new life. Human life is God's special sacred gift from the moment of conception to the moment of natural death. As a result, the Roman Catholic Church, as clearly represented by Pope John Paul II's encyclical, *Evangelium Vitae (The Gospel of Life,* 1995), both strongly condemns and prohibits sex for sake of pleasure alone, mechanical birth-control devices, abortion, human cloning, suicide, capital punishment, euthanasia and murder.

In all moral societies, unregulated human sexual freedom is considered to be a great source of moral, spiritual and societal evils. Therefore, all human societies have developed laws, customs or taboos to regulate sexual relationships and marriages. In most of these theocentric communities, the civil laws and religious regulations were synonymous.

These moral codes were imposed on people in the name of God. The moral codes and laws were theocentric, practical and social. They were designed to impose constructive societal limits and guidance for human freedom. This is essential in order to minimize the misuses of human causal freedom.

These limits minimize the potential for social chaos, conflicts, malice and proscribe moral evil, particularly, violence within the family and the community due to the culprits and criminals who use their freedom to do evil instead of good deeds. Contrary to some naive scriptural literalists, and destructive fundamentalist beliefs, these moral codes were not directly designed, written down and handed down by God to humanity through the prophets and other founders of the major world religions, such as Hammurabi, Moses, Jesus and the Prophet Muhammad.

As God's prophets, the religious and moral teachers (Rabbis) were holy men (religious patriarchs) who composed their moral and civic laws in the holy name of God. After the completion of that process, they wished to canonize and empower their religious and moral works with God's absolute authority. As a result, prophets like Moses and Muhammad, both anthropomorphically and theologically claimed that their works (sacred books) "had been physically written" or had been "given to them" by the transcendent holy God. This was considered necessary in order to engender their moral devised religious and moral codes with God's divine power, authority and supernatural moral sanction. Ultimately, in all these cases, the moral codes were carefully formulated, composed, written and imposed on the community in God's name, in order to protect the individual and the community from the harm and moral chaos due to misuse of freedom, drives and creativity.

The human beings are also freely endowed with God's divine nature and supernatural gifts, because they are also God's divinely appointed concrete ambassadors or visible representatives in the evolutionary, physical and historical world. As such, to see any true and obedient human being, such as a saint like Buddha, Krishna, Mary the Mother of Jesus, Jesus, Gandhi, or Mother Teresa is also to catch a glimpse of God's theophany (glory), and work of unconditional love, and grace in the redemption of the world into God's Kingdom.

In this respect, the world's scriptures, moral and religious codes were given to the people as ideal practical moral guides and religious paths to God, salvation, peace and happiness. The underlying assumption is that the unguided and unlimited human causal free and choice lead to evil and destruction. Moderation was the ideal, as Aristotle and Aquinas taught. Unlimited freedom or self-indulgence even in good things was considered to be the source of evil. Moderation in all things and the avoidance of extremes was considered to be the reliable practical moral guide in all moral decisions and actions in life. For instance, unregulated sex is considered evil in most societies. Therefore, rape, incest and prostitution were proscribed.

The opponents of sexual freedom and the legalization of prostitution and drugs are many. They condemn casual sex and prostitution. They contend that these sexual practices are serious social, moral, spiritual evils, and a medical menace to the local community and nation that condones the practice of these social evils and moral vices. They argue that prostitutes endanger the moral and physical health and general well-being of the community in which they hawk sex for sale, and sell their disease tainted merchandise of moral evil. The public and the community are at medical risk since the prostitutes often transmit deadly infectious venereal diseases, including herpes, hepatitis B and HIV. The presence of prostitutes also invites other kinds of moral evils and crimes such as illicit drugs peddling, robbery and armed violence.

Those who support the legalization of drugs, various forms of gambling, and prostitution as good ideas in order to decriminalize them as essential human services, both morally and socially fail to take into account the kind of destruction these activities bring to human families and the community. Alcohol was decriminalized for adults. Nevertheless, it is still responsible for many cases of violence within the homes, community, and fatal accidents on the American roads and highways.

Alcohol abuse remains a major menace to society and the family institution. It destroys many marriages, professions, people and their homes. Illegal drugs and prostitution also add serious burdens to the ailing institution of the family, and destroy the well-being of the community. The American innercity community where prostitution, drugs and alcohol are plentiful provides ample evidence to the nature of violence, homicides, fear, misery and destruction of both family and community as a result of these evils.

Society, peace and orderly life in the community would breakdown if each individual members of the community were left to judge for themselves what was good and right thing to do in every given situation. Laws and norms may not be according to every person's liking or standards, nevertheless, they are necessary in order to provide the essential fundamental boundaries for individual freedom and ideal moral guidelines for acceptable behavior and peaceful moral life within the community. By doing so, the fundamental liberties and human rights of each person within the community are both respected and protected. This is true inasmuch as the laws which are enacted by the respective society are themselves both morally sound and just or impartial for all the diverse groups as equal members and citizens of the moral community.

There would not be any peace, order, laws, culture, cooperation, values, civilization and societal institutions, such as families, nations, or states if there were no moral conventions and laws. If each person had the obligation to set normative his or her own laws and values or define and regulate what is good and right action as opposed to what is wrong or evil course of action to be avoided by all moral or responsible people, the community and state would be impossible. If the community or state was already in existence, it would sink into social chaos and political anarchy. That position would transform each individual person in the world into an autonomous moral agent, king, president and God. It is also analogous to an army composed of only the generals! That would be morally and socially destructive and unacceptable to the responsible and social intelligent people.

Even the amoral animals have found a natural way to define hierarchy, procedures and limits to behavior in order to live together in harmonious families, clans and orderly hunting groups. Some examples include: the whales, dolphins, wolves, lions, baboons, chimpanzees, elephants, hyenas, bees and ants. Elephants and hyenas as matriarchal societies respect the matriarch and look to her for guidance and protection. Bees and ants have evolved a complex social organization to a biological level and developed a "biological caste system." The ant and bee queen produces the offspring. The ant soldiers with their great mandibles protect the colonies and the workers do the tedious chores of gathering food, feeding the queen and the young, building and repairing the colony and cleaning the nests.

Within the human communities, religious moral codes, laws and cultural sex norms have been developed so as to protect all human life, especially within the essential family institution. Therefore, the various incest taboos and laws have been developed so as to ensure the full protection of the young females and males within their homes and families. If these sex taboos had not been developed, life for most young females and boys would been very difficult and insecure. This would have been even more traumatic since they would not have been safe even within their very own homes and families due to incest and sex-abuse and the correlative violence.

If left unchecked, the practice of incest would be socially destructive. It would probably provoke deadly violence and possibly murder within the family as a result of intense competition between brothers and fathers for unprotected and most vulnerable more helpless young females or males. In some cases, it may be conceivable that those family members who resisted sexual advances from an angry and stronger family member might have been killed off by that aggressive individual in both frustration and violent retaliation. Therefore, without the incest taboos and laws, the traditional human family and the expected unconditional love, protection and security that it provides to its members would have been impossible. This is partly because the practice of incest would have probably led to the elimination of any male rivals from the home by the father or his stronger sons. Biologically, family inbreeding would also lead to the physical extinction of some families due to some deadly hereditary diseases.

Jesus did not write down any new revelation from God as Moses did and taught much about marriage, sexual matters including homosexuality, incest and abortion, and the like. Christians have no direct material from Jesus as the Christ regarding these important topics of Christian ethics, religious debate, controversy and division within the Church. Remarkably, Jesus as the Christ of God did not teach any new material regarding sex and marriage. What St. Paul and Jesus taught on sex was based on the existing Hebrew scriptures and patriarchal customs.

On a topic of moral or theological controversy, most Christian ethicists, moral thinkers and theologians prefer to refer to the life and teachings of Jesus, rather the entire bible. When there is no direct teaching of Jesus on a topic of moral controversy, the Christian thinkers generally infer that since Jesus was a Jewish Rabbi, he accepted the law of Moses except in those matters where the teachings of Moses directly violated the moral essence and moral laws of God as Agape and "*Abba.*" However, other thinkers prefer to treat the entire bible as God's infallible revelation, and the definitive authoritative source for moral theology and regulations (Moral Law) for Christian private and public morally acceptable social conduct. As a result, many traditional Christian thinkers and opponents of sexual immorality, homosexuality and casual sex or other sex-related crimes often cite the law of Moses and the works of St. Paul.

In order to protect the security, well-being, and sanctity of the family, the Mosaic Law did not only prohibit adultery, incest, homosexuality, and bestiality, but also went into specific, detailed prohibitions and prescriptions of strict penalties for violations of those sex laws and moral inductions. For samples of the prevailing strict ancient Hebrew (biblical) sex prohibitions and sanctions, the Mosaic Law book of *Leviticus* provides many of provocative ones.

The religious prejudice and moral complexity concerning the emotionally charged moral and theological debates that are currently taking place in many American Christian churches concerning the ordination of practicing homosexuals and gay marriages is partly rooted in the writings of Moses (Gen. 18-19; Lev. 18-22) and St. Paul (cf. Rom. 1:17-32). This is due to the fact that we find some seriously debated - moral sexual practices in the USA, such as homosexuality. The Mosaic Law and Hebrew scripture specifically prohibited and condemned them as "unclean sexual behavior," unnatural, perverted, and disgusting sexual relationship. Rape, adultery, incest, homosexuality and bestiality were condemned and prohibited in the name of God. The penalty for the violation of these prohibitions was instant death! (Lev. 18,20). The following are examples of those forbidden sexual practices and their harsh penalties:

***1. Concerning Incest:***

The Lord gave the following regulations: Anyone who curses his father or mother shall be put to death; he is responsible for his own death. If a man commits adultery with the wife of a fellow Israelite, both he and the woman shall be put to death.

A man who has intercourse with one of his father's wives disgraces his father, and both he and the woman shall be put to death. They are responsible for their own death. If a man has intercourse with his daughter-in-law, they shall both be put to death. They have committed incest and they are responsible for their own death (cf. Lev. 18:6-18; 20:11-13;17-21).

***2. Concerning Homosexuality:***

If a man has sexual relations with another man, they have done a disgusting thing and both shall be put to death. They are responsible for their own death. If a man marries a woman and her mother, all three shall be burned to death because of the disgraceful thing they have done; such a thing must not be permitted among you (Lev. 18:22; 20:13).

***3. Concerning Bestiality:***

If a man has sexual relations with an animal, he and the animal shall be put to death. If a woman tries to have sexual relations with an animal, she and the animal shall be put to death. . . . If a man marries his sister or half-sister, they shall be publicly disgraced and driven out of the community. . . . If a man has intercourse with his aunt, both of them must suffer the consequences of incest. . . . You shall be holy, as my people, because I am holy (Lev. 18: 23; 20:15-16).

## 5. Need for Better Sex Codes, Community And New Family Values

Today's people need to develop their own culturally, socially, morally and legally relevant and appropriate sex codes and practices. These sex codes should be comprehensive enough in order to define appropriate sexual conduct and regulate moral sexual relations and conduct within the home, community, school, and workplace. This is essential in order to define, proscribe and eliminate sexism, sexual offenses and undesirable sexual conduct of other kinds.

Some of the obvious sexual offenses to be targeted by the law, include discrimination based on marital status or gender or sexual orientation, oppression of one sex by another, rape, incest, sexual harassment and other related offenses. At the same time, this complex task has to be accomplished without the infringement of the constitutional freedom of free speech and academic freedom for school teachers, college and university professors and their students. Obviously, in this venture, the Bible and the Qur'an may be of little help. The ancient Mosaic and (Old Testament) biblical sex moral codes and prohibitions were intended for the ancient Hebrews, whereas those in the holy Qur'an were intended for the ancient Arabs. They are not universally binding on people of other cultures and religions, such as Christians, Buddhists and Hindus.

Nevertheless, in some limited legal, social and medical perspectives, some of these ancient moral and religious injunctions are still relevant for non-Jews today. These sex moral codes were formulated not only to ensure holiness and sexual morality, but also to ensure the survival and the general social and physical well-being of the family unit and the community. The sanctity of the family institution needed to be protected in order to protect the community as a whole. This approach worked well because the family unit is the very universal and essential primary foundation of the human community and society in general. Subsequently, a healthy family life is the necessary prerequisite for any healthy community or society.

Therefore, this sexually moral code which proscribes all forms of incest was necessary not just to ensure the physical survival and well-being of the human family, but also the survival and well-being of the whole human community which is built on it. Consequently, the human community or any society which allows or encourages its family members to practice incest will eventually pay the heavy price for this immorality. This may occur in the tragic form of family disintegration, and the subsequent rise of generations of poorly socialized inhumane, brutal, violent and uncaring social misfits.

This is self-evident in the high increase of teen violence and mass murders committed by the young people. This is more so in the USA and the war-ravaged parts of Africa where the youths were recruited into the armies. Therefore, in the future, the countries such as Somalia, Rwanda, Liberia, Uganda and the Sudan will face serious forms of violence, crime and mass murders committed by these unloving, and uncaring dangerous armed young people (child soldiers).

Being socially uprooted, they have no identity and meaningful affinity or allegiance to humanity, society and its normative values. These people tend to be governed either by the natural instinct to survive by any means necessary irrespective of moral consideration of the means. For them, the end justifies the means. Like the amoral animals, they are driven and governed by the natural law which demands that personal physical needs must be met in order to maintain life. For them, the good is what provides for their physical needs of food, drink, shelter, and safety. This is one illustration of how the very disintegration, and dissolution of the family can lead to moral, social, economic, and political tragedy for the community, nation and the world.

The failure of the family institution can lead serious correlative social demise, political and destruction of the indifferent or uncaring, evil and immoral community or society itself that had fails to protect the human family as the foundation of the community and source of all personal and collective meaning, fulfillment, happiness, well-being and peace. This is the basic moral prophetic message of the Catholic Church, Evangelical and Conservative Christian groups in today's world of increasing moral relativism, apathy, materialism and moral decadence. This is judged by high number of abortions, divorces, murders, profanity in some people's casual speech, public entertainment, casual sex promoted by film industry, violent and indecent material on the Internet.

What happens to the family and members of that family finally happens to the community or nation. Likewise, it also both directly and indirectly affects all the members of that respective community or nation. The examples of the families and lives of Moses, Jesus, Buddha, Gandhi, the Kennedys, Desmond Tutu, Nelson Mandela, Malcolm X, and Martin Luther King are such examples. This is because all human beings in the community are interconnected in a web of growing, living and changing relationships. All human beings are also interconnected and linked together in the cosmic web of life, ideas, information and commerce.

Today, human beings are globally interconnected. This global human linkage occurs both indirectly, as well as directly through the global processes of mediated social interaction and mutual exchanges of ideas, goods, and technology. The global human connection also occurs through the exchange of either positive or negative invisible behavior changing psychic energies. Love, hate, and compassion are some of these forms of invisible shared energies that drive human behavior and actions in the local and global community. Accordingly Adolph Hitler's hatred for the Jews caused great suffering and millions of deaths for Jews and their sympathizers. Likewise, Idi Amin's hatred for the Jews and Asians caused great suffering for many people in Africa and beyond.

As a result of the need to teach love and tolerance for all people in the community, Church, schools, workplace and homes, there should be a reexamination and an inclusive positive reconstruction of essential societal and moral values. To this end, there should be an added emphasis on the need for openness, acceptance of diversity, compassion, and community service as essential moral, spiritual, political, social and civic noble virtues that should be required of all the people. The young people in the family and schools should be taught these important universal values of peace, love and inclusiveness.

We must protect the family institution and the community from acts of hate and bigotry. As loving and peaceful people, we should promote the desire to protect the well-being and integrity of the family unit. By doing so, we thereby act to protect ourselves, we pass laws to protect every person so that we too may be protected as citizens and members of the respective community. Subsequently, all societies and communities in one way or another, have universally instituted the important sex moral codes which proscribe both incest and adultery. The definition and scope of both incest and adultery may vary from culture to culture and society to society, but the prohibitions and taboos are universal, regardless of creed, culture, race, political ideology, and level of development.

Therefore, it is also not surprising that most cultural, ethnic, and racial prejudices and discriminations are sexually based and motivated.

For instance, until recently, many racist laws in South Africa had a clear underlying overtone and agenda of prohibiting sexual relations and marriages between the people of the different races, particularly, between Whites and Blacks. In India, the "Caste System" had also made it culturally and religiously illegal for marriages to take place across different castes. It is also a fact that in the USA, though the Black people are no longer slaves, they are still largely despised and illegally discriminated against on the account of their color.

Due to the deeply rooted personal and institutional racism and ethnic prejudice, many Whites still look at interracial dating and marriages with great disdain! Until the beginning of 2000, Bob Jones University in South Carolina, as a conservative Evangelical institution had regulations prohibiting interracial dating on the grounds that it was immoral and sinful before God. They theologically theorized that the good and just God who created people in different races and colors, rather than one color, race and ethnic group of people in the world did not intend them to mix and "crossbreed." This is an intrinsic Eurocentric or white-racism that is deeply rooted within whitesupremacy and fear of genetic annihilation by the majority of non-Whites in the world. The neo-Nazis and Ku Klux Klansmen characteristically represent the externally visible and vocal expression of this prevalent and insidious whitesupremacy and Western racism.

This phenomenon of white-racism and rejection for interracial dating and marriages seem to confirm Sigmund Freud's contention that much of the moral codes, human behaviors, neurosis and cultural ideals could be directly traceable to human sexuality, and fears of its misuse, particularly, the fear of incest. He used this thesis to explain racial segregation laws that were previously instituted in the USA and South Africa. They may also explain the laws and taboos that prohibit incest, adultery, bestiality, racism, or ethnocentrism.

For Freud, the theory also explained most of the human conscious and unconscious behaviors, moral codes, values, religions, secret desires, guilt, fears, anxiety and some major mental disorders. His famous writings and practice of psychoanalysis assumed that this theory was correct. Based on the American advertisements Freud is vindicated. It is a fact that much of the human socioeconomic work ethic, values and conflicts in most human and animal communities are gender and race based. For instance, in the USA, one can see this clearly in Hollywood's portrayal of sex ideals and symbols, films, comedies, advertisements, music, and dance.

To an moral observer of a morally corrupt capitalist society, sex can be observed to be the most desirable commodity that is attractively packaged and used to sell other new goods, such as cars, clothing and houses. Tourist destinations are advertised by seminude, and seductive sexy women. The majority of the public entertainment and television shows include a lot of sex and violence. When the secret ingredient to the entertainment's success is plenty of implicit or explicit casual sex and random violence, then Freud becomes vindicated in his observations concerning sex (Id) as the powerful unconscious force that drives most people's private and public behaviors. Based on observations about Hollywood and most college and university campuses, one can certainly say the Freud was correct in saying that sexuality appears to be the foundation of most human values, cultures, religions, and activities. From a Freudian perspective, sex-related issues also lead to many of the human conflicts, aggression and evils like envy, hatred, malice, crime, violence, murder and male-chauvinistic wars.

Consequently, if any human society or community is ever to survive meaningfully within the Global Community, it must find a constructive moral way to deal with human sexuality. The traditional solution has been to proscribe both incest and adultery. However, in today's society, especially in the USA, there are increasing reports of rape, incest, and child sexual abuse by parents and close relatives in the family home setting, and some child molesting teachers within the school setting. The increase of these reported crimes and moral violations may be due to several factors. These factors include a high rate of divorces and family disintegration. It may also be due to more awareness that these despicable immoral deeds are also crimes to be reported to the law enforcement authorities for prosecution and punishment of the evildoers and perpetrators.

Nevertheless, by all social and legal indicators, rapes, drug-abuse, pornography, abundant cases of adultery, and broken homes due to incest, adultery, homosexuality, and divorce are on the increase. Correspondingly, this negative trend has endangered the very essential stability, well-being, secure existence and survival of the human family, which is the essential universal fundamental societal foundation for all other human institutions, and essential social basis.

Therefore, unless there is an urgent slowing down and even a reversal of this destructive trend in the human family, the human secure traditional family will be destroyed. Corresponding destruction also occurs along with all the other important traditional societal institutions, such as religion, the Church, marriage, sexual moral codes, the economy, property rights, procreation, and childcare responsibilities. Without the viable necessary family structure, there would have to emerge a new socioeconomic and political order if human beings have to continue to exist, reproduce and rear children successfully without an institution comparable to our present family.

## 6. The Ethics of Genetic Engineering, Cloning And Power to Create New Humanity

The Roman Catholic Church has traditionally condemned some medical and social practices as moral societal evils. These condemned practices include abortion, artificial contraceptive means ofbirth-control, capital punishment, euthanasia, biogenetic engineering and the cloning of human beings. These are classified as moral and medical evils to be avoided by Christians and other God-fearing people. Most other conservative Christian churches, such as the Southern Baptist Convention concur and also teach the same basic moral values on most of these topics except on the subjects of birth-control and capital punishment which the Protestants allow. The reason for this moral position is that only God is the Creator of human life and its ultimate terminator.

Currently, the USA laws prohibit the cloning of human beings. Most other nations have no such laws. This is partly because their medical and biotechnology are still primitive, but developing rapidly. These nations also need to formulate laws prohibiting the cloning of human beings, since some unscrupulous opportunistic American or European medical researchers could go there to set up laboratories for the cloning and manufacturing of babies for childless Western couples. They could also manufacture babies for sale to governments or private organizations to be brought up to serve in the private armies or the Western military as the disposable, parentless, uncaring and conscienceless killing machines, mercenaries and assassins of foreign heads of states. This would be a misuse of biomedical research and technology. Nevertheless, Adolf Hitler's crude experiments in eugenics and attempts to create a super White race, serves as a cautionally lesson to the world about the possible misuse of DNA information and the biomedical technology by some unscrupulous politicians, military commanders and heads of states.

With the great success of the Human Genome Project (HGP), the human DNA sequencing and decoding we now have an accurate book of human life and instructions to clone a human being or make one. We now have the necessary genetic information, skills and technological tools to read the book of human life. As a result, we are now able to isolate and delete those inherited human characteristics we consider undesirable, such as the genes that cause some hereditary diseases, such as cancer and diabetes. This gene therapy is a medically beneficial and positive use of genetic engineering information and technology.

However, moral controversy becomes serious when biomedical technology is considered to be used to enhance those human characteristics which we aesthetically prefer, such as height, body-size or size of some desired parts of the body, skills such as capability to run very fast, color of eyes, hair-color or texture, intelligence and immunity to some diseases. The book of life is written using four letters and chemicals in thousands of different permutations, interfaces and combinations. The letters of DNA constituting the book of life are: G (Guanine), T (Thymine), A (Adenine), and C (Cytosine), simply referred to as GTAC. The DNA structure is composed of about 30,000-140,000 genes which define and determine the general personality of the human being.

Although, genetic engineering can be used to cure diseases and prevent others, improve the general human welbeing of people by providing better food products and more affordable medicines or cloned organs for human-transplant, thus improving and lengthening life, there are many are still opposed to biomedical technology despite these advantages. This is because these conservative and cautious people fear the potential misuse of biogenetic engineering. Those who know of Adolf Hitler's misuse of biomedical technology and his crude program of "eugenics" that was designed to produce a superior "Master White Race." This superior race of people was supposed to conquer and "master the world" by virtue of their supposed artificial superior intelligence and extraordinary management and technological skills. For some whitesupremacists, the Human Genome Project has succeeded to achieve what Hitler's scientists failed to accomplish. For some of them the question remains that of the discreet acquisition and usage of this HGP information and technology for their purposes as opposed to the previous mere use of mere violence and intimidation of their opponents.

As a result, these moral and social conservatives reject the HGP and other related programs of biogenetic engineering as potential sources of future human disaster. There is the real and historically founded fear that biogenetic engineering can also be acquired by some evil people, such as terrorists or ruthless leaders of hostile nations and be used for evil purposes, such as making biological bombs that target certain racial or ethnic groups or by producing the fiction-like Nietzsche's evil and terrorist "*UberMensch*" (Superman), Frankenstein's monsters or George Orwell's child-like Eloi community he encountered in his travels into the future by the *Time Machine*.

It is now foreseeable that unless there are laws to outlaw cloning and the manufacturing of babies in factories, that the family institution may be replaced as the institution in which children are born and reared. One can foresee some new forms of nonsexual reproductive procedures, such as the state owned or state controlled human cloning clinics and "baby order factories" may be set-up. These baby factories may then become the acceptable normal, reproductive, medical, procedural reality in the distant future evolution of the technological human community, and reproduction. In this advanced technological community, human cloning will replace the traditional natural sexual reproduction.

Human cloning may become the preferred, safe, clean, accurate and controllable mode of self-reproduction. Its popularity may be rooted in the fact that human beings are now able to play the role of God as they actually determine and design the desired ideal characteristics in their future child. And they control the timing and final biological outcome of the reproductive process, as if they were truly God the Creator of human beings.

It is also conceivable that some immoral dictators may imitate Adolf Hitler's white supremacist and political ideas for the creation of a "superhuman" White race that is biologically artificially designed, effectively engineered and created in the laboratory to become more intelligent and biologically stronger. Such human cloning and factory designed mass production of clones or "test-tube babies" with predetermined and set gender and genetically engineered and improved physical characteristics according to need, can be actualized as a reality in the future. Then, Hexley's *New Brave World* will ceased to be fiction; it will have become prophetic reality.

In this kind of artificial reproductive system, in which reproduction has become separated from sex, baby factories and other baby social institutions would have to be instituted. They would replace the shattered and discarded dysfunctional traditional family structures and the correlative family values. Marriage as the sacred institution entrusted with the divine task of human reproduction would be lost and become a mere subject of human history, social evolution and archeology! In place of the traditional family house, there would be instituted state or privately owned youth centers, and dormitories organized according to age, gender, intelligence, occupation, and other general interests.

As a matter of fact, the ants and bees evolved a model of reproduction and biological hierarchy and function based on this model. They created a biological caste system. If human beings imitate bees and ants, they will sacrifice human moral freedom, choice, responsibility, individuality and diversity. In turn, they will gain the perfection of law order, conformity, harmony, community and security. In this system, human beings would be reduced to merely intelligent biological robots! The loss of personal definitive freedom and individuality is too much sacrifice and unacceptably high cost for the creation of a perfect and harmonious community. Uniformity and conformity are not the desirable characteristics of human and social perfection.

Freedom, diversity and pluralism are essential characteristics of humanity and social perfection when seen in contrast and held healthy tension and essential complimentary relationship of one another. Therefore, religions and socioeconomic systems that reject human or cultural diversity and freedom in favor of uniformity and conformity are morally and theologically evil and unacceptable. This by virtue of the fact that in these systems, human beings lose their essential constitutive individual divine freedom and divine uniqueness. As a result, they are transformed into biological robots. They cease to exist and serve God and the world as the very responsible free moral agents that God had originally designed, intended and created them to become as his or her *imago Dei* (cf. Gen. 1:26-31) and responsible stewards in the world.

According to this scenario, it is also possible that the state would be an atheistic one which would not consider human life to be God's special gift and sacred in its essence. The atheist may consider the traditional theocentric family values and practices outdated, unsanitary, inefficient and undesirable as a means of human reproduction in a super-civilized era of advanced technology and human cloning for the "Cyberspace communications and bionic age." Eventually, all forms of traditional sexual reproduction may become outlawed as a dangerous, unhygienic primitive relics of the "superstitious and evolutionary past era."

The concept of God, religion, and sexual morality would be preserved forever in this scorned conservative group, as a testimony of God's love and saving grace in the disobedient evil human state of affairs in the world. This kind of group would, indeed, constitute the equivalent of a "Noah's Ark of divine salvation" amidst the sea of human moral evil and scientific godlessness, waiting for divine anger and destruction.

Fortunately, this kind of disaster will never occur as long as the world will obey God's commandments or moral law. It is necessary to observe the following normative universal moral principles for the imposition of moral limits on human freedom in order to guide their ideal moral action and define acceptable good social behavior.

Noble and acceptable moral codes of conduct that promote nonviolence, order, love, justice and peace as the ideal modes of human conduct are not arbitrary. In most communities, God is cited as the supernatural "Cosmic Designer," the "Maker of the world," "Giver of all good things," "the Moral Law Giver," "Cosmic Judge," the "Cosmic Enforcer of the natural law and the moral laws" of the society. The best example here is the Ten Commandments of God through Moses (Exod. 20). Regardless of where they are found, and irrespective of the human agents through whom they are delivered to the people, all God's true moral laws define the invaluable worth of life, and seek to protect it. These divine laws also define the moral community (Church and God's Kingdom), freedom, speech, the common good, virtue, vice (sin, and unholiness), property, rights to both life and property.

The moral codes are designed to achieve wholesome societal order, social harmony and a peaceful life within the human community. This is universally accomplished by setting boundaries for moral standards for human relationships, and the limits for human freedom. These conventional limits are considered positive guides for orderly and peaceful human interaction as the promotion of a Godly and loving mode of social life within an orderly, harmonious, and peaceful moral community. These moral codes and society's laws embody the following general moral social and moral principles:

1. To recognize God and honor him or her as the Eternal, holy Cosmic, Creative, All-Encompassing Living Spirit or the Cosmic Vital Force.
2. To honor the parents and elders;
3. Not to commit sexual offenses and violations of nature;
4. Not to engage in violent acts or kill without serious cause;
5. To honor other people's property and not envy them;
6. To observe justice and truth;
8. To avoid malice and falsehood;
9. To live peacefully with all neighbors in love, harmony, compassion, empathy and good will;
10. To take good care of the body and the rest of creation.

The traditional family institution and its structures will undergo modifications in order to most successfully adjust to the changing needs, times, economics, work-environment, cultures and values. The traditional family unit is seriously wounded, but it will recover unless out of apathy and carelessness, we fail take the necessary corrective measures in a timely manner. The family institution will finally recover its full central valuable role as the moral, cultural, educational, and socioeconomic basis of any sound society. The reinvigorated family institution will ultimately survive the shocks of the current wave of the sins of incest, adultery, rape, infanticide, and murders.

A strong and healthy human family institution is the necessary universal prerequisite for the survival of the community, nation, and ultimately, the survival of all the global human community. All these human institutions are correlatively and coextensively interrelated and reflect the socioeconomic condition and moral health of the family institution on which they are based. This is the case, irrespective of creed, color, nationality, race, ethnic group, class or economic status. That means that whatever happens to the family in Africa, USA, and China will also eventually affect those regions and ultimately, the whole world. For instance, Moses, Buddha and Jesus were creations of their own unique families. The world is better off because of these men and their families.

Without a happy, stable, healthy, functional strong family institution, there cannot be any truly good and morally responsible citizens. Without good citizens, there cannot be any stable, peaceful, healthy moral communities, a cohesive society, and viable nations. The demographic factors such as the number of births to unmarried single teenage mothers, deaths, marriages, and divorces reveal the health of the family and that of the nation. These factors also affect socioeconomic factors, religion, politics, and power structures at the local, national and the international levels. The well-being of the Church, schools, workplace, community, the nation and the world depends on strong healthy families and well-adjusted, virtuous, peace-loving and law abiding productive citizens.

Therefore, we must redeem and strengthen all our families and make them strong. Churches, schools and parents must become gender and culturally sensitive and tolerant of diversity. They must teach these values to the children as well as adults. This is essential in order to reduce the institutional vices of cultural and religious bigotry, and the vices of racism and sexism within the family, schools, community, Church, workplace, nation and the Global Community. People have to be taught to view each other respectfully as God's mosaic. Tolerance for diversity and inclusiveness also means the acceptance of people of different religions, cultures, races, genders and sexual orientations and sexual practices as fellow human beings and God's children. The world is richer and better because of diversity. It offers great contrasts and enhances beauty and the mysteries of life.

Therefore, any truly redemptive religion and sound systems of ethics should promote the intrinsic value, dignity and worth of each person. It should celebrate diversity as God's special gift. It should empower and build self-esteem in each person as a unique creature that is created unique in God's own image. Diversity and difference should be positively understood and celebrated as both God's will and a wonderful work in both creation and redemption. Insistence on traditional exclusive monolithic societal structures which have promoted institutional whitesupremacy, German Nazism, racism, tribalism and sexism along with the prejudice, injustice, ethnocentrism, bigotry and xenophobia should be condemned and repudiated as societal and moral evils.

Ultimately, religious, cultural and biological diversity are God's will and gifts to the world. As such, they should not be negatively viewed as tragic defects of nature or evolution. Diversity and differences are not imperfections in God's will, design or evolutionary processes of creation. Diversity and pluralism must be accepted and celebrated as God's special gifts. Diversity and biological differences or pluralism represent God's concrete supernatural processes for historical evolution and creation of life, including human beings. Ethnic and cultural diversity are part of the human being's divine freedom, creativity, choice and positive self-actualization in the world. It represents humanity's divinization into God's special unique finite incarnation and embodiment of God's mind and spirit within the historical and evolutionary world as the Kingdom. The cosmos is the mysterious sacred arena in which God's infinite creativity manifests itself in its rich colors of diversity and infinite pluralism.

# Chapter 9

# Society and Moral Education: Education and Humanization Of People into Moral Agents

All human beings are created by God through unmerited grace in God's own time or *"kairos"* and a chronological evolutionary process of life as God's physical means for special biological creativity to provide an infinite diversity of living beings within the physical world. Human beings are especially created by God to become his or her moral agents and ambassadors of creativity, knowledge, truth, positive action or redemption, justice, love, beauty, peace and harmony in the world. This special divine mission requires good socialization and education of all human beings. People without good education may remain "noble savages" and unfulfilled as human beings and God's special creative and redemptive free moral agents or divine ambassadors in the world.

## 1. Biology and Environment: Nature and Nurture Debate

Despite obvious human differences that are meant by God to enhance diversity, individual uniqueness and contrast, all human beings are created and born free and equal before God as the Ultimate Creator, Origin and Destiny of humanity and of all intelligent forms of life. Therefore, human beings should treat each other as equal. Likewise, the human society as God's temporal and evolutionary medium and divine agent as God's social and genetic and social, cultural and moral co-creator of human beings must transmit these truths and essential values to all its members. This is the basic core of all sound religion, moral values and ethics.

According to this understanding, the human community concretely serves as both an agent of God and as God in relation to each human being as its member. This occurs as the human community takes over the concrete or "mundane" process and responsibility for creating its various respective members according to its own image. This includes biological genetic heritage and it's own unique cultural and religious heritage. It also includes values, self-identity, religion, history, needs, fears, hopes for the future, education, sciences, socioeconomic system, ideology, world-view, physical environment and level of technological development.

As such, in the case of human beings, the Creator, Sustainer and Redeemer-God is effectively incarnate and inseparable from nature, humanity, community and the world. God is effectively experienced at all those levels. As a result, human religion, moral systems, values and ethics must also create respect for those realms as the holy temples and creative and redemptive arenas of God.

This is conscious process of religious and cultural hallowing and sanctification of life and the world is very important. This is essential since all human beings are born as religious, cultural and moral *tabula rasa* or moral and cultural clean slates, but possessing the potential for acquiring those cultural, religious and moral institutions. Moral values, conscience, religion and language are products of culture and society. They are not inborn, although there is an innate genetic potential for learning them.

Human moral and social values are acquired through the conditioning processes of cultural socialization and education. To this end, religion or the Church plays an essential central role as the foundation of sound, human and theocentric values of inclusive global justice, equity, equality, unconditional love, nonviolence, mutual respect, harmony and mutual peaceful-coexistence.

Nature or genetic heritage and nurture as environmental, cultural and social heritage are the essentially inseparable and permanently intertwined foundations and pillars of creaturely life, including that of animals and human beings. It is easier to see how the physical environment affects life, such as that of plants and other animals. But, it is not always easy for people to realize that human beings are akin to plants or other animals when it comes to dependence on both nature and the environment for nurture, good health and safety. For instance, if there is no rain as in the case of prolonged drought and there is not adequate irrigation system, the crops fail, wither, dry and turn into dust, and people both people and animals face food shortage or starvation. As a result, deserts are devoid of trees, grass and other plants because there is no water and soil to nurture them. Consequently, human beings and other animals also find it difficult to survive there.

Likewise, icy and cold snow-covered parts of the Earth are almost like deserts. Very little life survives there in the form of plants and animals. On the other hand, the warm tropics are teeming with an abundance of life including that of human beings, animals, plants, viruses and bacteria. Obviously, there is a very close relationship between biological heritage and the environment. Charles Darwin went further to conclude that the environmental factors direct the course of biological evolution. This accounts for ostriches with long legs and necks as well as the giraffe with its long legs and neck.

Both of these biological adaptations are related to the need for biological survival in the local environment. Likewise, the aquatic mammals have developed great layers of body fat for insulation against the cold, and have almost disposed of legs and feet as in the cases of whales, dolphins and manatees. They have developed flippers in to replace feet in order to help them swim better and navigate the oceans with greater ease, just as birds fly in the air using their special wings. Similarly, most land animals had developed legs and feet to enable them to run faster or travel long distances more comfortably and easily than the crawlers, such as worms and snakes.

In the debates on nature and nurture, there is need to recognize that nature of biological heritage alone with any favorable environment does not amount to any meaningful life of any creature. The DNA or the seed as a biological heritage that is planted in the desert as a harsh and unsuitable or hostile environment, gets roasted by the sun's intense heat and dies. Likewise, a good environment or a well-watered good soil without seeds is mere good nurture without anything to nurture, and does not lead to any growth of crops. Similarly, good human genetic heritage without the necessary nurturing environment of a good family and community will not amount to much.

A neglected, malnourished and sick child will never grow into a genius even when he or she may have inherited an IQ capacity of more than 170. Likewise, a well-nurtured imbecile will never turn into a genius. Both biological heritage and nurture must be adequate in order to compliment each other. And in a more meaningful manner be able to create an ideal human being. Both nature and nature are essential prerequisites for the creation of a normal and well-balanced human being as a truly free, moral, intelligent, knowing, thinking and responsible moral agent in the community and the world as God's evolutionary, concrete and effective visible representative (*imago Dei*) in the world.

Jesus as the Christ was the best example of this theosis and God's incarnation in both humanity and the world. Each human being is also called by God to become perfect incarnation of God in the world and fully divinized like Jesus. That is the true essence of Christianity at its sophisticated fundamental core. True Christianity has little to do with life after death! Conversely, it is a living and changing religion and moral system for living people. Christianity proclaims the world to be God's Kingdom or Fellowship of Love (Agape) for all God's obedient, just and loving people in the world as God's saints, redeemed sinners, God's representatives and as the loving members and citizens of Heaven or the Kingdom of God as the Children of God.

All human beings are born as incomplete, open beings with various kinds of potential for growth and development into various skilled experts and professionals. This potential exists as an open and undetermined capacity for abilities, skills and power for self-actualization and self-completion with the society's help.

The DNA is the special biological intelligent container and self-driven divine vehicle for God's supernatural special endowment and automatic transmission of God's individually designed supernatural gifts of life and unique potential for each living thing, including human beings. As such, DNA represents God's special creative design, power and supernatural gift for the individual creature or person's uniqueness, talents, potentiality and actualized accomplishments.

DNA's biological functions are locally limited or determined by the nature and quality of the nurturing environment also the mutual interdependence of nature and nurture. This mutual relationship clearly illustrates the key role that nature or biology and the environment (community/society) or nurture play in the creation and development of the human being as a unique, free, and responsible moral agent in the community and the world.

This is true inasmuch as the human being is an intelligent, thinking, cultural, religious, linguistic and moral social being that is produced and shaped by both genetic heritage and the social and cultural nurture by the loving and caring community and the self-fulfilling fellowship of caring and loving people. As such, as the temporal and evolutionary co-creators with God, good human institutions, such as the family and the community make true humanity possible, meaningful and rewarding. This includes culture, sense of belonging, social relationships, moral values, self-consciousness, moral consciousness, knowledge, education, technical skills, love, language, religion and self-identity.

The essential human institutions, such as the family, local community, state or nation, and the world are God's universal moral agents for human nurture, change and positive or negative transformation and fulfillment. They provide the various kinds of essential social and cultural environments in which the young person with his or her human potential is either positively nurtured to fruition or deprived of the necessary nurture and opportunity to develop and grow into a free, skilled, valuable, productive, good, just and loving responsible citizen.

Therefore, when a child is not properly culturally socialized, and intellectually nurtured or educated, the human potential becomes lost or stunted in growth just like a tree that is planted in the hot and dry desert. The tree withers and dies for lack of water and other essential soil nutrients. This is analogous to a child that is born with a good biological heritage, but gets neglected and does not receive the necessary cultural, social and moral nurture, such as love, support and guidance by the family and the community. That child will die due to neglect, a harsh and destructive environment in which it is born.

Despite the American ideal and the declaration that "all human beings are born equal" (*The American Declaration of Independence*), after birth, this supposed ideal human universal equality is permanently lost. The environmental factors, which may have determined how the child was conceived and born, include the parents, race, class and level of technological development takeover. The adults or powerful members of the community, both implicitly and explicitly acting as the representatives of God and the society, classify the newborn and begin the lifelong process of determining and shaping the new member's fate within the structure of that community's norms, and perceived ultimate destiny.

There has been a serious debate concerning "nature and nurture" in determining human intelligence, fate and destiny. Those who believe that biology is more important in determining intelligence and work performance are more likely to make prejudiced and racist judgements along the traditional characteristic racist stereotypes, racial profiling and whitesupremacy. These biological determinists and pessimist predestinationists wrongly assume that biology is destiny. DNA becomes the new crystal ball for the new breed of behaviorists and forecasters of human events based on the genetic make-up of any given person. These people wrongly assume that intelligence, work-ethic, disease, behavior and ability are biologically determined by genes, permanently fixed and race-based. They almost dismiss the major role played by the environment as a significant contributing factor in these important matters. This is one of the serious criticisms that the authors of the *Bell Curve* had to face.

On the other hand, the assumption that nurture or the environment (community) is the most important factor in shaping the nature, development of intelligence and abilities to perform certain tasks, as B.F. Skinner believed, is appealing to many liberal thinkers. This is because it is not race based. Therefore, it is not subject to the prevailing racialist views of biological determinism and racial bias and prejudice.

However, serious problems arise when biology is overlooked as an important factor that should be ignored or underrated when one seeks to carry out an objective study and analysis of human behavior and values. The healthy position may be the middle position which affirms that both nature and nurture interact and combine in various complex ways to shape and determine intelligence, personality, behavior and values.

Nevertheless, if a gifted, talented and highly intelligent child is abandoned at birth, there will never be any measurable intelligence and talent to be measured by those who sing the virtues of biology. The few legendary Tarzan-like human children that have been brought up by some animals did not have much human intelligence or language. They were almost like the animals that had reared them. Likewise, imbeciles cannot benefit from a middle class economic and intellectual environment. Similarly, a good college or university education would not improve their intelligence.

The environmental factors are so important that they determine class, language, culture, religion, nature or quality of education, gender roles, occupation, technology, civic virtues and moral values. These are essential components of the postnatal society's implicit and explicit environment. They are also various forms of societal determination and permanent conditioning of the human being as both a moral agent and citizen of the community. For instance, once the child is born, the society may decide to kill it in the name of gender selection or population control. They may also choose to deprive him or her of total development through slavery, poverty, discrimination, malnutrition, or lack of education.

This impoverished and deprived child may grow up to hate both society and people. They may seek opportunities to punish the members of the community for persecution, neglect and oppression. Being powerless to impose the traditional forms of punishment on the oppressor, the powerless and grieved citizen may resort to negative modes of revenge and punishment for the rich oppressor in power. Evil deeds of crime, such as: terrorism, armed robbery, rape, violence, homicides, kidnaping, arson, acts of vandalism, graffiti, civil disobedience, intimidation and criminal menacing are example of this reaction.

Several aspects of this kind of negative mode of life and socially destructive behavior can be seen in many American inner city communities. The poorly educated, unemployed and impoverished youths in these poor inner city communities, such as the metropolitan cities of Chicago, Houston, Detroit, Cleveland and Los Angles, often form violent armed gangs to fight police and the predominant White society. They consider these groups to be oppressors who must be resisted, and as enemies to be exterminated.

On the other hand, the child may be born to loving and caring middle class parents. The child may be showered with care, love and attention. That child may be well nurtured, educated and valued as a positive addition to the community and God's world. As result, he or she may become positively socialized, and effectively conditioned to become a self-confident, caring, responsible good citizen and a successful future leader of the community. In both cases, there is nothing inborn that is irreversibly determined and predestined about the disadvantaged children that are born within the innercity or urban slums to become hateful criminals, or the middle class children to turn into good citizens.

With good education and change of environment, the disadvantaged children can grow up to become good, well-educated, intelligent, productive and law-abiding citizens. This is the moral, economic and political challenge of every caring community, particularly, the Church and government.

Most of the above processes are a matter of social conditioning, religious and "social moral engineering." Therefore, if one reverses the socioeconomic settings and the environment of birth, the privileged children who are born to rich parents grow up to become good citizens and community leaders, would grow up in the inner city to become the criminals and hateful anti-establishment rebels, whereas the formerly disadvantaged children, are now the children of powerful and rich parents, and as expected grow up to become the intelligent and responsible middle class community leaders. B. F. Skinner was insightful in his theories that biology in itself is not sufficient to determine the human intelligence, behavior and destiny. However, Skinner was also wrong to assume that the environment and conditioning could transform any person into whatever he or she was conditioned to become. Adequate intelligence and good health are necessary prerequisites for Skinner's theory to work.

Human beings are not born morally, culturally, religiously, or economically conditioned or determined by God. On the contrary, human beings are born open and free. But, they are socioeconomically determined and mentally conditioned by society, nationality and the environment. Therefore, since racism and sexism are some of these major social, economic, religious, political and cultural environmental factors, then they far outweigh the genetic factors in the way they shape human life and both its well-being and destiny. In this case, B.F. Skinner was correct to affirm that environmental conditioning, more than genetic heritage, determines what people ultimately become.

This being the case, then if you are born Black in Africa or America, you are more likely to be poor due to historical factors of slavery, colonialism and racism. This is mainly due to the external realities of the economic, political and social factors, such as whitesupremacy and racial prejudice, rather than the fact that you are biologically non-White. Race, ethnicity and history in terms of socioeconomic and cultural factors may definitively determine a person's socioeconomic class and status within the community, nation and the world. Nevertheless, this state of affairs can be modified by laws that promote justice and social integration though equal access to good education and equal opportunity for employment based on the merits of education and qualification for work.

This state of affairs is not caused by genetic programming or inherent intellectual inferiority as the whitesupremacist literature and research such as that of Charles Murray and Richard Herrnstein, the authors of the *Bell Curve* (1995) erroneously claimed. For instance, if you are born white and male, the chances of becoming rich and famous are higher than those of a white woman or if you are black within the same nation, such as the USA and within the same socioeconomic class. This is due to the prevalence of the moral and social evils of sexism, whitesupremacy, racism and prejudice against non-white people.

Whitesupremacy or Western racism makes it tougher for the Black or non-white persons to compete equally and successfully in a racially prejudiced and predominantly White society. The non-white person has too many hurdles to jump over before he or she can be allowed to compete in the American system with its biased institutions, such as the educational system and the workplace. The Blacks are discriminated against most because within the Western dualism, they stand out as the antithesis of White people. As such, Jews, Asians and lighter skinned Hispanics are less targeted by the White racists and supremacists, except in those places where the Black people are absent or present in insignificant numbers.

The American Affirmative Action laws and policies have made institutional racism invisible by forcing it underground. Subsequently, today White racism on American college and university campuses is like a dangerous iceberg that is less than 10 percent visible on the surface and 90 percent is invisible since it is submerged in the water and hidden below the surface and therefore, posing great dangers to the unsuspecting people in the external world, above!

This invisibility and hiddenness make it more dangerous and destructive because it strikes its victims with little warning. This is a mere illustration of how vicious environmental factors are important in shaping people's fates more than their genes. If genes include racism, color prejudice and intellectual inferiority, then genes or race and skin-color truly play a dominant role in shaping the life, culture, socioeconomic status and destiny of the people. This is the message of Hollywood's presentation in the films "*The Birth of the Nation.*" Spike Lee's films and others like "*Amistad*" and "*Roots*" challenge that racist attitude.

Ultimately, DNA is not a person's destiny, although it sets limitations to the person's potential. This is because human beings are more free moral agents. They are more than mere complex thinking biological organisms or creatures. Human beings are born open, free, incomplete, imperfect, and helpless. They also design and determine their own destiny as they complete themselves through the positive or negative uses of freedom, by what they choose to do or not to do. Human beings are not biological robots that can be effectively programmed by nature or the environment.

Because of real freedom, the human being is capable of moral freedom and rebellion. That is what the myth of Adam and Eve, and the metaphor of "*the original sin*" clearly illustrate in good theology. Because of freedom, and in conjunction with biological inherited potential, the human beings determine themselves though choices and by their actions they shape themselves into the very people they become. At the center of self-realization and self-creation lies true freedom and the capacity, to act wisely and proper use of freedom by doing good, or to misuse freedom to do evil.

Therefore, human beings are responsible for their own fate and destiny because they are God's free self-determining moral agents in the world. They are good citizens and law abiding if they choose to do good and obey the law or criminal citizens when they choose to do evil. Who and what they become is largely due to the environmental factors, such as the nature of the family, society, or nation in which they are born. Some of them may rebel and refuse to be defined and determined by these genetic and environmental factors, including gender, race, color, socioeconomic class, nationality, and culture.

The affirmation of the universal permanent reality of God's efficacious grace as God's irrevocable supernatural gifts of redemptive grace are made within the above context of human freedom and biological limitations of that freedom. As such, God's grace is essential in the evolutionary process to empower and guide the human being to choose the good as that which is essential and positive for both self-fulfillment and self-completion in personal freedom as God intended it. To this end, God's *Logos* and Holy Spirit or unmerited grace are ever present within each person's mind and spirit as well as the community or the Church quietly directing the obedient people to seek and pray to God for divine guidance. God's *Logos* and the Holy Spirit are ever-present to facilitate the positive human-self completion and maximize, goodness, love, justice, freedom, happiness and transform potentiality into reality.

This human *a priori* openness to the cosmic mystery in positive faith, and indeterminate human nature as an open reality at birth, are central pillars of evolutionary humanity, redemptive or true religion and ethics. These affirmations of the reality of human moral freedom negated the traditional Christian doctrines of fatalistic or predestinationist, such as those of the Pauline and Augustinian pessimistic views of human nature for being completely corrupt or determined by God's providence.

The reality is that all human beings are to some varying degrees, both limited and determined by both external and internal factors. For instance, they are limited, shaped or determined to some significant degree by their own genetic heritage as well as environmental factors. But there is still room for both meaningful freedom and free human self-determination within those prescribed genetic and environmental fixed factors.

The natural human barriers of nature and biological limitations are analogous to some "stone walls" within which a person is free to do whatever he or she chooses to do. One person, being a pessimist, can say that since there are walls beyond which one cannot decide to go, therefore, there is no real freedom. However, another person, being an optimist, can decide that there is enough room for one's meaningful free activities and fulfillment within the valuable protection of the external walls and joyfully settle down in peace to enjoy that freedom. Both the pessimist and the optimist are looking at the same space and the same walls or external limitations to freedom of activity.

However, the pessimist and "hard determinist"is negatively preoccupied with the existence of the insurmountable walls. He or she allows the unchangeable factors of life to define him or her negatively. Meanwhile, the optimist is taking positive charge of the situation and positively defining himself or herself within the allocated space within the walls and assigning positive value and meaning to the activities within the walls and the walls, too. To the optimist, stone walls become positively viewed as the necessary protective devices, limits and boundaries on the frontiers of personal and collective freedom.

Within this analogy, "stone walls" represent various variables, such human nature within its finitude, and *a priori* givenness, such as gender, color, nationality, socioeconomic class, racial and cultural membership at the time of birth. Some of these variables can be easily changed, such as class and nationality. Nevertheless, there are other variables which are permanent and almost impossible to change without doing great harm or killing the subject that we seek to educate, change and redeem. These permanent human identifying factors include DNA and its biological inheritance, gender, color and race. For instance, artificially changing a woman into a man does not work out as God and nature designed males to function. The reverse is also true. Changing a man into a woman does not work well!

In short, all human beings are constituted of both their own biological and social or cultural heritage. Both of these two heritages, namely, nature and nurture are equally important and required in the making of authentic human beings and functional human communities.

When nurture in the form of one's own environment, religious, social, moral heritage or culture is seriously deficient, as in some cases of the impoverished and crime infested urban slums of many developing countries and some metropolitan innercity communities in Western cities, then, nature by itself fails to produce healthy, law-abiding, morally responsible, dependable, hardworking and productive citizens.

This is often the case, regardless of how wonderful the biological heritage happens to be in itself. Due to lack of ideal positive role-models and positive encouragement within the family and the community, a very intelligent child that is born within a very poor dysfunctional family and crime infested urban slum or innercity community may find it easier to become a clever criminal, such as a drug peddler or car-thief than an engineer or doctor. This partly explains why most people found in American jails are disproportionately poor Blacks and Hispanics who come from the impoverished American innercity communities.

Nevertheless, an ideal family in a middle class neighborhood and an ideal cultural or religious environment by themselves will also not transform a child that is deficient in intelligence or biological inheritance, such as an imbecile, into a successful professional, such as a doctor, engineer, lawyer, minister or teacher. Nature and nurture must be kept in an ideal mutual balance in order to produce ideal, healthy, well-educated, well-adjusted, moral and productive citizens.

Therefore, in order for the community, society and the world to produce healthy citizens, peace-loving and responsible moral agents, there must be a balance between a good biological heritage (nature) and nurture in the form of healthy families, sound moral communities, affordable good schools and peaceful neighborhoods. Class, education, language, religion, culture and civic values and virtues are secondary heritage through the community. As such, each person is mirror of both the parents (biology) and the community (culture and values). This human dual heritage is finally synthesized into a unique and meaningful human identity.

## 2. Human Processes of Socialization And Humanization

Some of the main differences between animals and human beings are intelligence and the capacity to teach and learn new things quickly and "become a fire-using technological animal!" Mere human biological heritage does not result in a human being, nor does the cultural heritage by itself result in a human being, unless there is a person to inherit it.

The process by which the young inherit their respective cultures, values, skills, traditions, language, and religion is known as "socialization." Animals do not have a sophisticated language or complex conventional system of symbols and sounds by which they can communicate new skills and concepts to others or transmit them to the young through education. Animals learn and discover new things. However, for lack of a higher intellect and a more developed language, these new discoveries are permanently lost because they are neither recorded nor communicated to others in spoken language. Thus, little technological change and progress are made within the animal society, except that of the human beings because they are able to speak and write!

If human beings did not have a sophisticated language and writing skills, human civilization would also be slow and even nonexistent! Cyberspace and electronic global communications have caused a global revolution in knowledge, technological development, and economic growth through international trade and instant money transfers by electronic means.

Time and distance have been mastered and transcended through cyberspace communication, instant electronic information exchange, and supersonic jet travel. Even photographs and other data can be faxed and downloaded via the Internet. Omniscience and glut of information are realities made possible by "the postmodern Cyberspace Information Age." In this respect, it can be said that "the human being has finally become like God!" This is also the same process which is variously known as "education," "humanization," and "civilization." It is linguistic and instructional. The process is often formal, as in the case of schools, institutes and other forms of planned education or instruction. But the process can also be informal as in most cases of the African or Native American traditional societies. The formal training was for doctors and periods preceding initiation ceremonies or rites of passage such as circumcision, marriage, and childbirth.

It is also by this same process of human socialization that the new, young members of the humankind and society are humanized and "tamed" into civilized, informed, technical, authentic, moral, responsible, humane, intelligent, and linguistic beings or people. In this respect, the socialization process of the young is like the social river providing continuity and linkage between the past, the present, and the future generations. This vital human process of socializing and humanizing the new, young members of the society and the global human race takes place primarily in the home in which the young are born and adopted within the social interactive context of the family, the community, and the larger society.

In other words, biologically the individual inherits directly from the parents the accumulated genetic material from past generations. Socially, however, the individual also inherits culture and civilization from past generations through the family and society's culture and civilization. The individual achieves this both informally and unconsciously. Socialization also occurs formally through education which is an organized formal method by which the responsible, knowledgeable adults transmit culture, values, and civilization to the young in order to socialize, educate and humanize them. This process is slow, gradual, free, and selective, whereas the biological process is a given, and therefore, swiftly appropriated within a short time, namely the moment of conception (initial creation).

However, unlike the human biological heritage (DNA) which is genetically determined and fixed, cultural heritage is flexible and fully changeable. Nevertheless, thinkers like Skinner theorized that education and socialization can be used to negate the limits of biology. This is important since this genetic heritage consists of a precise genetic programming code whose results and effects can now be scientifically and correctly predicted and analyzed in advance. The new information about DNA has given us the necessary genetic-engineering tools, genetic map and knowledge about the biological human nature and how to create it and modify it.

We now have the necessary biological genetic information, technological tools and capacity to create human clones. We can also create radically genetically altered future beings by medical and biogenetic intervention and genetic engineering and the manipulation of the DNA. We can create ideal people with the gender and physical or mental features which we may judge to be more ideal, healthy, aesthetically desirable and beneficial.

Hitler's dream and project for eugenics and biogenetic engineering has become a reality. The knowledge and technological power for creating an intellectually White superior race that can control the world has been obtained with the completion of the human Genome Project. The question why we should not do so is a matter of considerations made on the basis of biomedical ethics, theology, religion and politics. For instance, we must whether we should create these biogenetically engineered people according to our own designs and objectives or those of God. Is this to play God? Do we have the right to do this? Is it good for the world to clone people?

Furthermore, whom do we clone? Do we clone talented scientists like Albert Einstein, or bright politicians like President Bill Clinton? Or do we clone the beautiful women, like Princess Diana or the talented generals like Napoleon Bonaparte and Colin Powell and their brave soldiers? Or do we instead clone the talented entertainers like Elvis, Madonna, the Beatles and Michael Jackson, or do we clone the talented sports-persons like Michael Jordan? Or do we clone the moral saints and moral leaders or teachers, such as the Buddha, Jesus the Christ, the Blessed Virgin Mary, Gandhi, Mother Teresa and Martin Luther King? On what basis are we to judge what is socially, physically, or medically desirable characteristics to enhance and the undesirable ones to delete? Would this mean the elimination of some minority races such as the Blacks, Hispanics, or Jews whom we may not like? That is what Hitler tried to accomplish in the holocaust! We should learn from history that we must not repeat the tragic mistakes of the past!

However, socialization as humanization takes place in such a gradual and slow social, cultural, and educational process. Whereas it is most important during the childhood years when the child acquires basic human values, language, skills, self-identity, and gender roles, this process actually continues during adolescence and later maturing years. As a result, in some cases, socialization continues until death. That is, if it is properly understood to include learning new values and information that require social change and adjustment in one's way of life and social interactions so as to fit in a new role, or just to live a more adult, mature, social, humane, and satisfying life.

Since we affirm that learning is part of life as a component of a constantly changing evolutionary process of being alive, therefore, learning never ends until one's death. This must be true for religion and ethics, too. As such, people must realize that as long as this learning process continues, it will necessarily produce a corresponding moral evolution and spiritual growth. This moral education must continue to affect the learner's social behavior, and lead to more positive humanization, continued socialization, positive transformation, self-realization and self-fulfillment. This process is necessary if true happiness is to be achieved in this life and within the context of the world's historical and evolutionary processes.

This is more so in this Information Age of great increases in the scientific knowledge and new breakthroughs that have led to great successions of technological revolutions. These new great advances in the sciences and technology have profoundly affected human society with the result of rapid social changes, requiring innovations and renovations of jobs and life skills required to live in the Cyberspace Age and technological society. This is especially true in a society which is always rapidly changing and rendering the new information and technology obsolete as soon as it is off the manufacturing assembly!

Nonetheless, this constant and rapid changes in technological and information requires all human beings to keep learning and changing in order to remain current and marketable. Correlatively, this requires the necessary, constant, cultural, social, and personal and societal adjustments. This is necessary in order to keep up with the pressures of rapid technological and socioeconomic changes. This also involves doing so without being left behind or breaking down under the great pressures from constant changes and threats of inadequacies. This pressure for mastering technology is intrinsic in our Information Age. It makes it essential to learn new job skills quickly in order to retain or protect the job one already has. In this kind of situation, old work experiences, and job-training are inadequate. Constant job training and skills updating is the new feature of the Information Age and the "New Market."

As such, one has to keep on learning new information, new technological skills and being both technologically and socially adjusted throughout life in constantly changing society and evolving world. Past or old experiences are not adequate to meet the challenges of the "New Market," which is technologically based. The old experiences, systems of education and technology are inadequate to prepare the individual for "New Market" jobs which require new knowledge, new technology, new skills in problem-solving, and new and rapidly changing work conditions which require constant learning and adjustments.

Therefore, the most well-educated person is that person who is well-equipped with the necessary technological information, technological skills and knowledge required to make the most important personal adjustments quickly, efficiently, and easily in order to become an employed, law-abiding, peaceful and productive citizen. This being the case, then, the human society, both local and global, is best served when its respective constitutive members are well socialized, well-educated, well-informed, nonviolent, just, loving, caring and peaceful.

The good citizens of the local community, the nation and the Global Community must possess some learned and acquired noble moral and civic virtues. The well-educated and ideal citizen must be: humane, highly motivated, well-educated, hard-working, tolerant, cooperative, teamwork oriented, law-abiding, and technologically skilled, loving and caring considerate social, and healthy good citizens. Education, religion and ethics are relevant and useful only if they help to transform the human being into this kind of moral and socioeconomically ideal, well-adjusted and productive happy citizen of the community and the world.

Ultimately, the human being remains God's open, and incomplete work in historical development and evolutionary process. This is part of the cosmic human evolution and never ends or ever gets completed. This formative and learning process begins before conception and ends at death. As such, there is never a perfect human being since all human beings exist as open and incomplete realities that are constantly evolving, developing, changing and becoming either more perfect or worse based on the nature and quality of their knowledge, choices and deeds. Good deeds of agape help to make the human being more perfect like God, whereas those deeds of egocentrism, greed, selfishness, malice and hubris transform the human being into an evil destructive being or the devil in the world.

## 3. Negative Forms of Socialization And Criminalization

In repudiation of the antiquated "pagan" or fatalistic, spiritual, moral and biological determinist, as well as the predestinationist and pessimistic views of Augustine and Calvin, we positively affirm that no human being is ever born a sinner, a criminal, a sexist, a racist, or a thief! The corrupt community in which he or she is born brings him or her up negatively and conditions him or her through negative socialization or education to become a racist, a sexist or a criminal such as a thief, vandals, gangsters, illegal drugs-peddler and drug addicts!

The human community is also both negatively served and harmed by its poorly socialized members, poorly educated and unskilled citizens. These negatively socialized people are inhuman, social-misfits, and criminal-minded. Very often, they are also hateful, violent, brutal, ignorant, unskilled, poor, unmotivated, lazy, xenophobic, sexist, and racist. These individuals also happen to be criminals since they lack the essential noble values and virtues to keep them from the life of vice and crime. Some examples of this are: stealing, burglary, fraud, prostitution, drugs, rapes, vandalism, child abuse, violence, hate, blackmail and murder.

These poorly socialized individuals grow up to have families of their own and perpetuate the kind of undesirable socialization process which creates evil, uncaring, and violent human beings. This is due partly to inadequate and poor methods of socialization, education and poor and evil role-models inherent in bad, poor, criminal, violent and uneducated dysfunctional families, such as those found in the urban slums of any major on the outskirts of the Third World cities or the innercity communities of the USA metropolitan areas, such as Watts in Los Angles, and the South side of Chicago and Harlem in New York.

Since socialization as an informal system of education is a process which primarily occurs within the family context, the family becomes the universal microcosm of society and the Global Community. Therefore, bad or evil homes and families can only produce bad and evil children who in turn become bad and evil citizens of the community and the world. Many of these children become criminals, such as thieves and violent armed robbers of banks. Others become blackmailers and terrorists. In Africa, the "child soldiers" are recruited from such families and transformed in ruthless killing machines by rebel forces in Uganda, Rwanda, Congo, Somalia, Angola, Sierra Leone and Liberia. This is self-evident since these children get exposed to the daily evils of their own parents, and learn to accept and imitate them both consciously and unconsciously as an acceptable way of life.

Values, vices, and virtues are also unconsciously taught and learned within the home and the community. This is done both explicitly by words and implicitly by deeds, whether intended or unintended, in public or private. For instance, in a family in which parents steal either for survival or fun, children also learn to steal. They are sometimes directly taught by their own parents to steal. Others may simply imitate the examples their parents. Teaching can take many forms, being asked to stand a sentry and keep watch while the parents do the actual stealing, or being asked to lie or to conceal or sell stolen goods. Charles Dickens' "Artful Dodger" in *Oliver Twist* is an example of a product of a poor and dysfunctional family and how the disadvantaged children can easily be exploited immoral people, and be recruited into criminal gangs where they are taught to become criminals.

Oliver Twist as an unfortunate poor, homeless orphan was taught by Phagun and Billy Sykes how to pickpocket and steal in order to survive. These crooks served his moral and social mentors, foster family and parents. Amazingly, they were kind to him. Phagun served as their "Mafia Boss," "chief," "father," teacher, employer, and guardian of the homeless street children, whom he recruited into his family of crime and taught to steal. He paid them commission for their stolen merchandise and provided food and housing for them. Definitely, this is an example of organized crime in which the main criminals are the children from poor and dysfunctional families and runaway children from abusive homes.

The street gangs in American cities are organized in almost the same way as the family. They are an artificial family or a brotherhood/-sisterhood of criminals whose primary functions are social and economic well-being, as well as security and survival through collective self-protection. Dickens' books are insightful, good, moral, and socioeconomic commentaries on the social life of his time. But his works also provide insight into our own inner city problems and crime. Youth gangs in these harsh environments provide their members, often youths from broken, traumatized, and dysfunctional families, with a substitute functional family, security, acceptance and protection.

The values and behavior of the young are a fairly reliable reflective mirror for adult behavior and the values of the local community. Social thinkers and psychologists such as Freud, Skinner, Erickson, Piaget and others have clearly shown us how both family and child rearing practices are important for the society. This is in terms of what kind of adult human beings these children later become as a result of their family background, education, socialization methods and processes.

Socialization is, in some major sense, a form of social and cultural patterning and programming. This being the case, human beings tend to remain faithful to their own cultural heritage and social programming which often determines and governs most of the spontaneous human social behavior, gender roles, and relationships with friends, strangers and foes alike. Human beings who have been negatively conditioned and programmed by their own dysfunctional or evil families to hate and do evil will most likely succeed in producing social misfits and evil people (crooks).

Is it surprising, then, for us to find in the innercity communities of the USA a very high rate of poverty, crime, child abuse, divorce, unwed mothers, teenage pregnancies, school dropouts, drug problems, prostitution, illiteracy, lack of skills, unemployment, and con artists? These people have been neglected and isolated into some subcultures of poorly educated, unskilled, poor, and unemployed masses of dehumanized and hopeless people. They have very limited options for self-improvement, lucrative employment, self-fulfillment, and true happiness. Like in

Huxley's *Brave New World*, despair, boredom, and spitefulness have caused these people to resort to sex, drugs, and crime for leisure, pleasure, and recreation. In some cases, crime is intentionally committed in order to survive or attract public attention to the personal plight of poverty, neglect, and public indifference.

Society pays a heavy price in crime and correctional institutions (jails) for allowing some of its members to suffer from such socioeconomic evils of discrimination, neglect, and injustice. For instance, whereas the cost of state university education may be about $7,000-10,000 annually, it costs about $45,000-60,000 annually to keep a single dangerous criminal in a maximum security prison in the USA. Therefore, it is much cheaper to send all the potential criminals and poor people to college on state scholarships than to send them to jail. Nevertheless, many politicians prefer to build more jails than providing effective means to prevent crime including effective community policing to get rid of the prostitutes and drug-dealers from the innercity communities, free college education and medical care for the poor.

## 4. Problems of Teaching White Middle Class Values As Universal Social and Morals Values

The Western ideal values are characteristically upper White middle class in nature and standards. In general, these ideals tend to be Christian, patriarchal, and capitalist, and emphasize education, hard work, and teach that riches are God's reward and blessings for that hard work. They promote self-control and postponement of self-gratification. Conversely, the White middle class people tend to believe that poverty is God's punishment for ignorance, laziness, and lack of good work ethic and investment discipline.

In the middle class families, the young generally tend to receive positive socialization and humanization. Rewarding what is considered good or approved behavior and punishing undesirable behavior tends to be the method followed by many parents in this group. Good language, property rights, communication skills, decency, loyalty, time consciousness, and good job skills for marketability and success in the workplace are emphasized.

Subsequently, these young people get good educations and preferred professional or job training. As a result, they also are the ones who get good employment, earn plenty of money, and perpetuate their own middle class values and standards of living. In turn, they socialize and marry from their own middle class and raise their own children in the same middle class capitalist values and work ethic in which they were raised. They keep away from the lower class people whom they consider to be lazy, stupid, violent, vulgar, criminals, culturally unrefined and thieves. Most of these people live within slums or the innercity impoverished communities. In the USA, these impoverished people tend to be members of the racial minorities.

As a result, racial profiling by police is practically designed to catch these supposed criminals by looking at their color and race as reason to suspect them of crime before it has been committed. In this process the legal and moral principle that "You are innocent until you have been proven guilty in a court of law," is reversed for most of these impoverished racial minorities. This whitesupremacy and racial profiling by police has become a great source of police brutality, violence, injustice and breach of law. Examples of this includes many cities in the American South as well as cities and states in the North and Midwest, such as New York, New Jersey, Los Angles, Philadelphia, Pittsburgh, and both Toledo and Columbus, Ohio.

Christians can help to negate White prejudice and racism against non-Whites by teaching the moral ethic of unconditional love and free forgiveness for all people. In obedience to the commandment of unconditional love, they should be able to do more for the poor masses both at home and abroad in the Global Community. They ought to do this as a divine duty, incumbent upon them as the morally responsible, accountable, reliable, intelligent, and faithful stewards of God's world and treasures. They are "the chosen" (elect) and privileged custodians of God's creation, including the natural resources and wealth for the poor, the weak and the developing peoples of the world.

Subsequently, modern technology is not to be selfishly misused for mere personal gain and access to power, wealth, and dominion over the poor and the undeveloped nations of the world. Rather, technology gives us the means by which we can benevolently and freely develop more wealth to share both at home and abroad. This is also to help the undeveloped nations so that they, too, come into the international economic fellowship, mutual exchange, trade, interdependence, and ultimately, the fullness of a good, safe, and happy life for which all people hope and pray for.

## 5. The Global Ethic and Need for International Cooperation and Peace

Humanity is intrinsically social and interrelational. This being the case, then, humanity is only possible within the social context of the human family and the community as the extended family. The human community has several levels of relationships and functions. At each level there are different rules of how different people should relate to one another or work together. For instance, there may be regulations which prohibit dating and sexual relationships or drinking alcoholic beverages and smoking.

The extreme example is that of some East African traditional societies, such as the Banyankole and Bakiga of Southern Uganda where mothers in-law are not supposed to eat with their sons in law or travel in the same car or sleep in the same house. Inevitably, these rules must change to accommodate lifestyles within the modern society, such as allowing a son in law to give his mother in-law a ride to Church or the airport.

Today, we live in a local, national, and global human community. The destructive violent era of feudalism, tribalism, ethnic ethnocentrism and narrow exclusive ideas of divine election and exclusive nationalism is past. God is no longer perceived as a tribal God, feudal Lord, Patriarch, or local King as the ancient people once believed. God is the cosmic creator of all people and his Kingdom encompasses the whole cosmos! Nobody is excluded by God or God's election and predestination. That means that all human beings are God's chosen people, and therefore, fellow brothers and sisters in God's Kingdom!

Additionally, because of the cyberspace and efficient electronic global communications network, all human beings on the planet Earth have been truly interwoven in a global and interdependent community or "global village." What happens in the remote corner of the world affects us both directly and indirectly. The securities and stock markets all over the world react to the same world events. The news and shock waves from one part of the world now have an immediate impact on the Global Community and its affairs more than before. Even real wars are fought on live television. People see events and news as they unfold and happen in remote parts of the world, as if they were there as eyewitnesses. This is the revolution of the information era!

This becomes a moral obligation, because we are all God's children and moral agents in the world. As intelligent, social, humane and peace loving political beings, we are also obedient servants or the stewards of God. Therefore, we must view each human being as our brother or sister in God. Thus, we should lovingly seek to become each other's keeper without any conditions attached except the joy of self-sacrificial service as one's divine privilege and reward from God. This is because through this good work of self-sacrifice the saint has joined Christ and effectively participates in the redemptive life, work, passion, suffering and sacrifice of God in Christ to redeem the world.

The Church must seek to incorporate this ethical teaching and globalization of the socioeconomic responsibility in her teachings. It can also be introduced into the education and socialization process of the children born and reared in the Christian middle class families. This is because in the developed western societies, the middle class is the largest and the most powerful and influential class. It has the greatest numbers of well-educated and rich people in it. Consequently, it also has a greater socioeconomic impact on the world.

The Church can effectively transform the world by shaping the moral values and priories of the middle class. Members of this class can most easily work as God's ambassadors and the political and economic masters of the universe, as well as its moral conscience and diligent custodians. They are the effective moral creators, shapers, catalysts for peace, and the zealous advocates of international close cooperation, harmony, peace, and unity.

By this approach of inclusive, non-materialistic, non-imperialistic, positive socializing and educating people, especially the young to accept new inclusive global values, mutual cooperation, peace, interdependence, lasting global unity, harmony, and peace may be finally actualized in the world. Global cooperation and peace are important, and without them, this planet and its currently war-faring, divided inhabitants may actually destroy themselves in their mutual hatred, blindness, folly, and miscalculation.

Only the practice of tolerance and the diligent praxis of God's unconditional and universal acceptance and love for the neighbor can avert and prevent the dangers caused by xenophobia, bigotry, mutual intolerance, racism, imperialism and war. All people should be taught to love one another and work together for the human common good irrespective of culture, color and racial differences.

## 6. The Communities' and Parent's Central Role in Moral Education

Moral education is the responsibility of both parents and the community. The African proverb that "it takes a village or community to raise a child," is true in the case of education and socialization. The family can never accomplish this humanizing task unaided by the community.

The rearing and education of the young is a collective and collaborative venture. Parents cannot do it alone. But nor can the schools do it alone. Education is a responsibility of the parents, the community, and the state. The child is a citizen of the family, community, state, nations and Global Community. Sound education must incorporate values and content from these respective levels.

However, the parents and teachers must reinforce each other's teaching and peaceful living both at home and in the formal school environment. If there is violence and hatred at home or at school, it will negate the verbally or theoretically learned values of an unconditional acceptance, love, cooperation, and peaceful coexistence.

Nevertheless, all human beings are by nature finite and imperfect. Correlatively, all human institutions, knowledge, education, relations, ethics, and values are also imperfect. They will remain as such, until the unforeseeable future when human beings will become more humane and loving, instead of being greedy, selfish, self-centered, and imperialistic. Then, they will become more perfect than they are now! Ultimately, all human institutions and creations bear the stamp of creativity, aesthetics, limitations, sins, and imperfections of their human creators. This is the way it is. Therefore, it must be accepted as such because all human creators with God are responsible for these institutions, since they are the individual's or collective concrete expressions of their abstract humanity.

Responsible and caring people are the true local messiahs and effective instruments of God's moral action and deliverance for the oppressed people in the world. Therefore, they cannot ignore evil in the world, and overlook its perpetrators in the community. Just and loving people cannot let evil people terrorize the community or the world through apathy or cowardice. The moral people cannot sit idle and wait for a time when human beings will become perfect and morally upright in order to begin a global crusade for effective closer international cooperation and peace. This is true especially in fields of economic development and exchange, education, scientific research, technology, medicine, audiovisual and performing arts, communication, agriculture, trade, and tourism. It is also important in fights against war, crime, injustice, imperialism, terrorism, deforestation, environmental pollution, poverty, hunger, malnutrition, disease, and premature death.

To this end, there must be a closer knowledge, understanding, and acceptance of each other as real people and nations. To facilitate this process, there must be an initial mutual trust and goodwill to enable the rest to follow. In this initial quest for mutual knowledge and understanding, international studies are absolutely essential. These studies should include the world's history, cultures, geography, religions, politics, technology and trade. This kind of comparative education will reduce prejudice, ignorance, bigotry, and indifference. Subsequently, they should be able to create sensitivity to local, national and global human diversity, cultural and religious pluralism. Consequently, it will lead to international understanding, dialogue, cooperation, tolerance, peaceful coexistence and global peace.

Global peace can only become a reality and last when human beings realize their common humanity and common good as the mutual peaceful coexistence. These qualities are constituted by living together in unconditional acceptance and love of each other as fellow human beings. Peace also deepens the knowledge that one person's well-being and happiness consists in the happiness and well-being of all other human beings. It is in the well-being and happiness of others that our own is also both correlatively and coextensively truly found and experienced. This is because true happiness is indivisible. It is a collectively shared divine supernatural gift of God's salvation and state of heavenly existence in God's Kingdom which is coextensive with the authentic and fully humanized life of agape in this world.

Accordingly, based on the indivisibility of global moral theory of peace and justice, and agapic theological realization, Martin Luther King correctly proclaimed that all human beings in the world were inseparably morally, spiritually bound together and globally interconnected in the common web of life and well-being. As such, for Luther, "no human being is free until all human beings everywhere are free." Likewise, he always affirmed that "injustice anywhere is a threat to peace, everywhere," in the world. This truth is clearly illustrated by wars in the Middle East that also cause global hardships. For instance, the price of oil goes up when oil is used as a weapon against those who fail to support the Arab cause. Consequently, these destructive societal and moral evils must be rejected; peacefully resolved and prevented from recurrence.

As moral, responsible and intelligent beings, we must act as God's responsible ambassadors and saints in the world and its history. Caring, intelligent and responsible people must be empowered by obedience and faith in the supernatural transforming and redeeming power of God's and human agape (unconditional love), free forgiveness and justice. This positive faith and positive moral action are required in order for the human beings to transcend the limitations of finitude and evil. That is, the human being is divinized to become like God, and like God to be able to reject the evil temptations of greed, self-interest, hubris (pride and ego), and traditional negative conditioning to seek revenge (*lex talionis*) as the ideal form of justice and punishment.

Through this process of human deification or divinization by God and assimilation and participation in God's essence of Agape, free grace (*Sola Gratia*) and mercy, the finite human being is enabled to become perfect and divine like God. Like God, they are also transcendent over evil and divisive human barriers of sin. By truly becoming like God (*imago Dei*), human beings become divinely consecrated and empowered by God to serve as God's co-creators and co-redeemers in the world. Jesus was the best example of this case of true human perfection, divinization and obedience to serve as God's cosmic instrument of creation and redemption. However, for the Christians, Jesus as the Christ serves as the ultimate role-model and divine destiny for each obedient human being in the world as a "son" or "daughter" of God in the world.

Thus, empowered by the Creator and Redeemer God, the obedient saints of God and ambassadors in the world of all religions, races, colors, genders, socioeconomic classes, cultures and nationalities, universally become divinely authorized as his or her ministers and agents of love, peace, positive transformation, salvation and new creation. Without exception, they are all enabled to recognize evil despite its various social, academic, economic, political, social, medical, racial, religious and cultural disguises, in which it both resides and hides. Through the efficacious redemptive divine power of God's unconditional love, free grace, nonviolence, persuasion from evil and free forgiveness of sins, the majority of human beings in the world are redeemed. They are enabled to experience true and the most meaningful dimensions of the internal, personal, social and global modes of mutual harmonious mutual coexistence, interdependence, equitable sharing of the natural essential resources, justice, love, nonviolence, peace and happiness.

Peaceful mutual coexistence in love, is the true meaning and essence of supernatural salvation, peace and eternal life in God's Kingdom. This fellowship of love or "Heaven" is made possible by God's own free grace. It is activated by human cooperation through obedience, faith as a dynamic positive orientation to life and its mysteries, the praxis of agape and a life of nonviolence. God' Kingdom is God's free gift for all the obedient and loving human beings everywhere in the world. This is the testimony of the saints and the holy prophets like Aken Aton, Moses, Amos, Buddha, Jesus, Muhammad, St. Francis of Assisi, Gandhi, Janani Luwum, Desmond Tutu, Mother Teresa, and Martin Luther King.

Concerning the Kingdom of God, religious teachers and the prophets Jesus give his followers the following criteria to measure them:

> Enter [God's Kingdom] through the narrow gate, because the gate to hell is wide and the road that leads to it is easy, and there are many who travel it. But the gate to life is narrow and the way that leads to it is hard, and there are few people who find it.
>
> Be on your guard against false prophets; they come to you looking like sheep on the outside, but on the inside they are really like wild wolves. You will know them by what they do. Thorn bushes do not bear grapes and briers do not bear figs. A healthy tree bears good fruit, but a poor tree bears bad fruit. A healthy tree cannot bear bad fruit, and a poor tree cannot bear good fruit. And any tree that does not bear fruit is cut down and thrown in the fire. So then, you will know the false prophets by what they do.
>
> Not everyone who calls me 'Lord, Lord' will enter the Kingdom of heaven, but only those who do what my Father in heaven wants them to do. When the Judgement Day comes, many will say to me, 'Lord, Lord! In your name we spoke God's message, by your name we drove out many demons and performed many miracles!' Then I will say to them, 'I never knew you. Get away from me, you wicked people!' (Matt. 7:13-23)

# Chapter 10

# Problems of Patriarchal Religious Language: Myths, Metaphors And Symbolism for God

Religion has been universally dominated by various cultural patriarchal structures and their correlative patriarchal theology and priesthood. Subsequently, in traditional or Orthodox Judaism and pre-Reformation Christianity, all priests, major religious leaders and theologians were male. As a result, the theological language, liturgical and religious symbols also became correlatively male as their male creators.

Therefore, religious language, myths and symbols are religious, cultural and linguistic mirror-reflections of their patriarchal creators, rather than that of the transcendent holy God, whom they are supposed to mediate to the world. Nevertheless, these patriarchs were also convinced that God was a Cosmic Patriarch in whose image they had been created. As a result, they proclaimed to the world that their thoughts were the mediated thoughts and binding revelations of God. Moses, Isaiah, Amos, Jesus and Paul are examples of this religious phenomenon.

## 1. Religious Fundamentalism, Literalism, Bigotry, and Intolerance

All religions and their dogmatic doctrines are culturally relative systems of beliefs, and ritual practices in relationship to the holy Transcendent Creative and Redemptive Cosmic Mystery or God. Religion "speaks" or conveys its message about the unnameable Transcendent and

Infinite Creator-Redeemer God through the finite and imperfect human language. Religious language employs myth, stories, drama, hymns, poetry, dance, ritual, prayers, metaphors and symbolism in order to speak about this incomprehensible and "unspeakable God."Worship and the administration of sacraments are part of this holy language, drama, ritual and symbolism. They symbolize God's holy presence and communicate the efficacy of God's unmerited grace, unconditional love, forgiveness, holy fellowship, peace, salvation, entry into heaven and eternal life.

The majority of the religious scriptural literalists and fundamentalists misunderstand the nature of religious metaphorical language, myth and symbolism and take it literally as both prose and history. This is mainly due to the fact they are generally poorly educated, ignorant and narrow-minded people. They are confused by the theological nature of religion and it's figurative and mythological language. For instance, the literalists read the ancient Hebrew creation and fall religious myths found in the biblical book of Genesis as literal historical accounts of God's actual creation and fall of humanity.

Likewise, they misunderstand the stories of Noah's flood and the Tower of Babel as actual cosmic historical events. However, these kinds of misunderstandings and literalist errors have led to tragic religious confusion, bigotry, intolerance, and violence. The extreme examples are the destructive wars (crusades and jihads). Contemporary examples include religious wars in the Middle East, Northern Ireland, the Sudan and Nigeria.

All these interreligious wars and violence are neither "holy" nor morally unjustified as they often erroneously claim. God is neither a Christian nor a Muslim or a member of Judaism. Like other wars, religious wars are due to ignorance, and the sins of bigotry, ethnocentrism, xenophobia, injustice, hate and mutual intolerance. These problems occur in those parts of the world where religious fundamentalists, intolerant and ignorant people, zealously seek to exclude and discriminate against the people of different religions. Problems also arise when the members of the dominant religious groups try to force the conversion of the people of other beliefs or religions to their own religion or particular world-view and moral codes as God's revealed absolute and immutable universal redemptive truth.

Most of the religious fundamentalists are religious fanatics who also erroneously and tragically believe that their own religion is the only right, true, universal, redemptive, infallible religion, divinely revealed by God. Accordingly, they also affirm that it is God's universal mandate for them to convert people of other faiths and religions to their own religion. They also dogmatically regard it as the only true path to God, virtue, good deeds, salvation, peace and happiness.

As such, most of the religious literalists, fundamentalists and fanatics are also bigoted, religiously exclusive, intolerant and potentially both violent people. They may become dangerous to the people who hold liberal or different views from their own. They may think that they are doing God a favor by getting rid of "atheists" or "nonbelievers."This is mainly because they equate religious myths with historical reality and Holy Scriptures with history and science textbooks. Tragically, they confuse religious myths, stories and parables with real history and the sciences. As a result, some of these believers vigorously reject Darwin's teaching on human evolution because it contradicts the literal reading of the Genesis stories of God's "creation in six days" (cf. Gen. 1:1-31).

Subsequently, many devout religious people have reached the religiously destructive, intellectually absurd and erroneous religious conclusions that religion and science are incompatible. This error is largely due to poor education and a closed religious system of false doctrines and erroneous religious beliefs. In such a system, human symbolic and metaphorical religious language is equated with reality.

As a result, religion becomes confused with history and science. This happens when ignorant or poorly educated people confuse religious myths with history and science because they are found in the holy scriptures, such as the Torah, Bible and the Qur'an. This phenomenon includes: the story of the creation of the cosmos by God in "six days" and "God's rest on the seventh day" (the Sabbath); Adam and Eve's temptation, disobedience and original sin ("the fall"); Noah's story of the flood; and the sacred stories of the Virgin birth of Jesus, his resurrection and ascension into heaven (the sky).

Likewise, the names and metaphors for God as "Father" are sometimes taken as a literal biological and physical description of God as a "Man" or "Patriarch" and a male spiritual being like Zeus. Names like "Yahweh," "Jehovah," and "Allah" are taken literally as if there were many Gods with different names and religions.

As such, Christians tend to see Muslims as worshipers of a different God from that worshiped by Jews and Christians because the term for the same God in the Arabic language happens to be "Allah" and not "Yahweh." For instance, the Jehovah's Witnesses seem to be convinced that God can only be properly worshiped and served by calling him or her the correct name, namely, "Jehovah." This confusion arises out of the failure to perceive God as One, Cosmic Transcendent, Creative, nameless, Spirit and Mystery that we refer to as "God."

Metaphors such as "Father" and "Mother" are both anthropomorphic and anthropocentric efforts "to humanize God." "Naming God" also represents the universal idolatrous desire to understand God and "create God within our cultural, linguistic and physical images." The images of God which are curved out of wood, stone, clay and paint illustrate this human desire to "tame God" and "re-create the Transcendent God" in our own image. Accordingly, the commandments of Moses prohibit this form of idolatry. Nevertheless, it persists in many cultures and religions including Christianity, where many Christians who wish to deify Jesus, the man of Nazareth as God, the second Person of the Trinity, instead of the *Logos*, and Mary, the mother of Jesus, as the *Theotokos*, the Mother of God and "Queen of Heaven."

Ultimately, there is only One cosmic Creator, Sustainer and Redeemer God. This God embodies the entire cosmos as a pregnant mother embodies and gives life to her unborn-child. Yet, the child in the womb may not know how dependent he or she is on his or her mother. Although human beings are implicitly aware of their dependence on God, they are unable to gain the total knowledge and understanding of God as their transcendent and incomprehensible Cosmic Life-Giving Spirit and Parent ("Ancestor" as "Matriarch" or "Patriarch/*Abba*").

However, religious people are analogous to the proverbial blind men who went to see an elephant. Each blind man touched and felt a different part of the elephant, and in blindness and ignorance concluded that he had "seen" the whole elephant. They rejected the different competing testimonies and claims of truth regarding the same elephant, even when it was also true and correct, since they had felt a different part of the elephant. Just as the blind men could not see the whole elephant by virtue of their blindness, religious people can physically neither see nor perceive the totality of God's transcendence and infinite divine essence by virtue of their theological blindness, finitude and limited minds to apprehend the fullness of the Infinite and Transcendent Mystery or God.

## 2. God as the Cosmic Nameless Creative Spirit, Mind, Energy and Transcendent Mystery

As a result of the human finite knowledge about God and limited nature of the human language and symbolism, God is often perceived anthropomorphically and portrayed differently by different people depending on their own *a priori* local context. This religious and theological conceptual and epistemological context for the understanding and speaking about God consists of their own respective culture, language, class, gender, and level of technological development.

However, there is one transcendent Cosmic God and "not many different Gods" for the different people, various tribal groups and different nations or religions, as the "henotheism" falsely affirms. Henotheism is sometimes confused for monotheism because it affirms one God for the members of its religious community while affirming the reality of the gods of other surrounding religious communities. Some of the ancient Hebrews seemed to hold this concept of God rather than that of true monotheism as declared in the *schema* and the Islamic creed (*Shahada*).

The *Shahada* (*La ilaha illa Allah; Muhammad rasul Allah*). That is the affirmation that: "There is no god but the God (*Allah*) and Muhammad is his Prophet." This the public monotheistic creedal declaration and confessional opening statement for Islamic prayer and worship. It constantly and universally declares the cosmic unity and oneness of God and rejects all other divinities as mere idols and false gods. No images of God, prophets and saints are permitted.

The same one, cosmic Creator, Sustainer and Redeemer God is the same God variously worshiped by the Muslims as *Allah*, by the Jews as *Yahweh* and by the Christians as God (*Theos, Deus, Mungu, Katonda* etc). The one transcendent Cosmic Creator, Sustainer and Redeemer God being infinite and beyond the human intellectual grasp and complete understanding is variously perceived and understood differently by the people of different cultures and religions. Nevertheless, all these relative and finite perceptions of God contain some fragmentary revelations of God and partial finite truths regarding God's infinite mystery and the nature of God's ongoing supernatural activities in the cosmos.

The monotheists affirm the oneness and unity of God as the Cosmic Creative Force or Spirit, Sustainer and Redeemer. The best examples of the monotheistic world religions are Islam, Judaism and Christianity. The monotheists contend that the different manifestations of God as creativity and redeemer represent God's transcendence and complexity in terms of attributes and functions. However, some lay Christians are sometimes confused by the doctrine of the Holy Trinity. Some unsophisticated Christians may be guilty of tritheism and elevating some saints, such as the Virgin Mary the *Theotokos* (Bearer of God) into some kinds of gods. In the ancient pagan world, people of great importance were said to either gods or sons and daughters of God. Emperors and kings were worshipped as gods. As such, Jesus or Mary, his mother being worshipped as gods by new Christian converts from Greek and Roman paganism and the worship of human beings or images as gods, was natural. It was a continuation with their cultural and religious traditions.

However, strictly monotheistic Jews and Muslims reject the Christian doctrine of the Holy Trinity as tritheism and idolatry. They affirm that Jesus was mere devout Jewish moral and religious radical reformist Rabbi (teacher) who was crucified by the Romans on charges of sedition and then deified by his devoted disciples. The argument is that Christians have deliberately deified their martyred religious leader into a saint, "son of God" and God (cf. John 1:1-18). If this is true, much of Christian traditional Christology is also in reality part of human idolatry and polytheism which negate the teachings of any truly monotheistic religion, such as Judaism and Islam.

Polytheism was popular in the ancient pagan Roman and Greek cultures and religions in which Christianity was formulated by the Fathers of the Early Church. Polytheism is still preferred by many unsophisticated religious people in Africa, Asia and Latin America because it affirms the reality of many competing gods for human favor, service and worship. There are gods of weather, wealth, health, disease, wisdom, beauty, agriculture, water, lakes, rivers, forests, fire, love, safe travel, food, animals, mountains, fertility and the like.

The mediums and priests as religious experts help the people to worship and perform sacrifice to the right divinity! It is widely believed that the various gods punish the people who fail to recognize them and pay them their due respect. This is the explanation offered for most diseases and misfortunes that befall the people within these regions! The concept of germs and viruses as the causes of diseases are still alien to the many ignorant villagers in these undeveloped parts of the world. As a result, bacterial and viruses contagious diseases are rampant and the traditional healers still prescribe the traditional cures by sacrificing to the angry gods and the ancestral spirits.

It is by faith alone and real miracles that some of these sick people actually get healed by prayer and performing sacrifice to the gods and the spirits of the ancestors! In the absence of good and affordable modern hospitals and medicine, the traditional priests and healers must be properly trained to become more effective in their spiritual and medical service to the people. For instance, they traditional healers could be reacquired to instruct their clients in personal hygiene such as washing the hands after using the toilet and before they handle or prepare food for others, or before they eat.

The gods of water and food should become the guardian of this custom of personal "holiness" as cleanliness and hand washing before handling food and after using the toilet or coming from a public place and working in the garden. The god of water should be redefined to include personal holiness which is taught as comprehensive personal cleanliness and good hygiene. For the Christians, the holy sacrament of baptism must be used and taught to people in a manner that fulfil these healthcare ideals and priorities for enhancement of life and the well-being of God's people as part of God's offer of real supernatural salvation and eternal life now. Accordingly, for Christians in rural areas and developing countries, the sacrament of baptism could be explained within these healthcare and disease prevention guidelines. God and religion must be related to creaturely life as it is both experienced and lived in the world now.

Salvation and God's Kingdom must be positively experienced as God's unmerited, free and universal effective positive power for creation, the creatures' positive transformation or redemption, well-being, meaningful self-fulfillment and happiness. This need for human affirmation and experience of God's providence, continuing activities of creation and redemption of the world and its inhabitants constitute a rejection of *deism* as a doctrine which affirms that God created the world long ago and left it to be governed by the *natural law* as a watchmaker makes a watch and leaves it alone to run mechanically based on the laws of physics and powered by electricity or another source of energy, such as a swinging pendulum or solar energy coming from the sun.

Pantheism avoids the intellectual problem of the divine transcendence of God and confusion of multiplicity of the divine attributes and manifestation in the world by reducing God to nature and elevating nature to divinity as God. In this theological world-view Nature and God are identical. In pantheism, God is Nature and Nature is God. In this system, all things are divine fragments and God is the sum total of all things and beings in the cosmos.

Deism avoids all the above theological debates and confusion. Unlike atheism which rejects God or theism as a creative theory and an explanation for the cosmic existence, creation or origination of the cosmos and evolution of life, deism accepts this divine creative theory. But, deism suggests that God as the original creator of the cosmos may have existed at the beginning of evolution or as the initiator of the "big bang" after which he may have perished. This absent Creator-God is not the Sustainer of the world as mainline Christianity teaches. Rather, after the creation of the world, God is said to have left the world which he had made in charge of the "laws of nature" to govern it on his or her behalf.

This is the theory of the "clock maker" in that the universe is like a clock that had been designed to run by means of self-rewinding and self-correcting or cosmic cybernetics. Deism is not concerned with the names of God or the doctrines of God, such as providence, sustenance and redemption. God does not intervene in the world or relate to creatures in the world. That theory of God leads to naturalism and some forms of popular secular humanism, idolatry, materialism, capitalism, democracy, utilitarianism, Marxism and communism. In these moral theories there is no need for God or the names of God, except those of deified heros, such as Karl Marx, Joseph Stalin, Mao Tse Tung and Fidel Castro.

However, in traditional theism, the transcendent and Creative Mystery or Spirit that is called God is a reality and not an illusion. But, there is confusion about this transcendent God because he or she is an Incomprehensible Infinite Spirit, that is invisible and unknowable. Nevertheless, there are many popular names for this hidden, unnameable and unknowable mystery God. Idolatry is partly a human response and solution to this divine transcendence and hiddenness of God. Many people want to worship the God that they can see, understand and directly relate to or even manipulate and control! In some religions, people often idolatrously engage in ritualistic prayers and offer sacrifices as magical devices to accomplish this supernatural goal. For instance, praying to God to kill your enemy or make someone do what you want, falls within this category of magic, manipulation of God and idolatry.

It is also a form of idolatry to insist and elevate our own religion and claims as God's unique and absolute exclusive redemptive revelation. This is including the dogmatic claims concerning the names of God and revelation that the respective religion exclusively claims to be the only universally true, absolute, perfect, infallible, complete, immutable redemptive truth and true path to God and the supernatural salvation or the eternal life in Heaven or God's Kingdom. Before the reformation of the Vatican II, the Roman Catholic Church had traditionally taught this reprehensible doctrine by its dictum of *extra ecclesiam nulla salus* (outside the [Roman Catholic] Church, there is no salvation).

The Jehovah's Witnesses are good examples of the people who fail to see that the names of God are culturally relative and meaningless in a global setting except for the people who use those names. The unnameable God remains universally the same regardless of the names given to him or her and the doctrines formulated by human beings to define and control God's activities, such as those of unconditional love, free grace and cosmic salvation. Human beings cannot restrict God's free activities by imposing conditions on this transcendent God.

Human doctrines such as baptism, holy communion, monogamy as opposed to polygamy, and heterosexuality as opposed to homosexuality are meaningless to God and do not bind God and limit God's free grace and acts of salvation. Similarly, God does not prefer one religion or name over another. That is mere human preferences and prejudices which are anthropomorphically projected into heaven on God's and then, believed to be God's own true immutable attributes and essence.

Through this unconscious process religion and cultures create God in their own human image and values. As a result, the gods which are created in Asia look and sound Asian. Similarly, those gods created in Africa also look and sound African whereas those created in the West also look white, and sometimes also sound both capitalist and whitesupremacist! Gods are shaped in the image and according to the moral values and theology of their own human creators. Christianity is not an exception to this observation. In this respect, Buonarroti Michelangelo's paintings in the Vatican Sistine Chapel provide ample evidence. God and Adam look alike. They look like any handsome and strong Italian men.

This diversity of the names for God (*Mungu, Theos, Deus, Allah, Amun, Ra, Katonda* and *Yahweh*) and the seemingly mutually exclusive "divinely revealed religions" (such as Judaism, Christianity, Islam and Buddhism) and holy scriptures (*Torah, Bible, Qur'an* and *Vedas*) are not evidence of the existence or worship of many different Gods. Rather, they are evidence of the transcendence of God, and how different human beings only gain access to a mere portion of God's revelation and cosmic inclusive redemptive mystery.

The major tragic mistake that these people often make is to elevate their own limited, finite, fragmentary and partiality of their own access to God's revelation, mystery and knowledge to the absolute universality and totality of God's own essence (nature) and revelation. The second major tragic mistake is deeply rooted in the unconscious human failure to recognize the true limitations, fallibility and relativity of the finite nature of their own minds, conceptions of God, and scriptures as human relative perceptions of God's self-revelations.

These factors account for the subsequent correlative distortions in the understanding of God, errors in doctrines and moral teachings about God, and general imperfections and incompleteness of their own religions and religious and moral teachings. This includes the dogmatic assertions commonly found in these religions, such as, God is "*Abba*" (Father or Patriarch) and God's Trinity (Father, Son and Holy Spirit) as ontological divine realities and immutable truths.

For a long time, women were denied the sacrament of holy ordination on the mistaken doctrinal dogmas which asserted that God was male. Thus, females could not represent God at the holy altar as his holy priests and mediators of divine mysteries. They could not represent the supernatural grace of free forgiveness of sins and redemption as administered through the sacraments of the Eucharist and the restoration of the penitent (confession and absolution).

Yet, this fallacious Western characteristic form of patriarchal Christian theological logic, method and traditional formulation of Christian doctrines was too narrow and erroneous. It failed to take into account the real fundamental nature of God's free universal redemptive grace and cosmic mystery of God's inseparable universal free activities of creation and redemption through unmerited and unconditional love. Within this global Christian understanding, all the seven Christian sacraments (Baptism, Confirmation, Eucharist, Confession, Holy Orders [Ordination], Holy Matrimony, Holy Unction) are theologically rooted in God's primary universal redemptive sacrament of the holy Incarnation of God through the "holy Virgin [young woman] Mary!"

If the woman (Virgin Mary) was found by God to be holy and suitable enough as the vessel or medium of redemptive grace in the incarnation, and the apostolic Church is a result of this divine action through Mary, then, surely, all the women were duly cleansed by God through the incarnation and elected to become his holy instruments of divine revelation, grace, redemption, forgiveness of sins and reconciliation of the penitent! This is what true sacerdotal priesthood is about!

In addition, Mary as the Mother of Jesus, and all women as mothers, have more right than men or male priests to preside over the celebration of the body of her son as the symbolic holy atonement for sin for all those with faith that he was God's provision for the atonement and holy sacrifice for sin by his innocent death on the cross on behalf of all sinners! The Eucharist as a sacrament and holy ritual meal is best traditionally prepared and served by women as mothers, cooks and servers of the family food!

It is self-evident that traditionally the male or patriarchal Christian theologians have been the agents of great injustice and discrimination against women within the Church ministry and theology. This is due the to the dominance of patriarchy and intrinsic sexism within the institutional Christian Church and its affairs. In this case, prejudiced males have tragically failed to see the traditional value of the divine Incarnation of God's eternal *Logos* (Word) into the historical world, humanity, and cosmic violent history through the holy Virgin Mary. This is irrespective of the doctrine of the holy Virgin Birth which was widely accepted as part of the Christian dogma! Beyond this point, male language and religious symbols took dominated Christianity and theology.

Patriarchal religious language and symbolism effectively transformed *"Sophia"* which was a truly feminine attribute of God's essence into a masculine one. Women were further alienated from God and Christianity. Patriarchal society had no room for a God who included femininity in his essence, and symbolically, the correlative divine inclusion of women in salvation, priesthood and the redemptive ministry of God's Church in the world. Yet, the primary mission of God's redemption of the world had been effected though Mary as the obedient and holy Mother of Jesus (*Theotokos).* As such, Mariology has much redemptive value for both men and women, although it has been ignored by the Protestants. Likewise, women's redemptive ministry in the world remains truly God's will and mission in the world with Mary serving as the model.

Ultimately, God, humanity and the world are the focus of religion. God is the primary object or focus of mainline Christianity and other major world religions, such as Islam, Judaism, and Hinduism. Within this complexity, God is both mystically and functionally defined as the Infinite, Transcendent, cosmic holy Mind, eternal Spirit, Cosmic Creator-Sustainer and Redemptive Mystery.

Therefore, any God, other than the true Cosmic Creator, Sustainer and Redeemer is not the true God of monotheistic worship that is the focus of world religions. That kind of God is unable to offer true redemption to anyone. This kind of God is defined as a "man-made God" who is a mere idol. This human-made idol was the kind of God that Freud correctly rejected and denounced as a destructive "illusion" and deification of the males or revered patriarchs into God(s). The tendency for Christian deification of Jesus as a man of Nazareth, apart from the *Logos* that was incarnate in him, provides an example of male self-deification into God.

Religion based on this "man-made illusion" and idol for God is also what Karl Marx correctly identified as an "opium of the masses," and the tool for the capitalist or bourgeoisie exploitation of the poor. Christian theology and ethics reject idols and denounce the worship and obsession with other forms of Western idols or human-made gods, such as: money, wealth, fame, power, pleasure or addiction to sex and drugs. These are all considered sins and dangerous forms of societal idolatry, in which even the many religious people become unconscious victims.

"Idolatry" is rarely used by the clergy as the religious name or label for these moral evils and sins against God, because the Church and its membership themselves are often very guilty of them. As such, God as the holy divine Transcendence and infinite Cosmic Mystery is by definition and essence the essential, eternal "Great Mystery" (*Mysterium Tremendum*), who is beyond human intellectual grasp and understanding.

Yet, theology, religion, scripture, liturgy, doctrines and dogmatic affirmations often claim that they are speaking about God. In some cases, religions are so convinced that what they speak about God is the truth, that they call their scriptures and religious teachings God's self-disclosed truths and revelations. What is God-revealed is supposed to be true and without error, and God is also affirmed to be perfect and omniscient. The scriptures, as God's revealed books, are also often assigned the perfection, infallibility and inerrancy that is associated with the perfection and omniscience of God! History indicates that some misguided religious people became so convinced that they had been given God's total truth and redemptive revelation that they also we are convinced that other religions, and their scriptures and doctrines, were false, wrong and dangerous.

Subsequently, those religious bigots became so self-righteous that they believed God had called, elected and chosen them to go and convert the whole world to their religion as the only true redemptive path to God and the sole channel of God's efficacious, redemptive grace, revelation and salvation! Exclusive doctrines like those invented by Bishop Cyprian of

North Africa, which definitively declared that "*Extra Ecclesiam Nulla Salus*" (Outside the [Roman Catholic] Church, there is no Salvation) were formulated in this kind of sinful, exclusivist bigotry. They were accepted by the Church as God's universal and absolute truth, in the same sinful spirit of idolatry, hubris, ethnocentrism and exclusivism.

It is both idolatry and blasphemy to affirm that the transcendent Creator-Sustainer-Redeemer God or Spirit is universally bound or controlled by human religions, theologies and doctrines of God, salvation (soteriology), and judgement or eschatology. Such a God is the creation of human minds, imagination and doctrines. This limited God is an idol that is designed, created and determined by human beings according to their unfulfilled needs, hopes for the good life, existential anxiety and fears (*angst* and dread).

This is the kind of mental, linguistic, cultural, religious idol or the "human [male] made" patriarchal and tribal God that Feuerbach, Karl Marx, Freud and Emile Durkheim analyzed and correctly rejected as an illusion created by the human minds and projected into the sky (heaven) as the Creator, Sustainer and Preserver God. This is the kind of "man-made" patriarchal God that Mary Daly also correctly sought to castrate as the "patriarchal religious oppressor" and "rapist of women" in her radical feminist book called *Beyond God the Father*.

Mary Daly was right in pointing out that such a patriarchal, anti-female and antiblack "White-Male" as God was a mere "white man-made God" and an idol which needed destruction. This was the kind of idolatrous and false man-made patriarchal God Mary Daly was interested in treating indignantly, just as a mere object for mutilation, in the form of castration into an androgyny.

Daly also viewed this patriarchal anthropomorphic idol (God the Father) as an oppressive God that needed to be completely smashed and demolished. She also calls this smashing of the "man-made idols" as "the castration" and destruction of the patriarchal God. This radical feminist theological divine task is supposed to be carried out as a religious and moral crusade in the name of the one true God, who is the Transcendent Creator, Sustainer, holy Redeemer, and the nameless cosmic creative Mystery (*Yahweh*). As both Tillich and Karl Barth correctly taught in their many influential theological writings, the Transcendent Cosmic Creator-Redeemer God transcends all human minds, language, scriptures and religions. This is also the testimony of the Qur'an and true Islam.

Nevertheless, faced with the formidable task of teaching the ignorant and superstitious masses of his time, Jesus employed the language of myth, stories and parables, in order to talk about the mysteries of God's unconditional love, free grace, mercy, free forgiveness of sins, salvation and God's eternal Kingdom that was already present on the Earth and beyond. Jesus also personalized this divine Cosmic Creative Power as "*Abba*" so that human beings could feel at home and protected in the world as the beloved children of God and members and citizens of his Kingdom by birth. Human beings have this right, since they are the beneficiaries of God's Kingdom by virtue of their birth, and are thus heirs of God's world and Kingdom! Unfortunately, most theologians either completely missed or rejected the main point of Jesus' message about the arrival of God's Kingdom on the Earth through faith and practice of agape, free forgiveness of sins, nonviolence and peaceful existence with all people in God's world.

As fellow members of God's family and citizens in the Kingdom of love and peace on Earth, human beings were expected to practice these teachings (cf. Matt. 5-7; Lk. 17:20-21). Instead, they focused on his teachings about God as "*Abba*" as a biological reference rather than a theological metaphor, just like his other parables and metaphors for God as the "sower" or "farmer," "plantation owner," "king," "judge," "vine," "tree," "shepherd," and the like. That is a great tragedy indeed! These were some of the false teachers and prophets or "the blind guides" of other people that Jesus warned his followers about!

Ultimately, Jesus taught that we will know the obedient and true prophets not by their teachings, but rather by their good deeds of unconditional love and forgiveness (cf. Matt. 7:13-13; 25:31-46). Jesus himself had cursed a tree with good leaves to be without fruits as an illustration of what will happen to those people with mere faith or religious doctrinal confessions of God, but who are without any good moral deeds of love, grace and righteousness as part of their lives in the community and the world. Accordingly, Mary Daly is correct in her vicious denouncement and attack on the Western institutional patriarchal Christian Church that practices hate, injustice and the dehumanizing evils of sexism and racism against God's people, who are created in his or her own image and loved without any prior conditions.

For Mary Daly, as well as Tillich, Rahner, Hegel, Aquinas, Augustine, Paul and Moses, among others, affirm God to be essentially the nameless Cosmic, Creative Spirit or Energy whose primary "*essence is to be*" and whose primary divine attribute or essential function is to create or cause life and being to exist. The Creator God is not a being that exists as the greatest being among as other beings (*pares inter pares*). On the contrary, the true Creator-Sustainer and Redeemer God is "Being" or "Ultimate Reality" and "Life" itself. God as "Pure Being" and "Creativity" is the Cosmic, Creative Spirit or Energy that is both "medium of being" as well as "the self-generating Energy that is the Eternal Cosmic Power of being."

As Paul Tillich correctly realized, God is not a concrete thing or being that exists in time and space like all finite physical objects. As such, God is not subject to the limitations of natural law. This includes the physical laws of time (*chronos*), distance, speed (velocity), location and gravity. These laws and limitations do not apply to God. They do not describe or determine God, because God is their transcendent creator. God existed before he or she created them. God "Cosmic Being" and "Power to be" is also the cosmic "Medium, Energy, Principle of Order, Creativity, Reality, Love, Grace, Life, and Cosmic Unity" from which these dimensions, life, order, derive, and exist.

It is through God and the principle of *Logos* as Mind, Order, Agape, Peace and harmony, that the universe was created from a single point of God's creative *Logos*. It evolved, got organized, and became constantly coordinated as a cosmos or harmonious and well-balanced cosmic living system in respect to the planet Earth. The Earth as the living planet is the miracle of God's creativity, unmerited love, grace and providence.

The emergence of spirit, mind, consciousness and moral agency among human beings as God's chosen representatives in the vast cosmos of non-thinking matter is another puzzling miracle of God's unconditional deeds of unmerited grace and human free divine election in the cosmos. Human beings can only respond with joy, awe and thanksgiving for their unmerited creation and calling to become God's moral agents, stewards and concrete ambassadors of unconditional love, mind, freedom, creativity, beautification and redemption in the temporal world. The carpenters, engineers, farmers, prophets, scientists, teachers, doctors and saints are examples of these custodians of God's creation and ambassadors of God in the world.

Evolution is God's method for resisting entropy, chaos and nonbeing. Evolution as God's chosen extraordinary historical means and natural method for organizing the universe into a more harmonious system, where the negative and destructive, disorganized energy of chaos or entropy is balanced with God's positive energy for order and balance. In this mystery, God is the term for Einstein's Principle for which he knew to exist but could not prove through the scientific methods of mathematical equations. Mathematics is a good tool and language for science. But

God is not an object that can be measured or computed. This is analogous to the manner in which we speak of mind, spirit, and intuition, and yet we cannot measure them. We only see what they do and we know when they are absent.

Ultimately, for theology and religion, God is the cosmic unifying principle as well as the ground and medium for cosmic emergence, existence and sustenance. This is where faith, as a special intuition, can become a spiritual aid to theologians and religion in speaking about God positively, in the absence of scientific proof or knowledge. This is analogous to the intuitive manner in which we know the subjective reality and truth of love without any scientific evidence to substantiate it. Experience, relationships, intuition, faith and hope for fulfillment is all that we have for both love and God.

It is not surprising, therefore, that some of the New Testament writers employed the metaphor of Unconditional Love for God instead of the metaphor of *Abba* (Father). St. John defines God as Unconditional Love (*Agape*). Likewise, he defines true godliness and saintliness as the diligent practice of unconditional love toward all human beings in the world (cf. 1 John 4:7-21). Both these metaphors refer to the intimate nature and quality of relationship with God as their heavenly unconditional and loving Creator, Sustainer and Redeemer without any prior conditions as a good father or lover would relate to the child or the beloved in a mutually beneficial paternalistic manner of love, compassion, forgiveness and protection.

Like the Transcendent, Creative, Cosmic, Spirit or Energy that we call God, we know that love is not a concrete thing. However, although love is not a concrete thing, it causes real events to occur in history, relationships and within the physiological make up of those who are in love! Such people are healthier, happier and live longer! God as Energy or Spirit can still hold the universe together through gravity and "magnetism" of which he or she is the omnipresent center. This center can be uniformly experienced and accessed from any point within the cosmos. God being the positive Energy in the form of love, goodness and peace empowers us to do the same, and those who do are attracted to him. Those who rebel and do the opposite of goodness and agape, however, become negatively charged and are repelled by God.

This is the nature of the complexity God as the infinitely incomprehensible and cosmic Creative and Redemptive Holy Mystery that we call the "*Mysterium Tremendum.*" It includes the mysteries of God's power of creativity as Cosmic Creator (Originator), Sustainer and Redeemer of the cosmos and all its creatures. There is no partiality, except for the election of human beings to possess a special intellect and a portion of his mind in order to serve him and creation. They are his custodians of creation and the stewards of God's treasures in the universe.

## 3. God's Transcendence and Fallibility Of All Religions and Scriptures

"God" is the term or metaphor in the English language that we give to what Paul Tillich called the "Ground of Being." Thomas Aquinas in the *Summa Theologica*, also affirms God's existence as the implicit but nameless Cosmic Creativity, Creative Cosmic Energy or Spirit in the following five ways (proofs):

1. "The Ultimate Unmoved Mover" of all moving things is what is called "God" in both religion and philosophy.

2. "The First and Uncaused Cause" or the Cosmic Creator of all things that came into existence is, for Thomas Aquinas, what is called "God." That is another term for the Creator or God inasmuch as creation is God's essential work.

3. God is "the necessary Contingent Ground" which both originates and grounds all beings. This is analogous to the way in which life on Earth has emerged in the oceans and evolved into sophisticated animals. The thinking and knowing human being is the biological, evolutionary apex of evolution.

4. God is the "Highest Perfection." Thomas Aquinas affirmed that God was "Pure Perfection." Perfection meant pure essence or reality from which other realities emerge and derive their perfection. (This is a good argument for the Spinoza kind of "pantheism." If all things are rooted in God and derive their existence in God, then God is to some extent part of his own creation! Pantheism affirms that God and the world are identical and inseparable. The Judeo-Christian traditions affirm that God existed prior to creation and created the world *ex nihilo* or "out of nothing.")

5. God is for Aquinas, "the Designer, destiny and all creatures" or "final cause" of all creatures. God as the lure that persuades beings to come into being and actualize themselves fully is also what Whitehead claims in his complex book *Process and Reality*.

For St. Thomas Aquinas, God is the nameless cosmic creative and redemptive energy or transcendent Spirit and Mystery that Moses called

"Yahweh" (Nameless Mystery or "The I Am" cf. Exod.3:13-14). God is effectively known through nature by studying the nature of the cosmos through the sciences. His five cosmological proofs for God's existence are grounded in his understanding of the observable world.

Aquinas' concept of God has influenced Catholic theology and Western philosophy. In its modification, it is self-evident in the formulation of God as the cosmic creativity and "All-Encompossing Spirit" or "Ultimate Reality" that Martin Heidegger called "Being" and what Paul Tillich variously referred to in his monumental works on Christian systematic theology as "Being" itself, the "Ultimate Reality," and the inclusive holy and impartial, benevolent "Ground of being." However, longer before Tillich and Aquinas, St. Paul himself had realized this truth when he affirmed that "God is not a thing" or the greatest "being among other beings," that we could, see, touch and feel. On the contrary, he affirmed that God was the medium of being and existence in whom all things have their being and experience their total life (Act. 17: 16-24).

Furthermore, in the past, some religious people became so sure that they had the exclusive truth of God's essence and redemptive revelation, that they went out to convert other people by force to their own religious view of God! Jihads, the crusades and the inquisition are part of this religious tragedy! In reality, all human religious traditions in the world, including Christianity are incomplete and imperfect.

Each religion, irrespective of its claims to possess the definitive, final and complete fullness of God's absolute truth and revelation and correlative exclusive redemption, does not possess the full truth of God's revelation. Similarly, no single religion constitutes the absolute and exclusive redemptive path required for all human beings in order to gain access to God's Kingdom, truth, love, redemptive grace and God's salvation. On the contrary, each religion exists as an imperfect and incomplete religious or redemptive system, despite its actual dogmatic false religious claims to the contrary, especially those exclusive claims of possessing God's definitive redemptive special revelation as traditionally found in both Christianity and Islam.

Nevertheless, all religions only possess some varying degree of access to God's revelation, truth, God's redemptive grace and salvation. Therefore, each religion also exists in varying degrees of error, incompleteness, falsehood, escapism, self-deception and illusion. Therefore, each religion, including Judaism, Christianity and Islam contains mere fragments and teachings that are only small portions of God's finite revelations or self-disclosure in both nature and through the prophets.

No "revealed religion" or "natural religion" ever contains the complete fullness of God's eternal, universal, perfection of his infinite revelation and absolute truths! No single religion is ever complete or whole. No religion has that kind of supernatural capacity to contain God or apprehend God's complete infinite revelation as it exists in nature, communicated by God through his or her special agents. Perfect religion as the complete medium or encompassing container of God's totality would become God himself or herself! Therefore, no human-made or "revealed religion" is ever eternal, pure, perfect and absolute like God. Any religion that claims that exclusive perfection becomes guilty of idolatry. This is because all human religions are finite and fallible. Therefore, they cannot validly be equated with the transcendent God himself or herself, as the true universal embodiment of God's complete self-revelation to humanity and divine perfection.

All religions are culturally conditioned, relative and imperfect human creations in the name of God and instituted as holy institutions by their human priestly creators on God's behalf. As such, they embody the cultural and moral ideals, hopes, fears, world-view, technologies and cosmologies of their respective human creators. In short, all religions and their "revealed holy scriptures" are human-made in the holy name of God. The holy scriptures, including the Holy Bible and the Qur'an are written special religious works and moral codes of believing and inspired prophets and religious people.

These sacred texts are specially written and canonized by "men." As such, they only contain partial and fallible truths about God, humanity, history and nature. Likewise, these scriptures also contain mere finite fragments of God's revelation and moral law. Within this understanding, all doctrines of infallibility of the Bible, Koran, Church and the Pope are false and dangerous religious doctrines when taken as literal inerrant and absolute universal truths, to which the faithful religious people must subscribe without question, or dogmatically believe as an authentic expression or criterion of true religious faith.

Accordingly, the conservative Roman Catholics are in error when they affirm the literal infallibility of the Pope concerning the declaration of true faith and sound moral teachings. This literalism can make it nearly impossible for the Roman Catholic Church to accept errors in its doctrines and practices and take the necessary steps to correct them. The Catholic Church's 1992 reversal of the Church's condemnation of Galileo in 1669 during the Inquisition is historically unprecedented. Pope John Paul II's courageous action to correct a past theological and moral error of the Church illustrates the fallibility of the Church. At the same time, the Pope's action has redeemed the moral integrity the Catholic Church and restored its intellectual credibility within community of scholars. This action also set the necessary moral stage for the 1996 acceptance of Darwin's teaching on evolution as fact. It also set the context for the Catholic Church's atonement for its past sins of sexism, racism, discrimination against racial minorities due to religious intolerance and cultural ethnocentrism that was held on March 12, 2000, the request for forgiveness for these sins and others that had been committed by the Christian Church over the past two millenniums.

In contrast, the Evangelical Christians are also in serious error when they reject the infallibility of the Pope and instead dogmatically affirm the literal infallibility of the Holy Scriptures. This error comes from the Islamic like dogma concerning the nature of God's special revelation as some kind of mediated God's direct dictation of the contents which the human beings write down as holy scriptures. That is the affirmation or doctrine which teaches that the Bible as God inspired Word and book of holy Scriptures is God's eternal and inerrant holy Word (written *Logos*) and revelation that have been written down by God's inspired human scribes (secretaries).

However, in theological reality, all scriptures are religious literature of the religious community or Church. In the case of the Old Testament or Hebrew Scriptures, these are religious legendary stories of creation and human fall as told by the Hebrews. They are warnings of the prophets, the activities of Judges and Kings as God's agents who were chosen to lead the people of Israel into wars against their neighbors, the songs of praise to God (Psalms) and the like. These are obviously human literature, poetry, and history written from a theocentric or God-centered perspective. With the exception of the prophets, most people did not realize that they were either inspired or writing the scriptures!

The above observations are also true for the New Testament. God did not write the New Testament, and neither did Jesus. Most of the New Testament is about how the early Church was founded and how the apostles taught what they understood to be the message of Jesus about God. They taught the primacy of unconditional love and forgiveness for the neighbor as the keys for entrance into God's Kingdom.

Faith was stressed as important in the Church because it was required in order to believe what the Apostles taught about Jesus as the Christ or the expected Messiah of the Jews was true. They did not have any other evidence to prove it. Within the Hebrew world-view, eschatological expectations and theology, the Early Church's need for a theological construction and proclamation of new myths or stories of the resurrection and ascension of Jesus Christ were practical, cultural, linguistic devices, theological symbols for eternal life and metaphors for the reality of the presence of God's eschatological Kingdom on the Earth.

These myths or religious stories served the Christian Church in the same way in which the mythical stories of Adam and Eve had served in Judaism and the Hebrew Scriptures. They were later mistakenly taught as historical evidence of God's victory over sin, evil and death as its supposed primordial divine punishment for Adam and Eve's sin. The resurrection (human-transcendence over death) and ascension myths were created as new stories for human positive transformation (ascension) into a pure union with God-consciousness.

As pure Mind and Spirit, God does not require embodiment or the resurrection as prior condition for judgement, reward and punishment of human beings. One does not need a body in order to go into fellowship with God in heaven. On the contrary, the physical body may hinder the full spiritual union and fellowship with God, if God as eternal and cosmic Mind and Spirit. However, those people who wish to see evil people suffer in a literal eternal inferno or hellfire, may insist on a physical resurrection for this sadistic purpose and pleasure. As such, these kind of thinkers may find it theologically credible if they insist on the physical resurrection for the sinners and evil doers in order to be physically punished by God as they are both irrevocably and eternally sentenced to suffering in hell.

However, that teaching is contrary to God's essence as Creator-Redeemer that is eternal *Agape* (Unconditional Love) and *Sola Gratia* (Merciful and Compassionate). God as *Agape* and *Sola Gratia* loves and forgives all human beings without and prior conditions, and therefore, does not delight in sending people to eternal damnation and irrevocable suffering in hell. That kind of cruelty and retaliation against sinners and evildoers is immoral regardless of who does it. As such, God being holy and loving is more ready to forgive than to punish. As such, hellfire and Dante's inferno are human creations and imaginations of what they would have done if they were God, but far from God's truth, grace, unconditional love and redemption. God's sun shines of both good and evil people. Likewise, God's rain as the "living water of life" comes down on both the lands of the righteous people (saints) and those of sinners. Similarly, God's infinite love, mercy, unmerited free grace, forgiveness, redemption and eternal life or God's Kingdom and Heaven.

Buddha taught the same principle through his doctrine of enlightenment, self-transcendence and pure union with God in the spiritual state of beatific *Nirvana*. The resurrection is the Christian religious paradigm for newness of life and the eschatological triumph of good over evil; love over hate; forgiveness over retaliation; courage over the fear of death; faith over doubt and life over death. It was through his death on the cross and his expression of unconditional love for others, as was publicly demonstrated by his prayer to God for forgiveness of his executioners, that the Roman soldier encountered "the living love and grace of God" and declared that, "truly Jesus was the Son of God." The resurrection is also a religious metaphor and symbol for God's universal establishment of his eschatological Kingdom on earth in the present time. Death still takes place, but as in the case of the resurrection of Jesus, each human being is able to resurrect and become eternal in union with God's Spirit in God's eternal Kingdom.

Jesus had positively affirmed that God's Kingdom was within each believer, rather than being an external phenomenon. As such, ascension to God does not take place in a particular geographical direction, since God as the Cosmic and omnipresent Spirit is both within the human being as well as outside. The human spirit exists in God.

The "spiritual act of ascension to God" is therefore, to become like a *"Bodhisattva"* within Buddhism. It is the achievement of the highest mystical level of beatific, self-conscious vision of God and union or fellowship with the Eternal God from whom we all originated. As such, Jesus could confidently proclaim to the world that "My Father and I are one," and, "I am in the Father and the Father is in me," or that "Those who have seen me have seen the Father." (John 10:30). But Jesus also taught all his followers to pray to God as their Father in heaven and also to be perfect as God, their Father in heaven (cf. Matt. 5-7).

It is very significant that St. Paul wrote about 25 percent of the New Testament, and the Book of Acts records many of his activities in converting Christianity from a Hebrew-based religion to a Greek and more inclusive and universal religion. However, St. Paul himself was a not an eyewitness of Jesus Christ. Prior to his conversion to Christianity, Paul who was then known as Saul of Tarsus, was a dogmatic, unmarried, male-chauvinistic, Hebrew and patriarchal Pharisee. He had converted to Christianity through a miraculous divine intervention (cf. Act. 8:1ff.). Paul's religious conversion did not wipe out all of his Hebrew patriarchal religious heritage, cultural past conditioning, moral and social conditioning as a Hebrew and Pharisee.

Essentially, St. Paul was still Saul in many aspects of life and Hebraic patriarchal world-view. As such, both socially and culturally, St. Paul still remained a "male-chauvinist" after his conversion to Christianity due to his Hebrew patriarchal religious, social, moral and cultural conditioning.

However, St. Paul became a radical reformer of the original culturally exclusive Judaic form of Christianity. He proclaimed all baptized people to be equal and brothers and sisters in Christ, irrespective of class, race, gender and position (Gal. 3:28). Nevertheless, he did not put this ideal moral and theological revolutionary principle into practice. St. Paul made some allowances for some women's inclusion in the Church. This radical action was undertaken on an occasional and individual basis.

Socially, St. Paul remained conservative. This is illustrated the moral and religious principle for the subordination of women to men and slaves to their masters. He advised Christian slaves to remain slaves and loyal to their masters. He even sent Onesimus back to Philemon, his former master, from whom he had run away in search of freedom. Paul seemed to support Onesimus' status as that of a permanent slave. He merely counseled Philemon to treat Onesimus well as a slave, instead of asking him to set Onesimus free (cf. Philemon 1:8-20). Yet, this is in the same socioeconomic context in which Paul also declared that all human beings are one in Jesus Christ despite race, gender and class (Gal. 3:28). Even then, St. Paul being neo-Platonic and dualistic, did not mean that these kinds of physical, social and biological boundaries between men and women, Jews and Gentiles, and slave and slave-masters had become literally dissolved through the divinizing and unifying holy sacrament of baptism, except in mere spiritual sense! That, too, was only a reality after death and the dissolution of the body which divides God's people on the basis of gender, race, size, height, color, looks and age!

St. Paul wrote to the Churches he had founded in Greece and Asia Minor, saying that women should not hold positions of leadership in the Church, and that they should not speak in Church even if they had questions. Rather, they should wait and ask their husbands and fathers at home. Saint Paul claimed that this was God's command. But how did he know? He based this directive on the Hebrew patriarchal scriptures! He was willing to question circumcision and reject it as a prerequisite for entrance into the Church as the New Covenant. That was a good modification of the preexisting Hebrew religious tradition.

Circumcision as the divine symbol of the Hebrew covenant was a patriarchal and male-chauvinistic symbol which excluded women from union with God! Baptism as the symbol of the New Covenant was egalitarian, since it equally initiated both men and women into the mysteries, benefits and obligations of the New Covenant. As such, based on baptism, all men and women have been ordained into the universal "priesthood of all believers." Thus, all men and women have become equal before God and in the Church and its ministry.

Accordingly, the Church doctrines, language and theology should have been rooted in this sacramental priesthood and equality of all baptized people as equal members and fellow citizens in God's Church and Kingdom. But instead, the Church discriminated against women and developed a male-centered theology, christology, liturgy, ecclesiology and patriarchal religious language that alienated and excluded women from divinity, ordination process, priesthood and leadership in the Church. Unfortunately, this was done in the name of God, and was considered immutable, divine truth and God's universal revelation.

Muslims are in religious error concerning God's special revelation and the nature of holy scriptures, especially, the Qur'an. They dogmatically affirm that the holy Qur'an is perfect and inerrant because it is supposed to have been directly dictated by God to Prophet Muhammad through the Archangel Gabriel! As such, it is not to be translated from God's original holy language which is supposed to be Arabic! The holy Qur'an is dogmatically affirmed by Muslims to be God's infallible and final corrective for Judaism and Christianity.

The Qur'an contains some selected material from both the Jewish *Torah* which had been given to the Prophet Moses, and the *Ingil* (Gospels), which is supposed to be the holy book sent down to the world by God through "Prophet Jesus." Islam insists that Judaism corrupted God's original revelation to the world through "Prophet Moses," whereas the Christians corrupted God's revelation to the world through "Prophet Jesus." This charge of the corruption of God's revelation to the world through Jesus includes the charge of idolatry. Islam charges that whereas Jesus was the messenger of God's revelation and God's prophet, Christians mistook Jesus for God the Almighty in human form and worshiped him as God. That is, Christians deified and worshiped God's messenger, instead of worshipping the true Creator-Redeemer God who had sent him into the world to warn people against idolatry, disobedience, greed, materialism, unrighteousness and injustice.

Islam rejects the anthropomorphic language of Christianity, which called Jesus the "Son of God," instead of "God's holy prophet." Islam also rejects the Christian anthropomorphic and metaphorical language and model of the Trinity of God as "Father," "Son" and "Holy Ghost" or "Mother" as idolatrous and blasphemous. Islam says that God is not like a patriarch or the pagan gods who have sexual relationships with women and beget children!

Accordingly, Islam affirms that because of the human sin of idolatry, Jews and Greeks worshiped Jesus as God instead of worshipping God. They affirm that God had sent him as his prophet and entrusted him with his message of warning and repentance from evil, and sins of idolatry, hate, injustice and rebellion against the most holy, merciful and compassionate God.

Therefore, Islam challenges Christianity of its anthropomorphic idolatrous language, symbolism, art, doctrines and materialism. Islam accomplishes this by its rejection of images, art and anthropomorphic language about God. Islam affirms that God is so transcendent that as finite human beings we cannot even name that unnameable Ultimate Mystery. As a result, in Islam God (*Allah*) is assigned ninety-nine names and descriptive positive attributes, such as the "Creator," "Most Merciful" and "the Compassionate," and yet it goes on to express the disclaimer by saying that God transcends all of these terms and human-made names!

## 4. God's Holy Transcendence and Need for Mediators

God is both a holy and transcendent Creative-Redemptive Mystery whereas human beings are both finite and sinful creatures. There is a universal moral gap and epistemological problem between God and humanity. This gap is created by human sin, finitude and ignorance can be bridged by mediators, such as the prophets, angels, saints, priests, the Blessed Virgin Mary, the Pope as the "Vicar of Christ on the Earth," the Holy Spirit, and ultimately, the *Logos* that is incarnate in humanity, particularly, in Jesus as the Christ of God (cf. John 1:1-18).

Karl Barth was convinced that God was an eternal, hidden, holy Creative and Redemptive Mystery, and that this holy God was so transcendent and unknowable except by his own grace in self-revelation both in the Scriptures and in the divine Incarnation through Jesus Christ. Accordingly, for Karl Barth, God could only be truly talked about through the negative affirmations (*via negativa*).

Most of his famous works in theology, as found in the Church Dogmatics, is an elaborate development of this doctrine of divine transcendence in the remote perfection of heaven and sinful, finite and immoral mortals ("Man") who is exiled from God, here on the Earth! His view was that the holy God resides in heaven and sinful humanity resides on the Earth or in the supposed "evil and imperfect world!" His dualistic religious world-view of God and the world is characteristic of most Christians, especially the Protestants.

This gulf between the Hebrew Patriarchal God in heaven and humanity on the Earth was also reflected in religious language, theology, doctrines, liturgy, religious symbolism and art. Barth's theology is a recent example of what has always taken place in religion, from Moses, who found the Patriarchal God on the glowing top of Holy Mount Sinai, to David and the Hebrew prophets of Israel who were called by God to become his messengers and mediators to the people of Israel as his disobedient elect people. Israel as God's special covenant nation was itself unconditionally both chosen and elected by God to become his holy servant nation, mediator and temporal instrument of monotheism and codification of his explicit moral in the world. Even then, the high-priest served as the main mediator between the holy and transcendent God in heaven and the rest of the people of Israel.

Later, Jesus himself bridged the gulf created between God and the alienation of human sin and divine transcendence by claiming that God and his Kingdom were already truly effectively present in the world. Jesus went further, like Buddha before him, to affirm that God was inside each obedient person who believed his moral teachings and practiced Agape.

Since he was this perfect example of faith in God, obedience, contemplative mystic and perfect agent of God's Agape and free forgiveness of sins, Jesus was also correctly identified as God incarnate or historically manifested in humanity. As such, it was also religiously understood and theologically positively affirmed that he was the cure for human sin and disobedience to God's moral law. Therefore, he was the new concrete "High-Priest" or "Mediator between the holy God and sinful humanity" or "soteriological (salvific or redemptive) bridge" over the gulf between the holy God and sinful or rebellious and immoral human beings.

As the negation and reversal of human moral and spiritual evil, sin and imperfection, Jesus' self-sacrificial life, innocent suffering and death on the cross are considered as a perfect vicarious human sacrifice and acceptable atonement for sin before God. And therefore, considered being redemptive for all people in the world. This is a Christian theory of atonement or soteriology that was both conceived and constructed within the religious context of the Hebrew religious world-view and theology regarding God, sin and sacrifice. As in African Religion, Judaism also centered around the doctrines of sin as a pollution of the sinner and the community as well as being an offense before God. Sin could be atoned by restitution and sacrifice to the holy Creator God in order to atone for human sins and remove them and their pollution from the sinner, the community and the world.

Accordingly, the New Testament as the Christian holy scriptures contains significant amounts of Hebrew culture, theology, ethics or values, and religious language. As such, this material is almost irrelevant and meaningless outside its Hebrew context. This Hebrew context includes: Hebrew culture, religion, ethics and theology about God and the pessimistic understanding of human nature as fallen or sinful and ever standing in need and hope of God's eschatological special moral intervention or the coming of the Messiah to effect human redemption or salvation and establish God's Kingdom in the world.

Within this Jewish religious context, it was positively affirmed by Christians that Jesus provided an eternal and universal atonement and sacrifice for all human sins. This referred to the human sins committed in the past, and sins still to be committed in the future. Within the Hebrew context, and within the mythological stories of Adam and Eve who were supposed to have sinned against God and caused human downfall and alienation from God, it was also affirmed that Jesus had become the second Adam who was obedient, rather than disobedient to God and his moral law.

Subsequently, Christians affirmed this new theory of salvation and soteriological doctrine as not a mere theological formulation and religious speculation, but rather, as a new divinely revealed universal, redemptive truth. The requirement for salvation was changed from the moral observation of the Mosaic Law, whose center is the Decalogue (Ten Commandments). Instead, the new religious language and formulation of the soteriological doctrine by the Christian Church was that people would be saved by faith in Jesus as the Christ (Jewish Messiah) and Son of God. The atonement was identified with Jesus' holy life, obedience and moral actions in perfect union with God.

However, Jesus had himself taught that salvation was achieved through "treating other people with unconditional love and free forgiveness of sins in the same way in which they themselves wished to be treated." He spoke metaphorically of the *eschatological* (final) judgement by God as the "separation of sheep" (obedient saints) from the goats (rebellious sinners or evildoers). Again, in this parable and metaphorical religious language, "the saints would be rewarded by fellowship with God and bliss in heaven," whereas "the sinners would be permanently separated and alienated from God's fellowship of happiness and punished in hellfire." This is the metaphor for God's ongoing judgement, which occurs in the world today.

According to Jesus, we live within the "realized-eschatological era" of God's Reign and Kingdom in the world. In other words, God's Kingdom is already a present reality in the world as God's Reign through his obedient and loving people or saints (cf. Mk. 1:15-16; Lk. 17: 20-21). Jesus performed miracles as signs and evidence of the effective presence of God's Kingdom in the world. To this end, he healed the sick, opened the eyes of the blind and raised the dead to demonstrate God's effective creative and redemptive power that was effectively present as God's Reign or Kingdom in the world.

Therefore, contrary to the narrow and erroneous Protestant doctrines of salvation, such as "*sola fide*" (salvation by faith alone) and "*sola scriptura*" (salvation by Scripture alone), Jesus affirmed the criteria for God's universal judgement to be based on the obedience to the ultimate divine commandment of Agape and nonviolence.

Jesus' doctrine of salvation may be characterized as "*sola Agape.*" This doctrine is based on the idea of "*sola gratia,*" which is taught by the Catholic and the Methodist churches. God's grace empowers a free human being as a free and non-predestined moral being to choose to do good and not evil. According to Jesus, the ultimate moral and spiritually good is a result of obedience to God's moral law, which leads to the concrete external fruits of altruism and the praxis of Agape by which human beings are judged.

According to the reports of Jesus' teachings by St. Matthew (25:31-46), the self-sacrificial praxis of unconditional love in the center of true godliness and normative ethics. This includes the following external, concrete, and measurable criteria for concrete social manifestations of the inward invisible state of grace, faith, obedience to God, unconditional love, altruism, compassion and empathy: (1) Feeding the hungry; (2) Clothing the naked; (3) Healing the sick or providing for their treatment; (4) Providing shelter to strangers and the homeless; (5) Providing a caring ministry to those in prison; (6) Exercising free forgiveness of sins for all those who offend us, instead of seeking justice in the form of personal or legal retaliation (*lex talionis*) as Moses had taught (cf. Matt. 5-7; 25:31-46).

Because God is Agape, and Jesus practiced Agape to the highest possible degree and participated in the fullness of Agape, therefore, Jesus, as the Christ, became effectively united with God and inseparable from him. This is the theological essence of the affirmation by Jesus. He said: "My Father and I are one." Furthermore, there was the affirmation that whoever had seen him had also seen God his Father (*Abba*) in heaven. In this respect, Jesus became the "theophany of God" and the holy mediation of the transcendent and hidden God to humanity. Jesus Christ became a visible and tangible bridge for the human encounter with God, dialogue and reconciliation with God.

Jesus, as the Christ, affirmed that God, his heavenly Father, had sent him into the world to proclaim the Gospel of the Good News of the arrival of God's Reign or Kingdom. This "Reign of God" or "God's Kingdom" was based on the normative moral and spiritual principles of inclusive, cosmic, unconditional love of God. It included free forgiveness of sins for all sinners who repented of moral evil, rebellion against God's moral, hate, malice and sin.

Accordingly, Jesus did not preach new dogmas. Instead, he modified the teachings and laws of Moses based on normative principle of unconditional love as the new normative ethic for nonviolence as opposed to the Mosaic law of equal retaliation (*lex talionis*) as the ideal moral ethic for justice and godliness.

Jesus taught and proclaimed the universal message of God's redemptive free grace, unconditional love and free forgiveness of sins for all human beings, without exceptions. This should have been the central message and proclamation of the Church and all God's saints irrespective of denomination, religious tradition or creed! This is the true nature of the universal and inclusive salvation, religious community or Church of God. God's inclusive family is diverse and religiously and culturally pluralistic. What binds it together is God as Abba or Mother who creates, redeems, sustains, loves and forgives all human beings without conditions. God only asks all his obedient saints and servants in the world to do the same.

## 5. Divine Transcendence and Infinite Mystery: The Inadequacy of Finite Human Minds

God being the transcendent cosmic Mystery, is an invisible Creative and redemptive Spirit that is beyond the grasp and complete understanding of human finite minds, intellects and language. God is also completely inaccessible to the human senses of sight, sound, touch, smell, and taste. Therefore, the holy scriptures correctly affirm that: "No human has ever seen God." This is because God is an Eternal Creative Force or Energy and Spirit that is, by nature, invisible. Nature is God's direct effect and self-communication or divine revelation.

Therefore, scientists and theologians are engaged in the same quest for understanding God's activities in the world. They are trying to formulate ideal moral and physical guides for a good, satisfying, happy life. The scientists are engaged in the study of how the world came into being and how it functions. Theologians and philosophers, however, are engaged in the realm of why the world was created or came into being, and the meaning of human life and value in the world.

Theology and philosophy also prescribe the guidelines for how to live the good life and be fulfilled and happy in God's world and Kingdom. In this respect, Moses, Buddha, Socrates, Jesus and Muhammad were correct to affirm that ethics or morality were the goals of all sound knowledge and education. This includes the study of practical disciplines, such as economics, politics, technology, science and medicine.

Like religion and ethics, money, government, technology and good medicine are desired as the means to achieve the good life and live a happy and longer life. Traditionally, religious language and symbolism have formulated terms such as "salvation," "the beatific vision," "enlightenment," "eternal peace," "God's Kingdom," "eternal life," "union with God and heaven" or "*Nirvana*" as the positive "metaphors" for the ultimate good life and the destiny of a moral life.

Conversely, we speak of "hell," "damnation," "violence," "hate," "death," and "destruction of the wicked" as the undesirable and negative modes of human existence and destiny of evil people. These are the people who fail to love and forgive their neighbors without prior conditions, as God requires all obedient human beings to do.

In this religious language of myth and metaphor, "hell" and "heaven" are not physical locations or geographical places anywhere in time or space. They are religious metaphors for positive or negative modes of life and moral-spiritual qualities of self-actualization. Those people who choose evil as the lesser forms of the good are in hell, and will cause hell to befall others! Likewise, those people who are loving, caring and compassionate and choose the good and do it are in heaven. They live in the fellowship of love with their neighbors, themselves and God! They are nonviolent, and therefore, they live in peace with their fellow human beings and creation!

Despite the fact that the transcendent God is a colorless, genderless, invisible, Creative Energy or Spirit, we are still able to feel "his" or "her" or "its" presence and power and know "his" or "her" will. We can see the results of this divine Creative-Redemptive Spirit, in the same way in which we see the results of the invisible air which we breathe with joy, unless it has been polluted! Air in the form of wind cannot be directly seen, although we feel its force and see its effects on trees, grass, soil, buildings and the like. Likewise, God is the invisible cosmic Creative Force that has created the universe and guided the evolution of life, mind, language and moral consciousness through the Logos. The *Logos* (The Word) is God's cosmic principle of mind, life, knowledge, truth, virtue, morality, reason, order, design, creation and redemption of the universe.

## 6. Divine Transcendence, Mystery: The Inadequacy Of Finite Human Language to Express God

God as an incomprehensible, eternal and Cosmic Transcendent Mystery is not only beyond the grasp of the finite and limited human mind, but also the finite and limited human-made language, religious metaphors and cultural symbols. As such, the human beings are incapable of fully knowing God as he or she or it is really is, and we can only talk about God in an indirect and limited manner. We know that God is the Cosmic Creator, Sustainer and Redeemer. This knowledge is based on nature, history, reason, science, and experience. All human beings and their societies possess mere fragments of God's revelation and knowledge.

Ultimately, no one religion possesses a perfect revelation of God. Yet, out of the human sins of pride, ethnocentrism, cultural and religious hubris, as well as idolatrous bigotry and ignorance, the major Western religions have fought one another in the name of God, truth and missionary zeal. Northern Ireland and the Middle East illustrate this form of blasphemy and idolatry. There is also the problem of mistaking religious metaphor for reality as God's revelation. In this form of religious ethnocentrism and cultural bigotry, Christians forget that God is not a Western, White male (patriarch) Christian! Christians in Northern Ireland fail to realize the Jesus Christ was a Jewish Carpenter and Rabbi, and neither a Protestant nor a Catholic!

Jews also often forget that God (*Yahweh*) is a not a Hebrew Patriarch who is opposed to Arab Muslims. Muslims also fail to realize that God (*Allah*) is a compassionate God who desires peace (*shalom/salaam),* rather than holy war (*jihad*). Christians, Jews and Muslims worship the same God, but in different languages, ways (liturgies) and through different mediators, symbols, metaphors, cultural and mental imageries.

Judaism, Christianity and Islam have claimed exclusive possession of God's definitive and perfect revelation. That is idolatry. Human finite minds and languages are imperfect, and therefore, unable to comprehend God's totality, even if it were revealed either in nature or in the prophets and their messages (which were written down and later canonized as holy scriptures by the religious community or the Church.)

Like the proverbial "story of the blind men who went to see an elephant" and each got to feel a different part of the elephant, which they then declared to be the complete truth, all religions tend to have true fragments of God's divine truth and revelation which they mistake for the total truth! By the rejection of the fragments of religious, moral and spiritual truths which are present in other religions and moral traditions, irrespective of whether they call themselves religious or not, major religions remain divided, incomplete, acrimonious, mutually exclusive and competitive instead of being cooperative, inclusive and zealous of learning from one another about God's truth. Moral education is required to make each person and his or her community whole and morally sound.

In each religious tradition and moral school of philosophy and ethics, there is partial knowledge of God as learned from nature and special revelation through the messiahs, saints and prophets, such as Moses, Jesus and Muhammad. Their own understanding of God was also colored by their own patriarchal cultures and religions, primitive science, history and limited world-view of their own time. Because of the divine transcendence of God and the human inability to know God fully, religion communicates its revelation about God in an indirect manner. All religions, including Christianity and Judaism, package and communicate their respective central teachings and messages through the language of myth, stories, parables, proverbs, hymns, music, poetry, prayer, art, and symbolism.

The insurmountable problem for religion, theological and religious studies and worship is that of the transcendence of God and the limitations of the finite human languages, symbols, and cultures. The universal fundamental problems of religion, theology, the distorted human understanding of God, serious religious divisions, religious bigotry, intolerance and conflict, can be partly traced back to the nature of the diversity and confusion of human patriarchal cultures and world-view. This is addition to the universal intrinsic limitations and inability of finite human minds and languages to express God without serious distortions and misrepresentations of God. This is further complicated by the existence of human diversity of cultures, languages and experiences as tools and contexts in which to understand the nature and activities of God as the Infinite Transcendent Holy Creative Mystery.

This is the Cosmic Creative Mystery whom we often simply refer to as "God," or *"Allah"* if we are Muslims. God is used as a "term" and "nickname for the cosmic fundamental Spirit whom Karl Jaspers referred to as the "All-encompassing" creative reality, without any other qualifications. Paul Tillich calls the same God, "the Ultimate Reality" and "Ground of Being" who is better denoted by the verb "to be." Martin Heidegger also refers to God as "Being" (*Sein*) and correspondingly, refers to the human being as "Datum of Being" (*Dasein*).

Heidegger's *Dasein* is like the Hebrew concept of the human being as *imago Dei* (God's mirror or reflection). For Heidegger, the human being as *Dasein* "reveals God" as *Sein*. The human being's language or speech also "utters *Sein*" or God." In this Heideggerian understanding, humanity reveals God and human language also communicates (utters) God. Within this Heideggerian perspective, it is the human being who creates and reveals God within the human mind, religion, values and public affairs. The human being creates the images and revelation of God according to his or her own understanding. Because of this human perception, God's revelation and attributes as human creations of God by the patriarchs, religious leaders and theologians have become institutionalized in the human culture and language as God's revelation and immutable divine essence. Instead of God creating the human being, conversely, the human being has created God through his and her culture, language, scriptures, religion and values which are then attributed to God as his or her will and creations.

Since human evolutionary, historical, minds, languages and cultures are by nature ever finite and imperfect, likewise, the concepts, revelation and formulations of God within religion, language, culture, ethics or normative values are also correspondingly ever finite, evolutionary, imperfect and fallible. Major exclusive religious, cultural, moral and theological systems, such as Christianity and Islam arise from preexisting religions and take new radical and reformist forms in the name of God.

However, these imperfect human religious understanding of God and moral laws are attributed to the infallible and transcendent holy God as his or her exclusive revelation to the world. Subsequently, these religious and moral teachings are falsely assigned the definitive divine essence as God's universality, divine perfection, infallibility, inerrancy and immutability as God's own direct special revelation. This is the tragedy of the Evangelical doctrines of Biblical liberalism and inerrancy. This is also the problem with the Roman Catholic doctrines of Papal infallibility and the Muslim doctrine of the inerrancy and infallibility of the Qur'an as God's direct dictation and perfect revelation which supersedes the Hebrew and Christian scriptures. These Hebrew and Christian scriptures are said to have been corrupted by people as they substituted their theological teachings, interpretations of human history, moral and doctrinal formulations for God's original revelation. They also claim that further corruption of the original written revelation of God occurred through the processes of translation from one language into another.

As a result, God is affirmed to have dictated the Qur'an in God's own holy language, namely Arabic, and it is forbidden for the Qur'an to be officially translated into other languages. Arabic also remain the language of worship just like Latin was the language for the Roman Catholic mass and worship until the reformation of Vatican II (1962-1963) during the revolutionary and short reign of John XXIII (1958-1963). Since, by nature, the finite human being is incapable of complete comprehension of the Infinite Mystery, holy scriptures, religion, theology and ethics cannot validly claim to be based on God's will and revelation. They are human constructions and not God's direct activities and revelations. God as the Cosmic Encompassing Reality and Creativity transcends human minds, languages and constructions.

Therefore, one should also expect to see that the human being lives a life based on some epistemological and anthropological intrinsic paradox. For instance, the human being is both an evolutionary animal that is limited in abilities, and at the same time, is also a self-transcending divine being that is akin to God. The finite human mind is by nature incapable of fully understanding such a Transcendent Cosmic Creative Mystery, or God. Yet, at the same time, the finite human being is also the God's special creature in the world that is by intrinsic "*a priori*" divine Mystery as an *imago Dei* and most akin to God.

Therefore, the finite human being as God's evolutionary mind and spirit in the world as *imago Dei* is also the temporal creature that is ever open and attuned to God in order to hear "God's Word" of creation, life, forgiveness, restoration, redemption and salvation. As *imago Dei* (God's image/reflection and representative) in the world, the human is able to encounter God and have fellowship with him or her.

However, being finite, the human being is also unable to understand and write down accurately the fullness of God's infinite revelation and supernatural activities in the world. Nevertheless, the human being is able to communicate very intelligently and meaningfully to the finite world about God's transcendence, Divine Infinite Mystery, and to interpret and contextualize God's revelation and moral law within the given local religious and cultural context and limitations. This includes the relativity of the local human language, symbols, culture, world-view and values, including present fears and hopes for a better life now and within the time to come in the near and distant future.

In this respect, Karl Rahner's moral and theological teachings are very insightful, compelling and informative. In the *Hearers of the Word* and other works, Rahner strongly affirms that all human beings in the world are specially created by God to become the essential universal "hearers of God's Eternal Word" (*Logos*). As "God's hearers," human beings are also co-creators and co-redeemers with God in the world.

Furthermore, because of God's gifts of divinity in creation, all human beings are born with the supernatural gift of God's power of grace and divinity. This enables them to hear God speaking to them specifically, within their own context, history, experience, language, culture, philosophy, technology, values, needs, fears (anxieties), hopes and expectations for God's timely (*kairos*) supernatural intervention and miraculous deliverance from evil. This is the essential significance and meaning of God's election of local prophets and messiahs from among the people, the divine incarnation and the "Pentecostal experience," in which all the Christians in Jerusalem heard the Apostles speaking to them in their own local languages.

The Apostles were heard speaking about the good news of God's supernatural intervention in history to bring them supernatural salvation and the arrival of God's promised eschatological Kingdom on the Earth.

They discussed the life and ministry of Jesus. They speculated about the matters concerning the resurrection of Jesus as the Christ of God as God's victory over the curse of death. John made it clear that Jesus was the true historical and temporal embodiment of God's Logos who is God's cosmic principle for the divine creative and redemptive supernatural activities in the cosmos.

As such, the incarnate Logos of God became God's cosmic special agent of God's good news of God's forgiveness of human sins, divinization of humanity and salvation. This process of God's "re-creation" (redemption) and divinization of humanity through by God is accomplished through the *Logos* (Cosmic Christ) as God's eternal divine Medium for cosmic creation and redemption (cf. Gen. 1:1-31; John:1:1-18). Human beings also become willing and voluntary participants in this God's process of "re-creation" and redemption through their faith, obedience to God's moral law and the praxis of unconditional love and free forgiveness of sins for every believing and obedient people in the world (cf. Acts 2).

Due to God's incarnation in humanity and the world through the creative and redemptive *Logos*, all loving and obedient human beings everywhere in the world have become the redeemed saints of God. They have become positively transformed into God's moral agents of agape and active missionaries of God's peace in the world. This global peace is based on the moral and religious principles of unconditional love, free forgiveness of offenses and nonviolence.

All loving and just moral activists have become God's visible moral and spiritual saints in the temporal world. They are the redeemed Children of God and citizens of God's Kingdom in the present life in this world and also in the world that is expected to come in the future. By their strong practical faith, courage, unconditional love, obedience, hope and good works through the power of God's grace that is ever present within the indwelling Holy Spirit, these moral and spiritual saints have gained the beatific vision and heavenly fellowship with God as Agape.

The saints have also become God's participants in God's supernatural activities of creation and redemption in the world. These moral and religious saints have served as effective co-redeemers with God in the world by feeding the hungry, healing the sick, forgiving their offenders, loving their enemies, serving as the instruments of peace where there was war and violence, and became the advocates of justice, where there was injustice (cf. Matt. 5-7; 25:31-46).

# Chapter 11

# God's Transcendence and Human Distortions of God's Revelation In Religions and Scriptures

God's radical transcendence and infinite mystery present serious theological and philosophical epistemological problems to finite human beings. This is more explicit when they try to express, study and know God's true nature and supernatural activities in the world. This is because God is transcendent and the human beings and their languages, cultures, scriptures and religions are finite.

Despite the fact that the human being is an evolutionary animal, he or she is also by God's unmerited grace, election and special divine creation a divine being, an *imago Dei* that is most akin to God (Gen. 1:26). At the same time, being also an evolutionary animal, finite and mortal the human being is in this aspect also unlike the transcendent, infinite and immortal God. Therefore, the finite human being has limited intellectual, linguistic and symbolic capabilities for a complete mental grasp of God's infinite essence, transcendence and incomprehensible mystery. As such, no human being is ever able to understand fully and express the divine Mystery fully within the imperfect finite human language and symbols without serious distortions and misrepresentations.

## 1. Divine Transcendence and the Relativity Of Religious Language and Symbolism

God's transcendence and apparent impenetrable infinite cosmic Mystery often leads to the common universal human misconceptions about God. In turn, these misconceptions lead to correlative human distortions of God's revelation in the human being's mind, language, scriptures, religions, cultures and ethics. Human finitude causes these serious kinds of intellectual, epistemological, theological, religious and linguistic problems. This is particularly the case when it comes to the human being's attempt to study or understand the abstract Creative Cosmic Spirit or Mystery that we call God (*Deus/Theos*).

This cosmic transcendent creative holy Mystery is beyond human naming and the comprehension by finite minds. As a result, it is beyond infallible human formulations of doctrines. Finite human language and symbolism also present serious epistemological limitations and challenge of how to communicate or speak about this transcendent Mystery or God in a meaningful and accurate manner.

In order to resolve this apparent insurmountable theological problem, religion employs the symbolic language of myth, parable, story, analogy, metaphor, poetry, song, dance, drama, ritual, and prayer in order to talk indirectly about the hidden transcendent Cosmic Spirit of life and creativity or the Creative Mystery as the unnameable God. Religious worship or prayers, offering sacrifices, meditation and sacraments (rituals/rites) are part of this complicated religious language, communication and symbolism. This is the same holy Cosmic Mystery that the Moses and the Hebrews came to know as *Yahweh*. The ancient Egyptians among whom the Hebrews had lived for more than five hundred years prior to Moses' liberation and exodus, knew this same cosmic redemptive and Creative Mystery or God as "*Amun*" or "*Amen,*" whose symbol was the sun *(Ra*). Later, the Emperor Constantine declared the Christian's day of worship to be a public holiday as a "*Sunday.*"

This form of indirect speech or "mediated communication" and discourse about God through myth, ritual, symbol and metaphor is meaningful for liturgical worship and the believing religious community. However, the indirect mythological language, communication and discourses about God have failed to satisfy the serious intellectual quest for truths about God. This is especially in respect to truths as formulated in propositional logic in terms of what can be judged to be either true or false about some doctrines or propositions about the essence and functions of God. As such, speaking about God in religious myths, symbols and metaphors is often adequate for most religious people, liturgy and worship. However, it does not overcome the intellectual epistemological and pedagogical problems concerning the reality of God's transcendence, mystery and incomprehensible infinite nature and identity.

Subsequently, there is a constant universal human intellectual quest for a better understanding of God, better access to God's revelation, direct fellowship with God and salvation. There is also a correlative intellectual and theological quest for more adequate forms of religious language, symbols, metaphors, imageries, doctrines, systems of ethics or normative values, more meaningful religious rituals, relevant and meaningful intellectual and theological understanding of God's processes of unmerited free grace and unconditional love as they are universally manifested in God's holy mysteries of cosmic creation, sustenance and redemption.

God as the Infinite, Transcendent and Incomprehensible Mystery remains beyond the full grasp of human finite intellect, language, logic, philosophy and theology. Therefore, human beings as *imago Dei* of finite mirrors and imperfect reflections of God in the world ascribe the good attributes which they see in themselves to the Transcendent God. The doctrines of the incarnation of God in humanity is another way to affirm this principle. Conversely, within dualism, the evil human beings see within themselves is negatively ascribed to the work and presence of "the Devil." Nevertheless, in both dualism and monotheism, the finite human mind remains unable to fully understand the infinite nature of the Transcendent God or completely comprehend his or her supernatural revelation and works in both cosmic creation and redemption.

Correlatively, the finite and imperfect human language is incapable of being the theological tool for adequate formulation, expression and communication of God's essence, infinite mystery and transcendence. As a result, any speech and doctrines about God are never perfect, complete or infallible. That is impossible. The finite being is by nature limited and incapable of the full and perfect comprehension of the Transcendent and Infinite Cosmic Creative Mystery or God. The human being as an evolutionary finite creature in the cosmos is permanently incapable of gaining a complete understanding of its own infinite and transcendent Cosmic Creator or God!

Therefore, the human being can be only intellectually accurate about God when he or she talks about God in terms of what "God is not," rather than "what God is." Speaking about "what God is" means that we know God's essence in that specific divine aspect. Otherwise, religion employs the art of symbolic and figurative language of metaphors, parables, stories, myths, hymns, ritual, drama, prayer, metaphors, symbols and poetry. As such, Bultmann's call for "demythologization" of religion is untenable.

In his monumental theological works, *The Church Dogmatics*, Karl Barth stresses his new theological construction consisting of divine transcendence and human limitedness. As a result, Barth strongly affirmed that the human beings as finite beings can accurately only negatively and indirectly speak about God's essence. They can accomplish this by speaking in terms of *"what God is not"* (*via negativa*) since they can never be positively sure of *"what God is."* This doctrine assumes that we already know what is God is like in order to be sure about what God is not. Despite this apparent contradiction (paradox) many scholars find Barth's doctrine of God both intellectually meaningful and academically sound.

However, there are many Evangelical Christian leaders like Billy Graham and Jerry Falwell who strongly believe that Karl Barth was wrong. They strongly believe that through the Incarnation of God in Jesus-Christ as God's ultimate self-disclosure to the world and by the careful study of the holy Scriptures we come to know what God is truly like. They affirm the holy Scriptures contain the fullness of God's infallible revelation, and that therefore, we now most truly know both "*what God is*" and what "*God is not*!"

To some limited degree, these Evangelicals are also correct. For instance, based on the teachings of both Moses and Jesus we know God to be holy, good, loving or Agape, merciful, impartial, just, the cosmic Creator, Sustainer and Redeemer of the world. Nature constitutes God's "universal open book" of supernatural revelation that is universally accessible to all intelligent people everywhere in the world. They can accomplish this task through the uses of their senses and minds to do a careful scientific observation and investigation of nature. God's laws and truth discovered in this manner are never to be contradicted by the interpretation of God's revelation as written down by the prophets and God's chosen saints. This is because the "*truth is One.*" Truth comes from God and it is inseparable from God. Truth is a major attribute and essential component of God's essence.

Accordingly, Pope John Paul II correctly declared that "truth cannot contradict truth" as he affirmed theistic evolution to be God's chosen method for the creation of humanity. However, many Christians remain intellectually disinterested theological and scientific truths as they relate to the intellectual discourses on the nature of God's essence and debates on truths concerning creation by means of evolution, and the mechanics of "*cosmogenesis*," "*biogenesis*" and the nature of the human being as a finite being in God's evolutionary and finite world. They are only interested in simple truths that human beings are God's special creations and they are souls destined to either heaven if they do good or hell if they do evil. They seek to avoid hell and go to heaven by doing good. As a result, they do not pay attention to more complex explanations of the existence of the world, creaturely life and its divine purpose and destiny.

Moreover, most religious people do not engage in intellectual discourse about God or speak about God in propositional logic. The religious testimonies of religious people require the pious language of poetry, myth, song and prayer than that of logic. This academic language is meaningful in the departments of philosophy and theology and not in Church. Religious people are more interested in worshipping God and establishing a meaningful relationship of love, praise, fellowship and piety based on prayer and praise than logic and intellectual debate. St. Paul failed to convert the philosophers of Athens by his appeal to God's truth through intellectual discourse (cf. Acts 17). As a result, he warned his followers to shun philosophy as a missionary tool for teaching and evangelization of non-Christians. Unfortunately, the Protestants have taken this Pauline warning both literally and seriously that they hardly teach philosophy in seminaries as part of their theological education and training of the clergy. As a result, most Protestant clergy and their congregation members are intellectually unable to engage in serious discourse about God, the world, the nature of humanity and evil, unless they are based on the Bible.

Ultimately, most religious people prefer to speak about the transcendent God in terms of worship, prayer, liturgy, music, hymns, poetry, metaphors, myths and story because they are more appealing and meaningful. As such, it makes sense to pray or sing a song of love to either the "*Father*" or "*Mother in heaven*" than making a logical statement about God as the "impersonal cosmic creative force." Such a force does not pay attention to personal matters of human beings, since that has been delegated to God's power of natural law. The impartial natural may be actually closer to the truth concerning the mechanics of daily life than speaking about the guidance of the loving "God as Father or *Abba*," and the Holy Spirit. However, this scientific and naturalistic rendition of God's providence and supernatural activities in cosmic creation, sustenance and redemption is not conducive to religion. It strangles the love of God, quenches the need or spirit for worship, prayer and quest for fellowship with God as a loving Creator.

In this chapter, the difficult and complicated philosophical-theological task is to establish the fact that the eternal cosmic Creator-Redeemer God transcends all human modes of language and theological formulations of the doctrines about God's essence and cosmic activities. This includes our symbols for God in art, as well as the human mental and linguistic renditions of God. As such, traditional popular religious terms for God, such as "*Father*," "*Lord*," "*King*," and "*God's Kingdom*" are to be regarded as *mere patriarchal metaphors for God*, as opposed to being taken as literal biological descriptions of God as a spiritual male being or Divine Patriarch. God as a Spirit has neither gender nor color or nationality.

In order to accomplish this difficult theological task, God's radical transcendence and incomprehensible being must be first established. This task becomes easy and manageable when we first define what we mean by God. Within the Judeo-Christian tradition, one must begin with Moses, the founder of Western monotheism, and then work up to the present. It is very significant that Moses was not able to learn the name of God nor name and thus define God. This was partly because within the African and Hebrew religious and social understanding, naming something meant that one had an understanding and control of the named object. As a result, the people gave a name to all things, including cattle. However, God is often unnamed, but rather referred to as the "Creator." As such, Moses falls within this general African traditional epistemological and theocentric religious world-view.

Moses did not possess either the full understanding of God or the control of such a transcendent Cosmic Mystery. Therefore, Moses as a finite creature of God could not accurately name the transcendent God, apart from affirming him as his Creator, Sustainer and Redeemer. Later, Moses presented to the Hebrews this unnamed God as the cosmic Creator and Redemptive Mystery (*Yahweh)* who had redeemed them out bondage in Egypt. Symbolically, Moses presented this monotheistic concept to the Hebrews in association to the normative ethic centered on the Ten Commandments and the ritual of making a holy covenant with God at holy Mt. Sinai as a means of becoming God's (*Yahweh's)* special chosen, elect and Covenant People in the world. Unfortunately, this covenant ritual and the ideas that the Hebrews were God's chosen and elect, later became sources of great misunderstanding, religious persecution, violence and genocide.

Whereas Moses was clearly *monotheistic* and believed that there was only one (*monos*) true God that was the cosmic creator of the universe and all the people in the world, irrespective of the name they gave to this God, most of the Hebrews were either *polytheistic* or *henotheistic*. Most *henotheistic* Hebrews came to believe that *Yahweh* was their own exclusive tribal God, and that other tribes had their own valid gods.

However, these gods were considered to be inferior and subordinate to *Yahweh*, who was "the God above all other Gods."

Tragically, this concept of divine election of Israel was taken literally by some Hebrew religious fundamentalists. It was taken out of the religious context of religious language of myth and symbolism and taken to refer to sociological, political, ethnic and military physical reality election and superiority of the Hebrews as long as they remained faithful to *Yahweh* as their own tribal God that was also considered to be superior to the tribal gods of the people of other nations led to some misconceptions on the part of some exclusive and tribalistic Hebrews wished to believe that this God was their own tribal God who did not care about the Egyptians or people of other nations in whom the Hebrews found themselves, especially, the Palestinians. As a result, Joshua mistakenly thought that God commanded him to exterminate these polytheistic Palestinians and take their land and give it to the Hebrews as God's special gift. Today, this kind of action is considered a moral evil of genocide and injustice that cannot be justified on any religious, political, economic or racial and ethnic grounds.

Within this theological world-view, context and understanding, a God that can be named, understood and controlled is not God! That kind of God is a mere idol. The term "*Yahweh,*" which means: "*The Great I am*" or the "Great Mystery." It can also mean the verb "*to be.*" This includes the meaning of "*what is*" or "*Being*" and "*existential reality.*" These are some of the implications of the Great mystery or *the Great I am* that is conveyed by the term "*Yahweh*" (cf. Exod. 3:13-18). In Egypt, where Moses was born, raised and educated, the same cosmic holy Mystery and transcendent reality was denoted by the term "*Amun*" or "*Amen-Ra.*"

Characteristically, God revealed himself to Moses as a great creative and redemptive Mystery. God also revealed himself as a caring God who had created Abraham and made personal promises (a covenant) to him regarding his descendants and their redemptive mission in the world (Gen. 12:1-4). The Hebrew Bible itself begins by declaring God to be the Cosmic Spirit that is the Creator through his Word (*Logos*). The first creation by God was light (Gen. 1:1-3), and later, the sun and the moon were created. This story indicates that God is not an object that exists in space and time, such as the sun or moon or another object as some ancient people and "pagans" incorrectly thought.

For the Judeo-Christian tradition, God's essential functional definition is a "holy and benevolent Cosmic Creative Transcendent Energy, Spirit and Mystery." This is a monotheistic, functional definition of God, which both essentially affirms and declares to the world that "the true God is One" despite wherever and in whatever mode that God is experienced or reveals "himself" or "herself" or "itself!" This Creator, Sustainer and Redeemer-God is, by essence and essential nature, the only true Cosmic Creative Mystery that encompasses everything and also transcends complete human understanding and all the theological or philosophical doctrinal formulations.

God as the Cosmic Creator is the also the same cosmic, holy, nameless Transcendence of monotheistic religion focus and worship, and transcends all human finite minds, culture, language and symbols. As such, the finite human mind cannot fully comprehend the incomprehensible and Transcendent God. Likewise, the human finite language is imperfect and inadequate as a tool and medium for the formulation of the invisible and Transcendent God. It cannot be a perfect mediation and expression of God to the world.

This being the case, the true nature of religious language is that of indirect discourse about God and indirect mediation of God to human beings and the religious community through the language of myth, metaphor, symbolism, analogy, poetry, music, drama, faith, compassion, love, prayer and meditation (contemplation). The encounter and communion with God also takes place through positive action, devotion to duty and good works, worship, sacrifice, confession of sins and absolution or reconciliation to self, the community (neighbor and Church) and God. These are different channels by which obedient human beings can encounter, communicate with God, and also mediate God's goodness, essence, reality, unconditional love to the world. The liturgical form of prayer and communication with God takes the form of drama, song, prayer, confession of moral failure, wrong doing, omission of the good and sin.

Unfortunately, problems arise when religious myths, stories, parables, poetry and metaphors are read literary as prose and history! This is what has happened to many religious, mythological stories, hymns and metaphors in the Hebrew and Christian holy scriptures. This includes the mythological stories of the creation of Adam and Eve and their misuse of freedom to rebel against the Creator-God, thus sinning and causing the downfall of all humanity. This is the view which has shaped the Western world-view and religious consciousness.

The other myths and stories include: Noah's Ark and the flood, the Tower of Babel, the birth of Isaac, Jacob's wrestling match with an angel. The other famous biblical mythological stories include those of Jonah, Job, Samson, Balaam and his talking donkey, the ascension of Elijah, the book of Daniel, the infant narratives and the Virgin Birth of Jesus, some miracles of Jesus, the parables of Jesus, the resurrection and ascension of Jesus, and the book of the Revelation of John. Therefore, if any religious group takes these myths, stories, parables and metaphors as literal history, they create problems of reading poetry as prose and story as history. The appeal to faith to accept the religious rendition of poetry as prose and story as history is a misuse of religion and faith. That is to equate faith with ignorance and stupidity! Faith is the positive openness to life, love, mystery, God and the world.

Ultimately, faith is the power of acceptance of life, love, goodness and truth without evidence. Faith is not a substitute for knowledge, truth and education. The truth about life, God and our experience is often subjective and beyond words and the scope of the human language. This is also true for God's supernatural revelation and the human encounter with God, both within the inner mystical experience or the external experience during life in community, nature, history and the world.

This is the complex nature of the religious individual and collective experiences of God, love, goodness and forgiveness of sins. These blessings are variously mediated by God through the neighbor, clergy, saints, the community, the Church, nature, history, the world, religion and liturgy. Theology must try to formulate them within an understandable language and symbols. This is needed in order to be most effectively and meaningfully able to convey them to the religious community as meaningful and relevant doctrines about God, the Church, sacraments and liturgical (formal) worship. To this end, contemporary theology and ethics must employ contemporary religious language, metaphors, analogies and stories to communicate its teachings to the contemporary people within their given context, culture, language, values, science and world-view.

Unfortunately, many serious moral and theological problems often arise because these religious myths, poetry, hymns, stories, parables and metaphors are confused with prose, ontology, actual history and reality. For instance, some masculine metaphors, such as "King," and "Father," have been understood literally by many theologically naive and ignorant people as actual physical and real biological descriptions of God with tragic religious and moral consequences.

As a tragic consequence of a literal understanding of these patriarchal religious language, metaphors and symbols for God, women were traditionally excluded from the ordained priesthood of Judaism, Christianity and the religious leadership within Islam. This is partly because women were by gender excluded from these ancient patriarchal metaphors and symbols for God. God was in this patriarchal system portrayed as the Arch-Patriarch. Subsequently, the revered patriarchs were also considered to be his concrete and visible representatives within the family, community and religious gathering (Church, synagogue, temple or mosque).

Conversely, women and the matriarchs were either ignored or portrayed as subordinates and servants of men and the patriarchs. As a result, the founders of major religions, such as Moses, the founder of Judaism, Buddha the founder of Buddhism, Jesus the Christ, founder of Christianity and Prophet Muhammad, the founder of Islam, are all males. Jesus' chosen twelve disciples who later became known as the apostles, were also all men. This illustrates how a patriarchal society can institutionalize God as a male being and exclude women from the religious leadership of the patriarchal community. This problem leads to the widespread idolatry centered around male self-deification. This is best illustrated by both Buddhism and Christianity which have both deified and elevated their respective patriarchal founders into a god to be worshiped by their faithful followers.

The example is "Father" (*Abba*) as a metaphor for God. When it is taken literally as a physical attribute or description of God's ontological reality and essential historical nature, it means that God is a male person who is the primordial "Patriarch," and the physical Ruler or "King" of all the people in the world. Hence, we speak of "God's Kingdom" or "God's Reign" over the world. For most people, the metaphor for God as a "King" has been misunderstood. It has been taken literally to refer to God as the cosmic physical Being who is an actual cosmic "King" that rules over the world as "his Kingdom."

This becomes destructive when women are excluded from the ordained ministry on the theological grounds that God is male, and women, being females, cannot efficaciously physically represent Jesus or God the Father in the world or at the holy altar as his ministers. That kind of naive religious belief is analogous to reading poetry as prose and story as history. This tragic religious fundamentalism and literalism is absurd. It requires people to read the biblical metaphors of "God as Father" and "King" in terms of denotation instead of connotation.

Theological or religious language and symbols are created within a relevant historical, cultural and religious local context which is meaningful and valid for that time and those people, within that given local culture. Therefore, these locally conditioned religious symbols and linguistic or cultural terms and messages cannot be validly and meaningfully universalized to apply to all people, regardless of era, culture, historical and religious experience.

## 2. Higher Intellect and the Origination Of Human Language

The human being, who is, by nature, an intelligent and thinking being, is also, at the same time, both coextensively and correlatively a linguistic and religious being by special, essential divine-human essence. To be fully human, one has to be able to think, speak and become God-conscious and possess the Godlike freedom of existence in the unlimited state of divine Spirit and self-transcendence.

We are not very sure when and how language came into being, but we can speculate that it is as old as the human race itself. Indeed, some primitive societies associated language with God's essence as the "Omni-linguist" and "primordial Speaker" of his eternal *"Logos" (Word),* and as the divine creative and ordering principle of creation and evolution of the cosmos (cf. Gen. 1:1-31).

Within the Hebrew theocentric thought and world-view, "God spoke his Word" *(Memra)* and the world came into being. In that context, creation or the cosmos exists as God's ongoing creativity and "the precipitated Word of God" or "speech." Scriptures are part of this "Word." They take the "written form of God's Word." God's Incarnation in Jesus as the Christ takes another form of "God's Word," namely, the "Incarnate Word of God."

The apostolic proclamation about Jesus as the Christ of God or God's expected eschatological "Deliverer," the "Messiah" or "Savior," whose divine mission was to redeem all people from the evil and restore them to God's goodness, obedience and fellowship with God. This includes God's provision for the atonement and forgiveness of human sins of rebellion against God's moral law, hate, disbelief and apathy. This message is for Christians is also referred to as the "Proclaimed Word of God." This is what the Church proclaims as the "Gospel of Christ" or the "Good News of God's salvation." Human language, which is inseparable from the human culture, intellect, mind, and God as correlative eternal Speaker of his Word of creation, life, order, redemption, forgiveness, healing, consolation, happiness, blessings, peace and eternal life (cf. Gen. 1:1-31; John 1:1-18; Matt. 5-7).

Therefore, like the human intellect, mind and reason, the human language is projected back into God as the very divine origin of humanity in God himself or herself. Within this theological anthropology, God becomes the unifying principle of all human beings, religions, languages, races and ethnic groups in the world. The Eternal and Omnipresent cosmic God serves as the universal and local primordial Ancestor or Arch-Patriarch of all races, ethnic groups, cultures and religions of human beings in the world.

As a result, all groups of human beings are the concrete children of God in the world and God's Kingdom. They worship and pray to God in their own native language. It is the local divine language or the holy language for God's self-communication, holy speech (Word) and dialogue with them! This view affirms that each human language is a specially and supernaturally created, direct gift of God to the original human beings that God had personally, physically created in heaven or paradise. The story says God placed them on earth to take care of it on God's behalf, in the same way a steward takes care of the estate of his absent landlord.

The traditional African and Oriental "Creation and the Fall" stories fall into this category. For instance, the ancient Hebrews understood their God, "*Yahweh*," to be a God whose primary divine essence was to speak and to create by the "Word" alone. He created out of nothing, as opposed to the myths of the Greek gods who are more like great human beings. The Greek gods, being the imaginary creations of "men," are limited by time, space, distance, and physical objects, like their human creators. Like human beings, they also only create something new from the preexistent elements.

Within this understanding divine creation is akin to human creativity which consists of the transformation or remodeling new things or creatures from a recycled and improved preexistent matter. This mode of creation is like that of a sculptor or carpenter who creates new things by means of fashioning it out of the preexisting materials, patterns and ideas, such as making a chair or table out of wood. The carpenter can only make a chair or table but not wood. But in the Judeo-Christian doctrine, the reverse is the case. God can only create wood but cannot make a table or chair. That is left to the human beings to do, and in its specialized form, it is done by the carpenter.

However, unlike the carpenter whose tools are lines, nails, and hammers, God's tools are the mind, ideas and the Logos (or the Word). Surprisingly, those who insist that God became a real human being in the form of Jesus of Nazareth, also claim that God became a real carpenter. Jesus, like his father Joseph, was a carpenter by skill. He was also a Rabbi and prophet by God's calling. In this respect, the Creator of the wood, by the Word, could also fashion it by the carpenter's tools. This idea of the Incarnation bridges God's transcendence through the Logos or Word, who becomes God's instrument of cosmic divine creative and redemptive supernatural activities and presence in the historical world and its evolutionary processes. The Logos becomes the intrinsic creative and sustaining divine force immanent in nature. Consequently, nature can be correctly used to symbolize God's reality, creativity and order.

This is due to the fact that the creators leave their creatures or creations with their own signatures or marks. These marks reveal the creators' values, creativity, personality, ideas, skillfulness and purpose. This is as true of human beings as it is of God. The laws of cause and effect are at work in both cases.

However, it is reasonable to assume that God as the cosmic Creator and Redeemer can suspend these natural laws at will in order to perform an extraordinary creation. Such creations as the universe and the rational creatures that speak and possess the capacity to communicate with the rest of God's creation, including God himself or herself, are examples of this. Accordingly, in the book of Genesis we are told that God created the cosmos by his own words! So we read in Genesis chapter one:

> And God said, "Let there be light," and there was light . . . "Let the earth bring forth living creatures . . . Let us create human beings in our image, after our own likeness . . ." Male and female God created them in God's own image. (Paraphrase of Gen. 1:1-27)

Accordingly, in order to see, know and love God, one has to turn to human beings, both male and female. Subsequently, to see the authentic human beings is to see God. To know them is to know God, and to love them is also to love God. By virtue of being created in God's image and by virtue of the Incarnation, God has become inseparably bonded with human beings and their respective fate.

This is why Jesus as the Christ summed up the religious law into "Love your neighbor as you love yourself." God can only be served and loved as one serves and loves the concrete neighbor, for God has humbly become present in our world, incognito in each human being. In this respect, God is not only our Creator and heavenly "Ancestor," but is also our very neighbor and speaks to us daily in our human language.

We must listen to God within us and around us within the comic mystery in order to attain better, effective, and more meaningful communication and gain new insights of how to live more harmoniously, lovingly and peacefully with all people within this world as our fellow beloved brothers and sisters. This is essential in order to transcend natural barriers and the complexity of our own unique age of cultural, linguistic, scientific, religious, socioeconomic development, and political global diversity and pluralism.

## 3. God as the Primordial Cosmic Speaker And the Cosmos as God's Speech

According to the Bible, God is the primordial or quintessential linguistic Being. God speaks, and things happen! God is said to have spoken his or her primordial Creative Divine Word of command and the universe and its various systems and inhabitants came into being. They were created out of the divine Word itself, which they perpetually remain sustained by, namely as God's Cosmic Speech or Song and Drama. This Divine Song and Cosmic Dance can be said to be performed by God primarily for self-enjoyment and fulfillment as a personal creative expression. It is in this sense that the Prophets spoke of God's Word as a very potent power which accomplishes all that it has been addressed to:

> So shall my word be that goes forth from my mouth;
> it shall not return to me empty,
> but it shall accomplish that which I purpose,
> and prosper in the thing for which I sent it. (Isa. 55:11)

We are also familiar with the warning messages of the angels and the prophets, and with their claim to divine authority by their cries of: "Thus, says, the Lord." This prophetic cry together with the Genesis account of the cosmic creation by God through God's Word (*Logos*), bears the intrinsic, implicit message that God is the quintessential "*Speaker of the Divine Word*" (*Logos*) or "*Sender of the Message*" *(Logos)* and the messengers of God's Word (*Logos*). Prophet Isaiah also indicates that this Divine Word or Message, and God himself or herself is, by intrinsic nature, in free, self-communication with the world and the "Hearers of the *Logos* or God's Word"

In short, God's Creative and Redemptive Word is also both God and God's own Self-Consciousness in action. Thus, the Chinese designate these two correlative, creative divine principles as "*Yang*" (male or man) and "*Yin*" (female or woman), which unite and interact together to create or produce the universe as their child and mutual creation.

In this broad philosophical and theological perspective, God is not only the Cosmic Creator, but is also the Main Cosmic Speaker of the Cosmos. God's own Speech and Dramatic Love Song is for self-entertainment. This is done through the Cosmic Creative and the

Redemptive Word or the *Logos.* As such, God is the Ultimate Cosmic Sender of both creative and redemptive messages. The messengers, regardless of whether they are human, such as Jesus and prophets like Moses, Muhammad, Buddha, Gandhi and King, or spiritual beings, such as the angels serve God's various purposes and carry out God's creative and redemptive mission in the world.

Consequently, the recorded messages of the angels and the well known prophetic formulas of "Hear you, God's people," or "Thus, says the Lord," carry the essential intrinsic meaning that God is the "quintessential Speaker." Subsequently, the human being is also the correlative, quintessential "Hearer of this divine Word" or divine Message which is universally inscribed and expressed by God in creation or nature and the natural law. Therefore, Karl Rahner was correct to affirm that human beings, as the "Hearers of God's Word," are the universally elected, divine, cosmic ambassadors of God in all of God's creation or the Cosmos.

Having been created in God's image (*imago Dei*), all human beings are permanently attuned to "hear God's Word" *(Logos*) speaking to them from within their souls, minds, experience, conscience, history and experience. At this deep level, there is complete, immediate, direct apprehension of the message of God, and God's Word (*Logos)* is heard without the mediation of language and symbols. This true mystical union of God and humanity show how all barriers between God and the human being have been transcended! Jesus expressed this truth by the affirmation that: "My Father and I are one" and "I am in the Father and the Father is within me!" (cf. John 14:20).

This is probably the main explanation underlying the fact that all human beings have a religious inclination and need. It is in religious worship that most ordinary human beings are able to hear God speaking to them, his Word (*Logos*) of life and truth directly, whereas a few lucky ones tend to hear God speaking in all situations. They hear God speaking through nature, the earthly historical events, ordinary people, and the ordinary cosmic processes of life, such as love, success, failure, friends, the preacher, the holy scriptures, prayer, teachers, nature, child birth of a healthy child, sickness and death. For these people, the silent Word or Message of God can be found imprinted on everything in the created universe, for everything bears the divine seal of God as its creator.

Therefore, a scientific study of nature as God's creation, reveals that nature or the cosmos both intrinsically and explicitly bears and tells the divine story of the creative, cosmic Mystery, beauty and wonders which in religion we associate with God's essence as Cosmic Creativity, Being and Order, or the Intelligent Designer, Creator and Sustainer of the cosmos. This observation is in harmony with the material in the prologue to St. John's Gospel when it affirms that: "In the beginning was the Word, and the Word was with God, and the Word was God." The Greek translated English as "the Word is the Greek word: "*Logos*." The term *Logos* represents an ancient Greek philosophical concept with a very complex, metaphysical explanation and complicated theological implicit doctrine. For instance, the term *"Logos"* has the implications that God is not just linguistic, but also rational, creative and male!

It is self-evident that human language is not neutral in terms of culture, content, metaphysics, world-view, values and meaning. The human language is conditioned and relative to the local cultural context and values. All human languages have a culturally conditioned meaning, values, a particular metaphysics and a local world-view already built into it, either implicitly or explicitly. As such, all moral cultures censor vulgar forms of language, particularly, the references to private parts, reproductive activities and elimination processes of body waste matter.

In the final analysis, what is being said here is that God is the quintessential linguist and indeed, omnilinguist. He or she has to know and speak all the human languages, for they belong to the people whom he or she has created in his or her image. We have already seen them to be constitutive of both masculine and feminine characteristics as evidenced by the creation of both male and female human beings in God's image and likeness. Therefore, it is logical to assert that, in this respect, language is both human and divine. It is a divine gift from God, like the very intellect and thought or cognitive processes themselves.

Subsequently, it would also follow that to participate in either a linguistic or thinking process is to participate not only in a natural human activity, but also in a divine or supernatural act. Language and the mind or intellect are more than just natural, since they are divine qualities and ultimately flow to us from God as unmerited gifts. We are his or her special creatures in the world, charged with the responsibility of being the created custodians or stewards of this created universe.

As a result, we can always measure, judge, classify, identify, accept or reject people on the basis of their own language, for apart from human deeds, there is no perfect way to judge a person except by their own words or language. Therefore, bad language is supposed to express the hidden evil nature of the speaker, whereas good language is supposed to express noble intentions and good nature of the speaker regardless of circumstances. For instance, when Jesus was in pain as he was being nailed on the cross, he never cursed his executioners and tormentors. Instead he prayed for them to be forgiven.

In short, like the invisible God is known through self-disclosure both in creation and his Word as revealed through the prophets, a person's innermost invisible nature and mystery is also concretely expressed externally and made visible to the world by the speaker's own self-revelation in language, actions and mode of life. As such, a person is his or her language and actions! That is one of the primary reasons why most of our professional education is oriented to the "manufacturing" and acquisition of useful or "good skills" and a prestigious "professional language" with its highly specialized vocabulary.

Nevertheless, this positive affirmation of language as God's divine gift to humanity does not mean that the human language as it is now, or as it was in the past, was in itself ever created by God. No language is ever directly created by God in terms of vocabulary, grammar, structure or intonation and symbolism. As such, without any exception, all human languages are imperfect, finite and evolutionary. They are both correlatively and coextensively with the emergence and evolution of the human mind, culture, knowledge and technical tools for communication. Therefore, language especially English, as the medium of thought and communication is constantly being changed, improved, revised, and being created according to need.

The English language has been revised to become more inclusive of women and members of the racial minorities. This applies to those areas where language has been patriarchal, sexist and demeaning to women, or racist and degrading, and dehumanizing to racial and ethnic minorities. Therefore, what is given to us by God is the capacity for language, in the same way and slow natural processes through which God has acted to bestow on us the capacity for intellect and thought. Language is also revelatory of both God and hidden moral, intellectual, and spiritual essence of each person. The human language both in its verbal and nonverbal symbolic forms is the medium for thought, creativity, memory, relationships, work, worship, study, reflection and self-expression.

The arts perform this complex function of human communication and celebration of life within its rich diversity as God's special gift. Poetry and dance express love much better than oratory or science and mathematics. Without language, the communication of truths, knowledge and experience would be nearly impossible. Without language, religion, ethics, education and civilization would be also impossible. Animals which have no language must have experiences and discoveries to share but cannot for lack of a language. For instance, when dogs and cats come rushing to greet their masters after a period of separation, they may have witnessed events that need reporting. But for lack of a language, they may be content to bark and wag their tails in the case of the dog, and to mew, purr and rub herself on her master's leg in the case of the house cat.

For lack of a better universal common language and culture as the media to communicate with all human beings in the world, God chose and sent local people as his elect prophets and messengers to each ethnic group. God conveyed his or divine message in the local context of each culture and language. Therefore, the prophets were chosen by God from the local people so that they could speak and relate to the people in the meaningful context of their own local language, culture, history, religion and moral values. Moses was sent to the Hebrews, Buddha to the Hindus, Jesus to the Hebrews and Muhammad to the Arabs. Nevertheless, the Christians teach that in reality God sent his Logos to become incarnate in humanity in the form of Jesus and therefore, by so doing, God became incarnate in each human being to speak directly to the heart and soul of each human being as an *imago Dei* and child of God.

These God's supernatural gifts of intellect, intuition, language and conscience are all made possible by the evolution of a superior human brain. The brain has the intrinsic capacity for critical thinking, moral agency, language, great creativity and self-transcendence both in thought and benevolent, loving, moral actions on behalf of others. However, this extraordinary human condition has come about through the natural and ordinary laws of evolution.

This is the very humble yet divinely ordained process by which the Holy Transcendent God acts secretly and incognito in the finite and mundane ordinary world. Subsequently, God's silent Creative and redemptive Word is eternally at work within the entire universe. God's *Logos* (Word) works in the world quietly and incognito by the apparently humble natural laws.

Therefore, natural law is part of God's silent *Logos* at work to effect God's divine creative and redemptive supernatural activities within the cosmos. God is omnipresent, incognito, in the entire cosmos through natural law or the *Logos* and the Holy Spirit (creativity) to create, sustain, redeem and fulfill the cosmic historical processes, creation and especially, the intelligent moral creatures, such as the human beings. Yet, like the fish which live in the ocean without the necessary divine gift of self-consciousness or self-transcendence and ever knowing that they are fish and live in a large ocean, some people live in this world unaware that they are the unique embodiments of God's mind, self-transcending spirit, freedom, moral agency, self-consciousness and creativity within the historical evolutionary processes and temporal cosmos.

## 4. The Imperfection of the Human Language And Inadequacy of Religious Symbols

Human cultures, languages, scriptures and symbols are relative to the culture, era, world-view, science, technology, class, education, race, color, gender, theology and philosophy of the people and society that create them. Therefore, culture, religion, language, philosophy, and scriptures are imperfect tools to study the infinite and Transcendent God and formulate accurate doctrines about God's essence and attributes. These doctrines cannot be true, absolute, and immutable for all times and binding on all people of every age and culture! Like religion and scriptures, no human language and culture is the perfect, direct creation of God, but rather an indirect or direct creation of the human being who is imperfect. Subsequently, we should also expect to find human culture and language and the correlative religious symbols also to be correspondingly imperfect, to the same degree as their imperfect human creators.

As a result of human imperfection, human culture and language are ever undergoing review and modification in their evolution and slow change, just like the human being's creative spirit. This change should also be reflected in the religious language, in terms of the formulations of the liturgy, composition of new inclusive hymns and the translation of scriptures to make the language more inclusive, and less patriarchal and exclusive of women or racially offensive to non-Whites.

Furthermore, since all languages are imperfect creations of finite, imperfect, human beings, therefore, no human language is ever perfect or holy enough to become the universal, normative exclusive language for the worship of God, scriptures, and the liturgical literature.

Consequently, any given human language is a fit and holy vehicle for the divine revelation, holy scripture, liturgy and religious worship! This means that Hebrew, Greek, Latin and Arabic are also as ordinary as the contemporary English or the "Bushman's" language. None is holier or better for the liturgical worship of God.

Each person must worship in the language of his or her community, since it is as holy, divine and beatific as any other. All people and all languages are equal before God, who understands all of them. This statement is also, by nature, a denial and a refutation of some old-fashioned, religious fundamentalist views found in Islam and some poorly educated Christians who claim that God speaks only either in Arabic or in the King James Bible Version English! However, God does not have a special language to communicate with us, nor does he or she have any preference for Latin or English when it comes to liturgical worship.

Therefore, each human language is a fitting language for the worship of God. In reality, apart from the evil and sins of ethnocentrism and hubris, no language has the advantage over any other when it comes to God. God loves his or her people unconditionally as they are, for all of them are his or her own beloved children, and all of them are sinful and imperfect along with their languages which they have created in their own sinful and imperfect reflection or image. It would have been self-contradictory had the imperfect human being, with a limited intellect, succeeded in creating a perfect language. It is impossible for an imperfect creator to create something more perfect than himself or herself.

The analytical philosophers of language such as Benjamin Lee Whorf, C.G.E. Moore, Betrand Russell and Ludwig Wittgenstein have very clearly pointed out in their controversial scholarly works how this imperfection of the human language has been responsible for the major problems and flaws in metaphysics, epistemological or cognitive processes, logic and religion. Obviously, the inadequacy of the finite human language makes it an imperfect tool for theological and religious formulations of the doctrines of God and salvation. Due to the religious problems of unexamined epistemological or ontological assumptions and prejudices in human language, serious errors have crept into religious and confessional theological constructions of the doctrines of God, humanity, sin, sacraments, Church, grace and salvation.

The Apostles and Nicene Creeds which are the central Christian baptismal covenants, and the Christian doctrines of Trinity, Virgin Birth, the resurrection and ascension of Jesus into heaven are all good examples. For instance, the Nicene creed affirms that Jesus "descended into hell" and rose from there on the third day. Where is hell? What is it? Why did Jesus go to hell, if it is a place for sinners receiving divine punishment for their sins? Obviously, we are dealing with antiquated religious and theological language here.

Definitely, the Nicene creed meant something meaningful for the Bishops who met at Nicea in 325 C.E. However, this ancient ecumenical Christian creed is largely meaningless and irrelevant for us today! The Nicene creed belongs to another world-view of mythology, theology, superstition, and ancient metaphysics. Greek myths and metaphysics have been replaced by physics and other branches of sciences. They are no longer valid for us as a form of epistemological or theological reference. Today, we make references to evolution and astrophysics.

Yet, the Nicene creed is still recited regularly, as the universal standard guide for true Christian faith and doctrine in most mainline churches! Obviously, they need to be either revised or discarded as foundations of sound Christian doctrine. The antiquated ancient language of these patriarchal, theological dogmas and philosophical world-view of God as "Father," Church, Trinity and a three storied universe no longer applies. To ask intelligent and well-informed people to affirm these errors as truth on the basis of their faith is an absurd religious request. It represents a distortion of God's truth, nature and intentions in the world.

Bishop John Spong's book, *Why Christianity Must Change or Die: A New Reformation of the Church's Faith and Practice* constitutes a very important ecclesiastical call for a new Church's reformation according to this New Age of science and technology. Bishop Spong has been courageous and bold in challenging the antiquated and erroneous traditional teachings of the Church. He has also been insightful in calling for a new reformation of the traditional ecclesiastical religious language, and a reformulation of the Christian central message for a post Darwinian evolutionary world-view and "cyberspace electronic information age."

Jesus reformed Judaism for his time. Likewise, St. Paul reformed Jewish Christianity for an intellectual global community, beginning with the Greeks and then the Romans. By doing this, Paul transformed an originally Jewish religious cult based upon Jesus as the expected eschatological Jewish messiah, into a world religion.

In a hellenized Christianity as a new world religion, Jesus and his mission were also correspondingly universalized and reinterpreted by Paul and his followers, especially, St. Augustine and Martin Luther. In this hellenization and universalization process of the "Jesus Christ Cult," Jesus became proclaimed as the *Logos* and incarnation of God "the Father" in human history. The incarnation was declared to be necessary in order for God to reconcile the alienated humanity with "himself" as its original source of its moral and spiritual power, as well as the source of ultimate meaning for human existence (cf. John 1:1-18). St. Augustine and Thomas Aquinas completed this task for their respective cultures, intellectual context and time in history. Martin Luther and John Calvin revised the material for their own era and cultures. John Wesley made further adaptations and modifications of the Christian tradition, and so did the Baptists and Pentecostals.

Ultimately, the Christian teaching, faith, message and tradition cannot become frozen in time. To do that would finally cause the decline, death and extinction of Christianity and the Church. This is the case since the Christians are living and changing beings who are not frozen in time. Their religion, theology and values or ethics must also become dynamically alive and changing along with the people. This is essential if these doctrines and teachings are to remain important and relevant moral and spiritual guides for the people.

Each era and generation needs to reform Christianity, doctrines, ethics, rituals and canonical laws for its age and specific context. Indeed, Vatican II (1963-65) and Pope John Paul's 1992 formal reversal of Galileo's condemnation in 1616, as a heretic for teaching a Sun-centered cosmological world-view, and his 1996 declaration that Charles Darwin's teachings on evolution were fact. Theistic evolution can be accepted as God's method for the *cosmogenesis* and *biogenesis* (creation). These papal declarations have proved to the skeptical world that even the traditional and conservative Catholic Church can very effectively both reform and renew herself in order to remain current and meaningful to the contemporary society.

Therefore, in order for Christianity and the Church to remain meaningful and relevant, and therefore, survive within a scientific and technological world, they must constantly undertake the endless task for continual critical self-examination, self-reformation, and self-modernization according to God's continuing activities of self-disclosure, creativity and redemption in the world.

Examples for this continuing self-critical examination and reformation of the Church include: the debates concerning the sensitive and controversial issues of women's ordination, inclusive religious language, socioeconomic justice, racism, sexism, homosexuality, sex without marriage, abortion, euthanasia and family values. Moral and cultural relativism are the center of this theological and moral debate and reformation. As long as there are no agreed universal moral codes and religious absolutes as God's unchanging revelation on which to base these moral and theological formulations, serious religious debates on these moral issues will remain part of the religious traditions, dissent and call for moral reformation within the religious community and the world.

# Chapter 12

# Finite Nature and Supernatural Functions of Human Language

The possession of a complex spoken and symbolic language, and the capacities to speak are divine attributes and special supernatural gifts of God's unmerited grace and unconditional love. They are freely and unconditionally universally bestowed on humanity by God through the process of human evolution and special divine creation.

This extraordinary process for divinization of the human being by God, takes place through the human access and participation in God's essence of intellect, mind and speech. It takes place naturally through God's mysterious process of special creation of bestowing the divine attributes of intellect, mind, spirit, self-consciousness, self-transcendence and moral agency upon humanity through the ordinary historical process of human evolution in the world. Language and the capacity to speak are correlative and coextensive with this divine cosmic process of the human special creation or the divinization of the evolutionary primate into a human being, the *imago Dei* and child of God.

## 1. The Problem of Language, Symbolism and Reality

God is the Ultimate, Eternal, Cosmic Divine Speaker and God's speech is the cosmic creation. The human language is evolutionary, culturally relative, diverse, finite and imperfect. Yet, simultaneously this imperfect human language is also supernatural both in its ultimate origins and function. The human being as "*imago Dei*" is the finite, evolutionary historical cosmic spirit and "hearer of God's Word (*Lo-*

*gos*)." God as the eternal "Speaker of the Word" and the human being as the "hearer of God's Word" are bound together in dialogue and fellowship by "God's Word" (*Logos*). The *Logos* is the eternal bridge or mediator of God to humanity and the cosmos and also the perfect advocate of humanity and the world or cosmos to God. This is the essence and central meaning of God's incarnation in the world in humanity through the *Logos* (cf. John 1:1-18). As such, God's incarnation is not a result of human sin. It is a result of the intimate relationship and affinity between God (*Dei*) and humanity (*imago Dei).*

Therefore, the evolutionary human being as a composite of finite spirit and mind that has historically emerged within the cosmos, is coextensively also God's echo, partial self-reflection and finite embodiment within the evolutionary cosmos and its historical processes. As such, the human being is also both "the finite speaker" and "respondent" to God's creative and redemptive Eternal Word or the Λογος (cf. Gen. 1:26-31; John 1-3), that is universally incarnate in the world.

The human language is complex in its syntax or grammatical construction, meaning, abstract references, metaphorical and symbolic nature. The human being is relative, finite and imperfect. This is true even when its respective users may not be consciously aware of such limitations, especially when it is in reference to the Holy Scriptures (Bible and the Qur'an) as God's specially revealed, inspired and inerrant "Word." To ascribe infallibility to Scriptures is to ascribe infallibility to the Religious Community or the Church that wrote and canonized them.

All human languages and knowledge of God are relative, culturally conditioned and imperfect. Human beings use language to name things and to construct a mental reality that may not have any corresponding existence in the ontological world. As such, language is the mirror of the abstract mental, social and a cultural world expressed in words and symbols rather than serving as the mirror of the physical world and its objects. Language does not in itself contain some self-existing intrinsic reality or truth beyond the social, cultural or religious symbols it names.

Language is a human conventional tool for communication. It employs conventional names for ordinary objects. Language describes the nature, location and assigned symbolic value of people and objects. The names and value of objects and people are assigned by human beings within the context of their own cultures, religions, fears, desires, hopes, class and technology. For instance, the term "good" assigns some positive value to an object or person or the person's action.

However, the term "good" by itself is meaningless, unless it is accompanied with more detail about the object, person or action. The term "good" does not necessarily bear any intrinsic relationship to the object, person or action described. The term is relative to the speaker's own values of what "good" is. For instance, when a criminal describes some criminal action as "good," it may be described as "evil" by a moral saint. Is the criminal wrong and the saint right? Is "good" and "evil" a mere matter of opinion and emotional judgement without some independent objective reference or validity?

To answer this question, the Christian moral thinkers must refer to God's revelation in the holy Scriptures or Christ's teachings on *Agape as the ultimate universal measure* of what is "*good*" or "*evil*." The Muslim may refer to the Qur'an and the *Shari'a* (Islamic Law) and members of Judaism may refer to the *Torah* (Mosaic Law) and Scriptures for measures of goodness in any given thing or action. What is "good" would have to conform to God's essence and attributes. These include goodness, unconditional love, free forgiveness, mercy, compassion, patience, order, justice, holiness, peace, benevolence, life and creativity.

What is good is what God approves or likes because it is in obedience to God's commandments or conforms to God's attributes. Similarly, Socrates posed and answered the question of why the gods like holy things by affirming that "the gods like holy things because they are holy." This is analogous to why the saints do good things. Therefore, language and words, such "good" or "holy" is only meaningful depending on the speaker and the context. "Good" and "holy" as uttered by the saint or prophet have different meanings and influence by the same words uttered by a criminal, hoodlum in the slum or a child on the playground.

The utilitarians may use the term "good" and then try to measure the action by the number of people it benefits and makes happy! The utilitarians wrongly assume that what is good will be liked by the majority of the people or that it will benefit the majority. In that case, the crucifixion of Jesus would qualify as a "good thing" since many people have become Christians as a result of that innocent death on the cross. Likewise, the slavery of masses of Africans would falsely and outrageously morally qualify as a good thing on the grounds that it enabled economic development of America.

Likewise, the common term, "God" is a social, religious and linguistic construction although it has great reality in the mental world and emotional experience of religious people. "God" as both a popular and powerful term has no corresponding physical reality or reference within the physical world. Idolatry is the human attempt to create and provide concrete and visible physical reference for an invisible God, who intangibly and invisibly only exists in the abstract spiritual realm of the mind *(nous)* and spirit *(pneuma)*. The human language performs several essential human communicative, organizational, moral, religious, philosophical, and socioeconomic functions in the human community and the world. Language possesses the intrinsic divine power to create, classify, bless, curse, name and dominate people and things.

Therefore, the human language is also the cultural linguistic medium and power to name, classify, identify, empower or disenfranchise and dominate powerless groups of people and their institutions to exploit their resources. In the Western patriarchal societies, men (Adam) have invented language, and named God, things, women (Eve), animals, elements and the outsiders in order to dominate them. By so doing, the Western society became the "Whiteman's society" in which the majority of the women and non-White racial minorities were both discriminated against and excluded from power and full economic participation.

The patriarchal or male language provides evidence for this religious and social exclusion as well vilification of Black people. For instance, "male" such as "Father" and "King" came to symbolize God. At the same time, white came to symbolize purity, good and God, whereas "black" came to symbolize evil. Examples here are "black market," "black sheep," "black cat," "black devil" and "black attire" for funerals or mourning.

Women and Black people felt insulted by this kind of prejudiced sexist and racist language. They correctly realized that language was part of externalizing the demonic forces and realities of the Western patriarchal sexist and racist culture, religion and society. It was a societal powerful mental, religious, cultural, symbolic and political medium and tool for oppression of women and racial minorities. As a result, both women and racial minorities have sought liberation from the degradation of sexism and racism by seeking to reform the patriarchal oppressive society by the reformation of language and transvaluation of the traditional White-male values and systems, so as to include women and racial minorities.

This is true for the Church. God's Church should have been at the forefront in fighting sexism and racism, but instead it was the source and perpetrator of these social and moral evils. Religion sought to justify the subordination of women on the basis of the myth of Eve and the original sin. Whitesupremacy was also justified as God's will in creation, namely, that Whites were created as superior people to the rest of the nonwhite people. In *God Beyond the Father*, Mary Daly has correctly asserted that the phallic or patriarchal symbols, myths and language were invented by the patriarchs and employed to deify the White male. Conversely, they were also designed to degrade women and non-Whites to lower, subordinate status and inferior class of humanity.

It is through language that human beings think, formulate, encode and communicate the instructions to be carried out for events or implementation of other important societal tasks and functions. Language is essential for effective social organization, education, thought, communication and implementation of necessary events. It is also necessary for vital societal functions, which are required for societal organization and the maintenance of an advanced form of human life, technological, and sophisticated quality of human existence as we know it today.

For the less intelligent and nonthinking animals, having a less complex form of communications, political, and socioeconomic organization, have little need for a complex verbal, abstract and symbolic language. As such, chemical forms of communication may be sufficient in some cases, whereas in other cases, a few different vocalizations and noises for: "I am lost," "where areyou?" "here I am," pain, fear, warning, food, mating call, happiness or contentedness maybe sufficient. More intelligent animals such as the chimpanzees, dolphins and elephants may have a more complex form of language and communication symbols that are not yet deciphered by human beings. Those engaged in research in the fields of biological sciences, animal psychology and behavior may one day discover them.

However, the human being as both mind and spirit, as well as the most intelligent animal, thinks in very complex abstract language and symbols. The human being also communicates with others and God in the same manner. Thus, for human beings to speak is to be like God (cf. Gen. 1:1-3). It is also to cause a new creation or new events to occur in both nature and history. The human speech is the universal primary societal tool for effective organization of an orderly, cultural, technical and moral life in the community. It is the human instrument for teaching, learning, social transmission of information or knowledge that enables human creation of culture, complex social systems, religions, technology and civilizations. Even human families would be impossible without the language to communicate love, needs, instructions for work and express happiness.

The human being's information, thoughts, history, experience, culture, values, laws, religion, knowledge, and technology are also processed in abstract language and symbols, communicated to others that way, and stored in that complicated form of abstract language and symbols. These symbols include pictures, metaphors, sounds, colors, smells, numbers, maps and diagrams.

Nevertheless, for many unsophisticated people, language is taken for granted to be the same as ontological reality. Very often, human beings mistakenly equate names of things, logical philosophical-theological or religious formulations of doctrine and liturgical language with ontological reality. Despite the fact that language is not reality in itself, as Ludwig Josef Wittgenstein mistakenly claimed in the *Tractatus* and the *Notebooks*, it mirrors mental reality. As such, language is a very important tool for mental processing of perception into mental reality.

Language is the medium for abstract mental reality as consists in mental activities, such as perceptions, thinking, memory, judgement and communication. Therefore, language is the essential cultural, social and mental medium for human processes of epistemology and ontology. Mental reality is relative and may be erroneous. Mental reality is subjective and does not always correspond to "actual reality." For instance, a child's mental reality or that of the insane people may have little correspondence to "actual reality." The insane people have a distorted view of the world and reality. They may "see" God, people, spirits or "hear voices" where there none to be seen or heard. This is the realm of the hallucinations and delusions of which Sigmund Freud had plenty to excavate through psychoanalysis.

Language is the linguistic and mental mirror of what people perceive to be reality. Language is employed to map out mysteries or data and process them into intelligible material in order to arrive at a mental portrayal and description of reality. Knowledge, being a social and shared truth, is encoded and communicated from one person or group to another in the abstract medium of language. Numbers, images, sounds, and colors are some examples of the symbols and codes of this abstract nature of language. Technology helps to encode and decode these codes in order to facilitate effective and accuracy of communications between the sender of the message (speaker) and the recipient (audience). Drums, bells, smoke, trumpets, loudspeaker, telephones, fax machines, computers (Internet, e-mails), letters, newspapers, radios, and television are some of these examples of communication technology that facilitate human communication.

Language paints some imaginary mental pictures of reality. This is why poetry, stories, parables and myths are effective tools for the communication of transcendent realities like those of God, religion and love. Shakespeare's story of *Romeo and Juliet* communicates love as truth without being a historical account! The story of Noah and that of Job communicate the mysteries of sin, pain, death and divine judgement! We feel their great message and moral teachings about faith in God, even when they are non-historical!

We fail to appreciate the great value of language, metaphor, stories and myths when we mistake them for historical realities. Likewise, we misuse language if we try to name the unnameable realities like God, or when we misrepresent metaphors for God such as "*Father*," "*Mother*," "*King*," "*Judge*," and "*Patriarch*" or "*Ancestor*" as real biological realities and historical truths. Tragically for both religion and theology, this is what has happened with these myths of creation, fall or original sin and metaphors for God. As a result, many Christians understood God in literal anthropomorphic terms. They understood the Cosmic Creator to be "*God the Heavenly Father*" or a kind of "Zeus," the Greek male god who was the divine Arch-patriarch and head of the Greek pantheon. This was the error of many unsophisticated, poorly educated and superstitious early Christians. For most of them, Jesus was also understood anthropomorphically to be the biological "Son of God," just like Hercules was the son of Zeus.

Like Hercules, Jesus was said to be the Son of God who was brought to the Earth by the earthly foster parents, Mary and Joseph. The "*Virgin Mary*" became the surrogate "*Mother of Jesus the Son of God!*" This is the essence of the traditional Roman Catholic doctrine of the "Virgin Mary" as the *Theotokos* (Mother of God). The Christian misunderstanding of religious myths, analogies, parables, hymns, poetry and metaphors as figurative and symbolic religious language is the origin of serious heresies in the Christian Church's doctrines and liturgy. These erroneous doctrines and heresies are self-evident in doctrines dealing with the divine Incarnation of God (*Logos*), the Virgin Birth, the resurrection, ascension into heaven by Jesus, the Holy Trinity, the Kingdom of God and the return of Christ!

Obviously, it makes a great difference if one takes this religious language literally as biology or historical truth as opposed to being merely metaphorical and figurative. The literalists would expect Jesus' ascension to be similar to being rocketed into space by NASA, without a spacecraft. The questions of destination and gravity do not worry these people. The fact that Jesus would suffocate for lack of oxygen or freeze to death or disintegrate because of gravity and excessive, unregulated speed in outer space never occurs to them.

These kinds of irrational forms of religious literalism make a mockery of the deeper religious and spiritual meaning which is communicated by the stories of the resurrection as God's triumph over sin and power of the fear of death! It is in the openness to life in the presence of suffering and death that true life and happiness are found! This is what the Buddha formulated as one of his noble truths: "Life is *Dukkha*."

Buddha declared that life is by nature inherently sorrowful! This is the truth that requires faith in God in order to be fully embraced and accepted. Jesus taught the same truth when he invited his followers to carry their own crosses and follow him. That was an invitation to the truth of life as lived in the midst of suffering and death. Jesus used special language to communicate complex ideas and teach the divine transcendent truths in metaphors, parables and stories. These religious media became a source of misunderstanding by his illiterate audiences, and later, the early Church.

Unfortunately, Christianity has inherited these problems and religious epistemological errors caused by complicated religious stories. Biblical mythological stories such as those of Adam and Eve, Noah's flood, the virgin birth, the resurrection and ascension have been incorrectly portrayed as actual historical events that took place in cosmic history.

Likewise, the figurative language and metaphors, such as "God the Father," "God's Kingdom," "Heaven,""Adam and Eve," "Original Sin,""Virgin Birth," "Resurrection," and "the Ascension of Christ," have been erroneously proclaimed as literal, historical and physical realities. This is an illustration of the misuse of the religious language through the historicization and literalization of symbolism and metaphors into nonexistent historical realities or absurdities. Taking the stories of Adam and Eve or the Virgin Birth as history is like taking the story of Job and the parable of the Good-Samaritan as history. Some of these functions and tasks performed by language are directly related to the subject under discussion, and therefore, will be dealt with within this complex social, moral, philosophical religious and theological context.

## 2. Language as the Medium of Humanization Socialization, Worship and Education

Language is an essential tool for communication. It is the medium and means for accomplishing important social and mental tasks, such as thought and telling stories. It is the means for planning and designing new things and communicating them to others. Language as the tool for thought, consciousness and communication is also the means for discovery, teaching, learning and revelation.

Mathematics is an example of a perfect tool at the level of designing things, such complex machines and tall buildings. It can be used to convey complex abstract concepts and build models of invisible realities with great accuracy. Nevertheless, mathematics cannot convey our deep feelings of love and care to the person we love. At this level of communication, the language of poetry, song, dance, story, metaphor and symbolism is ideal and best equipped to accomplish the desired task in the most meaningful manner.

Language is a necessary organizational, social, societal and communicative tool for human beings in their incessant quest for a better form of existence in which leisure, pleasure and happiness are maximized. This is one of the reasons why no human society has ever been found lacking in this most essential human tool that is in itself an abstract essential, constitutive element of the human being. This is simply another way of saying what has been said before that the nature of the human being is essentially linguistic. However, being human and a tool for the humanization of the newborn, language has to keep up with the societal changes in which the newborns are socialized into civilized members of the community.

If language fails to do what society wants it to do, then it is either discarded gradually in favor of a new one, or modified with the addition of new words, professional vocabulary, slang and new idioms. Examples of dead ancient languages include Koine Greek, Latin, and the King James English! Languages are not static and unchangeable. Languages are as alive, flexible, evolutionary, growing and changing as the people who use them. Therefore, when a language becomes static, that language also dies. It is replaced by a more dynamic and contemporary one. This is part of the universal law that governs biological, cultural, social and linguistic evolution. Some of these dead languages include Koine Greek,

Aramaic, Syriac, Celtic, ancient Hebrew and Latin. This is also true for music, religion, culture, values, technology and the sciences. One can see the clear evidence of this truth by visiting a museum of natural history and the sciences.

The museums provide an evolutionary historical record of these disciplines. The modern cars and fashions of today are tomorrow's museum antiques. This is true for all aspects of evolutionary human life, including language, cultures, religion, ideas, sciences, technology and ethics. They all exist in the constant process of constant evolution and change. The only problem is that the people involved in these processes are often unaware that they are active participants in an evolutionary process and change. They rarely see it as it happens. Instead, they see it in retrospect by looking at history or photographs taken some years before.

Human beings rarely see themselves growing even when that is a biological fact. This is true also of other aspects of their evolutionary and ever-changing life. For instance, you are not the same person as when you started reading this book! It has changed you and I am not the same person as the person that wrote this book. I have already grown older, wiser and changed accordingly! Some of these views you are now reading may have already changed, too, as a result of this evolutionary process of constant growth, positive transformation and change! Life is improved and enriched by this process irrespective of the fact that it brings us closer to death! Therefore, some people believe in the resurrection and human reincarnation in order to experience this exciting process of life and positive spiritual transformation through death and rebirth to life again as better and wiser reincarnated spirits.

A modern theology must employ modern concepts of eternal life based on modern science and technology. For instance, death, immortality and rebirth or the resurrection could be reaffirmed using modern concepts such as those of water, matter and energy. Matter and energy are interchangeable states of matter. Ice and clouds are also interchangeable states of water ($H_2O$). The various states and cycles of water ($H_2O$) from a sold (ice, snow) state to liquid (lakes, oceans, rivers, rain), gas (steam, vapor, clouds) when heated and back to liquid as it freezes offers an interesting analogy for human life as body and spirit that can go through several stages of physical and spiritual existence without being destroyed, in as much as spirit and matter are two dimensions of the same substance, such as clouds and oceans are two states of existence and locations of the same substance namely, water ($H_2O$).

In new theology, contemporary myths and language, human life could be affirmed to be analogous to water in its various different states of physical existence and functions. In order to use it for shelter, you need it as a solid in the form of ice or snow and you need it as a liquid in order to use it for bathing, cooking, drinking and transportation (lakes, rivers and oceans). You need it as moisture in the air in order to keep the lungs and the body healthy. Human life as spirit and mind is also essential for human self-transcendence, thought, contemplative player, happiness, peace and eternal life in union with God who is the All-Inclusive Cosmic Spirit and Mind.

As culture and sciences change, languages must also undergo a corresponding change. Subsequently, we see new vocabulary and language usage come about as a result of the felt need to think and communicate better. For example, we have new "high-tech" words such as "mouse," "modem," "bug," "debug," and "log on," which have been invented to describe some essential computer communications, functions and malfunctions.

This is an example of how professional language has become so specialized that different branches of knowledge can hardly be accessed and utilized by the scholars from other disciplines. This is mainly because of too much formidable, technical jargon employed in that particular discipline. This is also partly due to the fact that some misguided scholars and technical experts very absurdly seem to think that the more professional or technical vocabulary that is employed in one's speech, lecture or written work, the more scholarly and prestigious it appears!

This pitiful position equates the mastery and usage of mere technical jargon and professional language with the measure of the validity and scholarship of the subject matter and truth content of the work or presentation. This is absurd, because it turns academics into polemics, jargon and mere linguistic studies. This is also to equate the medium with the message itself. In the entertainment and political arena, that may well be true. However, it is false when it is applied to the academic world, where content is more important than the manner of its delivery or presentation, as long as effective communication takes place. This means that professors and preachers have to concentrate on the truths of their message rather than the dramatization of their message or content.

The danger here is that some students merely dwell on the drama, rather than on the content of the drama.

However, what should not be forgotten in this situation is that, ultimately, language is basically a medium for communication. Good communication takes place when the language, symbols, signs, gestures, sounds or codes used are familiar and known by both the originator of the message, such as, the speaker, sender, writer, preacher and communicator, and his or her intended recipients or audience.

In short, communication only effectively takes place if the communicator and the audience speak the same language, irrespective of whether this language is verbal or nonverbal. This includes the Native American smoke signals, the Chinese picture language, modern sign language, computer language and mathematics, as well as the African talking drums.

## 3. Language as the Chief Medium for Thinking, Communication and Social Organization

Since the human being is, by nature, essentially both a relational and social being, therefore, the major functions of language are essentially those of communication, socialization, education, information sharing, and community building. These functions are aimed at the creation of good interpersonal networks of social relationships and the building of an orderly society or *"polis."*

It is in this way that language truly becomes a medium of humanization. Our humanity, identity and self-worth are gained from our society and social networks of relationships. For instance, we may see ourselves through the linguistic mirrors of our society. We see ourselves as wise, kind, beautiful, great or vice versa, if we have been constantly told by those around us that we are these things! We, too, see others in linguistic, mental images as good or bad.

Unfortunately, these linguistic terms are so relative and fluid that we rarely agree on what they mean! This is one of the great problems of language. Words derive their specific meaning from the particular context, and are less meaningful without the original context in which they were used. For instance, the word "space" will mean one thing to a housewife in a small kitchen, and mean another thing to a psychologist, and mean yet another thing to a physicist or philosopher! This is what was probably meant by McLuhan, the great communications expert, when he made the now famous statement that "the medium is the message."

This also means that not only are the words and nonverbal expressions important and very meaningful, but even more so is the very structure of the sentence, and ultimately, the structure of the given language itself. This is because language is itself the mirror and the accessible reflection of the mind, culture, philosophy, religion and technology of those people who created the specific language. They are the ones who continue to use and modify the given language, according to their own specific needs, philosophy, world-view and technology of the times.

To this end, the human language is an essential tool for human work, action, thought and creativity as a computer is essential for many professionals, particularly those in sciences. As such, if language does not serve our essential purposes, it has to either be modified, so as to serve our needs better, or be discarded on the trash heap of history and subsequently be replaced with a more relevant and functional one that is meaningful for the respective times. This is true for the ever changing scientific language, as well as for the more static and dogmatic religious and theological language. In the flux of the finite world, no language ever become perfect, absolute and remain dogmatically static.

Within this evolutionary and ever changing world, the only absolute truths are God, creaturely finitude and the absoluteness of change for all created and finite beings and their own institutions. This includes, human beings and their institutions, including cultures, language, religions, ethics, values and technologies. For instance, women have been ordained as clergy and bishops in many Protestant churches, whereas, in the past this was considered blasphemous and unthinkable because of the prevailing traditional patriarchal hegemonic religious structures and doctrines.

In this finite and constantly changing world of both people and things, language is employed as a finite and changing tool and means to communication. It is used by people to express themselves to others and even to themselves, in thought, action, art, music, dress, dialogue, fellowship, conversation, debate and argumentation. Language is also used by humans to express themselves to God in private prayer and corporate liturgical worship, in fellowship with the religious and the worshipping Ecclesial Community or the Church. Language is, for most people, important and valued primarily because it enables them to express themselves to their fellow human beings. It facilitates essential interpersonal relationships through speech, love songs, poetry, and writing.

Language is also the means by which we think and communicate with God in prayer and worship. It is through the medium of language that we also communicate with other people, creatures and the intelligent machines in the world. Therefore, human life and the correlative human community would cease to exist if there were no languages or communications to make them possible.

This is necessarily the case because humanity and community are merely interrelated components of God's Word and Speech in the Cosmos. Therefore, they exist correlatively and coextensively together most fully when or where good human language and communications take place. This is also the case because the human community is a result of mutual good communications in the presence of God as the Creator and Sustainer of the God-dependent, finite human being. The human being as God's earthly image also means that just like God, the human being is also quintessentially a linguistic being whose essence is to hear God, other people, the world, and also to speak in response to the various messages and the ultimate questions of life.

## 4. Language as a Cultural Tool and Weapon

Whereas language is the divine expression of a higher intelligence that makes the evolutionary animals or the *Homo sapiens* into real human beings. Therefore, like mind, intellect and thinking, language is also inherently good.

Nevertheless, language can be misused to inflict harm on our enemies. It can be used by evil, hateful and racist or sexist people as the powerful tool and weapon to exclude, isolate, insult and dehumanize and inflict social or psychological harm on people. Name calling, mud slinging, slander, malicious misquotation, insults, character assassination, profanity, dirty jokes, evil gossip, telling lies and falsehood belong to this category.

However, in these and other human problems, our counter weapon is the teaching of good language to the young so that they grow up with respect for language and other people with whom they come in linguistic contact. In the Church, the usage of exclusive, male dominated language in terms of nouns and pronouns for both God and humanity has been common. As a result, many women have felt personally excluded from the Church, its Scriptures, and its liturgical worship whose language is heavily influenced by this male dominated, patriarchal language. This is the language that refers to God as "Father," "Lord," "His," "King," "God's Kingdom," and refers to Jesus as "Son of God," "Son of Man," "a man," "Prince of peace and Lord of Lords," "Lord," "Master, and "his Kingdom."

These are some of the theological words and thinking underlying what feminist theologians seek to exorcize from the Bible, liturgical books such as prayer books and hymnals, as well as from all forms of public religious discourse in the form of sermons, lectures and Sunday School instruction for the young and the adults. This is the noble motivation behind the positive, but highly controversial *NCCC (National Council of Christian Churches) Inclusive Lectionary* and other new inclusive hymnals, prayer-books and liturgies. The more theologically sophisticated and liberal churches, such as the Episcopal, Methodist and the Presbyterian churches have embraced the women's liberation movement. They have ordained women into the priesthood and the episcopacy. The ordination of women requires new inclusive titles for the clergy, new inclusive liturgical language in reference to God.

The process of transmission of culture, language, education and the humanization of the young into the community must include inclusive language and the positive values of equality and justice. These new normative values are required in order to negate personal and institutional evils of sexism and racism. This process also creates thinking members of the community who will use language for the purposes of cognition and thought.

This being the presupposition, language then becomes the perceived weapon with which the linguistically excluded, oppressed and dehumanized members of the human female gender defend themselves from such abuses, and correct the sexist situation which has given rise to this offense. Again, the underlying assumption is that linguistic semantics do affect human thinking, philosophy, world-view, religion, and ultimately, human existence in general.

Subsequently, it follows that the Churches' attempts to reverse and change the traditional, exclusive, male oriented and male dominated religious language are also attempts to change humanity itself. This is the case since human beings will be subsequently influenced and shaped by this new inclusive language to become more inclusive in their own thinking and actions.

Therefore, language is a double-edged sword which can be used as either a lethal weapon for self-defense, or an effective lethal offensive weapon with which a merciless and harsh critic can effectively employ to silence opponents or dissect their various targeted victims' valuable work into worthless pieces of junk to be thrown away onto the decomposing trash dump of the indifferent cosmic history. Since our society tends to identify, judge and evaluate us by our language, then our language is more than a mere societal communications tool. Our language is ourselves in self-abstraction, and self-expression or self-communication to others, God, and the world around us. Our language is our moral, social and linguistic identity.

Ultimately, we are our own language, thoughts, choices and deeds. Our language, just like our own works, is the external cultural mirror that reveals who and what we are inside. Language reveals who we are as both individuals and collectively as a particular group of people. Language provides our identity to the external world. To this end, our education, profession, class, nationality and moral values can be very well revealed by our own language and its usage. For instance, if someone shouts obscenities in a particular accent on the street or a public place, one could probably conclude correctly that the person is angry or lacking in self-control, moral or civic virtues and public decency.

Based on common stereotypes, scientific observations and published research in the field of race, class and ethnicity, one could also classify the person as having poor social skills, poor education and low socioeconomic class, if the person lacks sound moral values as measured by the middle class Christian ideals, in the case of the Christian Western nations. One may also conclude that that person has been raised in a poor and morally deficient environment, if he or she lacks the necessary moral background to govern him or her live a good moral life, irrespective of income. This is more visible with some athletes from some urban slums who have attained fame and a lot of money, but lack the true values and cultural refinement of the upper middle class where their high income would naturally place them.

Some rich athletes have engaged in public behavior that is truly embarrassing to sports and their sponsors. These include rape, indecent language, assaults of their coaches or members of the public. This is a clear example that money alone, without proper moral and liberal arts education does not necessarily confer a higher class!

One can argue that in the USA, the more refined upper-middle class values and etiquette are required of that class, in the same manner that the royal family and the aristocracy were expected to behave as role models. They were expected to behave in a civilized, compassionate and dignified manner. Low class behavior, such as foul language (swearing, cursing, obscenities), public indecency, drunkenness, disorderly conduct, overeating and unkept property or uncleanliness and the like would be a source of disgrace for royalty or members of the professional classes (upper middle class).

*My Fair Lady* and Spike Lee's films center's film, "*Do the Right Thing,*" are good illustrations of this sensitive socioeconomic, moral, cultural, educational and class differences. The poorly educated and unemployed inner city men on the street were the living embodiment of the "ghetto subculture." In both cases, language, both verbal and nonverbal, was the main vehicle of this interesting class drama. The loud music and its lyrics are a very important part of this language.

Subsequently, the racial tension between the Whites and Blacks in Lee's films center around lower class crude forms of vulgar language and loud music as its expression. Consequently, when the irritated and enraged White businessman, armed with a heavy club, violently attacked and destroyed the irritating "boom-box" that produced the loud Black music, it inadvertently amounted to the symbolic White people's attack and destruction of the Black people's culture and identity as symbolized by the Black music and "noisy boom box."

The consequences of this mutual cultural intolerance were portrayed to be indeed very tragic and destructive to the society. It was also shown how in the time of trouble and crisis, those people of the same color and the same language tend to act together, including the members of the police force themselves. It also showed how exclusive racial slurs can be quickly vocalized further to isolate the minorities who are already sufficiently outnumbered and intimidated.

In this racial tragedy, color and language seemed to define peoples' identity, socioeconomic class, behavior and the kind of treatment they were accorded from the public. Tragically, the justice system itself failed to remain color-blind and unaffected by the people's class, gender, race, creed, language and accent as the law requires. Justice was administered by imperfect, sinful human beings, and was used to pass evil laws based on language, gender, and race in order to exclude those who are different.

The racist system of apartheid in South Africa is a good example of this. Many of the White supremacists in South Africa "blasphemously believed" that God was a "White Man" like them. Subsequently, they also tragically concluded that God, being a White Patriarch, could not have originated or created the Black people (or other racial minorities). That was because they, too, would have been created in God's own image! The idea that Blackness could represent God was repugnant to them, because for them, "Blackness" represented evil and the Devil. And could not validly be the same as its very antithesis, namely, the most holy God. When Bishop Desmond Tutu became the Archbishop of the Anglican Province of Southern Africa, many Whites left the Anglican Church in protest. They called him a "monkey" and a "baboon."

Characteristically, the White Afrikaners had also required every student in South Africa to learn Afrikaans, the national and official language. This is the language which is spoken by the Afrikaners. It had been declared by them to be the Constitutional, official language of South Africa. The then White minority rulers of South Africa imposed their own language on the majority people as the official language, even when it was a language of the small minority (less than 15 per cent) of the nation. This is an example to illustrate the linkage between language, culture, values and political power. The dominant group, rather than God, imposed its language, culture, religion, values and identity on the rest of the people. Language became the vehicle for the transmission of the values and culture to create new cultural symbols and forms of collective self-consciousness and identity.

It is not surprising, therefore, that the ancient people identified and named tribes and races according to their spoken language! For instance, in general, *you were French if you spoke French*. Likewise, you were considered *English if you spoke English!* But this categorization does not apply today because we have learned to speak other languages other than those of our own parents. As a result, some of us now speak both French and English, yet we are neither French nor English. Subsequently, we tend to forget that the human language is still an essential part of our own identity, cultural and intellectual heritage, without which knowledge, education, religion, complex societies, human civilizations, interpersonal communications and self-transcendence would be impossible.

## 5. Problems of Religious Language And Symbols

The human language as an imperfect human cultural creation is at times also underdeveloped, vague, equivocal, and inadequate for some specialized disciplines of study or description of new inventions in medicine, the natural sciences and technology. New names have to be created to designate new inventions and new procedures, such as "*mouse*" as a name for an electronic device to point to positions and items on the computer screen or "*bug*" for computer problems and "*debug*," as the term for fixing the computer ailment. "*Internet*," "*cyberspace*" and the "*information highway*" are other examples of new technological names to describe new realities, services and technologies which did not previously exist in both reality and language, as such.

In the academic study of religion, theology and ethics, theological language presents us with the another example of such a problematic phenomenon of language, difficulties in naming objects and epistemology. The main problem facing religion, theology and philosophy is that of limitation of the human language due to its imperfection, semantics and inadequacy. However, we can also continue to create new words and symbols to name God, divine revelation, values, new spiritual understanding of ourselves and the world.

Human language is finite, yet its object, content and subject claim to be divine, and as such, infinite in nature. It is therefore a great problem for the finite ever to have a full grasp of the infinite and fully express it without distortion. It is indeed a contradiction for us to claim that God is an infinite Mystery, and yet insist that we can have the right theological understanding and doctrinal formulation about this incomprehensible Creative Mystery we call God. Yet, most Churches claim absolute doctrinal truth, and subsequently, any questioning of their theological language and doctrinal formulations is viewed grimly as a question of unbelief, Ecclesial insubordination and demonic rebellion.

This being the case, in most religious establishments, theology, religious language and liturgy have not been given the creative expression they need. Consequently, religious dogma and creedal statements of faith have come to dominate our religious lives. As a result, those independent or rebellious people who did not comply with the Church dogma have been either censured and silenced or forced to leave their respective conservative and intolerant ecclesiastical institutions. For instance, in 1989, Fr. Charles Curran was terminated from his tenured position as professor of theology and ethics at the Catholic University of Washington, due to his failure to comply with the conservative dogmatic teachings of the Roman Catholic Church on controversial moral issues, such as abortion, euthanasia, and homosexuality.

However, some of those who stayed have sometimes tried to reform the religious language, theology and the liturgy from within. The translation of the scriptures, the Protestant Reformation, the Evangelical Revivals, and more recently the NCCC Inclusive Lectionary, the Episcopal Prayer Book, and The New United Methodist Hymnal are just a few examples of this courageous group. Since the object and content of religious or theological language is abstract, infinite and incomprehensible, the human finite language is inadequate and unable to embody and express this divine, cosmic, creative Mystery called God.

Nevertheless, many Christian thinkers strongly disagree with Wittgenstein who suggested that since language mirrors reality, that which cannot be grasped and expressed in language should be consigned to silence and the realm of the nonexistence. He was wrong in as much as language only mirrors mental reality rather than the actual ontological reality as it really is in-itself. The finite human mind and the human language are too small and too limited to grasp the infinite scope of what there is to know as the scientific truth and reality. As such, myths, hymns and poetry express truths and realities which are beyond language. Matters of love and God are mysteries and realities which we cannot adequately formulate in verifiable propositions. Doing so, is to confuse logic with ontology, and language with physics or reality.

With the exception of mathematics, language is symbolic, conventional and figurative, but does not necessarily mirror physical or spiritual reality. In general, the human language mirrors the thinker and speaker's own mind, culture, philosophy, technology, values, education and knowledge. Within this theological, philosophical and epistemological understanding, language is nothing more than a conventional system of codes and symbols of any given group, culture, society, discipline, school, profession and the like.

In this respect, therefore, religious language is no exception. Religious language does not in any way contain the reality it describes or claims to represent. In order for us to speak humanly yet meaningfully about the supernatural God, who is the main object of religious worship and theology, we have to realize that human language is finite and relative. As such, we should remain open to the question of relativity in our own religious beliefs, liturgical language, scriptural translations, theological knowledge, and doctrinal formulations including our traditional creeds and dogmas. This has not been always the case. As a result, most people have come to equate myths, metaphors and figurative religious language with the Absolute Truth and ontological reality! This serious mistake of confusing language with reality has led religion to serious doctrinal errors of scriptural literalism, anthropomorphism, and idolatry!

For instance, many people have failed to appreciate the nature of the mythological, parabolic, symbolic, poetic, figurative and metaphorical nature of the religious language found in the Bible, and have uncritically and tragically interpreted it literally as factual descriptions of real ontological, scientific and historical realities. As a result, the biblical book of Genesis is read as if it were a sacred textbook of science and history containing literal historical records of the primordial events regarding God's physical creation of the cosmos within six days or 144 hours.

This is true inasmuch as each day was measured by the rising and setting of the sun despite the fact that the sun, moon and stars are reported to have been created on the third day (cf. Gen. 1:14), a day after God had created green plants and grass! Obviously, the story teller had scientific idea that the solar system depends on the sun for its existence and gravitational orbital balance. It is clear that biblical story teller, like most ancient people and many religious fundamentalists erroneously believed that the sun, moon and stars rotated around the Earth.

Likewise, the mythological account of Noah's Ark and the flood that destroyed every living thing that was not aboard Noah's Ark of salvation, is also literally read as a real historical record of a catastrophic global flood destroyed life on the entire Earth about 6,000 years ago. Therefore, they have fallen into this deadly trap of confusing language with ontological reality. As an example, some people believe that God is a supernatural Man, a kind of super man or cosmic king, just because the scriptures refer to God in male terms, such as "our Father who art in heaven," "King," "Lord," and "the Father of our Lord Jesus Christ." But all of these are simply human metaphors, analogies, figures, and imageries for the infinitely transcendent, abstract and incomprehensible Creative cosmic, holy Mystery we call God.

Therefore, if we take literally these human metaphors, analogies, and figures and treat them as sacred symbols, we will be guilty of idolatry, for we have been forbidden to make images and any other representations of God! Subsequently, "maleness" alone does not adequately represent God any more than "femaleness" by itself.

God includes male and female attributes in the wholeness and totality of God's own infinite divine essence and mystery. For that matter, God created humanity as both male and female in his or her own image (Gen. 1:26-27). As such, for those within the Judeo-Christian tradition, the true *imago Dei* is a balance of male and female qualities. Therefore, no single gender by itself is ever truly adequate to represent God even if this representation was acceptable, as has been the case in the Western traditional patriarchal Christianity and the correlative traditional patriarchal theology. This as it is traditionally characterized by Thomas Aquinas for the Catholic Church, and Martin Luther, John Calvin and Karl Barth for the Protestant churches.

However, we should never give in to the suggestion of great theologians like Rudolf Bultmann, who claimed that the religious and theological language have become more of a hindrance than an aid in the understanding of the faith, and therefore, it should be demythologized in order to make the hidden religious meanings become plain and clear to all.

The problem consists in the fact that myth, itself, is religious content, since it has religious meaning which cannot exist apart from itself. In other words, religious myth is itself the medium and the very message. A good analogy here is the relationship between the human body and the mind. In this respect, demythologization of religion would be like killing a person in order to analyze his or her mind! Myth, parable, symbolism and mystery constitute the heart of religion and subsequently, its language, beliefs, scriptures, and liturgy.

For instance, can you visualize a Church devoid of its symbolism of the cross, water, bread, wine, light, colors, vestments, music or the Bible? Are sacraments themselves not ecclesiastical symbols pointing to the sacred which they embody in a religiously meaningful manner? Are they not part of the Christian central myth and mystery which cannot be demythologized without the destruction of the spiritual meaning and symbolic nature of the Christian message itself? Its center is Mystery whose human, linguistic, metaphorical religious embodiment is myth itself.

The fact that every human race has its myths about the ultimate origins, meaning and destiny of creation, particularly that of human beings themselves, is a case in point. In this respect, Christianity is not unique, although Christianity tends to be more exclusive than the other universal religions. Furthermore, Christianity, like Judaism and Islam, was born in the same region, around Palestine and the surrounding Arabian desert. This region not only gave birth to these religions, but it also gave rise to all the major canonical religious books or scriptures of these religions.

Since the people of this region were patriarchal, their understanding of God and the scriptures they wrote down were subsequently influenced and expressed in their own languages which were male-dominated in its gender nouns, pronouns, metaphors, and imagery. This was, of course, acceptable to these patriarchal cultures in which women were generally supposed to be of inferior gender, and therefore, to be subordinated to men who were considered to be of a higher and better gender.

However, in our society, today, the sexes claim equality before God, the law, employment, and also before the Church. Therefore, women now demand that the Church change its official language so as to be equally included in scripture readings, hymns and the liturgy. They are God's people, equally chosen and redeemed, just like their male counterparts. After all, it is mostly the women who come to Church in large numbers.

Therefore, when they come to worship, they should not to be insulted by male-chauvinist ministers and their patriarchal religious language and symbolism for God, which *exclude women and render them invisible and powerless in both Church and society*! Women should not be insulted by both being excluded from the Church's liturgical activities and by being referred to in exclusive male terms.

These masculine terms, such as "men" or the generic "man," and the male pronouns, "he" and "his," which are used in the male-dominated religious language both in sermons and liturgical worship alienate, insult and offend many intelligent women, especially the feminists within the Church. Ultimately, women are not men. Women were never created by God to become men as part of their perfection as human beings. "Maleness" or patriarchy is not the true measure of authentic humanity. The *praxis* of *agape*, free forgiveness of sins, compassion and exercise of justice for all human beings, irrespective of gender, race, ethnicity, color, class, nationality and handicap are the true universal measures of authentic humanity. These criteria are gender neutral.

Therefore, they should not be subjected to male chauvinistic patriarchal religious language in the bible and prayer-books which refers to them in the generic terms of "man," and "mankind." These terms could easily be inclusively translated as "men" and "women" or "humanity." Most women are proud of being women and they constitute the majority of the Christians attending the Church services on most occasions. Therefore, they should not be alienated from the Church which they love and diligently serve more than their male counterparts. Women should feel at home in their Church as their own redemptive community and meaningful holy space in which to encounter God in prayer, worship and fellowship with God's people.

*The NCCC Inclusive Language Lectionary* was meant to redress and facilitate the inclusion of women in the Church and remove the evil and religious linguistic abuse and exclusion of women from the scriptural readings and the liturgy. As expected many conservative Christians of both genders have opposed the proposed inclusive language within their churches. It poses a great challenge and threat to the security of the old sexist and racist religious language they are familiar with. Some of them consider it the holy language of God. Some of these people have anthropomorphically used it to identify God as "Father," and "King" as an ontological divine reality.

Some of them have mental images of a White God who looks like a strong, long bearded, stern and graying muscular Whiteman. The Greek myths of Zeus, Santa, and Michelangelo's depiction of the creation in the Vatican's Cystine Chapel have become the main Western sources of these popular traditional anthropomorphic mental images for God within Christianity. Obviously, these mental images for God constitute idolatry in as much as those who create and hold them, insist that they definitive are descriptions or real mental photographs of God.

Therefore, for these kinds of people, changing the familiar religious images and language for either the Scripture or the liturgy is negatively viewed as tantamount to the destruction of their own religion, God and religious security which had been built on these idols! They lack the necessary faith to believe in the reliable, salvific power of the incomprehensible, transcendent and infinite God who abides within the cosmic mystery, and has chosen to reveal himself or herself through the human imperfection and the cosmic historical process by means of the Divine Incarnation of the *Logos* of God into a real human being, Jesus the Christ.

In this respect, the fear of life and its constant evolutionary processes which make changes inevitable as part of life itself, amounts to the sin of faithlessness in God's providence. God has out of unconditional love and unmerited free grace ordained natural law and the processes of cosmic, evolutionary, and creative activity to bring the cosmos, order and life into being on the Earth. Through these processes and providence, God is ever actively engaged in the supernatural activities of creation, sustenance, and renewing creation as new things are created, including the human beings and their cultures, religions and languages.

God's ongoing activities creation and redemption exist within the constant evolutionary and changing processes of birth, growth, decline, death and recyclement into new and improved spirit or mind for rebirth to life again. Languages also undergo this same processes. The ancient Egyptian heliographics have been replaced with computer programming codes and conventional symbols which differ greatly, yet retain some similarities, especially, in the case of road signs and menus in some restaurants where pictures accompany the menu being described. Many people order according to the pictures rather than the words describing the meal depicted in the picture. Similarly, when driving, the pictures on the road signs are more important and easily understood than the words that accompany them, if any.

The proverb that a picture is worth a 1,000 words may be true for the ancient Egyptians as it is for most of us today. In some cases, the picture cannot be replaced by words. The picture of my childhood or parents' wedding or that of my own children cannot be adequately replaced by any number of words. The nonverbal language is sometimes more expressive and cannot be formulated adequately into language. This includes the kiss from a lover or making love. No language or poetry can adequately capture it and express if fully and as perfectly as the actual event itself.

As it was clearly taught by Moses, Buddha, Jesus and Prophet Muhammad the human divine experience of the encounter with God is divinizing. This truth is also attested to by the saints. All these saints and prophets positively affirm that their experience of God also consists of their mystical fellowship and spiritual union with God as part of this divine encounter. It cannot be adequately expressed in words.

Hymns, poetry, myths, stories, music and dance come very close to the reality of the experience, but also fail communicate it fully. That leaves each person to be inspired to experience for himself or herself that religious and spiritual truth and experience that is within reach, but, yet almost defies full expression and communication in language. As a result, many saints and sages remain silent, not just to pray and listen to God speak to them, but also because they find words inadequate to express their own encounter and experiences with God.

Silence as God's language, and that of that wise saints and noise as the language of sinners was instrumental in the popularity of monastic life, especially in the medieval era. Monasteries and convents have survived as testimonials for this powerful religious tradition. The New Age with the culture of urban and electronic noise has to relearn to find God and joy in silence, including the silent retreats into the quiets parks, churches, convents, monasteries, camping grounds, wilderness, mountains, deserts, beach, lake and river banks. This discovery will bring healing to the body, soul or spirit and mind which are constantly bombarded by harsh urban noises. A lot of stress and diseases are caused by this cacophony and noise pollution and the impersonal life within the overcrowded noisy and dirty metropolitan cities.

## 6. The Problem of Patriarchal Religious Language, Myths and Symbolism: A Summary

All human languages and cultures are imperfect creations of human beings. Likewise, the scriptures as sacred books are not the perfect and inerrant creations of God, as some misguided religious leaders have both falsely and fraudulently proclaimed to the world. On the contrary, like human language, religion and culture, the holy scriptures, their religious language and subjective truths are all relative and human creations in the name of God. The leaders erroneously and falsely communicate to the ignorant believers that they are God's directly revealed, inerrant, infallible, universal, absolute and immutable divine, redemptive revelation.

Islam, which proclaims the holy Qur'an to be a direct, perfect dictation of God from a permanent record of God's Scriptures in heaven supposedly carved in stone tablets, is one extreme example. The Evangelical Protestants, with their infamous doctrines of the "verbal inspiration of the Bible," "inerrancy" and "infallibility" of the Bible in "matters of faith and morals," is another example.

The Roman Catholics correctly insist that the holy scriptures are the product of the Ecclesial Community. They claim that they are part of the Church's oral tradition which was written down by inspired Christians and canonized as scripture by the Church's leaders (bishops) sitting in ecumenical councils. The Catholics thus have the best position on this matter. As a result, for the Catholic Church, scriptures are part of the Church living and changing tradition.

The infallibility is placed in the Church and symbolically in the Pope as the visible head of the Church. The Church, or the Pope speaking officially on behalf of the Church (*extra cathedra*) in sermons, proclamations and encyclicals which define the official Church's teachings on *matters of faith and morals*, is supposed to be inspired by God and infallible. The keys of St. Peter are also invoked to make the teaching conform with the teachings of Christ (cf. Matt. 16:17-19).

The religious principle of "infallibility" is a theological and religious quest for certainty in the midst of pluralism, uncertainty and confusion or competing opposite claims to divine truth. It is also a search for the possession of God's definitive and redemptive revelation. The Protestants affirm that this need for truth and certainty is met through the study of the holy Scriptures as God's infallible and inerrant revelation. The Roman Catholics disagree and place their infallible moral authority and need in the Pope as Head of the Apostolic Church. The Pope as the successor of St. Peter and Jesus Christ is positively affirmed to be the living mediator of God's ongoing revelation, grace and redemption in the world. The Catholic Church affirms that the Pope is "the Vicar of Christ on Earth." That is, the Pope is the visible moral, spiritual, ecclesiastical Representative of Christ, and the efficacious temporal link between Jesus Christ and God in heaven and the sinful mortals on the Earth.

The chain of mediation of God's grace, forgiveness and beatitude is long. It goes from God to Christ, then from Christ to the Pope as the successor of Peter, from the Pope to the bishops as the successors of the Apostles, from the bishops to the priests and deacons, and finally, from the priests and deacons to the lay people. The saints, particularly the blessed Virgin Mary (*Theotokos*), also find some linkage within this Catholic chain of mediators! Within the Protestant doctrine of religious egalitarianism and universal priesthood of all believers, the Bible is considered infallible. But without a hierarchy to interpret it, the infallible Bible being antiquated in language and imagery, leaves the Protestants in confusion and divided on the real nature and message of the scriptures.

Within Protestantism and ecclesiastical chaos and division, each individual believer becomes a Pope to himself or herself, and declares that his or her version of understanding the Bible is definitively true and other people are wrong! As a result of the lack of a central power to interpret the Bible and declare the truth regarding faith and morals, as the Pope does for the Roman Catholic Church, there is great diversity of conflicting theological and biblical views. They have led to a familiar phenomenon of endless divisions and the proliferation of Protestant denominations. The Protestants and Catholics should learn from one another what is good and what works well, and then share those elements.

Ultimately, the Church has the correct theological view of the scriptures and the relationship between the Church and the scriptures. The Catholic Church correctly affirms that the Church is the inspired writer and interpreter of holy scriptures, and that the Church also has the religious and moral duty to translate the scriptures and reinterpret them to meet today's moral and spiritual needs.

Apart from these scriptures or sacred texts of the Religious Community or the Church, there are no other scriptures. This is true for all religions, particularly Christianity, Judaism and Islam. Unfortunately, these religions have mistakenly sealed their religious canons of holy scriptures as if God has stopped speaking and sending his holy prophets and messiahs into the world with new revelations and relevant messages for today's world, sins and problems. African and other religions which have open living scriptures and religious traditions are able to become more flexible in their adaptation to today's world and changing needs!

The human language itself is a creation of the ever evolving, changing human beings, and thus, it cannot be perfect enough to become divine, immutable or static. Indeed, the human being, along with the rest of God's creation, is still undergoing this evolutionary process, change and transformation. Therefore, the human institutions must keep undergoing corresponding changes at the same speed at which the human beings change. As such, these institutions can remain essential, meaningful, and helpful to the versatile human being in his or her endless search for knowledge, meaning, fulfillment and happiness.

Consequently, if any of the human institutions resists change and remain retarded in matters of change, growth and development, they will subsequently get discarded as meaningless historical relics to be thrown away on the trash heap of fossilized history. Religions, philosophies, theologies and languages are no exception to this principle. Any genuine religious attempts at self-examination, self-reformation, and redirection in faith, prayer, study and guidance of God's redemptive Spirit of Truth, revelation, creativity, and divine renewal, should be encouraged by all those who love God. These are people whose faith in God is strong and mature enough to believe that our Creator God is still creating new things today, and that this Redemptive Creator God is also the God of Change, residing right at the heart of turbulence so as to call creative order right in the midst of chaos. Our God is the God of Babel (Diversity) as well the God of the Pentecost (Unity)!

In the new redemptive and unitive spirit of the Pentecost, let Christians welcome the noble efforts of those who are trying to make sure that God's holy Word will be heard in their own language! This is the message of the divine Incarnation, the meaning of the Pentecost. It is also the meaning and motivation of all scriptural translations, including the new NCCC Inclusive Language Lectionary and the new ventures in Bible and liturgical revisions. These all serve to bring about inclusiveness in theological and liturgical materials and practices.

Inclusive theological language and imagery is essential because all human beings are created by God and in God's own image. This is regardless of gender, skin-color, race and nationality. Therefore, God should not be portrayed in sexist terms as exclusively male or in racist terms as White. Equating holiness with white while equating evil with black, dark, or female is wrong. For instance, Eve, evil, or devil sound too much alike to be mere coincidences. This is especially when one takes Genesis and Paul's anti-feminist theology into account.

The new NCCC Lectionary is not perfect in its translation, new references, and metaphors for God, but it represents a noble venture of making the Christian faith relevant and meaningful to female members of the Church, who constitute the bulk of its membership. This Lectiona ry translation is therefore a very timely prophetic, religious and social venture in faith. It is a witness to the continued presence of the Holy Spirit, which Jesus promised would guide the Church into further truths.

The main moral problem in every age is whether people will hear God's new revelation and truth and obey, or kill God's prophets, just like God's rebellious people have often done in the past! God's incarnation in Jesus as the Christ and his redemptive Gospel truth are ever globally true and relevant in every era and culture, *only if they become reincarnated* and expressed in that respective local culture, language and world-view. This is essential if they are to be heard in the contemporary language, symbolism, imagery and culture of the people of that society and that era. This is the ultimate meaning of the divine incarnation both during the time of Jesus and for each cultural and linguistic group of people today.

Our society today and new age is that of postmodernist human equality, democracy, global inclusiveness, internationality or borderless (seamless), instant, electronic cyberspace information, and "virtual interactive communities." It is noteworthy that within this postmodern era, the traditional barriers of nationality, gender, race, age, class, color and physical disability are completely transcended. God has to speak to us in our own language of evolution in the biological sciences and technology.

The cyberspace technology and the Information Age have enabled us to create new mutual openness, acceptance and inclusiveness within this new global electronic community. Subsequently, the Church and other Religious Communities need to create and formulate a new, inclusive, meaningful, contemporary theological language and metaphor, in order to be able to communicate more meaningfully the eternal, timeless truths to the people of our era. New Age enthusiasts may have the solution. The feminists do not lead there, in as much as they are content to become reactionaries to White-male sexist theologies and male oriented religious language, symbols and metaphors in mainline traditional religious scriptures, the liturgy, sermons and worship.

Therefore, we need a reformation of the traditional theology and the Church in order to create a gender and racial inclusive religious language, nonracist and non-sexist Church in leadership, doctrine and liturgy. That requires a religious reformation or revolution from within the religious establishment! The Catholic Church needs a Vatican III. The Church needs a new era of the new inclusive religious language, symbolism, metaphor and Church practice. Christians also need a new revolutionary inclusive translation of the Bible. This new Bible should include the exorcism of the traditional Hebrew myths of disobedience and the divine curse on all humanity due to the mythological moral failure of Adam and Eve as historical people. Genesis 2-11 should be cut out of the new Bible and be printed in the Apocrypha. These texts should not be used as valid divine revelation on which to build Christian doctrines, ecclesiology and ethics. These texts and stories have been misunderstood and misused to develop an oppressive system of sexism, an exclusionary theology and practices which have victimized women. Women are not "Eves" any more than men are "Adams." Both males and females are created in God's own image. They compliment each other in their various roles and biological diversity.

The derogatory Deutro-Pauline material about the inferiority and subordination of women to men as God's will in matters of Church and State should also be exorcised from holy scriptures (1 Cor. 14:34-40; Eph. 5-6). This passage also condones the ancient practice of slavery as God's will! Obviously, to this ideal democratic and inclusive future, traditional religious values are barriers. They are like chains which seek to keep God's people in the bondage of male chauvinism, patriarchal power, and exclusion of women from important positions of leadership both in Church and State. To this noble end, Protestant Christians should not look to the antiquated religious language and male-chauvinistic symbols of the scriptures in the traditionally popular King James Bible. This version of the scriptures is notorious for its exclusive male chauvinistic and patriarchal language in reference to God and people as if women were either not God's people or supposed to read the Bible.

The ancient religious and theological language of the neo-Platonic, Patristic theological formulations, political, theological language of the Nicene and the Apostles' creeds, is outdated, meaningless and confusing for the Christians today. Bishop Spong is correct to demand that these patriarchal forms of religious language and Christian doctrines should be promptly revised or discarded. They are inadequate to speak about God, humanity, Christ, sin, redemption and the Church.

In theological terms and religious actuality, both the Apostles Creed and Nicene Creed can be objectively judged to be antiquated, blind and worthless misleading guides for theology, Christian faith and orthodoxy today! They may have been adequate guardians of the orthodox doctrines two thousand years ago. However, today the Church needs a contemporary reformulation of the same divine mysteries, grace and redemption by God. The Church must employ today's world-view, anthropology and modern scientific information in order to reformulate its essence, mission and doctrines.

The much cherished creeds were relevant and meaningful for that pre-scientific era and the neo-Platonic world-view that prevailed at that time. Unfortunately, after two thousand years of evolutionary Christian history and theology, these ancient Greek philosophy-based creeds and formulations of Christianity have largely become meaningless, religious relics of the past. They are outdated in their theological and philosophical definitions God, Jesus, life and Church, as well as the formulations of the universal orthodox Christianity and essential Christian doctrines.

Therefore, if we do not make religion and its theological language meaningful to our era, the modern, scientifically minded and secular generation may either reject religion as meaningless, antiquated superstition and mythology, or dismiss it as mere cultic social drama and entertainment. Consequently, we must keep up the search for new and better religious inclusive language, expressions, metaphor, imagery, analogies and theological formulations. However, this human religious, finite venture has to be undertaken in humility, courage and prayer for God's guidance.

To this end, the *NCCC Inclusive Lectionary* and the United Methodist Church's new inclusive hymnal are good theological, religious, and prophetic examples. They challenge and witness to God's ever present Holy Spirit, working tirelessly to inspire God's Word of Salvation, meaning and fulfillment in our own day. The United Methodist Church has set for us an ideal example to follow by providing us with a truly inclusive religious language which removes military, chauvinistic, sexist and racial linguistic expressions and metaphor from our hymnals, liturgical language, Lectionary and prayers.

Ultimately, God is a Cosmic Creative and Redemptive Spirit without gender or color. God is not a "White male or patriarch." Conversely, evil and sin or the Devil is not a "Black male" or woman (or black being/thing). These kinds of destructive, evil, racist and sexist language and symbolism has no place in God's true holy and inclusive Church or its wholesome theology. Meaningful religious and theological language must also become truly inclusive, to be like God.

New inclusive Christian moral theories and religious doctrines be formulated in a non-sexist and non-racist religious language. It is also liturgically appropriate since God is Spirit with neither gender nor color. Likewise, God's inclusive Church must become androgynous or gender inclusive in its language, theology and symbols for God. God's redemptive, and catholic (universal) Church must become open and inclusive of all people of all races, colors, cultures, languages, genders, classes, ideologies, ages and different levels of socioeconomic development.

To this end, the Church and its members must remain humble and repentant. The Church must seek justice, protect the weak, serve the poor as part of mission and praxis of Agape. The Church must become the voice of the voiceless and the conscience of the wealthy and powerful people in the world in order to persuade them to share their God-given wealth with God's poor and the needy people in the world. The people, Church and the nations must confess their sins and failure to love:

> Most merciful God, we confess that we have sinned against you in thought, word and deed by what we have done and left undone. We have not loved you with our whole heart; we have not loved our neighbors as ourselves. We are truly sorry and we humbly repent. For the sake of your Son Jesus Christ, have mercy on us and forgive us; that we may delight in your will, and walk in your ways, to the glory of your Name. Amen
> *(The Episcopal Church's Book of Common Prayer, 360).*

# Chapter 13

---

# Good Education and Sound Ethics: Knowledge, Virtue and Happiness

A "good life" of happiness is found in an existential state of peace, contentedness, satisfaction and fulfillment. This is a heavenly state of mind and concrete existence made possible by God's grace within this seemingly ordinary world. It is God's supernatural gift and reward to his or her obedient, just and loving people. It is a correlative joint result of human obedience and cooperation with God's free universal redemptive grace working everywhere in the world through sound moral education, good citizenship within a caring, just, peaceful and happy moral community.

## 1. Good Education, Religion, and Ethics: A Threefold Path to God, Virtue, Good Life and Happiness

In all the major world's "civilized" human societies, human beings and the community have valued redemptive religions, sound moral values and good education. This is because these institutions have promoted correct knowledge, moral and civic virtue, and enhanced personal, spiritual, social, societal well-being and peace. These essential human institutions also confer the necessary moral and social skills on how to live the good, moral, spiritual, satisfying peaceful and happy life within the community and the world.

Subsequently, in these societies, religion, moral law and education were positively viewed as the inseparable triple pillars of any well organized moral community, happy and enduring society or nation. These institutions were considered the essential divine media, as well as the societal conventional means for God's indirect method for effective communication of God's will and revelation for sound values for the good life, knowledge, truth, peace and happiness.

Happiness and peace are the goals of the spiritually and morally mature, intelligent, and free wise creatures or moral agents, such as the human beings. However, according to most major religions, the true and lasting peace and happiness can only be found in God. This is relationship characterized by a loving and harmonious fellowship with God, obedience and in living a peaceful life of virtue, unconditional love, justice and nonviolence on the Earth as God's Kingdom.

Accordingly, Buddhism affirms that everlasting peace and happiness are to be found in union with God or *Nirvana*. But a more relative form of peace and happiness can also be obtained by living a life consistent with moral and spiritual virtues based on the following six perfections: (1) *Charity (2) Self-discipline (3) Patience (4) Right and consistent Effort (5) Calmness [courage and nonviolence in face of adversity] (6) Wisdom*. These are excellent attributes of a saint in any moral or religious tradition, irrespective of the religion's name and exclusive truth and dogmatic soteriological claims of that tradition.

There are many paths to God, virtue, a good life and happiness. These paths include education, religion or piety and ethics. A good life is that which is virtuous, successful, productive, social, loving, peaceful, and a happy life is both the explicit and implicit goal and objective of any good and sound liberal arts and theocentric education.

This noble, ethical objective and humanistic quest of the good and happy life is, to some explicit and implicit degree, a quest for God and salvation. This is mainly due to the human existential reality, namely that any truly virtuous, successful, loving, and harmonious or peaceful and happy life is what we mean by a redeemed mode of human life and "authentic human existence." This social and moral ideal peaceful mode of human life in the world is coextensive with both supernatural salvation and God's Kingdom.

Within this theocentric system of education, salvation or sound moral values and peaceful human coexistence with each other and the rest of creation, is the ideal goal of a good education. This is as opposed to the secular forms of education, whose primary objectives are merely the acquisition of scientific knowledge and technological skills. However, secular education should not be rejected. It confers good and useful skills that are used as essential tools for the efficient and profitable exploitation of nature so as to extract natural resources and get rich, or to get rich by providing technical services to industries and other groups. Technical and scientific knowledge must be included in good theocentric education. It must be treated as a good tool to enhance the quality of human life and to unlock God's mysteries in creation or nature as God's universal revelation.

These skills were also employed in the production of wealth and building of projects, such as the great pyramids of Egypt, temples, erection of obelisks, great cathedrals, and the like. The integration of religion and science in both education and life as a whole is best illustrated by the ancient Egyptian society. Science and technology were employed in the service of God, humanity, and nature. This is self-evident in the building of elaborate temples, great pyramids and irrigation canals in the name of God, life and religion.

With the possession of skills and knowledge of both advanced science and technology, the human being was able to become a more efficient representative of God in the world and custodian of creation by sound education in sciences and technology. Within a sound theocentric system of education, there is no separation of religion from science. As such, evolution is correctly viewed as God's method for the intertwined and inseparable divine twin processes of natural and supernatural (special) cosmic creation. Science is a significant tool for religion to be effectively employed in the study of God's cosmic creation and wonders in creation, sustenance, and redemption. Physics, astrology, and astronomy are examples of how these subjects have been central in religious discourse about nature, its ultimate origins and destiny.

Both religion and education have served as the society's most explicit, purposeful, and carefully designed or structured, formal, and orderly transmission of positive moral values. These essential social and moral values are prerequisites for producing civilized, virtuous, morally responsible, peaceful, harmonious, productive, and happy citizens and communities. As a result, all ancient and Medieval forms of education were essentially religiously based.

These systems of education were, to some high degree, similar to traditional African, Native American and Oriental systems of education in terms of being holistic, theocentric, and aimed at both sound moral values as a way of life and the attainment of God's approval, salvation, and eternal happiness. The ancient Egyptian, Babylonian, Chinese, and later, Hebrew theocracies, religion, education and government are the best illustrations of these theocentric systems of education. The Roman and Greek systems, which came later, were revisions and innovations in education and ideas which were based on these ancient theocentric systems in education, philosophy, science, ethics, and religious foundations.

In this respect, education through school, the academy or university, was religious education since these institutions were formal religious extensions and instruments of the Church and its divine redemptive mission in the world. They were the official institutional means of evangelism, missionary activity, and instruction in the religious faith and moral values that are based on religious sacred books or the special revelation in the scriptures and God's natural revelation in nature or the cosmos. As such, natural sciences were taught as part of God's redemptive self-communication in creation, sustenance of creation, and evolutionary positive moral transformation of human beings as free moral agents who are capable of both choosing to do good or evil.

Evil was and is still considered to be a result of any imperfect or negative choice and the correlative imperfect action which is made in ignorance or greed and self-centeredness. Instead of looking to God as the true source and measure of true goodness, evil thus results from choosing or performing the lesser good action, as opposed to the higher good, loving, altruistic, and more beneficial deeds. Evil deeds are due to ignorance of the good or rebellion against God's goodness, unconditional love, grace, truth, and justice.

Within this understanding, evil is as both Augustine and Aquinas correctly defined it as the "corruption of the good" or "defect in the good" and "a deprivation of goodness." In that case, sound education means teaching people to recognize the good and to aim at choosing the best alternative and doing the best that can be done in any moral or social context. This moral principle helps the moral agents to minimize evil in the world by choosing the best possible alternative in any given situation.

The moral principle of choosing the best alternative in any situation, based on agape, justice, and the best ideal outcome, includes what has been described as "situation ethics." It maximizes goodness in the world. As such, it is God's concrete means of effecting his activities of free grace, redemption, and salvation from evil in this cosmic, evolutionary and ever-changing world. To this end, the obedient moral agent requires the possession of correct knowledge and truth.

Correct information as knowledge and truth are required in order for the thinking moral agent to be able to recognize good from evil choices and to predict the positive or negative consequences of their choices. In this manner, the moral agent as a free causal being is able to choose the best course of action and implement it. In utilitarian terms, the best course of action is that which causes maximum good and brings maximum happiness to the self, the neighbor, and the maximum number of people in the community. This moral action stemming from the previously learned, accepted and internalized positive values is the ideal moral state for any mature and responsible moral agent. This is ethical principle known as "*teleological ethics*" as opposed to "*deontological ethics*" which is a system that governs the less mature and responsible moral agents based on external moral authority and fear of punishment for violation of the moral codes. The fear of God, hell and jail are examples of how deontological systems of the ethics are enforced.

In contrast to the internal moral principle of "*teleological ethics*," where the free moral agent is the best judge of what is good, just, right, and loving to be done in the given situation, "*deontological ethics*" is based on the principle of following the "external moral." The external moral authority and definitive reference for moral action includes: God, the Church's dogmas, the Pope, the scriptures (Torah, Bible, Qur'an and Veda), the Ten Commandments, the state laws, *Shari'a* (Islamic Law), constitutions, professional codes, and peers and parents' regulations.

Failure to follow the laws or moral codes set by a serious moral authority leads to direct punishment by the cosmic Eternal Moral Authority or God. The African Traditional Religionists, the Roman Catholic Church, Evangelical Protestants, Muslims, and Orthodox Jews are examples of deontological ethics. Their moral values and actions are governed by dogmas, scriptures, God's commandments, and the fear of God. The doctrines of God's eschatological (final) judgement and the punishment of sinners in the hellfire are a logical extension of deontological ethics, where God is the ultimate moral giver, enforcer or police, King, cosmic judge, and disciplinarian or "punisher!"

In deontological ethics, a few people do good because it is the right thing to do, by virtue of being good, just and loving or for the love of heaven! Most people do good because they fear punishment! This is a negative motivation or intention for doing good. As a result, Immanuel Kant was led to the affirmation that a moral act should be judged on the basis of its intention as well as its outcome.

According to Kant, all moral and true good deeds must be rooted in the obligation of love (agape), duty and justice. Like Jesus, Kant, strongly affirmed that the true virtues of duty and justice are rooted in the moral imperative of unconditional love for the neighbor. This is as opposed to being rooted in greed, pride, or fear of punishment by God or another moral authority that is locally acting in the world on God's behalf. Kant based his ethics and moral teachings on the imperative commandment of Agape. Jesus Christ commanded his followers to love and serve the neighbor out of unconditional love and free forgiveness of sins.

All forms of education were essentially religious and theological in both objective and content. As a result, in the Middle Ages, Thomas Aquinas could validly declare that "theology was the queen of the sciences." There is no conflict between science and religion since they complement each other in their quest for knowledge, truth, and the secrets of life and how to live a good and satisfying life in the world.

Ultimately, both theocentric education and true religion are inseparably bound and completely intertwined in nature, fundamental objectives, and essential societal functions. Both education and religion serve the same fundamental moral and societal functions. Both institutions enhance the "*summum bonum*" (the highest good). That is, they served as the moral and spiritual true path to God, fellowship, and union with God. The state of the good life or "*summum bonum*" is coextensive with the human life that is faithfully lived according to positive faith, optimistic openness to God's goodness in life, wonder, beauty, meaningfulness of life, and delight in the joys and mysteries of creation.

Ultimately, the good, satisfying, meaningful, and redeemed life is correlative with God's Kingdom (Reign) in the world. It is coextensive with concrete life that which is lived in positive faith, unconditional love, and obedience to God's will. This is a saintly or good life characterized by: correct knowledge, truth, goodness, virtue, contentedness, peace, harmony, tolerance, wisdom, agape, patience, justice, nonviolence, compassion, forgiveness, moral and spiritual perfection, divine salvation and eternal happiness! Buddha, Socrates, Jesus, Gandhi, King, Julius Nyerere, Nelson Mandela, Mikhail Gorbachev, Archbishop Tutu of South Africa, Archbishop Janani Luwum of Uganda, Archbishop Oscar Romero of El Salvador, and Mother Teresa are some examples of this positive, loving, social and morally responsible mode of human life.

## 2. God and Religion as Universal Contexts For Sound Education and Values

Sound, redemptive, relevant and meaningful religion is inclusive of all disciplines of natural and social sciences, philosophy, especially ethics and "metaphysics" as tools for the study of God's revelation in nature and the scriptures. Natural law is God's moral law that functioned impartially and the same in all the universe and in all societies.

The natural sciences, especially physics, are part of true theology in that they uncover nature and correctly reveal God's intricate mysteries of cosmic creation and order. Mathematics, especially geometry, reveals the perfection of God's mind and principles for God's design of the immense and orderly cosmos and its galaxies and planetary systems. Orbits of planets follow precise laws, and gravity balances the systems in such a way that they rarely collapse upon themselves. Copernicus, Tycho Brahe, Johannas Kepler, and Galilee Galileo are some of the Christian mathematicians and astronomers who described the glory of God in scientific and mathematical terms going beyond the Psalmists who sang their own glory of God's greatness in cosmic creation both in poetry and song.

Among the Ancient Egyptians (*Kemites*), Hebrews, Ancient Greeks, and later, the Christians and Muslims, formal education was moral, religious and both theocentric and holistic. The main goal and objective was to impart the necessary correct "secret" or "privileged knowledge" as keys which were required to open the mysteries of life and attain the necessary moral virtues and social, interpersonal, and technical skills on *how to live a virtuous and "good life."* As a result, the Hebrew Psalmist attributes human moral evil and corruption to ignorance, foolishness, and disbelief in God. He writes:

> The fool in his [or her] heart:
> "There is no God!"
> They are corrupt.
> They do abominable deeds.
> There is none among them
> That does good.
>
> God looks down from heaven
> upon the children of men,
> to see if there is any
> that acts wisely,
> and seeks after God.

They [the fools] have all gone astray.
They are all alike, corrupt.
There is none that does good.
No, not one [among the fools].

Have they no knowledge,
all these evildoer?
They eat up my people,
like people eat bread.
They do not call upon the Lord.

The fools will be in great terror
because God is on the side of
the righteous people.
They will try to confound the
plans of the poor.
But God is their refuge.
(Psalm 14:1-5)

Without exception, the good life was identified as the mode of life which was approved by God. That is one of the reasons why atheism was not accepted by the Greeks who condemned Socrates to death. They charged him with the moral corruption of the young by discrediting traditional Greek doctrines of the gods which were the basis of Greek religion, ethics and civic virtues.

As in present day America, the ancient people associated the good life and sound moral values to be those approved by God. The good life could not be atheistic. It was considered to be a life of faith in God. It was a life of obedience to God which was lived in pure goodness, altruism, love, peace, contentedness, and peace with oneself, the neighbor, creation, and God. As such, all sound education had a moral and ethical primary objective. Its implicit and explicit or intrinsic noble end was the full attainment of sound knowledge, truth, and skills of how to do good works and live in harmony, peace, happiness in the fellowship of God and fellow human beings.

In other words, education was pursued as a religious quest for God, goodness, truth, and supernatural salvation. In this respect, ancient systems of education, science, philosophy, and ethics were theocentric (God-centered) and religious in origin, expression, and ends. Education, science, ethics, and philosophy were part of the human religious quest for "the good life and supernatural salvation," to the extent that they were inseparable from religion and ethics.

Like religion, this mode of theocentric education was the primary means to gain the necessary knowledge of God, sound moral values, theocentric humane civic virtues of love, justice, and ethical skills, virtues, and social ethics of how to live a peaceful and happy productive life on Earth as God's Kingdom or theocracy. To this end, the happy life was perceived to be a divine quality achieved by living virtuously, according to the knowledge of goodness, justice, truth, correct knowledge, compassion, and love, just like God.

Hegel's evolution of knowledge, mind, spirit, and God-consciousness which is coextensive with moral consciousness, virtue, compassion, justice, and nonviolence, is a good example of how education, knowledge, and truth are associated with God-consciousness, religion, ethics, and virtue. Socrates himself had declared that "knowledge was virtue" and that vice was due to ignorance of the good.

According to Socrates, Plato, Aristotle, Buddha, and Jesus, human ignorance, and not sin or the imaginary "Devil" or mythological "original sin," was the real cause of human moral evil. As such, moral evil and vice could be effectively cured and removed from society if true and correct knowledge or reality and truth became known by the human being. For instance, greed for material gain and profit is based on the false assumption and illusion that wealth is the source of happiness, instead of the fellowship and union with God, who is the ultimate source of wealth and embodiment of true love and eternal happiness.

Accordingly, Jesus taught his disciples and the unsophisticated masses about God's essence and infinite mysteries of unconditional love, unmerited redemptive grace and free forgiveness of sins for all penitent sinners. He was convinced that the attainment of the knowledge of the truth was necessary for the spiritual and mental liberation of men and women. Following the example of Jesus, Christians have built schools and universities to teach correct knowledge and impart God's truth. This leads to the true human liberation through faith and repentance of sin and moral evil, and the decision to lead a new mode of transformed and supernal life at a higher level of union with God through faith and love. This further leads to a just, loving, nonviolent, and humane life, which is in accordance with God's will, moral laws, justice, and agape.

## 3. Education, Class, and Moral Values

Traditionally, education was a privilege of the aristocratic class or the ruling elite, the rich, and the clergy. In the past, almost all formal education, with the exception of the military and specialized business or technical training and apprenticeship, was provided by the Church or religious community.

In the past, the clergy, particularly the Catholic priests, monks, and nuns, were the teachers, professors, and scientists. The present day academic dress in gowns, caps, and hoods goes back to this era of the clergy or priests as the professors of knowledge and its teachers to the lay initiates and the catechumen. The university academy and training of the clergy also went hand in hand.

Until the twentieth century, almost all universities in the world were Church founded, supported, and operated. Only the clergy and lay Christians of that denomination held administrative and key faculty teaching positions. The departments of religion and philosophy were the centers of the university curriculum. Every student had to take one or two compulsory courses in religion, ethics, and logic. The languages were important, and the natural sciences came next in importance. Some good American universities and colleges, such as Harvard, Yale, Princeton, William and Mary, Kenyon, Ohio Wesleyan, Pontifical College, Notre Dame, Catholic University of America, Duke, Vanderbilt, Emory and the University of the South were started by religious bodies based on denominational lines and traditional religious rivalry.

By essential nature and deliberate curricular design, most of this education was religious, moral, and confessional. The primary educational mission was to produce a virtuous Christian and productive citizen. This mission was important and unopposed, since there was not yet, any alternative secular or "humanistic education" whose primary function and mission was not to foster moral values, instead of knowledge and technical skills.

The noble religious and moral educational general objectives and mission of these Church founded schools, colleges and universities were to provide the necessary moral and spiritual or civic training, technical skills and knowledge needed for the graduate to become a good, morally responsible and productive citizen in the community, Church and nation. This morally educated person would be able to recognize the good and live the good and satisfying, happy life. This is in line with Socrates, the famous philosopher, made it most plain to his generation and era that the greatest evil which threatened the well being, peace, and happiness of the nation and the world was *ignorance*.

Therefore, it is noteworthy that the Church's redemptive mission in the world has, indeed, correctly incorporated the provision of education as a fundamental tool to fight the evils of ignorance, vice, crime, poverty, bigotry, injustice and both racial and cultural intolerance in society. The racial integration of schools has been part of this moral crusade against racial injustice, whitesupremacy and racism in the society. This is, particularly, true for the late 20th century United States and Southern Africa where there were still state laws that mandated racial segregation in public schools, accommodations and civic activities. Yet, the makers and enforcers of these evil laws were self-confessed Christians. Clearly, they lacked a good moral education.

Lack of good education and correct knowledge leads to ignorance. Ignorance of the truth and what is good and virtuous leads to vice and a negative mode of life, which is dominated by falsehood, violence, fear, prejudice, and superstition. The solution for this moral and spiritual problem was found in good education that taught the young as well as adults, the soldiers and political leaders, slaves and free people, Greeks and non-Greeks, and the religious and the superstitious (pagans) how to think critically and ethically.

Socrates did not claim to teach or have new, special knowledge which was not already available. His chief claim was that he taught people to think more analytically and critically about what they were previously taught as the truth and lived by as the right guides to correct moral behavior and happiness. By so doing, he said these people learned to discover what was true and what was false.

However, the Greeks were not alone in this quest for correct knowledge, virtue, and a good moral life and happiness. Indeed, the Egyptians and the Hebrews had been engaged in this pursuit for hundreds of years and had written quite a lot on this subject. This had occurred before the Greeks themselves had even become civilized or had organized themselves into viable city states, which enabled the luxury of philosophy, performing arts, democracy, and the rule of the law to flourish.

Furthermore, the ancient major Greek philosophers, such as Socrates, Plato, and Aristotle, were persecuted for teaching controversial foreign doctrines. They were forced to flee Greece, with the exception of Socrates, who refused to escape and was subsequently executed for his controversial religious, ethical, and philosophical teachings. Therefore, it makes good sense to trace these new philosophical teachings from

Egypt in Africa with which they were in close political, cultural, and economic contact.

In fact, Aristotle later moved his own academy to Alexandria in Egypt in Africa, where there was an already flourishing Egyptian research university and a large library. The research library contained Egyptian scientific, philosophical, medical, and religious books, going back thousands of years of Egyptian civilization. These books had resulted in engineering feats, such the building of the great pyramids, erection of tall unsupported obelisks and networks of irrigation canals. Aristotle and his students both utilized and translated some of these ancient Egyptian books into Greek without proper credits to their original Egyptian authors.

As a result, many of these ancient Egyptian works have been erroneously attributed to their Greek translators as their original authors in the same way the biblical books of Mark, Matthew, Luke and John were erroneously attributed to the Apostles of the same names as their real authors. This is also the manner in which some people have erroneously attributed the first five books in the Hebrew Bible to Moses as their real authors, whereas, he only wrote the commandments and some of the moral expansion of these commandments.

In the era when copyright laws were absent, these translators wrote their names down and the books were later ascribed to them as the authors, rather than crediting them with the mere translation of the material into Greek. This worked in the same fashion in which Jerome translated the Hebrew scriptures and Greek New Testament into Latin. The translation is sometimes referred to as the *Jerome Bible* as well as *The Vulgate*. Likewise, some naive Christians erroneously believe that King James wrote the Bible which he authorized to be translated from the Hebrew, Greek, and Latin versions of the Bible.

Therefore, it is conceivable that Aristotle carried out a similar translation and revision, as part of his task of research carried out in the Egyptian manuscripts and books at the Alexandrian library. It is also possible that some of these translated Egyptian works and books were then mistakenly accredited to him as their real author. This does not mean that Aristotle had no great personal original research and writings of his own. His works *Nicomachean Ethics* and *On the Soul* are definitely his own. The notion that the human being is a composite of soul, body, and mind, which disintegrate at death and cause the permanent loss and extinction of the person, is neither African (Egyptian) nor Platonic. It is uniquely Hebrew! In this case, he may have borrowed it from the Greek speaking Jews who lived in Alexandria prior to his establishment of his academy there in 322 BCE.

Definitely, a careful examination shows that what has been credited to Greek philosophers included some African material. Failure to accept this glaring truth constitutes some unacceptable academic dishonesty, which Afrocentrism and Africanist studies have begun to point out, more to the displeasure of the traditional Eurocentric scholars. In today's academic standards, much of what Socrates and Aristotle taught without proper African credit for their sources would constitute some deliberate acts of academic dishonesty, and illegalities of plagiarism and copyright infringement.

However, there were no copyright laws then and we should not hold these philosophers to today's academic standards. Buddha, Moses, and Jesus themselves taught material which they got from other prophets and books. Most often, they never cited their sources.

In the case of Moses, he metaphorically cited God as the source of the Ten Commandments, even though these were summarized from Egyptian and Babylonian sources! Is this an academic and religious form of dishonesty? Some naive people mistakenly, literally believe that God physically wrote the Ten Commandments because Moses said so! It never occurs to these literalists that God as pure Spirit has no literal hands by which he could have written these Commandments. During the late 1960s filming of *The Ten Commandments*, the ingenious Hollywood solution to this anthropomorphism was to use a laser beam to write the Ten Commandments on the tablets of stone. However, for many young people that became the historical divine rendition of the Decalogue!

Nevertheless, we need to correct these kinds errors in scripture and Western scholarship by doing more careful research into the African and Mediterranean religions and philosophies from the time of Aken Aton to the present. We must correct previous errors or prejudiced omissions of data by giving proper credit to the ancient Egyptians (Africans) for the origination of monotheism, the law (Ten Commandments), philosophy, ethics, mathematics, and engineering skills which were the basis for the building of the huge pyramids without machinery and the cutting, curving, and erecting of the huge and tall obelisks without cranes and other modern mechanical devises for aid.

It is important that some Old Testament scholars are beginning to credit Egypt with a good portion of the material that is now found in the first five books of the Bible known as the Pentateuch or the Books of Moses (Torah). The Dead Sea Scrolls confirm the continuity of Egyptian or African Religion and the Old Testament. This is one of the main reasons why prejudiced Eurocentric scholars would prefer to begin writing sections on European civilizations with the Greek civilization, particularly, Socrates and Plato rather than beginning with Moses in Africa (Egypt) and the Hebrew Scriptures (the Old Testament).

Most of these scholars correctly view Moses and the Old Testament as predominantly African or Egyptian in both origin and content. For instance, the Africans still practice the customs described in the Old Testament, such as blaming women for the original sin and the downfall of humanity (Nnambi and Mumbi stories in East Africa). Circumcision as a religious initiation, animal and human sacrifice for atonement for sin, sacrificial altars, polygamy, patriarchy, male-priesthood, prophesy and visionaries. Tragedy, and misfortune are seen as God's punishment for human sin and rebellion or secret malice.

Until recently, education was always part of the Church, temples, and mosques, where the priests were the professing masters of divine knowledge and scientific and artistic, creative skills required for a wholistic and integrated, enlightened, virtuous life of knowledge of God and God's will. Consequently, one could thereby live the good life, which is the necessary prerequisite for true happiness that all human beings constantly crave and try to achieve in whatever they do, whether good or inadvertently evil. That is to assert that nobody does evil knowingly unless there is some form of perceived good to be derived from it, even if it may only be finite, limited, and short-lived.

This universal human quest for good education and knowledge as the means to the good life and happiness is also the human quest for divine eternal knowledge, virtue, supernatural salvation, and eternal bliss. This is true for Christianity, Judaism, and Islam, as well as Hinduism, Buddhism, and the African Traditional Religion. In other words, education, knowledge, and divine salvation have always been intertwined as correlative and coextensive temporal divine realities.

The evidence for this traditional, indissoluble, and correlative relationship between education and salvation is the fact that ancient universities were mere extensions of the clerical education and were also located on Church, temple, and mosque grounds. These religious places of worship also served as the very halls of knowledge and learning. They are the halls for lectures, ethical sermons, and centers of higher education directly under the expert, "professional" guidance of the clergy (priests and ministers) who were the privileged few "professors" of knowledge.

In most cases, the clergy were professors of knowledge and mysteries. They were "seminary" or "university" graduates. They had been the previous students of more famous masters in whose esoteric or mystical knowledge they had to be initiated by both ritual and obedient, disciplined study of the divine, revealed mysteries. They were carefully guided by the testimony, expertise, skill, knowledge, and religious or ethical codes of life and behavior, which were a necessary preconditions for initiation and subsequent education.

Egypt had such an elaborate system of education, which was duplicated in Judaism where the priests are the Rabbis (professors, teachers, and masters of knowledge), and in Christianity and Islam, where the clergy and the monks are the traditionally recognized teachers, lawyers, judges, healers, and counselors. In this respect, religious terms such as "deans," "professors," "masters," and "preceptor" have remained part of modern secular education.

In addition, most universities still begin their academic year with a religious service known as "Convocation Service" and end with a "Baccalaureate Service." Many universities, especially the private ones, are still expected to provide chapels, chaplaincies, and the academic departments of religious studies and philosophy.

The former popular conservative USA President Ronald Reagan and his conservative Republican right wing disliked the constitutional separation of Church and State. Subsequently, these conservatives constantly proposed the amendment of the USA Constitution in order to permit the religious practice of holding public prayers in state and other publicly funded schools, colleges and universities. Their main "religious feeling" and argument was that "God had been expelled from public schools when public prayer in public schools was outlawed" by the US courts.

Nevertheless, whether these people knew it or not, this was a request to return to the traditional university system of the pre-Enlightenment Era. It was also a return to pre-Rationalism which brought the split between religion and science, based on the new skepticism which regarded all knowledge as suspect myth unless it could be rationally proved or empirically verified with scientific experiments.

# 4. Need for Well-Integrated Education For Virtuous Life and Happiness

Virtue is a result of self-discipline based on sound knowledge and moral training in matters of truth, love, compassion and socioeconomic justice. Unlike the Western secular or public and fragmented systems of education, the Church or religiously based educational systems are traditionally theocentric, well-integrated and wholistic in their curricula. As a result, they have produced many graduates who are morally sound, responsible, productive citizens, good community and national leaders.

In contrast, the American public educational systems, have institutionalized the separation between Church and State and have rejected the teaching religious moral values and religion in the public schools. These public schools have promoted education as the attainment of knowledge and skills, have excluded values as part of education. This has been for fear of teaching religious values and violating the constitutional divide between Church and State, or offending someone who does not agree with the stated values or their basis. This position ignores the fact that human beings are by nature free moral agents.

Any sound, practical and useful system of education anywhere in the world has to include appropriate values of discussion of a sound moral judgement and its basis given certain conditions. For instance, a doctor should never be allowed to graduate or be licensed without taking a course in biomedical or professional ethics courses. The doctors' and nurses' training in biomedical or professional ethics courses should be rigorous, comprehensive and diverse in both content and scope.

The ethics courses must include extensive discussion of the following topics: informed consent, patient-doctor relations, racism, sexism, sexual harassment, incompetence, abortion, euthanasia, doctor-assisted suicide, environmental issues, poverty and malnutrition, teenage pregnancy, contraception, chemical and biological weapons, population control, greed, malpractice, cloning, gene-therapy, cosmetic surgery, organ transplants, confidentiality, triage, AIDS, equity, insurance and the uninsured patients, compassion, "*pro bono*" (free) community service, and the like, must all be discussed. The same material can be modified for other professionals, such as: attorneys, teachers, engineers, counselors and social workers.

Ultimately, there is no sound education that can be truly defined as "value-free education." "Value free education" is worthless and destructive to the human being as a moral agent and citizen of the Moral Community. A person without any human values is not a true moral agent or a true human being! If moral values are not taught, then the law and the justice and correctional system become meaningless forms of retaliation against evildoers (*lex talionis*).

Instead of putting emphasis on crime and punishment, we must shift emphasis to the deterrence of crime. This includes the provision of an affordable good education, job-skills training, elimination of poverty and child-abuse. Instead of emphasizing justice as equal retaliation and harsh punishment for criminals as a deterrence to crime, it must be correctly shifted to reformation and the moral rehabilitation of criminals, including the medical treatment habitual sex-offenders and counseling for the drug-addicts.

Jail as the place for mere punishment or torture of criminals does little to reform the criminal and prepare him or her for a peaceful re-entry into the society and living a normal life within the community as a law abiding citizen. This is why there are many angry ex-offenders who willingly repeat offenders as part of their own form of revenge and retaliation against the uncaring that would rather lock them away instead of helping them to become rehabilitated, gainfully employed, self-reliant, reintegrated and productive members of the community.

Deterrence to crime can also occur earlier in the educational and socialization process of young people. For instance, it can occur through an early-life sound moral education and positive conditioning to shun evil and violence and do good works of love, altruism, compassion and justice. The Church and state can also intervene in the chaotic life of a dysfunctional family life and dynamics in order to break a destructive vicious cycle of violence, crime and child-abuse. That will save the community from the horrors of crime and the tax burden of building more jails and keeping the criminals locked away from society.

In the USA, long jail sentences and death penalty are popular forms of societal imposition of "existential hell," control and punishment on criminals. The system empowers society and disempowers criminals. Many people like this form of justice system and pay taxes to support it. This is partly because these people enjoy the collective exercise of power that this system of crime and punishment confers upon them as if they were truly God. In reality the jury often has a person's fate in its hands as if the jury members had become God. This is a form of idolatry which has led to the deaths of many innocent people who have been wrongly convicted and sentenced to death.

The Catholic Church is right to condemn capital punishment as a moral evil and state murder of the criminal. Murder or the killing of people is wrong regardless of who does it. It does not make it right when the state or police officers kill people, including criminals, trespassers and traitors, any more than when individuals, such as mothers, husbands, and vigilante groups do it.

The confinement of criminals in jail effectively removes human freedom because that freedom had been misused to commit crime. This protects society from the irresponsible people who misuse their freedom to cause harm to other people or violate their rights and freedom. However, some people may not have been well trained in the proper use of their freedom. Such is the case of an ignorant, immature or retarded persons. As such, they are not responsible, free moral agents.

Therefore, in order to be fair and just, jail systems should only be reserved for habitual criminals and those violent criminals who pose a danger to the society. Young people who kill or commit other horrible crimes, should be sent to reformatory schools instead of traditional jails where they may be raped, killed or taught to become worse criminals. They may be products of dysfunctional families that abused them and taught them negative values. They can be morally rehabilitated, unless they are genetically programmed to become irreformable psychopathic killers. The death penalty where it exists should only be reserved for such violent and dangerous criminals who may kill other prisoners or prison guards. Otherwise, the death penalty as a retributive punishment is morally unacceptable. "State murder"of criminals is not a virtuous deed.

The less dangerous criminals should be punished by payment of fines and damages in restitution for their offenses. They should be reformed through moral education and public service while they are on moral probation, rather than by sending them to jail! Jails embitter the souls of those sent there, and unsophisticated criminals learn to become sophisticated career criminals from the habitual and master criminals they find in jail. Ideally, jail systems should only receive less than 10 percent of the budgetary support committed to public schools, colleges, and universities in that state.

It is morally embarrassing that some people are willing to pay their taxes to support building more jails and hiring more police officers than building more schools and providing sufficient fiscal supporting education, job training programs, national health insurance and welfare programs for the unemployed and the poor. These are more the constructive and morally sound methods of crime prevention than merely paying for a larger police force and expanding jail systems to accommodate more prisoners.

The American system of education, which has separated moral education and values from the rest of education, has partly caused moral harm to the American society as a whole. Violence within the innercity public schools and some suburbs where major incidents of mass shooting have taken place, such as that of Columbine High School in 1999, in the suburb area of Denver in Colorado, provide a good illustration for this moral problem of teenage violence. Public education has obviously produced citizens who are knowledgeable, but lack in civic virtues and sound moral values.

Bad systems of education also correlatively produce bad and criminal citizens. For instance, many graduates of bad public schools, especially, those in the innercity communities, tend to be self-centered, greedy, selfish, hedonistic and violent against anybody or anything that stands between them and their need for instant self-gratification. As such, teachers and school administrators as well as police may be attacked by these kinds of youths, without thinking about the consequences for their actions, until after the event has taken place. Some of them are anti-establishment and anti-moral authority. They mistakenly perceive them as their enemies. Yet, these people are the future citizens and leaders of the local community and the nation.

There is a direct correlation between poor education and criminal activity. The American prison population clearly proves that. American jails are disproportionately populated with people of low socioeconomic class and poor education. Based on these demographic factors, most of the people in prison are also racial minorities, such as Blacks and Hispanics. As such, good education in schools is the single most effective deterrence to crime within the local community as well as in the larger society. Crime is an external manifestation of a sick mind, troubled and impoverished spirit, low self-esteem, dehumanization, and a state of inner decrepitude.

This is especially true for people who are nonreligious. The majority of the criminals often have no meaningful relationship with God and the Church or religious community. Their own family members and close friends also tend to be dissociated from the Church and the activities of the religious community in their own area. For instance, gang members have friends from their own gang. Obviously, this is not morally helpful. In this case, the common or group shared values are those of a criminal nature. There is peer pressure to become violent and commit crime than to avoid it. Unfortunately, some students in some public schools belong to gangs. They recruit their classmates into these crime oriented and violent gangs promising them a unique sense of power, group identity, and protection from the other people.

The ultimate and most effective remedy for American urban crime and violence is not building more jails and providing more police. On the contrary, it consists in teaching good values of civic virtues, positive work ethic, justice and godliness. This includes the virtues of compassion, patience, sharing with the needy, peaceful conflict resolution, tolerance, equality, justice, delaying self-gratification, and openness to racial diversity. It must teach and encourage hard work, and acceptance of reality as opposed to escapism through drugs, food, sex, and wealth.

Public education must teach nonreligious forms of ethics and values which promote justice, democracy, humanism, utilitarianism, Marxism, good citizenship, societal harmony, and peace. These systems of ethics should be taught from kindergarten through graduate and professional school. The United Nations Charter for Human Rights can be used to teach these moral values. It is a sound, neutral, nonreligious document of universal and inclusive human rights and moral values. It can be used instead of the Bible, Torah, Shari'a, or other kinds of scriptures.

The traditional systems of education, being essentially religious or Church based, were also well integrated and holistic. Unlike modern Western secular education, particularly the European and American systems, these theocentric systems of education were not divorced from moral values. In a theocentric system of education what is important is not the mere acquisition of information and skills in order to compete successfully in the job market and get a well paying job with attractive fringe benefits.

In a theocentric system of education, value or worth of what is important is measured in terms of the good technical, moral quality of education and the kind of virtuous, compassionate, just, peace-loving and productive citizen it produces. That is, the affirmation that a well-educated person must be able to live a full, integrated, ethical life in the community, relating well in a civil and cultured manner with their fellow citizens and playing a major role as moral leaders of the community and also as a good role model for the young.

Therefore, in essence, the traditional theocentric educational system seeks to enable graduates to love both God and their fellow human beings and seek to serve them well. Subsequently, it also seeks to make a positive contribution and thus to make a positive difference in the world. This system further stresses the accountability and responsibility of human beings as God's moral agents and concrete intelligent representatives in both creation and the cosmos. This education shows that equipping the individual with mere technical information and skills without imparting moral values, accountability, and responsibility to both society and Almighty God the Creator, is to create a dangerous, immoral, clever, technological monster capable of destroying us, along with the rest of God's creation. Therefore, most scientists and leaders need this traditional, holistic system of education which emphasizes ethical values, the love of humanity, and the love of God.

Being in agreement with Plato's concept of education for leaders as the Philosopher Kings as advanced in *The Republic*, one can strongly argue that both leaders and modern scientists need to undergo this kind of holistic and ethical education. This is because these leaders have greater influence on society and the world in their decisions and deeds.

The leaders must be well educated and trained in order to equip them with Godlike moral consciousness and justice, so that they are fully enabled to make good, sound, moral, and ethical decisions on behalf of humanity, creation (animals, plants, water, air, soil), and God. As such, these leaders need all the necessary intellectual, humanistic, moral, religious, ethical, political, economic, scientific, and technological education and information in order to make sound decisions in all these important perspectives.

Whereas teamwork is important in providing the above mentioned essential expertise, it is important that the leaders and those who make key decisions in any society, especially among the super powers, are well educated and well informed. This is in order to be fully accountable and responsible to both humanity and God in their important decisions, which tend to have both cosmic, concrete ramifications and irrevocable consequences. It was in this respect that Plato declared that there will not be any meaningful peace in the world until philosophers become rulers (or kings) and rulers become philosophers. For Plato, philosophy was a systematic inquiry and study that included all branches of knowledge. Accordingly, he recommended holistic systems of education for all those destined to become good leaders and global peacemakers. Ignorance, shortsightedness, naive egocentricity, parochialism, and ethnocentrism are the greatest obstacles and enemies to good leadership, wise governance, and global peace.

## 5. The Ancient Egyptian Theocracy And Theocentric Education

The Ancient Egyptian society was theocratic. God was considered to be the Creator and King of the Universe. The Pharaoh was considered to be God's temporal representative in the world. As such, the Pharaoh was the Vicar of God or God's visible High-Priest and Divine Agent on the Earth. His political and religious holy role and position in relationship to God and the people was like that of the Pope today.

The primary objective of the Ancient Egyptian (Kemetic) system of education was human attainment of God's salvation. This supernatural salvation, constituted the coveted ideal life in God's Kingdom. It was believed to be attained through sound moral and religious education. This education conferred on the enlightened person well safeguarded, divine secret mysteries or knowledge which was expected to lead to moral and civic virtues, as well as both moral and spiritual perfection.

As illustrated by Moses' special encounter with God, conversion and free transformation by God through a vision of fire in the form of the "the burning bush" (setting sun behind a bush) on holy Mt. Sinai, and St. Paul's conversion and transformation on the road to Damascus through the vision of God in the encounter with a bright light that made him temporarily blind, God was clearly associated with light. Like Moses, the Egyptians believed that God was the Eternal Light and the Sun was the symbol for God. This light enlightened all human beings who sought after knowledge and truth through education, religion, and a personal prayerful, holy life.

Moses, Socrates, Jesus, Paul, and St. John's teachings are to some great extent in harmony and continuity with the Egyptian mystical traditions as taught in the secrets of salvation knows as "the Divine Mysteries." These Egyptian divine mysteries were the foundation of the popular "Mystery Religions" around the Mediterranean region and Gnosticism. These Egyptian or African religious ideas influenced the teachings of Christianity, including the doctrines of the sacraments of Baptism as a "rite of washing away sin, regeneration, and initiation into the holy redemptive mysteries of God in the crucified, dead, and risen Christ," and the Eucharist as the "ritual of immortality" and "holy communion with God."

The Bacchus ritual and the Dionysus cult in Greece were partly a Hellenization of some portions of these African cults of holy communion sacrifice. These were central in some versions of these African Mystery Religions. Wine was invented in Egypt for religious reasons and ceremonies. Perhaps wine was used in worship as peyote is used in the Native American Religion, and wine is used in the Christian sacrament of the Eucharist and the Jewish feast of the Passover!

God's universal divinizing and beatific supernatural knowledge transformed the enlightened person into the true "Son" or "Daughter of Light" of God, whose symbol was the Sun. This "*beatific vision*," as the illumination by God's knowledge and truth, also transformed this person into a new being that was effectively spiritually and morally empowered to live and attain a moral good life. This ideal moral life of spiritual perfection and union with God was lived in obedience to God. This perfection of the divinely illumined and redeemed life was lived in accordance with the divine decrees, righteousness, justice, love, happiness, growth in personal knowledge, and divine or supernatural illumination, culminating in the union with (*Atum Amen Ra)* God, and thus, supernatural salvation.

Like the rest of Africa, the Ancient Egyptian education had as its primary objectives, human deification and salvation. Subsequently, this Egyptian system of education, like the one Moses introduced to the Hebrews in the form of Judaism (which was itself a modified form of the Egyptian system of the divine mysteries, traditionally combining both education and religion), had no boundaries between secular education and religious or theological education. For such a distinction did not exist in life itself. Life was viewed and perceived as a whole. And as such, unlike the modern Western times, there was no distinction between the sacred and the secular realms.

Consequently, both secular and sacred studies were combined in general or wholistic systems of education known as "The Divine Mysteries." They were kept secret and hidden away from the lay people and all those who were not trained, disciplined, and initiated into the cult and knowledge of these Divine Mysteries by the authorized masters who were also temple priests of God (*Atum Amen-Ra*), the One Supreme God of Egypt and the whole world.

This ancient Egyptian or African, God-centered system of education was designed not only to ensure a virtuous life, but also a skilled life in the world. It also ensured harmony, peace, and happiness as a blessing from God. This came as a reward for virtue, the disciplined search for knowledge, and the spiritual enlightenment that transformed the knower or the enlightened initiate into the "Son" or "Daughter of Light."

The Egyptian wholistic, integrated, and theocentric educational curriculum covered a lot of subjects in theology, the humanities, languages, and the natural sciences. The curriculum consisted of language (both Grammar and Rhetoric), Mathematics, Engineering, Architecture, Astronomy, Music, Geography, Divinity and Philosophy (locally known as "The Mystery of the Secret Word"), Political Science, Law (also known as the "Mystery of Pharaoh"), Communication, and Teaching Skills (known as the "Mystery of Teachers"). It is to be noted that it was at the highest level of learning, in the Mystery of Teachers, that the secret mystery language and hieroglyphics were taught.

Since much of what was taught in these Egyptian or African holy mysteries was secret and to be only taught to the initiates, the priests, teachers and initiates were strictly prohibited from writing down these mysteries and disclosing them to the uninitiated public. (This prohibition still goes on today in some parts of Africa where initiation into cultic mysteries and activities cannot be disclosed to the outsiders.) In ancient Egypt the publication of books on these secret teachings was prohibited, except by some temple priests in order to keep secure and accurate the secrets of the knowledge and keys to eternal life (immortality), God's eschatological judgement, the resurrection to life again and salvation.

However, the Temple Chief Priest could, from time to time, commission some of the scholars to study certain subjects and write down their findings in book form. It is also known that long before Moses was born, there were many books and libraries in Egypt, which inspired the Hebrew Scriptures and Moral Law through Moses, and later, the Greek philosophy. Later, some of these libraries were both plundered and burned down by the invading foreign armies (or the barbarians), although the one that later became known as Alexandria following the Egyptian conquest of Alexander the Great in 332 BCE, remained fairly intact and turned into the first great world university. It even attracted notable Greek philosophers such as Aristotle, who moved there with his whole academy and helped to translate some of these Egyptian scientific books into Greek.

According to this understanding, the first scientists, mathematicians, and philosophers were not the Greeks, as we tend to think here in the West. On the contrary, the Ancient Egyptians were the true pioneers in these subjects. These subjects were unknown until the Egyptians invented them. They were not yet developed in the West or Europe. Between 5,000-450 BCE Europe was nonexistent. What we now know as Europe was still largely "primitive and barbarian, including the Greeks and the Romans themselves."

In this case, it was a case of civilization and enlightenment from Egypt in Africa to these still benighted people. This continued though the first four centuries of Christianity. Most of the Christian doctrines which are now accepted as Western and Catholic, were actually developed in Alexandria by thinkers such as Clement, the founder of the first Christian University, Origen the pioneer in Christian systematic philosophical-theology, and Athanasius who formulated the Nicene and Athanasius Creeds.

Christian theology was also developed in North Africa by thinkers such as Tertulian, who formulated doctrines of the Trinity, Cyprian who doctrine of *extra ecclesiam null salus*, and St. Augustine, Bishop of Hippo (now Libya) who became one of the most influential Christian thinkers and Fathers of the Church doctrine and systematic theology. St. Augustine serves as the theological foundation for both the Roman Catholic and Protestant churches. As such, St. Augustine is validly claimed by both the African and Western theologies and civilizations. He was a man of both worlds.

Monasticism was also started in Egypt by Pachomias and St. Antony. It is a major feature of Western Christianity. However, this African positive influence came to an abrupt end in 641 CE when Arab Muslims overran Egypt and North Africa. This Arab invasion of Africa plunged Africa into a "Dark Age." Christianity was outlawed and became extinct in North Africa, despite having had great bishops such as Cyprian and St. Augustine. Their writings survived in Europe whereas they were destroyed in Africa by the invading Arab Muslims and their militant jihadism. In Egypt, the Arab Muslims embarked on a crusade to destroy all the temples, statues, and monuments as dangerous idolatry. The Arabs called this period of Egyptian civilization the "*Jahariyya*" (the Era of Darkness).

Fortunately, the Greeks had written down what they found in Egypt, including the record of history and religious and philosophical teachings. These Greek records have been used by Africanist scholars to reconstruct the ancient history of Egypt and the surrounding parts of Africa. The Greeks are duly credited with the more systematic development and actual writing down of these Ancient Egyptian mysteries, which are the foundations for the theological understanding of Judaism, Greek philosophy, Christianity, and Islam.

All of these religious systems and civilizations have greatly theologically, philosophically and scientifically benefitted from the heritage of the Egyptian holy mystery religions, culture and technology. What has been called the Mediterranean religious mysteries are actually largely African or Egyptian mystery religions. It is not a historical accident that Greek civilization, Judaism, Christianity and Islam all emerged within this theological, cultural and philosophical richness and intellectually vicinity of Egypt. It is self-evident that we can trace all religious systems and civilizations from the ancient Egyptian mysteries. This is also where the Hebrews were held in bondage and subjected to Egyptian religious and cultural inculturation for about four hundred years before Moses liberated them and gave them a new religion called Judaism.

However, because of prejudice and racism, the West has preferred to ignore the great Egyptian civilization, just because it was African. Subsequently, the West has sought to begin courses on Western Civilizations with the "Ancient Greeks," rather than with the great "Ancient Egyptian Civilization." Similarly, the West has chosen not to begin with the Hebrews. This is because the Hebrews point us back to Egypt, their origin, and the origin of their corporate civilization and religion through Moses, the Egyptian priest, prince, and professor who turned into the Hebrew Liberator or Messiah.

Unfortunately, most people often deliberately ignore the truth when they do not like it. They also reject the truth when it puts them in bad light by exposing falsehood they believe or proclaim as truth. Truth is often brushed aside when it validates the claims of their rivals, enemies or opponents to be true and valid. This applies to the claims and teachings of the African Traditional Religions and African history which were rejected by Western imperialists and colonialists as too "primitive" and "pagan" to be of any value.

The Western destructive imperialistic, whitesupremacist and racist devaluation of the precolonial Asian, American and African religions, history, ideas, social and political institutions was done in order to justify their colonial acquisitions in Asia, America and Africa, and their oppressive colonial treatment of the local people as "benighted savages." This was part of the justification of their colonial and Christian missions.

These European imperialist invaders and conquerors had to show the world a moral justification for their military and missionary activities in these foreign lands. They declared that the local people needed the Europeans to come and save them from their own destructive "evil," "primitive religions and cultures," and bring them civilization, education and salvation by converting them to Christianity as the superior religion, being the only revealed and true redemptive religion in the world. In some cases, some people choose to believe a lie because the truth ruins their own comfort and the false sense of superiority and security they obtain from their own unfounded myths and fears. This is especially true of the myth of the intellectual, moral, religious and technological superiority of the White race over the nonwhite people.

This destructive form of racism is best illustrated by the crude claims and affirmations of some whitesupremacist and white racist groups, such as the Neo-Nazi and the Ku Klux Klansmen. But some academic whitesupremacists also exist, such as those who had claimed that the Africans were inferior people who had contributed nothing to the world civilization or those who insist that ancient Egypt, Sudan (Nubia), Ethiopia and North Africa were European civilizations, regardless of the fact that these civilizations predated the European civilizations by several millenniums in the case of Egypt.

The kingdoms, empires and civilizations of Eastern Africa, Zimbabwe and West Africa have been also attributed to the presence and activities of the some Europeans rather than the creation of the Africans themselves. This is one of the reasons that created the genocide of the Tutsi people in Rwanda in 1994 and Banyamulenge in Zaire. The former Belgian colonial masters in these areas had indicated that these people were "Black Europeans." The local agriculturalists wanted to get rid of them permanently as the foreigners whom they had been said to be. As such, one can conclude that the phenomenon of European imperialism and colonialism in Africa, Asia and America was deeply rooted in European nationalism and whitesupremacy.

Subsequently, most people in the West, were ethnocentric and perceived Africa, Asia and the Pre-Columbian America as primitive continents inhabited by primitive and inferior people who could be massacred and their land and wealth taken over by the Europeans. The natives were also viewed as potential commodities for capturing and selling as slaves to provide free cheap labor to the Europeans who had settled on those continents to farm the land. Even today, some whitesupremacists are still filled with some racial prejudice and conviction that nothing good can come out of Africa, Asia and Latin America except cheap raw materials, minerals, and cheap labor in the form of poorly paid migrant workers.

Therefore, the Human Genome Project (HGP) which affirms that all human beings are essentially members of the same race with a common ancestry and evolutionary birth place in Africa is not popular among these conservative racists. The findings of the HGP are rejected because the truth is embarrassing to these whitesupremacists and racists. This scientific affirmation of the essential unity of the human race is blow to the whitesupremacists who proclaimed that there were many races of humanity and the white race was superior to the nonwhites who were said to be members of an inferior human race.

Those who reject and disgrace the nonwhite people as members of an inferior separate race of people will inevitably disgrace the whole human race. This is because the human race is essentially one and indivisible before God. Color is simply skin deep. Skin color is not definitive of race or intellectual ability or moral behavior. Therefore, each time we allow racist degradation and dehumanization to be directed against the nonwhites, such as the Asians and the Africans, eventually we are all disgraced and dehumanized. This is to our mutually shared common biological human heritage as members of the same human race.

Therefore, what happens to one ethnic groups will eventually affect another group because humanity in closely interconnected in the web of life and the socioeconomic networks of the human Global Community. Christ's commandment of agape as the moral obligation for love the neighbor without any conditions, is the universal moral foundation, God's means and guarantor of justice and human rights for all human beings in the Global Community as God's children.

Biology in terms of "ethnicity," "race" and "gender" cannot by itself become the exclusive means of human classification and discrimination. Culture, education, class and religion are better alternatives for the social classification of people. They are voluntary and more descriptive of the personality of the people more than race or biology by itself. For instance, if my computer breakdown, I do not care about the color, race, gender or religion of the person who comes to fix it. All a care about is that the person who comes to fix it is a well trained professional and knows what to do to have it running smoothly, again.

The Egyptian princes, like Moses, priests and teachers, such as Moses, were well-trained at the highest level in the secret knowledge of the mysteries of life and immortality. The highest level of training was called the "*Mystery of the Teachers*." The most advanced qualification attained at this educational level was equivalent to our doctoral degree. The second stage of training that was equivalent to the masters degree was that of "*The Order of the Mystery*." All the teachers themselves had to first be successful *initiates*.

The initiates were extensively trained and examined in the mysteries before they were qualified and promoted to higher levels of training to the masters level or the "Order of Mystery." This extensive education and training was required in order to teach these Mysteries. Most of this training was by memorizing the information disclosed by the "Master." They had to learn all the mysteries they were to be initiated in.

The initiates were required to learn everything and master it by heart. This was essential before they could communicate it and teach it to others largely from memory, and accomplish this pedagogical task without any distortions or variance with what they themselves had been taught. Mastery and accuracy of knowledge and skills were important. They were regarded as the manifest evidence of true godliness, moral and intellectual perfection and union with God whose mysteries the priest or teacher had attained, mastered and now carefully guarded as God's enlightened representative, servant and Child in the world. The highest in the hierarchy of these divine messengers and representatives in the world was the Pharaoh. The Pharaoh represented God's embodiment to the world. The pyramids provide evidence for that belief.

Because these divine mysteries were completely secret, in order to preserve this secrecy, the divine mysteries were not supposed to be written down without permission. Moses was, therefore, free to write them down and disclose them to the world because he had been expelled from Egypt, and he no longer felt bound by his vows to keep them secret! This was his ultimate vengeance on Egypt. There are still secret mysteries in Africa which have not yet been written down. This is true for both West and East Africa.

Authentic examples of this kind of oral traditional education, oral transmission of knowledge, and religion still exist in nonliterary cultures of Africa. In these societies, history and other skills, such as medicine, religion, philosophy, moral codes of conduct, laws, handicrafts, and cooking are all transmitted in an oral manner. These are carefully communicated orally from one expert to another by means of apprenticeship, and from one generation to another.

These Egyptian masters or teachers, having attained the highest level of knowledge and training in the mysteries and divine knowledge for both spiritual and intellectual enlightenment, were regarded as God's direct representatives, mediators, priests and saints. They were considered to be very close to God.

This was supposed to be achieved through the deification process of divine knowledge, a disciplined, virtuous, or holy life, and ultimately, through divine illumination that is correlative of correct moral or ethical knowledge of what is true and what is false, right and wrong, and important and trivial. This process of human deification into divinity through knowledge and illumination was later appropriated by the Greek neo-Platonic philosophers under the term "*theosis,*" which literally translates into "divinization," "deification," or "Godfication."

It is also to be noted that Africa, South of the Sahara, still deifies its heroes today. Heroes are given the rank of "gods." This rank is beyond the rank of the "ancestors." In the Western Christian world-view and theology, the ancestors are equivalent to Saints within the Catholic Church. However, they are subordinate to the One Supreme Creator and Redeemer-God. This Supreme and Creator-God is regarded to be above all gods. Within this African hierarchal conception of monotheism, the subordinate gods are merely God's mediators, cabinet ministers and departmental representatives in God's vast spiritual Kingdom and Reign over the universe (creation).

Traditionally, the good African ancestors were regarded as saints and got periodically defied and elevated to divinity to become some essential spiritual component parts of the long hierarchical chain or ladder of mediators between people and the radically transcendent God. The good African ancestors are part of God's visible immanence in the immediate social world. These defied ancestors and secondary gods are considered to be subject to God's power and control. This is the case, although a considerable portion of the divine power has been effectively delegated to these subordinate gods, saints, ancestors, priests, and holy people to be exercised in the world on God's behalf.

Healing and miracles effected by God's people in prayer and blessings are part of this explicit manifestation of God's mediated power in the world. It can also be negatively used to cause harm through curses and witchcraft when it is accessed by undisciplined, proud, evil and malicious men and women. The same divine power is used by the Church to redeem sinners through the sacrament of reconciliation of the penitent, pronouncement of forgiveness of sins to the penitent and exorcism of evil from the possessed and those afflicted by guilt due to sin. But, this same divine power can also be used to curse and excommunicate notorious sinners from the Church and the eternal fellowship with God.

In this respect, God's power is a double edged sword which can be used for good or evil purposes depending on the moral and spiritual state and nature of intentions of the person accessing and utilizing God's mediated power that is abundantly available both in nature and people, everywhere in the world. The evildoers, such as evil ancestors, are not part of this mediation chain. They are the dreaded evil spirits. In most areas, the priests are trained in trapping these evil spirits and getting rid of them, just like the "Ghost Busters" of Hollywood and the Africanized local level of rudimentary technology. The African "Ghost Busters" use drums, lights, calabashes, and pots in their hunt for the evil spirits or ghosts! The priests serve as God's holy warriors in the fight and destruction of moral and spiritual evil.

As a result of God's delegation of divine power to these subordinate mediators and departmental gods in African Traditional Religion, some outsiders have tended to be prejudiced it. Very often, they have ethnocentrically and negatively viewed the traditional Africans as primitive polytheists and pagans in need of God's redemption through the work of the Western Christian missionaries, instead of seeing them as members of a different redemptive "monotheist religion."

If one had to employ the same theological criteria and measure for African Religion as for the Roman Catholicism with its cults of Mary and the saints, statues, and long chain of mediators, the Africans would qualify to be called monotheistic. The two religions are almost the theologically the same. This factor accounts for the ease with which the Africans have converted to the Roman Catholic Church without abandoning their Traditional African Religion. Because of this cultural sensitivity, the majority of Christians in Africa are Roman Catholics.

The Protestant missionary strategy was to turn the Africans into European or American Christians. This has left most of them alienated from their African culture, religious values, identity, and history! This is thus a good breeding ground for future atheists, greedy capitalists, corrupt leaders and criminals! Crime is becoming a serious problem in Africa, especially in the urban areas. This is partly because Christianity has despised and waged war against traditional values to be viewed as pagan and superstitious. Yet, Western Christianity having "desacralized the Africans," has failed to replace traditional taboos, spirituality and theocentric values with an effective spiritual and moral equivalent.

As result, the police will have to do for the Westernized modern Africans what the Traditional African Religion and moral conscience effectively did for the traditional Africans. This is in terms of cultural, social, spiritual and moral power for deterrence against moral evil, injustice and crime within the traditional African community. In traditional Africa, conscience was a sufficient deterrence against moral and social evil.

An African moral conscience was an internalized positive spiritual and moral power to choose and do the good and shun evil. It was the effective personal police and deterrence of sin as moral and social evil. It was also effectively deontologically policed and reinforced by the Traditional African Religion, cultural and moral codes and values of the African community. There were no police officers or jails to enforce the moral and social laws, yet it functioned very well.

Nevertheless, the elders, priests, kings, chiefs, and ancestors served as God's local and compassionate secondary police officers and moral enforcers of cultural and moral values. They punished evildoers, atoned for sin and evil in order to purify the sinner (moral violator) and cleanse him or her together with his or her community from the social, moral and spiritual pollution caused by the evildoer in the community. These moral enforcers were omnipresent everywhere in the community and world. Therefore, the traditional Africans had great spiritual and moral incentives to internalize the community's ideal spiritual and moral values and diligently live a holy, social, just, peaceful, loving, charitable and moral life according to them.

However, with this religious and moral institution destroyed by Western Christianity, a Western style of crime prevention must be found and implemented. As such, in a new Western oriented Africa, the police officers will have to act as the moral authority and public conscience of society unless Christianity becomes appropriately inculturated within the essential African traditional moral values and spirituality to make Africans whole, again, as responsible moral agents who fear offending God and the ancestors than they fear the police and going to jail.

As a matter of fact, most traditional Africans feared to commit crime in private because the omniscient and omnipresent God who sees everything would see them and punish them or their relatives. Misfortunes were interpreted as God's punishment. With the Christian missionaries teaching the Africans that their African Traditional Religion and beliefs were false superstition, the African moral conscience was freed from the fear of God, and the traditional moral values as they knew them and traditionally practiced them. As a result, new crimes, such as murder, rapes, vandalism, and violent robberies are on the increase in all African cities where Western Christianity and secular values have gained a strong foothold.

For the Egyptians, all those people illuminated and divinized by God and the people through this traditional human purification and deification process through initiation, study, knowledge, self-discipline, and the mastery of the mysteries. These initiated and God's illumined people were variously referred to as "The Sons of Light" or "The Sons of God," if they were male. They were referred to as "Daughters of Light" and "Daughters of God," if they were female. This initiation into light represents spiritual, moral and intellectual enlightenment that embodied in God's truth and eternal essence. God as "*Atum Amen Ra*" or as *Kazooba Nyamuhanga* as in the case of the Upper Nile in Uganda, is symbolized by both the golden light and the never-failing brightness and warmth of the African sun. The sun embodies light, order, warmth, life, truth, creativity and well-being.

Along the Nile Valley Civilization, culture and religion, stretching from Egypt on Mediterranean Sea to Uganda around Lake Victoria (Nyanza), the sun was the symbol of the Creator, Sustainer and Redeemer-God. This is partly because it shines everywhere, drives away the darkness and insecurity of moonless dark and scary night, and ushers in a new day with its renewed hopes of new life, another day for celebration of life, promises of success, a better life and happiness. In addition, the sun was considered an appropriated symbol for God, because without it, our planet would cease to be in its orbit and life on this Earth, as we know it today, would cease to exist.

These Egyptians may not have fully known the scientific theories of how gravity worked, but they built great pyramids, erected tall obelisks, and constructed irrigation canals with water elevation systems (*shaduffs*). They also knew that the sun, as well as the water, were appropriate symbols for both God and life on this planet. Subsequently, some African groups still view God through these primordial symbols of light, fire, air, and water (rivers, lakes, and oceans).

The Egyptian system of education was not open for everyone. The inquirers had to be instructed in the need and function of divine knowledge. The prerequisite conditions were self-renunciation, self-discipline, and purgation. Those passing the test and the hurdles of rigorous self-discipline were then initiated into the Secret Mysteries of God in the Temples by the appropriate ranks of the priests.

As we have already seen, the Egyptian curriculum was designed to make the student whole. Therefore, all students had to learn mathematics not just to be able to count, but to be able to carry out sophisticated engineering projects like building canals, houses, temples and sphinxes. Probably most imposing and lasting of all, they had to learn the construction of the great pyramids to immortalize and externalize the deceased Pharaohs and humanity which these Pharaohs both embodied and symbolized, both in life and death.

It was also in this tradition that Plato and Aristotle, his successor, required of their philosophy students to be masters of mathematics, science, language, and logic before they could advance into metaphysics and ethics. Ethics and metaphysics were viewed as the epitome and crown of both knowledge and philosophy and life itself. This was because ethics or virtue, the good life, and happiness were regarded as the necessary fruits of both knowledge and the correlative divine salvation, as well as the goal and state of the good life in which happiness is a permanent attribute.

For these ancient Egyptians or Africans, the main problem was ignorance and how to know what is good and right, rather than the problem of weakness of the will and the failure to do what one knows to be both right and good. Consequently, this moral and ethical standpoint is found both in Judaism and Greek philosophy, which inherited it with little modification from the Egyptian ethical teachings.

It is only in Christianity, particularly the Pauline letters, that we find a strong emphasis on God's free, redemptive grace. This is due to the weakness of the human will to save the human being by choosing and doing good works, without God's necessary help of supernatural free redemptive grace. Subsequently, St. Paul, Augustine, and Calvin agree about the universal human moral and spiritual failure to live a good and happy life of virtue based on one's knowledge of God's moral law as found in the Ten Commandments, as well as in the teachings of Jesus Christ.

This Christian teaching of God's universal, redemptive grace is a needed corrective for the ancient Egyptian Mysteries, Gnosticism, Greek philosophy, and Islam on the question of education as a path to salvation, because it confers knowledge, truth, virtue, a good life, and salvation.

The problem of salvation through truth and knowledge of the good is that of the will and power to do what the person knows to be virtuous, good, and beneficial. For instance, there are many doctors and nurses who know that smoking is a bad habit which causes bad breath, respiratory diseases, cancer of the lungs, and premature painful death. And yet, they smoke, despite their possession of this knowledge and truth. Similarly, most of us know that overeating and becoming obese is bad for our health. Yet, many people continue to overeat and become overweight (fat)!

It seems as if Socrates was only partially correct when he affirmed that "knowledge is virtue." Jesus himself also affirmed and taught this moral principle. For instance, he said: "Know the Truth and it will set you free." Obviously, unless the Truth here refers to God the Creator and Redeemer, the truth by itself, without God's power of grace for positive action and positive transformation, is also like the knowledge of the good without the moral power to do the good. Addiction to evil and the easy way of doing things is also another problem that inhibits positive moral and spiritual action.

## 6. Judaism and Christianity: Education for Justice, Righteousness and Salvation

It has been pointed out already that Moses modified the Egyptian mystery teachings, and introduced them to the Hebrews as a new religion that we now know as Judaism. Atum Amen Ra, the God identified with fire, water, and the sun in Egypt, was introduced to the Hebrews as Yahweh, who was known to Moses through "the burning bush" on Mount Sinai.

Again, the well known system of an elite, professional priesthood which was to be the physical, intellectual, and moral custodians of the Torah, reveals a continuity with Egypt. In Judaism, the Priests, and later the Rabbis, were the educators of the community. They, too, taught all the subjects, including physics, astronomy, medicine, religion, mathematics, geography, history, ethics, engineering, philosophy, theology, art, architecture and technology as holy mysteries concerning God's truth, essence and the world as his or her creation.

As in Judaism, Islam, Buddhism, Hinduism, Native American religions, within the ancient Egyptian or African world-view and systems of education, religion and politics, there was no boundary between the secular and the sacred. All were sacred and God Reign or Kingdom included everything within the cosmos. There was no distinction between Church and State. God's Kingdom could not be limited to a mere portion of his or her creation. God was transcendent and the Cosmic King over the entire universe. The earthly rulers, such as the Pharaoh were the visible divine finite embodiment and local representatives of God's cosmic order, power, moral authority and rule over the world. Today, according to the Roman Catholic church tradition and teaching, the Roman Pontiff (His Holiness the Pope) has taken over this religious, moral, spiritual and political role and effectively serves as "*the Vicar of Christ on the Earth*" and God's temporal representative in the world.

However, in Judaism, unlike the Egyptian Mysteries which were secret, God's sacred mysteries were disclosed to all Jews as members of God's covenant or redeemed people. Education was open to all males who wanted to learn the law. It barred women from this pursuit. But it also has to be noted that for the patriarchal Hebrews, God was also perceived as male, and the covenant contracts had always been made between God and the Patriarchs. This was in the notable absence of women, including the wives. Circumcision, too, which was the initiation rite into the covenant and which it was also regarded as the symbol of the covenant did not include the females. And there was no equal alternative ceremony to incorporate them into the covenant community and its obligations.

As a result, Judaism, like Islam, almost became a male religion, since it excluded women from the inner part of the temples and mosques. It also barred them from becoming priests and ministers or studying the law, which in both cases covered civil matters as well as religious and moral matters.

This is how religion, in the name of God, elevated and deified the male gender, while subordinating, subjugating, denigrating, and ultimately, dehumanizing those of the female gender as weak, inferior, and defiled beings because of their menstrual periods. Up to this day, some churches which strictly follow the Mosaic Law and the Pauline Epistles in the New Testament, in the name of God, still bar women from the ordained ministry.

The problems of gender bias and exclusion of women from religious leadership, as found in the Bible, can be easily summed up as follows:

1. The Patriarchal Hebrews had a male dominated culture.

2. The Patriarchal Hebrews had a male oriented language.

3. Patriarchal Hebrews had a male oriented religion and priesthood.

4. The Patriarchal Hebrews despised women as weak, defiled and inferiors of men. Women's menstrual periods were considered a source of religious impurity and spiritual pollution.

5. The Patriarchal Hebrews viewed God as a Patriarch or male, warlike, and good.

6. The Patriarchal Hebrews viewed female and "femaleness" as un-God-like and evil who could not represent God.

7. The Patriarchal Hebrews viewed men as the beneficiaries of God's covenant, and therefore male circumcision became the symbol of the Mosaic Covenant with God. Only the people with the phallus could be circumcised. This covenant symbolism left out women, just on the basis of their God-given gender.

Given this kind of background, it is easy to see how and why Eve is the one who is supposed to have caused the original disobedience and sin in the world. This is despite the fact that the commandment was only given to Adam and not Eve, who was not yet created when God commanded Adam not to eat from the tree of knowledge of the good and the bad as well as death (Gen. 2:5-17). This divine command is significant not because it led to the primordial human rebellion, disobedience, and sin against God, but because it clearly testifies to the fact that the knowledge of the good and the bad is primarily a supernatural, divine quality.

Therefore, to possess this moral knowledge and consciousness is a divine privilege which human beings can only gain and enjoy by divine permission and benevolent divine tutelage for the human being's enlightenment. This leads to a good, habitual state of life of virtue, self-discipline, harmony, peace, and blissful happiness.

In this sense, it is through the human "a priori" divine intrinsic attributes of self-transcendental, greater mental capacity for infinite intellectual activity, free thinking, reasoning, value judgement, moral consciousness, good education, and knowledge by which human beings truly become Godlike (or become God).

Subsequently, following Eve and Adam's disobedience and eating of the forbidden fruits of the tree of knowledge and death, God is reported to have said the following:

> "Now the man has become like one of us and has knowledge of what is good and what is evil. He must not be allowed to take fruit that gives life, eat it, and live forever." So, the Lord God sent him out of Eden and made him cultivate the soil from which he had been formed (Gen. 3:22-23).

Therefore, within Judaism, just like the Egyptian Mysteries, it can be said that knowledge is supernatural and divine, and its quest is also the quest for salvation, the supernatural, and the divine. Subsequently, its possession does not only confer wisdom, but also divinity, salvation, virtue, right judgment, righteousness, goodness, peace, and happiness.

Therefore, in these monotheistic religious and philosophical systems, God can only be God because he or she is the omniscient source of knowledge, creativity, providence, perfection, and salvation in the world. As a result, the Whiteheadian finite and ignorant God would be utterly rejected as meaningless, since he/she was unable to create, direct, and save at will and at any time, both in history and eternity. After Moses and the Sinai Covenant between Yahweh (God) and the people of Israel, the Torah or the Law of Moses began to be the Hebrew foundation, focus and center of education. Indeed, God himself is credited with the command to teach this law, especially to the young so that they would grow up in the fear of the Lord and the observance of his moral code as was given to Israel through Moses. On this subject, Moses is reported to have said:

> These are the laws that the Lord your God has commanded me to teach you. Obey them. . . . As long as you live, you and your descendants are to honor the Lord your God and obey all his laws that I am giving you so

> that you may live in that land a long time. . . . The Lord and the Lord alone is our God. Love your God with all your heart, with all your soul, and with all your strength. Never forget these commandments that I am giving you today. Teach them to your children so that they observe them when they grow up. Repeat these commandments when you are at home and when you are away, and when you are resting and when you are working. (Deut. 6:1-7)

And, as we have already seen, the priests, scribes, rabbis, and Pharisees later became the highly esteemed, privileged, authoritative, and expert teachers, developers and interpreters of the Law (Matt.23:1-3). Most of the lay people were derogatorily known as "the common people" or "sinners," and lived a life which was generally oblivious to the details of the Mosaic Law. Therefore, they were also unable to become serious in matters of religion and the ritual observance of the Law.

By the time of Jesus, the religious "priests," such as the Pharisees, avoided contact with the ordinary populace. It was strongly believed that the religiously pure would become contaminated and defiled by physical contact with those who did not know the Law, such as foreigners and those who did not strictly practice or observe it. If such physical contact took place, the Pharisees had to purify themselves with a ritual of hand-washing up to the elbows.

This is the kind of Pharisaic legalism that Jesus denounced and repealed by his own inclusive ministry, moral and religious teachings. Indeed, it was this very neglected large group of common and ordinary people, which the Pharisees shunned as defiled "sinners," that Jesus primarily sought out, taught, and ministered to (Luke. 4:16-21). Jesus also explicitly affirmed that it is the sick that require a physician for healing, the lost that need to be found, the blind that need restoration of sight, the lame that need to walk, the ignorant that need teaching, and the sinful that need forgiveness and restoration to wholeness. It was for this supernatural and divine redemptive work that God through the Incarnation in Jesus, came into the world (cf. Mk. 1:21-2:12).

Nevertheless, Jesus himself knew the divine quality of knowledge and the redemptive and divinizing value of his ministry, which was almost entirely devoted to the essential teaching of the ignorant masses in the open fields and on lake shores, so as to reach the previously unevangeliz ed masses of people. He sought to teach them God's moral law, and to impart to them God's redemptive knowledge and message of the good news of the availability of God's free salvation in God's own free loving and saving grace. This is for all human beings who turn to him in faith and need of this supernatural salvation and divine restoration to wholeness, harmony, unconditional love for all people, peace, and happiness.

Therefore, it is in obedience to Jesus Christ's examples and command to his followers to carry out his uncompleted work, reach out to all human beings on earth and teach them what Jesus taught about God's unconditional love, forgiveness, nonviolence, peace, and salvation that the Church today should be the primary instrument of education. This is particularly the religious, moral, and ethical education is necessary, if there is to be any normative moral values, meaningful global harmony and lasting peace.

The fact that Jesus saw education and knowledge as part of salvation and theosis or divinization of the active and obedient knower, is clearly stated and illustrated in the following encounter and discussion between Jesus and a teacher of the Mosaic Law:

> A teacher of the Law was there who heard the discussion. He saw that Jesus had given the Sadducees a good answer, so he came to him with a question: "Which commandment is the most important of all?"
>
> Jesus replied, "The most important one is this: Listen, Israel! The Lord our God is the only Lord. Love the Lord your God with all your heart, with all your soul, with all your mind, and with all your strength. The second most important commandment is this: Love your neighbor as you love yourself. There is no other commandment more important than these two." The teacher of the Law said to Jesus, "Well done, teacher! It is true. . . . It is more important to obey these two commandments than to offer on the altar animals and other sacrifices to God."
>
> Jesus noticed how wise his answer was and so told him: "You are not far from the kingdom of God." (Mk. 12:30-35)

Therefore, it is self-evident from this passage that according to Jesus, all those who wish to be godly and to become his redeemed and obedient disciples, and thus, the children of God and enter God's Kingdom, must not only love both God and their fellow human beings as the universal neighbor, but must also study God's law and God's works in nature. They must do so to prove wise and to live more meaningfully according to God's Law, goodness, holiness, truth, justice, and unconditional love, which only occur where there is good and godly education.

It was for this kind of good and holistic education that Christian churches founded all the ancient universities in Europe and America. Good universities like Cambridge, Oxford, Harvard, Yale, Princeton, Duke, Vanderbilt, Emory, Ohio Wesleyan, Fisk, Notre Dame, and others were all founded by Christians or Churches. This was in obedience to

Christ's command to teach all nations and make disciples of men and women for God's universal kingdom, both in heaven and here on earth.

Subsequently, these universities and others have a moral obligation to provide godly education. This is essential in order to increase the unconditional love for both God and human beings everywhere. Subsequently, this will facilitate global understanding despite cultural and ideological pluralism, as well as international cooperation, tolerance of diversity, a life of harmony, disarmament, and global peace. To do otherwise would be tantamount to the negation of the essential teaching of Jesus, the true Church of Christ. Therefore, it would be to also negate Christ's message of love and reconciliation. And as such, to negate their own primary mission and the very reason for being as Christians and the followers of Jesus Christ.

## 7. The Ancient Greek Education System: Knowledge, Virtue, the Good Life, And Happiness

The Western intellectual tradition, logic, theology, ethics and system of education are heavily rooted within the ancient Greek secular epistemological system and intellectual tradition. This secular world-view is exemplified by the Athenian tradition, which produced great philosophers, thinkers, scientists, and academicians like Socrates (469-399 BCE), Plato (427-347 BCE), and Aristotle (384-322 BCE). However, some of the other Greek city states, namely militaristic Sparta, commercial Corinth, and Thebes, were less intellectually inclined.

The latter mentioned Greek city-states were more interested in other practical affairs, such as the acquisition of military and commercial power, superiority and domination of the region. This militarism, tension and rivalry eventually led to the protracted, destructive, Peloponnesian wars beginning in 431 BCE. These only ended in 4O4 BCE with the overthrow of Athens by a coalition of Sparta, Corinth, and Thebes, primarily out of jealousy and fear of its growing moral, intellectual, military power and imperialistic expansionism in the region.

As we have already seen, Greek philosophy did not merge out of an intellectual vacuum. This is the case since the intellectual traditions of both Egypt and ancient Israel were readily accessible in the Mediterranean region. However, the Greeks did a great job of systematizing the existing ideas into various intellectual disciplines, like metaphysics, ethics, logic, and natural sciences or geometry, as Plato referred to it, and required of all his students.

It is also to be noted that for these Greeks, the term "*philosophia,*" which we translate as philosophy, has the exclusive meaning which covers all branches of study and knowledge. It is literally and more correctly translated as the "love of wisdom." This is why the highest academic degree that Western universities offer is a PhD (Doctor of Philosophy), regardless of the field of study.

The Greek intellectual tradition, both before and after Socrates, the first greatest Greek philosopher, thinker, and teacher, remains very diverse and pluralistic. For instance, the Ionians had primarily engaged in what we would call natural science, in trying to determine the primary stuff or elements of which life and things were constituted.

Thales had concluded that the world was made up of water; Anaximander had said it was made up of fire instead; and Anaxamines had disagreed and said it was made up of air. Pythagoras (58O-497 BCE), the great mathematician and philosopher, had himself speculated the universe was composed of numbers and ratios. Pythagoras' religion-philosophical brotherhood and mystic community had been established to live in accordance with his philosophy.

Plato himself had also speculated on this metaphysical problem. The result was his famous doctrine of abstract "Ideas" or "Forms" as the basic essence of the physical, spiritual and mental dimensions of reality. The visible world was taken as mere transitory phenomena or appearance and illusory, whereas Ideas or Forms were immutable, permanent, universal, perfect, and most real.

For Plato, God (Demiurge) was the chief organizer of these Forms, so as to create the world of phenomena out of them. This was following the Idea or Form of the "good," which is supposed to be the chief and most perfect, as well as inclusive, of all these Forms. Subsequently, for Plato, all human knowledge, choices, life, and will are required to be in line with the "good" in order to be correct, acceptable, and satisfying to the community, the doer, and God.

In other words, true human virtue, a good life, and its coextensive happiness are only possible when the human being discovers the "good," does it, and lives by this knowledge and the doing of the "good" deeds. This is "the good life" made possible only by a state of virtue which is itself a result of correct knowledge.

It is, therefore, within this understanding that Socrates taught that "true knowledge was virtue," since it inevitably led to virtue. Ignorance and false knowledge on the other hand, led to vice and an unauthentic form of existence, being unrelated to both truth or reality and the good.

As a result, for Socrates and Plato, no ignorant person would live a good life; and subsequently, no ignorant or foolish person is able to live a life of habitual virtue and correlatively to live a happy life. It is very clear that this Greek form of education and philosophy had supernatural salvation and human deification through knowledge, correct moral life, and good deeds as its primary function and chief priority. This is because to possess correct knowledge conferred a life of virtue, self-control, satisfaction, and happiness on the philosopher, who would thus become like God or the gods.

Socrates' moral philosophy and dialectics consisted of an ethical call for self-examination, and diligent search for the knowledge, truth, beauty and virtue. This was opposed to falsehood, ignorance, acceptance of the cultural moral norms without question, and following one's base or sensuous desires without self-discipline and self-control. He further warned against blindly following corrupt moral teachers, such as some sophists like the famous Protagoras (481-411 BCE) who taught that "Man is the measure of all things."

According to Protagoras, regardless of whether things are good or bad, "man" is the one that measures and classifies them as such. The human being's knowledge and self-interests are the subjective criteria measures for good and evil. Subsequently, Protagoras taught that whatever was good for "man," was therefore, also to be regarded as essentially and intrinsically good. Conversely, whatever was bad for "man" was also essentially and intrinsically evil.

This is the kind of irresponsible, extreme epistemological and moral principle of relativism that Socrates, Plato, and Aristotle had to fight against. For instance, if the society ever followed Protagoras' extreme moral relativism theory, no human being would judge anything as bad or evil. This is because there would not be any common moral law and normative values for moral guidance. It would also be difficult to enact civil laws due to lack of a common moral understanding, knowledge and agreement of what is right and what is wrong, in as much as there were doers for each deed who claimed that it was good. But, even after Socrates, the Greeks still followed different moral philosophies. For instance, unlike Stoicism, Epicureanism taught that bodily or sensuous pleasures were desirable as a countermeasure and cure of pain, stress and boredom. Pleasures of the body were to be celebrated as highest natural good. As such, pleasures from food, drink, sex and other forms of self-indulgence were to be aimed at as the guiding goals, moral and existential principle for living happily in the body with its natural pleasurable senses. This is the essence of hedonism.

For many hedonists, a good life consists of pleasure and happiness is attained through the sensory celebration of the body and the world. This position affirms that: "Let us celebrate! Let us eat, drink, make love and be happy now before we die!" This is the extreme position of hedonism. However, Epicurus (342-270 BCE) himself never taught this kind of blatant hedonism, which is sometimes erroneously credited to him as its chief exponent. He even taught that too much pleasure could itself cause the pain that was the main evil to be avoided. His followers corrupted his teachings and created an extreme hedonistic world-view that has dominated much of the world.

On the other hand, there were the contemplative, responsible, serene, and dignified, tranquil Stoics. Zeno (336-263 BCE), the founder of Stoicism, being himself a Jew, combined the ethical principles of Judaism with those of the Hellenic culture, to create this great philosophy which taught that the human being was a privileged creature. Though having an animal or earthly body filled with earthly requirements, needs, and desires, the human being was also thought to have a divine soul, which is part of the cosmic inclusive soul that is God.

This being the case, to be Stoic is to face life courageously and to try to live a sober life filled and permeated with tranquility and transcendental peace of both the mind and the body. This is regardless of what the environment is and the earthly events which will happen according to preestablished laws.

Therefore, one has to learn these natural causal and involuntary laws, accept them, and live peacefully according to them. Consequently, one has to courageously, peacefully and willingly accept whatever comes in one's way as essentially divinely predestined, and therefore, inevitable, definitive, essential, and leading to the hidden ultimate destiny.

Nonetheless, this Stoic position was very different from that of the naturalists like Diogenes (412-323 BCE), who taught that human beings should live simply, just like the rest of the other animals. He even suggested that human beings should be completely naked if the weather allowed, and mate in public, just like the other creatures, such as dogs.

Stoic philosophy enables its adherents to view themselves as part of the irreversible, natural, and supernatural process to which they must surrender themselves. This is true if they are to live meaningfully in this world of historical events, human voluntary actions, disasters, pain, time, change, finitude, and death. This position brings to mind the author of

Psalm 23 who is ready to trust in God and leave the rest to God, including personal death itself.

We also find some kind of Stoicism in the Pauline Epistles, and through Paul, Stoicism entered Christianity itself, but in a very modified manner. This is mainly true for the mainline churches. This is especially true for Catholicism, Eastern Orthodox, and Anglicanism.

This should not be surprising, since the early Church Fathers themselves deliberately studied Greek Philosophy, especially Neoplatonism, with its strong emphasis on the doctrine of the "Logos." As a result, the doctrine of the Logos was readily accepted and appropriated by the Christian philosophers and theologians. It was readily appropriated and adopted as a suitable tool for formulation and teaching of the complex Christian doctrines of the pre-existence of Christ prior to the incarnation.

The Logos, or Word of God, became defied as the preexistent Christ through whom all things were made by God. At God's appropriate time (*kairos*), the Logos became incarnate in the world as a perfect human being to redeem human beings from evil and self-destruction, due to the misuse of personal freedom and rebellion against God's commandments and moral law. The Logos became incarnate in humanity to show all human beings what authentic humanity and authentic human life lived in positive faith in God's goodness, agape, forgiveness of sins, and complete daily openness and obedience to God is truly like (cf. John 1:1-18, 3:16-21). He showed that to become a perfect human as *imago Dei* is to become like God and to be united with God!

There is also a tendency for Protestant Christian groups to become attracted to radical fundamentalism, scriptural literalism, and dualism. Subsequently, Protestants tend to view the world and the body negatively, as evil. The body is viewed as evil because it embodies sensual feelings. These bodily senses expresses troubling insatiable physical needs and sensuous desires. As such, holiness is equated with the denial of the bodily senses and desires.

Holiness and spiritual purity are equated with a self-disciplined life that is ascetically purged by the self-disciplined, self-denial of the bodily sensuous pleasures. Hedonism is rejected as a deadly sin. This is because hedonism equates happiness with the pleasures and gratification that come with the fulfillment of these desires. In Protestantism and mysticism, the bodily sensual craving for pleasures and self-gratification are rejected as bondage to evil. The body and all its desires are purged, extinguished, and transcended in order to reach God through intellectual contemplation, and divine illumination, and union with God.

To some significant degree, this Christian tradition of asceticism and mysticism is due to the Neoplatonic influences and Oriental philosophy, especially that found in Buddhism. In the West, the African derived monastic and mystical traditions came to influence the West through the works of St. Anthony, and more significantly through the works of St. Augustine, Bishop of Hippo in North Africa (354-430 CE). St. Augustine was a very prolific writer of theology and works of spirituality and doctrines.

St. Augustine's theology, philosophy, and ecclesiology have very fundamentally shaped the theology and doctrines of the Western Church, both in its Catholic and present Protestant expression. The Christian doctrines of the original sin, grace, sacraments, and predestination are very Augustinian. This is more so for the Calvinist and Reformed traditions.

However, the Catholic Church has preferred, since the thirteenth century to adopt Saint Thomas Aquinas (1225-1274) as its normative theologian, teacher, and philosopher. And by so doing, the Catholic Church has strongly embraced Aristotelian philosophy in which Thomas Aquinas had grounded his Christian works, both the logical and philosophical. In fact, the *Summa Theological* and *Contra Gentiles* are so steeped in Aristotelianism that one can hardly understand them without the necessary background in Aristotelian *Logic, Metaphysics, and Ethics.*

The works of Aquinas seem to be more of a Christian commentary on these Aristotelian works and their Christian appropriation for a new age and the Church than anything else. This does not deny that Thomas was one of the greatest original thinkers that the world has ever known, but rather also affirms that he was one of the greatest Aristotelian Christian teachers and systematizers.

Definitely, the main external, intellectual, ritual, and expressive differences between Catholicism and Protestantism can be mainly attributed to the great differences between Platonism and Aristotelianism. This is both in metaphysics and ethics, which these two Christian traditions have inherited from these two main schools of Greek philosophy.

The Evangelical and Protestant emphasis on heaven and hell, sin and virtue, God and the devil, Spirit as opposed to the evil desires of the body, death and resurrection, and self-denial can all be said to be due to this Platonic, dualistic influence with its teaching on the two unequal and opposed worlds. The first is regarded as good and ideal, being of the essences and perfection, and the other is seen as imperfect, physical, and of phenomena or becoming, and subsequently characterized by constant change. For Roman Catholicism, following Aristotelian philosophy, the world is an integrated whole composed of spirit, intellect, form or essence, and matter or substance.

In matters of Ethics, again, following Aristotle, who taught that virtue and the good life are in the middle of two opposing extremes, Catholicism advocates and teaches a life of moderation for most of its members. Protestant emphasis, on the other hand, is on bodily negation, self-denial, and a puritanical life of asceticism, rather than that of moderate Aristotelian self-indulgence and a life of habitual virtue and goodness.

Therefore, the Greek influence on Western intellectual and religious life is very great and almost immeasurable. It extends beyond Hellenic Fraternities and Sororities on Western university campuses into general education. It also grounds and underlies much of the Western philosophy and the Christian theological and dogmatic formulation and teachings, such as democracy, ethics, logic, and ideas like the Logos, Christology, the Incarnation, God's Perfection, Creation, Evil, Mind, Body, Heaven, Virtue, Morality, Truth, Eternity, and Immortality.

Subsequently, in the West, in order to study the classics, theology, and philosophy, one also has to learn ancient or Koine Greek in order to read the original texts and commentaries. Thus, one can dynamically perpetuate the ancient Greek intellectual life and traditions into the present, just like the Church and synagogues that have also preserved the Judeo-Christian intellectual and moral tradition. They have reinterpreted it for today's modern generation and is more attuned to the future, space age, and the wide cosmos than the past with its parochial and restrictive, rigid moralism.

Consequently, the modern generation needs modern, moral, and ethical codes and guidelines that are broader, global, flexible, pluralistic, scientifically based, inclusive, humane, and practical. The next section tries to deal with this specific problem.

It is contended that apart from God as Creator and Redeemer, nobody can make another mature person, especially an evil one into a virtuous or morally responsible one. This is the case regardless of coercion, threats of punishments, and pain, such as arrests, fines, and the imprisonment of habitual criminals. However, it is also generally recognized that just like cancerous cells contaminate, infect, and destroy a previously healthy body, likewise, the evil people also contaminate their friends and cause great harm to the community if they are not removed from society or adequately reformed.

In addition, it is also positively affirmed that good, holistic education, good early correct child-rearing, socialization, and instruction in good, humane, moral, and ethical values and providing good moral and responsible role models will more effectively facilitate the learning of both the positive moral values and virtuous ethical moral codes. There is also the need for necessary moral support from the local community to which belong, so that they can become positively transformed into its well integrated morally conscious members and responsible social beings and productive and law abiding citizens. This is as true in the city as it is true in the rural areas.

Consequently, due to humanistic individualism, greed and relativism, ethics, values and morality are as much an individual affair as they are a collective and public affair. This is because in an interdependent, good and harmonious community, whatever affects an individual, eventually affects the whole community. Conversely, what affects the community also affects the individual members of that community. This happens because the individual and the community are inseparable.

In other words, the individual and his or her community are two intertwined coextensive and correlative social realities. The individual and the community are irrevocably interdependent twin realities of the human life, and meaningful, organic, human social existence. That is, all human beings are invisibly linked together in the sociobionic web of life, as interdependent creatures both within the local and global community. For instance, a general without an army is an insignificant military force! Likewise, cities and civilizations are possible because human beings work together in organized teams and networks of communication.

The biblical story of the Tower of Babel (Gen. 11:1-9) illustrates the Godlike human potential and capacity for great accomplishments. This occurs as long as the people are united, speak a common language and are collectively well organized as a harmonious community. In contrast, there are many tragic examples of human division, violence, genocide, powerlessness and poverty in Africa which occur because of mere linguistic and cultural differences. Africa has allowed itself to be permanently divided, and underdeveloped because the traditionalist Africans have no moral desire, insight and the courage to seek a broader, Pan-African common identity which transcends the destructive ancient feudalist divisions and systems of local power that were locally based on the limited parochial identity and support of the extended family, clan, "tribe" or ethnic group.

The local identity and both privilege and power that were based on it were locally determined by kinship, the local language, culture and patronage. This is the fundamental breeding ground for Africa's problems of nepotism, tribalism, corruption and military conflicts, in countries like Somalia, Rwanda, Congo, Uganda, Liberia, the Sudan, Sierra Leone, and Nigeria. For instance, in Somalia, the clan loyalty and patronage of the clan leaders destroyed the integrity of the Somali nation.

This Somali nation disintegrated despite of the fact that there are shared common national cohesive forces of history, ethnicity, religion (Islam) and the Somali language. Likewise, the genocide in Rwanda took place in 1994 in a uniquely integrated nation which shared a common history, language, and religion (Roman Catholicism). It was designed to exterminate the Tutsis. The powerless majority Hutus wanted to eliminate the minority aristocratic Tutsis who had traditionally exercised political and military power over the agriculturist Hutus for hundreds of years. Yet, the Tutsis and the Hutus share much in common including history, language, religion and even biological kinship. Definitely, this kind of senseless mass murders of people and genocide is not the solution for racial and ethnic differences and tensions in Africa, Europe, Asia, the Middle East and some parts of America.

The enlightened future leadership and caring citizens of these diverse countries and troubled continents must broaden their vision and concepts of an ideal community, nation, race and ethnicity. They must see ethnic, religious and cultural diversity as a good thing and as asset for economic success within a diverse and pluralistic Global Community and its economy.

The leaders of Africa and Asia have to a great deal to learn from the political and social experimental success of the United States of America (USA). This is a great nation where every race, ethnicity, culture, religion are represented. Therefore, instead of reinventing the wheel, the leaders of developing nations may choose to imitate the more successful multiracial and multicultural experiment of the USA. The USA has all races of the world represented, and yet evolved into a world's most powerful nation on the Earth. This great American success is a result of its unique composition of racial and ethnic diversity. Following the American example, the bitterly divided and feuding "feudalistic" and "tribalistic people" of Africa could also form a new and successful United States of Africa, and thereby, be able to transcend tribalism, powerlessness and poverty which have seriously hindered meaningful national and Pan-African political integration and economic development.

In the case of Africa, Pan-African unity must be attained first before the local and regional differences can be minimized. Antiquated forms of tribalism and feudalism have no place within the New Age. The New

Age must become the inclusively diverse, multiracial, open and culturally tolerant global community. Unity is both the destiny and tool of Africa's mature nationalism and self-consciousness as one great and diverse country!

Within Pan-Africanism, the individual's essential form of identity and reference become the whole of Africa, rather than the local tribal land. This would both elevate and positively transform the individual's self-consciousness and identity in new Pan-African ways. The United States of America offers the best example of this self-evident truth. The diverse races and ethnic groups of Americans represent the world, yet, the majority of the people in America positively view themselves with pride as "Americans."

A good constitution is that which guarantees democracy, observation of human-rights, and separation of Church and state. The USA Constitution is a good example of an ideal constitution that guarantees these essential freedoms and human rights. It has made these positive developments possible in America. Other countries consisting of racial and ethnic pluralism can adopt the American-like federalist constitution and laws which protect the equality, justice and human rights for all the citizens, irrespective of color, race, religion, gender, ideology and disability.

The national constitutions and laws can be modified according to the own local conditions and needs. For instance, they can be redesigned in order to protect the specific rights of the local racial, ethnic, cultural or religious minorities. God as the cosmic Creator of all people in his or her own image, irrespective of gender, color and race, abhors the systems and acts of violence, discrimination and injustice that may be directed against any given groups of people on the basis of color, race, gender, religion, ideology, culture or ethnicity. God as the impartial Creator, Sustainer and Redeemer of all people does not get involved in the egocentric corrupt practices and evils of hubris, ethnocentrism, tribalism, nationalism, favoritism (inclusion) and discrimination (exclusion) as prejudiced and sinful people commonly get tempted to do.

Ultimately, for the unconditionally loving, just and eternally forgiving God, all people and creatures are included in his or her Kingdom of unconditional love and life God's own unmerited universal redemptive grace. This eternal Kingdom of God in the world is evolutionary, complex and incompletely realized by the creatures at each stage of its unfolding in the history of the world. It consists of the intertwined, simultaneous and ever ongoing and changing twin evolutionary and creative process of God's unfolding process of supernatural cosmic creation and redemption. God's process of creation is both correlative and coextensive with God's divine process supernatural redemption and salvation.

God's processes of creation and redemption are two sides or dimensions of the same divine process of creation, sustenance and fulfillment or renewal of creation! They are as inseparable as the sun's heat and light or God from creation. The life in the world and the redeemed life in God's Kingdom for the loving and obedient people as God's saints are coextensive. Similarly, the life of damnation and existential hell for the rebellious and evildoers, is also coextensive with the life in this world. God's constant processes of creation and redemption in the present moment, are also coextensive with God's time as *kairos,* God's Kingdom and eternity. This is why the hungry must be fed, the sick healed, the naked clothed, strangers made feel welcome, the lonely visited, those in jail ministered to, the bereaved comforted by God's caring and loving people as part of God's redemptive ministry (cf. Matt. 25:31-46).

Finally, the cosmos is to be positively viewed from the new standpoint of a "realized eschatology." That is the realization and affirmation that God's Kingdom, heaven and eternal life in concrete self-manifestation within both God's time as *kairos* and *chronos* as cosmic history are a present efficacious reality. That is, the positive affirmation that heaven is effectively present in God's world now, since heaven is wherever God exists and wherever people live in obedience to the reign of God, by obeying God's moral law and the Ten Commandments. This reality requires the eyes of faith and both mental and spiritual divine illumination (enlightenment) by God's Logos and Holy spirit in order to see and recognize it, as such. This is the essence of the divine revelation and redemptive message as preached by both the Buddha and Jesus as the Christ (cf. Mk. 1:14-16; 4:9-12; Lk. 17:20-21).

# Chapter 14

# Christian Ethics and Education For Justice and Peace Within a Pluralistic Society

We now live in a very exciting Global Community. It is characterized by cultural, linguistic, religious and moral pluralism. These factors are themselves grounded within the complexity of both racial and ethnic diversities that inhabit the Earth.

Therefore, people must be given the necessary moral and cultural training and preparation in order to live and work peacefully and successfully within this pluralistic Global Community. Without this cultural and moral education, it will become very stressful to live within this kind of diverse and pluralistic community. Without the appropriate cultural, religious and moral education and sensitivity training, the vices of cultural or religious ethnocentrism, bigotry, racism, imperialism, mutual intolerance and violence can take place and destroy the possibility of any meaningful cooperation, peaceful mutual coexistence and peace.

## 1. The True Nature and Measure Of Sound Education

In general, education is a complex process of acquisition, processing, adaptation, and utilization of information, knowledge, technology, and skills to solve the problems of life, society, and community building. Good education is measured by pragmatic socioeconomic, technical, and moral criteria. It must equip the human being to become a sound moral agent as a free, creative problem solver, moral thinker, and a responsible, caring, humane, social, peace-loving, law-abiding, and a productive citizen in the local as well as the Global Community.

Education is essential for a life of virtue and happiness. Good education provides good preparation for a sound, moral, productive, and happy life. It is also the means by which the human as a moral agent and a problem-solving moral being learns and develops new skills and solutions for life's problems. This is essential for the human being to be able to adapt most successfully to new modes of life and changing environment. To this end, the human being constantly acquires new information, modifies it, and uses it to meet the pressing needs and solve new problems which constantly arise in the evolutionary process of history and constantly changing life.

Therefore, successful human beings are open-minded, flexible, rational, advanced technological users, information oriented and good problem solvers. They are efficient data gathering and processing creatures who generate new ideas, knowledge, truths, theories, inventions, treatments of diseases, new ways of doing things, and the like. As a result, in this "information age" there is an explosion of knowledge, new ideas, and new inventions. People are interconnected mentally through cyberspace and computer networks, and they have thereby, transcended time, space, ethnicity, race, color, gender, nationality, and other traditional barriers.

According to this measure of sound education, a well-educated person should be a well informed, creative, and a responsible moral agent that is emotionally balanced, compassionate, caring, well-informed, non-prejudiced, and considerate. He or she should be an independent intelligent thinker that is technologically efficient, social, inclusive, God-conscious, environmentally conscious, productive citizen, cooperative, responsible, and a peace-loving person.

This informal and formal process of both learning and education begins while the unborn who are still in the womb, and lasts throughout the process of the person's normal life. Those people who fail to learn or stop learning new facts of life or knowledge, truths, skills and adjusting to the changes of life and environment soon die. Alternatively, these become miserable social misfits and outcasts of their own respective societies and die prematurely. This is a natural law. Creatures must constantly learn to adjust to the changing conditions of life and the environment or die. For instance, creatures eat when they are hungry and seek shelter when the weather gets too hot or too cold.

Human beings are better at this educational and adaptation process more than the other creatures because they are the most intelligent and therefore, most creative problem-solvers. The use of fire to cook food and provide heat during cold weather is the best unique example of human creativity and problem-solving technology that have enabled the human being to colonize and live on most parts of the Earth. The advanced inventions in technology, mass food production, food processing and better medicine, make human life more exciting and heavenly, compared to the life of the other creatures in the wild.

This life is part of God's Spirit. It is fluid, ever flowing through matter to animate it. It is also ever changing and transforming the world and its creatures, moving them toward self-fulfillment and perfection. God's universal absolute natural law is that of impermanence and change of all created or evolutionary beings and systems. This includes plants, animals, human beings, societies, nations, planets, stars, suns and galaxies. All forms of evolutionary systems and life on this planet exist imperfectly in a transitory state.

Human beings being the most intelligent evolutionary creatures, possess the intrinsic unique capacity for intuitive *a priori* knowledge or God's revelation, self-contemplation, self-consciousness and acute awareness of themselves as evolutionary and finite beings. This supernatural capacity and knowledge create existential anxiety and fear of an avoidable phenomenon of an undated future death.

This universal knowledge and acute awareness of human finitude troubles the human being. It is the basis of most escapist religions, which emphasize the immortality of the soul or the resurrection of the body and God's reward with a better life in heaven, after the physical death. As a result, some people prefer religious escapism in order to live happily in a religious state of denial of the meaning and finality of death. That religious and moral position is immoral and intellectually dishonest.

## 2. Knowledge and Truth about Life: Accepting the Reality of Death

A good education adequately prepares a person to live a good and productive moral life within the context of the family and the community. This education must include the correct knowledge about the nature of human beings and their moral nature. Death as a universal truth must be taught to all mature people. This is essential in order to ensure that they live correctly and die peacefully without regrets rooted in ignorance about the nature of life and the mode of life that they chose to live as compared to the available alternatives.

The denial of the reality of death, also constitutes a denial of the truth regarding the nature of God, essential nature creatures as finite beings and the world as a historical occurrence in time. Death is part of God's providence for evolutionary creatures. Natural death is not a result of sin. On the contrary, it is an essential component of evolution and therefore, parts of God's original creation before the emergence of human beings, disobedience against God or the "the fall." For instance, before the emergence of human beings through the evolutionary processes, creatures killed each other and plants for food. Creatures, such as animals and plants were born or came into being, grew old and finally died and decayed to become the fertilizer for new forms of creatures, such as trees and the grass.

The absolute law of nature that governs all creatures, everywhere in the universe is that whatever comes into being in time is finite and is subject to the processes of chronological time, will soon or later, also die or perish in time and cease to exist in its current form. The stars and planets in the cosmos came into being and will also finally die, just like the earthly creatures regularly do. This is not God's punishment. Only unnatural and premature death which is a result of moral evil, such as abortion, suicide, murder, capital punishment, death due to environmental pollution or degradation, or lack of access to good healthcare can be considered evil and results of human sin. Otherwise, natural death is good as God's providence for purification of life, evolutionary improvement of creatures and as a means of providing food and nutrition for more developed forms of animal life.

As such, death is part of the ontological nature of all living and non-living finite things. Natural death insures that all potential living beings have their own turn and to come into being and enjoy God's unmerited supernatural gift of life. History is the cosmic stage of this drama of creation or evolution of life, birth of creatures and their self-realization of life and finally their death as the exist from this stage of life to the next stage of "non-living existence" as matter or material for God's creation of new life.

It seems an ironic paradox that death and life are inseparably intertwined as two mutually interdependent components that constitute the complex process of animal and human life. The mystery of life in this physical world is that death of some creatures must take place in order for others to live. Life feeds on itself in order to perpetuate itself. This is most visible in the case of carnivores and cannibals. A carnivore such as a lion kills creatures, such as, antelopes and wildebeests in order to live. Lions, like any carnivores cannot eat grass and digest it. They must kill other animals in order to live. It is mostly the plant life form that is self-sufficient in terms of producing its own food without killing other plants or animals in the process of its food production.

Plants need water, minerals, light and air in order to manufacture their own food. In turn, the herbivores, such as cows, wildebeest, antelopes and elephants eat the plants in order to live. In turn, the carnivores hunt and kill the plant eaters and in order to feed themselves and their families. The human being is lucky in that he or she can feed on both plants and animals. He or she can live without killing animals. But, the carnivores cannot live without killing other animals for food. This will remain true unless God chooses to recreate them into herbivores. That requires to redesign their teeth, stomachs and digestive system, including the necessary enzymes to be able to digest grass and turn it into some a healthy nutrition and source of energy.

In the final analysis, death or perishing for all finite or created beings, is an absolute reality. Death will come to all living and non-living things will also finally perish. Only the transcendent and eternal God is immortal and not subject to the limitation of space and corrosion of time, which are two of God's primordial creations. The mortality of all creatures and death are truths which must be universally accepted as God's will and providence for all finite things. Even sinners and saints die in time. Kings and slaves become equalized before God in death. They all return to dust from which God had created them. The Egyptian Pharaohs who sought to escape death through building great pyramids and having their bodies preserved with their treasures, only became tempting targets for grave robbers. Their power and great wealth could not protect them from the finality of death.

The Pharaohs would have been wiser if they had given away their great wealth to the poor, instead of being buried with it. In the spiritual world, physical treasures are both worthless and useless. Wealth is only of value in this world in order to facilitate a good social life. Wealth may be used to postpone death in terms of buying better medical insurance and paying for the best medical treatment, but death will finally come.

Ultimately, natural death is not punishment for poverty and sin. This is the case since, the wealthy people, kings, poor people, sinners, the saints and the sinless people, like Jesus the Christ, all finally die. Fame, power, wealth, and saintliness cannot buy immortality for mortal beings. Mortal beings suffer and die. That is the nature of life and finitude. Buddha discovered the noble truth that "life is *Dukkha*" (suffering/-sorrowful). Buddha learned the essential truth that life involves suffering, loss, pain and death because that is how it is.

As a result, Buddha taught that life must be accepted in its givenness of finitude. That is, life must be accepted as a supernatural gift in which one will experience pain, suffering, growing old, losing a loved one, disease, uncertainty, anxiety, fear and death. He taught that the fear of pain and death can be minimized by living a clean life that resists desire for wealth and pleasure through a bodily self-gratification. A contemplative and self-discipline based on a moral law almost similar to the Decalogue, in addition to nonviolence and avoiding intoxicating drinks, was supposed to be one of the major remedies for fear of living life in face of pain, uncertainty and death.

The empirical reality and universal truth is the fact that all created or evolutionary beings are finite and their existence, precarious. Mountains get eroded by wind and water, grasslands become deserts, rivers and lakes dry up. Earthquakes, lightening ignited fires, asteroids hitting the Earth, droughts, tornadoes, floods and volcanoes create new landscapes and kill people, animals and plants indiscriminately, in the process. These horrifying and destructive natural events become classified as natural evil by self-centered and self-referencing human beings because of the life loss and destruction of property.

Nevertheless, this is how God creates a new world or new beings in cosmic history through the natural and impartial processes of natural law. The existence of all creatures is delicately suspended in the dimensions of chronological time, space and the dynamic, impersonal, cosmic, evolutionary creative processes. Likewise, the correlative essential learning needed to keep abreast with life in a constantly changing society and the world, is also an evolutionary and flexible one.

Sound education and learning must consist in an ongoing process that never stops as long as a person is alive. In this process, the art of moral reasoning and the learned virtues of compassion, unconditional love, altruism, justice, patience, hard work, truthfulness, and peacemaking are more important than the specific information on which these skills and moral virtues are to be applied. The enduring moral principles of reasoning and skills of making sound moral judgement in any given situation, and displaying ethical behavior are the primary objectives of any sound education.

The sound and good education is that flexible system for information delivery and training process which adequately equip the learner with the necessary information, training, problem solving skills and other essential survival tools. These essential tools and skills include the mastery of essential technical and social skills to become an informed and well adjusted productive member of the local community, nation and the world. Dangerous rebels and violent socioeconomic misfits, such as the criminals are often removed from society. This is done by either sentencing them to long jail terms or to death. This is done in some societies where capital punishment is still legally practiced, such as the United States of America.

Teaching the necessary critical thinking skills and good moral reasoning will positively shape the formation of a peace-oriented, loving and humane moral conscience. This is a well-formed and highly developed human moral conscience that is rooted in the knowledge, moral consciousness, justice and unconditional love for all human beings as the highest moral good and virtue. This moral virtue and skill will help the moral agent to become a true, thinking, and responsible free ambassador or representative of God in the world.

This kind of obedient moral agent and effective ambassador of God in the world is empowered by God from within. He or she is enabled by God to recognize the good and right and very correctly distinguish it from evil, which may pose goodness or cover the good to hide it. The wise person is able to distinguish the good from evil, and the illusion of the good. The illusion of the good is that which possesses aspects of the good. But, in reality, it is an evil that exists in the disguise of the good in terms of appearance and false promises. Jesus condemned this moral deception. He equated this moral disguise of evil with "a wolf in sheep's clothing" that tries to sneak into the flock, unseen.

The person has to learn new information and use it well in order to solve a new problem of life, or determine how to adjust to changing times and circumstances. A person who fails to learn new information and skills becomes frozen in the past. He or she becomes unable to fit into life, since life is a constantly changing evolutionary process. Yesterday's impossibilities become today's alternative choices, and the vices of yesterday may become the virtues of today, and vice versa!

Ethics is a branch of applied knowledge and critical moral education. It deals with human values, the norms of behavior, knowledge, experience, and other factors governing human moral judgements and choices, such as racial, color, religious, ideological, cultural, socioeconomic, and class prejudice.

Therefore, ethics is for everyone who makes any values, moral judgements, and choices. This is necessarily the case because all human beings are by nature called upon to become moral agents in the world. This is the virtue of their superior brains and subsequent great mental capacity to think, process information or data, memorize, and possess knowledge.

Consequently, the human being is able to make sound moral judgments and decisions based on the availability of goodwill, experience, God's moral guidance (scriptures, commandments, natural law), tradition, moral training, and correct knowledge or information. This comes as a result of these unique divine gifts which make him or her the most highly developed intellectual and free moral agent within the known cosmos. Subsequently, the human being is able to become a true moral, free, responsible, well-informed, flexible and a constructive moral agent. This God-like position within the universe is due to this special evolution and free divine endowment of superior brain structure, intellect, and special reasoning abilities. Descartes defined the human being in terms of this special aptitude as a creative and analytical abstract thinking being (*res cogitans*).

In this manner, Descartes was the predecessor of Hegel. Hegel affirmed that all reality was mental or rational. As such, a sound moral agent is that rational person who gains access to true knowledge and the truth through education. Furthermore, if that person were able to gain absolute knowledge and truth, he or she would become omniscient, good, virtuous, and eternal like God.

In short, such an obedient person would become united with God and become God or indistinguishable from God. Obviously, Hegel was also in the Socratic and Platonic model of reality (metaphysics), epistemology, and ethics. For these moral thinkers, correct knowledge and truth were the keys to any true virtuous life, the good life in fellowship with God, and true eternal happiness. This is in contrast to Jesus, John, and Paul who affirmed that moral virtue and union with God consisted in obedience to God and the devoted praxis of Agape to the neighbor and in faith in God's goodness in cosmic creation.

St. John could also positively affirm that God is Agape, and whoever has practiced Agape, knows God and has both participated in God and is united with God. In this respect, Jesus became the incarnation of God's Agape or became God by practicing the purity of Agape and free forgiveness for all his enemies and everyone in the world, both in the past and the future. In this manner, Jesus' self-sacrificial death as the cosmic atonement for sin became positively viewed as God's manifestation of self-sacrificial unconditional love for the world that was manifested in Jesus' innocent death and forgiving words on the cross.

However, within traditional Western and Eastern schools of mysticism, enlightenment, the beatific union with God, salvation, and eternal happiness are rooted in this school of the theory of knowledge, truth, virtue, and union with God or *theosis* (divinization). This in complete contrast to Aristotle, who rejected dualism and idealism and proposed virtue to be a mere moderation in one's actions and way of life. Aristotle was convinced that *virtue consisted in "moderation"* or "*the middle* of two opposed extremes." According to Aristotle, this *via media* moral principle of ethics was applicable to all dimensions of human life and behavior. This includes religion, work, politics, economics, exercise, food, drink, sex, and civic duties or commitments. Excesses were condemned as sources of imbalance in society or person's life and led moral, economic, political and social evils.

For Aristotle, this *via media* moral principle of ethics was applicable to all aspects of human life, choices and actions or behavior. This is includes religion, work, politics, economics, exercise, food, drink, sex, and civic duties or commitments. Hedonism does not bring lasting or any meaningful happiness to the overindulgent. Instead, it brings destruction in the form of pain, misery, addiction, depression, disease, suffering, despair, and in some cases, it leads to suicide. Some young college students who misuse their newly attained personal freedom from their parents, and become tempted to overindulge in these vices of hedonism suffer the above evils and their grades also suffer. Some of these morally irresponsible and pleasure seeking students get expelled for poor grades or breaking the college or university's moral codes of conduct.

As a free, creative and analytical moral thinker, the human being possesses the moral capacity to evaluate information, and make sound and free judgements. The free human being is also capable of putting his or her choices into action. Because of the reality of human freedom, the human being makes consequential choices and moral decisions for which he or she is both fully morally accountable and legally responsible. The human being, as a free moral agent in the community, nation and the world, is God's co-creator of institutions and history. Subsequently, the human being is God's servant and chosen representative as local moral a causal agent that is indirectly responsible for all the secondary effects as the subsequent consequences resulting from these choices or decisions and their corresponding actions.

Ultimately, as a free, creative and analytical moral thinker, the human being possesses the moral capacity to evaluate information, and make sound and free judgements. Because of the reality and causal efficacy of the human freedom, the human being makes consequential choices and moral decisions which affect the individual's well-being and destiny as well as that of the community, nation and the world. Irrespective of the moral theories of determinism and the religious teachings of predestination and fatalism, in most societies all mentally competent and mature people are considered to be both morally accountable and legally responsible. The human being, as a free moral agent, is the causal agent that is indirectly responsible for all the secondary effects as the subsequent consequences resulting from these choices or decisions and their corresponding actions.

## 3. Human Beings are Created to Become Voluntary Moral Agents in the World

Human beings everywhere in the world are created with an intrinsic special religious and moral structure that universally anchors religion, moral consciousness and conscience. Karl Rahner identified this God-given free supernatural gift and *a priori* universal special human structure as the "*supernatural existential.*" This divine structure of unmerited grace within the human being acts a supernatural antenna that is permanently oriented to God's Word *(Logos)* of creation, life, meaning, happiness, order and positive resistance against chaos, resistance to entropy or sustenance, positive transformation, healing, restoration to wholeness and redemption.

According to Karl Rahner and the Roman Catholic Church, this is the structure of God's universal and free grace that is implanted in all human beings in the world by God, at the moment of special creation by God. In this respect, it serves both as the human soul and God's grace and human-divine bidirectional antenna and receiver that is ever tuned to hear God's Word *(Logos)* and broadcast to the person in whom this structure of God's grace resides. This structure of grace within each person also serves as the seat of God's Holy Spirit and moral conscience. This structure of supernatural grace leads human beings everywhere in the world to an existential mode of inner state of faith. This contentless state of faith exists within the person in the world as a structure of God's grace for a fuller life of love, courage, believing, positive self-actualization and salvation. It exists in each normal human being as an *a priori* positive orientation to life and God as the Cosmic Creative Mystery and the Ultimate embodiment of life, order, truth, meaning, values, goodness, love, justice, peace, happiness and human destiny.

The above realization leads us to emphasize the special creation, evolutionary nature, divine role and moral duty of human beings within the cosmos. This theory of human nature, purpose and destiny is rooted in the theological understanding that all human beings are created to become responsible religious or spiritual beings and God's representatives or moral agents within the local community and the world. In this capacity, all human beings are created to serve as the evolutionary and historical channels of God's supernatural grace of special creation and redemption within the cosmic history of the intelligent creatures. As the universally most intelligent, thinking and knowing religious and moral agents, all human beings are created to become the special instruments of God's creation, preservation and redemption in this world. They are the local and historical embodiments of God's *Logos* and therefore, the effective representatives of God in the local cultural history and cultural context as the Jesus the Christ was for the Hebrews.

In the past, in a crude theological understanding, human beings were perceived to be "gods" or "sons or daughters of God." This was especially true for the patriarchs, kings, queens and powerful emperors. The examples include the Egyptian Pharaohs whose pyramids still stand as eternal temples and tombs to externalize them. The Roman emperors declared themselves gods and part of the religious, moral and political duties of the Roman citizens included the worship the Roman emperors and the performance of sacrifices to their statues. The powers of the Roman Emperor's of life and death of their subjects was for many people analogous to that of God, and more visibly so than that of God.

All free, intelligent and mature human beings are obligated to act as free and responsible moral agents. They have the divine capacity to cause good or evil in the world through their free moral choices and actions. If more people are too lazy to choose the good and do it, due to the fact that the good moral deeds require more positive effort than negative or destructive ones, then it also naturally follows that there is a visible accumulation of evil in the form of negative actions and negative energy which is emitted by these evil people.

As a result, the human beings may experience their community or society being threatened by an oppressive external evil in the form of these externalized negative deeds and evil energy. Some people metaphysically, dualistically and anthropomorphically referred to this external and internal negative force or energy as "*the Devil*" or "*Satan*." The dualists referred to it as "the Devil" that created caused the human rebellion against the good and the positive in the world.

The dualists blamed the "Devil" for causing them to choose and do the less good or evil and the negative deeds instead of doing the good and positive deeds. For these spiritual dualists and moral escapists, ignorance was not the cause of evil since they knew both good and evil and still chose to do evil. They believed that evil was a moral and spiritual evil or sickness caused by the "Devil."

Within spiritual and moral dualism, the moral agent has to fight the Devil with God's help in order to choose and do the good. Within dualism, morality is perceived as a spiritual battle-ground between God (Goodness) and the Devil (evil). This Greek and Babylonian pagan dualism has found its way into mainline Christianity through the influential Christian thinkers and writers, such as St. Paul and St. Augustine. It is very popular among the less well-educated Christians because it makes more sense as an explanation and scapegoat for the presence of sin and evil in the world. They blame the Devil, instead of the Creator-God for the occurrences of natural disasters, innocent suffering, pain and death and death in the world.

St. Paul, for instance, refereed to this negative human experience of human energy and evil force exerted by evil deeds as the demonic force and "principalities" of darkness (cf. Rom. 8:38; Eph. 6:12; Col. 1:16). St. Paul also referred to this "evil force" or "moral and spiritual oppression" as "the flesh" and "greed for money" and "the world." This moral evil was negatively referred to by Jesus as the failure to love, and also as materialism or "*Mammon*." "*Mammon*" can refer to greed and the materialistic love of money, wealth, and power.

Modern forms of idolatry center around greed for wealth, power, fame, sex, beauty and pleasure. These obsessions are idolatrous and equivalents of "*Mammon*." No one can serve them and serve God at the same time. These forms of idolatry are antithetical to true godliness, equality, justice and a life of virtue. These vices are popular among many people who regard them as the essential foundations and ingredients of Western capitalism, politics, materialism and hedonism. The prophetic Church must condemn these vices in order to promote true godliness based on the teachings of Jesus and Christ's example of a simple, non-materialistic spiritual and prayerful life.

Ultimately, human beings are not condemned to a certain way of life by fate either by the star of their birth or by what the mythological Adam and Eve are supposed to have done in the garden of Eden! And nor are human beings slaves of gender, race, color, and culture, as the false prophets of sociobiological determinism like Arthur Jensen and Charles Murray have erroneously claimed.

Human beings, as free moral agents, make moral decisions each day of their active, normal lives. They make these moral judgements without first consulting an expert on ethics and moral theology. Consequently, each person, is by essential nature, a voluntary moral agent whose definitive, moral authority is the Holy God, and as a moral consequence to some degree, an ethicist, since he or she wills, intends, chooses, and acts one way or the other. In addition, he or she makes these moral judgements constantly regarding what is right and wrong, true and false, the beautiful and ugly, good and bad, appropriate and inappropriate, beneficial and harmful, important and trivial, moral and immoral, and just and unjust. The moral agent must also do the right or the good voluntarily out of one's intrinsic, habitual, moral virtue and goodness.

These kinds of decisions are of great ethical and moral significance, not only for the individual person making these decisions, but also for the local human community. In some cases, these individual moral decisions can have both national and global significance. For instance, an Arab's decision in Beirut or Tehran to take an American or a Soviet citizen hostage, so as to prove his own loyalty to the fundamentalist and jihadist Shi'ite Islamic teaching, can cause actual global, military alertness, conflict, and serious destruction in terms of human life and material property.

However, many people fail to receive the necessary wholistic education, correct information, and essential good moral training to equip them well in order to live a good moral, loving, just, peaceful and happy life within the community. They fail to acquire the necessary information and skills required for making these important daily, ethical, and moral decisions. Yet these moral choices, decisions and actions determine the quality and shape the nature of their own lives, their community, nation, and ultimately, the world. A good example is that of the people of Florida and how their choices and actions both at the local and state level determined the outcome of the 2000 USA Presidential Elections. In turn, this political outcome has a direct impact on the American and global politics, since the USA is the leading global military and political power.

It may well be true, as Plato insightfully prophesied that, "there will not be peace in the world until philosophers have become kings or rulers, and rulers have, conversely, become philosophers." However, there is enough evidence to support the view that there will not be lasting peace on the Earth until human beings have learned to become benevolent, just, humane, loving, tolerant, nonviolent and peace-loving moral agents in the community and the world. It is not just the philosophers or well educated people who have learned to respect each other's relatively different intellectual, cultural, and pluralistic religious positions, but also the common people who are able to respect and love each other without conditions.

As a result of this moral education, rehabilitation and positive transformation people will be led to realize the need for a voluntary acceptance of God's offer of a peaceful life in his or her Kingdom based on the praxis of agape and nonviolence. By God's grace and through the work of the *Logos* and the Holy Spirit, human beings will be able to listen to each other with interest, and live with each other in mutual harmony and enjoyment of each other's differences and similarities as a source of intellectual, moral, religious, and cultural enrichment. This is opposed to the current Western practice of avoiding the different and viewing it as either inferior or as a threat. This has been the prevailing prejudice in respect to non-Western religions, cultures, philosophical systems, and other systems of education.

This may be largely due to the exclusive nature of the Judeo-Christian tradition, which claims superiority over other traditions and the finality of God's word, divine revelation, and supernatural salvation. Western modern technology tended to confirm this position until recently, when Buddhist Japan and the former Communist Soviet Union began to catch up and even threaten to supersede the West. In this case, the claim of the West to be superior is merely based on prejudice, ethnocentrism, racism, and sin, rather than God's will and election.

Unfortunately, this is equally true in the USA, where the nation is composed of several different races and many ethnic groups of people. These people are trying hard to live together in equality, harmony, and peace. For instance, many Blacks had become disadvantaged because their ancestors had suffered enslavement and had worked for Whites without pay. Thus, they had received a reversal of the negative effects through Affirmative Action Programs.

It is true that these programs did not always reverse the effects of centuries of discrimination against the Blacks, but it was a legal statement of need for some kind of bridging of the gap between Whites and Blacks in terms of education and access to jobs. This is in contrast to South Africa, where the Whites still claimed to be "the elect" and "chosen people of God." Until 1992, when President Nelson Mandela came into power, the Black people in South Africa were still largely regarded as a biologically inferior people and treated with great brutality as if they were wild beasts.

Therefore, it is extremely important that all human beings be given access to a free universal primary and secondary school education. This education must be provided by the governments and religious organizations. The United Nations must provide funding for this education in the case of very impoverished developing countries which cannot yet afford to provide it unaided by external funding and low interest loans from the wealthier countries.

As part of this essential education, the students must be required to take basic courses in moral reasoning, moral education, and practical training in ethics. This is basic education that is necessary to promote essential skills and correct knowledge that are required for making sound moral judgements. These forms of moral education and training in good moral decision making processes are necessary. All human beings should undergo this kind of essential moral training. This is because all human beings make these important moral judgements and decisions, and most people do it without essential knowledge, or the necessary correct information, analytical thinking skills and training in problem solving.

As a result, today we have many unnecessarily harmful global problems and products which are created by well intentioned, but ignorant people. Tragically, some people create greater and more harmful problems in the process of solving simpler and less harmful problems. "Thou shall do no harm," must be the ideal guiding principle in problem solving processes. This is especially required in medicine, relationships, maintenance of equipment or service, economics and our care of the environment.

Ignorance is the worst enemy that our world has to face today. For instance, it is due to public ignorance that we have the deadly problem of ideological and religious conflicts in the world. In the era of the Cold War, the superpower arms race was funded by the tax paying masses who, in ignorance, believed that the other, supposedly "evil power" was out there plotting to invade them and impose its own ideology on them by force of arms.

It was also falsely believed that nuclear arms build-up on land, water, and space instead of peace treaties and disarmament, was the best method to provide protection and insurance for victory or deterrence by the fear of "mutual destruction." The fear of mutual destruction did not work, and there was a massive arms build-up beyond the capacities of these superpowers to sustain. As a result, the Soviet Union became bankrupt, and the empire dissolved into war-faring smaller nations, while the USA suffered serious economic deficit.

Within this respect, ignorance is twofold. First, there is the mistaken belief by each group that the other is not peace-loving, and is planning a surprise attack. Secondly, there is the mistaken belief that nuclear arms build-up will ensure global stability and peace, rather than stimulate more military technological research to invent even more deadly weapons, and subsequently, lead to more and more military competition producing a deadly arms race.

In the past era of the Cold War, the real dangers of nuclear confrontation, war, mutual annihilation, and global destruction in a nuclear holocaust seemed to become a more likely human self-imposed eschatological hell-like reality. Movies like *Judgement Day* portrayed the deadly aftermath effects of nuclear radiation. Astrophysicists like Carl Sagan have also focused on a possibility of deadly global nuclear winter as a result of thick clouds of dark smoke from city buildings and forest fires which would be ignited by the bomb. These thick, dark clouds of smoke from burning buildings and green vegetation would block out the sun for considerable months. Then, this would usher in a corresponding freezing period on earth, which Carl Sagan, a famous anti-nuclear war proponent, called suicide.

According to Sagan, this nuclear winter would be like another ice-age, in which most of the earth's creatures froze to death and perished "*en masse*." The dinosaurs are a good example of this mass extinction of a widespread species of dominant creatures on the Earth. Their extinction must provide a lesson to human beings today as they carelessly compete with each other to dominate and exploit the natural resources of the Earth. The dinosaurs' temporary success did not ensure their future survival. The Inca Civilizations of pre-Columbian Latin America provide examples of empires and civilizations which arose and then, became extinct.

Humanity may also inadvertently commit suicide through deadly nuclear or biochemical weapons. Doctrines of "assured mutual destruction" are therefore ill-advised, dangerous, a waste of resources, anxiety inducing and suicidal. Life is God's special gift, and therefore, we should never do anything selfish, cruel, and unloving to endanger it!

## 4. Mass Moral Education as a Prerequisite For Democracy and Global Peace

Many religious people prefer theocracy to democracy as the ideal form of government. In theocracy God's rule or Kingdom is mediated through human beings as his ambassadors in the community and the world. Divine kings, pharaohs, Popes, and priests have in the past ruled people in God's name and over God's theocracy.

However, these theocracies have tended to be tyrannical. God's moral law can not be compromised. As such, God is not considered a traditionally considered a democratic divine Monarch. God is often portrayed as a Cosmic Dictator whose moral law must be obeyed always obeyed without question. Those who fail to obey must be judged and thrown into the hell-fire!

This is the kind of crude theological and moral reasoning that underlies the medieval construction of the theology of hell as a hot and nasty place where God sends sinners to be tortured for eternity! Dante's *Inferno* is rooted in this kind of theology. Theocracy still remains a very attractive idea. The affirmation of the reality of God's Kingdom in the world now, is part of this theological idealization, or utopian sanctification and construction of pure moral perfection in the world. The saints and popes are part of this tangible presence of God's Kingdom in the world. Therefore, the Papal Encyclicals carry the weight of God's moral law for the faithful and obedient believers, everywhere, within the Roman Catholic Church.

Ancient Egypt, Ancient Israel, the Holy Roman Empire, and Islamic governments are examples of these theocracies. The rule by the holy religious laws, such as the *Torah* (Israel) and *Shari'a* (Islamic nations), is the explicit and conscious imposition of God's Reign or Kingdom over sinful people. Since human governments tend to become tyrannical and unjust, republican and democratically elected governments offer a better chance for more meaningful human freedom, tolerance of religious diversity, cultural pluralism and self-governance by common consent of the governed people. This common consent is publicly expressed in constitutions and laws agreed to too by the majority of the people.

In a theocracy, majority rule has no place because the majority are sinful people whose will may also be tainted by their own sinful desires, ambitions, and moral values. For instance, the majority could vote to enslave or exterminate the minorities. The past evils of slavery of the Africans and the holocaust of Jews clearly illustrate how the majority will can become evil and destructive. As Plato, correctly realized, the majority will and rule of ignorant and evil people could degenerate into chaos and anarchy as a rule by an irresponsible mob. Kierkegaard also despised the crowd as an amoral mass of directionless and irresponsible mob. This partly accounts for many of the destructive behaviors as seen in mob riots. People in the mob lose their individuality, moral center and personal conscience. They become faceless components of the crowd or mob whose collective conscience and moral center shifts constantly like debris tossed about in a rough lake or river.

Nevertheless, true democracy can be imposed on the people by a benevolent dictator or group of leaders in the community or nation. For any true democracy to work, the masses must be well educated. This is because in a democracy, the government is by the people, for the people, and for the common good of the people who elect and empower it. In a great democracy like the USA, where the public vote is important for the elected public officials, including the president, the senators, and the members of Congress, these officials have to rule according to the will of those who elected them; otherwise, they may be voted out of office. As a result, even if the President was well qualified as Plato's Philosopher King, without a well educated subjects and a moral citizenry to support him in his noble and paternalistic programs of "national welfare" and international cooperation and peacemaking initiatives, he will become isolated, powerless, and ineffective.

This was undoubtedly the case with the former President James Carter, whose noble foreign policy of human rights and global peacemaking initiatives were greatly applauded abroad, especially in Africa and the Middle East, but were never appreciated at home. On the other hand, the former President Reagan's call for a stronger American military shifted from former President Jimmy Carter's American foreign policy of peaceful, diplomatic, peacemaking initiatives in the world, to that of an aggressive superior forceful military presence in global affairs.

President Reagan's view was that an invincible and strong military combat force was the true and effective moral and political means to ensure international peace. This militarism got him elected into office. President Carter's humanitarian peace and justice policies, including strong welfare programs to eradicate poverty and Affirmative Action Programs to eradicate racial imbalance and discrimination in employment or at the workplace and at home, as well as the strong advocacy for global peacemaking initiatives and international programs, were rejected by the American electorate in favor of the opposite policies which had been proposed by Reagan.

Consequently, Carter was voted out of office largely by the anti-peace and anti-Agape conservative "American Evangelical Christian" voting masses. Obviously, these voting masses were not ethically nor intellectually sophisticated enough to see the folly and great expense of militarism in the nuclear military technology and Cold War militaristic policies of "assured mutual destruction."

International terrorism, American troops, Jihadist bombardment, American hostages in Beirut, escalation of war in Central America, the bombardment of Libya, the invasion of Grenada, "Star Wars," and the Iran Arms Scandal were some of the results of this militarism. This is in addition to the *highest record deficits and debt despite Reagan's ironic campaign promise to balance the budget within the first few years in office!*

Yet still, the American voting masses could not see that they had made a mistake to support a larger military budget expenditure at the expense of essential domestic programs of welfare, public health, environmental protection, medical research, and educational programs. The public could not see that the nuclear arms build-up they had supported could only result in unnecessary international military provocation for arms race, international military hostility, and terrorism. This occurred as a negative counter military response to what was perceived to be the renewal of American global militarism, imperialism, and threat to the global military balance of power and peace, especially the so-called "moral majority."

Unfortunately, even some religious preachers have failed to preach the central message of Christ. This central Christian message or Good News of God's salvation and arrival of God's Kingdom is that of love, peace and nonviolence. People in any era and everywhere in the world could become true citizens of God's Kingdom by virtue of obedience to God's imperative commandment of Agape or unconditional love.

This commandment of Agape is the universal imperative for all God's redeemed people, including the Christians. The praxis of agape is implicitly God's universal will and moral imperative for all obedient human beings everywhere in the world, and every age. This is essential for them, if they are ever to live together in peace, love, and free forgiveness of sins for all human beings, irrespective of race, color, creed, ideology, gender, class, culture, and language. These preachers are not able to see the real un-Christian nature and dangers of militarism and nuclear arms race, and have supported blindly the arms race, ironically doing so in the name of God. These preachers see communists not as men and women created and loved by God, but as evil atheists to be destroyed.

Tragically, for both Christianity and the world, these kinds of demagogues and preachers of war are the false prophets in our time. They have negated the true nature of the Gospel and Agape that Jesus taught and commanded his followers to practice as evidence that they were his disciples. Christianity calls for the unconditional love and forgiveness of everybody, including one's own enemies.

Then, how can we, as Christians, morally support a government which spends too much money on military technological research and the refinement of nuclear arms. These arms are specifically designed to attack and indiscriminately kill God's people, of whom we are commanded to love in the same way we love ourselves? Since I would love to live a long, happy, and independent life, how can I then, support the government that tries to invade or support nations which invade and subjugate other independent nations?

As a loving and caring Christian, how can I support freedom and free thinking, and yet support war to punish and silence other nations just because they have chosen a different political ideology or economic socialist (and communist) structure which may suit them best? Aren't people free to choose their own political and economic destiny without interference from Western greedy capitalists and ethnocentric Christian cultural and religious imperialists? Should we not let people and nations freely choose what ideology, economic system, and religion is most functional and meaningful for them and their own nations, within their own unique local cultural conditions, technological level of development, historical experience, and socioeconomic context?

Since I value my own intellectual and religious beliefs, if I love others as I love myself, how can I then, in clear conscience, despise their religions and try to convert them to my own? Is this love or religious and intellectual imperialism? *Can I love others without changing them first and creating them in my own image?* And if I successfully convert others to be just like me, will I have done them any good, since I am myself imperfect and sinful?

Christian missionary activity is not to bring God to people without God. God is everywhere and God's revelation is universally found in nature and the mysteries of the cosmos. Constructive and meaningful Christian missionary activity should be ideally directed toward converting all violent people and non-Christians to the praxis of the redemptive virtues of Agape, nonviolence, socioeconomic justice and peace which Jesus Christ taught. In this manner, God and Jesus Christ as the Incarnate *Logos* of God in nature and cosmic history are well served. People should follow his perfect example of a holy life, unconditional love, forgiveness, and nonviolence. Christians should invite the new converts to walk and follow Jesus with them in mutual fellowship of love, faith, and sharing each other's burdens of life, in the name of Christ.

The Christian missionaries should always remember to be humble because, before God. They are no better than the people they are sent to minister to evangelize by "word" and "good deeds." In Christ the missionary and the people they have just converted to God through Christ, are all equal. In God's family, all obedient saints are equal. They are all fellow brothers and sisters in Christ, and fellow pilgrims and seekers of the good life, truly everlasting happiness, harmony, and peace. As human beings, we seek all these positive modes of life and heavenly experiences for ourselves and our friends.

However, as loving and obedient saints of God, we should also seek all this for all our fellow human beings. This must be done indiscriminately, irrespective of color, gender, class, education, race, nationality, and creed. This is essential since all people are all our neighbors as God's children, created in his or her own very image, just like us. They are all members of God's Family and therefore, our brothers and sisters both trough the preincarnate Christ (*Logos*) as well as the incarnate Christ (*Logos* cf. John 1:1-18).

In short, in whatever I do to my fellow human being, I must begin from an understanding that he or she is my very own brother or sister in God. In God, we share a common origin, humanity, need, parenthood, neighborhood, purpose, meaning, and destiny. In order to bring the positive transformation of agape, free acceptance, and unconditional free forgiveness of sins to the world, it is necessary to start with the self.

Michael Jackson was prophetic. Unless each person acts to correct injustice and acts of hate or violence, nobody will. We are the people of God. We are also the victims and perpetrators of evil. We are the sinners and saints. As the saints of God, we are able to save the world in God's name and power. Conversely, as sinners and hateful evildoers, we able to transform God's good world into an ugly, evil and hellish place of torture, unnecessary pain, suffering and premature death.

Jackson was correct to call us to begin "with the man in the mirror." Our own positive reflection will also be reflected back to us and the other people in the world. This is what Christian positive "witness and evangelism" are about. The moral dictum that "Actions speaker louder than words" is true for Christianity in its true mode of the praxis of Agape. In this altruistic and beneficent starting point, there is the underlying, fundamental vivid awareness and understanding that the other human being needs unconditional, intellectual, practical, socioeconomic, and emotional acceptance.

Furthermore, there is the need to begin from the theocentric view that other people are real human beings and persons just like me who need to be loved, valued, and needed. Similarly, they are in need of personal well-being and protection from all manner of harm, whether bodily, mental, or socioeconomic. For Christians, there is Christ's universal commandment and moral imperative of agape. This requires Christians to accept the other people unconditionally as true sons or daughters of God, irrespective of religion, culture, gender, sexual orientation, race, ethnicity (tribe), color, nationality, creed, ideology and socioeconomic class.

## 5. The Rejection of Racism and Jungle Ethics: Profiling, Violence and Retaliation

According to the teachings of Jesus, the highest level of moral and spiritual development and concrete expression is that of nonviolence, peace-loving, unconditional love for all human beings as the neighbor and free forgiveness for offenses committed including those of enemies. This important moral teaching required concrete good actions (deeds) as fruits of the true obedience to God and true faith and godliness. Faith in God as a result of God's universal grace had to lead the believer to good works of obedience and grace. These include feeding the hungry, clothing the naked (destitute), healing the sick, providing shelter to the homeless or welcoming strangers, prison ministry and consoling the bereaved, serving as pacemakers where there is violence (cf. Matt. 5-7; 25:31-46).

In this manner, Jesus effectively reversed some of the teachings of Moses which were based on natural revelation, such as the law of equal retaliation (*lex talionis*). According to Jesus, human beings are required to become as loving, forgiving and perfect as God, their heavenly Parent.

Therefore, human beings are not mere evolutionary animals who are predestined to behave irrationally based on mere biological programming and physiological needs. As such, A.H. Maslow's famous and insightful hierarchy of needs and motives for behavior is a mere good guide to determine and understand human and animal behavior. But, it is not determinative and fully predictive of human behavior. His hierarchy of needs, starting with the basics and ending with the moral, intellectual and spiritual are:

1. Physiological (food, drink and sex).
2. Safety (shelter, job, and laws).
3. Belongingness and love (family, friends, clubs, spouse or lover).
4. Self-esteem (feeling of value, pride, and meaning).
5. Self-actualization (creativity, spirituality and achievements).

The most important human needs and how to meet them are not programmed by genes as in the case of the animals. This also applies in cases of the basic needs for reproduction as well as physiological, psychological and physical safety or survival. For human beings, the community must teach and help the infants and adults to meet some of these essential needs.

In general, the amoral and lower animals perform at an innate or genetic biological programming level. But, normal mature human beings do not behave naturally like the animals. Human beings live according to moral, cultural, social, religious and legal conventions. This is universally the case, except for the very young, the extreme cases of the insane or severely mentally disabled people.

The insane and imbeciles are abnormal and amoral people. They may function at the level of other unintelligent, instinct-directed and amoral animals. This is not their fault. This mental and moral aberration is part of the reality of the imperfection of the evolutionary processes of life and glitches in natural law. They are to be considered God's will or punishment for sin of the parents or the victim. Physical and natural imperfection or evils are God's punishment or due to God's moral's imperfection or powerlessness over evil. They are part of the evolutionary physical and natural life.

The evolutionary processes of life are impartial. It is filled with many dead ends, biological errors, and corrections of errors through death and extinction of the genetically weaker, defective or environmentally unadaptable mutants and unfit creatures. This is true among lower forms of life as it is true for higher forms of life, including human beings. In some cases, the environment, the activities of parents and genes combine to explain these mishaps in the evolutionary process and creation of defective human beings. Until biogenetic engineering becomes affordable and accessible to all families, these biological problems will continue to plague the human community.

Within biological determinism or predestination, one can say that for those born less intelligent, biology becomes the ultimate determining factor in life or destiny. They are unfortunate accidents of nature and the environment that produced them. Although, they are innocent victims of nature, they are predestined to a life of hardship, social and moral inferiority. They are also destined to become dependent on their family members, relatives and society for their livelihood, protection, guidance and general well-being. They are not responsible moral agents to be held accountable for their own moral choices and actions. Like young children, the custodians or guardians of these mentally incapacitated and incompetent people are held accountable for the actions of their clients.

Because of the well developed human intellect, freedom, culture and religion, the human being's life and conduct cannot be fully programmed by education or conditioning and physiological needs. Environment, heredity, education, family background, gender, history, socioeconomic class, race/ethnicity, age, nationality, culture, religion, health and the like come together to shape the person's consciousness and destiny. For instance, in the past, more poor people born within the innercity communities of America were also disproportionately poorly educated, unemployed, violent and criminally oriented, as compared to those born within the richer American middle-class communities. The difference may partly be explained in terms of environmental and economic factors. The members of the impoverished innercity communities were sometimes driven to crimes of prostitution, selling illegal drugs, theft, and robbery in order to acquire the essential resources needed to survive in their own harsh, impoverished and brutal environment.

Some of these poor people confess that they steal in order to meet their basic physiological needs for food, shelter and physical survival. These basic physical needs drive the people, just like any other creature, to meet them, regardless of cost. This is in as much as the cost is less than death, itself. Desperation for food can lead to a good person to steal money to buy food or steal food to ensure personal survival and that of his or her family. This is not a sin before God. Personal survival and a higher good and virtue that overrides the lesser good in terms of moral laws, commandments and social conventions. The dead are unable to serve God or repent of their sins. Saving a life is a higher good than protecting property or property rights and laws. Property, including money and food, comes from God and its essential value and function is to promote, preserve human life and serve humanity. To do otherwise, is to commit idolatry and dehumanize people into servants of *Mammon*.

That is why the essential safety net of welfare and "food-stamps" (food coupons) must never be taken away from the poor. By so doing, innocent lives are put at risk, especially, those people who work in communities of the desperate poor people who may have nothing to lose by killing a shop owner in order to rob money to buy essential items. Some desperate poor people may even prefer life in jail where meals and shelter are provided than face starvation, homelessness and hopelessness on the cruel and cold streets of most cities.

However, there are many others who choose to live a decent, nonviolent and honest life despite this kind of environment and poverty. As such, biology and environment are not destiny, nor predictive of human all behavior in every situation. In their quest to provide effective crime prevention, some White police officers have often used these kinds of prejudiced, racial and ethnic stereotypes as accurate profiles of people and to identify potential criminals before they commit crime.

In this process, racial profiling and crime prevention, many innocent Black and Hispanic people have been unfairly targeted and harassed. This method of crime prevention has many times resulted in police perpetrated crimes of hate, injustice and racism that are directed against the racial and ethnic minorities, instead of preventing them. The more widely publicized police related accidents of brutality and racism are those that have happened in Los Angles, New York and several cities in New Jersey in the 1990s. However, other cities are guilty of this evil, including Columbus in Ohio and Pittsburgh in Pennsylvania, which were investigated by the US Government and charged with violations of human rights, including those of racial minorities.

The powerless racial and ethnic minorities and poor Whites are the people who fit well the prejudiced police profiles for potential criminals. Clearly, in this process, race, ethnicity and class are employed in a destructive manner. They are generalized for all members of the targeted minority and ethnic groups for the purpose of profiling the potential criminals, and because of this racism and prejudice, many innocent people get wrongly suspected of being criminals and then, get treated as if they were actually criminals who needed to be arrested unless they could prove that they were not indeed criminals.

Many professionals members of these targeted groups have sometimes endured humiliating and embarrassing moments having to prove the ownership of their own cars after they had been stopped on the public highways on suspicion that their expensive cars may have been stolen from some other White middle class people, who could afford to buy them! Stories abound about some Black professionals mowing grass in their lawns being mistaken for servants of the supposed White owners of the house, or being stopped for walking in their own neighborhoods. There are many reports of racial profiling by the police and other law-enforcement officers. For instance, it has reported in the media that Black motorists are sometimes stopped and searched on the American highways on suspicion of car-theft or illegal drug-dealing, just because they are black people driving fancy cars.

Profiles of criminals may be helpful in some cases in aiding the police to arrest some dangerous criminals, but if not carefully utilized can become a great source of civil and human rights abuses, for people of ethnic and racial minority groups. For racial and ethnic minorities and some poor Whites, the constitution and presumption of innocence until proven guilty is arbitrarily suspended by the some police officers and other law enforcement groups. It was because of this kind of White prejudice and racism against Blacks, that African American radical nationalists like Malcolm X (*Malcolm X Speaks)* and writers like Richard Wright (*The Man Who Lived Underground*) concluded that in the eyes of most White Americans, Black people are born guilty of a crime. The crime is being "born black."

These African-American separatist nationalists believed that racist White America perceived blackness as an an evil human quality to be rejected. They convingly demonstrated that most White Americans profiled "blackness" as a crime, external evidence of low intelligence and a physical indication of potential future criminal behavior! Being born black was the necessary evidence for all that innate evil, original sin and moral guilt. Personal character did not count! Racist White Americans saw "*a nigger*," before they saw credentials or character, Malcolm X claimed. He mocked the people that extolled King's dream of "the beloved community" in which people would be "judged by the content of their character" and "not the color of their skin." Ironically, the hate crimes directed against African-Americans, including more the burning of more than 375 predominantly Black churches and White Police racial profiling of Black motorists for harassment have proved Malcolm X right. Some schools are also becoming racially resegregated, once more.

Wright's works made it clear that the fundamental moral assumption of White America, the police and law courts was that the Black people were inherently criminals, over-sexed, lazy, and dishonest people who could not be trusted. As such, for Malcolm X, all Whites were to be viewed as the enemies of Black people. He condemned Dr. King's programs for social and racial integration in schools, workplace and the public spheres of life. Malcolm X advocated for voluntary racial separation. He believed that racial integration would be accomplished at the political, cultural and social expense of Blacks.

Institutional White racism is self-evident when the most of the high-ranking police officers are White and the victims of police brutality are Black or non-White. This was especially the case in the USA and former whitesupremacist South Africa. Victims of police brutality and racial profiling in the 21st century in the USA are still predominantly Black and other ethnic minorities or lower class Whites if the racial and ethnic minorities are absent. This is a kind of racial and class warfare that the law enforcement seem to be quietly waging in the cities of America based on the false assumption that racial and ethnic minorities and poor Whites are the natural perpetrators of crime.

In this process of identification of potential criminals through racial profiling by the police officers, the factors of minority race and ethnicity as biological categories are vilified as part of the potential for criminal behavior. Blackness or membership in another conspicuous ethnic or racial minority group becomes equated with potential criminal behavior. That is morally wrong. In this manner, Blacks and Hispanics or other racial minorities are judged to be guilty and treated as such until they prove their own innocence! This is contrary to the US Constitution and other nations' laws which requires that all people must be assumed to be innocent until they have been proven to guilty of the alleged crime.

In addition, because of racial profiling for criminal behavior, emphasis shifts from crime to race or color as the indicator of crime. In this process, the true causes of crime are ignored and not solved. The major (yet sometimes overlooked) true causes of urban crime are many and complex. They include: the economic and environmental factors, such as poor education, overcrowding, unemployment, White racism and discrimination against racial minorities in hiring, training, evaluations for retention and promotion. Some of these institutional discriminatory and racist practices are major sources of hidden anger, desperation and rage that drives some people to aggression against the law enforcement officers and the society that has rejected them.

Other forms of aggression and quest economic for survival outside the conventional structures, may sometimes, take the form of illegal activities, such as illicit drug-trafficking, prostitution, burglary, bank robberies, embezzlement of public funds and gambling. These poor and unemployed dehumanized people are unprotected by the safety net of welfare and free food distribution, they become reduced to the animal physical needs for survival and may be forced to behave violently like any other animals when they feel that their safety and survival needs are threatened.

Unlike the idolatry of secular humanism which enthrones the human being as a god, and utilitarianism which affirms that the good is done when the deed brings maximum happiness to the majority of the people, the true Christian ethic of agape differs radically from these two moral theories. The Christian central moral principle of agape is positive and humane in respect to each person. All human beings are treated as objects of concern, justice, compassion, love and forgiveness. It does not less if the people to be served are members of the majority or minority group. Numbers are irrelevant. Each soul is valuable and treasured by God and God's people.

The principle of Agape has its starting point in God as Agape. From God's Agape, the moral principle of agape mandates the best service and highest respect to be accorded each person or each individual as a beloved child of God in whom God is incarnate and ever present. Agape is rooted in the ethics and human interpersonal relationships of obedience to Christ's universal imperative commandments of agape, nonviolence, non-retaliation, justice, and peace. There is injustice if the majority oppresses the minority group, as in some cases of Western systems of democracy and utilitarianism.

Plato rejects the principle of democracy because he saw the inherent danger of the tyranny of the majority group and oppression of the minority group. Tyranny and oppression are serious moral evils and sins before God, irrespective of who perpetrates them. Majority tyranny and the oppression of the minority groups are best seen in the Nazi Party and the attempted extermination of Jews in Europe during the World War II. Ultimately, *might or majority power does not make wrong into right, except in "the jungle" or Animal Kingdom.* Survival of the fittest (powerful or cunning) is the natural law of jungle ethics and the animal kingdom, but not in God's Kingdom, the Church, and the moral community. *In God's moral community, the strong has the divine mandate to protect and defend the weak.* This is the true justification for any morally acceptable war or use of military force and violence. This is also the foundation of the Augustinian and Thomistic "just war theory."

Nietzsche, the famous German nihilistic and atheistic philosopher, realized the centrality of agape within Christian ethics as Jesus, John, Paul, and Kant had correctly taught the essence of agape as divine redemptive grace and virtue. Nietzsche tried to negate this by his doctrine of the "*Ubermensch*" as the "superman" whose only moral guiding principle is might or force and "will to power."

This Nietzschean, evil superman could pillage, rape, rob, and kill at will. Nietzsche's rejection of the central Christian ethic of unconditional love was based on the idea that it was "an invention of the weak to ensure that they were not destroyed by the strong!" This was the conventional human device for the preservation and survival of the weakest among the human community! This moral process is applicable to the local community as the microcosm of the macrocosmic national and global communities and in creation as a whole. The Christian moral ethic of agape overwhelmingly rejects the anachronistic and atavistic "jungle and beastly normative ethics" which are grounded in the natural norm of the survival of the fittest, where "might makes right," and weakness is regarded as a defeat and thus is not tolerated.

Natural life in the jungle is extremely dangerous. As Thomas Hobbes correctly argued in *The Leviathan*, this life in the wild was short, brutal and filled with anxiety. This is particularly true for the small, the weak, the young, the slow, the old, and the infirm, who all become easy prey for the strong. Subsequently, in "jungle ethics" of violence, vices are mistaken virtues. In this great moral inversion and tragic reversal of human virtue, animal virtues are equated with swiftness, strength, large body size, sharp horns and teeth, good sight, ability to camouflage and hide. In addition, the ability to bite, sting and inject poison or spray foul smelling gas as a chemical weapon to discourage predators, or body armor and spikes for self defense and protection against predators are essential for surviving the brutal life in the jungle.

The untamed life in the jungle is characterized by violence, existential anxiety and premature deaths. Nevertheless, different species of violent predators rarely kill and eat their own kind. However, very often the animals kill each other in competition for food or other rights, such as a dominant position in the hierarchy, so as to control access to power, mating rights, territory, shelter, food and water.

Unlike the brotherhood and sisterhood of some animals, such as the peaceful Bonobo chimpanzees of the Congo, and the African Central Republic, human beings seem to be slower in learning the most important natural lesson in survival than these less intelligent animals. This lesson is that any species of animals on this or another planet that actively and indiscriminately kills or preys on its own kind will inevitably face extinction sooner or later. This is necessarily the case because personal survival is intricately intertwined with the collective survival of others. This is especially, most true in respect to one's own family, community, nation, and ultimately, one's species and the world.

These support structures and mechanisms are essential for any meaningful human life and survival. As such, the moral and social conventions of justice for all, nonviolence and peaceful mutual coexistence are both local and international obligations. Obedience and praxis of Christ's moral imperative of Agape effectively transforms Christians into God's temporal co-redeemers of the world with God. They cooperate with God to redeem the world from self-destructive and negative forces of moral chaos or evil and sin, particularly, those of greed, hate, injustice, selfishness, hubris, intolerance, malice, violence and retaliation that threaten to destroy it.

This is also because nobody can survive meaningfully alone, for no human being can become a "true and complete human being" if he or she exists alone, like an isolated island in the middle of the sea. Whereas an island may exist indifferently out in the sea far from another piece of land, no single human being could ever live and survive alone meaningfully and happily on such a lonely island. The human beings derive their humanity, meaning, value and completion and fulfillment from both God and the human community. Despite its various imperfections, evils and sins, the concrete human community mediates God, life, love, happiness and salvation to the individual person. Without the community, human beings lose their value, purpose, meaning and identity as human beings.

To be an authentic human being requires one to become a free, social, humane, caring, loving, productive, informed, intelligent, creative, thinking, peace loving and responsible moral agent in the world. This means that an ideal human being is intrinsically social, caring and interactive with other people, and belongs to society, beginning with the family, a particular community, and a nation.

Yet, for many people today, the sense of belonging and being social or humane has been forgotten. Consequently, the results are tragic, inhumane, antisocial acts, such as violence, murder, theft, rape, unprovoked mass killings, vandalism, arson, suicide, sabotage, child abuse, aggression, and war.

These kinds of crimes, evils, and malicious deeds disturb the community and threaten societal peace, harmony, and the well-being of the community. If crime is not successfully checked or eradicated, crimes and their evil perpetrators can also threaten the very existence of the family and the community which condones evil or crime and the criminals. Yet, these are the very institutions in which human life and a virtuous community are rooted.

Without the integrity and well-being of the family and the local community, sound family and social values, human beings are socially, morally and spiritually lost. Without the necessary strategies and sound ethical measures taken to rehabilitate the family and community, which are the primary institutions for the creation of healthy people and well adjusted citizens, the human species may become self-destructive and ultimately, extinct. It is conceivable that some reckless and extremely violent people can arise and think of committing mass and global so as to usher in a new era, a good idea. They may cause a fatal global catastrophic disaster by initiating a nuclear war in the name of God, Christ, Armageddon, White-supremacy or another doomsday ideology. In that tragic manner, humanity may become another extinct species just like the dinosaurs or the so-called "prehistoric man."

Suicidal people and foolish militarism may actually lead to a global human catastrophe. If some evil and psychopathological leader, like Adolf Hitler and Idi Amin, starts a Third World War, it will become a global nuclear nightmare. Massive radiation may lead to the extinction of life, including the human species, due to global radiation contamination. Massive toxic pollution would make normal human life on this planet impossible. Therefore, God's obedient people everywhere are called to become the prophets of justice and peace. To this end, they must condemn violence and hate injustice and war:

> Let wars cease! Turn your tanks and nuclear reactors into electrical plants instead of nuclear bomb factories! Let those with ears hear God's word of warning and turn away from injustice and violence. Practice unconditional love and act appropriately to check evils of hate, intolerance, and violence.
>
> Shun the love of war and money which are global threats to life, agape, and peace. Act wisely, and learn how to live together in peace; lest like fools, you all perish together through the destructive acts of hate, intolerance, genocide, and deadly wars which destroy life, property, and the environment. (*Twesigye's combination of Amos and Jesus' Sermon of the Mount, Matt. 5-7*).

## 6. Obedience to God's Commandment Of Unconditional Love and Justice

In order to avoid foolish and tragic self-destruction, we must obey God's commandment through Jesus' teaching and requirement of unconditional love for God and our fellow human beings. This is true regardless of whether they are already friends or enemies whom we would have naturally preferred to fight and destroy instead of loving.

This commandment of universal unconditional love of the neighbor has to become our imperative starting place, grounding of our ethics of life, and normative measure of what is morally right and wrong, just and unjust, good and bad, appropriate and inappropriate, and godly and evil and sinful. The ethical norm and rule here is do to others the good that one would seek for oneself, in order to enhance maximum personal worth, maximize a good life, and realize true happiness.

This normative ethical rule is required in order to banish the evils and vices of greed, hate, malice, selfishness, exploitation, or oppression of others for personal gain and profit at the expense of others. Unchecked greed and self-interest were positively viewed by some evil people as the justification for slavery, capitalism, imperialism, and colonization of Africa and Asia which were already populated.

Capitalism also creates two opposed extremes or classes of people that Marx characterized as the privileged rich people or "the haves" and the poor masses as "the have nots." The class of "the haves" was composed of the privileged, few rich individuals who "owned and controlled the means of production." These factory and business owners employed and controlled the poor masses or "the have nots," whom they employed at very low wages in order to exploit them and maximize profits.

Marx noted how the employers could hire and fire the poor masses at will. The factories were very hazardous. Yet, the laborers worked very long hours under poor lighting, ventilation and sanitation. "The haves" even "get richer" at the expense of the poor masses. The poor masses ("have nots") "get even poorer" in a correlative proportion to which the rich get even richer! Marx believed that the Aristocratic ruling class and the *bourgeoisie* (capitalist class) were morally insensitive against the terrible dehumanizing conditions and suffering of the industrial working and poor masses (have nots).

In his prediction of the communist revolution which would be led by the disgruntled, exploited, and poorly paid factory workers (*the proletariat*), Marx had not expected the emergence of the middle class and powerful labor unions. This powerful middle class provides an effective buffer zone between the poor and the factory and business owners. The emergence of a rich middle class absorbed the potential for communist revolutions as Marx had predicted them. The middle class provides hope for the poor to be uplifted from poverty and be incorporated into the fluid middle class economic structure. The top member of the middle class are rich and elitist members. They enjoy special political and socioeconomic privileges and prefer to keep the "*status quo*."

The rich and powerful middle class quells the potential for rebellion and communist or socialist revolution among their subordinate poor employees below them. This is because they benefit most from being the "middlemen" of the flow of wealth from the lower class to the small, upper rich class that controls everything by its vast resources and wealth in "immoral" economies where "money speaks" and people just listen! This is the tragic idolatry of Western capitalism, materialism, and obsessive love of money and wealth which the Bible denounced as evil or *mammon* and the root of all evils.

Who then is the master, money (*mammon*) or the people? What is the good end or the good life? Is money or wealth the end or a mere means to some noble end? Is technology the means for those who possess it to create more wealth for themselves by exploiting those who are technologically not yet developed? Or is technology the human tool for the advancement of knowledge and the improvement of industrial and agricultural production, so as to meet the needs of the world's people, improve their quality of life, the standards of living, and the provision of medical and healthcare?

A good medical and healthcare system must include a comprehensive national medical insurance program for the poor. This would positively enhance the local and global, human general well-being, and would also eventually lead to health-filled longevity, peace of both body and mind, and as such, the attainment of a good life and happiness. This is because a healthy mind and soul need a healthy body in which to reside. The body is therefore, the holy temple of God as St. Paul called it. At the same time, the health body also the temporal embodiment of both a healthy spirit and mind. As such, the physical state and health of the body correspondingly affects the health and state of mind and spirit or the soul. The proverb which states that a "healthy mind is a healthy body" is a good prescription for the universal existential reality and truth in this correlation of the medical and spiritual relationship between the state of the mind and that of the body in which the mind and spirit are both emergent and residents.

If technology and money are viewed not as the means to this noble end, but rather as the destiny in themselves, then inevitably, humanity faces some future catastrophe. This doom is self-imposed. It will be due to the fact that humanity will have abdicated its position as master in favor of money and wealth. If the human moral agency is replaced by greed for money and wealth of which they have become the slaves and the worshipers, this serves as the new God.

Having replaced the true God with this idol of the love of money or wealth as found in extreme cases of materialism and godless capitalism, then there will be a corresponding "trans-evaluation" of traditional ethics. A new form of capitalist ethics will emerge where "money makes right." Likewise, poverty and the lack of money would be considered by the majority to be a tragic curse to be avoided at all costs. For these people, the end justifies the means. As a result, the cost of escaping poverty may include moral corruption and crime. These evil ways to attain wealth include: fraud, theft, cheating, robbery, slave-trade, smuggling and selling illegal drugs, counterfeiting money, murder, pornography and prostitution.

This is the kind of inevitable moral depravity and rampant vice prevailing in the kind of society whose "God" is money and pleasure. The end of such a godless, materialistic, immoral society is lawlessness, crime, immorality, misery, hate, murder, and self-destruction. This is because human beings, having been created in God's own image, try hard to find God so as to be like him or her. God is the ultimate role model. Therefore, as Bishop Stephen Neil correctly noted, human beings can only be as good as the God they admire, worship, and seek to imitate in their own lives in the quest to become like him, her, or it. Therefore, the ethical and moral ideals and the values of each individual human being are closely correlated and intertwined with the individual's ideas of God, the good, justice, love, forgiveness, happiness, the neighbor, sin, and oppression.

## 7. Faith, Grace and Good Deeds of Love

Jesus' teachings stress faith, obedience, and good deeds as the path to salvation and union with God who is Agape (cf. Matt.5-7). But the Protestants chose just to stress faith as the only sure means for salvation. That presents a serious departure from the teachings of Jesus, Paul, John, and James. Like Jesus, St. James himself was forced to denounce those Christians who said that they had faith in God and were saved or redeemed even though they had no corresponding transformed mode of new life, which is externally expressed in the concrete works of agape as good works of altruism.

Jesus himself said that we would know the saints and true prophets not by their words, but rather by what they did in real life in terms of their deeds. Jesus called people's moral deeds their fruits! The tree which had no fruits was cursed by Jesus to demonstrate the need for fruits or good deeds by his followers.

God's Kingdom is built on Agape, and good deeds of grace and faith in God's goodness, and the notion of every person as a child of God. According to Jesus, any tree or branch that does not bear fruit is pruned and thrown into the fire (hell). (Cf. Matt. 57; 25:31-46; John 15). The final judgement is also based on good deeds as opposed to only faith as the Protestants erroneously teach (cf. Matt. 7:13-23; 25:31-46; Jam. 2:16-26).

The Protestant doctrines of "*sola fide*" (salvation by faith alone) and "*sola scriptura*" (salvation based on scriptures alone) originate from the

Protestant Reformation of the sixteenth century. The Reverend Professor Martin Luther who taught systematic theology and New Testament theology was one of the first anti-Catholic reformers who rejected the traditional doctrine of sacrifice, and good works, in favor of Pauline doctrine of salvation based on "justification by faith alone" *(sola fide).* Luther's doctrine was conditioned by his experience of inadequacy of his good works, love for God, confession of sins, and his failure to accept absolution and God's removal of personal guilt and inability to trust God's work of redemption.

Through personal experience, he found that the doctrine of salvation by "faith alone" in Christ gave him the assurance of salvation which the liturgical and traditional sacramental confession, good works, and absolution could not give him. What Luther failed to realize that good works, like faith, were all actually based on God's unmerited grace *(sola gratia)*, unconditional love and goodness that made them possible. As such, as Jesus taught about this moral issue, they are truly inseparable. Faith and obedience to God is only visible and measurable in terms of quality and quantity of good deeds of grace or agape (cf. Matt. 5-7; 25:31-46). The separation of faith from God works has led to great distortions of the teachings of Jesus and abuses within Christianity. Agape, justice and care for the poor have been forgotten. Yet, these are the central teachings of Jesus as the Christ and the reason for the incarnation of God in Christ and ministry (cf. Lk. 4:16-21).

Therefore, Christians must remember that it was because Christianity had failed to live to its divine calling and God's redemptive mission that Karl Marx (1818-1883) rejected it and sought to replace it with communism. His dialectical materialism by itself, does not explain Marx's view of religion, especially Christianity, without looking at the social, economic and political conditions of Europe and the Church in the nineteenth century. The poor masses had become alienated from the land, political and economic processes. They only had been left with religion in the form of uncaring Christianity about their economic plight and moral predicament.

In the nineteenth century, Christianity had become aligned with wealth factory owners, materialistic, corrupt and miserably failed its mission as the religion of justice and unconditional love for the neighbor that Marx was led to denounce it in the last century as an "opium of the people." The Church had failed to respond positively to the plight of the poor. The Church had failed to help to find creative solutions for the serious major problems created by the industrialization in Europe and the creation of the landless, urban, poor masses. The masses of landless poor masses whose livelihood and plight were tied to the availability of work in the factories, where they worked long hours in unhealthy and hazardous conditions for very little pay became the concern of Karl Marx and his friends, particularly, Friedreich Engels (1820-1895).

Marx's solution was the unification of the workers and revolutionary seizure of the factories which they would collectively win and control. Since then, Russia, China, and Cuba have undergone this communist revolution; others may soon follow suit if the West does not come to terms with both God and the unconditional love of the neighbor that ensures impartial treatment and justice for all human beings. These beliefs also lead to the correlative equitable distribution of natural resources according to need, instead of being based on color, race, military strength, or superior technology. An unfortunate case of this at the moment is with the people of color and those without modern technology who still get either cheated or given the leftovers and castoffs by people in wealthy and developed countries.

Subsequently, these two groups are viable candidates for communism, unless the West changes its socioeconomic structure so as to include them fully as equal partners in whatever ventures, advances, planning, successes, and losses that happen to be of importance.

In addition, the Church cannot afford to keep quiet about the important issues today, such as nuclear arms race, wars, injustice, sexism, racism, poverty, hunger, and disease. To do so would be to make the same kind of mistake as the Church has made over the previous hundreds of years by siding with the rich, kings, rulers, imperialists, slave traders, and other kinds of oppressors. Furthermore, it would be to neglect its prophetic and redemptive mission in the world. As a result, the Church would also to become an accomplice with evildoers, negative forces and therefore, partners with the evil forces or the "Devil."

Therefore, if there is to be meaningful peace in the world, Christians and the Church must become its vanguard, for it is the Church which has God's explicit commandment given to it and all its members to love each other and all human beings, including enemies, unconditionally.

Agape requires the Christian to be nonviolent and nonretaliatory. According to Jesus, agape requires one to "turn the other cheek," when hit, instead of violent retaliation. Agape demands of the Christian and moral saint to "turn the other cheek" and walk the extra mile. It demands that the obedient people become the salt and light of God in the dark world of sin and injustice. Agape requires us to become the apostles of the good news of God's salvation. This redemptive divine mission is accomplished through the persuasion of men and women to accept God's positively transforming power of grace, pragmatic faith and free unconditional love and free forgiveness of sins.

Agape calls and persuades us to become the peacemakers in the world of strife in order to bring the reconciling and healing power of God's grace through unconditional love, free forgiveness of sins, and the correlative divine removal of its barriers of pain and guilt. Within this perspective, the Christian's redemptive divine mission of love and peacemaking in the world is probably best summed up in the words of the famous prayer of Saint Francis of Assisi (1182-1226). His prayer reads as follows:

> Lord make us instruments of your peace:
> Where there is hatred, let us sow love;
> Where there is injury, pardon;
> Where there is discord, harmony;
> Where there is doubt, faith;
> Where there is despair, hope;
> Where there is darkness, light;
> Where there is sadness, joy.
>
> Grant that we may so much seek to be as consoled
> as to console;
> To be understood as to understand;
> to be loved as to love.
>
> For it is in giving that we receive;
> it is in pardoning that we are pardoned;
> And it is in dying that we are born to eternal life. (St. Francis)

It is self-evident that St. Francis is praying for a practical Christian life and the faithful manner, in which it is to be lived out daily in the world. It further illustrates our own failure to live by the Gospel, God's commandments, and Christ's teaching. For Jesus taught us to pray that "God should forgive us in the same way we forgive others," and that judgement will be given according to how we respond to the need of the poor, hungry, oppressed, sick, homeless, naked, and falsely imprisoned (cf. Matt. 25:31-46). St. James puts it drastically as follows:

> My brother, what good is it for someone to say that he has faith if his actions do not prove it? Can that faith save him? Suppose there are brothers or sisters who need clothes and don't have enough to eat. What good is there in your saying to them, "God bless you! Keep warm and eat well!" - if you don't give them the necessities of life? So it is with faith: if it is alone and includes no good action, then it is dead.
>
> But someone will say, "One person has faith and another has actions." My answer is, "show me how anyone can have faith without action. I will show you my faith by my actions. . . ." You fool! Do you want to be shown that faith without actions is useless? (Jam. 2:14-20).

Indeed, the Christian problem is that, unlike St. James, we have concentrated on the preaching and requirement of faith as the necessary prerequisite for Christian adult baptism and supernatural salvation.

Subsequently, we have tragically tended to ignore and neglect to emphasize that faith alone without corresponding personal discipline of good, just, godly, loving, and charitable deeds is dead and worthless, just like a fruit tree which never yields any fruits is worthless.

Therefore, mere unfruitful faith is neither holy nor redemptive. Such a faith is a mere empty, hypocritical confession of Jesus Christ as Lord. Meanwhile, it ignores his essential and definitive commandment to love God and one's fellow human beings without any conditions, and to minister to the needy, hungry, weak, poor, homeless, sick and oppressed.

As a result, most Western Christians have most ironically and sinfully identified themselves, their values, and style of living with those of the rich, greedy materialists. Subsequently, they have become evil partners with the imperialists, slave-traders, colonialists, exploiters, and oppressors. They have tragically succumbed to this dehumanizing moral evil mainly because of their uncontrolled greed and avarice. Fatefully, their love for money, power, and supremacy have sadly outweighed their love for God and Jesus Christ's call to the way of justice, honesty, simple living, and suffering for God's righteousness sake.

Ultimately, these kinds of greedy and egocentric people have in essence most tragically rejected God's free redemptive call in Christ, which is ever inviting all human beings everywhere to hear, positively respond, and become God's own essential and authentic temporal representatives in the world. As such, humans can become active instruments of God's unconditional love, salvation, caring, fellowship, peace, and happiness in this world of self-centeredness, sin, selfishness, greed, strife, division, hatred, unhappiness, and self-destruction.

## 8. Basic Contemporary Moral Issues

The extreme moral relativists like Protagoras and "New Age" advocates have rejected traditional forms of authority, including the established canons, and have tended to teach that morality is a personal and a private affair. As such, that morality cannot be legitimately legislated or taught.

This was based on the false assumption that there is no truth or a virtuous moral good deed that is universal. Furthermore, it was assumed that there was no meaningful agreement on what is morally good and evil, or morally right and wrong. This was based on another ethical assumption that what is considered morally good and right by one person may be viewed as morally wrong and harmful by another depending on one's background, gender, age, upbringing, socialization, intelligence, education, socioeconomic, class, creed, race, and culture.

For instance, some Christians in the USA saw slavery as being morally wrong and a social evil to be fought against and abolished. They thus mobilized other men and women of goodwill and moral conscience to oppose this reprehensible practice of slavery. At the same time, slavery was being religiously and morally defended vigorously in the South for being both divinely ordained and the destiny of the Africans, who were considered inferior people created by God to serve Whites as slaves and servants.

The Christian preachers in the South positively affirmed in God's name from the pulpits that slavery was moral and economically beneficial, and therefore, desirable and justified enough to be forcefully defended by resorting to war and secession. As a result of this moral dilemma, disagreement on racism, slavery, segregation, and oppression led to the historic American moral and military civil war. They further led to the aftermath of moral issues relating to the newly emancipated slaves, who also happened to be racially African and black, and thus, to be readily identifiable.

These are academically very interesting moral issues and ethical dilemmas to analyze for ethical normative judgements and moral values. It is very clear that for some people, slavery was viewed as morally wrong, repugnant, and not to be tolerated since it meant the brutal degradation and material possession of one human being by another. This fundamentally affected the master who brutalized the slave. At the same time, it also dehumanized the slave into some kind of thing or object by virtue of being held and categorized as valuable material property, just like the farm work animals, particularly the mules, horses, and cattle. The descendants of former slaves are still trying to overcome the trauma of slavery and forgive the descendants of the slave-masters.

Slavery is morally and ethically viewed as one of the greatest forms of human degradation, and hence, an extreme evil. Slavery led human beings to be abused by other fellow humans by capturing, selling and enslaving them. They slaves were often reduced to the status of the beast of burden, such as a horse, mule and an oxen. This morally reprehensible of slavery and dehumanization of people was carried out of greed for the selfish evil motive and purpose of exploiting, utilizing, and reducing them to the status of beasts of burden to produce wealth and profit for the slave masters.

Slavery became a great temptation for the rich and the powerful because it provided a physical means of cheap labor and production in the fields, factories, and at home "*in lieu*" of other appropriate cheap animals of burden and machines. In addition, the slaves were most often physically mistreated, overworked, and not paid for their hard labor, or allowed to share in the profits of what they produced for their idle parasitic masters. This illustrates the problem of moral theory of experience and pleasure for the majority.

From this extremely dehumanizing moral problem of slavery, which is the worst moral act one group of people can do to another, there are also other horrible moral evils which human beings do against one another. These evils include senseless war and destruction of both life and property. They also include some cases of genocide, such as that committed by Nazi Germany against the Jews, the Hutu massacres of the Tutsi people in Rwanda, and the Serbian Christian massacres of the Muslims.

Ultimately, regardless of the scriptures and the commandments, based on reason and nature, normal moral, rational, and thinking human beings as moral agents are able to view life as sacred. As such, they should see it as that which is not to be abused either by slavery, arbitrary arrest, confinement, discrimination, violence, rape, torture, starvation, abuse, neglect, degradation, and murder. This is not only true for human beings, but also to a certain extent for the rest of life in creation.

In this respect, the environmentalists seek to protect animals, plants, air, rivers, and lakes from careless human abuse, misuse, pollution, and destruction. These varied and sometimes conflicting religious and moral perspectives of how to view God's creation, nature, and the environment are, indeed, very much moral issues, as are murder, rape, greed, stealing, abortion, and capital punishment. This is true, because they all deal with both life and property on which this life is based. If killing is morally wrong and evil since it eliminates life instead of enhancing it, then pollution of the environment is also morally wrong and evil since it destroys the very environment that enables life forms to exist on this unique planet. This is unlike Venus, which is too hot to support life, and Mars, which is too cold to support any life forms.

But without proper moral and legal controls, the human beings may just concentrate on making money with the factories and products while ignoring the problem of increased emission of carbon dioxide, carbon monoxide and sulphur oxide, which are responsible for air pollution, acid rain, and destruction of vegetation. They also lead to the warming the atmosphere and creation of destructive seasonal changes like the recent failure of rains and subsequent fatal droughts in Africa and India.

If carbon dioxide increases drastically due to uncontrolled factory and car emissions in the atmosphere and forest and vegetation are destroyed, this planet may warm up and lose its water to the air and become a hot and lifeless planet just like Venus. This environmental issue is fundamental, and therefore as morally important as the nuclear arms race, which is similarly capable of destroying life on this planet. This would be in either a direct immediate nuclear holocaust or the aftermath massive radiation and thick smoke clouds which would turn the earth into another lifeless iced up planet, like Mars, through human bigotry, belligerence, and stupidity.

Consequently, in view of the unprecedented global dangers and threats to life as we know it today in this fragile planet, we have to reject destructive traditional ethical theories such as those based on Stuart Mill's utilitarianism. The utilitarian moral principle works for the majority and leads to the oppression of the minorities.

Utilitarianism measures value, the good and happiness in terms of the majority served and made happy. Its proponents advocate the maximization of pleasure for the maximum number of people. Utilitarianism shifts the emphasis back to axiological ethics which insists on the value or goodness as measurable in terms of a large quantity of measurable good results of an action. That is, if that action or deed is to be judged as morally sound and good. This moral theory also compels all moral agents to do good deeds. They also avoid causing harming to other people or nonhuman creatures. This moral theory is in line with the teaching of

Jesus who taught that a good tree bears plenty of good fruits whereas the bad tree bears only a few or none. As a result, Jesus cursed the tree without fruits to illustrate this point. He also taught that true teachers and prophets are not judged by their confessions or teachings, but rather, they are judged by what they actually do (deeds cf. Matt. 7:15-23).

Personal intrinsic moral authority is a result of correct knowledge, personal goodness, and virtue. Rewards are realized in doing the right thing for its own sake. They are not material rewards to be realized in monetary terms or praise and glory to be received from others. In this understanding, Kant's moral imperative for doing the morally right as a divine duty out of love and moral obligation is the best expansion of this theory. This Kantian categorical moral imperative to moral duty provides a necessary ideal corrective and radical negation to the recklessness of the pleasure principle and moral expediency.

In other words, what is morally right and just is not what is necessarily the most pleasurable or the most expedient. In fact, very often, the reverse is the case. That is why there is always a moral crisis for most people, because what is morally correct and just is often unattractive, unpleasurable, and less profitable in terms of money, wealth, fame, and prestige. It is probably for this very reason that for many people, it has appeared that politics and morality, and commerce and morality, do not mix and that they are diametrically opposed.

However, it would be very tragic for any just, democratic, moral and responsible people and society to separate morality from economics and to separate morality from politics. To do so would create a monster for a government that cares less about the human rights of its citizens and those of others in the international community.

Therefore, the politicians, legislators and community leaders must become the good public examples and ideal role models of good, moral, responsible, law abiding, and caring citizenry to emulate. They should not become the lawbreakers, robbers, public scandals, and terrorists of the public. As a result, the people of the developing countries must get rid of their corrupt leaders in order to create a new leadership and new society with better moral values and higher chances of a more rapid economic development. Public officials have the moral obligation, duty, responsibility, and chance to become the moral guiding shining stars of their own generation, nations, and the global community, which is shaped by their significant moral or immoral decisions and actions.

Subsequently, it is a divine imperative that nations should seek to elect into key public offices and support the most educated, moral, caring, and responsible people among them. For it is a great tragedy when people elect the immoral and the unjust to lead them, just because they are either rich, powerful public speakers, or manipulative, unscrupulous, and shrewd political actors. This is the kind of tragic situation which Jesus denounced as "blind guides of the blind" who will lead themselves and their blind followers into the pit or over the cliff and into destruction.

It is also in this context that Plato called for a Philosopher King or ruler if there was to be global enlightenment, goodwill, and lasting peace, instead of ignorance, prejudice, poor judgement, strife, and wars which characterize our untutored world. This world is still heavily steeped in barbaric and naive mutual ignorance, suspicion, injustice, hostility, strife, hatred, and war. In this respect, Socrates' teaching that "knowledge is virtue" and ignorance the source of evil ravaging human beings and the world, has proved to be true.

Therefore, in order to reduce human evil in the world and facilitate peaceful interpersonal and international communication and cooperation, good international and moral education are essential prerequisites. Jesus' commandment of mutual unconditional love and acceptance is the necessary bedrock which this global system of education, communication, and cooperation must be grounded. Otherwise, very little will be accomplished, and, as in the past, and tragic global consequences will inevitably follow.

If human species have to continue to survive on this increasingly "shrinking" plant, human beings have got to learn to live together in harmony and peace as loving, caring, responsible, sharing, moral agents, and as brothers and sisters in the one global family of God.

Subsequently, prejudice, racism, slavery, imperialism, ethnic or religious bigotry, fraud, exploitation, deceit, poverty, disease, injustice and warfare have to be eliminated. They are all moral evils. They do not enhance global mutual life nor do they create the ideal conditions conducive to mutual trust, justice, mutual acceptance in unconditional love, a good life, happiness, and peace. These are the good and positive aspects of life for which the human being deeply yearns and strives constantly to achieve in whatever he or she does, regardless of whether it is noble, good, just, selfish, evil, or unjust.

Even in doing evil, the evildoer sees in it some desirable good and personal fulfillment. However, due to ignorance and lack of goodwill, the evildoer is evil and dangerous to himself or herself and the society because of this hazardous ignorance and malevolent lack of goodwill to do the good where it is clearly known. This option for the evil doer to do the less good instead of the better alternative cumulatively and ultimately threatens to overwhelm human affairs with human evil and its consequent misery and pain to both the doers and community.

This is why it is both an individual and collective moral obligation for human beings of moral conscience and goodwill to act both alone and together to fight evil, especially sadism, discrimination, ignorance, sexism, oppression, dictatorship, abuse of human rights, crime, poverty, exploitation, militarism, violence, and war wherever they exist on this globe. To this end, the United Nations Universal Declaration of Human Rights and Amnesty International have been very helpful.

This is why it is important for the USA not to withdraw its membership from the UN and its important educational programs and other joint activities in protest against the so-called socialist and terrorist organizations' infiltration of those organizations. This would amount to capitulation to communism, and therefore, an unwise and unconstructive action. Beneficence is of greater global moral significance than holding the world hostage with military, nuclear, and economic threats and sanctions. Furthermore, nations, just like individuals, have a right of speech, freedom of self-determination, self-governing, and self-development without reference either to the systems of the USA or the Soviet Union. The superpowers have to learn to live together in mutual peace, and have to accept that military, economic, ideological, and religious or cultural imperialism in the modern world is not favorably viewed as a moral thing to do.

Finally, for the individual, national and global responsible freedom, harmony and peace are the highest and most valued virtues and the main objectives of all morally, ethically and critically thinking good-willed, godly, moral, and peace-loving people everywhere on this most blessed living planet. Unfortunately, many of its inhabitants have not yet discovered how unique and most blessed they are. Subsequently, we all still need to learn to live together lovingly in godly peace in order to enjoy most fully God's special beauty in creation and life. There are unique heavenly blessings to be seen and enjoyed on this planet and nowhere else in this wide but largely lifeless cosmos.

## 9. The Moral Prerequisites for a Just And Peaceful Human Society

For any human community or society to exist in a state of peace and endure in this ideal condition of harmonious existence, it must necessarily become one which fosters virtue and ideal moral values among its members. That community or society must become a caring and moral community which both *values and promotes justice, harmony, and peace for all its law abiding citizens.* This must be observed for all its members, irrespective of gender, marital status, sexual orientation, creed, ideology, handicap, age, color, class, racial or ethnic identity, and political and religious affiliation.

Inclusiveness and acceptance of diversity are the good foundations of justice in any pluralistic society. The evils of valuing monolithic systems are characterized by racism, sexism, tribalism, and genocide in Africa and some parts of Eastern Europe. These are the same evils which are the causes of violence and wars in the Middle East and Ireland. On the other hand, diversity has been the main strength of the United States of America. Africa and Europe can learn a great lesson from the American experiment despite its imperfections. The USA is an ideal model for the global community. It represents all the colors and races of humanity! It is a microcosm of the future global macrocosm!

The just and moral community is that which encourages its members to become ideal voluntary moral agents. They are desiring, willing, and aspiring to do their best and to achieve the best in whatever they do, whether in public or in private. Therefore, it must legislate against and proscribe evil deeds which are motivated by extreme self-love, self-interest, selfishness, self-centeredness, greed, ignorance, prejudice, individualism, envy, malice, and hate.

This must be the case for these deeds and evil expressions are not motivated by God's Holy Spirit and the *Logos*. These deeds are grounded in the positive intention and the reconciling and redemptive divine spirit of mutual unconditional love, acceptance, togetherness, goodwill, justice, sharing, and cooperation. Yet, these are the basic essential moral requisites for the existence of any viable moral, enduring, just, harmonious, and peaceful human family. They are the wider macrocosmic community of which the family is the basic foundation and microcosm.

Consequently, the moral foundation of the viable local community, as well as the larger human community, both national and international, is the good and morally sound human family. It is in the human family that all individuals are born, raised, socialized, educated, humanized, and inculturated as human beings and as members of the human race, which is the larger global human community, of which the local human community is an essential and integral constitutive member or part both at the local and global levels.

Subsequently, it is quite clear that no individual and no human community can be either moral or healthy unless the human family itself is healthy since it is the primary societal foundation. As such, the human family is the human "co-creator" with God, as well as the protector, educator, and socioeconomic safeguard of the individuals created in the world through it and the community based on it.

Therefore, a weak and morally unhealthy family is a great societal tragedy. This is particularly true for some families where proper sex behavior and sex roles are absent. The absence of these sound and normative moral values in this family setting leads to destructive incest, adultery, and fornication. Due to this unchecked sex out of wedlock, there are many children who are born out of wedlock. Most of these unfortunate children grow up without ever knowing their real biological fathers. This is also the situation in which most children are brought up by young, poor, uneducated, unmarried, promiscuous, single mothers.

These poor people live on public assistance and welfare, and live in dirty, crowded public housing projects either with their parents or alone. This is currently the unfortunate case of most Black American poor families in the inner city communities.

Children in these settings grow up abused, neglected, violent, and crime-oriented. Many of them drop out of school, commit violent crimes, such as armed robbery, and serve long sentences in prison. In this respect, prison is a natural extension of the miserable life in the ghetto or poor and crime-riddled inner city violent communities. Life there is comparable to life on the front line, because of drugs, gangs, and armed wars in these hellish neighborhoods. These conditions are socioeconomic, and not genetic, as Richard Hernstein and Charles Murray erroneously concluded in their racially biased book, *The Bell Curve*.

These kinds of families represent a multitude of past and present socioeconomic and political evils of slavery, oppression, discrimination, and dehumanization. They are the victims of prejudice, oppression, poverty and crime. Therefore, these families represent divine judgement and a societal hazard. The local community and the nation will have to pay a very heavy socioeconomic and political price for having allowed such inhumane and immoral conditions of poverty and moral degradation to exist within its borders.

The community and nation that permits such economic and educational injustice and moral degradation to occur among its own members will inevitably pay heavily for this evil in terms of an increase in crime, particularly theft, rape, break-ins, robberies, arson, larceny, fraud, assault, and vandalism. These kinds of crimes are usually committed by people who have been wronged by society, either economically or socially, through parental neglect, abuse, hunger, and poverty as they were growing up. Subsequently, as adults, these people sometimes turn to a life of crime because of psychological problems, negative values, programming, revenge, sadism, indifference, poverty, lack of marketable job skills, survival compulsiveness, and habit.

As a matter of fact, some of these homeless, poor habitual criminals are sometimes better off in jail than on the unfriendly streets with no home or caring family and relatives. In jail, they are sure of a free roof over their heads, free utilities, and daily food.

However, this is in no way to suggest that all criminals should be kept locked up in prison in order to protect the community from moral and physical harm. The real care for criminals and crime prevention is not long jail sentences, and nor is it barbaric capital punishment, since capital punishment does nothing to reform the crime or reduce homicides and other crimes of passion.

On the contrary, a more meaningful and effective Christian means for lasting crime prevention is the global eradication or drastic reduction of poverty by a more moral, loving, just, Christian, unconditional, and beneficent equitable redistribution of natural resources, wealth, and property. Thus, nobody is forced to resort to a life of crime or stealing in order to live. In addition, the provision of a more holistic liberal arts education is important, for it cultivates the free mind and ability to think more analytically and critically about life and existence, and to make informed sound moral choices and decisions with responsibility for the consequences.

Nevertheless, since the family remains the basic foundation of the community, if the community is to thrive and endure in a meaningful and peaceful manner, it has to ensure the healthy endurance, moral well-being, and socioeconomic integrity of the family. As a result, the society must assist families to stay intact both morally and socioeconomically.

To this end, casual sex, teenage pregnancies, single parentage, and causal marriages and divorces must be strongly discouraged. The sanctity of sex, the seriousness of sexual relationship, and the sanctity and permanence of vows and the marriage bond must be reaffirmed by the Church and the community. Today's threat of deadly sexually transmitted diseases may be God's way of warning and punishing people for their irresponsible sexual practices which reject God's laws of the sanctity of sex, marriage, and monogamy. Accordingly, in the Hebrew Scriptures (the Old Testament) there are prohibitions against adultery, fornication, homosexuality, bestiality, and incest as immoral, unclean, social, and medically hazardous practices (cf. Lev. 18-20). These sexual evils harm both the perpetrators and the community.

Consequently, if the ancient divine warning against sexual aberration, promiscuity, and immorality is not seriously heeded in good time, in the face of new deadly sexual diseases like AIDS, we can easily become another proverbial Sodom and Gomorrah. These cities are said to have been destroyed because of their sins of disobedience against God and hedonism in the form of sexual immorality (adultery and fornication) and homosexuality (Gen. 18:16-19:29; cf. Rom. 1:18-32).

Some people have erroneously thought that, due to the sexual revolution of the 1960s and 1970s, many people engage in premarital sexual relations or live together in trial marriages, commit adultery, engage in homosexuality, abort or have children out of wedlock, and divorce in large numbers, that therefore, these practices should be subsequently viewed as morally acceptable for our generation, including the Church. The presupposition and moral theory behind this kind of moral argument is the mistaken extreme moral relativism and "situation ethics."

The moral view that whatever the majority decides or does is morally right, and that whatever feels good and expedient is in fact good and morally acceptable is false and dangerous. The majority can be wrong since all people are finite, sinful and fallible. Therefore, the moral theory which equates right with the democratic vote of the majority, must rejected and condemned by mainline Christian ethics. Jesus warned that the road to hell is very wide and the road to truth, God and eternal life is very narrow, and many people fail to find it (cf. Matt. 7:13-23). Extreme moral relativism, human-centered and defective moral theories lead to false moral conclusions and ideas, such as the idea that the "majority is always right." This idea erroneously assumes the majority will constitutes truth, and determines the common good as well as whatever is moral and ethical for that community! Undoubtedly, this is the kind of proverbial "mass gate" that leads to evils of sexual immorality, ethnocentrism, racism, imperialism, oppression, sexism, hedonism, genocide and destruction.

This kind of moral teaching can only come from an evil or sinful desire to commit evil without being morally sanctioned either by personal moral conscience or the community. However, the fact remains that right and wrong, moral and immoral, and sin and evil are not grounded in the "maximum number theory" of moral utilitarianism and pragmatism. Instead, they are grounded in God's eternal truths, natural laws, and moral laws as found outlined in the Decalogue and Jesus' teaching and commandment on the imperative unconditional love for both God and one's fellow human beings or the neighbor.

Therefore, according to traditional Christian teachings and ethics, even if everybody cheated, committed adultery or fornicated, engaged in homosexuality or if some people found bestiality more appealing, it would never make these acts ethically and morally correct or right. Likes and dislikes have very little to do with Christian ethics. The majority vote does not define what is good, right and moral. What is good and right may be considered evil and wrong by evil people. For instance, the fact that at one time most European and American Christians saw nothing wrong with slavery did not make slavery good and morally right. These Christians may have thought that it was morally acceptable, but it was not. Righteousness corresponds to the good, truth, reality, and God's Moral Law as both revealed in nature and moral consciousness, nature and the various scriptures.

Therefore, from an axiological and deontological perspective, it could be argued that it was for this reason of moral instruction and guidance that God sent the prophets into ancient Israel. Their divine public mission was to denounce its prevailing immorality, lawlessness, idolatry, greed, exploitation, injustice, oppression of the poor, and corruption and pervasion of justice through bribes. They also denounced the rich people's excessive greed for money and property at the expense of the poor who were becoming increasingly disposed and poorer. Prophets like Amos, Habakkuk, Hosea, and Isaiah vividly addressed these moral issues and promised God's severe punishment to the nation due to these sins.

It is to be noted that God and the prophets never accepted these sins and evil deeds as moral and acceptable just "because everybody did them." Instead, "because everybody did them," therefore everybody was to be punished, including both the religious and political leaders who out of love for popularity and material wealth, did nothing to stop these evils being committed in their nation.

Subsequently, what we need most today are more dedicated prophets of God who will speak out boldly in the name of the most holy, loving, redemptive, and righteous God who will tolerate our sins only to a certain point without punishing us. These kinds of prophets should be above the temptation of money and material wealth, for Church leaders and religious ministers have been already largely silenced by the world and evil through corrupting them by bribery of money, cars, property, and sex, and then effectively holding them hostage with threats of blackmail, scandal, and public disgrace.

Nevertheless, the family as the primary foundation of society remains with the primary "creation" of human beings, socializing them into the ethical values of living most meaningfully and peacefully together with others in community. Furthermore, the community and its well-being are possible by each individual's moral duty and obligation to protect the other members so as to be protected themselves. This protection is especially needed by the young and the weak.

There must be also teaching on the virtues of faithfulness, honesty, loyalty and reliability. People must be taught to keep promises and vows made to one another or to God. People must be taught that personal integrity requires that these promises are kept irrespective of whether they are made in public or private, and involves honesty, loyalty, truth telling, and not telling lies or gossip about other people since it harms them and the welfare of the community. There is also the responsibility not to steal, but rather to share one's property freely with others in need. Furthermore, there is also the need to observe all the rules both written and customary on the right behavior and social interactions so as to facilitate harmony and peace within the community.

It is clear that the moral paradigm for this kind of positive socialization, unconditional love and ethical, beneficent moral imperative duty follows that of the Good Samaritan. The idea is to produce positively, morally conditioned citizens through correct socialization. Love and justice must become internalized and imprinted by God and the community on the person's soul as a habitual state of personal moral virtue and beneficent goodness. In this way, each human being as an adult member of the community is truly an authentic moral agent who knows, desires, and seeks to do what is good, just, and morally correct, without any conditions or expectations for personal reward apart from the personal intrinsic moral satisfaction that is derived from doing well one's moral duty and obligation.

This concept of categorical moral obligation to duty and work is similar to the Hindu concept of "*Karma Yoga.*" This is the path to God through doing one's work dutifully. As such, good work is part of prayer and practical quest for God and meaning through one's obligations of ordinary work and duty. As such, God is as effectively and redemptively present in the kitchen, garden and office as God is present in the temple or Church. "*Jnana Yoga,*" is the alternative spiritual straight and difficult path to God through education, contemplation, and acquisition of redemptive secret knowledge of God's mysteries of salvation.

This acquisition of moral and ethical knowledge leads to the virtuous life that is pleasing to God. Knowledge makes possible an explicitly expressed life of holiness and virtue that is externally manifested in both good deeds and holy speech or words of wisdom and counsel to other people. In this respect, the holy person is also a moral teacher, who teaches people about the sacred mystery of life and the world. And teaches them how best and most meaningfully they can live in this world.

The saints provide good examples of how to live in this world in peace as a good, caring, loving, and productive citizen. Their secrets to a good moral and spiritual life can be successfully learned and imitated by other people. Jesus, Mary the Mother of Jesus and the Buddha provide some of these best examples of a simple, prayerful, spiritual, moral, loving and nonviolent good life that can be learned and followed successfully by all obedient and God-loving people.

Unlike these Hindu moral teachers, many parents are ignorant and poorly educated. Subsequently, they are not able to adequately or effectively socialize well their young ones without help from the community and the larger society. Since many parents are also poor moral agents, and therefore, poor moral role models for their children, it is reasonable that the community should use the school classroom opportunity to impart the necessary essential ideal, universal, social, and ethical values to the young. These ideal humane and civic virtues as well as basic technical and social skills that are required for a successful, productive, and peaceful life and work in the community, should be part of the central education that the schools and communities impart on the young. Good education and moral training should adequately equip the student with all the skills and moral and social virtues which are required for the student to learn how to cooperate and live together with others in harmony and peace, regardless of the inevitable differences of gender, color, race, creed, and nationality.

These global human moral values cannot be omitted. They are essential for the proper functioning of the Global Community. Therefore, moral education and training in civic virtues cannot be entrusted to families alone. The families can only do a partial job in imparting these essential values to the young during the socialization process. This is partly because they require a well informed, trained, objective and sensitive teacher to teach them, as well as the essential exposure to different people of different races and ideas, just like the way it is in real life in this pluralistic world.

The cooperation between the community and the family is essential in order to provide good services and education to the children. When these institutions are working together, they will find new ways to do an excellent job in children's essential education as an intellectual, moral and social positive conditioning to live a good and happy life. It is necessary mental, social, spiritual and moral equipment for living most meaningfully, morally, productively, socially, peacefully and happily in this pluralistic world of interpersonal relationships and potential for strife and breakdown.

The well socialized, educated, and integrated moral agent or well humanized person should also be able to love, honor, forgive, and accept himself or herself in order to be able to love, honor, forgive, and accept others unconditionally. This unconditional acceptance and love for the self is the necessary basis for the person to love, accept, and forgive others in unconditional redemptive love. This unconditional love reconciles, heals, and restores alienated groups or relationships. Agape makes authentic personal and collective life with the neighbor through both a possible and fulfilling reality. In short, it is a human moral obligation to love oneself as God's good creation unconditionally in order to love others divinely in the same manner as we love ourselves, and to do this cheerfully in full obedience to the Lord Jesus Christ's teaching and commandment of gratuitous redemptive love for all human beings as God's own beloved children.

Finally, the "*Law of Karma*" or the law of moral causality, must be respected and taken into account. This moral principle correctly affirms a person reaps what he or she sows in the moral and spiritual realm, just like people reap what they sow in their gardens. For instance, if we sow corn, we harvest a plentiful crop of corn if the weather and soil are right. We do not harvest a crop of rice where we sow corn. Similarly, if in relating to others we sow the seeds of hate, we will also reap the violent fruits of hate. If we sow the seeds of unconditional love, harmony, and peace, likewise, we will reap the fruits of love, harmony, and peace. Subsequently, we will be able to realize the true fruits of a good life and its coextensively correlative true human happiness, which all thinking, normal human beings crave and yearn for as their most desired divine fulfillment and ultimate destiny in God's divinizing eternal presence.

This ultimate divine and happy destiny in God is also traditionally described as "eternal life," "immortality," "beatific vision," "heaven" and God's Kingdom." For most Buddhists, this heavenly and blessed state is called the state of "*Nirvana*." *Nirvana* is typically characterized by the personal experience of God. For Christians, Jews and Muslims, this is called "God's Kingdom" or "Heaven."

*Nirvana* as Heaven or God's Kingdom is both simultaneously experienced as it is mediated by God's unconditional love, fellowship, forgiveness, righteousness, holiness, beauty, glory, eternity, peace, and happiness. This is accomplished through God's revelation, creative and redemptive work of God's *Logos* that is eternally incarnate and at work in the world (John 1:1-6). These divinizing attributes and redemptive powers of unmerited grace conferred on obedient human beings by God are also the very moral virtues and universal ethical values and moral prerequisites for a viable, strong, moral, healthy, harmonious, peaceful and happy life and the human community here on the Earth.

Ultimately, true peace, joy, and happiness of heaven is accessible here in the present moment. They are present here on the Earth. Indeed, the praxis of agape is the key to this God's Kingdom. The praxis of agape also creates a peaceful Global Community. Through agape people can live together in mutual acceptance and tolerance of each other as brothers and sisters, and as members of God's Family and the Kingdom.

# Chapter 15

# Religion, Values and Christian Ethics for A Pluralistic World: A Summary and Conclusion

Whereas the world of the past two millenniums has been that of feuding ethnocentric small communities and militant feudalistic nations characterized by tribalism, nationalism, racism, sexism, violence and wars, the world of the Third Millennium is hopefully that of an interwoven pluralistic and interdependent, tolerant, inclusive and peaceful Global Community. It is a Community of a highly evolved freedom, and moral consciousness. It is characterized by the new human global collective self-consciousness and new inclusive and collective-identity as humanity and members of one diverse common evolutionary human race, rather than many.

## 1. The Importance of Human Collective Self-Consciousness and Identity As Brothers and Sisters in God's Family

The new democratic and utilitarian Global Community must become pluralistic and diverse as the ideal, rather seeking to become monolithic. It must be rooted in the new understanding that all human beings belong to the same race of humanity and that they are all merely different brothers and sisters who belong to the same God's extended cosmic family. As such, quarrels and conflicts within the brotherhood and sisterhood must be amicably settled within the spirit of brotherly love and compassion that are truly characteristic of any ideal and caring members of the brotherhood and sisterhood in the world. This includes conflicts between Jews and Arabs, Christians and non-Christians, Black and White, men and women, the poor and rich people or nations.

The past nationalistic quests for national monolithic communities have sadly led to crimes of racial or "ethnic cleansing" and genocide. The Nazi attempt to exterminate the European Jews during the World War II is the worst example of fascism. This Jewish holocaust represents an extreme example of a national quest for racial purity, condemnation and collective social intolerance for cultural, ethnic, moral or religious diversity and pluralism.

Other examples of this public and collective moral and social evils include the Serbs' attempted extermination of the Slavs in Kosovo in 1994-1998, and the 1994 Hutu attempt to exterminate the Tutsi people of Rwanda provide other recent examples of this moral, cultural, social and political evil. As such, the universal acceptance of cultural, linguistic, religious and ethnic pluralism and diversity is the necessary basic strong societal and moral foundation for the new inclusive Global Community.

Like a strong and long-lasting Egyptian pyramid, this new Global Community must be supported by the strong societal theocentric values and strong pragmatic trinitarian pillars constituted by the inclusive global moral principles of: (1) human mutual peaceful coexistence, (2) free trade and (3) technology assisted cooperation and joint ventures. This peaceful Global Community is grounded in a new inclusive and better academic understanding of human biology, culture, religion, politics and economy. Good education is required to ensure that mutual respect, tolerance for diversity, pluralism, nonviolence, justice and peace continue to prevail within this new Global Community.

There is a strong collective human self-consciousness or common identity as the *Homo sapiens* that unifies people everywhere in the world as the uniquely intelligent, thinking, linguistic, fire-using, self-transcending and free creatures that are like God. This is universally true despite the artificial environmental originated biological differences of skin-color, hair-texture, various facial features and the environmental factors, such as the diversity of cultures, pluralism of religions and languages.

The more geographically isolated people are, the more these environmental factors determine and shape both the life and destiny of those ethnic or tribal groups. This reality is self-evident in the precolonial Africa, America and Asia. The more geographically, educationally, economically and politically the people interact together, the more culturally and linguistically they become similar, and tolerate the differences of gender, color, religion and ethnicity. The USA provides the best example of this phenomenon of a cultural and ethnic "melting pot." Otherwise, without human technological and political interference, the biological evolution and diversity are largely determined, shaped, directed and driven by environmental factors.

Consequently, the human race that evolved and originated in East Africa, later developed different color, hair text and facial features in response to environmental factors and biological needs for survival in those different environments. This is similar to the mammals, such as whales and manatees that left land to live in the oceans and how they lost their original legs and feet and instead developed flippers in their place to facilitate better navigation of the oceans. Likewise, the Khoisan and the Batwa of Africa are smaller and shorter because of the environmental factors.

Since these people are small, they also require less food to survive. The Batwa who live in impenetrable tropical forests in the Congo and the surrounding countries, also found that short and small stature were great assets in going through the dense jungle. Once, they mix with other people in a different environment, and with better diet, they will eventually also become taller and bigger! This claim is based on the North American observation which seems to indicate that affluence leads to people's eventual increases in body size, height and life expectancy. This is largely due to better diet, health and improvements in the general quality of life.

As a matter of fact, most well-educated and well-informed people already correctly know and accept the historical and biological evolutionary truth that all men and women in the world are descendants of the original human beings who evolved in Africa, more than one hundred thousand years ago. Based on these historical truths and anthropological data, then, it also naturally follows that by virtue of biological evolution, all modern human beings in the world today, also share a common African biological heritage. This is true since human evolution began in Africa and human beings emigrated from there to other parts of the world, where they attained their present distinctive physical appearances and environmentally appropriate technologies and cultures as part of their successful adaptation to the local environment.

This tropical geographical and environmental factor partly explains why the people who live in the tropics also naturally live in God's proverbial "Garden of Eden." Accordingly, they never had the natural need to develop more sophisticated technologies for agriculture, food processing or building schemes of permanent buildings in order to survive. This is unlike the people who live in cold climates to the north or south of the equator who needed to these technological developments and services in order to survive in their harsh environment.

Life in the tropics was so easy, and life outdoors in God's natural gardens was the ideal. Life in the tropics also provided plenty of vegetables, fruits, wild-game and plenty of clean and fresh water. In the tropics, every day is a summer day! Every day is a day for the outdoors. Similarly, each day is also a good day for working in the garden, playing in the water or the sand on the beach, climbing trees or playing hide and seek in the tall grass, while cattle, goats and sheep graze in the green pastures.

According to this process of evolution, all human beings in the world, irrespective of apparent ethnic and color differences are essentially brothers and sisters. They share a common divine spirit, stream of consciousness, mind, identity, life, origin and destiny that are universally grounded in the same creative Cosmic Spirit, Mind, Energy, Ordering Principle and holy Mystery that we call God.

Human beings constitute a single biologically and socially interrelated and inclusive global human community, and God's family. This is an important scientific truth that will change the religious and moral values of many prejudiced and racist people. The teaching of science, religion and anthropology have to stress the fact of human biological unity despite the external human factors of skin-color, diversity of human facial features and cultures. This is an essential component of good education for grounding sound ethics and religion for the harmonious global human community.

This universal truth regarding the essential biological unity of all modern human beings in the world is important as a common basis for a global ethic of unconditional love based on this universal "brotherhood" and "sisterhood." Based on the Human Genome Project and DNA analysis, all human beings are essentially biologically related as some distant cousins and members of one race. This is true regardless of "superficial traditional barriers" and "conventional human divisions" based on geographical location, color, nationality, class, gender and religious affiliation.

The knowledge and realization that the concept of race is a cultural, political, religious and conventional creation originally constructed to classify people and confer privileges on those identified as one's kinsfolk and exclude those classified as the outsiders, is an essential tool in education that is needed to create an open and tolerant Global Community. This knowledge and truth will become powerful instruments and sources of liberation from ignorance, hate, bigotry, intolerance and racism. This is the necessary social and moral antidote against the traditional teachings of biological whitesupremacy and the correlative exclusivist white racism.

If "one drop" of an African or Black person's blood in one's ancestral heritage ever truly makes that person an African or Black person as most American whitesupremacists, such as the members of the Ku Klux Klan (KKK) and other White racist groups have in the past very naively claimed, then, by virtue of biological evolution, all human beings can be said to be Africans or essentially Black! That kind of truth may actually lead these racists to carry out more desperate and destructive acts of racism, whitesupremacy and attempts of genocide directed against the Blacks and other non-White ethnic groups. Hitler's crude whitesupremacy and programs of eugenics and genocidal acts directed against the German Jews provide extreme examples of this innate White people's overwhelming fear of being racially diluted or genetically annihilated by the non-Whites whom they generally regard as genetically, racially, intellectually and culturally inferior.

The past era racist laws of racial segregation and prohibition of interracial dating and marriage in the USA and South Africa during the era of apartheid, provide clear evidence of this case. These racist and segregationist laws were based on the fear of the social integration that would lead to intermarriages between Blacks and Whites. In the USA, the offspring of a Black and White couple was automatically classified as Black, irrespective of the child's personal skin-color. Obviously, in this case, racial classification did not mean much, since some people classified as Blacks were as by skin-color as white as any Europeans.

Therefore, Karl Marx was correct to reject race as the most important socioeconomic and political factor in society of his time and the future of the world. Factors of clan, tribe and race may have been important in the primitive historical past, especially during the feudal era of the Middle Ages, but their socioeconomic and political importance as forces of social mobilization, politics and economic development were fading very fast.

Marx correctly realized that race, ethnicity and skin-color were not the ideal factors for a meaningful analysis of society. This includes the existence, nature and functioning processes of the social, economic, political, cultural and religious institutions. Marx profoundly understood that class, rather than race or ethnicity was the better and more meaningful cross-cultural objective instrument for the analysis, classification, and mobilization of all people anywhere in the world. Marx regarded this to be universally true irrespective of color, race, ethnicity, nationality, ideology, language, religion and socioeconomic class.

Subsequently, the Latin American Christian liberation theology and ethics thinkers have employed Marx's tools for social analysis in order to prescribe more appropriate and redemptive theological programs, doctrines and ethics for the oppressed people of Latin America. James Cone and Cornell West have tried to do the same in their liberation theologies and ethics for North America.

In general, social analysis of society based on race tends to end-up in a racist treatise and discourse, such as that of Charles Murray and Richard Hernstein' *Bell Curve*. On the other hand, a class based analysis of society, tends to ignore race and color as factors which cause real discrimination and socioeconomic injustice. Well educated Blacks and Hispanics are still subjected to police racial profiling, discrimination in hiring, retention, promotion and poor evaluations by their racially prejudiced superiors and resentful subordinates. They live in an a kind of special existential hell created by white institutional racism around them.

As a result, they constantly live in a state of stress and distress. Their immunological system becomes weakened because of this stress caused by social stress that is rooted in whitesupremacy or racism. Accordingly, their life expectancy is lower than that of their White colleagues who do not have to live under comparable stress. For instance, the Blacks and Hispanics are more likely than Whites to die younger due to opportunistic diseases, strokes, cardiovascular complications, diabetes, and a variety of cancers, when compared to Whites with similar education, occupation and incomes. This phenomenon is not genetic. It arises largely due to environmental factors, such as, stress, distress and existential anxiety due to racism, discrimination and harassment on the job or within the community. It can be changed by the elimination of racism in the workplace and the community as a whole.

The elimination of racism, sexism, injustice and poverty must become the new Christian moral crusade of the Third Millennium. The last millennium successfully fought against the evils of slavery, colonialism, imperialism, religious wars and tyranny. Some of these evils still persist in some developing countries. However, they are no longer a threat to the civilized world. Nevertheless, it is now our own turn for a moral crusade and duty to fight against the evils within us, the community, nation and the world inasmuch as they constitute intolerance, racism, sexism and socioeconomic injustice.

Here, the proposed form of liberation from racism is based on idealism that is rooted in common biological heritage, shared global space, mutual knowledge, collective human consciousness, social experience of life and reality of mutual interdependence. This realization will positively shape the human consciousness and awareness of this reality, so as to minimize the destructiveness of racism. This is particularly essential in the prevention of unfounded concepts of racial purity, and whitesupremacy. These destructive vices and evils promote racial violence and acts of genocide.

The worst examples of these cases, include those of Adolf Hitler, who sought to exterminate the so-called people of inferior races, the Serbs in Yugoslavia who wanted to cleanse the land of non-Serbs, and the Hutus of Rwanda who wanted to cleanse the land of the Tutsis. In Rwanda, the Hutu and Tutsi people have tried to exterminate each other, based on the perceived economic, class and political differences. Nevertheless, in reality these two Rwanda's ethnic groups are biologically similar and culturally interrelated as cattle-keepers in the case of the Tutsi and predominantly agriculturists, in the case of the Hutu. In some cases, the two groups are almost indistinguishable from one another. Yet, they still fight each other because of the perceived ethnic and cultural differences.

In contrast, the Middle East situation is complicated by religious, cultural and the perceived ethnic differences. The fact that the Jews and Arabs tend to view each other as different races rather than brothers and sisters who have adopted different religions and cultures based on those different religions is part of the main political and military problem in Palestine. As a result, these racially related Semitic people and descendants of Abraham have failed to live together in mutual tolerance and peace as different brothers and sisters. Instead, they have resorted to mutual intolerance and acts of hate, violence and vicious wars of mutual destruction. This is tragically similar to the self-destructive Northern Ireland Irish people who have waged destructive wars against each other based on the fact that some of them are Roman Catholics whereas others are Protestant and politically affiliated to England.

The awareness that cultural and religious differences are superficial and that all human beings are biologically the same people is essential truth that leads to the necessary human mutual acceptance as brothers and sisters in God's inclusive global family. They must become conscious of the fact that they are all constituent members of God's inclusive global Kingdom and therefore, should also be civil, loving and mutually tolerant of one another as fellow citizens of heaven and God's Kingdom. This moral consciousness and theological inclusive understanding is necessary in order for different races, ethnic groups and religions to coexist together in the Global Community on the Earth within the ideal state of harmony and mutual peace.

This would also create the essential ideal conditions for peace in the Middle East and the "Holy Land" where religious and ethnic bigotry and mutual exclusivism are at their worst negative and destructive extremes. In this region, despicable acts of hate, injustice, intolerance, violence, war, death and attempted genocide are self-evident among the violent extremists on both sides of this ethnic and religious tragic conflict. Tragically, many of these crimes and evil-deeds have been done, both ignorantly and blasphemously, in the holy name of God! At least, the more intelligent people should realize that God is neither a Jew nor an Arab!

This is analogous to the feuding Christians of Northern Ireland, who do not realize that Jesus and God are neither Catholics nor Protestants. For that matter, the world has still to realize that all human beings, irrespective of gender, skin-color, race, ethnic or "tribal" group, religious affiliation, socioeconomic class, and nationality are all created in God's own infinite image (*imago Dei*). This theological and moral understanding of the common unity of humanity is affirmed by the Hebrew scriptures. Adam and Eve are regarded as the ancestors of the human beings in the world. Nevertheless, the Jews later developed categories of distinction between "Jews" as "members of God's elect people" and "the covenant" as opposed to the "Gentiles" who were regarded as the idolatrous and perishing people outside God's covenant and Community of Redemption ( or Church).

Both Jesus and St. Paul, later negated this distinction between Jew and Gentile. Jesus' parable of the "Good Samaritan" was supposed to achieve this effect. St. Paul's declaration that in Jesus Christ, all people had become one family and there were no longer the divisions based on the traditional categories of Jew, Gentile (Greek), free and slave people (Gal. 3:28) were his noble attempts to actualize in his own time what is now happening in the world during this third millennium! This moral and religious evolution has taken a very long time to arrive at this practical acceptance of human equality before God, universal human rights, equal justice for all, democracy and nondiscriminatory inclusive global human ethic.

Yet, at the same time, this millennium will still be filled with many widespread, conservative resistance, cultural and ethnic struggles for self-identity, dominance and survival. It is also an era for tragic renewed religious conflicts between Christians and Muslims. This is primarily because there are many culturally and religiously conservative, ignorant and intolerant people who are forced to become part of the new inclusive "global village" or "Global community."

Due to technological advances in information and communications these conservative, xenophobic, racist and intolerant people are forced to come into close contact with the people of other races, religions, cultures, and values. Therefore, this forced globalization is a major source of stress, and serious conflict for many conservative, sexist, bigoted and racist groups of closed minded and intolerant people.

Xenophobia and whitesupremacy have complicated the nature and content of the central moral issues in Western religion and ethics. Whitesupremacy and ethnocentrism have sometimes tragically transformed the traditional Western systems of ethics and religion into a destructive form of exclusive Eurocentric cultural ethnocentrism, white racism and claims of white superiority. The nineteenth century Western ideas and practices of colonialism, imperialism and missionary activities in Africa, Asia and Latin America were deeply rooted in this Western whitesupremacy and racism. Nationalistic and militant liberation wars and theologies that emerged in these regions in the twentieth century were part of the local responses in these regions to this dehumanizing Western whitesupremacist racism and imperialism.

## 2. Some Positive Forces of Globalization And Negative Forces of Resistance

The forces of global trade, travel, tourism, Internet exchange of information, movies, news and television entertainment have broken down the traditional national, ethnic and racial borders! People of all races, cultures, religions and values are becoming closely interdependent and interwoven into a network of the global community. However, due to lack of preparation and good liberal education, many people may experience the inevitable cultural shock, during mutual contact and interaction.

Unfortunately, many cultural or religious traditionalists may organize themselves into militant "missionary" or "paramilitary" groups. These groups try to impose their own values on those with whom they come into contact. They may try to convert them, and may even feel offended enough and declare "a holy war" (*jihad* or crusade) against them as immoral infidels (nonbelievers) and blasphemers. This is more probable with the Islamic fundamentalists than the Christian ethnocentric, racist, and whitesupremacist bigots, such as the Ku Klux Klan (KKK), the White Identity Church members and the Neo-Nazis.

Most of the readers of this book are people who live in a Western pluralistic and secular society. The world or the human global community is not a religious, cultural, or linguistic monolithic community. Monolithic cultures, languages, and values are of a bygone era. This is the tragic nature of tribalism and feudalism like those which have destabilized much of Africa.

The West is no longer a religious or cultural monolithic society. This is true despite the presence of Christianity as the dominant religion. Soren Kierkegaard, the famous existentialist philosopher, moral teacher, and theologian, correctly lamented that the West had become a secular society that he described as a "pagan Christendom." For Kierkegaard, the West had turned Christianity into a cultural and civil religion with the essential Christian values and virtues, such as: faith, a self-sacrificial praxis of Agape, and free forgiveness of sin of those who offend us, according to the normative teachings and commandments of Jesus Christ.

Kierkegaard affirmed that the good life in the world was both found and lived in complete faith and obedience to God's moral of love (Agape). This was a self-conscious and informed mode of faith, or what Kierkegaard called "subjective truth." For Kierkegaard, faith was a dynamic form of power, and a subjective consciousness of being in union and fellowship with God. The "leap of faith" and acceptance of the truth of having been freely loved, forgiven of sins, and redeemed by God by virtue of his unconditional love and grace alone is an example of this.

The obedient human is enabled, by God's power of grace working in the world through the Holy Spirit and the Logos-Christ, to live a new life of holiness, obedience, faith, and praxis of Agape. These actions are toward both God and the neighbor, who is the concrete expression, incarnation, and representative of the invisible God in the world. In this incarnational understanding, God is present and works incognito in the world thorough obedient servants like Jesus the Christ.

Ultimately, all forms of good education should serve as good training in moral and ethical wholesome ways of living responsibly, socially, morally, peacefully, and productively in the world. In this respect, all forms of sound education are ethical or moral and ultimately religious! This is true because a good education is identified as that which equips the educated person with all the necessary virtues and skills to live a meaningful and good life in peace, love, harmony, and happiness in the world with his or her fellow human beings. This is because the good life, (meaning true love (Agape), peace, and happiness), is only found in God.

## 3. The Absence of a Single Normative Moral Center And Problems of Protestant Moral Relativism

Due to the nature and reality of global cultural diversity and religious pluralism, ethics and moral values have suffered from extremist forms of cultural, moral, and religious relativism. As a result, there are some students, teachers, and parents who argue that there is no need to study religion and ethics, since there is no central moral authority to define what is universally normative, true, good, and beneficial.

In the absence of such a deontological or strong external normative moral principle or authority such as an infallible Pope, a common religion, infallible scripture as God's directly revealed and God's Written Word, or reliable authoritative code of virtues and conduct, each individual becomes a free moral agent that has the responsibility to define what is truly good and virtuous! This kind of moral anarchy can cause confusion, moral evil, and chaos in the community, society, and the world or Global Community. For the Roman Catholics, the principle of Papal infallibility in defining matters of faith, doctrine, and moral teachings is a good global solution and Christian antidote against the Protestant tendency toward moral relativism, confusion, and anarchy.

The Protestant doctrine of the *infallibility* and *inerrancy* of the Holy Bible as a reliable and divinely inspired guide to doctrine and moral values is a poor substitute for Catholic Papal Infallibility, the Torah for Orthodox members of Judaism, or the guidance of the *Shari'a* for fundamental Muslims. The trouble with the Protestant doctrine of egalitarianism and priesthood of all believers, is that there is a direct individual access to God without the mediation of the Church or priests and saints (as is the case in the Roman Catholic Church and African

Traditional Religion.) This leaves each individual to assume the infallible role of the Pope.

That means that each Protestant almost believes that his or her version of interpretation of the Holy Bible is the right one, and that other views are unacceptable and wrong! This is one main reason, according to David Barret, there are more than 20,000 Protestant "denominations" or different Churches in North America and more than 6,000 in Africa! Some of these Churches have incorporated into independent organizations, but sometimes they have just a few members! In the Protestant religious paradigm and community where each person is a Pope, there cannot be agreement on moral values, religious doctrine, and practices. As result, there is no meaningful religious unity, harmony and peace!

Accordingly, "the Protestant faith" and disunity are the main breeding grounds for disbelief, atheism, moral relativism, moral confusion, nihilism, and anarchism. Extreme forms of oppression and societal moral evils, such as slavery, capitalism, racism, sexism, nationalism, imperialism, whitesupremacy, and genocide are often more associated with the Protestant groups of Christians than with the Catholics! The problems of moral education, ethics, partisan religious values, and public education in a pluralistic and secular society are very great and almost overwhelming.

## 4. Confusion about the Life, Mission, Teachings And Death of Jesus

The meaning and legacy of the teachings, mission, arrest, torture, suffering and death on the cross depend on how the person views and believes *"who"* and *"what"* Jesus *"was"* or *"is."* Accordingly, the meaning and mission of Jesus is different if one perceives and believes that Jesus was a mere Jewish prophet or Jewish radical reformist rabbi or Jewish political messiah. The meaning and mission of Jesus in the world is radically different and cosmic in nature, if like St. John, one truly believes that the man Jesus was the historical and symbolic human embodiment of God's *Logos* who become historically incarnate into humanity, specifically in the person of Jesus the carpenter and man of Nazareth (cf. John 1:1-3; 14:6,9-21; 15:1-10), the son of Mary and Joseph.

However, if one only believes that Jesus was put to death merely for crimes of treason against Rome and died as a political activist or political messiah against the imperial jurisdiction of Rome, then, one only perceives Jesus in narrow Jewish historical political terms and Jewish messianic expectations. He or she may see Jesus as a political failure as most Jews of his day did. This kind of person does not have to believe in the spiritual or moral theory of the efficacious cosmic atoning death of Jesus on the cross. He or she may reject the idea of Jesus' death as God's provided human perfect atonement and efficacious sacrifice for the sins of the whole world.

For some skeptics, Jesus' mission and death could also be academically viewed like those of any other false Jewish messiahs that had arisen in Palestine before and after Jesus. Most Jews still take this position. Consequently, they reject as erroneous and falsehood the Christian central truth and doctrines of God's final revelation and redemption of the world through Jesus as the Christ. Like Muslims, most Jewish rabbis and scholars question and reject the validity of the Christian claim, belief and teaching that Jesus was the promised and awaited eschatological Jewish Messiah that was sent by God into the world to redeem both Jews and believing Gentiles.

Whereas the Muslims accept the divine mission of Jesus in the world. They only affirm Jesus as God's prophet and reject the idea that he was a Son of God and God incarnate in humanity. Whereas, some Jews may wish to view Jesus as a radical rabbi, they reject the idea that he was God's messiah sent to deliver them from sin and evil. In any case, it is a matter of historical record that Jesus as the Christ or Messiah did not liberate the oppressed Jews of his day from the political evils and economic burdensome oppression of Roman imperialism. Instead, he taught the imperative moral obligation of unconditional love for enemy, free forgiveness, nonviolence and "turning the other cheek," when unjustly attacked. He rejected and negated the traditional moral duty of self-defense and equal retaliation (*lex talionis*). Moreover, in 70 CE, the Roman imperial power finally destroyed the Jewish temple in Jerusalem, and sent into exile the main leaders of Israel.

As such, it takes what Soren Kierkegaard called "a leap of faith" for Christians to affirm that Jesus was more than a mere moral teacher, prophet and reformer of Judaism. It is by faith alone *(sola fide)* that Christians affirm that Jesus was the Christ, the Son of God and the embodiment of God's *Logos* or God incarnate. Then, who and what was Jesus? The answer to this question is completely based on faith and not history or science. This is the case since there is no adequate historical or scientific data about the Jesus of history.

However, there is some sufficient evidence scattered within the Roman official court records and correspondences, such as the 112 CE letter of Pliny, Governor of the Bithynia Province, to Trajan, the Roman Emperor, asking for an imperial clarification of the nature of crime Christianity constituted and the right punishment for Christians, prove that Jesus existed. These sources indicate that he was considered to be a radical Jewish rabbi and a moral teacher of monotheism and nonviolence, and that he was crucified. His followers (the Christians) were persecuted for their religious beliefs and refusal to join the Roman army or worship and offer sacrifices to the "pagan" Roman gods and the statues of Roman emperors. The Christians were also mocked by many Roman and Greek pagan writers for refusing to worship the Roman Emperor as a god, while "they worshipped a man called Jesus as their God," risen Lord and Savior.

The Christian apologists (defenders of Christianity), such as Clement, Justin Martyr, Eusebius, Origen, Tertullian and Irenaeus tried to answer some of these Roman and Greek pagan main misunderstandings and objections to Christianity. The Christian thinkers were forced to develop an intellectual doctrine of Christology within the context of Greek philosophy, epistemology and logic. In this process, they positively affirmed that unlike the Roman emperors, who mere moral men, Jesus was outwardly a man, but inwardly, he was true God incarnate in humanity. Accordingly, the Christian apologists argued that the Christians were not guilty of idolatry when they worshipped Jesus as God, since Jesus was God.

In contrast to the Roman and Greek religious beliefs and practices, they argued that whereas the "pagan Romans and Greeks" were really guilty of idolatry for worshipping the Roman emperors as gods. They affirmed this to be the case, since the emperors were only men, and not the true incarnations of God like Jesus the Christ was in reality. Based on this christological claim of God's historical incarnation in Jesus, the Church Fathers later developed the correlative doctrine of the Holy Trinity.

This unique complex Christian Trinitarian doctrine that distinguishes Christianity from both Judaism and Islam, affirms monotheism within a Triune Godhead composed of God, *Logos*/Son and the Holy Spirit. It affirms the essential co-eternity, coequality and co-activity of *God the Father as Creator*, God the *Logos* or *Son as Redeemer* and God the *Holy Spirit* as the divine Medium for the supernatural divine activities of creation, redemption, revelation and fulfillment. The same Holy Trinity that is referred to in non-anthropomorphically and gender-free terms as: God the *Creator, Sustainer* and *Redeemer*.

According to this Trinitarian doctrine and the creeds, matters of God's Kingdom, religion, Church, faith, grace, sacraments, inspiration, scriptures, doctrines, wisdom and salvation are located within the realm of the Holy Spirit. God's Kingdom exists as the Reign of God's Holy Spirit in the world and its history. For instance, the Divine Incarnation is accomplished by God's Spirit (cf. Lk. 1:26-35). Likewise, at the baptism of Jesus, the Holy Spirit descends upon Jesus to anoint and declare him "Son of God."

The Holy Spirit empowered Jesus to preach the "Good News" (Gospel) of the arrival of God's Kingdom and redemption in the world (cf. Mk. 1:7-15). Jesus' acts of mercy and healing, and his definitive teaching of the fundamental moral principles of unconditional love, free forgiveness of sins, nonviolence and peace as God's imposed new universal moral law and the moral duty of all truly obedient people or the saints, anywhere in the world, is part of this apocalyptic and eschatological new era of God Kingdom.

Ultimately, the New Testament material presents the "Christ of faith" as opposed to the "Jesus of history." The Gospels writers have struggled with the question of "who and what was Jesus?" Therefore, what we read in the New Testament are their own personal answers to that spiritual and theological question. Their fallible and tentative answers about the nature, mission and identity of Jesus are different and vary a great deal. They include the following: "*Jesus is the Son of God;*" "*Jesus is a Faith-healer;*" "*Jesus is a Rabbi;*" "*Jesus is a Prophet;*" "*Jesus is an anonymous Jewish Messiah;*" and John reaches the conclusion that *Jesus is an anonymous Incarnation of God's Logos* in the person of Jesus (cf. John 1:1-3).

Jesus still invites each person and community to reflect on his own life, teachings and works, and then, seek to answer the following question for themselves: "*The other people have said that I am. . . . What about you? Who do you say that I am?*" (Cf. Mk. 8:27-29). Every Christian and every Christian community has to be personally confronted by Christ and this central question. "*Who do you say that I am*?" At this fundamental personal spiritual level, any imported or other peoples' borrowed answers are worthless. At this spiritual level, the central christological question has become spiritually and morally personal. It demands personal answers from a personal spiritual life and experience of God. *Theophany* as the personal encounter God through the person of

Jesus Christ, as the pure embodiment of God's *Logos,* Agape or God's free redemptive grace, restoration to wholeness through healing, the free forgiveness of sins and removal of paralysis caused by guilt and self-alienation from God, self and the community is the Apostolic Christian proclamation as the Good News of God's Kingdom.

These answers are based on faith, experience and salvation history. Most Christians have chosen to adopt some of these collective answers about "who Jesus is" as their own. The main problem has been that most of the churches and Christians who have chosen either to affirm Jesus as God incarnate in humanity or a mere prophet and moral teacher, have done so, assuming that their own particular answers were based on actual history rather than faith of the Early Church, as testified to by the writers of the Gospels. As such, they transformed the faith-based theologies of the Gospels into biographies and the history of Jesus as the Christ.

Thus, many uncritical Christian theologians and Church leaders erroneously and dogmatically historicized the New Testament and its theological doctrines of the Christ, instead of seeing their own doctrines of christology and those of the New Testament being merely statements of personal faith in God's unconditional love, grace and redemption as Jesus did and taught his followers. This is why theology is ever an evolutionary and an ongoing endless task. The theology of the past provides answers for the people of the past and not for the people of today.

The people of each era and culture need their own moral and theological questions answered by God. God's meaningful and relevant answers must be meaningfully and effectively communicated within the local context. That is, it must be communicated by God within the local people's own contemporary worldview, culture, history, experience and language of those people. As such, theology of each community and each era must be appropriate for culture, values, problems and questions of those groups in their time and situation.

To this end, the scriptures, history, tradition, past doctrines and creeds are only helpful guides. They enable reason to be effectively guided by the Holy Spirit to see God's *Logos* and God as revealed in nature (science), history and the experience of the Religious Community (Church), today. Equipped and enabled by God's Spirit and the *Logos,* the Church leaders and Christian thinkers can fully and more constructively be able to undertake a meaningful and fruitful theological or moral reflection upon these sources in relationship to any current moral or spiritual problems, doctrinal, social or ethical questions. Subsequently, the contemporary Church may be able to provide an adequate contemporary answer or solution for a vexing moral or religious problem, and so confidently in the name of God.

However, the Church's contemporary or new moral or spiritual answers may actually contradict and reverse the answers that were previously given to similar problems by the Church, but under different circumstances. In this respect, moral and religious truth is evolutionary, relative and flexible in order to be applicable to new problems or changing moral and cultural contexts. Questions of evolution, abortion, the ordination of women, divorce and remarriage, homosexuality in the Church, premarital sexual intercourse, cloning, euthanasia and doctors assisted suicide provide some these examples which in each different era, the Church has provided different answers because of changing social, cultural, legal, religious, moral, economic, political and educational contexts.

History and society are not static institutions. They are both evolutionary and constantly changing. This must become true for the religious and educational institutions as well in order to keep pace with the changing world, institutions and social realities. For instance, it was once considered morally acceptable to enslave Africans and discriminate against them. Today, slavery is considered both a moral evil and a sin against God and humanity. Likewise, discrimination based on race or gender is treated as a crime and moral offense in many socially advanced and democratic nations of the world. Religious persecution has almost ceased, except within the conservative and fundamentalist Islamic nations, such as Iran, the Sudan, Saudi Arabia, Afghanistan, Morocco and Pakistan. Religious pluralism and diversity have also become acceptable in many developed and democratic nations.

Ever since the trial, conviction, and execution of Socrates, the great Greek moral philosopher, in 399 BCE on the moral charges of atheism and corruption of the young, moral philosophers, religious teachers, and writers everywhere have had to contend with the mass public outcry of crimes like "heresy," "treason," "atheism," "blasphemy," "communism," and "revolution." These terms incite the public into an irrational motion of frenzy and denunciation and rejection of new ethical values. This is the case even if they are godly, based on God's eternal moral laws in nature, and deductive, intellectual, eternal truths that transcend all finite barriers of era, time, culture, and established religious and moral beliefs and practices.

Jesus himself was another great example of a religious and moral teacher whose moral teaching was rejected. Jesus' ideas were not rejected because they were wrong, but rather because what he taught and preached was religiously and morally uncomfortable. It was true, right, and just, and threatened the traditional world-view, moral values, and religious doctrines about God, righteousness, and salvation. It shattered the contemporary religious and moral illusions of the time.

As expected, Jesus' religious and moral teachings were counter-cultural, prophetic, spiritual, agapic and theocentric. These new teachings and the reformation of the Mosaic Law caused great stress to the traditional religious establishment and threatened its religious and moral authority to interpret teach religion and formulate moral laws. As a result, there was serious opposition from the traditional religious leaders and rabbis, who were the traditional religious and moral teachers, authorized interpreters and guardians of the Mosaic Law.

Jesus Christ's new moral teachings and ethics had challenged and denounced the prevailing social, moral, political, and religious complacency for being corrupt, unjust and lacking in both mercy and compassion. Jesus also rejected the prevailing greed, materialism and obsession with money, riches, material comfort, and wealth as evidence of God's favor or election and blessings (cf. Lk. 6:20-34; 18:18-25). Like Amos and Karl Marx, Jesus believed that wealth was often ill-gotten and robbed from the defenseless and the poor masses, who were constantly cheated and exploited by the rich so they may become even richer, whereas the poor became poorer and more desperate.

As a result, Jesus as the Christ taught the poor ignorant masses, healed their diseases, and fed them when they were hungry. He also declared: "Blessed are the poor and the pacemakers because the Kingdom of God will be their inheritance." The poor and the oppressed were the people whom he had come to minister to and redeem from their plight (cf. Luke 4:16-21). Subsequently, Jesus uncompromisingly denounced these rich priestly groups and the self-righteous Pharisees, who were so legalistic that they shunned mixing with the rest of the people for fear of moral, spiritual, and ritual contamination.

In addition to the universal and non-negotiable definitive moral principle of agape, Jesus also taught the correlative moral principle of nonviolence and free forgiveness of offenses. He gave his followers the commandment of unconditional love, which he said must be deliberately extended to the enemies. This did little to endear him to some sinful people whose moral philosophy, theory of justice and ethics were firmly grounded in the Mosaic Law. Most of the Jews preferred the morality of equal retaliation for offenses and injuries (*lex talionis*), summed up as "life for a life, an eye for an eye, and a tooth for a tooth" (Exod. 21:24).

For most Jews, the Law of Moses was straightforward. If you killed someone, you also got killed as a punishment for your crime. However, it was almost impossible to fulfil when it came to the regulations regarding daily life, such as clothing, personal ritual cleanliness or hand washing, food, land, agriculture, economics, and social relationships. Jesus lessened the burden of the Mosaic Law. Later, St. Paul abolished it for Christians and set them free to become loving and compassionate people rather than legalistic moralists, like the Pharisees.

The Gospel writers affirm that it was due to the fact that Jesus' moral and religious reformation posed a threat to traditional Judaism and its dogmatic doctrines concerning ritual holiness as godliness, that the religious leaders of Judaism wanted to arrest and get rid of him. The evangelists write that the Jewish religious establishment wanted to silence Jesus. They sought to accomplish this mission by arresting him and trying him in their religious courts and condemning him for crimes of blasphemy and disrespect of the established religious laws and traditions of Judaism.

Subsequently, these Jewish religious leaders, namely, the moral teachers of Judaism (Scribes and Rabbis), and the Pharisees banded together in a coalition against the new moral teachings of Jesus. According to these Gospel writers, the Jewish religious leaders charged Jesus with the moral and capital offense of blasphemy against God and impiety. They condemned him to death according to the Law of Moses, but since Israel was under Roman imperial jurisdiction, only Rome could impose the death penalty on Jesus or any other Roman colonial subject.

The Gospel writers allege that the Jewish religious leaders mobilized the ignorant masses to agitate for his death as a dangerous false messiah. Fearing a riot, Pilate the Roman Governor of the Roman Province of Judea is reported to have ordered the torture of Jesus and when this action failed to please the mob, he signed the requested death sentence against Jesus. Nevertheless, the Gospel writers blame the Jewish religious leaders for the death of Jesus, rather than the Roman imperial government in Palestine. This has been a major source of anti-Semitism in Christianity.

The Gospel writers report the fact that Pilate was reluctant to put Jesus to death because he found him innocent of treason against Rome, and he refused to try him on charges of blasphemy since the charges did not violate Roman laws. Blasphemy was covered under the Jewish religious and moral laws and Rome had no interest or jurisdiction in matters of Jewish religious and moral law.

Pilate is reported to have authorized an inscription to be placed on the cross of Jesus saying: "JESUS THE NAZARENE, THE KING OF THE JEWS" (John 19:19). This inscription would have been politically designed by Pilate to signify that Jesus' death was a political execution and not a religious martyrdom. It would have been done to send a political message that no future Jewish messiahs or acts of treason (military resistance to the Roman imperial rule), would be tolerated by Rome in Palestine or any in other part of the Roman Empire.

However, the Jewish Religious Community (Judaism) and later, the Christian Community (Church) perceived and interpreted the crucifixion and death of Jesus on the Roman cross in religious terms. The Christians saw the innocent suffering and death of Jesus on the cross during the Passover, as a holy sacrifice and an efficacious atoning death for the sins of all the sinners in the world. The body of Jesus had become the symbolic lamb that is sacrificed to God, slain, roasted and eaten as part of God's provided atonement for sin and deliverance from oppression, sin and evil.

The Christian sacrament of the Holy Communion still contains the reference to this holy mystery of eating the "body of Christ" and "drinking blood of Christ" as the sacrifice for sin and the food of eternal life. Jesus, John, Paul, Athanasius, Augustine, Irenaeus, Aquinas and other Christian thinkers have regarded the Eucharist as the symbolic divine vaccination against sin and death. As such, it is the mystical holy medicine that produces the desired spiritual immortality among the mortal human beings who come in faith and in hope for eternal life, partake of the Eucharistic meal in fellowship with God, the risen Christ as Lord and with all the saints, both living and dead (departed).

Therefore, for all God's saints and obedient people of deep faith in God's providence and goodness, death is not the meaningful final end of human life. According to the traditional doctrines of the Church, death is the gate to a spiritual realm of God's Kingdom and eternal life in the joyous fellowship of love with God and the saints.

The medieval Roman Catholic Church doctrine of transubstantiation was to some great degree designed to affirm and communicate these holy mysteries. But, it created the crude literalist problems of Christian cannibalism. Vatican II found it prudent to adopt the more Anglican and Lutheran doctrine of symbolism and "real presence of Christ" in reference to the Eucharist, rather than the physical and literal transformation of the consecrated elements of bread into the physical body of Christ and wine into the real blood of Christ, as the crude doctrine of transubstantiation implied to many literalist Christians.

Ironically, Jesus, who was the most innocent, God-fearing, nonviolent moral teacher of imperative unconditional love for both God and all of one's fellow human beings, was ironically executed on the cross. He had been convicted of the same evil crimes of hate and violence that he had denounced and negated by his life of unconditional love and forgiveness for all human beings, irrespective of their sins, socioeconomic status, creed, race, and nationality.

However, Jesus had warned his followers to take up the cross if they wanted to follow him. He had also warned them that since a disciple is not greater than the master, they too, would be persecuted and even killed like he was if they remained faithful to his teaching. St. John reports that Jesus predicted that this Christian persecution would follow because "the world hates love, truth, and justice" (cf. John 16). Instead, the evildoers in the world prefer to cause injustice, hate, suffering, chaos and failure.

These evildoers also prefer falsehood, illusion and injustice, and ultimately, they teach the exploitation and oppression of the weak and the defenseless as the path to power, profit, and wealth. As a result, there are many fraudulent schemes that evildoers invent and promote as truth to rob the uninformed trusting public!

These kinds of evildoers have caused the problem of skepticism and cynicism among some people. Their faith in people has been badly shaken, and in some cases the damage is irreparable. In these unfortunate cases, it is difficult for the moral teacher to teach the moral value of faith, unconditional love and forgiveness. Yet, these are the same kinds of people that need this renewal of faith, trust, unconditional love, and free forgiveness of sinners. This is partly why some people find Jesus' moral saying true that: "It is easier for the camel to go through the eye of the needle, than for a rich man to enter the Kingdom of God" (cf. Lk. 18:25). Like Jesus, Gandhi and King's moral teachings of unconditional love and nonviolence have likewise been rejected. These moral teachers and social prophets were also both violently hated and killed by evildoers, just like Jesus.

## 5. The Indivisibility of God's Revelation in Nature Or Science and Truth in Religion

Science and religion represents two mutually complimentary ways of viewing the world and complex realities around us. Science and technology give us the tools to study and understand God's revelation in nature. Religion gives us the spiritual insight on how to view the world and discern the real value and spiritual or moral meaning of life. Science tells us "*how*" things function and religion tells us "*why*" things exist. Therefore, we should never collapse science into religion or reduce religion to science. Religion and science serve two different societal functions. They are both necessary and can coexist peacefully as the instruments of "God's natural revelation," in the case of science or reason, and "God's special revelation," in the case of religion or the Church.

Like all moral virtues and divine attributes of goodness, agape and justice, Truth is an attribute and essence of God. Truth is also universally one and indivisible. It ultimately comes from God, who is the Truth and cosmic embodiment and source of all fine truths. As such, wherever, goodness, justice, agape and truth are found, they are of God and they come from God, regardless of whether their local agents know it or not. What matters is that these supernatural and divine gifts are present and that they are extended to all people within the community.

However, these divine gifts are not always received by people with joy and in the spirit of thanksgiving. As a result, many people reject agape, justice, goodness and truth. The Hebrew prophets were rejected, assaulted with rocks and assassinated by kings because the people and their kings could not bear to hear the truth, or hear their secret evil deeds publicly exposed and condemned.

Therefore, instead of repentance, the people and their corrupt leaders killed the prophets, moral teachers and messengers of truth and justice. Jesus was killed because of his prophetic and moral teachings of unconditional love, mercy, compassionate justice, nonviolence and free forgiveness of sins. Mahatma Gandhi, M.L. King, the archbishops Janani Luwum of Uganda and Oscar Romero of El Salvador, were also killed for teaching similar moral and spiritual principles.

Even today, there is evidence that many people in the world still prefer violence, ignorance and falsehood to the real truth. This is more likely to be the case, if the truth does not confirm some people's traditionally held religious, scientific, and moral beliefs. This was the case with Copernicus, Galileo and Darwin. Accordingly, Galileo was forced by the Roman Catholic Church officials to recant his scientifically well-researched, verified and clearly documented findings, scholarly writings and teachings. For instance, Galileo had proved that the sun was in a stationary orbit as the gravitational center of the solar system. He had also established the fact that the Earth was not the center of the universe. Its orbit took it around the sun.

Yet, without examination of Galileo's scientific evidence and sound proofs for his teachings of a sun-centered universe, the Church had tried him. The Inquisition or Church court had found him guilty of teaching material that was contrary to the official teachings and dogmas of the Church. Obviously, it was the Church that had seriously erred by its failure to examine the nature of the data and scientific proofs that Galileo had discovered in the cosmos and carefully completed and presented to the world as God's truth. The Church had feared the truth because that truth effectively negated the Church's own erroneous teachings and dogmatic formulations of doctrines.

Galileo's discoveries and teachings challenged the Church's traditional dogmas regarding God's creation, the nature of the world, the position of the Earth within the universe. The truth required the Church to admit its own fallibility and that of the scriptures. This admission of human fallibility requires the acceptance of the correlative fallibility of all human institutions, including the Church and all its doctrines, teachings and writings, including the scriptures, creeds, decrees, canons, council or convention decisions, letters, "Papal Bulls" and encyclicals.

Instead of the Church's gracious acceptance of the truth and congratulating Galileo on his observations and discoveries, the Church arrested Galileo. Tragically, the Church's authorities in charge of the inquisition threatened Galileo with torture and execution for his scientific findings and teachings that had been theologically judged to be dangerously secular, irreverent to the Bible, and therefore, irreligious. Fortunately, on October 31, 1993, Pope John Paul II, the Pontiff of the Roman Catholic Church, remorsefully reversed the Church's condemnation of Galileo and his scientific teachings in the seventeenth century.

In addition, the Pope effectively declared that there were two centers of God's true revelation and truth. He also declared that God's truth does not contradict itself. As such, truth as found in God's universal revelation in nature cannot be contradicted by God's special revelation in holy scriptures, history, experience, faith and the like.

Therefore, the two centers of God's revelation of truth in nature and the Church or the Religious Community (Covenant, scriptures, doctrines, messiahs, prophets, popes, bishops and theologians) must never be in conflict. If the truth declared by special revelation based on faith contradicts, the divine truths in nature as proved by science and critical thinking, the divine revelation based on God's revelation in nature must prevail, since it is the more universal and accurate truth that can universally be demonstrated to be valid and true, whereas, the truth based on special revelation or faith has no validity beyond the faith of the believer or his or her Religious Community. As we know, this faith based revelation can be misunderstood, miscommunicated and erroneous.

It is self-evident that the first and most important universal center of God's revelation and truth is that found in nature. This divine revelation is open to be read and studied by every intelligent creature in the universe. Indeed, many animals carefully organize their lives based on it. For instance, squirrels harvest nuts in the fall and carefully store them away for food during the hard times of the winter.

The cosmos exists as God's effect or creation. It effectively reveals the essence of God as the "creative cause of the world or the Cosmic Creator." The study of an effect bears knowledge that is relevant concerning the unknown cause of that effect. There is a reliable degree of causal relationship and identifiable connection between cause and effect.

St. Thomas Aquinas' five arguments or proofs of God's existence are cosmological. They begin with the world (cosmos), nature or creation as God's effect. He affirms that "God is the Unmoved Mover" or the creative and Ordering Cosmic Principle that acts as the "Prime-Mover of the cosmos." Secondly, God is the Uncaused Cause of the world. Today, St. Thomas would have argued that the "big bang" was initiated by God as this Uncaused Primordial Cause or the Cosmic Originator of all finite or created (originated) original things within the cosmos. Thirdly, St. Thomas maintains that God is also the necessary "Grounding" or the Ultimate Reality or "material cause" that grounds all finite realities or contingent beings. As such, nature, natural law, and finite beings are rooted in God as their Grounding Reality. They cease to exist if alienated from God, like fish taken out of the water or ice left out in the hot sun.

Aquinas' fourth argument or proof for God's existence is that God is the "Perfection" that exists and serves as the eternal source of the gradations of perfections found among the finite or created things. Finally, St. Thomas argues that God is the eternal creative cosmic intelligent Mind, who is the Intelligent Purposive Designer and final Destiny of all things as their final cause.

It is self-evident that Thomas Aquinas regarded nature and science as more important than faith and the scriptures. For St. Thomas, religion and science were compatible and complimentary to one another. He even claimed that theology was the meta-science or queen of the "Queen of the sciences." Theology was grounded in *metaphysics* which was the science of physical realities and *ontology* or the nature of being (existence).

It is self-evident that St. Thomas Aquinas would have become a zealous student of Galileo and Darwin, instead of being a source of their rejection, judgement and condemnation as the theological officers of the Church Inquisition erroneously did. Subsequently, Pope John Paul II was clearly theologically rooted within the theological and philosophical tradition of St. Thomas Aquinas when he declared that science and faith (religions) constitute two compatible and complimentary centers of God's revelation in the world.

Accordingly, Pope John Paul II was right to reverse the erroneous Church's condemnation of Galileo in 1616, and to embrace Darwin's teachings on evolution as God's method for the creation of the cosmos, and thereby, rejecting the atheistic interpretations of biological evolution, such as those of Feuerbach, Marx, Nietzsche, Freud and their followers. This is a good example of the Church's contemporary theological and moral reflection and reformulation of the ancient doctrines within the current understanding of the world based on contemporary science. This is the kind of intellectual leadership role of the Church in moral, social and religious affairs of the world that St. Thomas would be happy to engage in and reformulate for the world. Karl Rahner tried to accomplish this task on St. Thomas' behalf, or in his scientifically-based theological and philosophical spirit, as his many books and 25 volumes of *Theological Investigations* clearly illustrate to any careful and patient reader of complex topics in philosophical and contemporary theology and ethics.

God's cosmic creation through evolution bears the universal stamp of God's power and creativity. This divine natural revelation of God is universally accessible through the scientific study of nature and the mind or reason. The tools for uncovering this divine revelation of God in nature include technology, research, experimentation, mathematics, and intellectual formulations of the theories of knowledge in testable hypotheses or propositions.

The second center of God's revelation is that of faith and special revelation. This special revelation is centered around the scriptures, messages of prophets, saints, messiahs, angels (God's messengers in whatever form), and ultimately, God's special revelation in the Incarnation. In the Incarnation, God has entered human history and time, and God's *Logos* has become partly embodied in the man form of Jesus as the Christ of God.

This center of God's revelation does not negate the truth learned about God through nature and science. It is on this basis that Pope John Paul II, again, on October 24, 1996, declared to the world that Charles Darwin was correct and that evolution is God's method for creating the cosmos, including the emergence of human beings as *the Homo sapiens*. This timely and Papal definitive definition of true faith and declaration effectively puts an end to the three-century debate between religion and science about the nature of the cosmos and how it came into being.

In the beginning, religion and science were not in conflict; therefore, it is good for them to be reconciled again. In the beginning, the scientists were priests, and scientists were also Christian researchers and teachers. God is inseparable from creation, nature, the world, and humanity. Human beings, as the *imago Dei*, should look at themselves or look at any true humanity to catch a glimpse of the invisible God as the Cosmic Creative Spirit (Consciousness), Mind, and Eternal Energy. The apparent debate and rejection of science by some religious people were based on ignorance and the misunderstanding of holy scriptures as science and history!

Three centuries after Galileo, Darwin's theory of evolution would be simply rejected by the Christian Church, just because it contradicted the ancient and pre-scientific "mythological accounts" of creation as recorded and found in the book of Genesis, chapters 1-3. These Hebrew creation myths were monotheistic alternatives to other creation myths and legends, such as those of the Greeks, Romans, Babylonians, and Africans (Egyptians). These Hebrew creation stories, legends, and myths simply stated that God created heaven and earth through a period of "six days," of which three days are said to have actually occurred before the actual creation of the sun itself! The existence of the Earth without the sun is a silly creation story if viewed as a literal historical account of what God did!

Just several decades ago (July 10-21, 1925), John Thomas Scopes was tried and convicted in Dayton, Rhea County in Tennessee, for teaching the theory of evolution during a biology class. He was fined a token sum of $100 and admonished not to teach the theory of evolution as a historical fact or true science. The State Constitution of Tennessee prohibited teaching of evolution in schools as scientific truth. In 1986, again, the Tennessee Hawkin's County Board of Education was sued unsuccessfully by "fundamentalist" Christian parents for teaching evolution and international studies in schools.

The conservative parents objected to these and some textbooks, and literature courses as a source of atheism, moral corruption, and vice. The team of conservative, Christian, rural parents suing the school was composed of three families. They felt morally justified to wage a Christian moral crusade against the moral corrosive "Godless and secular education." They sued the County Public School System on the legal and moral grounds that public school education had violated their religious and moral values.

The conservative Christians argued in court that this violation had occurred by teaching their children the un-Christian theory of evolution, feminist values, witchcraft through literature that mentions witches and wizards, and religious and moral relativism in education and values. They objected to what they saw as a secular, moral, and religious relativism.

These angry parents claimed that it was un-American, unpatriotic, anti-Christian, and blasphemous to hold and teach the view that all religions are equally valid, meaningful, and true for the people who practice them. They also argued that globalism, international interdependence, and the essential need and moral obligation for richer nations to aid the underdeveloped poor ones, rather than encouraging parochial patriotism, ethnocentric nationalism, missionary activity to convert the heathens, and aggressive militarism to achieve global superiority, was immoral, unchristian, and unpatriotic.

These infamous religious lawsuits against teachers of science, and specifically against the idea of evolution as the agent of "secular humanism" and atheism in the public school system, are absurd and anti-intellectual. The past unsuccessful frenzied and widely publicized trials of teachers and Public School Boards of Education officials in several states of the USA clearly indicate that the American educational system is still intellectually tied to religious fundamentalism and backward. This is true inasmuch as it produces these kinds of biblical literalists, intolerant religious fanatics, bigots, racist, ignorant parents, politicians and public officials.

The teaching of evolution as a science and virtues of tolerance of cultural, religious and ethnic diversity must become a compulsory part of the curriculum in Public Schools in order to fight and negate the these evils of ethnocentrism, religious bigotry, racism and cultural intolerance both within the educational institutions and the community as a whole. Private schools, colleges and universities have been specifically established and well equipped in order to accomplish this special moral and religious educational mission.

However, on the positive side, one can note that the heated debate and controversies concerning the teaching of evolution and moral values in American Public Schools also clearly indicate that the American educational system is open and democratic. These debates demonstrate that the American Public School systems are flexible enough to recognize the central role of parents and families in the education of their children.

This social educational concern with the school curriculum also demonstrates the fundamental concept and awareness that the parents are essentially the primary educators and role-models for their young children. There is also the recognition that parents are also the primary judges of the curriculum in terms of moral, religious, social, and educational and moral values, and essential skills considered for wholesome development and good education of their own children.

Nevertheless, in 1988, the State of Tennessee intervened in extremely Christian conservative family-based schools in the Montgomery and Stewart counties on the boarder with the conservative Christian County of Kentucky. The parents had refused to enroll their children in public schools based on the charge that the schools taught atheism, since it allowed the teaching of evolution in public schools. Yet, these semi-literate and ignorant parents were not adequately educated and equipped to provide an acceptable form of education for their home-schooled children.

In protest, the Tennessee State Board of Education took ten children away from their parents on legal grounds of child-abuse. The children had alleged that their parents had refused to allow them to leave their homes and go to school to study and socialize with their friends. This example provides good evidence that the community and the state are sometimes positively aware of their constitutional obligations to provide sound education, healthcare, and protection for all their respective citizens. As such, the state is also often equally concerned about the nature of moral and educational values of the growing children, since these are the society's leaders and adult citizens of tomorrow. Subsequently, to educate and shape them well in the right moral values, civic virtues, and responsibilities, is to educate and shape the moral values and course of the world tomorrow.

Therefore, if we truly desire to create an ideal or better moral community, a just society, and a peaceful world, we have to create it today through a system of sound moral education and dedication to restructure society. We need values that promote equity and socioeconomic justice. This moral ideal calls for a self-sacrificial global cooperation in the spirit of compassion, equality, mutual free acceptance, agape, and altruism. We must, by our own resolute and moral dedication to the wholistic liberal arts education, denounce selfishness or greed as the basis of action (objectivism).

Objectivism as the moral principle of self interest and greed, positively viewed as the basis of ideal behavior and moral conduct, is destructive to the local and global community. This is the essence of the tragic moral vice in Africa in terms of destructive tribalism and exclusive nationalism in the West. The two world wars were started by this kind of ethnocentrism, militaristic ethnic nationalist and parochialism.

The teaching of the essential positive cultural values associated with religious pluralism and ethnic diversity is essential in order to transform good education into the effective cure for the moral and social evils of racism, sexism, cultural and religious bigotry and intolerance. This moral education will also provide the necessary additional moral remedies for the social stress and violence associated with these moral and social evils.

Legislation against these moral and social evils is essential. But, by itself, it will not get rid of these moral and social evils. The effective remedies must include good education to convert or positively transform the conscience of the people in order to see and realize that the hate crimes of injustice, racism and sexism which they perpetrate are serious crimes, despicable moral evils, and sins committed against God, the community and the victims who are also God's beloved people. The people must be correctly taught that ethnocentrism, "tribalism" and nationalism are evil manifestations of collective greed and narrow self-identity, which lead to ethnocentrism or hubris, collective self-deification as God's special elect or "God's chosen people," exclusivism, and cultural intolerance of pluralism. This includes cultural, religious, ideological, and economic diversity.

By introducing sound moral education, we will implement moral reformation and correct moral education, and therefore, positively reshape conscience and moral values. This can be accomplished through moral training in sound *teleological* or *consequentialist* and *deontological systems of ethics*. We must concentrate on the moral education of the young and their parents. Children are still open and receptive to new ideas and values of *moral duty*, as opposed to their own parents and other adults whose values are already firmly set and consciences fully formed. The children are the hope for a more inclusive society. They are tomorrow's leaders and active responsible citizens.

Therefore, we must train the young people now concerning how to live as good, just, loving, humane and peaceful citizens of the local and Global Community. They must become the "detribalized" global citizens. They must be effectively correctly taught to accept the divine *moral imperative* and duty to practice love unconditionally and the unconditional acceptance of each person in the world, as God's child. And do this well, irrespective of color, creed, nationality, class or gender. Thereby, each person will be treated well, as a beloved brother and sister, and a fellow member of God's global family and Kingdom. Ultimately, all people must learn to serve each person with love and reverence, treating him or her as the physical incarnation of God in the local community and the world. This is the essence of the Christian doctrines of the *imago Dei* and the Divine Incarnation.

## 6. Sound Family Values as the Basis for Sound Moral Education and Virtuous Citizens

It has already been established that sound moral education and moral training begins at home in the ideal two parent family setting. Unfortunately, the ideal traditional family structure of mother and father has been badly damaged. Correlatively, so have been the traditional family values and the nature of moral training imparted to the young people.

The traditional family moral units consisting of a father as the main breadwinner and mother as the childcare provider have been eroded and largely destroyed. About 50 percent of the American marriages end in divorce! This high divorce rate negatively affects the health, growth, cognitive and moral development, education, social and moral education, and well-being of the child. Broken, violent, and poverty prone homes also produce less academically successful children who are aggressive, hostile, violent, and crime-oriented.

This relates to negative environmental conditioning than genetic programming for failure and low IQ, as Arthur Herrnstein and Charles Murray have erroneously concluded in their racially biased book, *The Bell Curve*. Intelligence measures are known to be biased to high income and middle class culture, language, and values more than the street language and logic or symbolism of the lower socioeconomic classes who live in the crime riddled inner cities.

In this *angst* and existential hell constituted by abject poverty and crime in the inner city, there is no time or suitable quiet facility for homework and parental assistance and general support with school work and projects. Additionally, in many cases, these students and many of their poorly educated single-parents are morally irresponsible and immature in their moral judgements, voluntary choices and actions. Many of their moral or voluntary actions are often irrational and self-destructive. These actions are often based on mere personal feelings of good as pleasure, opinions, peer pressure and basic animalistic drives in the form of instincts for personal survival, sex, food, (alcoholic) drink, and aggression. Rough forms of sports take care of some instincts for aggression and violence. Meanwhile, in the inner city, due to poverty and crime, the hungry kids resort to stealing, shoplifting, selling drugs, sex, and prostitution, instead of doing homework.

The conservatives claim that in America, the traditional family institution has been almost destroyed by divorce and sexual immorality. The traditional family institution has suffered from socioeconomic hardships, poverty and high rates of divorce. Traditional moralists and religious teachers have blamed the sexual revolution of the 1960s and 1970s and the liberation of women and feminism for these evils and the breakdown of the family. The tragic result is a higher rate of increasing numbers of single parents and numbers of children born out of wedlock to unemployed, impoverished and poorly educated teenage mothers.

Ultimately, society has to take an increasing role in the moral education and training of the children in a formal classroom set-up, despite protest from some parents, especially when it comes to sex education and moral family values, property, rights, and gender roles. If the school must do it, then the teachers must become the ideal moral role models in place of the irresponsible or nonexistent parents, particularly the male role and father-figure for children who come from undisciplined, lower socioeconomic class, female-headed, single parent homes within crime infested urban slums and the innercity communities.

In addition, sex or family education teachers should always be mature, well informed, sensitive, moral, and responsible adults, since this role has been traditionally reserved for responsible parents, ministers, and marriage counselors. Good moral family values and sex education should include the traditional moral values and rationale for insistence on abstention from sexual intercourse until marriage. It should teach the biology of the reproductive system, the proper function of these organs, how children are created, child spacing, child adoption, and the positive use of contraceptives and how they function to prevent unwanted pregnancy and sexually transmitted diseases.

Good education must also include the teaching of moral solutions concerning the moral and social problems of abortion and sexually transmitted diseases, the sanctify of marriage as an honorable covenant and the importance of waiting until one is emotionally, physically, and financially ready to be sexually active within a monogamous relationship under the protection of the marriage bond and the covenant of mutual obligations to each other and the offspring.

It should be pointed out that most Churches, particularly the Roman Catholic Church and the Southern Baptists, condemn all forms of abortions as crimes of murder and sins before God. In addition, the Catholic Church also condemns the use of artificial and mechanical birth control devices. Sex is positively viewed as God's special gift for reproduction. Therefore, the indulgence in sexual activity as a mere source of recreational pleasure is condemned by the Catholic Church as a mortal sin of lust, moral impurity and hedonism. This is also the basic moral reasoning and some of the main reasons that the Roman Catholic Church traditionally gives for its vehement moral condemnation of homosexuality as an unnatural, corrupt, and unclean sexual practice that constitutes a deadly or "mortal sin" and destructive moral evil. It is to be shunned by all the moral, obedient and faithful religious people.

The main objective of sex education is therefore to bring about moral sexual awareness and responsibility for one's moral choices, decisions, and alternatives to sexual encounters. This can reduce the high incidences of unplanned teenage pregnancies and school dropouts, and prevent or reduce the destructive sexually transmitted diseases, particularly the deadly HIV.

Good sex education should promote moral reasoning about sexuality and it's acceptable or moral uses. It should also facilitate moral responsibility for one's moral decisions when tempted to engage in premarital sex. Correct information and good moral training are important in all moral decision making processes including those involving personal, social, and sexual relationships. Subsequently, ignorance, trial and error, and the hazards correlated with them will be greatly reduced, if not entirely banished.

## 7. Schools, Colleges, and Universities: Problems of Moral Education and Public Education

However, when it comes to religious values, public schools should never try to present one religious system as being religiously and morally better or superior to another. To do so would be to select, favor and establish one religion over the other religions. This is expressly prohibited in the USA by the constitution as part of the separation of Church and State spheres of operation.

Moreover, this principle negates religious ethnocentrism, prejudice, subjectivism and bigotry, since there is no scientific or objective basis on which such a determination could be made. The teaching of religion is best left to private schools, colleges, universities and seminaries. People who seek admission into these religious institutions, go there knowing in advance that they will sacrifice some of their personal rights and privileges in order to follow the religious regulations of those institutions as stated their educational mission and religious principles.

In contrast to the religiously affiliated private schools, colleges and universities, the American public schools, colleges and universities cannot teach religion and theology. They can only offer and teach religion and philosophy from a strictly academic, non-sectarian and comparative point of view. This academic approach must seek to present to the students the critical analytical understanding of the truth not a mere moral judgement, as opposed to the propagation or indoctrination of faith in respect to anyone religion. In this critical study and presentation of religion, there is no room for faith and dogmas.

On the contrary, religious faith, beliefs and dogmas are the topics and contents of an academic, comparative and critical analysis and study of religion. For instance, topics such as the virgin birth of Jesus, resurrection and ascension are subjected to rigorous scrutiny and analysis from a purely academic point of view as informed by history and the sciences.

The conclusion may be that these are mere Christian pious stories or myths which have no real historical truth or scientific validity.

Obviously, the seminary's pedagogical approach to the study and teaching of these religious topics is very radically different. It starts from the point of faith that these topics present truth and the historical and religious faith and experience of the Early Church. Instead of dissecting the religious dogmas, the seminary pedagogical religious and theological approach seeks to reaffirm them.

The challenge to be resolved by academic is research how to find and devise better contemporary meaningful ways for effective understanding, reformulation and communicating these ancient Christian holy mysteries, Christian statements of faith, creeds and dogmas as God's holy mysteries or miracles to the believers. Academic research in theology and ethics also seeks better ways in which to most effectively communicate them as "the Gospel" or "Good News" to nonbelievers in order to convert them to Christianity. As such, the mission of private schools, colleges, universities and seminaries are quite different from the secular educational mission of public schools, colleges and universities, when it comes to the teaching of values and religion or religious studies.

Subsequently, the Christians, Muslims, Hindus, and atheists can all sit together in the same religions course and do well in it, merely as an intellectual exercise and an open academic analysis of the religious material as religious literature and philosophy. This neutral academic approach to the study of world religions is essential if all people have to learn to live together in harmony and peace as one family of God.

Ultimately, all forms of effective and good education and knowledge must also result in a correlative, visible, or measurable effects and changes and modification of behavior, values, concepts, beliefs, and practices. A diverse number of great scholars and moral teachers like Socrates, Plato, Aristotle, Jesus, Augustine, Thomas, Luther, Descartes, Calvin, Hume, Locke, Kant, Rousseau, Jefferson, Marx, Freud, Jung, Kierkegaard, Tillich, Barth, Whitehead, Skinner and Piaget have all taught that good education and correct knowledge is important. They all agree that knowledge is essential in making the knower whole, integrated, virtuous, moral, self-confident, dutiful, skilled, peace-loving, and happy.

Since all human beings are born without any rational knowledge and experience, therefore, all moral values, knowledge, and beliefs are learned after birth. They are not innate in human nature. They are not intrinsic components of the intellect, mind, spirit or soul. Instead, they are both learned and acquired through the unconscious, unthematic, and conscious cognitive processes of both structured, formal and unstructured, informal education and socialization.

Informal and unstructured education as a main form of socialization and humanization takes place all the time, everywhere, unlike the formal education, which takes place in planned settings and with preplanned curricula in schools, colleges, universities, and churches.

Whereas the former takes place anywhere and anytime, some settings are most ideal for it, particularly at home and within the social and cultural interaction within the family context. Here, parents, siblings, grandparents, and neighborhood peers and playmates play a key role as the informal teachers and role models.

In addition, these days, the mass media, particularly television, has also taken a very significant role in this educational and socialization process. The cartoons and other video game actors have become the ideal new role models presented to children by the mass media. Unfortunately, these new mass media role models are often immoral, violent characters who cheat and violently fight each other most of the time.

The public media, especially, the Internet and the television can be a source of vice, casual sex, and violence. It can also become a source of misunderstanding that it is morally and socially acceptable to be tough (machoistic), violent and kill one's opponents. Most popular films and cartoon characters are violent. They include some degree of sexual content and violence, such as fighting, shooting and killing of enemies as an ideal goal in fighting. But whereas the cartoon characters do not die even after being pushed over very high cliffs or after being shot at very close several times, real human beings will often die when they are pushed off cliffs or shot. Yet, the children are not taught this moral message while they are being conditioned to view strife, rivalry and violence as normal acceptable ways of human life. Some American school shootings by young people are direct results of this American culture of violence as communicated to the young people through the violent computer video games, cartoons and films on television and movie theaters.

Subsequently, parents, schools, and other good willed people need to protest violence and sexual indecency in the mass media. The Southern Baptists have provided a good example by calling for the boycott of Disney and its programs until violent and sexually explicit material has been removed from the children's programming, cartoons, music and other forms of public entertainment. Therefore, responsible parents and other caring people of moral conscience must come together and form effective moral coalition to exert moral and political consumer pressure against public indecency in the media, film and music entertainment industry.

The Hollywood film industry, television program sponsors and producers can make sure that more positive moral characters are created for the television viewing audience, especially the young. They must also clean up the violence from the electronic games, cartoons and other children's entertainment programs. These children are the future citizens and leaders of the nation and the world. The society must not condition and program them to accept casual sex, violence and war as normal or acceptable ways of behavior and life in the community and the world. This includes domestic abuse, child abuse and some cases of elective abortions, involuntary euthanasia and capital punishment as state retaliation for crimes and serious violations of the law.

Violence and war must not be portrayed as normal or ideal methods for personal, collective or state problem-solving. Violence or threats of violence and war cannot solve significant problems or bring about peace. Violence creates more violence in retaliation or as a counter-response (retaliation), self-defense, and retributive punishment for the initial use of violence. In his famous book, *The Prince*, Niccolo Machiavelli (1469-1527) realized and also advocated the use of brute force and violence to conquer and utterly crush the spirit and will of the conquered masses.

Machiavelli counseled the necessity of the use of violence to keep the conquered masses from rebellion. He advocated constant use of total military power to suppress the conquered people and keep them under constant military vigilance, intimidation and coercion if the imperial conqueror or colonizer wished to retain power over the conquered people. This use of military violence against enemies and to quell uprisings was visible in the Roman Empire and Napoleon's French Empire. More recently, this dehumanizing Machiavellian military and political treatment of opponents has been witnessed in the Middle East, especially, in the Israeli-Palestinian conflicts.

According to the Machiavellian military and political principle of imperial and colonial military occupation, the uprisings were utterly militarily crushed with great brutality in order to deter future rebellions and to teach other people a lesson of what would happen to them if they rebelled against the emperor or the occupying conquering powers.

Ultimately, all forms of violence are evil and must be condemned by the moral community and God's people, as Jesus did. Violence is destructive to the local community as well as the Global Community which is rooted within the individual local communities and nations. The public education network channels are already doing a good job of setting a good example for the commercial networks.

Sesame Street, Mr. Roger's Neighborhood and the Muppets are excellent programs for children to view. They are educational and provide good moral role models for all children to see and seek to emulate. It is also good that many preschools and elementary schools utilize these programs in formal classroom settings as part of their formal processes and programs of education. Character animations of the story and the book being read is a valuable educational tool and pedagogical method of teaching the young people and keeping them interested in the subject and moral of the story. For adults, poetry, hymns, proverbs, drama, sermons, story telling, films, role-play, essay writing, debates and discussions accomplish the same pedagogical goal.

Whereas the private schools and colleges have no legal constraint in what subjects they teach, including religious education, Bible knowledge, moral education, and ethics and moral philosophy, the public schools and colleges are legally bounded and constrained from teaching religion and partisan, sectarian, moral values. This is because it would amount to a breach of the American constitution that prohibits the favor and government establishment of any religion or denomination.

Therefore, teaching moral values in the public schools and colleges is a more tricky and complex task. Yet, it has to be done. However, it must be done in a non-sectarian and nonpartisan manner if it is to succeed and go unchallenged by both parents and law courts for constitutional legality and conformity.

To this end, schools can introduce civics and ethics courses whose basic texts can be the *Decalogue*, *Shari'a*, the *American Declaration of Independence*, the *USA Constitution*, and the *UN Universal Declaration of Human Rights.* The documents can be studied for their view of humanity, God, human rights, moral values, obligations of individuals to the State, and the obligations of the State to the citizens such as protection, law enforcement, material welfare, the provision of basic education, and medical and economic services.

Formal courses programs and educational events must include moral education. This moral education must involve academic debates, seminars, workshops, and outside speakers on current moral issues. These topics should include: AIDS and its prevention, capital punishment, abortion, genetic engineering, organ transplant, euthanasia, suicide, nuclear war, international terrorism, world hunger, poverty, disease, Darwinism or evolution, "nuclear winter" or deadly nuclear pollution, creationism, homosexuality, marriage, divorce, the ordination of women to the ministry, inclusive language, racial profiling, and problems of institutional racism and sexism. Experts should be asked to volunteer their time as part of their community service, and lead the discussions, give lectures, provide reading and research data, answer questions, and chair and moderate debates.

However, the students should always be allowed to make up their own minds on what is moral for them on the basis of the data and presentation. They should never be compelled or coerced to change their moral views except on the basis and level of moral, logical, critical reasoning based on objective data and accumulated experiences and facts. Any form of indoctrination is not part of any good education and should never be tolerated in a public education system. This is true because it turns students into irresponsible social and moral robots unable to think ethically and critically for themselves on important moral issues of life.

Good liberal arts education and moral critical thinking are the essential cures to this problem. Ignorance, the lack of a free-thinking mind, and the absence of positive moral role models and reinforcement for good moral actions and habits are the greatest dangers for a community and the world's well-being, harmony, peace, and happiness. This is the case, because it is easier to do evil than it is to do good. Also, doing evil is often more immediately rewarding. But, this reward is often a lesser good and negative when compared to the rewards and long term positive effects of doing good.

Furthermore, there are more evildoers who hate the good and the morally right, and sometimes benefit from crime and corruption. That is, the main reason why honest, good people and the vocal advocates of justice and morality are often violently hated and subsequently killed by bad and evil people. Evil cannot afford to stand against the contrast and opposition of the good without being exposed for what it truly is.

Therefore, evil people try to recruit and corrupt the good people. If this move fails, evil people may then resort to the use of violence and seek total elimination of the good people. This happens in the war against organized crime, such as the "mafia," drug-dealers, smugglers and gangsters. The police and other law-enforcement are sometimes bribed and corrupted by the criminals. In turn, the corrupt police protect the criminals from arrest and hinder prosecution by getting rid of the key incriminating state evidence against the criminals.

Subsequently, in the moral crusade against evil, the incorruptible and uncompromising great moral teachers like Socrates, Jesus, Gandhi, and King, and the prophets of justice and divine holiness, were all killed by sinful and hateful, evil men and women. The death of Jesus on the cross stands as a permanent remind to the world of this tragic nature of moral crusade against evil. This is why the resurrection, rather than the innocent and unjust death of Jesus on the cross, is for most Christians held to be the moral and spiritual center of Christianity.

According to the New Testament, the resurrection of Jesus was the main driving power of the Apostolic proclamation of the Good News of God's triumph over human acts of hate, injustice, innocent death, sin and evil in the world. The Apostles perceived the death of Jesus as on the cruel cross as the triumph of evil against goodness and the triumph of the Devil against God. But, with the resurrection, this scenario is reversed. There is a triumph of good over evil and God triumphs over he Devil!

Ultimately, the students have to learn the real unpleasant truth that being morally upright and virtuous is not a popular social option. They must learn that it may lead to both rejection and persecution by their peers. Therefore, they must be taught to be fully prepared to accept the cost for moral integrity. They must learn that being a moral saint requires courage to face ridicule, temptation, suffering, rejection and even death. This can be taught comparatively in terms of the dramatic trial and execution of Socrates and Jesus and the violent assassinations of Gandhi and King. Excellent educational films and books exist on the lives, work, death, and significance of these great moral teachers, whose teachings have irreversibly changed the world from barbaric hate, retaliation, and violence to the moral universal requirement of moral knowledge, mutual acceptance, unconditional love, forgiveness, nonviolence, and peace.

In order to excite students and bring some of the moral issues to life, the teacher should devise actual moral dilemma simulations, such as a mock United Nations' (UN) debate on the American military action in Libya in order to punish Khaddafi for his alleged role in international terrorism and bombing of a Pan-American passenger airliner over Scotland on December 21, 1988, killing over three hundred people. The UN sponsored international, national, state, and district forums on ethics and public policy can be created to discuss and debate the problems of education, environmental destruction, global warming, human-rights, democracy, freedom of press, poverty, development, debtor nations, cultural and gender bias, nuclear and biological or chemical weapons of mass destruction, and war. These UN sponsored forums can also be used to find and discuss effective solutions for these serious problems.

A mock debate can include people on the panel who may be assigned to represent an opposing view, such as that of Russia, China, Iran, Libya, or Iraq. That forces moral ideals from all perspectives to be examined and evaluated. The same legal reasoning can be done about other controversial issues, such as human cloning, as the US Supreme Court did in the abortion case of Roe vs. Wade. On January 31, 1973, the US Supreme Court declared that abortion was a legitimate and legal woman's moral right and choice. Similarly, the US Supreme Court could on the same grounds declare that euthanasia is a right for each person to enable him or her to die peacefully in dignity and painlessly with an a doctor's assistance. People assisting the terminally ill to commit suicide or die in peace would not be tried for murder or any crimes related to this act of mercy.

Therefore, Dr. Jack Kevorkian's crusade for the legalization of euthanasia and doctor assisted suicide as a legitimate legal medical procedure and moral act on behalf of the terminally ill must be positively legally reviewed by the courts, accepted and legalized. Other related laws and medical regulations of euthanasia must be correspondingly enacted by the states as necessary moral and legal safeguards to prevent abuses of euthanasia as a medical procedure by doctors, insurance companies and the patients' family members.

Academic debates can also be organized on important topics and issues of confidentiality and laws governing them. The merits and demerits for the legal and moral imperative to disclose confidential information when human life is endangered or when injustice is about to be committed, refusal to undergo medical treatment, and the moral value dilemma of truth telling and self-incrimination or self-endangerment should be debated and reevaluated. These all should be discussed and debated in a structured classroom setting.

This kind of approach is important, because it confronts the individual with real life moral conditions and moral choices and decisions to be made. Consequently, the learner's moral awareness is greatly aroused. He or she is positively motivated and challenged to employ his or her ability and skills to make a moral evaluation of available data and weigh alternative choices and their consequences in order to arrive at the most appropriate choice. The student must also make the most relevant decision and also take the responsibility to accept the consequences for one's decision and deeds. Moral maturity requires taking responsibility for all of one's decisions and actions. This moral process is better learned by going over all the essential stages in all moral judgements and moral decision making processes which characterize human life, since all human beings are by nature essentially moral agents.

This is the "*a priori*" moral condition which is the essential moral requisite for being human. It cannot be otherwise, although the human being can rebel against his or her essential nature, and in ignorance, self-negation, and self-destruction, live an immoral life of vice in the ever present torment of daily guilt of failure to do the good and the right when it is clearly known. Consequently, authentic humanity is essentially constituted by moral uprightness or virtue, love, justice, and humane kindness, which are moral requirements for personal integrity, wholeness, general well-being, peace, and happiness.

## 8. Key Roles of Church, Religion and State in Moral Education, Ethics and Public Education

There is a central role that can be played by the responsible religious community of the Church in the moral education of the young and adult citizens. Islam and Judaism do this in a more formal and dogmatic manner. The Roman Catholic and Evangelical Churches also do a good job compared to the liberal traditions. Most people prefer a canon and moral guidelines, because they find them comforting and reassuring in their own moral quest for God and the good and happy life both "on the Earth and in heaven after death." Good instruction, faith, and obedient practice of the good are the keys to all moral values and ethics, since nobody is ever born moral or virtuous.

Correct knowledge, truth, and skills are the necessary tools for positive moral action, civic moral virtue, and positive transformation of the individual and his or her community and the world. All schools, churches, and religious institutions have a moral obligation to educate their members in ideal religious moral values, such as justice, unconditional love for all human beings, and charity and concern for the poor, the homeless, the oppressed, the hungry, and the sick and dying.

Ideally, education in this religious context should not be by the methods of preaching, indoctrination, and intimidation. Instead, the Christians should be carefully taught why the Church teaches the very values and commandments which it promotes and teaches as God's holy will and universal ordinances.

Moral education for all people is essential because people will become better and more responsible moral agents when they know the reason why they believe certain moral beliefs or doctrines and hold certain religious values. Good moral education fosters the following virtues: critical thinking skills, positive and nonviolent creative problem solving skills, hard-work, personal responsibility, team-spirit, courage to resist evil influences, personal discipline, integrity, justice, charity, honesty, accountability, cleanliness, good personal habits, compassion, considerate care for other people and the environment, good citizenship, enthusiasm for peace, order and harmony within the community.

Those people that are rooted in the correct knowledge of the good, will not be as easily tempted, swayed or threatened when they meet and live with other people who do not share their own moral values or religious beliefs. This is the main reason why religious fundamentalists tend to feel very insecure with their moral values and religious beliefs when they are exposed to the academic challenges and scrutiny of the sciences, especially the theory of evolution as opposed to the literal, interpretation of the Genesis mythical accounts of creation.

Therefore, in a pluralistic society such as the USA, where there is a clear constitutional separation of Church and State affairs and spheres of operation, there is also religious and academic freedom for all people, irrespective of creed and ideology. There is also the necessary legal safeguard for religious values and ethics based on the Church's doctrinal teachings and rigid dogmas which the various religious communities or churches have formulated established over their own jurisdiction. This includes their respective obedient members, churches and educational institutions that function as the conduits for these values and religious teachings.

Subsequently, it is wrong for churches and their Christian followers to be pressing for legislation to allow public schools to teach religion and religiously based moral values since this would be an unconstitutional political and moral advocacy. The democratic and pluralistic state does not exist in order to serve any religious tradition or promote one religion over others, since there are many competing valid religions in the world.

Any state that promotes a single religion at the expense of other religions, as in the case of the *Shari'a* based Islamic nations, eventually becomes the missionary tool of religion. Correlatively, the state that establishes religion becomes a major source of moral and religious confusion and conflicts. Very often, that state also becomes a major source of religious persecution and oppression of the members of less favored religions. This happened in the Christian Roman Empire, the Spanish Inquisition, England after becoming Anglican (Protestant) and Uganda where King Mwanga of Buganda martyred more than five hundred Christians in 1885-1877, most of whom were burned on the stake at Namugongo hill on June 3, 1886.

The divine kings of Uganda had invited the European Christians missionaries to come teach and evangelize the people within their kingdoms. They also strongly believed that they could expel the Christian missionaries, criminalize the Christian religion and execute its members, if the European Christian missionaries and Christianity as a new religion failed to unite the people in the clan-divided kingdoms or ceased to serve the king's own political, social, military and economic agenda.

As a poorly educated and devout Muslim, President Idi Amin of Uganda (1971-79), also believed this to be the case. As a result, he also viciously persecuted Christianity, killed the Janani Luwum, the Anglican Archbishop of Uganda in 1977 along with two cabinet ministers for being loyal Anglican Christians. Idi Amin is responsible for the deaths of about 1 million Ugandan Christians, most of whom were Anglicans. Christian persecution still takes place today in some fundamentalist Islamic nations, especially, Pakistan, and the Sudan where more than 2 million Christians in Southern Sudan have been martyred by Muslims over the past 30 years, and the war between the Christian south and Islamic north still goes on.

Therefore, instead of states establishing religions, there should be a constitutional separation of Church and State spheres of operation. Accordingly, religious organizations or churches must be encouraged to establish Sunday Schools and the Church-related schools, colleges, and universities, in which they can teach the desired doctrinal, moral, ethical, and religious teaching needed and in the manner most desired by the particular Church or Religious Community.

However, this should never be expected or asked of the public school system or the government sponsored public institutions of higher learning. As a result, public prayer in these public school systems would be very unconstitutional and religiously divisive, since public institutions are open to people of all creeds, religions, philosophies, and even to those who are either agnostic or self-confessed atheists.

It is that Jesus as the Christ taught the universal imperative and theocentric moral obligation of agape (unconditional love), nonviolence, nonretaliation and the free forgiveness of offenses. Therefore, the obedient and morally responsible Christians should never use force, deceit, legislation, or threat to compel anyone to be converted to Christ, for Jesus himself rejected and overcame the very same temptations of the use of power, force, and miracles at the beginning of his ministry to convert people to God. Instead, Jesus as the Christ of God, chose to employ the humble but humane and loving method of moral teaching and gentle persuasion.

Like God, Jesus also fully respected the freewill and freedom of each human being as an intelligent, self-determining and self-fulfilling creature. He recognized that by freedom and free choices and actions, the human being co-self-creates himself or herself with God into the very person that the person eventually becomes. Jesus wanted men and women to hear God, understand, and make a personal moral choice and consequential decision to obey his call and teaching, and to follow him even if this obedience might lead to personal rejection, suffering, and death at the hands of hateful and sinful men. It is also his promise that all those who would obey and follow him would become immortal, since God would raise them to eternal life if they were killed for righteousness and for Christ and the Gospel's sake.

Consequently, all those people of goodwill do good works in the name of God and love their fellow human beings unconditionally and seek to become God's moral ambassadors and ministers in the world. All obedient human beings and God's saints are to become God's ambassadors of love, reconciliation, nonviolence, harmony, unity, peace, and happiness. It is the Christian hope and traditional affirmation that even if the saints are killed because of their prophetic message, they will be raised up by God to eternal life, and their legacy will continue to live, shaping men and women and the world long after they have died. Jesus, Gandhi and M.L. King are good examples of this truth.

Therefore, let God's loving and caring people everywhere in the world be encouraged to mobilize any willing men and women of moral virtue and goodwill to rise up and stand firm for justice for all people, irrespective of color, race, nationality, class, sexual orientation and gender. Let us encourage God's moral saints to "carry their crosses" courageously and faithful as the shining torches of truth, socioeconomic justice, moral well-being and praxis of the divine imperative of unconditional love. This is the love which we are to express to all our fellow human beings and the world. The world and its people are already tired of hate and evil, and therefore, eagerly waiting for the Gospel of unconditional love, mutual acceptance, forgiveness, unified cooperation, and peace.

Let God's people humble themselves to God's transforming power of love, grace, hope, faith and prayer. Let the people pray that God may transform us into His or Her effective representatives and ambassadors of love, peace and healing in the world. This is the true meaning of God's redemption and salvation for the world, torn apart by the human moral evils of greed, self-centeredness, selfishness, strife, hate, and war. Let God's loving and obedient saints of all religions work together, so as to bring God's own unconditional redemptive love, harmony, peace, and happiness to the world.

Then, together and united in faith, hope, and prayer with all the saints we can most effectively and meaningfully pray for global peace, success and happiness. When God's loving and obedient saints, everywhere in the world work together with all God's peace-loving people and any people of goodwill, anywhere in the world, they can very effectively and practically transform positively this world into God's Kingdom. To this end, and in hope of miraculous expectation, God's people can answer with a resounding, "Yes" or "Amen!"

This is God's invitation that is ever extended to God's obedient people in the world. They are all called to become just and nonviolent. And to become God's active and effective societal courageous divine mediators and the instruments of unconditional love, socioeconomic justice, nonviolence and peace in the world. Let them go out into the world in God's name to love and serve their fellow human beings. Let them work hard as empowered by moral imperative of agape and God's free universal redemptive grace to accomplish the unconditional loving works of God through the spirit of charity and justice. Let them become the concrete representatives of God in the world by becoming the willing and active peace makers everywhere on earth where there is constant strife, conflict, or war.

Jesus himself commended peacemaking as God's redemptive divine mission in the world. He declared: "Blessed are the peacemakers, for the Kingdom of God belongs to them" (cf. Matt. 5:8). This mission of agape and peacemaking in the world is reason for being of any true religion, sound system of education and ethics. The promotion of love, well-being and peace in the local community and the world is the ultimate, universal, moral and religious divine mandate and mission of every sound, good and redemptive religion and system ofbeneficial ethics. This is also the true universal criterion measure of any truly sound and redemptive religion as well as that of any sound moral theology or ethics.

It is self-evident that the more developed, humane, worthy and redemptive systems of religion become evolved, universally, they also inevitably promote personal and societal modes of life that promote human positive transformation, love, healing, acceptance of sinners, forgiveness of sins, well-being, nonviolence and peace. This is in addition to the cultivation of good habits of grace and the virtues of agape as they express themselves in humility, creativity, peacemaking, hard-work and continuing quest for intellectual and moral development through sound education, and openness to change according to the new knowledge and truths as they are gained through study, prayer, meditation, science, research and reason.

Ultimately, very conservative, static and closed systems of religion and ethics which do not accomplish the above noble moral task are worthless and must be discarded. They are fraudulent and dangerous to their adherents and the society in which these people live. Examples of this danger is represented by the fraudulent religious cults, such as that of the Rev. Jim Jones' People's Temple which ended in a mass suicide in 1988, the Heaven's Gate which ended in a mass suicide in 1997, and The Movement for the Restoration of the Ten Commandments of God, which also ended in a mass suicide in a deliberately set church fire on March 17, 2000 in the rural town of Kanungu, in South-Western Uganda.

The evil and self-centered cult leaders convince their members that this world is an evil place and that a self-sacrificial death in a holy war (*jihad* and crusades) or mass suicide is the gate to escape from evil in the world and to enter into the blessedness of God's Kingdom, on another more peaceful and holy planet! Such an escapist and fraudulent religions, and systems of ethics fail to represent the transforming and redemptive power of God's unconditional love and free unmerited grace. These kinds of cults and religions are the ones that Freud and Nietzsche truly condemned as destructive and whose God and heaven were mere human made imaginary creations and mental illusions without any objective reality. Indeed, the leaders of such destructive religious cults are often men and women suffering from mental illness, such as schizophrenia, hallucinations, depression, paranoia and anxiety neurosis.

By remaining static and changeless in an evolutionary and changing world, they also misrepresent the living and All-embracing, creative Cosmic Spirit that is actively disclosing himself or herself in the world as the "All-Inclusive," transcendent Cosmic Creative Spirit. This is the genderless, and colorless cosmic Creator-Sustainer and Redeemer God whose unconditional and unmerited benevolent cosmic activities of creation, revelation and redemption are ever ongoing and in which we participate. They are the external embodiment of his or her unconditional love, universal free grace that are manifested to us in both God's processes of cosmic creation and redemption. As such, God creates the cosmos as part of his or her essence as creativity and redeems it as part of his or her divine essence of unconditional love, grace and salvation.

For all these unmerited divine activities, the human being can only respond positively in cooperation with God in these activities of creation and redemption of the world and thereby become like God. Then the human being is able to become the most effective divine instrument for God's supernatural activities in the world through politics, religion, science, medicine and technology for the benefit of both humanity and all creation.

In this existential sense and spiritual reality and Christian teachings and faith in God's omnipresence in the cosmos as both Creative and Redemptive Spirit or the All Encompassing Ultimate Reality, God's Kingdom is truly present in the cosmos and effectively established here on the Earth. It is both mystically correlative and intertwined and inseparable from daily life, humanity, truth, mind, goodness, justice, order, acts of compassion, the manifestations of unconditional love in good altruistic deeds and peace in the world.

God's process of human salvation and divinization into the original and authentic *imago Dei,* or Jesus as the most true incarnation of God in the world is both correlative and coextensive with the manner is which human beings live in the world in complete openness and obedience to God's *Logos.* This obedience to God and the corresponding inner state of spiritual grace, deep faith in God, faith, godliness, moral perfection and divinization or union with God is both correlative and externalized manifested by good deeds of unconditional love, compassion, free forgiveness of sins, nonviolence and peace.

Therefore, all truly redemptive religions, regardless of the religious name or label they have chosen for themselves, and all sound moral systems must teach their members to produce these saintly fruits of moral and spiritual perfection which effectively transform this world into God's Kingdom for all God's creatures. Within this understanding, God's cosmic processes of historical, biological, cultural, moral, religious and technological evolution provide to God's intelligent creatures freedom and the necessary power of God's unmerited and free supernatural creative and redemptive grace for self-determination, self-co-creation and co-redemption with God.

Through the process of evolution, God provides and infinitely open future dimension of potential realities for the intelligent creatures. The free and intelligent moral creatures are presented with many alternative potential choices by God through a constantly unfolding alternative potential choices for moral, physical, biological, spiritual, social, technological, political cultural, economic and technological self-actualization. These are ever evolving and changing opportunities for self-determination, self-improvement, self-perfection, self-completion, ultimate fulfillment, peace and happiness. This is the true nature of human life, divine invitation at the moment of conception. This is also the true nature of any human authentic moral and spiritual journey or divinization process for each normal human being for evolving into God's true moral agent or the *imago Dei* as God's responsible temporal representative and custodian of creation.

Within this evolutionist and theocentric understanding of humanity, each human being is affirmed to be a special creation in order to become the temporal embodiment of mind, spirit, truth, thought, knowledge, language, creativity, religion, love, compassion, moral conscience, responsibility, beauty, order, freedom and self-transcendence as God's Son or Daughter in the world. For the Christians, Jesus as the Christ of God provides the best human example and role model for human life of nonviolence, perfection in obedience to God, prayer, embodiment of Agape, and free forgiveness of sins. Jesus provides the best example of how each human being can live in love and peace with the neighbor and thereby become the perfect true *imago Dei*, effective God's representative and divine incarnation as God's Son or Daughter or the obedient embodiment and agent of God's *Logos* in the world and its temporal institutions and divine process of creation and redemption.

# Appendix A

# THE UNITED NATIONS DECLARATION OF UNIVERSAL HUMAN RIGHTS

**PREAMBLE**

Whereas recognition of the inherent dignity and of the equal and inalienable rights of all members of the human family is the foundation of freedom, justice and peace in the world;

Whereas disregard and contempt for human rights have resulted in barbarous acts which have outraged the conscience of mankind, and the advent of a world in which human beings shall enjoy freedom of speech and belief and freedom from fear and want has been proclaimed as the highest aspiration of the common people;

Whereas it is essential, if man is to be compelled to have recourse, as a last resort, to rebellion against tyranny and oppression, that human rights should be protected by the rule of law;

Whereas it is essential to promote the development of friendly relations between nations;

Whereas the peoples of the United Nations have in the Charter reaffirmed their faith in fundamental human rights, in the dignity and worth of the human person and in the equal rights of men and women and have determined to promote social progress and better standards of life in larger freedom;

Whereas Member States have pledged themselves to achieve, in co-operation with the United Nations, the promotion of universal respect for and observance of human rights and fundamental freedoms;

Whereas a common understanding of these rights and freedoms is of the greatest importance for the full realization of this pledge;

Now, therefore,

The General Assembly

Proclaims this Universal Declaration of Human Rights as a common stand of achievement for all peoples and all nations, to the end that every individual and every organ of society, keeping this Declaration constantly in mind, shall strive by teaching and education to promote respect for these rights and freedoms and by progressive measures, national and international, to secure their universal and effective recognition and observance, both among the peoples of Member States themselves and among the peoples of territories under their jurisdiction.

ARTICLE 1: All human beings are born free and equal in dignity and rights. They are endowed with reason and conscience and should act towards one another in a spirit of brotherhood.

ARTICLE 2: Everyone is entitled to all the rights and freedoms set forth in this Declaration, without distinction of any kind, such as race, colour, sex, language, religion, political or other opinion, national or social origin, property, birth or other status.

ARTICLE 3: Everyone has the right to life, liberty and the security of person.

ARTICLE 4: No one will be held in slavery or servitude. Slavery and the slave trade shall be prohibited in all forms.

ARTICLE 5: No one shall be subjected to torture or cruel, inhuman or degrading treatment or punishment.

ARTICLE 6: Everyone has the right to recognition everywhere as a person before the law.

ARTICLE 7: All [people] are equal before the law and are entitled without any discrimination to equal protection of the law. All are entitled to equal protection against any discrimination in violation of this Declaration and against any incitement of such discrimination.

ARTICLE 8: Everyone has the right to an effective remedy by the competent national tribunals for acts violating the fundamental rights granted him by the constitution or by law.

ARTICLE 9: No one shall be subjected to arbitrary arrest, detention or exile.

ARTICLE 1O: Everyone is entitled in full equality to a fair and public hearing by an independent and impartial tribunal, in the determination of his rights and obligations and of any criminal charge against him.

ARTICLE 11: 1. Everyone charged with a penal offense has the right to be presumed innocent until proved guilty according to law in a public trial at which he has had all the guarantees necessary for his defense.

2. No one shall be held guilty of any penal offence on account of any act or omission which did not constitute a penal offence, under national or international law, at the time when it was committed. Nor shall a heavier penalty be imposed than the one that was applicable at the time the penal offence was committed.

ARTICLE 12: No one shall be subjected to arbitrary interference with his privacy, family, home or correspondence, nor to attacks upon his honour and reputation. Everyone has the right to the protection of the law against such interference or attacks.

ARTICLE 13: 1. Everyone has the right to freedom of movement and residence within the borders of each State.

2. Everyone has the right to leave any country, including his own, and to return to his country.

ARTICLE 14: 1. Everyone has the right to seek and enjoy in other countries asylum from persecution.

2. This right may not be invoked in the case of prosecutions genuinely arising from nonpolitical crimes or from acts contrary to the purpose and principles of the United Nations.

ARTICLE 15: 1. Everyone has a right to a nationality.

2. No one shall be arbitrarily be deprived of his nationality nor denied the right to change his nationality.

ARTICLE 16: 1. Men and women of full age, without any limitation due to race, nationality or religion, have the right to marry and to found a family. They are entitled to equal rights as to a marriage, during marriage and at its dissolution.

2. Marriage shall be entered into only with the free and full consent of the intending spouses.

3. The family is the natural and fundamental group unit of society and is entitled to protection by society and the State.

ARTICLE 17: 1. Everyone has the right to own property alone as well as in association with others.

2. No one shall be arbitrarily deprived of his property.

ARTICLE 18: Everyone has the right to freedom of thought, conscience and religion. This right includes freedom to change his religion or belief, and freedom, either alone or in community with others and in public or private, to manifest his religion or belief in teaching, practice, worship and observance.

ARTICLE 19: Everyone has the right to freedom of opinion and expression. This right includes freedom to hold opinions without interference and to seek, receive and impart information and ideas through any media and regardless of frontiers.

ARTICLE 2O: 1. Everyone has the right to freedom of peaceful assembly and association.

2. No one may be compelled to belong to an association.

ARTICLE 21: 1. Everyone has the right to take part in the government of his country, directly or through freely chosen representatives.

2. Everyone has the right of equal access to public service in his country.

3. The will of the people shall be the basis of the authority of government. This will shall be expressed in periodic and genuine elections which shall be by universal and equal suffrage and shall be held by secret vote or by equivalent free voting procedures.

ARTICLE 22: Everyone, as a member of society, has the right to social security and is entitled to realization, through national effort and international co-operation and in accordance with the organization and resources of each state, of the economic, social and cultural rights indispensable for his dignity and the free development of his personality.

ARTICLE 23: 1. Everyone has the right to work; to free choice of employment; to just and favourable conditions of work and to protection against unemployment.

2. Everyone, without any discrimination, has the right to equal pay for equal work.

3. Everyone who works has the right to just and favourable remuneration ensuring for himself and his family an existence worthy of human dignity, and supplemented, if necessary, by other means of social protection.

4. Everyone has the right to form and to join trade unions for the protection of his [or her] interests.

ARTICLE 24: Everyone has the right to rest and leisure, including reasonable limitation of working hours and periodic holidays with pay.

ARTICLE 25: 1. Everyone has the right to a standard of living adequate for the health and well-being of himself and of his family, including food, clothing, housing and medical care and necessary social services, and the right to security in the event of unemployment, sickness, disability, widowhood, old age or other lack of livelihood in circumstances beyond his control.

2. Motherhood and childhood are entitled to special care and assistance. All children, whether born in or out of wedlock, shall enjoy the same social protect-ion.

ARTICLE 26: 1. Everyone has the right to education. Education shall be free, at least in the elementary and fundamental stages. Elementary education shall be compulsory. Technical and professional education shall be made generally available and higher education shall be equally accessible to all on the basis of merit.

2. Education shall be directed to the full development of the human personality and to the strengthening of respect for human rights and fundamental freedoms. It shall promote understanding, tolerance and friendship among all nations, racial or religious groups, and shall further the activities of the United Nations for the maintenance of peace.

3. Parents have a prior right to choose the kind of education that shall be given to their children.

ARTICLE 27: 1. Everyone has the right to participate in the cultural life of the community and its benefits.

2. Everyone has the right to the protection of the moral and material interests resulting from any scientific, literary or artistic production of which he [or she] is the author.

ARTICLE 28: Everyone is entitled to a social and international order in which the rights and freedoms set forth in this Declaration can be fully realized.

ARTICLE 29: 1. Everyone has duties to the community in which alone the free and full development of his personality is possible.

2. In the exercise of his rights and freedoms, everyone shall be subject only to such limitations as are determined by law solely for the purpose of securing due recognition and respect for the rights and freedoms of others and of meeting the just requirements of morality, public order and the general welfare in a democratic society.

3. These rights and freedoms may in no case be exercised contrary to the purposes and principles of the United Nations.

ARTICLE 30: Nothing in this Declaration may be interpreted as implying for any State, group or person any right to engage in any activity or to perform any act aimed at the destruction of any of the rights and freedoms set forth herein.

# Appendix B

# Normative Christian Ethics And Moral Social Principles: The United Methodist Social Principles[1]

**PREAMBLE**
We, the [Christian] people called United Methodists,[2] affirm our faith in God our Creator and Father, in Jesus Christ our Savior, and in the Holy Spirit, our Guide and Guard.

We acknowledge our complete dependence upon God in birth, in life, in death, and in life eternal. Secure in God's love, we affirm the goodness of life and confess our many sins against God's will for us as we find it in Jesus Christ. We have not always been faithful stewards of all that has been committed to us by God the Creator. We have been reluctant followers of Jesus Christ in his mission to bring all persons into a community of love. Though called by the Holy Spirit to become new creatures in Christ, we have resisted the further call to become the people of God in our dealings with each other and the earth on which we live.

Grateful for God's forgiving love, in which we live and by which we are judged, and affirming our belief in the inestimable worth of each individual, we renew our commitment to become faithful witnesses to the gospel, not alone to the ends of earth, but also, to the depths of our common life and work.

## I. THE NATURAL WORLD

All creation is the Lord's, and we are responsible for the ways in which we use and abuse it. Water, air, soil, minerals, energy resources, plants, animal life,, and space are to be valued and conserved because they are God's creation and not solely because they are useful to human beings. Therefore, we repent of our devastation of the physical and non-human world. Further, we recognize the responsibility of the Church toward lifestyle and systemic changes in society that will promote a more ecologically just world and a better quality of life for all creation.

**A) Water, Air, Soil, Minerals, Plants:** We support and encourage social policies that serve to reduce and control the creation of industrial by-products and waste; facilitate the safe processing and disposal of toxic and nuclear waste and move toward the elimination of both; encourage reduction of municipal waste; provide for appropriate recycling and disposal of municipal waste; and assist the clean-up of polluted air, water, and soil.[3]

We support measures designed to maintain and restore natural ecosystems. We support policies that develop alternatives to chemicals used for growing, processing, and preserving food, and we strongly urge adequate research into their effects upon God's creation prior to utilization. We urge development of international agreements concerning equitable utilization of the world's resources for human benefit so long as the integrity of the earth is maintained.

**B) Energy Resources Utilization:** We support and encourage social policies that are directed toward rational and restrained transformation of parts of the non-human world into energy for human usage and that de-emphasize or eliminate energy-producing technologies that endanger the health, the safety, and even, the existence of the present and future human and nonhuman creation. Further, we urge wholehearted support of the conservation of energy and responsible development of all energy resources, with special concern for the development of renewable energy sources, that the goodness of the earth may be affirmed.

**C) Animal Life:** We support regulations that protect the life and health of animals, including those ensuring the humane treatment of pets and other domestic animals, animals used in research, and the painless slaughtering of meat animals, fish, and fowl. We encourage the preservation of all animal species including those threatened with extinction.

**D) Space:** The universe, known and unknown, is the creation of God and is due the respect we are called [by God] to give the Earth.

**E) Science and Technology:** We recognize science as a legitimate interpretation of God's natural world. We affirm the validity of the claims of science in describing the natural world, although we preclude science from making authoritative claims about theological issues. We recognize technology as a legitimate use of God's natural world when such use enhances human life and enables all of God's children to develop their God-given creative potential without violating our ethical convictions about the relationship of humanity to the natural world.

In acknowledging the important roles of science and technology, however, we also believe that theological understandings of human experience are crucial to a full understanding of the place of humanity in the universe. Science and theology are complementary rather than mutually incompatible. We therefore encourage dialogue between the scientific and theological communities and seek the kind of participation that will enable humanity to sustain life on earth and by God's grace, increase the quality of our common lives together.

## II. THE NURTURING COMMUNITY

The community provides the potential for nurturing human beings into the fullness of their humanity. We believe we have a responsibility to innovate, sponsor, and evaluate new forms of community that will encourage development of the fullest potential in individuals. Primary for us is the gospel understanding that all persons are important – because they are human beings created by God and loved through and by Jesus Christ and not because they have merited significance. We therefore support social climates in which human communities are maintained and strengthened for the sake of all persons and their growth.

**A) The Family**: We believe the family to be the basic human community through which persons are nurtured and sustained in mutual love, responsibility, respect, and fidelity. We understand the family as encompassing a wider range of options than that of the two-generational unit of parents and children (the nuclear family), including the extended family, families with adopted children, single parents, step-families, and couples without children. We affirm shared responsibility for parenting by men and women and encourage social, economic, and religious efforts to maintain and strengthen relationships within families in order that every member may be assisted toward complete personhood.

**B) Other Christian Communities:** We further recognize the movement to find new patterns of Christian nurturing communities such as Koinonia Farms, certain monastic and other religious orders, and some types of corporate Church life. We urge the Church to seek ways of understanding the needs and concerns of such Christian groups and to find ways of ministering to them and through them.

**C) Marriage:** We affirm the sanctity of the marriage covenant that is expressed in love, mutual support, personal commitment, and shared fidelity between a man and a woman. We believe that God's blessing rests upon such marriage, whether or not there are children of the union.

We reject social norms that assume different standards for women than for men in marriage. Ceremonies that celebrate homosexual unions shall not be conducted by our ministers and shall not be conducted in our Churches. [See Judicial Council Decision 694, *Book of Resolutions*].

**D) Divorce**: When a married couple is estranged beyond reconciliation, even after thoughtful consideration and counsel, divorce is a regrettable alternative in the midst of brokenness. It is recommended that methods of mediation be used to minimize the adversarial nature and fault-finding that are often part of our current judicial processes.

Although divorce publicly declares that a marriage no longer exists, other covenantal relationships resulting from the marriage remain, such as the nurture and support of children and extended family ties. We urge respectful negotiations in deciding the custody of minor children and support the consideration of either or both parents for this responsibility in that custody not be reduced to financial support, control, or manipulation and retaliation. The welfare of each child is the most important consideration.

Divorce does not preclude a new marriage. We encourage an intentional commitment of the Church and society to minister compassionately to those in the process of divorce, as well as members of divorced and remarried families, in a community of faith where God's grace is shared by all.

**E) Single Persons:** We affirm the integrity of single persons, and we reject all social practices that discriminate or social attitudes that are prejudicial against persons because they are single.

**F) Women and Men:** We affirm with Scripture the common humanity of male and female, both having equal worth in the eyes of God. We reject the erroneous notion that one gender is superior to another, that one gender must strive against another, and that members of one gender may receive love, power and esteem only at the expense of another. We especially reject the idea that God made individuals as incomplete fragments, made whole only in union with another.

We call upon women and men alike to share power and control, to learn to give freely and to receive freely, to be complete and to respect the wholeness of others. We seek for every individual opportunities and freedom to love and be loved, to seek and receive justice, and to practice ethical self-determination.

We understand our gender diversity to be a gift from God, intended to add to the rich variety of human experience and perspective; and we guard against attitudes and traditions that would use this good gift to leave members of one sex more vulnerable in relationships than members of another.

**G) Human Sexuality:** We recognize that sexuality is God's good gift to all persons. We believe persons may be fully human only when that gift is acknowledged and affirmed by themselves, the Church, and society. We call all persons to the disciplined, responsible fulfillment of themselves, others, and society in the stewardship of this gift.

We also recognize our limited understanding of this complex gift and encourage the medical, theological, and social science disciplines to combine in a determined effort to understand human sexuality more completely. We call the Church to take the leadership role in bringing together these disciplines to address this most complex issue. Further, within the context of our understanding of this gift of God, we recognize that God challenges us to find responsible, committed, and loving forms of expression.

Although all persons are sexual beings whether or not they are married, sexual relations are only clearly affirmed in the marriage bond. Sex may become exploitative within as well as outside marriage.

We reject all sexual expressions that damage or destroy the humanity God has given us as birthright, and we affirm only that sexual expression which enhances that same humanity. We believe that sexual relations where one or both partners are exploitative, abusive, or promiscuous are beyond the parameters of acceptable Christian behavior and are ultimately destructive to individuals, families, and the social order.

We deplore all forms of the commercialization and exploitation of sex, with their consequent cheapening and degradation of human personality. We call for strict enforcement of laws prohibiting the sexual exploitation or use of children by adults. We call for the establishment of adequate protective services, guidance, and counseling opportunities for children thus abused. We insist that all persons, regardless of age, gender, marital status, or sexual orientation, are entitled to have their human and civil rights ensured.

We recognize the continuing need for full, positive, and factual sex education opportunities for children, youth, and adults. The Church offers a unique opportunity to give quality guidance and education in this area.

Homosexual persons no less than heterosexual persons are individuals of sacred worth. All persons need the ministry and guidance of the Church in their struggles for human fulfillment, as well as the spiritual and emotional care of a fellowship that enables reconciling relationships with God, with others, and with self. Although we do not condone the practice of homosexuality and consider this practice incompatible with Christian teaching, we affirm that God's grace is available to all. We commit ourselves to be in ministry for and with all persons. [See Judicial Council Decision 702, *Book of Resolutions*].

**H) Family Violence and Abuse**: We recognize that family violence and abuse in all its forms -- verbal, psychological, physical, sexual -- is detrimental to the covenant of the human community. We encourage the Church to provide a safe environment, counsel, and support for the victim. While we deplore the actions of the abuser, we affirm that person to be in need of God's redeeming love.

**I. Sexual Harassment:** We believe human sexuality is God's good gift. One abuse of this good gift is sexual harassment. We define sexual harassment as any unwanted sexual advance or demand, either verbal or physical, that is reasonably perceived by the recipient as demeaning, intimidating or coercive. Sexual harassment must be understood as an exploitation of a power relationship rather than as an exclusively sexual issue. Sexual harassment includes, but is not limited to, the creation of a hostile or abusive working environment resulting from discrimination on the basis of gender.

Contrary to the nurturing community, sexual harassment creates improper, coercive, and abusive conditions wherever it occurs in society. Sexual harassment undermines the social goal of equal opportunity and the climate of mutual respect between men and women. Unwanted sexual attention is wrong and discriminatory. Sexual harassment interferes with the moral mission of the Church.

**J) Abortion:** The beginning of life and the ending of life are the God-given boundaries of human existence. While individuals have always had some degree of control over when they would die, they now have the awesome power to determine when and even whether new individuals will be born. Our belief in the sanctity of unborn human life makes us reluctant to approve abortion. But we are equally bound to respect the sacredness of the life and well-being of the mother, for whom devastating damage may result from an unacceptable pregnancy.

In continuity with past Christian teaching, we recognize tragic conflicts of life with life that may justify abortion, and in such cases we support the legal option of abortion under proper medical procedures. We cannot affirm abortion as an acceptable means of birth control, and we unconditionally reject it as a means of gender selection. We call all Christians to a searching and prayerful inquiry into the sorts of conditions that may warrant abortion.

We commit our Church to continue to provide nurturing ministries to those who terminate a pregnancy, to those in the midst of a crisis pregnancy, and to those who give birth. Governmental laws and regulations do not provide all the guidance required by the informed Christian conscience. Therefore, a decision concerning abortion should be made only after thoughtful and prayerful consideration by the parties involved, with medical, pastoral, and other appropriate counsel.

**K) Adoption:** Children are a gift from God to be welcomed and received. We recognize that some circumstances of birth make the rearing of a child difficult. We affirm and support the birth parent(s) whose choice it is to allow the child to be adopted. We recognize the agony, strength, and courage of the birth parent(s) who choose(s) in hope, love, and prayer to offer the child for adoption.

In addition, we affirm the receiving parent(s) desiring an adopted child. When circumstances warrant adoption, we support the use of proper legal procedures. We commend the birth parent(s), the receiving parent(s), and the child to the care of the Church, that grief might be shared, joy might be celebrated, and the child might be nurtured in a community of Christian love.

**L) Death with Dignity:** We applaud medical science for efforts to prevent disease and illness and for advances in treatment that extend the meaningful life of human beings. At the same time, in the varying stages of death and life that advances in medical science have occasioned, we recognize the agonizing personal and moral decisions faced by the dying, their physicians, their families, and their friends.

Therefore, we assert the right of every person to die in dignity, with loving personal care and without efforts to prolong terminal illnesses merely because the technology is available to do so.

## III. THE SOCIAL COMMUNITY

The rights and privileges a society bestows upon or withholds from those who comprise it indicate the relative esteem in which that society holds particular persons and groups of persons. We affirm all persons as equally valuable in the sight of God. We therefore work toward societies in which each person's value is recognized, maintained, and strengthened. We support the basic rights of all persons to equal access to housing, education, employment, medical care, legal redress for grievances, and physical protection.

**A) Rights of Racial and Ethnic Persons**: *Racism* is the combination of the power to dominate by one race over other races and a value system that assumes that the dominant race is innately superior to the others. Racism includes both personal and institutional racism. Personal racism is manifested through the individual expressions, attitudes, and/or behaviors that accept the assumptions of a racist value system and that maintain the benefits of this system. Institutional racism is the established social pattern that supports implicitly or explicitly the racist value system. Racism plagues and cripples our growth in Christ, inasmuch as it is antithetical to the gospel itself.

Therefore, we recognize racism as sin and affirm the ultimate and temporal worth Of all Persons. We rejoice in the gifts that Particular ethnic histories and cultures bring to our total life. We commend and encourage the self-awareness of all racial and ethnic groups and oppressed people that leads them to demand their just and equal rights as members of society.

We assert the obligation of society and groups within the society to implement compensatory programs that redress long-standing, systemic social deprivation of racial and ethnic people. We further assert the right of members of racial and ethnic groups to equal opportunities in employment and promotion, to education and training of the highest quality; to nondiscrimination in voting, in access to public accommodations, and in housing purchase or rental; and [access] to positions of leadership and power in all elements of our life together.

We support Affirmative Action as one method of addressing the inequalities and discriminatory practices within our Church and society.

**B) Rights of Religious Minorities:** Religious persecution has been common in history of civilization. We urge policies and practices that ensure the right of every religious group to exercise its faith free from legal, political, or economic restrictions.

We condemn all overt and covert forms of religious intolerance, being especially sensitive to their expression in media stereotyping. We assert the right of all religions and their adherents to freedom from legal, economic, and social discrimination.

**C) Rights of Children:** Once considered the property of their parents, children are now acknowledged to be full human beings in their own right, but beings to whom adults and society in general have special obligations. Thus, we support the development of school systems and innovative methods of education designed to assist every child toward complete fulfillment as an individual person of worth. All children have the right to quality education, including full sex education appropriate to their stage of development that utilizes the best educational techniques and insights.

Christian parents and guardians and the Church have the responsibility to ensure that children receive sex education consistent with Christian morality, including faithfulness in marriage and abstinence in singleness. Moreover, children have the rights to food, shelter, clothing, health care, and emotional well-being as do adults, and these rights we affirm as theirs regardless of actions or inactions of their parents or guardians. In particular, children must be protected from economic, physical, and sexual exploitation and abuse.

**D) Rights of Youth and Young Adults:** Our society is characterized by a large population of youth and young adults who frequently find full participation in society difficult. Therefore, we urge development of policies that encourage inclusion of youth and young adults in decision-making processes and that eliminate discrimination and exploitation. Creative and appropriate employment opportunities should be legally and socially available for youth and young adults.

**E) Rights of the Aging:** In a society that places primary emphasis upon youth, those growing old in years are frequently isolated from the mainstream of social existence. We support social policies that integrate the aging into the life of the total community, including sufficient incomes, increased and non-discriminatory employment opportunities, educational and service opportunities, and adequate medical care and housing within existing communities.

We urge social policies and programs, with emphasis on the unique concerns of older women and ethnic persons, that ensure to the aging the respect and dignity that is their right as senior members of the human community. Further, we urge increased consideration for adequate pension systems by employers, with provisions for the surviving spouse.

**F) Rights of Women:** We affirm women and men to be equal in every aspect of their common life. We therefore urge that every effort be made to eliminate sex role stereotypes in activity and portrayal of family life and in all aspects of voluntary and compensatory participation in the Church and society. We affirm the right of women to equal treatment in employment, responsibility, promotion, and compensation.

We affirm the importance of women in decision-making positions at all levels of Church life and urge such bodies to guarantee their presence through policies of employment and recruitment. We support Affirmative Action as one method of addressing the inequalities and discriminatory practices within our Church and society. We urge employers of persons in dual career families, both in the Church and society, to apply proper consideration of both parties when relocation is considered.

**G) Rights of Persons with Disabilities:** We recognize and affirm the full humanity and personhood of all individuals with disabilities as full members of the family of God. We affirm the responsibility of the Church and society to be in ministry with children, youth, and adults with mental, physical, developmental, and/or psychological disabilities whose different needs in the areas of mobility, communication, intellectual comprehension, or personal relationships might interfere with their participation or that of their families in the life of the Church and the community.

We urge the Church and society to receive the gifts of persons with disabilities to enable them to be full participants in the community of faith. We call the Church and society to be sensitive to, and advocate for, programs of rehabilitation, services, employment, education, appropriate housing, and transportation. We call on the Church and society to protect the civil rights of persons with disabilities.

**H) Equal Rights Regardless of Sexual Orientation:** Certain basic human rights and civil liberties are due to all persons. We are committed to supporting those fights and liberties for homosexual persons. We see a clear issue of simple justice in protecting their rightful claims where they have: shared material resources, pensions, guardian relationships, mutual powers of attorney, and other such lawful claims typically attendant to contractual relationships that involve shared contributions, responsibilities, and liabilities, and equal protection before the law.

Moreover, we support efforts to stop violence and other forms of coercion against gays and lesbians. We also commit ourselves to social witness against the coercion and marginalization of former homosexuals.

**I) Population:** Since the growing worldwide population is increasingly straining the world's supply of food, minerals, and water and sharpening international tensions, the reduction of the rate of consumption of resources by the affluent and the reduction of current world population growth rates have become imperative. People have the duty to consider the impact on the total world community of their decisions regarding childbearing and should have access to information and appropriate means to limit their fertility, including voluntary sterilization.

We affirm that programs to achieve a stabilized population should be placed in a context of total economic and social development, including an equitable use and control of resources; improvement in the status of women in all cultures, a human level of economic security, health care, and literacy for all.

**J) Alcohol and Other Drugs:** We affirm our long-standing support of abstinence from alcohol as a faithful witness to God's liberating and redeeming love for persons. We support abstinence from the use of any illegal drugs. Since the use of alcohol and illegal drugs is a major factor in crime, disease, death, and family dysfunction, we support educational programs encouraging abstinence from such use.

Millions of living human beings are testimony to the beneficial consequences of therapeutic drug use, and millions of others are testimony to the detrimental consequences of drug misuse. We encourage wise policies relating to the availability of potentially beneficial or potentially damaging prescription and over-the counter drugs; we urge that complete information about their use and misuse be readily available to both doctor and patient.

We support the strict administration of laws regulating the sale and distribution of all opiates. We support regulations that protect society from users of drugs of any kind where it can be shown that a clear and present social danger exists. Drug-dependent persons and their family members are individuals of infinite human worth deserving of treatment, rehabilitation, and ongoing life -

changing recovery. Misuse [of alcohol and drugs] should be viewed as a symptom of underlying disorders for which remedies should be sought.

**K) Tobacco:** We affirm our historic tradition of high standards of personal discipline and social responsibility. In light of the overwhelming evidence that tobacco smoking and the use of smokeless tobacco are hazardous to the health of persons of all ages, we recommend total abstinence from the use of tobacco. We urge that our educational and communication resources be utilized to support and encourage such abstinence. Further, we recognize the harmful effects of passive smoke and support the restriction of smoking in public areas and workplaces.

**L) Medical Experimentation**: Physical and mental health has been greatly enhanced through discoveries by medical science. It Is imperative, however, that governments and the medical profession carefully enforce the requirements of the prevailing medical research standard, maintaining rigid controls in testing new technologies and drugs utilizing human beings. The standard requires that those engaged in research shall use human beings as research subjects only after obtaining full, rational, and uncoerced consent.

**M) Genetic Technology:** The responsibility of humankind to God's creation challenges us to deal carefully with the possibilities of genetic research and technology. We welcome the use of genetic technology for meeting fundamental human needs for health, a safe environment, and an adequate food supply.

Because of the effects of genetic technologies on all life, we call for effective guidelines and public accountability to safeguard against any action that might lead to abuse of these technologies, including political or military ends. We recognize that cautious, well-intended use of genetic technologies may sometimes lead to unanticipated harmful consequences.

Human gene therapies that produce changes that cannot be passed to offspring (somatic therapy) should be limited to the alleviation of suffering caused by disease. Genetic therapies for eugenic choices or that produce waste embryos are deplored. Genetic data of individuals and their families should be kept secret and held in strict confidence unless confidentiality is waived by the individual or by his or her family, or unless the collection and use of genetic identification data is supported by an appropriate court order. Because its long-term effects are uncertain, we oppose genetic therapy that results in changes that can be passed to offspring (germ-line therapy).

**N) Rural Life:** We support the right of persons and families to live and prosper as farmers, farm workers, merchants, professionals, and others outside of the cities and metropolitan centers. We believe our culture is impoverished and our people deprived of a meaningful way of life when rural and small-town living becomes difficult or impossible. We recognize that the improvement of this way of life may sometimes necessitate the use of some lands for nonagricultural purposes.

We oppose the indiscriminate diversion of agricultural land for nonagricultural uses when nonagricultural land is available. Further, we encourage the preservation of appropriate lands for agriculture and open space uses through thoughtful land use programs. We support governmental and private programs designed to benefit the resident farmer rather than the factory farm and programs that encourage industry to locate in non-urban areas.

We further recognize that increased mobility and technology have brought a mixture of people, religions, and philosophies to rural communities that were once homogenous. While often this is seen as a threat to our loss of community life, we understand it as an opportunity to uphold the biblical call to community for all persons.

Therefore, we encourage rural communities and individuals to maintain a strong connection to the earth and be open to: offering mutual belonging, caring, healing, and growth; sharing and celebrating cooperative leadership and diverse gifts; supporting mutual trust; and affirming individuals as unique persons of worth, and thus to practice *shalom*.

**0) Urban-Suburban Life:** Urban-suburban living has become a dominant style of life for more and more persons. For many, it furnishes economic, educational, social, and cultural opportunities. For others, it has brought alienation, poverty, and depersonalization.

We in the Church have an opportunity and responsibility to help shape the future of urban-suburban life. Massive programs of renewal and social planning are needed to bring a greater degree of humanization into urban-suburban life-styles. Christians must judge all programs, including economic and community development, new towns, and urban renewal, by the extent to which they protect and enhance human values, permit personal and political involvement, and make possible neighborhoods open to persons of all races, ages, and income levels.

We affirm the efforts of all developers who place human values at the heart of their planning. We must help shape urban-suburban development so that it provides for the human need to identify with and find meaning in smaller social communities. At the same time, such smaller communities must be encouraged to assume responsibilities for the total urban-suburban community instead of isolating themselves from it.

**P) Media Violence and Christian Values**: The unprecedented impact the media (principally television and movies) are having on Christian and human values within our society becomes more apparent each day. We express disdain at current media preoccupation with dehumanizing portrayals, sensationalized through mass media "entertainment" and "news." These practices degrade humankind and violate the teachings of Christ and the Bible.

United Methodists, along with those of other faith groups, must be made aware that the mass media often undermine the truths of Christianity by promoting permissive lifestyles and detailing acts of graphic violence. Instead of encouraging, motivating, and inspiring its audiences to adopt lifestyles based on the sanctity of life, the entertainment industry often advocates the opposite, painting a cynical picture of violence, abuse, greed, profanity, and a constant denigration of the family.

The media must be held accountable for the part they play in the decline of values we observe in society today. Many in the media remain aloof to the issue, claiming to reflect rather than to influence society. For the sake of our human family, Christians must work together to halt this erosion of moral and ethical values in the world community.

**Q) Right to Health Care:** Health is a condition of physical, mental, social, and spiritual well-being, and we view it as a responsibility - public and private. Health care is a basic human right. Psalm 146 speaks of the God "who executes justice for the oppressed; who gives food to the hungry. The Lord sets prisoners free, the Lord opens the eyes of the blind." It is unjust to construct or perpetuate barriers to physical wholeness or full participation in community.

We encourage individuals to pursue a healthy lifestyle and affirm the importance of preventive health care, health education, environmental and occupational safety, good nutrition, and secure housing in achieving health. We also recognize the role of governments in assuring that each individual has access to those elements necessary to good health.

**R) Organ Transplantation and Donation:** We believe that organ transplantation and organ donation are acts of charity, *agape love,* and self-sacrifice. We recognize the life-giving benefits of organ and other tissue donation and encourage all people of faith to become organ and tissue donors as a part of their love and ministry to others in need. We urge that it be done in an environment of respect for deceased and living donors and for the benefit of recipients, and following protocols that carefully prevent abuse to donors and their families.

## IV. THE ECONOMIC COMMUNITY

We claim all economic systems to be under the judgment of God no less than other facets of the created order. Therefore, we recognize the responsibility of governments to develop and implement sound fiscal and monetary policies that provide for the economic life of individuals and corporate entities, and that ensure full employment and adequate incomes with a minimum of inflation.

We believe private and public economic enterprises are responsible for the social costs of doing business, such as employment and environmental pollution, and that they should be held accountable for these costs. We support measures that would reduce the concentration of wealth in the hands of a few. We further support efforts to revise tax structures and to eliminate governmental support programs that now benefit the wealthy at the expense of other persons.

**A) Property:** We believe private ownership of property is a trusteeship undergo, both in those societies where it is encouraged and where it is discouraged, but is limited by the overriding needs of society. We believe that Christian faith denies to any person or group of persons exclusive and arbitrary control of any other part of the created universe.

Socially and culturally conditioned ownership of property is, therefore, to be considered a responsibility to God. We believe, therefore, governments have the responsibility, in the pursuit of justice and order under law, to provide procedures that protect the rights of the whole society, as well as those of private ownership.

**B) Collective Bargaining:** We support the right of public and private (including farm, government, institutional, and domestic) employees and employers to organize for collective bargaining into unions and other groups of their own choosing. Further, we support the right of both parties to protection in so doing and their responsibility to bargain in good faith within the framework of the public interest.

In order that the rights of all members of the society may be maintained and promoted, we support innovative bargaining procedures that include representatives of the public interest in negotiation and settlement of labor/management contracts including some that may lead to forms of judicial resolution of issues. We reject the use of violence by either party during collective bargaining or any labor/management disagreement. We likewise reject the permanent replacement of a worker who engages in a lawful strike.

**C) Work and Leisure:** Every person has the right to a job at a living wage. Where the private sector cannot or does not provide jobs for all who seek and need them, it is the responsibility of government to provide for the creation of such jobs.

We support social measures that ensure the physical and mental safety of workers, that provide for the equitable division of products and services, and that encourage an increasing freedom in the way individuals may use their leisure time. We recognize the opportunity leisure provides for creative contributions to society and encourage methods that allow workers additional blocks of discretionary time. We support educational, cultural, and recreational outlets that enhance the use of such time.

We believe that persons come before profits. We deplore the selfish spirit that often pervades our economic life. We support policies that encourage the sharing of ideas in the workplace, cooperative and collective work arrangements. We support rights of workers to refuse to work in situations that endanger health and/or life without jeopardy to their jobs. We support policies that would reverse the increasing concentration of business and industry into monopolies.

**D) Consumption:** Consumers should exercise their economic power to encourage the manufacture of goods that are necessary and beneficial to humanity while avoiding the desecration of the environment in either production or consumption. Consumers should evaluate their consumption of goods and services in the light of the need for enhanced quality of life rather than unlimited production of material goods.

We call upon consumers, including local congregations and Church-related institutions, to organize to achieve these goals and to express dissatisfaction with harmful economic, social, or ecological practices through such appropriate methods as boycott, letter writing, corporate resolution, and advertisement. For example, these methods can be used to influence better television and radio programming.

**E) Poverty:** In spite of general affluence in the industrialized nations, the majority of persons in the world live in poverty. In order to provide basic needs such as food, clothing, shelter, education, health care, and other necessities, ways must be found to share more equitably the resources of the world. Increasing technology, when accompanied by exploitative economic practices, impoverishes many persons and makes poverty self-perpetuating.

Therefore, we do not hold poor people morally responsible for their economic state. To begin to alleviate poverty, we support such policies as: adequate income maintenance, quality education, decent housing, job training, meaningful employment opportunities, adequate medical and hospital care, and humanization and radical revisions of welfare programs. Since low wages are often a cause of poverty, employers should pay their employees a wage that does not require them to depend upon government subsidies such as food stamps or welfare for their livelihood.

**F) Migrant Workers:** Migratory and other farm workers, who have long been a special concern of the Church's ministry, are by the nature of their way of life excluded from many of the economic and social benefits enjoyed by other workers. Many of the migrant laborers' situations are aggravated because they are racial and ethnic minority persons who have been oppressed with numerous other inequities within the society.

We advocate for the rights of all migrants and applaud their efforts toward responsible self-organization and self-determination. We call upon governments and all employers to ensure for migratory workers the same economic, educational, and social benefits enjoyed by other citizens. We call upon our Churches to seek to develop programs of service to such migrant people who come within their parish and support their efforts to organize for collective bargaining.

**G) Gambling:** Gambling is a menace to society, deadly to the best interests of moral, social, economic, and spiritual life, and destructive of good, government. As an act of faith and concern, Christians should abstain from gambling and should strive to minister to those victimized by the practice. Where gambling has become addictive, the Church will encourage such individuals to receive therapeutic assistance so that the individual's energies may be redirected into positive and constructive ends.

The Church should promote standards and personal lifestyles that would make unnecessary and undesirable the resort to commercial gambling including public lotteries – as a recreation, as an escape, or as a means of producing public revenue or funds for support of charities or government.

## V. THE POLITICAL COMMUNITY

While our allegiance to God takes precedence over our allegiance to any state, we acknowledge the vital function of government as a principal vehicle for the ordering of society. Because we know ourselves to be responsible to God for social and political life, we declare the following relative to governments:

**A) Basic Freedoms:** We hold governments responsible for the protection of the rights of the people to free and fair elections and to the freedoms of speech, religion, assembly, and communications media, and petition for redress of grievances without fear of reprisals to the right to privacy; and to the guarantee of the rights to adequate food, clothing, shelter, education, and health care. The form and the leaders of all governments should be determined by exercise of the right to vote guaranteed to all adult citizens.

We also strongly reject domestic surveillance and intimidation of political opponents by governments in power and all other misuses of elective or appointive offices. The use of detention and imprisonment for the harassment and elimination of political opponents or other dissidents violates fundamental human rights. Furthermore, the mistreatment or torture of persons by governments for any purpose violates Christian teaching and must be condemned and/or opposed by Christians and Churches wherever and whenever it occurs.

The Church regards the institution of slavery as an infamous evil. All forms of enslavement are totally prohibited and shall in no way be tolerated by the Church.

**B) Political Responsibility:** The strength of a political system depends upon the full and willing participation of its citizens. We believe that the state should not attempt to control the Church, nor should the Church seek to dominate the state. "Separation of Church and state" means no organic union of the two, but it permits interaction. The Church should continually exert a strong ethical influence upon the state, supporting policies and programs deemed to be just and opposing policies and programs that are unjust.

**C) Freedom of Information:** Citizens of all countries should have access to all essential information regarding their government and its policies. Illegal, and unconscionable activities directed against persons or groups by their own governments must not be justified or kept secret even under the guise of national security.

**D) Education:** We believe responsibility for education of the young rests with the family, the Church, and the government. In our society this function can best be fulfilled through public policies that ensure access for all persons to free public elementary and secondary schools and to post-secondary schools of their choice. Persons in our society should not be precluded by financial barriers from access to Church-related and other independent institutions of higher education.

We affirm the right of public and independent colleges and universities to exist, and we endorse public policies that ensure access and choice and that do not create unconstitutional entanglements between Church and state. The state should not use its authority to promote particular religious beliefs (including atheism), nor should it require prayer or worship in the public schools, but it should leave students free to practice their own religious convictions.

**E) Civil Obedience and Civil Disobedience:** Governments and laws should be servants of God and of human beings. Citizens have a duty to abide by laws duly adopted by orderly and just process of government. But governments, no less than individuals, are subject to the judgment of God.

Therefore, we recognize the right of individuals to dissent when acting under the constraint of conscience and, after having exhausted all legal recourse, to resist or disobey laws that they deem to be unjust or that are discriminately enforced. Even then, respect for law should be shown by refraining from violence and by being willing to accept the costs of disobedience.

We do not encourage or condone, under any circumstances, any form of violent protest or action against anyone involved in the abortion dilemma. We offer our prayers for those in rightful authority who serve the public, and we support their efforts to afford justice and equal opportunity for all people. We assert the duty of Churches to support those who suffer because of their stands of conscience represented by non-violent beliefs or acts. We urge governments to ensure civil rights, as defined by the International Covenant on Civil and Political Rights, to persons in legal jeopardy because of those non-violent acts.

**F) Criminal Justice:** To protect all citizens from those who would encroach upon personal and property rights, it is the duty of governments to establish police forces, courts, and facilities for the confinement, punishment, and rehabilitation of offenders. We support governmental measures designed to reduce and eliminate crime that are consistent with respect for the basic freedom of persons.

We reject all misuses of these necessary mechanisms, including their use for the purpose of persecuting or intimidating those whose race, appearance, life-style, economic condition, or beliefs differ from those in authority; and we reject all careless, callous, or discriminatory enforcement of law. We further support measures designed to remove the social conditions that lead to crime, and we encourage continued positive interaction between law enforcement officials and members of the community at large.

In the love of Christ, who came to save those who are lost and vulnerable, we urge the creation of genuinely new systems for the care and support of the victims of crime and for rehabilitation that will restore, preserve, and nurture the humanity of the imprisoned. For the same reason, we oppose capital punishment and urge its elimination from all criminal codes.

**G) Military Service:** Though coercion, violence, and war are presently the ultimate sanctions in international relations, we reject them as incompatible with the gospel and spirit of Christ. We therefore urge the establishment of the rule of law in international affairs as a means of elimination of war, violence, and coercion in these affairs.

We reject national policies of enforced military service as incompatible with the gospel. We acknowledge the agonizing tension created by the demand for military service by national governments. We urge all young adults to seek the counsel of the Church as they reach a conscientious decision concerning the nature of their responsibility as citizens. Pastors are called upon to be available for counseling with all young adults who face conscription, including those who conscientiously refuse to cooperate with a system of conscription.

We support and extend the ministry of the Church to those persons who conscientiously oppose all war, or any particular war, and who therefore refuse to serve in the armed forces or to cooperate with systems of military conscription. We also support and extend the Church's ministry to those persons who conscientiously choose to serve in the armed forces or to accept alternative service.

## VI. THE WORLD COMMUNITY

God's world is one world. The unity now being thrust upon us by technological revolution has far outrun our moral and spiritual capacity to achieve a stable world. The enforced unity of humanity, increasingly evident on all levels of life, presents the Church as well as all people with problems that will not wait for answer: injustice, war, exploitation, privilege, population, international ecological crisis, proliferation of arsenals of nuclear weapons, development of transnational business organizations that operate beyond the effective control of any governmental structure, and the increase of tyranny in all its forms.

This generation must find viable answers to these and related questions if humanity is to continue on this earth. We commit ourselves as a Church to the achievement of a world community that is a fellowship of persons who honestly love one another. We pledge ourselves to seek the meaning of the gospel in all issues that divide people and threaten the growth of world community.

**A) Nations and Cultures:** As individuals are affirmed by God in their diversity, so are nations and cultures. We recognize that no nation or culture is absolutely just and right in its treatment of its own people, nor is any nation totally without regard for the welfare of its citizens. The Church must regard nations as accountable for unjust treatment of their citizens and others living within their borders. While recognizing valid differences in culture and political philosophy, we stand for justice and peace in every nation.

**B) National Power and Responsibility:** Some nations possess more military and economic power than do others. Upon the powerful rests responsibility to exercise their wealth and influence with restraint. We affirm the right and duty of people of all nations to determine their own destiny. We urge the major political powers to use their nonviolent power to maximize the political, social, and economic self-determination of other nations rather than to further their own special interests.

We applaud international efforts to develop a more just international economic order in which the limited resources of the Earth will be used to the maximum benefit of all nations and peoples. We urge Christians in every society to encourage the governments under which they live and the economic entities within their societies to aid and work for the development of more just economic orders.

**C) War and Peace:** We believe war is incompatible with the teachings and example of Christ. We therefore reject war as an instrument of national foreign policy and insist that the first moral duty of all nations is to resolve by peaceful means every dispute that arises between or among them; that human, values must outweigh military claims as governments determine their priorities; that the militarization of society must be challenged and stopped, that the manufacture, sale, and deployment of armaments must be reduced and controlled and that the production, possession, or use of nuclear weapons be condemned.

Consequently, we endorse general and complete disarmament under strict and effective international control.

**D) Justice and Law:** Persons and groups must feel secure in their life and right to live within a society if order is to be achieved and maintained by law. We denounce as immoral an ordering of life that perpetuates injustice. Nations, too, must feel secure in the world if world community is to become a fact.

Believing that international justice requires the participation of all peoples. we endorse the United Nations and its related bodies and the International Court of Justice as the best instruments now in existence to achieve a world of justice and law. We commend the efforts of all people in all countries who pursue world peace through law.

We endorse international aid and cooperation on all matters of need and conflict. We urge acceptance for membership in the United Nations of all nations who wish such membership and who accept United Nations responsibility. We urge the United Nations to take a more aggressive role in the development of international arbitration of disputes and actual conflicts among nations by developing binding third-party arbitration. Bilateral or multilateral efforts outside of the United Nations should work in concert with, and not contrary to, its purposes.

We reaffirm our historic concern for the world as our parish and seek for all persons and peoples full and equal membership in a truly world community.

## VII. OUR SOCIAL CREED

We believe in God, [the] Creator of the world; and in Jesus Christ, the Redeemer of creation. We believe in the Holy Spirit, through whom we acknowledge God's gifts, and we repent of our sin in misusing these gifts to idolatrous ends.

We affirm the natural world as God's handiwork and dedicate ourselves to its preservation, enhancement, and faithful use by humankind.

We joyfully receive for ourselves and others the blessings of community, sexuality, marriage, and the family.

We commit ourselves to the rights of men, women, children, youth, young adults, the aging, and people with disabilities; to improvement of the quality of life; and to the rights and dignity of racial, ethnic, and religious minorities.

We believe in the right and duty of persons to work for the glory of God and the good of themselves and others and in the protection of their welfare in so doing; in the rights to property as a trust from God, collective bargaining, and responsible consumption; and in the elimination of economic and social distress.

We dedicate ourselves to peace throughout the world, to the rule of justice and law among nations, and to individual freedom for all people of the world.

We believe in the present and final triumph of God's Word in human affairs and gladly accept our commission to manifest the life of the gospel in the world. Amen.

*(It is recommended that this statement of the Social Principles be continually available to United Methodist Christians and that it be emphasized regularly in every congregation. It is further recommended that "Our Social Creed" be frequently used in Sunday worship.)*
*This material is reprinted with permission.*

---

## Emmanuel Twesigye's Notes and Commentary

1. This material is reproduced in this book with the kind permission of the United Methodist Publishing House © Copyright 1996.. The *Social Principles* are found in the United Methodist *Book of Discipline 1996*, paragraph numbers 67-70, and also in the *Book of Resolutions 1996*. The Social Principles were originally adopted by the 1972 General Conference of the United Methodist Church, and have been revised by the 1976, 1980, 1988, and 1996 General Conferences.

These *Social Principles* are important Christian moral guides in a constantly changing social world. They remain an open canon that continues to be open to God's continuing revelation through his Holy Spirit and the Word (Logos) as they continually work in the Church, community and the world to inspire us, and reveal God's new truths or God's will for our "New Age" through the *Holy Scriptures, reason/mind, history/tradition*, and *experience*.

Our moral, social, spiritual and existential experience today is very different from that of Moses, Jesus and his twelve apostles. Therefore, God's living revelatory and redemptive Word (*Logos*) has to be heard continuously, obeyed and reinterpreted within the context of the lives, values, cultures, realities and experiences of people, today. God alive today and not dead. As such, the living God is revelation and moral law are not limited to the past revelations as recorded in the scriptures and the moral laws of Moses. This was part of Jesus' central message and teaching. As such, he was able to transcend and negate some of the repressive and violent the laws of Moses (cf. Matt. 6:38-48).

2. "The United Methodist Church has a long history of concern for social justice. Its members have often taken forthright positions on controversial issues involving Christian principles. Early Methodists expressed their opposition to the slave trade, to smuggling, and to the cruel treatment of prisoners.

The *Social Principles* are a prayerful and thoughtful effort on the part of the General Conference to speak to the human issues in the contemporary world from a sound biblical and theological foundation as historically demonstrated in United Methodist traditions. The *Social Principles* are a call Christians to live an upright moral life of a prayerful, studied dialogue of faith and practice." There were no revisions made to these principles at the 2000 General Conference that was held in Cleveland, Ohio, USA.

3. In order to simplify the complicated text, and highlight the main points for students or other readers, yet without alteration of the content, some very complex paragraphs have been subdivided. This makes it easier for readers to sport the key affirmations in the text.

## Appendix C

# God's Kingdom is Here On the Earth Now; Not in the Sky or Distant Future[1]

By The Reverend Professor Paul Nicely
Emeritus Professor of Pastoral Care, Methodist Theological School in Ohio, Delaware, OH 43015

The beginning of the good news of Jesus Christ, the Son of God: (Mk 1:1) This is the topic sentence of the Gospel of Mark: Jesus came to Galilee, proclaiming the good news of God and saying, "The time is fulfilled, and the kingdom of God has come near; repent, and believe in the good news. . ." (Mk. 1:14b-15). In the Gospel according to Mark, these are Jesus' first recorded words. This is the theme of Jesus' ministry.

"The Kingdom of God is at hand; repent, and believe in the Gospel." *THE KINGDOM OF GOD "IS." And Not "WILL BE." The Kingdom "IS here now!"* The whole of humanity and history (our history) have been changed by God. The Kingdom of God is here. Now. Not tomorrow. *Not in some far-off promised land. Not pie in the sky, by and bye*. The Kingdom of God is at hand. Here. *Now.* And what is God's rule like? It like as if someone should scatter seed on the ground, and in effect forget it and let it go and grow. According to the creator's processes, the earth produces of itself; the sower does not know how. The kingdom grows quite by itself. Human beings don't need to fuss with it. The parable sounds to me somewhat like a perennial flower which re-seeds itself without anyone's making it so.

What is God's Rule [Kingdom] like? The book of Esther in the Hebrew Scriptures is a wonderful tale of political power shifts, deceit, and courage. Esther had become the apple of the King's eye, and he made her his Queen, not aware that she was Jewish. Later, one of the king's major political and military advisors proposed a scheme to destroy not just one Jewish troublemaker (who incidentally was Mordecai, the man who had raised Esther), but rather, to massacre all the Jews. This was Esther's opportunity to prevent that and possibly in the process come clean about her heritage.

Mordecai sent a message to Esther: "Do not think that in the king's palace you will escape any more than all the other Jews. For if you keep silence at such a time as this, relief and deliverance will rise for the Jews from another quarter, but you and your father's family will perish . . . ." Esther, you can help save and deliver your people. That's in keeping with the Kingdom of God. But the Kingdom doesn't depend on you. If you fail, someone else will do God's will. The kingdom grows quite independently of any single human being's doing. You don't have to fuss with it. It will find a way. It will find others to be faithful. It is inexorable, like the seed that grows of itself.. Now I want you to notice how this understanding of the Kingdom of God turns conventional wisdom on its ear.

The challenge to "bring in the Kingdom" — perhaps in our generation – has inspired and motivated many Christians over the years. But if the thrust of Mark's Gospel is to be believed, it is not for us human beings to bring in God's Kingdom. It's already here. God is already in charge. God reigns over all his\her creation. God has shown us already what the rule of God's unconditional love, free grace and forgiveness of sin looks like through Jesus Christ.

Look at another popular rallying cry: "Let's build community." It sounds so needed and so possible, and gives persons of good will a constructive motivation to be doing something useful. But if the thrust of Mark's Gospel is to be believed, it is not for us human beings to build community. It's already built. The Kingdom of God is at hand. Here! Right now!

The Gospel I'm preaching this morning is offensive, I think— Not good news. If there's nothing we can do or need to do to bring about the Kingdom of God, then the message I'm conveying threatens to undercut human activity and positive initiative. Now that *offends* our conventional wisdom. Doesn't it? We are proud of human ingenuity, human invention, and human agency which make things happen.

We heard the Old Testament lesson. We heard from Ezekiel how the nation which blows up its image with huge pride will be cut down like the great cedar of Lebanon which thinks itself superior to all else, and is cut down exactly because of its pride. I think there's a message here for [fathers on] Father's Day. I'm a father. I'm a man. Like the vast majority of men in our society, I'm programmed to earn my self-respect by doing good things, by making things happen, by action. The negative slang for this is being "macho." The positive side is making a contribution to family and society and being a responsible, earnest Christian. But all those positive initiatives and good works are flawed because of pride.

To be *"macho"* seriously requires the illusion that I am or we are bringing in the Kingdom of building community or making our families what they are supposed to be, or causing the workplace to be a genuine community hospitable to humane values, and so on. When I or we seem to succeed, we fill with pride because we seem to have exercised power and control effectively. When I or we seem to fail, we define ourselves as failures because we seem to have lost control and become powerless.

Don't you see? We've overstepped our role. We've taken over, or have tried to control and perform God's action. It is God who has brought in the Kingdom.

It's already here. It is not for us to usurp God's power. Which, by the way, is the strange alluring power of love, not the conventional power which compels and controls.

Well, I guess we're left with the preacher's advice simply to be passive. But wait! There was one more sentence in Mordecai's message to Esther. Yes, he said that if she failed to come through, relief and deliverance for the Jews would arise from another quarter.

But then he added, "Who knows but that thou art come into the kingdom for such a time as this." She had, and we have, a chance to be ***responsible participants in the Kingdom*** which *God* is already building. St. Paul concluded his reflections on life and death, driven as always by his desire to be with God, by reminding his friends in Corinth that "all of us must appear before the judgment seat of Christ, so that each may receive recompense for what has been done in the body, whether good or evil." What we do has consequences. We can choose to be responsible participants in the Kingdom which *God is* already building.

I take it that once we are freed from the impossible task of doing God's thing of bringing in the Kingdom, then we are empowered to behave in the light of the Kingdom. To do our part; empowered to live under God's rule. Empowered to live responsibly, not by our own strength or for prideful self-gratification, but by the grace of God living as children of God and inheritors of the Kingdom. No longer are we motivated to enhance our own pride. The new powerful motivation is service and obedience to the Rule [or Kingdom] of God, out of gratitude for God's infinite grace, forgiveness, and power.

It's not for us to bring in the Kingdom. It's for us to live as if it's already here. Lives that are blessed. Blessed are the poor in spirit; those who mourn; the meek; those who hunger and thirst for righteousness; the Merciful and the pure in heart; the peacemakers; and those who are persecuted for righteousness sake. It's not that such persons will be blessed in the future as a reward for their sacrifices. It's that such persons, when we humble ourselves to be that faithful, are blessed now. And who knows but that we are brought into the kingdom.

Conventional wisdom is turned on its ear!

The Kingdom of God is at hand. Here! Now! Repent! That is, turn around from conventional wisdom, and believe this Good News.

---

1. A sermon preached on July 13, 1997 (Fathers' Day) at St. Peter's Episcopal Church, Delaware, Ohio. The sermon is reproduced here with the kind permission of the Reverend Professor Paul Nicely.

## Appendix D

# Christian Moral Values And Civic Virtues: Finding God in Daily Life And Work

A Sermon Preached at St. Peter's Episcopal Church, Delaware, Ohio, USA on June 6, 1997
by The Reverend Dr. Thomas Van Brunt, Rector
(Reproduced with permission)

(***The Lectionary Scripture Readings for the Day***: Proper 5B; 3 Pentecost Psalm 130; Genesis 3:1-21; 2 Corinthians 4:13-18; and Mark 3:20-35).

I have been working on two books . . . . The first is an attempt to compile the story sermons I have written about the mythical town of Chicago Junction, Ohio . . . . The other book is born out of frustration and some anger. My anger is provoked by statements like this:

> [The Episcopal Church] has been moving away from traditional, classical, and orthodox faith, morality, piety, and liturgy towards an increasingly obvious form of liberalism. At the core of this liberalism has been the setting aside of the authority of the Holy Scripture in and over the Church, and the treating of the Bible as if it were just any kind of ancient literature." (The Rev. Peter Toon, editor of *Mandate*, the Society for the Preservation of the *Book of Common Prayer*: Vol. 16 #2 p. 3).

This supposed loss of Biblical values depends on the author teamed with a decline in American values, fundamental Christian morality, and family values. . . .The confrontation of Jesus with members of his family in today's Gospel gives me an excuse to share some of what I believe to be family values for Christians, not just at the turn of the new millennium, but forever. First I want to give you a list of moral values and virtues that I believe are fundamental to Christianity and sound ethical modes of life:

1. **Go to Church every Sunday**: Exodus 20:8; Deut. 6:4-5; Joshua 24:14-15; Psalm 95:6; Jonah 1:9; Luke 4:8; Exodus 20:10 and 31:14; Matt. 22:37.
2. **Raise your children in the [Christian] faith**. Help other people's children grow up in the faith: Exod. 12:24-27; Deut. 6:1-2; 6:7; Matt. 19:13-14.
3. **Care for the needs of others before your own:** Matt. 5-7; 25:31-46.
4. **Especially care for the those in need**: the poor, the stranger, the prisoner, the hungry, the thirsty, and the naked: Ps. 72; Deut. 10:19; Matt. 25:31-46.

5. **Do not kill other people**. Violence and killing are wrong: Exod. 20:13; Lev. 19:18; Matt. 5:9; 26:50-53.

6. **Stay married and faithful in marriage**: Gen. 2:18-25; Matt. 5:27-30.

7. **Work hard at your job**: Eccl. 3:22.

8. **Treat all your employees fairly**: Matt. 20:1-16.

9. **Do not waste what you have been given by God**. Christians are good stewards of time, worldly goods, money, and the environment. Voluntary simplicity is a Christian moral virtue: Gen. 1:28-30; Heb. 13:5.

10. **Admit you are wrong when that is true** (confession of sin and restitution): Exod. 20:16; Jam. 5:16.

11. **Leave punishment to God**. Only God can truly give the judgement and do the punishing: Deut. 32:35; Rom. 12:19.

12. **Take care of your physical body**. Eat, drink, and exercise moderately; observe moderation in all things: Dan. 1:8-17; Tim. 4:8.

The task of Christian ethics and values is more difficult than simply making a list. For example, do not drink, smoke, play cards, dance or associate with those who do. Because we [Episcopalians] do not share some views of another group of Christians does not mean that we are not Bible believing. It does not mean that we are guilty of being (O horror of horrors) *LIBERALS*!

If anyone can make a list of virtues and defend it from the Bible, does that mean there is no truth — no absolutes? The truth is not in statements in either English, Greek, or Hebrew. Truth is in people and relationships. Jesus' family and enemies tried to pin his down to explicit statements of truth, but he maintained that "*I am the Truth*."

Genesis chapter three is not about how sin leaked into the world, the activities of the first two human beings, or why snakes slither on the ground or bite. It is most certainly not about sex between Adam and Eve as the origin of all sin, or how we continue to sin through the act sex and procreation. It is not even about the Fall of Mankind or the Original Sin.

This deeply psychological story is about the primacy of relationships. It is about our personal connections to each other and our connection to God and to God's creation. Relationships are fragile; we easily and too often crack and break them. The fact that this story has such a prominent place in scripture is because our Jewish forebears knew that the fundamental values of human life revolve around the nature and quality of our relationship to God and our faithfulness to the Creator-Sustainer-Redeemer God who is faithful to us. Please notice the final verse of today's reading. God the seamstress made garments for her people!

. . . . But I know the most important thing I want to say. . . I want to proclaim to the world that *God loves us so unashamedly that "She" will make us new clothes right after we have lied to "her."* God will ignore "his immediate family," Joseph and Mary's family, to include us as "mother," "brother," and "sister." God has already given his only begotten Son, Jesus Christ to us, and we live in the joy of knowing and experiencing that most wonderfully enlightening and redemptive "Fundamental Truth."

# Appendix E

# Kwanzaa and Seven Normative Principles for Building Successful And Peaceful Black Communities

**By Professor Emmanuel K. Twesigye**
**Ohio Wesleyan University, Delaware, OH 43015**

## I. INTRODUCTION

The Black family and community in the USA are currently facing a serious moral, spiritual, social and economic crisis. In the past era of American racial segregation, the Black Church used to play an important central role in shaping the moral, political, educational and economic values of the Black family and community. In this era of integration, the Black Church no longer serves as the fundamental social center and essential moral pivot of the Black community.

With the educational, social, and religious integration of the 1960s and 1970s in America, the traditional Black Church lost its essential central moral position in Black affairs and institutions. Despite its essential moral pivotal position, with the American racial and institutional integration, the American Black Church was demoted in importance and became socially marginalized. In the 1980s and 1990s, the American Black Church became one of the many American competing institutions for Black membership, loyalty, leadership and guidance.

Having been deposed from its former powerful and influential traditional pivotal role in the Black community, and become marginalized, the Black Church no longer provided the necessary vital moral guidance for many Black youths. The marginalization of the Black Church was the same correlative process that also marginalized the Church's societal power to serve as the essential moral, spiritual, social, educational, economic, political foundation and cohesive center for the both the Black family and community. As a result, there are many Black people who have lost their essential moral and spiritual center and self-esteem that the Black Church traditionally provided to its members and the Black community as a whole. Unlike the dualistic Western world-view, and the White community which values the dualistic separation of life into the secular and the sacred realms, the "Africentric" (African-centered) world-view is essentially monistic and religious.

Therefore, the marginalization of the Black Church created a corresponding phenomenon of social, moral, spiritual, economic, and political disorientation, disintegration and destruction within the Black family and the community. Significant increases in the rates of violence, divorce, drug abuse, poverty, low self-esteem, child-abuse, homicides, teen pregnancy and children born out of wedlock within the Black community correlate with the increased secularization and integration of schools of the 1970s and 1980s. With increased secularization and spiritual alienation of many Black people (especially those within the innercity communities), new forms of moral and spiritual outreach need to be created to reclaim the alienated Black youths who now find acceptance, fellowship and values in joining the community of violent gangs, drug peddlers, pimps, prostitutes, and other underground illegal forms of life and commerce.

One way to reach these kinds of morally, socially and spiritually alienated young people is to return to voluntary segregation of education by building private Black or "Afrocentric schools." These schools may provide the necessary Black community to rebuild Black pride that is rooted in the African moral world-view, values and cultural heritage that emphasize humaneness, love, peace, community, care for the neighbor, harmony and collective work ethic.

The second alternative is to encourage every Black person to rediscover his or her intrinsic central moral and spiritual values. The Africans and their descendants in the diaspora are known to be inherently religious in both world-view and values. The American "Negro Spirituals," "Gospels," the "blues," beliefs in voodun, witchcraft and magic, clearly demonstrate this self-evident truth.

In order to practice conventional or traditional religious spirituality and moral values, the non-religiously affiliated Black people must make the necessary life-transforming, positive moral and spiritual choice to return to their traditional Black Church or convert to the Nation of Islam. These Black religious institutions have traditionally provided the essential meaningful redemptive messages and values to their loyal members. They have effectively supported positive, wholesome, self-empowering and the effective socially and morally transforming modes of positive, loving and nonviolent modes of life within the Black communities.

The third alternative is to practice an inclusive African cultural form of generic civil religion which does not require religious affiliation to either Christianity or Islam. This inclusive Africentric cultural spirituality can be accomplished through the seven moral and social principles of *Kwanzaa*.[1] The principles of *Kwanzaa* are moral and spiritual, yet are free from the traditional forms of religious dogma and religious affiliation. They constitute a non-threatening outreach moral, social and economic program to the nonreligious as well as religious Black people in African diaspora.

It is significant to note that *Kwanzaa* is based on African language (Swahili), culture, spirituality, and philosophy of both existence and economics. The seven normative moral and societal principles of the African-American Community are borrowed from Africa. They are stated in Swahili which is the dominant African language of East Africa (Kenya, Tanzania and Uganda). Swahili is also spoken in Somalia, Rwanda, Burundi, Congo, Zimbabwe and Southern Sudan.

These moral and societal principles are incorporated into the current practices of "*Kwanzaa*."[2] *Kwanzaa* is the Black cultural holiday, which was created in 1966. It was formulated by Dr. Maulana Karenga, a California professor of African-American Studies. *Kwanzaa* was first celebrated by Dr. Karenga's cultural organization, and has since been observed by Black Americans around the country. It is a "nonreligious" cultural celebration and social holiday. According to Professor Karenga, *Kwanzaa* was created not to take the place of Christmas. Rather, it was created to reinforce the bonds of brotherhood, sisterhood and unity among the people of African descent.

Festivities last seven days from December 26 through January 1. *Kwanzaa* is symbolic of the "first-fruits harvest celebrations" of Africa. It is a time of "*kairos*" to strengthen family consciousness and social solidarity while educating children in social and moral principles of love, generosity, charity, peaceful mutual interdependence, and positive skills for community building.

Black, red and green are the symbolic and cultural colors of *Kwanzaa* and for most African-Americans. In Africa, most Africans also use yellow or gold to represent the sun as the cosmic king and symbol for God. They also use green to symbolize "Mother Earth" and the life she bestows on creation. Libation is poured on the Earth to honor her and nourish the departed ancestors. Black is for the African Black people, red for brotherhood, as well as the continuing struggle and the blood shed in the process of justice and liberation.

Traditionally, non-Blacks were deliberately excluded from the celebrations of *Kwanzaa*, despite the fact that there are many Africa-Americans who are actually married to people of other races or ethnic groups. This controversial African-American exclusion of Whites and other non-Africans has been challenged as an unethical form of reverse racial discrimination and self-segregation. Some Blacks were of the moral view that those who have experienced the injustice of the legacy of slavery, racial discrimination and bigotry, should not become the new champions of cultural and racial discrimination themselves.

However, the discriminatory practice of *Kwanzaa* has been defended by Karenga and other Black cultural nationalists on the moral rationale that *Kwanzaa* was explicitly designed to unify the divided, oppressed, culturally disinherited, and socioeconomically disadvantaged African-Americans. The desired cultural, social, political and economic unity was to be accomplished by the Black people themselves through their own efforts. *Kwanzaa* was the tool for community building. It was also the means of mobilization of the Black people for the family and collective group celebration of the uniqueness of Black experience, blackness and African cultural heritage and Afrocentric moral values. White people as former slave-masters and continuing oppressors of the African people were considered either as spies or distractions at these African-American cultural festivals. As such, they were consciously and deliberately excluded from these celebrations by Karenga when he designed *Kwanzaa* and its main principles in 1966.

In order to enhance the African cultural affinity and consciousness as well as both beauty and symbolism, African attire, mats, fruits and other African cultural objects are used as aids in this Africentric cultural, social, moral, spiritual and economic celebration. This celebration is wholistic in the same way that the African world-view is wholistic. That is, contrary to the Western dualism, the African world-view does not divide the world into secular and sacred realms. The whole of life and the world are considered God's work and therefore, a sacred realm or God's Kingdom.

These African spiritual and cultural celebrations and the community that celebrates them are based on the seven moral and societal principles. They are the necessary foundational pillars which are necessary to support the societal, economic, political, social and spiritual moral systems for building and sustaining a sound Black community both in America and abroad, including Africa. These seven socioeconomic, social, moral and spiritual African principles of *Kwanzaa* are discussed in more detail below.

## II. THE SEVEN PRINCIPLES (*NGUZO SABA*) OF *KWANZAA*

"*NGUZO SABA*" is Swahili for the seven normative African principles on which *Kwanzaa* was founded. They constitute the essential societal moral guidance for an economically successful, united and peaceful Black community.

### 1. *UMOJA* (Unity, Dec. 26)

In order to achieve social, political, cultural and economic unity, Professor Karenga, maintained that the Black people had to strive for and maintain the essential unity of the family, community, nation and Black race. At dinner, the importance of Black people's unity is explained to the children. The children are sometimes asked to recite the principle: "If we embrace Unity and believe in ourselves, our families and our leaders, we will be victorious in our struggles as individuals and as a race."

Indeed, the Black community is so badly divided and wounded either by past injustice of slavery or colonialism, discrimination, oppression and exploitation, and therefore, needs healing, reconciliation and unity. This is true for America, as well as Africa where division has taken ethnic and religious lines. Accordingly, ethnic violence has caused great tragic civil wars and attempts of genocide in Rwanda, Burundi, Congo, Nigeria, Liberia and the Sudan. Pan-Africanism is the solution to Africa's division, underdevelopment, poverty, corruption, violence and wars. Black people in the diaspora are also as divided as those left on the continent. W.E.B. DuBois, Marcus Garvey, Kwame Nkrumah, Malcolm X, Julius Nyerere and Yoweri Museveni are some positive examples of leaders who sought to unify Africa and other Black people abroad into a viable Pan-African family.

**2. *KUJICHAGULIA* (Self-Determination, Dec. 27)**
This is the principle of self-definition and self-determination as free, thinking, intelligent, moral and responsible individuals and collectively, as Black people. Karenga framed the power, means, and courage to "define ourselves, name ourselves, create for ourselves and speak for ourselves rather than allow others to do these things for us." On this day, many people chose African names for themselves. Karenga goes on to define this principle as "to celebrate our determination as a race to define, name and create a better world for ourselves than we could possibly imagine."

Self-determination, self-naming and naming the world is part of this principle. "Naming" implies control over what is named. Accordingly, in Hebrew patriarchal society where men perceived themselves to be gods (*imago Dei*). These men taught that men or males were created by a male God ("the Father") "in his own image" (*imago Dei*) to "name," "tame," "control" and to rule over the world, (including all women, children, animals, plants, and wealth), and accomplish this divine task in God's own name, as his ambassadors and concrete representatives in the created world (cf. Gen. 1:28-31; 3:1-27).

As such, the Hebrew biblical mythological book of *Genesis* ("*In The Beginning*") declares that God created the world and names the creatures in it. In the second account of creation Gen. 2:4-3:27), the creation story claims that God created the world and handed it over to *Adam* (man) and gave him the power to name and govern everything in that world, including *Eve*, the first woman!

Adam's (man's) alleged divine power for "naming" and "governing of God's creation" including Eve ("the woman"), has led to destructive male chauvinism and oppression of women in the world by men. Yet, men have perpetrated these evils, including those of racism and sexism in God's holy name. This has been accomplished by religious men, including Christians, Muslims and Jews whose patriarchal theologies of priesthood, ministry and anthropology declares that men are superior to women, and that it is God's will for them to represent God in the world, the temple or Church and religious ceremonies.

It is this kind of destructive patriarchal theology which has led to the tragic idolatrous male-self-deification, slavery, sexism, racism, oppression and exploitation of the world. This was the tragic case in the West because the White male was considered the representative of God.

Women and non-Whites were considered inferior because they were considered to be un-God-like. Subsequently, racism has been targeted against the Black people, particularly, the Black males because they were the antithesis of White males. That is, if the "White males were gods," then the Black males as their antithesis were, likewise, negatively considered to be the "black devils," and natural enemies of White males!

The evidence lies in the disproportional numbers of Black males in American jails! The 1993 beating of Rodney King, a Black motorist, by Los Angles White-policemen, and the 1995 international notoriety of O.J. Simpson trial case for alleged murder of his White wife are just a couple of illustrations of this complicated racial-syndrome.

In patriarchal societies, the males are the symbolic representation of their societies. In this symbolism, the present high rate for incarceration of Black males by a predominantly White American law enforcement and judicial system is in some respects a modern version of Black male the antebellum American lynching and "symbolic castration of the Black male" along with his family and the Black community. Because of this suffering, the Black males should never become the perpetrators of sexism, racism, oppression and exploitation because they know how these forms of injustice injure the soul and the body as they destroy self-esteem, and the will either to live or work hard to succeed in a hostile world.

Nevertheless, despite all these odds and institutional barriers erected by White-racism and whitesupremacy, the Black people still desire to survive, hope to thrive, and succeed. Therefore, they wish to regain the power to determine their own destiny, both as individuals and collectively, united as a "Black Nation." The correct identification and naming of the real enemies and evils that confront the Black people is the first necessary major step in the process of struggle needed to fight and overcome them. One cannot fight some unknown or invisible enemies and win!

Therefore, good education, knowledge, technological and problem solving skills are the keys and weapons for the effective struggle and liberation of the oppressed and impoverished Black people, or their oppressed people, regardless whether they are in the Americas, the Caribbean, Africa, Asia or other countries.

Self-naming means self-definition, self-identification, self-empowerment, and self-determination in responsible free exercise of personal freedom and free choice. Slaves, racial minorities, and oppressed people, including women and children as victims of male-chauvinism, rarely have the freedom for self-naming, free choice and self-determination.

Malcolm X is the best example and advocate for Black people's freedom for self-naming and self-determination. He discarded his name of "Little" as a slave name imposed on his ancestors by their slave-masters. He positively transformed himself from a life of ignorance and crime to that of a learned, productive, articulate, law-abiding citizen, respectable and highly effective moral and spiritual leadership within the Black community and the world.

African names taken by the Black nationalists of the 1960s and 1970s were means of self-empowerment and recovery of self identity. In the former French and Belgium colonies in Africa, the "Negritude Movement" had also led to the rejection of French and European systems and cultures which had been imposed on Africa during the colonial era. The French colonial policy of both cultural and racial assimilation of Africans had led to the de-Africanization and destruction of the Africans systems, religions, languages, and cultures. Karenga's *Kwanzaa* being formulated around the African Swahili language and cultural principles is part of this process of mental, cultural, moral, spiritual and linguistic decolonization, African-self renaming and self-recovery.

**3. *UJIMA* (Collective Work and Responsibility, Dec. 28)**
The *UJIMA* principle was stated by Karenga as being: "To build and maintain our community together, to make our sisters' and brothers' problems our problems and to solve them together." This is the stated noble principle of *UJIMA*. The individual, and collective mutual love, respect, trust, responsibility and care for one another are the values that the Black community needs most. It needs these moral and social values more than it needs money and employment.

No viable human or animal community can exist without its respective members' essential mutual care, protection, respect, love and trust. Urban gangs are appealing to the urban youths from dysfunctional families because they provide these basic needs for community, love, sense of belonging, pride and protection which their families have failed to provide. As a result, they are loyal to one another and die to protect each other and their territory or property.

**4. *UJAMAA*[3] (Cooperative Economics, Dec. 29)**
The collective principle of African work and economics was defined by Karenga as: "To build and maintain our own stores, shops, and other businesses and to profit from them together. We all profit from our collective efforts. We can build and maintain our communities with Black-owned stores, restaurants and other service businesses. (*Mazao*) Fruits and vegetables symbolize the rewards of our collective productive labor."

This is what the African-American community, and the African divided nations need most. This is a good principle which needs to be adopted by individuals, families and groups of people in order to bring about their own economic liberation and development. It is a venture rooted in faith and desire for economic freedom and well-being.

Cowards and unbelievers are condemned as evildoers by all revealed and most traditional religions. This is mainly because the cowards and unbelievers are considered to be lacking the necessary power of faith and grace as the necessary social, moral and spiritual power for undertaking risky, yet necessary good and positive social or political actions that would transform the world into a safer, better and just place to live and work in peace.

Investments on Wall Street stock market are not just a gamble, but also a venture of positive faith and courage. This is also true for most other economic investments and ventures. Accordingly, the year 2000 closed with the worst losses in the USA stock markets, particularly, the technology sector which lost about 40% in capital investments. But without the risk for loss, there is no possibility for gain! The higher the potential for gain, also comes the higher risk for loss! That is the true nature of life. Therefore, life must be courageously faced in joy and lived as a venture of faith.

Ultimately, the Black people must pool their resources together in order to build their own economic businesses. There is already enough capital earned by Black entertainers and professional sports players in basketball and football. For instance, Michael Jackson, Michael Jordan, Oprah Winfrey, Eddie Murphy, Bill

Cosby, Lou Rawls, Denzel Washington, and James Earl Jones already earn considerable billions of dollars which could be used for building a Black economic empire.

However, before this economic dream can become realized as a concrete societal reality in Africa or in America, the Black people must first effectively mobilize themselves into a viable nationalistic Black community that is grounded in the common good and unity of purpose, vision and Black nationalism or Pan-Africanism. W.E.B. DuBois, Marcus Garvey, Malcolm X, Kwame Nkrumah, Julius Nyerere, Nelson Mandela, Jesse Jackson, Yoweri Kaguta Museveni, Kofi Annan and Colin Powell provide good resource materials and examples of how this political, social and economic unity can be variously achieved. The Black people must overcome the colonial economic system, mental conditioning, and "politics of divide, conquer, and exploit" the conquered peoples' economic resources at will.

This Western imperialism and colonial system worked for the great political and economic benefit of the European colonial masters of Africa and Asia. Today, colonial mentality among African leaders, consumerism, and neocolonialism still work for the economic benefit and profit of the European community at the expense of the African nations and the impoverished African masses.

The burden of debt is carried by Africa which borrows from the West in order to buy Western consumer goods! This colonial economic system keeps Africa poor, in debt and economically dependent on the West, in the same manner in which slaves were dependent on their masters. Yet the slave master profited at the expense of the hard-working slaves who remained poor, dependent, and in bondage.

The Black leaders and their people in both America and Africa must learn to overcome deeply ingrained destructive unconscious colonial brain-washing, or conditioned slave or colonial mentality, in order to achieve any true personal or economic freedom and self-determination. Ultimately, the Black people must regain their moral and social courage to trust one another and work together in business investment ventures in order to better their economic condition and to provide employment for the other less fortunate and economically disenfranchised Black people and other racial minorities.

**5. *NIA* (Purpose and Meaning, Dec. 30)**

"To make our collective vocation the building and developing of our community in order to restore our people to their traditional greatness. Let us concentrate on the principle of purpose so that we can achieve our vision," is the positive affirmation of this principle of life and condition of meaningful or happy existence, anywhere in the world.

*Babe* is Hollywood's insight that like human beings, animals themselves also need a worthy purpose for living a satisfying life, apart from eating. Despite the fact that *Babe* was born a pig, she found her own purpose, meaning and reason for living by adopting a lifestyle of a sheepdog. For all practical purposes, *Babe* the pig, became a good "sheepdog," despite her own biological heritage and limitations as a pig. In this witty manner, the commonly held scientific and deterministic behaviorist concept and mythology that "biology is destiny" is both directly and indirectly challenged and debunked by the film. The popular concept of absolute biological determinism that is held by most people (the crowds) is portrayed as a popular, but baseless and erroneous tradition based on both myth and superstition.

Indeed, world history clearly illustrates that without a clear purpose and vision for being, or how to cope with changes within the environment, any group of people will finally perish. The purpose or reason for being provides the necessary vision for life and how or why its should be lived.

People without vision or reason for living drift through life tossed here and there aimlessly like rubbish tossed into the stream of life is tossed here and there down stream by the current! A noble vision of life, and significant purpose for existence or living provide the essential and ideal focus for life. They also provide life's ultimate meaning or fundamental goal for a satisfying good life, and happy mode of existence or living out one's life in this world. In addition, a noble and worthy vision of life, significant noble goal of life provide an ideal reason for living. They also both guide and call people to move courageously forward when they travel through a dark path on their moral and spiritual journey of life or face a moment of crisis.

The noble moral and spiritual principles of creativity and faith help us as finite human beings to keep us positively motivated, energized and ever going forward despite hostile opposition, stubborn obstacles, defeat and adversity. These principles empower us and push us constantly to go forward, even when the going gets tough and hazardous.

Giving up or going back is never an option. In any case, going back is never a wise option since life is a one time venture or personal occurrence, and entry on "the one way highway" on the single journey of life. Life is by God's design and natural law, a "one way" stream, down the "highway" of existence, flowing toward the lake, and finally the distant ocean or God.

God as the cosmic ocean of life, is the Life-Force in whom all the major cycles of life both originate and finally return to complete the "great cycle of life," or begin a new one. Once placed on the highway of life through birth, as the only entry point on this highway and journey of life-time, there is only one final official and permanent exit on this one way highway of life. The official exit foe each person reads: "DEATH." The newspapers' obituary section, hospitals, funeral homes, and cemeteries provide ample evidence on the reality and nature of these individual permanent exists and permanent rest from the tiring travel on the seemingly endless highway of life.

On the highway of life, there are many voluntary entry points or unofficial exits. Even the poor, the tired and the injured are not allowed exit on the highway of life unless their own right permanent exit has been sighted and correctly labeled on the horizon. Otherwise, once on the highway, one can only travel forward.

Voluntary exit may occur if one deliberately drives off the highway over a precipice and the void below. But that kind of violent exit or suicide is often believed to be condemned by God. Most religions or moral traditions also condemn and reject it as suicide and eternal self-destruction. The deliberate or consent to throw another person over the cliff into the abyss and nonbeing or death either because he or she is in pain or has lost the will and courage to live, is also rejected as murder. This includes acts of active euthanasia.

The mainline Protestants, the Anglican Communion and the Catholic Church condemn euthanasia as murder, regardless of whether it was solicited by a patient or not. Ironically, many governments punish murderers by sentencing them to the same fate as the people these murderers killed! That does not make any moral sense. It is an act of revenge and retaliation (*lex talionis*) if one kills a murderer for killing some other person! Revenge is not a good moral act of justice.

On the contrary, according to the teachings of Jesus, both revenge and retaliation are both ungodly and immoral acts of violence, destruction and death. This is Jesus' central teachings of on God as the unconditionally loving and merciful Father (*Abba*), who requires the moral and spiritual obligation of unconditional love, nonviolence and free forgiveness (Matt.5-7).

There are rest stops and refueling stations on the highway to keep the travelers in good health, but the stops are short and the journey goes on day after day with one's eyes fixed on the horizon where the individual's exit may suddenly come into focus. It is by faith that meaningful and satisfying life is lived. The slaves were able to survive their hardship through faith in God's future redemption alone. That is also true for the Jews in the concentration camps during the holocaust in World War II.

Those people who survived the horrible and dehumanizing conditions of these tragic concentration camps were fortunate men and women of great personal faith and courage. According to Dr. Victor Frankol, an eminent psychiatrist who survived the holocaust, these people survived the horrors of the camp because they had found an energizing significant reason and essential future obligation for which they had to keep on living today in order to fulfill after they were liberated. That fundamental faith, courage and reason for being kept them alive despite the odds and adversity confronting them daily. Like John Bunyan, through the holy pilgrimage in life, one has always to choose wisely and go forward on the journey of life with its unknown many wonders and adventures.

The Black people are on the moral and spiritual highway of life. They should learn to desist from violence that destroys life and property in the Black community. Acts of retaliation and violence in the Black community should be negated and prevented by reiteration of Dr. Martin Luther's teaching on collective nonviolence, noncooperation with evil and non-retaliation as the effective strategies to deal with a violent group and racist society. Tragically, most acts of homicidal violence within the Black community are perpetrated by violent gangs of ignorant and uncaring Black male youths against other young Black people and their families.

These poverty stricken and socioeconomically disadvantaged innercity Black youths have lost faith in America and have correlatively failed to find the humanizing love or acceptance by the majority of people. As such, they have not acquired any ideal noble vision of life, ideal moral purpose and reason for being, and care little about the lives of other people or their property. They need our collective love, care, counseling and healing in order to effect in them and their traumatized communities, social, spiritual and moral rehabilitation, and reconciliation.

The Black community cannot afford to discard these people and leave them as the problems of the state or federal government agencies to deal with. Jail sentences finally come to an end, and the criminals return to society untreated, unrepentant, unreformed, angry and in quest of revenge. They are worse and more dangerous criminals than when they were originally sentenced to jail. Tragically, the less violent and unsophisticated juvenile offenders learn to become hardened and expert criminals from the career criminals whom they find in jail.

As such, the Black community has to become proactive in the prevention of youth crime. This is essential in order to save the integrity of the Black family and preserve law, order and peace within the poverty stricken innercity communities. The Black community should devise programs of family and youth education which teach social and personal skills of good communications, nonviolent conflict resolution, mediation, peaceful mutual coexistence and the promotion of non-materialistic modes of life. In addition, fathers should be urged to take care of their children that are born both within or out of wedlock. Males without male-role models should be assisted by the Church's provision of a substitute father figure for an ideal, faith, perseverance, hard-working, loving, caring and nonviolent male role-model.

### 6. *KUUMBA* (Creativity, Dec. 31)

This principle affirms the following ideals: "Always, to do as much as we can, in any way we can, to leave our community more beautiful and beneficial than when we inherited it. When we celebrate this principle, we can give thanks for the wonderful fruits of our creative powers."

Karenga had argued that the African-Americans needed to put together a celebration that would be remembered for years by preparing a simple, nourishing meal; by making gifts that come from their own hearts; and by sharing their homes, food and music with their friends, family and neighbors, as their African ancestors did at harvest time. He urged the Black Americans to rejoice together and apply their individual and collective creative minds in order to fashion new ways to nourish, nurture, heal, unify and re-build the African-American community, and at the same time, build an economically powerful Pan-African Black Nation.

The third millennium requires great creativity, increased technological training, and new skills for macro-socioeconomic organization in order to ensure survival and success within the global community. Ethnic and tribal nationalism as bases of operation and socioeconomic organization are antiquated and meaningless in the macro-socioeconomic and political systems of the global community, and international pluralism and inclusive diversity. Africa's inclusive Pan-Africanism and great cultural, religious, linguistic, ideological, tribal, ethnic and racial diversity can become the right global training ground for global tolerance, harmonious and successful modes of life within the global community of the third millennium.

Human diversity is a divine gift to beautify the world and provide color and contrast to life and its cultures, religions, ideas, languages and other systems. As such, human diversity calls for celebration, rather than a repressive quest for the creation of a monolithic structure, such as Adolph Hitler attempted to create and impose on the world. Creativity and beauty are direct results of diversity.

The USA is great nation, partly because of its racial, ethnic, cultural, ideological and religious diversity. As such, the USA provides an ideal practical model of inclusive diversity to the world, and its diverse people. Africa will become a new nation and new international economic power when its tribalistic and politically divided people stop fighting useless ethnic wars and unite.

Africa can accomplish this essential political task by learning from the United States of America, and unifying its nations to form the United States of Africa. Good leadership, Pan-African nationalism, positive self-determination and desire for self-development will be the foundations and positive driving force of the United States of Africa. Without this unity, Africa will remain divided, backward, underdeveloped, poor and politically unstable due to ethnic conflicts and border wars.

**7. *IMANI* (Faith, Jan. 1)**

"*IMANI*" is the moral and existential principle of faith and courage to be a finite and mortal being in a seemingly capricious and transitory impersonal world. Africans and their descendants are essentially religious people whose implicit and explicit forms of faith are their foundational and sustaining power. Because of this power of faith, the African slaves were able to withstand slavery, and its horrors. They never lost hope that God would eventually send them a deliverer (Messiah) to set them free from their bondage.

Lincoln, and later, Martin Luther King, were perceived as God's messiahs who were sent to deliver the Black people in America from the evils of slavery and oppression. Like Moses and Jesus who were not accepted by all the people to whom they had been sent by God, so were also Lincoln and King. Obviously, it takes an act of faith for people to recognize a messiah or prophet, and to believe that what they see is part of reality, and not an illusion. As such, without faith, miracles are not sufficient evidence to convince a skeptic that a miracle, indeed, took place. They are more inclined to explain it away as an illusion or accident of nature.

Faith is the primary source of supernatural power for all human beings, especially, the powerless and the oppressed. Without faith in a good Creator and Savior God, many African slaves would have been overwhelmed by despair and depression. Most of them would have committed suicide out of desperation.

According to this moral principle, faith and courage must be harnessed as the essential power "to believe with all our hearts in our God, people, our parents, our leaders and the righteousness and victory of our struggle." It is the tradition to celebrate the principle of Faith on the last day of *Kwanzaa* by pouring out libation in celebration of the first fruits of the harvest in the New Year. Water is placed in the communal cup and poured out in the direction of the four winds (north, south, east and west) to sanctify, honor, bless and call into mystical union and fellowship with God, the ancestors, people and all the good spirits in the universe.

## III. PROCEDURES, SYMBOLS AND MEANING OF *KWANZAA*:

In the same way Christian holidays, such as Easter and Christmas have their symbols and ritualistic procedures, so does *Kwanzaa*. The symbols, rituals and procedures of *Kwanzaa* are kept simple. The masses are able to practice the principles of *Kwanzaa* without much instruction or clergy to led the ceremonies. An elder within the community or family head is considered worthy enough to preside over the ceremonies.

1. **A STRAW MAT** symbolizes tradition and history because it is an African object (the other symbols can be placed on it). **FRUITS** represent the African festivals and celebrations of harvests of crops.

2. **The CANDLE-HOLDER** symbolizes parenthood. Seven candles are placed in the candle-holder. One candle is lit on each day of *Kwanzaa*.

3. **CORN**: Have one ear of CORN for each child in your household (and even if you have no children, one ear should represent African-American tradition of extended family). **GIFTS** should be given mainly to children and must include two different items. These items must include a book as the key to the secrets of knowledge and success. The second item must be a heritage symbol, such as a poster, African art, a framed family photograph, or a suitable black doll.

4. **The UNITY CUP** is used to toast to the ancestors. The UNITY CUP serves the same function that the chalice serves within the Anglican and Catholic Eucharistic sacramental communion with each other and the departed ancestors or saints.

5. **SPECIAL AFRICAN GREETING**: ***HABARI GANI***? This is the African-American customary *Swahili* greeting during the period of *Kwanzaa*. It means "What's happening?" or "What is the news?" During *Kwanzaa* the greeting is answered with the name of the *Kwanzaa* principle of that day. (This is a technical *Kwanzaa* usage of the African greeting. It deviates from the African normal usage of the same greeting and its responses.)

6. ***HARAMBEE*** is a call for African unity, collective work, self-reliance, community service and struggle for a common good. This call includes building projects, such as roads, wells, schools and hospitals, or cleaning the neighborhood and disposing of trash and abandoned cars.

## IV. CONCLUSION

Like the people in Africa, the African-American community is faced with many serious problems. These problems include external factors, such as oppression, exploitation, unemployment, racism, violence, and discrimination in the work place as well as in schools, colleges, universities, hospitals, and housing. But they also face the internal problems such as those of low self-esteem, self-hate, division, disease, poverty, anger, addictions to drugs and alcohol, violence, crime, homicides, spousal and child abuse, poor work ethic, welfare-dependency, laziness and apathy.

Some of these serious problems of the Black family and community are essentially both moral and spiritual. As such, they require both a moral and spiritual remedy or solution, rather than a mere provision of a material solution, such as money or employment.

Spiritual and moral problems require corresponding moral and spiritual treatment for both truly effective and meaningful or lasting solutions. Likewise, material problems require material solutions, instead of spiritual or moral ones. Apart from moral and spiritual counseling, the Black community needs to turn itself into a viable work force and investment block. This means that the community must fight crime and vandalism which prevent outside businesses from locating and investing within the Black innercity areas.

Ultimately, the Black people will redeem themselves from their own current trend of moral, spiritual, socioeconomic crisis and the correlative dehumanizing conditions of poverty and violence within the innercity communities by working together against these destructive forces of evil. The Black community will rediscover its essential moral and pivotal spiritual center in the spirituality and healing refugee of the traditional Black Church.

There is nobody who worships in a joy and spirit filled Black Church, and who hears both the angelic music and dramatized spiritual sermons, and fails to be encountered by the healing and redemptive presence, grace and love of the Creator-Redeemer God. The innercity's criminals and troubled youths will find a cheaper treatment for their bad attitude, violence, anger, low self-esteem, temptations for robbery or burglary, if they go to a Black Church, rather than going to jail or an expensive therapist. Black preachers are traditionally good counselors, teachers, psychiatrists, role-models, advocates for the poor and the voiceless. They are the essential Black community builders, leaders, protectors and saviors.

Finally, economic redemption will inevitably occur if the Black community either in the USA or Africa adopts a strong Pan-African nationalism, unity and people join together in noble ventures of self-help collective work, economic development and financial investments. This is bound to happen in the future, despite the many racist and neocolonial forms of "politics of divide and conquer," and other serious obstacles that must be constantly fought against and overcome.

To this end, American Jews, Asians and other racial minorities provide excellent examples and practical models of successful family owned small and large businesses that the Black people can adopt and adapt to their own conditions. America is a capitalist society and capitalism only respects capital, money, wise investments and hard work.

Black people have to join in this capitalist venture it they wish to become free of poverty and dependency on White or other people for employment, livelihood, and general well-being. This is hazardous due to the fact that racism is still a major factor in American affairs, including the hiring, promotion and retention practices in the work place.

To begin with, the local neighborhood people can mobilize themselves through the local Church or mosque resources into a visible force of unity for the purposes of cleaning their communities, prevention of crime and finally, building up their own fully owned and controlled institutions and businesses. Despite the problems of anti-Semitism, the American Black Muslims under the direction of the controversial Reverend Louis Farrakhan and Benjamin (Muhammad) Chavis (the former President of the NAACP and leading Black Christian minister in Cleveland, Ohio, USA prior to his conversion to the American Black Nation of Islam in 1996), have provided a good example for the rest of the Black community in these societal aspects regarding the promotion of economic self-sufficiency, and building both crime and drug free viable Black communities.

---

## NOTES:

1. *Kwanzaa* was founded by Professor Maulana Karenga of California. As both outlined and celebrated in the USA by African Americans, *Kwanzaa* is an African-American invention that is unknown in Africa. However, the main elements that are celebrated are African in both origin and nature. It combines many African ideas and festivals, particularly the harvest cerebrations. This is the right time (*kairos*) for communal festive religious ceremonies in thanksgiving to God and the ancestors for providence, and the divine blessings of good weather, good health, fertility, abundance, well-being and peace. This occasion marks the joy, fellowship and peace of God's existential heaven on Earth, and within the mediation of the happy, loving and festive peaceful community!

2. The seven principles are those of Karenga, but the explanation is that of Professor Emmanuel K. Twesigye. The seven principles of *Kwanzaa* are found on posters, and in many forms of "public domain" publications. For instance, they are annually published in the *BOUND NEWSLETTER*, Ohio Wesleyan University, each December. The 1997 version was edited by Amanda Dawney. Dawney cited Professor Karenga and the *Essence Magazine* as the original sources for the principles.

3. President Julius Nyerere of Tanzania tried to mobilize the whole of Tanzania into "*Ujamaa Villages*" and cooperative farms. The state sponsored socialist experiment failed in the same way communism would later failed leading to the sudden collapse of the former Soviet Union in 1992. People became too lazy and unmotivated to work for a common good, and equality on collective farms! Instead, they preferred to work on personal farms for gain and

personal profit! They were not interested in the socioeconomic common good, equality and justice for all! They overwhelmingly rejected this utopian universalist ideal of equity, justice and equality for all people.

As such, the future Black community should avoid similar utopian dreams of equality for all people like President Julius Nyerere tried to implement in Tanzania. Human beings seem to favor an economic, social or moral hierarchy of some kind, with God at the apex. They place themselves next to God and in God's name empower themselves with God's supernatural authority to govern the rest of the creatures and finite beings in God's creation. Plato's Republic is a good illustration of this universal human hierarchical tendency in repudiation of utopian egalitarianism, equality and true direct mass participatory democracy.

Unfortunately, it is also because of this universal human tendency and preference for stratification and hierarchy that makes the Blacks in America as identifiable racial minorities, the targets for racism and discrimination. These are examples of the injustice and evils of White racism, sexism, whitesupremacy and police racial profiling. Justice and agape demand that all people should be treated equally in society and given the same opportunities for employment, pay, leadership and recognition for what they do. They should be treated the same before the law and within God's Community or the Church. They are all brothers and sisters in God's world and Kingdom.

# Appendix F

# The Anglican Bishops' Lambeth Conference Resolution on Homosexuality and Sexuality

## 5 August 1998

On August 5, 1998, the Lambeth World Anglican Bishops' Conference approved the following resolution on homosexuality and sexuality by a vote of 526 in favor and 70 against [mainly from North America and Europe], with 45 abstentions [mainly from North America and Europe].[1] This [Global Anglican Bishop's] Conference:

a) commends to the Church the subsection report on human sexuality;

b) in view of the teaching of [the Holy] Scripture, upholds faithfulness in marriage between a man and a woman in lifelong union, and believes that abstinence is right for those who are not called to marriage;

c) recognizes that there are among us persons who experience themselves as having a homosexual orientation. Many of these are members of the Church and are seeking the pastoral care, moral direction of the Church, and God's transforming power for the living of their lives and the ordering of relationships, and we commit ourselves to listen to the experience of homosexual people. We wish to assure them that they are loved by God and that all baptized, believing and faithful persons, regardless of sexual orientation, are full members of the Body of Christ;

d) while rejecting homosexual practice as incompatible with Scripture, calls on all our people to minister pastorally and sensitively to all irrespective of sexual orientation and to condemn irrational fear of homosexuals, violence within marriage and any trivialisation and commercialisation of sex;

e) cannot advise the legitimising or blessing of same-sex unions, nor the ordination of those involved in such unions;

f) requests the Primates and the ACC [Anglican Consultative Council] to establish a means of monitoring the work done on the subject of human sexuality in the Communion and to share statements and resources among us;

g) notes the significance of the Kuala Lumpur Statement and the concerns expressed in resolutions IV.26, V.1, V.10, V.23, and V.35 on the authority of

Scripture in matters of marriage and sexuality and asks the Primates and the ACC to include them in their monitoring process[2]

---

## NOTES

1. There was a bitter debate prior to the vote concerning condemning the homosexual practice as a sin against God, nature and the community. The African bishops denounced the European and American bishops for supporting homosexuality, and asked them to repent of "sin" and "cultural moral evil." One Nigerian bishop tried to exorcize "the evil spirit of homosexuality" from a European bishop! Previously, Bishop John Spong of New Jersey had condemned the African bishops as bible literalists and theological conservatives.

2. On January 29, 2000, in Singapore, some representatives of the conservative African and Asian Anglican bishops ordained the Rev. Charles H. Murphy III and John H. Rodgers Jr. of the United States as Missionary Bishops to the USA Episcopal Church to preach against its sins of homosexuality. However, the rest of the Anglican Communion has condemned these episcopal consecrations as being both canonically illegal and invalid. It is self-evident that the Anglican Communion may split over the moral and theological issues regarding the acceptability of homosexuality within the Church for both laity and the clergy. The United Methodist and the Presbyterian churches are also facing similar moral and theological dilemmas within their own churches and ecclesiastical governing bodies.

The United Methodist General Conference of May 5-12, 2000, that was held in Cleveland in Ohio, USA, overwhelmingly rejected the practice of homosexuality by a huge majority vote. Again, like the Anglican Church, the African conservative bishops and delegates were the main vocal opponents of homosexuality. They condemned it as a moral evil, anti-biblical immoral sexual custom and sin before God. They were ready to secede if the Conference had voted in favor of homosexuality and the ordination of homosexuals.

## Appendix G

# Twelve Steps and Principles Of Alcoholics Anonymous Self-Treatment[1]

1. **An admission of an existence of a serious problem:**[2] "[We] admitted we were powerless over alcohol -- that our lives had become unmanageable."[3]

2. **Faith in God's power for restoration:** "[We] came to believe that a Power greater than ourselves could restore us to sanity."

3. **Decision to yield the control of life to God:** "[We] made a decision to turn our will and our lives over to the care of God *as we understood Him.*"

4. **Making a moral inventory:** "[We] made a searching and fearless moral inventory of ourselves."

5. **Confession of moral failure:** "[We] admitted to God, to ourselves, and to another human being the exact nature of our wrongs."

6. **Readiness to remove moral defects:** "[We] were entirely ready to have God remove all these defects of character."

7. **Prayer for God's help and forgiveness:** "[We] humbly asked Him [God] to remove our shortcomings."

8. **Contrition (repentance) and seeking forgiveness from those wronged:** "[We] made a list of all persons we had harmed and became willing to make amends to them all."

9. **Making reparations:** "[We] made direct amends to such people wherever possible, except when to do so would injure them or others."

10. **Moral growth:** "[We] continued to take moral inventory and when we were wrong promptly admitted it."

11. **Meditation and prayer for the knowledge of God's will and power to act on it:** "[We] sought through prayer and meditation[4] to improve our conscious contact with God *as we understood Him*, praying only for knowledge of His will for us and the power to carry that out."

12. **Living a positively transformed life based on the practice of these moral principles:** "Having had a spiritual awakening as a result of these steps, we tried to carry this message to alcoholics, and to practice these principles in all our affairs."

## NOTES AND COMMENTARY by Emmanuel K. Twesigye

1. The material in quotation represents the original principles of the American "Alcoholic Anonymous" (AA) program for self-empowerment, self-help and treatment as originally formulated in 1934. The AA principles are grounded in spiritual, moral and ethical principles for promotion of self-discipline, self-motivation and self-empowerment to confront, fight and overcome the serious destructive problem of alcoholic dependency and addiction. In this respect, alcoholism is looked at as a disease and addiction as opposed to condemnation as mere sinful behavior and moral evil due to a free self-indulgence in alcoholic drinks, and moral failure to control oneself.

2. Denial of the problem is the greatest barrier for alcoholics in seeking treatment. Admission of the existence of the problem is a prerequisite for any effective problem-solving. The material within the **bold** type are part of Twesigye's commentary and analysis of the twelve principles and steps of Alcoholics Anonymous programs.

3. Alcoholics and drug addicts tend to live a self-destructive life of denial of the reality and seriousness of their addictions. There is a denial of the existence of the problem or sickness to themselves, family members and close friends, even when these people know the real truth, and often offer to help. Therefore, the moral courage to admit the existence of the problem or condition of addiction and helplessness or recognition of dependency on these substances, is a major step in the process of healing. It empowers the person to confront the sickness and to seek help, support, professional counseling and treatment.

4. Prayer and meditation are essential components of healing of the human body, soul or spirit, mind, and society. Both prayer and meditation are essential universal accessible sources and supernatural resources for an effective positive supernatural power for a meaningful, contentedness, and a healthy human life. Both Jesus and the Buddha provide good examples of a prayerful life, meditation and joyful contemplation of life, God, the world and the meaning of life given the existential reality of pain, suffering and death.

Prayer and meditation reduce stress, bring peace of mind and body, well-being, harmony and healing to the body, mind and community. These benefits do not depend on going to Church. Rather, these healing and redemptive benefits depend on faith, living a peaceful simple life of contentment, love, dedication to duty or one's work, prayer, meditation and positive orientation to life and its mysteries.

Job, Buddha, Socrates, Jesus, Gandhi, Janani Luwum, Nelson Mandela, M.L. King, Desmond Tutu and Oscar Romero are good examples of positively transforming personal deep faith, moral courage and a redemptive contemplative prayerful life. This ideal moral and spiritual perfection and godly mode of life mystically usher into the world God's Kingdom as characterized by the transcendent peace of mind and spirit while one lives in the midst of persecution, pain, finitude and threat of death.

For those interested in questions of theodicy or God's providence and meaning in personal life and history will find it helpful to read, Harold S. Kushner, *When Bad Things Happen to Good People* (New York: Shocken books, 1981), and Viktor E. Frankl, *Man's Search for Meaning: An Introduction to Logotherapy* (New York: Simon & Schuster, 3rd Edition, 1984). Finally, one should read the tragic biblical stories of the persecution and crucifixion of Jesus as a criminal, despite the fact that he was an innocent holy man, a Jewish moral reformist teacher (Rabbi), God's special prophet or messiah (Christ), and messenger of God's moral law of unconditional love, nonviolence and free forgiveness of offenses.

## Appendix H

# Human Finitude, Hubris And Death:

The Wisdom of Solomon

The ungodly by their words
and evil deeds summoned death;
considering him a friend,
they pined away
and made a covenant with him,
because they are fit to belong
to his company.

For they reasoned unsoundly,
saying to themselves,
"Short and sorrowful is our life,
and there is no remedy
when a life comes to its end,
and no one has been known
to return from Hades.

For we were born
by mere chance,
and hereafter we shall be
as though we had never been,
for the breath in our nostrils
is smoke,
and reason is a spark kindled
by the beating of our hearts;
when it is extinguished,
the body will turn to ashes,
and the spirit will dissolve
like empty air.

*The ungodly said in their evil
hearts and thoughts:*

Our name will be forgotten
in time, and no one will remember
our works;
our life will pass away like the
traces of a cloud,
and be scattered like mist
that is chased
by the rays of the Sun
and overcome by its heat.

For our allotted time
is the passing of a shadow,
and there is no return
from our death,
because it is sealed up
and no one turns back.

Come, therefore, let us enjoy
the good things that exist,
and make use of the creation to
the full as in youth.

Let us take our fill of costly
wine and perfumes,
and let no flower of spring
pass us by.

Let us crown ourselves
with rosebuds before they wither.
Let none of us fail to share
in our revelry;

everywhere let us leave signs
of self-enjoyment,
because this is our portion,
and this our lot.

Let us oppress the righteous
poor man;
let us not spare the widow
or regard the gray hairs
of the aged.

But let our might be our law
of right, for what is weak
proves itself to be useless.

Let us lie in wait
for the righteous man,
because he is inconvenient
to us and opposes our actions;
he reproaches us for sins
against the law [God],
and accuses us of sins
against our training.

He professes to have knowledge
of God, and calls himself a child
of the Lord [God].

He became to us a reproof
of our thoughts;
the very sight of him
is a burden to us,
because his manner of life is
unlike that of others,
and his ways are strange.

We are considered by him
as something base
and he avoids our ways
as unclean;
he calls the last end of his life;
for if the righteous man
is God's child, he will help him
and will deliver him
from the hand of his adversaries.

Let us test him with insult
and torture,
so that we may find out
how gentle he is,
and make trial of his forbearance.

Let us condemn him
to a shameful death,
for, according to what he says,
he will be protected.

Thus they reasoned,
but they were led astray,
for their wickedness blinded them,
and they did not know
the secret purposes of God,
nor hoped for the wages of
holiness, nor discerned the prize
for blameless souls.
(*The Wisdom of Solomon* 1:16-22).

# Appendix I

# Twesigye's Commandments for Critical Thinking And Moral Problem Solving

1. Thou shalt not create a problem where one does not exist. Instead, provide creative, peaceful, moral acceptable, affordable and constructive solutions to existing problems.

2. Thou shalt not create a greater problem in the process of solving a simpler one! "Never do harm" in the process of solving a problem. Refer the problem to the experts if you cannot resolve it without creating new problems, or causing an equivalent or greater harm in the process!

3. Thou shalt not attempt to solve a problem which has not yet been clearly identified and carefully studied for real causes and possible alternative solutions.

4. Thou shalt not point a gun at what you do not intend to shoot or kill! Guns are not toys to play with. You may cause some unintentional harm, or get shot by the other party or police in a justifiable self-defense!

5. Thou shalt not tell what should be kept secret. Once disclosed, it is no longer a secret. You never know who is listening in or taping your private conversation for blackmail or sale to the highest bidder! Remember the lesson of Monica Lewinsky and Bill Clinton. They were betrayed by those they trusted. Only priests and counselors are sworn to keep secrets!

6. Thou shalt think twice before you speak or act. Your thoughts are your own secrets and private property until they are made public in speech or action. Public evaluation may lead to punishment for evil disclosed, and reward good deeds.

7. Always remember that your own mind is God's best and highest supernatural gift to you and the world. Respect it. Use it well to bring glory and goodness to you, God, the community and the world. God has placed us here as his or her concrete supernatural representatives and custodians of creation. Therefore, think deep thoughts and do good to become God-like *(imago Dei)*! Descartes discovered that he was alive through thinking.

8. Thou shalt not argue on anything of which you are ignorant. Asserting falsehood as truth is a great evil. It is self-damnation.

9. Thou shalt not assume that something is true because somebody says it is true. Gossip is not truth. False stories destroy good and innocent people who get entangled the deadly web of lies and distorted truths.

10. Thou shalt not assume that it is true because it is written down in a holy book *(Bible, Torah* or *Qur'an*), textbook, or newspaper, unless it can be proved by independent or objective evidence. Remember that faith alone and the religious claims to truths as evidence or fact are not acceptable empirical forms of evidence. Illusions, dreams or visions, myths and beliefs are not facts or true as God's revealed and objective truths.

11. Thou shall not worship a book as God or God's infallible holy revelation. That is idolatry. Remember that all sacred books or scriptures *(Bible, Torah, Qur'an* and *Vedas)* are mere man-made books that have been declared to be inerrant or infallible holy books, despite glaring errors and contradictions about God's revelation and truth in nature and history!

Remember, the Truth of God does not contradict itself, and God does not write books! Nature is God's universal holy and reliable book (or universal holy revelation) for all people to read and study carefully as God's true revelation as recorded by God in events of creation and redemption!

12. Thou shalt not appeal to the infallible authority of your religion or supposed inerrant holy religious book(s) to establish scientific, empirical, and historical truths. Treating scriptures as historical or scientific books is both idolatry, blasphemy and ignorance.

Biblical literalism misuses both religion, sacred books and gods. This is true unless the gods are able to speak for themselves to the contrary regarding this debate. The Living God still speaks his or her creative and redemptive Word today. We hear it and see it in both nature and the cosmic historical processes. We need the tools of faith, technology and science to see more clearly God's supernatural activities and Mystery in the world and its evolutionary processes.

13. Thou shalt not invoke the sacred name of God in order to validate your invalid argument, unsupported beliefs and falsehood as divine truth. Remember that God is the same cosmic Mind and Creator who gave you the supernatural gifts of mind and intellect so that you could become knowledgeable and know the truths like God. Therefore, in God's name, verify the truth through the sacred activity of the mind in vigorous research, orderly analysis of facts, creative, analytical and free critical thinking processes. God is Truth. To find the Truth is also to find and glorify God as Truth, Mind and Ultimate Reality.

14. Thou shalt not assume that what you say or intend to be heard is what is actually said or heard and understood by your audience. Therefore, always repeat the same message or information in various ways and in different words. Then seek an honest feedback in order to ensure effective mutual communication or else speak to the trees and the sky.

15. Thou shalt not assume that difference and diversity denote something evil or inferior. God did not intend to create a monolithic world. Variety, diversity and contrast provide the beauty of life. They are the ideal spices of life. Therefore, learn to appreciate differences and diversity as God's supernatural gifts to break the boring monotony of a monolithic life.

16. Thou shalt learn to recognize thine own ignorance, prejudice, and limitations, in order to be able to transcend and change them. Thou shalt not become like the alcoholics and drug addicts whose denial of the reality and truth become the main secondary causes of more moral and social evils when falsehood and illusions are believed and projected to the public as reality and truth. Live by the instruction of Jesus: "Know [and accept] the Truth and the Truth will set you free!"

17. Thou shalt learn to recognize thine own ethnocentrism, prejudice and bigotry in dealing with other people. Remember the "Golden Rule" of agape in dealing with the people of another nation, religion, class, race, color and gender.

18. Thou shalt learn to listen to others in order to hear, learn, understand, and become wise. This is a basic principle required to facilitate effective mutual communications and relationships. Nobody can communicate to anybody when everybody is talking, with nobody listening to anybody.

19. Thou shalt not speak in a language that is foreign to your audience unless there is a capable interpreter available. Remember that even God speaks to human beings through their own local prophets, cultures, languages and world-view. To the Hebrews, God spoke to them through Moses and Jesus; to the Asians, God sent Buddha, and to the Arabs, God spoke to them in Arabic through the great Prophet Muhammad.

Therefore, Hebrew, Greek, Latin, and Arabic are not God's own exclusive holy preferred languages. Before God, these languages have the same merit as Chinese, Swahili and English or any other language!

For God, no human culture or language is ever holier, superior and more important than another one! Like God, we too, must speak to people in their own language and cultural context in order to communicate with them more effectively and show them respect. Vatican II recognized this divine truth and decreed that Mass conducted in other languages, other than Latin, was valid and efficacious before God as Mass conducted in Latin.

20. Thou shalt not assume that other people see the same "world" and the same "reality" that you see when looking at the same scenery. The human perception of the world or nature, events, history, people and reality are very personal, subjective, diverse, partial and radically differ from one person to another. Yet, each person may claim total truth as a witness to an event.

You must recognize the epistemological law of an evolutionary world and finite humanity, namely, that knowledge and the truth is never absolute. They are evolutionary, partial and mediated to the mind through the imperfect senses and relativity of sensory perception. Human perception is filtered through experience, intellectual aptitude, knowledge already possessed, gender, history, state of health, senses, expectations, education, age, culture, language, religion, science, nationality, class, race and neighborhood.

These factors filter and shape what a person perceives to be the truth. Even God's Word, messages and revelation are processed and filtered through epistemological processes and factors. As such, what is heard and affirmed as God's Word is often "the human interpretation and word about God." In other words, what is visible and sensible to us is subjective reality, and the objective reality is never fully available to our subjective experience, for it is infinite and transcendent.

Therefore, be humble during debates about the nature of the world, truth, and reality, for these debates about the nature of the world tend to be analogous to debates about the nature of the shapes of clouds. Thou shalt remember that there is no absolute reality or truth that is directly available to the grasp of the finite human mind, and the subjective senses of the body.

21. Thou shalt not fight a war or kill your opponent because of a verbal or an intellectual disagreement. Physical violence is not an appropriate response to an intellectual threat of inadequacy, ignorance or mental inferiority. American jails are filled with people of low mental aptitude, poor education and poor problem-solving skills. Moreover, violence only provokes more violence, and counter-violence, and therefore, violence is never a constructive solution for human problems since. Often, it creates more serious problems than it solves.

However, in the absence of good willed, great creative minds to provide creative, nonviolent and humane global problem solving skills, violence remains a viable solution to global problems. Violence as a solution for problems appeals most to unthinking and unintelligent beasts. Similarly, violence appeals to the less intelligent, poorly educated, poor, and the ignorant masses who lack the necessary knowledge, intellectual skills, training and moral capability to effect nonviolent mediation of conflicts and accept peaceful solutions to problems of life. Nonviolence is the highest level of moral and spiritual development. Therefore, imitate the examples of Buddha, Socrates, Jesus, Gandhi and M.L. King.

22. Thou shalt not instruct or argue with a fool. It is an absolute waste of valuable time and may become a source of irritation for the fool. The fool will hate you for it and reject the good advice you give him or her. However, if you charge the fool a high fee, he or she may value and respect your advice because of the value attached to the cost of the advice. Therefore, charge a high tuition cost, if you must instruct a fool! Charge an entrance fee for religious services and Sunday School, and you will have better behaved and more eager members!

23. Thou shalt not assume that one race or religion is superior to another. This ethnocentrism is an erroneous assumption and a major source of many serious global human problems of violence, wars and other great evils. God does not care which nationality, race, gender, and religion you belong to. God only requires that you live a peaceful, loving, just, honest, holy or clean, productive and responsible social life within the community and the world.

24. Thou shalt do unto others what you want them to do unto you in a similar situation. This is the true universal practical guide and criterion measure of functional unconditional love, compassion, forgiveness, godliness and justice.

25. Thou shalt not love thyself and others in the same way unless it is wholesome and unconditional love. Thou shalt remember that free unconditional love for the self and others is the key to both happiness and meaningful global harmony, peaceful human coexistence and mutual fulfillment. It is through the diligent praxis of agape (unconditional love) that human beings are divinized and united with God or Agape (cf. 1 John 4:7).

26. Thou shalt always remember to smile. It is a revelatory and healing divine event. In unconditional love, a smile enlightens the world with God's supernal light of love and healing. A smile costs little than frowning. Yet, it is the sunshine of love in a gloomy world starving for unconditional acceptance, love and forgiveness and healing. A smile is the best peaceful weapon and means to win over enemies, permanently, without firing a single shot! Smile and laugh to heal yourself, depressed people in the community and the world.

27. Thou shalt not abuse or oppress the weak and the defenseless. Human strength is truly measured in good deeds and not in evil accomplishments.

28. Thou shalt not desire to be another person; for God made you to become a unique and special person in the world. Therefore, you can only be truly happy when you find your own true identity, special role, meaning, and appreciate the authentic and unique self or person that you were specially designed and created by God to become.

To be happy, you must become your unique true self. You cannot aspire to be another person, and yet be happy. Remember, grass only looks greener the other side of the fence! Some people may envy you while you envy them!

29. Thou shalt not confuse religion with science. This naive confusion has been the main source of many religious evils, violence and misery in the world. The church threatened to execute Galileo and rejected Darwin's theory of evolution because of this confusion.

Remember the truth: sound religion is a conventional system of faith and practices. It is based on sound ethics, faith, reason, nature and science. Science tells us *how* the cosmos came into being. It gives us the *tools or technology* to enable us to study, appreciate and harness the laws of nature for our benefits. Religion tells us *why* the world and the things in it came into being.

Religion teaches us *how best to live in the world both in harmony and peace with the neighbor and all God's creatures*. Religion is not science and science is not religion; they have complimentary functions. Therefore, the Bible is not a textbook for either history or science. It is book of religious myths, stories, parables, and religious moral teachings of the past era.

30. Thou shalt not accept a bribe. It is the perfect conventional disguised blindfold for unsuspecting foolish greedy victims, being "set up" for an eventual terrible day of destruction. Remember, the true worth of a human being is not measured in material goods, wealth and material possessions, but rather, in the

individual's personal moral values and responsibility as a thinking moral agent capable of acting in a manner that will enhance goodness, beauty, justice, love and tender care, in the indifferent world.

31. Thou shalt not entertain any sexual temptations for immoral or unlawful self-gratification. Uncontrolled sexual drives have been the main sources of human misery, blackmail, dirty politics, loss of job and dignity.

Sex has created a mess on the broad street of hedonistic pleasures. It has led to both unhappiness and destruction for many civic leaders, clergy and laity. Samson, King David, Solomon and President Bill Clinton and Monica Lewinsky learned their lessons the hard way. Besides, AIDS has no mercy on those who have no room for self-control and respect for safe sex.

32. Thou shalt not postpone to tomorrow what needs to be done today. In reality, tomorrow is God's time and secret which never comes! Tomorrow is just today's dream, fantasy and shelf to pile on postponed work by lazy people. There is only today in which mortals can do the good works to make the future and the world a better place, as God's actual Kingdom. God's Kingdom as reality is effectively present here today. God does not postpone it!

33. Thou shalt not take love or friendship for granted. That is the sure way to abuse and lose it.

34. Thou shalt not say anything in private about any person, that you could cannot say in the presence of that person. This is an ideal universal practical guide for truth-telling, love and civic virtues in the world.

35. Thou shalt not do evil in order to bring about good! Evil only produces evil. Only the good is capable of producing a greater and lasting common good.

36. Thou shalt not solve a political problem by means of military violence. Political problems require a political solution, just like a medical problem requires a medical solution. Hence, major global socioeconomic and political problems can be solved through education, justice, charity and democracy.

37. Thou shalt not forget that many deadly and savage wars have been mistakenly fought in the name of the Loving Almighty God, superiority, freedom and liberation.

Thou shalt not forget that the victorious liberators often become the new corrupt evil oppressors to be overthrown, for having succumbed to the evil temptations of power, wealth, sex, technology and idolatrous hubris.

Therefore, always remember that true human liberation will not come until the oppressors and the oppressed have both become liberated and reconciled to one another in peace. The liberators also must learn that true lasting human liberation, global freedom and peace consist in the dual liberation of the oppressor and the oppressed from mutual fear, distrust, prejudice and hatred.

38. Thou shalt remember that true liberation consists in living a positively transformed mode of life that is characterized by love, justice, free (voluntary) community service and empathy for other people. In this a mode of liberated life, people must be freed from the invisible evil chains of ignorance, greed, selfishness, pride, ethnocentrism, racism, color-prejudice, discrimination, sexism, class

consciousness, materialism, idolatry, violence, hate, injustice, oppression, malice, envy, sadism and both religious and ideological bigotry.

39. Thou shalt love without condition and do good if you wish to find love and goodness in the world; for what you sow is what you reap many times over! Love and good deeds, like evil deeds are the boomerangs we throw out into the world, eventually return to us as God's blessings.

40. Thou shalt learn to accept the truth that we are free and responsible moral agents in the world. Our deeds are definitive of our lives and direct the course of world history. We are immediately transported to a life with God in Heaven or the misery of Hell by the moral nature and quality of our deeds.

Remember, the Devil has little to do with our own freely chosen fate, or misuse of freedom and moral failures! We invent scapegoats to blame for our moral irresponsibility and failures. Likewise, men invented Eve as a moral scapegoat for moral evil! People also invented a spiritual and moral personification of evil and scapegoat, called "the Devil." This is moral and spiritual escapism from the responsibility for use of freedom, choice and moral actions. Hence, "The Devil made me do it," says the idiot, and the morally and spiritual immature or irresponsible person. Wisely, the society sends the real Devil to jail for doing evil. It also praises the heros and saints who do good deeds of love.

41. Thou shalt learn the universal redemptive secret truth that God's creation or the world is God's good work in progress and continually unfolding Kingdom! Nobody is excluded from God's Kingdom! The world or creation as God's Kingdom is governed by God through the impartial laws of evolution, and natural law, resulting in cause and corresponding effect (*Karma*).

Therefore, live as an informed, wise, good and obedient citizen in God's Kingdom, respecting the laws of God, Church and the society. Oppose evil and injustice everywhere in the world. Ultimately, learn to love and work peacefully together with other people of goodwill in God's redemptive mission to keep the world peaceful, clean and free from the impurities and defilement of human moral evils and ecological degradation.

42. Thou must not defile God's world, creation and Kingdom. As God's obedient, loving, and responsible moral saints you must prevent the evils of: greed, suicide, dooms day cults, injustice, exploitation, materialism, war, racism, sexism, bigotry, violence, ignorance, neglect and ecological contamination by hazardous industrial chemicals, farm and industrial or military nuclear waste.

43. Know when to form alliances to solve a problem. And know when and how to dissolve them amicably. This excludes most marriages!

44. Live by the moral code of Agape, nonviolence and peace. If you are not yet ready for this moral perfection, then live by the moral code of Moses. As a practical process of moral purification accept the moral authority of God; shun idolatry; shun misuse of God's name; honor the Sabbath; honor your parents; avoid senseless killing; shun sexual immorality; honor property rights; shun falsehood/slander and envy/coveting.

45. Live in contentedness and peace to attain true and lasting happiness.

46. Learn and teach people the divine creative art of making love, instead of the art of making war! Love creates a world and community, whereas war brings violence and destruction of life and property. Remember, *God is Agape* (Unconditional Love)! People become like God by the praxis of agape.

47. Do not reinvent the wheel. Learn from history to build on past successes, discoveries and knowledge. And avoid past failures and mistakes, and the pain they cause. Only the fool insists on repeating the mistakes of the past by a refusal to learn from history and the experiences of others!

48. Remember that strength, development and success come from knowledge, unity, technology, cooperation and hard work. Laziness is a disgrace to humanity. People are what they do! They are good if they do good, and evil if they do evil! But, "they are nothing, if they do nothing!"

49. Remember that the good and evil we do are like a boomerang! They eventually return back to reward us or harm us! Therefore, it is always good to do good for goodness sake, even when there is nobody there to reward us! Ultimately, we are there and God is there, too! We are our own witnesses, cheerleaders, judges, jury and executioners! Guilt is a self-imposed sentence in existential hell-fire!

50. Even when you find yourself in living in existential hell, you must member the reality of God's Unconditional Love and free redemptive grace for all sinners and evil-doers. You must take courage and renew your faith in God and forgive yourself and others when mistakes are made. Mistakes are part of the learning process and experimentation. They keep us humble, and we learn to become better and more perfect. Learn from nature, history, experience, the scriptures, the saints and wise teachers.

Consult a priest or another moral or spiritual advisor or counselor to pronounce and assure you of God's unconditional mercy, love, grace and forgiveness. Make appropriate restitution to correct wrongs and facilitate moral, social and spiritual balance, healing and peace!

# Bibliography

## A Selected Bibliography and Further Reading


Abelson, Raziel and Friquegnon Marie-Louise. *Ethics for Modern Life*. New York: St. Martin's Press, Third Edition, 1987.

Adams, Sheri. *What the Bible Really Says about Women.* Macon, Ga.: Smyth and Helwys, 1994.

Albrecht, G. *The Character of our Communities.* Nashville: Abingdon, 1995.

______ . *America's Original Sin.* Washington, D.C.: Sojourners, 1992.

Arthur, John, ed. *Morality and Moral Controversies.* 4th ed. Englewood Cliffs, N.J.: Prentice Hall, 1995.

Ashe, Arthur. *Days of Grace.* New York: Knopf, 1993.

Ashley, Paul. *Oh Promise Me But Put It in Writing.* New York: McGraw-Hill, 1978.

Ashmore, Robert B. *Building a Moral System.* Englewood Cliffs, N.J.: Prentice Hall, 1987.

Bahm, Archie, J. *Comparative Philosophy: Western, Indian and Chinese Philosophies Compared.* Albaquque: World Books, 1977.

Barbour, Ian G. *Earth Might Be Fair.* Englewood Cliffs: Prentice Hall, 1972.

Barndt, Joseph. *Dismantling Racism.* Minneapolis: Augsburg Fortress, 1991.

Barnette, Henlee. *The Church and the Ecological Crisis.* Grand Rapids, Mich.: Eerdmans, 1972.

_______. Exploring Medical Ethics. Macon, Ga.: Mercer University, 1982.

Barret, William. *The Irrational Man*. New York: Anchor Books, 1962.

Barry, Vincent. *Moral Aspects of Health Care.* Belmont: Wadsworth, 1982.

Batchelor, Edward, Jr. *Homosexuality and Ethics,* New York: Pilgrim, 1980.

Bates, Ulku. *Women's Realities, Women's Choices.* New York: Oxford University Press, 1995.

Beach, Waldo. *Christian Ethics in the Protestant Tradition.* Atlanta: John Knox, 1988.

Beach, Waldo and Niebuhr, Richard, H. *Christian Ethics: Sources of the Living Tradition.* New York: John Wiley & Sons, Second Edition, 1973.

Behrman, Jack N. *Essays on Ethics in Business and the Professions.* Englewood Cliffs, NJ.: Prentice Hall, 1988.

Birch, Bruce C. and Larry L. Rasmussen. *Bible and Ethics in the Christian Life*. Minneapolis: Augsburg, 1976.

Bloch, Abraham *P. A Book of Jewish Ethical Concepts.* NY: Ktav, 1984.

Bloesch, Donald G. *Freedom for Obedience.* N Y: Harper and Row, 1987.
Boff, Leonardo, and Clodovis Boff. *Introducing Liberation Theology.* New York: Orbis, 1987.
Bornkamm,, Gunther. *Jesus of Nazareth.* New York: Harper and Row, 1960.
Borowtitz, Eugene B. *Understanding Judaism.* New York: Union of American Hebrew Congregations, 1975.
_______, ed. *Reform Jewish Ethics and the Halakhah.* West Orange, N.J.: Behrman House, 1994.
Brody, Baruch A. and N. Tristram, Engelhardt, Jr. *Bioethics.* Englewood Cliffs, NJ.: Prentice Hall, 1987.
Brooks, Roy L. *Integration or Separatism?* Cambridge: Harvard Univ. 1996.
Brown, Robert McAfee. *Liberation Theology.* Louisville, Ky.: Westminster, John Knox, 1993.
________. *Making Peace in the Global Village.* Philad.: Westminster, 1981.
________. *Religion and Violence.* 2nd ed. Philadelphia: Westminster, 1987.
________. *Saying Yes and Saying No.* Philadelphia: Westminster, 1986.
Brunner, Emil. *Man in Revolt.* Philadelphia: Westminster Press, 1948.
________. *Moral Man and Immoral Society.* New York: Scribners, 196O.
________. *The Divine Imperative.* Philadelphia: *Westminster, 1947.*
Buber, Martin. *I and Thou.* Translated by Walter Kaufmann, New York: Scribners, 197O.
Cahill, Lisa Sowle. *Between the Sexes.* Philadelphia: Fortress, 1985.
Cahill, Lisa Sowle, and James E. Childress. *Christian Ethics.* Cleveland: Pilgrim, 1996.
Cannon, Katie G. *Black Womanist Ethics.* Atlanta: Scholars Press, 1988.
Carter, Jimmy. *Talking Peace.* New York: Dutton, 1993.
Cecil, Andrew R. *The Third Way.* Dallas: University of Texas, 1980.
Chardin, de Teilhard. *The Phenomenon of Man.* New York and London: Harper & Row, 1975.
Cobb, John B. Jr. Is *It Too Late?* Beverly Hills, Calif.: Bruce, 1972.
Cochran, B. H. et al. *Task Force Report on Same-Gender Covenants.* Raleigh, N.C.: Pullen Memorial Baptist Church, 1993.
Cohon, Samuels. *Judaism-A Way of Life.* Cincinnati: *Union of* American Hebrew Congregations, 1948.
Cone, James H. *A Black Theology of Liberation.* Twentieth *Anniversary Edition.* New York: Orbis, 1986.
________. *For My People.* New York: Orbis, 1984.
________. *My soul Looks Back.* New York: Orbis, 1995.
________. *God of the Oppressed.* New York: Seabury, 1975.
Council of Bishops of the United Methodist Church. *In Defense of Creation.* Nashville, Tenn.: Graded Press, 1986.
Countryman, L. William. *Dirt, Greed, and Sex.* Philadelphia: Fortress, 1988.
Crites, Laura L., and Winifred L. Hepperle. *Women, the Courts, and*

*Equality*. Newbury Park, Calif.: Sage, 1987.
Crook, Roger. *Introduction to Christian Ethics*. 3rd edition. Englewood Cliffs: Prentice Hall, 2000.
Cullmainn, Oscar. *The State in the New Testament*. NY: Scribner, 1956.
Cutler, Donald R., ed. *Updating Life and Death*. Boston: Beacon, 1969.
Dailey, Robert H. *Introduction to Moral Theology*. New York: Bruce, 1971.
Daly, Herman E. *For the Common Good*. 2nd ed. Boston: Beacon, 1994.
Daly, Lois K., ed. *Feminist Theological Ethics*. Louisville: John Knox, 1994.
Deckard, Barbara Sinclair. *The Women's Movement*. 3rd ed. New York: Harper and Row, 1975.
Delangue, Nicholas. *Judaism*. New York: Oxford, 1986.
Dewolfe, L. Harold. *Crime and Justice in America*. NY: Harper-Row, 1975.
_______. *What Americans Should Do about Crime*. NY: Harper-Row, 1976.
Deyoung, Curtiss; Paul. *Coming Together*. Valley Forge, Pa.: Judson, 1995.
Donaldson, Thomas, and Patrick H. Werhane. *Ethical Issues in Business*, 3rd ed. Englewood Cliffs, N.J.: Prentice Hall, 1988.
Dosick, Wayne. *Living Judaism*. New York: Harper, 1995.
Drinan, Robert E. *Beyond the Nuclear Freeze*. New York: Seabury; 1983.
DuBois, W.E.B. *The Souls of Black Folk*. New York: Bantam, 1989.
Englehardt, H. T. *Bioethics and Secular Humanism*. London: SCM, 1991.
Erickson, Brad, ed. *Call to Action*. San Francisco: Sierra Club Books, 1990.
Fletcher, Joseph. *Morals and Medicine*. Boston: Beacon, 1960.
_______. *Situation Ethics*. Philadelphia: Westminster, 1966.
Farley, Edward. *The Ecclesial Man*. Philadelphia: Fortress, 1975.
Freeman, Jo. *The Politics of Women's Liberation*. New York: McKay, 1975.
French, Peter, A. and Brown Curtis, eds. *Puzzles, Paradoxes and Problems: A Reader for Introductory Philosophy*. New York: St. Martin's, 1987.
Foucalt, Michael. *The Order of Things: An Archaeological of Human Sciences*. New York: Vintage Books, 197O.
Freund, Richard A. *Understanding Jewish Ethics*. San Francisco: Edward Mellen, 1990.
Friedan, Betty. *The Feminine Mystique*. New York: Dell, 1963.
Fromer, Margot Joan. *Ethical Issues in Sexuality and Reproduction*. St. Louis: Mosby, 1983.
Funk, Robert W. and Roy W. Hoover. *The Five Gospels*. New York: Macmillan, 1993.
Gardner, E. C. *Biblical Faith and Social Ethics*. NY: Harper-Row, 1960.
Geyer, Alan. *Christianity and the Super Powers*. Nashville: Abingdon, 1990.
Gonsalves, Milton A. *Fagothey's Right and Reason*. 8th ed. St. Louis: Times Mirror/Mosby, 1985.
Guroian, Vigen. *Life's Living Toward Dying*. Grand Rapids: Eerdmans, 1996.
Gustafson, James M. *Ethics from a Theocentric Perspective. Vol. 1, Theology and Ethics*. Chicago: University of Chicago Press, 1981.

_______. *Ethics from a Theocentric Perspective. Vol. 2, Ethics and Theology*. Chicago: University of Chicago Press, 1984.

_______. *Protestant and Roman Catholic Ethics.* Chicago: University of Chicago Press, 1978.

Guthrie, W.K.C. *The Greek Philosophers: From Thales to Aristotle.* New York: Harper & Row Publishers, 195O.

Gutierrez, Gustavo. *A Theology of Liberation.* Rev. ed. Maryknoll, NY: Orbis, 1988.

Haring, Bernard. *The Law of Christ.* Westminster, MD: Newman P., 1966.

_______. *Toward a Christian Moral Theology.* Notre Dame: University of Notre Dame, 1966.

Harmon, Gilbert. *The Nature of Morality.* New York: Oxford University Press, 1977.

Harrelson, Walter. *The Ten Commandments and Human Rights.* Philadelphia: Fortress Press, 198O.

Haselden, Kyle. *The Racial Problem in Christian Perspective.* New York: Harper, 1959.

Hauerwas, Stanley. *Against the Nations.* New York: Harper and Row, 1985.

Hauerwas, Stanley, and William H. Willimon. *Resident Aliens.* Nashville, Tennessee: Abingdon, 1989.

Hawley, Robert, C. & Hawley, Isabel L. *Human Values in the Classroom: A Handbook for Teachers.* New York: Hart Publishing Co. Inc. 1975.

Hayes, Diana L. *And Still We Rise.* New York: Paulist, 1996.

Hayes, Richard B. *The Moral Vision of the New Testament.* New York: Harper Collins, 1996.

Healey, Edwin F. *Moral Guidance.* Chicago: Loyola, 1943.

Heidegger, Martin. *The Question Concerning Technology and Other Essays.* New York/London: Harper & Row, 1977.

Hessel, Dieter, ed. *Theology for Earth Community.* New York: Orbis, 1996.

Hewlett, Leslie. *A Lesser Life: The Myth of Women's Liberation in America.* New York: William Morrow, 1986.

Hidalgo, Hilda; Travis Peterson and Natalie Jane Woodman, eds., *Lesbian and Gay Issues.* Silver Spring, Md.: National Association of Social Workers, 1985.

Higginson, Richard. *Dilemmas.* Louisville, Ky.: Westminster/Knox, 1988.

Hollenbach, David. *Justice, Peace, and Human Rights*. New York: Crossroad, 1988.

Hopkins, Dwight, N. *Black Theology USA and South Africa: Politics, Culture, and Liberation*. New York: Orbis, 1989.

Hospers, John. *Human Conduct.* New York: Harcourt B. Jovanavich, 1972.

Houlden, *J. L. Ethics and the New Testament.* NY: Oxford University, 1977.

*Humanist Manifestos I and II.* Buffalo, N.Y.: Promethus Books, 1973.

Hunt, Corton. *Gay.* New York: Pocket Books, 1973.

Hunter College Women's Studies. *Women's Realities, Women's Choices.* 2nd ed. New York: Oxford, 1995.

Jackson, Dare. *Dial 911: Peaceful Christians and Urban Violence.* Scottsdale, Ariz.: Herald, 1981.

Jacobs, Louis. *Jewish Personal and Social Ethics.* West Orange, N.J.: Behrman, 1990.

Jones, H. Kimball. *Toward a Christian Understanding of the Homosexual.* New York: Association Press, 1966.

Kammer, C. L. *Ethics and Liberation: An Introduction.* NY: Orbis, 1996.

Kaufman, Gordon D. *Theology for a Nuclear Age.* Philadelphia: Westminster, 1985.

Kilner, John E; Nigel M., De S. Cameron, and David L. Schiedermayer, eds. *Bioethics and the Future of Medicine.* Grand Rapids: Eerdmans, 1995.

King, M.L. Jr. *Stride toward Freedom.* New York: Harper and Row, 1958.

_______. *Why We Can't Wait.* New York: Harper and Row, 1964.

Kitano, Harry, and Roger Daniels. *Asian Americans: The Emerging Minority.* Englewood Cliffs, N.J.: Prentice Hall, 1988.

Kurtz, Paul. *In Defense of Secular Humanism.* Buffalo: Prometheus, 1983.

Lammers, Stephen E. and Allen Verhey, eds. *On Moral Medicine.* Grand Rapids, Mich.: Eerdmans, 1987.

Lehmann, Paul. *Ethics in a Christian Context.* NY: Harper and Row, 1963.

Lester, Andrew D. *Sex Is More Than a Word.* Nashville: Broadman, 1973.

Levine, Martin P., ed. *Gay Men.* New York: Harper and Row, 1979.

Linzey, A. *Christianity and the Rights of Animals.* NY: Crossroad, 1987.

Loesch, Judi. "Unmarried Couples Shouldn't Live Together." *U.S. Catholic,* July 1985, *16-17.*

Long, Edward Leroy. *Peace Thinking in a Warring World.* Philadelphia: Westminster, 1983.

Luper, Steven, ed. *Living Well: Introductory Readings in Ethics.* New York: Harcourt Brace, 2000.

MacIntyre, Alasdair. *After Virtue. Notre Dame*: University of Notre Dame Press, 1981.

Malloy, Edward A. *Homosexuality and the Christian Way of Life.* Washington, D.C.: University Press of America, 1981.

Marmor, Judd, ed. *Homosexual Behavior.* New York: Basic Books 1980.

May, William F. *Testing the Medical Covenant.* Grand Rapids, Mich.: Eerdmans, 1996.

Mbiti, John S. *African Religions and Philosophy.* London: Heinemann, 1969.

Mcdaniel, Jay B. *Of God and Pelicans.* Louisville: John Knox, 1989.

McKenzie, Steven L. *All God's Children.* Louisville: John Knox, 1997.

McLemore, S. Dale. *Racial and Ethnic Relations in America.* Boston: Allyn and Bacon, 1980.

______. *War and Conscience in America.* Philadelphia: Westminster, 1968.

McCormck, Richard A. "Abortion," *America,* June 19, 1965: 898.
Mcneill, John J. *The Church and the Homosexual.* Boston: Beacon, 1988.
Meeks, M. Douglas. *God the Economist.* Minneapolis: Fortress, 1989.
Meilaender, Gilbert. *Bioethics: A Primer for Christians.* Grand Rapids, Mich.: Eerdmans, 1996.
Mitchelson, Marvin. *Living Together.* New York: Simon and Schuster, 1980.
Moltmann, Jurgen. *Man: Christian Anthropology in the Conflict of the Present.* Translated by John Study. Philadelphia: Fortress Press, 1979.
Moore/McCann/McCann. *Creative and Critical Thinking*. Boston: Houghton Mifflin Co., Second Edition, 1985.
Niebuhr, Reinhold. *Moral Man and Immoral Society*. New York: Charles Scribner's Sons, 196O.
_______. *The Nature and Destiny of Man*. (2 Vols.) NY: Scribners, 1964.
Niebur, Richard H. *Christ and Culture*. New York: Harper & Row, 1951.
Mott, Stephen Charles. *Biblical Ethics and Social Change.* Part I. New York: Oxford University Press, 1982.
Mount, Eric, Jr. *Professional Ethics in Context.* Louisville: John Knox, 1990.
Nash, Rodericy Frazier. *The Rights of Nature.* Madison: University of Wisconsin, 1989.
National Conference of Catholic Bishops. *The Challenge of Peace: God's Promise and Our Response.* Washington, D.C.: National Conference of Catholic Bishops, 1983.
______. *Economic Justice for All.* Washington, D.C.: National Conference of Catholic Bishops, 1986.
Pannenberg, Wolfhart. *Human Nature, Election and History*. Philadelphia: Westminster Press, 1977.
Paris, Peter. *The Social Teaching of the Black Churches*. Philadelphia: Fortress Press, 1985.
______. *What is Man?* Philadelphia: Fortress, 197O
Parker, William R. and Aldwell, Enid. *Man: Animal and Divine*. Los Angeles: Scrivener & Co., Third Edition, 197O.
Paul II, Pope John. *The Gospel of Life [Evangelum Vitae]*. New York: Random House, 1995.
Perkins, Hugh V. *Human Development and Learning*. Belmont, Ca.: Wadsworth Publishing Co., Second Edition, 1974.
Pittenger, Norman W. *The Christian Understanding of Human Nature*. Philadelphia: The Westminster Press: 1964.
Rahner, Karl. *The Evolutionary Origin of Man as a Theological Problem.* New York: Herder & Herder, 1965.
_______. *Foundations of the Christian Faith*. New York: Seabury, 1978.
_______. *Spirit in the World.* New York: Herder & Herder, 1968.
_______. *The Hearers of the Word*. New York: Herder & Herder, 1966.
_______. *Grace in Freedom*. New York: Herder & Herder, 1969.
_______. *Theological Investigations*. 25 Vols. NY: Herder, 1960-1985.

Reale, Giovanni. *The Systems of Hellenistic Age: A History of Ancient Philosophy*. Edited and Translated by John R. Catan. Albany: State University of New York, 1985.

Ring, Merrill. *Beginning with the Pre-Socratics*. Palo Alto: Mayfield, 1987.

Sanders, Cheryl J. *Empowerment Ethics for a Liberated People.* Minneapolis: Fortress Press, 1995.

Schell, Jonathan. *The Fate of the Earth.* New York: Knopf, 1982.

Sellers, James. *Theological Ethics.* New York: Macmillan, 1966.

Shannon, Thomas A. *Bioethics: Selected Readings.* 4th ed. Mahwah, N.J.: Paulist, 1993.

________. *An Introduction to Bioethics. 3rd* ed. New York: Paulist, 1997.

Simmons, Paul *D. Birth and Death: Bioethical Decision-Making*. Philadelphia: Westminster, 1983.

Simpson, George E. and J. Milton Yinger. *Racial and Cultural Minorities.* 5th ed. New York: Plenum, 1985.

Skinner, J. B. *About Behaviorism.* New York: Knopf, 1974.

________. *Beyond Freedom and Dignity*. New York: Knopf, 1971.

Smedes, Lewis B. *Choices.* New York: Harper and Row, 1986.

________. *Mere Morality*. Grand Rapids, Mich.: Eerdmans, 1983.

________. *Sex for Christians.* Rev. ed. Grand Rapids: Eerdmans, 1994.

Smith, Adam. *An Inquiry into the Nature and Causes of the Wealth of Nations.* Chicago: University of Chicago Press, 1976.

Smith, Harmon *L. Ethics and the New Medicine.* Nashville: Abingdon, 1971.

Smith, Rachel Richardson. "Abortion, Right and Wrong." *Newsweek,* March 15, 1985, p. 16.

Stegenga, James A and Axline, Andrew W. *The Global Community: A Brief Introduction to International Relations.* New York & London: Harper & Row, Publishers, Second Edition, 1982.

Stone, Glenn, ed. *A New Ethic for a New Earth.* NY: Friendship, 1971.

Storer, Morris B., ed. *Humanistic Ethics.* New York: Prometheus, 1988.

Stout, Jeffrey. *Ethics after Babel.* Boston: Beacon, 1988.

Taylor, Paul *W. Respect for Nature.* Princeton: Princeton University P., 1986.

Thielicke, Helmut. *The Ethics of Sex,* New York: Harper and Row, 1964.

Thomasma, David *C. Human Life in the Balance.* Louisville, Ky: Westminster/John Knox, 1990.

Thurman, H. *The Luminous Darkness.* New York: Harper and Row, 1965.

Tillich, Paul. *Systematic Theology*. 3 Vols. Chicago: Chicago U Press, 196O.

_______. *The Dynamics of Faith*. New York: Scribners & Sons, 1961.

_______. *The New Being*. New York: Scribners, 1955.

Twesigye, Emmanuel K. *Common Ground: Christianity, African Religion and Philosophy.* New York: Peter Lang, 1987.

_______. *African Religion, Philosophy, and Christianity in Logos-Christ: Common Ground Revisited*. New York: Peter Lang, 1996

______. *The Global Human Problem: Ignorance, Violence, Injustice and Hate*. New York: Peter Lang, 1988.

______. "Positive Affirmation of Evolution and Need for New Theology," *Ohio Academy of Religion Papers*. OWU/OU, Athens, April, 2000.

______, ed. *God, Race, Myth and Power: An Africanist Corrective Research Analysis*. New York: Peter Lang, 1991

Twiss, Harold L., ed. *Homosexuality and the Christian Faith*. Valley Forge, Pa.: Judson, 1978.

Umbreit, Mark. *Crime and Reconciliation*. Nashville, Tenn.: Abingdon, 1985.

Velasquez, Manuel G. *Business Ethics*. 2nd ed. Englewood Cliffs, N.J.: Prentice Hall, 1988.

Wallace, Ruth A. *Gender in America*. Englewood Cliffs: Prentice Hall, 1985.

Walters, James W. *War No More?* Minneapolis: Fortress, 1989.

Weeks, L. B. *Making Ethical Decisions*. Philadelphia: Westminster, 1987.

Welch, Sharon D. *Communities of Resistance and Solidarity: A Feminist Theology of Liberation*. New York: Orbis, 1985.

Wellman, Carl. *Morals and Ethics*. 2nd ed. Englewood Cliffs, NJ.: Prentice Hall, 1988.

Werkmeister, W. H. *Historical Spectrum of Values Theories*. Lincoln: Johnson Publishing Co., 197O.

West, Cornel. *Race Matters*. New York: Vintage, 1994.

White, Mel. *Stranger at the Gate*. New York: Penguin, 1994.

White, R. E. 0. *Biblical Ethics*. Atlanta: John Knox, 1979.

Wicks, Robert J.,Parsons, Richard D. and Capps, Donald E. eds. *Clinical Handbook of Pastoral Counseling*. New York: Paulist, 1987.

Whitehead, Alfred North. *Adventures of Ideas*. New York: MacMillan Publishing Co., 1983.

______. *Science and the Modern World*. New York: MacMillan, 1925.

______. *Religion in the Making*. New York: MacMillan, 1926.

______. *Process and Reality*. New York: MacMillan, 1978.

Will, James E. *A Christology Peace*. Louisville: John Knox, 1989.

Wittgenstein, Ludwig. *Philosophical Investigations*. Third Ed. Translated by G.E.M. Anscombe, New York: Macmillan, 1968.

Wogaman, J. Philip. *Christian Perspectives on Politics*. Philadelphia: Fortress, 1988.

# INDEX

# ABOUT THE AUTHOR

Emmanuel Twesigye is the Aden S. & Mollie Wollam Benedicts Professor of Christian Studies at Ohio Wesleyan University, and an adjunct Professor of Christian theology at the Methodist Theological School in Ohio, Delaware, Ohio, USA. He teaches courses in Christian theology and ethics.

The Rev. Professor Twesigye is an Anglican/Episcopal Priest, who was forced to flee Uganda on April 4, 1977 as a result of a confrontation with President Idi Amin, a semi-literate Muslim fanatic, who persecuted Christians in Uganda 1971-79, and assassinated the Anglican Archbishop Janani Luwum on February 17, 1977. Archbishop Luwum was Twesigye's immediate superior and friend. The Rev. Twesigye was the Anglican Chaplain and Head of the Department of Religious Education, at the National Teachers' College, Kyambogo, Uganda. Twesigye's experience of Christian persecution and violence of the State against the Church has shaped his theology and ethics into those of nonviolence, justice and agape based on the teachings of Jesus and the "golden rule" of doing to others what you would like them do to you under similar circumstances.

Professor Twesigye is the former Director of Black World Studies, at Ohio Wesleyan University. He is the current President of the Ohio Academy of Religion. He has taught at Makerere University, and the Uganda National Teachers College, Kyambogo in Africa. Twesigye served as Professor and Chair of Religion and Philosophy Department at Fisk University 1983-1989. Professor Twesigye has taught the gifted and talented in the Governors' School for International Studies at Memphis

State University 1986-1992. In 1984 he served as a fellow at Princeton University, and in 1995, he was a fellow at Harvard University.

Professor Twesigye has published a number of major scholarly books. These books include: *Common Ground: African Religion, Philosophy and Christianity* (1987); *The Global Human Problem: Ignorance, Hate, Injustice and Violence* (1988); *God, Race, Myth and Power: An Africanist Corrective Research Analysis* (1991); *African Religion, Philosophy, Christianity in Logos-Christ: Common Ground Revisited* (New York: Peter Lang, 1996); Editor, *Mission Theology & Partnerships: A Handbook* (National and World Mission Commission, Episcopal Diocese of Southern Ohio, 1999); Editor, *The Ohio Academy Religion Papers,* 1999 (OAR, 1999; 2000); Editor, *Zumari Journal* (BWS); he is currently working on a book manuscript entitled, "*Church and State Conflicts in Uganda*." He spent the summer of 1998 in Uganda carrying out research for the book.

Professor Twesigye holds the following degrees: Dip. Th. (UEA 1970); B.A. (Hons.) in History (MUK, 1973); Dip. Ed. (MUK 1973); M.A. (Hons) in Cultural Anthropology and Communications (Wheaton Graduate School 1978); STM (U of the South 1979); M.A. in Philosophy and Religion (Vanderbilt U, 1982); Ph.D. in Theology and Philosophy (Vanderbilt U, 1983).

Professor Twesigye has been listed in the following honorific publications and directories:
*"Who's Who in the World;" "Who's Who in the Mid-West;" "5,000 Personalities of the World;"*
*"The International Who's Who of Intellectuals;" "Men of International Achievement."*